SEXUAL HARASSMENT

Issues and Answers

Edited by

LINDA LeMONCHECK
JAMES P. STERBA

New York   Oxford

OXFORD UNIVERSITY PRESS

Oxford University Press

Oxford   New York
Athens   Auckland   Bangkok   Bogotá   Buenos Aires   Calcutta
Cape Town   Chennai   Dar es Salaam   Delhi   Florence   Hong Kong   Istanbul
Karachi   Kuala Lumpur   Madrid   Melbourne   Mexico City   Mumbai
Nairobi   Paris   São Paulo   Shanghai   Singapore   Taipei   Tokyo   Toronto   Warsaw

and associated companies in
Berlin   Ibadan

Library of Congress Cataloging-in-Publication Data

Sexual harassment : issues and answers / edited by Linda LeMoncheck, James P. Sterba.
        p. cm.
    Includes bibliographical references.
    ISBN 0-19-514299-3 (alk. paper)—ISBN 0-19-513481-8 (pbk. : alk. paper)
    1. Sexual harassment of women—United States—Case studies. 2. Sexual harassment of
women—Government policy—United States. 3. Sexual harassment of women—Law and
legislation—United States—Case studies. I. LeMoncheck, Linda. II. Sterba, James P.

HQ1237.5.U6 S485 2000
305.42'0973—dc21   00-040653

Printing (last digit): 9   8   7   6   5   4   3   2   1

Printed in the United States of America
on acid-free paper

Contents

Preface   xi

Acknowledgments   xiii

Introduction   1

I   THE NATURE OF SEXUAL HARASSMENT

1. Sexual Shakedown: The Sexual Harassment of Women on the Job   29
   Lin Farley

2. Sexual Harassment of Working Women: A Case of Sex Discrimination   42
   Catharine A. MacKinnon

3. Understanding Sexual Harassment at Work   50
   Barbara A. Gutek

4. The Definition of Sexual Harassment   62
   Jan Crosthwaite and Graham Priest

5. Why the Fight Against Sexual Harassment Is Misguided   77
   Mane Hajdin

II   VARIETIES OF SEXUAL HARASSMENT

6. What's Sex Got to Do With It?   85
   Deborah Tannen

7. Tailhook: Scandal Time   93
   Eloise Salholz and Douglas Waller

8. The Military Culture of Harassment   95
   Linda Bird Francke

9. Sex Bias Persists in L.A. County Sheriff's Department   103
   Tina Daunt and Anne-Marie O'Connor

10. Mitsubishi Plant Split on How to Define Writing on the Wall   106
    Stephen Braun

11. The Lecherous Professor   110
    Billie Wright Dziech and Linda Weiner

12. Failing at Fairness: How Our Schools Cheat Girls   118
    Myra Sadker and David Sadker

13. Caltech Student's Expulsion Over Contents of E-Mail
    Raises Concerns   124
    Amy Harmon

14. So Many Choices, So Little Time   127
    Jan Buckwald

15. Court Says Law Covers Same-Sex Harassment   129
    Joan Biskupic

III SEXUAL HARASSMENT AND THE LAW

16. Basic Facts About Sexual Harassment   135
    U.S. Equal Employment Opportunity Commission

17. The History of Sexual Harassment on the Job   136
    Susan L. Webb

18. Legal Update   145
    William Petrocelli and Barbara Kate Repa

19. The Legal Context of Sexual Harassment on Campus   146
    Robert J. Shoop

20. Speaking Truth to Power   150
    Anita Hill

21. Making Sense of Our Differences: African American Women on
    Anita Hill   159
    Beverly Grier

22. Race, Gender, and Liberal Fallacies   165
    Orlando Patterson

23. The Fall of Bob Packwood   168
    Allan Freedman

24. U.S. District Court, Arkansas, Western Division,
    Jones v. Clinton   172

25. Feminists and the Clinton Question   181
    Gloria Steinem

26. Mitsubishi to Pay $34 Million in Sex Harassment Case   184
    Stephen Braun

27. Guilty If Charged   187
    Richard Bernstein

28. The Silva Case at the University of New Hampshire   194
    Mary M. Clark

29. The Reasonable Woman: Sense and Sensibility in Sexual
    Harassment Law   207
    Kathryn Abrams

30. Closing the "Bisexual Defense" Loophole in Title VII Sexual
    Harassment Cases   214
    Sandra Levitsky

IV CURRENT DEBATES OVER SEXUAL HARASSMENT

31. Understanding, Explaining, and Eliminating
    Sexual Harassment   231
    James P. Sterba

32. Bared Buttocks and Federal Cases   245
    Ellen Frankel Paul

33. Reckless Eyeballing: Sexual Harassment on Campus   249
    Katie Roiphe

34. No Law in the Arena   260
    Camille Paglia

35. The Power of Sexual Stereotypes and the Sexiness
    of Power   264
    Linda LeMoncheck

36. Sex Is the Least of It: Let's Focus Harassment Law on Work,
    Not Sex   269
    Vicki Schultz

37. Heterophobia   274
    Daphne Patai

38. Academics' Shame: Our Failure to Confront
    Sexual Harassment   287
    Jeannette Oppedisano

39. The Myth of Male Power   294
    Warren Farrell

V MULTICULTURAL AND INTERNATIONAL ISSUES

40. Race, Sexual Harassment, and the Limitations of the
   Feminist Paradigm   305
   Kimberlé Crenshaw

41. Anti-Lesbian Harassment   307
   Celia Kitzinger

42. Immigrant Latina Domestic Workers and Sexual Harassment   315
   Diana Vellos

43. Japan Abuzz Over Sexual Harassment   324
   Nicole Gaouette

44. Sexual Harassment of Working Women in India   327
   Ramni Taneja

45. Shameful Silence: Professional Women in Mexico Are Talking More
   Than Ever About Sex Harassment   332
   Pia Hilbrert

46. The Regulation of Sexual Harassment in International
   Treaties and Documents   336
   Gaby Oré-Aguilar

VI SELECTED LEGAL DOCUMENTS AND COURT CASES

47. Title VII of the U.S. Civil Rights Act of 1964
   (as Amended in 1991)   345

48. Title IX of the Education Amendments of 1972   349

49. Equal Employment Opportunity Commission, Guidelines on
   Discrimination Because of Sex: Sexual Harassment   351

50. U.S. Department of Education Office of Civil Rights, Sexual
   Harassment Guidance   352

51. U.S. Supreme Court, *Meritor Savings Bank v. Vinson* (1986)   361

52. U.S. Supreme Court, *Franklin v. Gwinnett County
   Public Schools* (1992)   366

53. U.S. Supreme Court, *Harris v. Forklift Systems, Inc.* (1993)   370

54. U.S. Supreme Court, *Oncale v. Sundowner Offshore
   Services, Inc.* (1998)   373

55. U.S. Supreme Court, *Faragher v. City of Boca Raton* (1998)   376

56. U.S. Supreme Court, *Gebser et al. v. Lago Vista Independent School District* (1998)   383

57. United Nations Convention on the Elimination of All Forms of Discrimination Against Women (1981)   391

Selected Bibliography   399

❖ Preface

Sexual Harassment: Issues and Answers is a collection of contemporary popular and scholarly writing on the subject of sexual harassment. The book is designed to clarify and enrich our understanding of a topic that in recent years, especially in the United States, has been the subject of contentious debate in the media, the law, and the academy. The book's variety of political analysis, legal theory, philosophical debate, multicultural and international perspectives, regulatory documents, and Supreme Court case law is unprecedented in any single text on the subject. Chosen for their readability, concise presentation, and contribution to current debate, the book's fifty-seven selections examine the most compelling and perplexing questions surrounding sexual harassment, posed by scholars, activists, researchers, and the lay public alike: What counts as a case of sexual harassment? Is it a case of sexual attraction gone wrong? A cultural expression of male dominance over women? How persistent or severe must the conduct be? Can women sexually harass men? Can men sexually harass other men? What is wrong with sexual harassment? Is it an abuse of power? A clumsy attempt at a sexual overture? An instance of sex discrimination? Who is liable under the law for sexual harassment and how should they be held accountable? Should employers be liable for the sexually harassing conduct of their employees? Should universities be liable for the sexually harassing conduct of their faculty? How do victims seek redress when they are harassed outside of work or school?

A comprehensive introduction offers a summary of each selection, including relevant discussion topics for teachers and students. Selections on the nature of sexual harassment, varieties of sexual harassment, sexual harassment and the law, current debates over sexual harassment, multicultural and international issues, and selected legal documents and court cases are grouped by section to facilitate research and understanding of the issues surrounding sexual harassment. A selected bibliography is included for further reading. No other anthology on the market combines this comprehensive and pedagogical approach to understanding sexual harassment. The anthology is useful as an undergraduate text, a popular reader, and a sourcebook, all in one.

In putting together this anthology, we have benefited from the advice and help of many different people. In particular, we would like to thank Catharine MacKinnon, Camille Paglia, Katie Roiphe and the following reviewers: Bonnie Steinbock, Anita Superson, Rosemarie Tong, Louise Antony, and Anthony Weston. We would also like to thank Robert Miller, Senior Editor, and Justin Collins, Project Editor, at Oxford University Press.

Acknowledgments

Pages xiii–xiv constitute an extension of the copyright page.

Selection 1. Reprinted from *Sexual Shakedown: The Sexual Harassment of Women on the Job*. McGraw-Hill/Warner Books, 1978.

Selection 2. From *Sexual Harassment of the Working Women*. Reprinted by permission of the author and Yale University Press.

Selection 3. Reprinted from "Understanding Sexual Harassment" by permission of *Notre Dame Journal of Law, Ethics and Public Policy*.

Selection 4. From "The Definition of Sexual Harassment." Reprinted by permission of the *Australasian Journal of Philosophy*.

Selection 5. From *Sexual Harassment*. Reprinted by permission of Rowman & Littlefield.

Selection 6. From *Talking from 9 to 5*. Reprinted by permission of HarperCollins Publishers.

Selection 7. From *Newsweek* 1992 © Newsweek Inc. All rights reserved. Reprinted by permission.

Selection 8. From *Ground Zero*. Reprinted by permission of the author and Simon and Schuster.

Selection 9. From "Sex Bias Persists in L.A. County Sheriff's Department." Copyright © *Los Angeles Times*, 1999. Reprinted by permission.

Selection 10. From "Mitsubishi Plant Split on How to Define Writing on Wall." Copyright © *Los Angeles Times*, 1996. Reprinted by permission.

Selection 11. From *The Lecherous Professor*. Reprinted by permission of Beacon Press.

Selection 12. From *Failing at Fairness*. Reprinted by permission of Simon and Schuster.

Selection 13. From "Caltech Student Expelled Over Contents of E-Mail." Copyright © *Los Angeles Times*, 1995. Reprinted by permission.

Selection 14. From *Sexual Harassment: Women Speak Out*. Reprinted by permission of the Crossing Press.

Selection 15. Reprinted from "Court Says Law Covers Same-Sex Harassment." © 1998, *The Washington Post*. Reprinted with permission.

Selection 17. *Step Forward*. Reprinted by permission of the author.

Selection 18. Reprinted from *Sexual Harassment on the Job*, 4th edition. Reprinted by permission of the publisher, Nolo.com. Berkeley California.

Selection 19. From *Sexual Harassment on Campus*. Reprinted by permission of Allyn & Bacon.

Selection 20. From *Speaking Truth to Power*. Reprinted by permission of the author.

Selection 21. From *Race-ing Justice*. Reprinted by permission of Simon and Schuster.

Selection 22. From "Gender, Race, and Liberal Fallacies." Reprinted by permission of *The Black Scholar*.

Selection 23. From "Fall of Bob Packwood." Reprinted by permission of the *Congressional Quarterly*.

Selection 25. From "Feminists and the Clinton Questions." Reprinted by permission of the *New York Times*.

Selection 26. From "Mitsubishi to Pay $34 Million in Sex Harassment Case." Copyright © *Los Angeles Times*, 1998. Reprinted by permission.

Selection 27. From "Guilty If Charged." Reprinted by permission of the *New York Review of Books*.

Selection 28. From *NWSA Journal*. Reprinted by permission of Indiana University Press.

Selection 29. From "The Reasonable Woman: Sense and Sensibility in Sexual Harassment Law." Reprinted by permission of *Dissent*.

Selection 30. From "Closing the 'Bisexual Defense' Loophole in Title VII Cases." Reprinted by permission of the *University of Minnesota Law Review*.

Selection 31. From "Understanding, and Explaining and Eliminating Sexual Harassment." Reprinted by permission of the author.

Selection 32. From *Society* (1991). Reprinted by permission of Transaction Publishers.

Selection 33. From *The Morning After*. Reprinted by permission of Little, Brown and Company.

Selection 34. From *Vamps and Tramps*. Reprinted by permission of the author and Alfred A. Knopf.

Selection 35. From *Sexual Harassment*. Reprinted by permission of Rowman & Littlefield.

Selection 36. From "Sex Is the Least of It." Reprinted by permission of *The Nation*.

Selection 37. From *Heterophobia*. Reprinted by permission of Rowman & Littlefield.

Selection 38. From *NWSA Journal*. Reprinted by permission of Indiana University Press.

Selection 39. From *The Myth of Male Power*. Reprinted by permission of Simon and Schuster.

Selection 40. From *Race-ing Justice*. Reprinted by permission of Simon and Schuster.

Selection 41. From *Rethinking Sexual Harrasment*. Reprinted by permission of the Pluto Press.

Selection 42. From "Immigrant Latina Domestic Workers and Sexual Harassment." Reprinted by permission of the author and the *American University Journal of Gender, Social Policy and the Law*.

Selection 43. From "Japan Abuzz Over Sexual Harassment." Reprinted by permission of *The Christian Science Monitor*.

Selection 44. From "Sexual Harassment of Working Women in India." First published in the International Bar Association Section on Legal Practice Journal. *International Legal Practioner*. December, 1999.

Selection 45. From "Shameful Silence." This article was first printed in Business Mexico, a monthly publication of the American Chamber of Commerce of Mexico, A.C.

Selection 46. From "Sexual Harassment and Human Rights in Latin America." Reprinted by permission of Fordham University Press and the author.

:• Introduction

Who put this pubic hair on my Coke?

> *—Comment allegedly made by Clarence Thomas, director of the Equal Employment Opportunity Commission, within earshot of office employee Anita Hill. In 1991, on the basis of this and other allegations, Hill accused Thomas of sexual harassment.*

[D]escribe a belly dancer: Take a bowl of Jell-O, stick it on a plate, hold a vibrator underneath it, and watch it jiggle. . . . How many of you have tried this?

> *—Example of a "working definition," allegedly given during class by University of New Hampshire Professor J. Donald Silva. Citing several forms of alleged sexual misconduct, some of Silva's female students accused him of sexual harassment in 1993.*

Well, I don't want to make you do anything you don't want to do. . . . You are smart. Let's keep this between ourselves.

> *—Statement attributed to Governor Bill Clinton of Arkansas by state employee Paula Jones. Jones alleged that Clinton, with his pants unzipped, requested that she "kiss it" in Clinton's hotel room where she claimed she was invited to visit. Jones testified that she refused Clinton's request. In 1998, Jones filed a lawsuit against Clinton, accusing him of sexual harassment.*

As we enter the twenty-first century, allegations of sexual harassment have become more public, more widespread, and more controversial than ever before. The allegations described above reflect a trend that shows no signs of abating. Navy Secretary H. Lawrence Garrett stepped down from his military post in 1992 after allegations that he failed to fully investigate the sexual harassment of at least twenty-six women by scores of male naval officers at the Navy's 1991 Tailhook Convention. Senator Bob Packwood resigned in 1995 after repeated allegations of his sexually harassing conduct toward several congressional staff members became public knowledge. In 1998, Mitsubishi Motors settled a $34 million sexual harassment suit filed by 350 of its female workers, the largest such settlement against a U.S. corporation. That same year, the Supreme Court decided more sexual harassment cases than at any other time in its history.

The current public concern over sexual harassment is a recent phenomenon. In the mid-1970s, feminists such as Lin Farley and Catharine MacKinnon were naming and writing about sexual harassment with relatively little public support, despite their extensive documentation that men's sexual harassment of women is an entrenched and long-standing feature of the U.S. workplace. Feminist legal and political activism eventually encouraged women to file lawsuits against their harassers, resulting in the Supreme Court's recognition in 1986 of sexual harassment as a violation of federal antidiscrimination law. However, Anita Hill's 1991 public accusations of sexual harassment by Supreme Court Justice nominee Clarence Thomas during his tenure as Director of the Equal Employment Opportunity Commission (EEOC) galvanized the nation, and the world, to look more closely at a phenomenon whose precise description and remedy remain contentious to this day.

Sexual Harassment: Issues and Answers is a collection of contemporary popular and scholarly writing on the subject of sexual harassment. Chosen for their readability, concise presentation, and contribution to current debate, the book's fifty-seven selections examine the most compelling and perplexing questions surrounding sexual harassment, posed by scholars, activists, researchers, and the lay public alike: *What counts as a case of sexual harassment?* Is it a case of sexual attraction gone wrong? A cultural expression of male dominance over women? How persistent or severe must the conduct be? Can women sexually harass men? Can men sexually harass other men? Can students sexually harass their teachers? *What is wrong with sexual harassment?* Is it an abuse of power? A clumsy attempt at a sexual overture? An instance of sex discrimination? *How extensive is the problem?* Is sexual harassment limited to the workplace? Is it limited to the United States? Is it a case of feminist exaggeration and a few boorish men? Is it a pervasive and institutionalized means for the oppression of women? *Who is liable under the law for sexual harassment, and how should they be held accountable?* Should employers be liable for the sexually harassing conduct of their employees? Should universities be liable for the sexually harassing conduct of their faculty? How do victims seek redress when they are harassed outside of work or school? *How should we prevent sexual harassment from occurring?* Should we put harassers in jail? Assess them damages? Assess their employers damages? Offer workplace and campus counseling? Are voluntary public policy guidelines better than legal sanctions?

Perhaps the most significant question for a twenty-first century faced with the challenges of a new global politics is: *Whose decisions count in answering the important questions raised by sexual harassment?* If the power to define and implement sexual harassment policy for a multicultural, indeed international, community remains primarily in the hands of affluent, Anglo-European, heterosexual men, then we must look to other cultural voices and contexts if we are to get a comprehensive and fair accounting of what is at stake. The question is also complicated by the fact that not only do liberals differ from conservatives and feminists from their critics in their understanding and analysis of sexual harassment, but those of the same political persuasion often differ among themselves as to how to resolve the many issues involved. Conservatives may agree that Title VII of the Civil Rights Act of 1964 prohibiting sex discrimination in the workplace is unsuited to the task of addressing the legal wrong of sexual harassment, but they may disagree over whether and how the law should address it. Liberals may agree that the Equal Employment Opportunity Commission should be given authority to issue regulatory guidelines to employers and legislators on what constitutes sexual harassment, but they may disagree over precisely what the guidelines should say. Many feminists may agree that the underlying problem with sexual harassment is its discriminatory stereotyping of male and female sexual roles, but they may disagree as to how to implement the social changes necessary to bring about a culture-wide reconceptualization of gender.

THE NATURE OF SEXUAL HARASSMENT

Thus, the anthology is organized to reflect both the variety of questions raised and the variety of ways that any one question about sexual harassment may be addressed. Part I (The Nature of Sexual Harassment) reveals how competing philosophical presuppositions about sexual harassment complicate any attempt to reach consensus about its meaning. Selection 1 is an excerpt from Lin Farley's groundbreaking 1978 book, *Sexual Shakedown: The Sexual Harassment of Women on the Job.* Farley was among the first feminists to identify and theorize sexual harassment in the workplace in terms of men's economic oppression of women. Farley describes in historical detail how men's sexual harassment of women—from unwelcome staring, touching, and sexual comments to sexual extortion and rape—forced women out of the jobs men wanted and drove women into female job ghettos where wages and job security were lowest. Farley's exposé made visible some of the inner workings of an institutionalized system of male dominance aimed at ensuring that economic power remained in the hands of men. Farley urged women of all cultural backgrounds to refuse to accept men's harassing behavior, believing that because women are socialized under patriarchy to be deferential to men and to acquiesce to their demands, they may too readily accept the treatment they receive. However, Farley defined sexual harassment as *male* behavior that asserts a woman's sex role over her function as worker; she also referred to sexual harassment almost exclusively in terms of the organizational power of male employers to coerce their female employees. Thus, it remains unclear how we are to understand women's harassment of men at work or how we are to assess a coworker's harassment of another coworker, the so-called hostile environment harassment that is the most common form of sexual harassment in the workplace.

Selection 2 is taken from Catharine A. MacKinnon's *Sexual Harassment of Working Women: A Case of Sex Discrimination,* published in 1979. MacKinnon points out the economic advantage men reap from men's sexual harassment of women and from women's socialized acquiescence to their harassment. However, MacKinnon goes further to argue that sexual harassment must be understood as sex discrimination, that is, as discrimination against women *because they are women,* stemming from men's (and women's) well-socialized expectations that men should dominate women sexually and women should acquiesce to male desire. MacKinnon argues that sexual harassment in the workplace is a form of the unequal treatment of women disadvantaged by the "social realities of sex," specifically the discriminatory sex roles that put women in the socially and economically subordinate position of sexual object. MacKinnon's work is extraordinarily significant because her analysis of sexual harassment as sex discrimination was used by federal court to allow women to sue for sexual harassment as a violation of Title VII of the Civil Rights Act of 1964 prohibiting sex discrimination in employment. Critics of MacKinnon's analysis have argued that sexual harassment is a private matter between individuals that has nothing to do with prejudicial attitudes about women as a class and thus should not be adjudicated under federal antidiscrimination law.

Sociologist Barbara A. Gutek agrees with both Farley and MacKinnon that there is something importantly sex-based about sexual harassment. In Selection 3, Gutek describes a host of research surveys designed to determine exactly how people define sexual harassment and how common it is. Noting that the vast majority of sexual harassment victims are women and that men are much less likely than women to label a given behavior as sexual harassment, Gutek suggests that sexual harassment is the result of what she calls "sex-role spillover" in which socialized and stereotypic expectations about women as sexual objects carry over into the workplace. Such expectations encourage both women and men to think of women solely in sexual terms, making it impossible to consider women as sexual beings and as workers. Such role expectations are to be contrasted with men's sex role stereotype as "organizational beings" whose competence and initiative in the workplace are not shrouded by the specter of their sexuality. Gutek does not make MacKinnon's claim that the dominance of men as a class must be understood in terms of the sexual dominance of men over women, only that men's desire for power and control in the workplace can be explained in terms of sex role stereotypes. However, based on Gutek's analysis, we are left without an explanation of women's sexual harassment of men if there is no male stereotype of sexual object to "spill over" into a woman's workplace, or how men might harass other men on this model. And as in MacKinnon's analysis described above, Gutek offers no analysis of sexual harassment in other areas of women's lives besides the workplace.

In Selection 4, Jan Crosthwaite and Graham Priest argue that sexual harassment "is any form of sexual behaviour by members of a dominant gender group towards members of a subordinate gender group whose typical effect is to cause members of the subordinate group to experience their powerlessness as a member of that group." The authors freely admit that their analysis precludes women from sexually harassing men. According to their model, we can identify true cases of sexual harassment by their capacity to oppress women as a class: Sexual harassment causes women to feel powerless *as women*. According to the authors, this account of sexual harassment fits a wide variety of cases of sexual harassment, from coercive sex to off-color jokes, wolf whistles, and pornographic pinups. The authors also argue that their definition has the advantage of explaining women's humiliation at their harassment, the asymmetry in frequency and reaction to sexual harassment between men and women, and the incidence of sexual harassment at home, school, or work. The authors also suggest that the harassing treatment of men by other men in prison fits their model because harassment victims in prison become feminized by their harassers as a way of asserting individual dominance and control over other inmates. Male employees may feel powerless when they are summarily fired by their female employers or be annoyed or embarrassed at a female employer's attempt to coerce them into sex. However, the authors argue that (free) men who live in a patriarchal society will not be reminded of their own powerlessness *as men* by such actions and so will not be truly harassed by them. Nevertheless, there may be quite a few readers who would argue that women wield their own fair share of sexual power over men; one may also question whether organizational power always plays second fiddle to the power of gender.

Mane Hajdin suggests that the entire concept of sexual harassment should be rejected as unhelpful and confusing in assessing the wrongness of the conduct in question. One of the arguments he offers for this conclusion is given in Selection 5, in which Hajdin argues that many, although not all, instances of what is called sexual harassment are in fact instances of adultery, promiscuity, or insensitivity to another's feelings. Because, according to at least some people, adultery, promiscuity, and insensitivity are all instances of wrongful conduct, Hajdin argues that we should let the so-called harassing conduct be evaluated morally and legally on those grounds. Instead, by calling the conduct sexual harassment, we obscure the grounds of its wrongness and end up making the conduct into something it is not, such as an instance of illegal sex discrimination or an instance of inappropriate sex stereotyping. Feminists who are critical of this line of reasoning have asked whether it is not the adultery, promiscuity, and insensitivity to another's feelings in some instances of sexual harassment that obscure the institutionalized wrong that constitutes discrimination against women. Indeed, the feminist aphorism "the personal is political" is meant to expose the privatization and normalization of the sexual oppression of women that many believe have legitimized sexual harassment for so long.

VARIETIES OF SEXUAL HARASSMENT

Part II (Varieties of Sexual Harassment) describes the diversity of contexts in which sexual harassment occurs. In Selection 6, Deborah Tannen describes sexual harassment in government, business, and medicine to show how men use sexual harassment to establish and maintain authority. Former Senator Bob Packwood allegedly propositioned his congressional aides and campaign workers on a regular basis or lunged at them lustily in parking lots or elevators (see Selection 23). Tannen recounts how she deftly removed herself from the hotel room of the editor of her first book, who, after reviewing her manuscript, began undressing in her presence. Gynecologists and psychiatrists have been known to sexually abuse patients made particularly vulnerable on an examining table or therapist's couch. Tannen also suggests that by calling attention to a woman's sexuality, a man can remind a woman of her physical vulnerability and secondary status as sexual object, even when she is in a position of organizational power. Thus, for example, a male visitor to a congresswoman's office can make her wary simply by signing the daily log as "Dick Hurtz, 131 Penis Drive." Male patients can unnerve their female physicians by attempting to grope them during an appointment, requesting unneeded genital exams, or sending sex-related objects and letters. Some female physicians report being sexually assaulted by their male patients. Tannen describes how she was the target of an obscene phone call when she was the featured guest at a television call-in talk show. In Tannen's view, by associating women and sex with vulnerability and subordination—and by associating men and sex with power and aggression—sexual harassment becomes an effective tool for maintaining gender hierarchy.

Selection 7 by Eloise Salholz and Douglas Waller describes the pervasive sexual misconduct by naval aviators at their 1991 Tailhook Convention. The convention was held at the Las Vegas Hilton ostensibly for networking and continuing education but became, in the words of one officer, an "animal house off the high seas." The most widely reported sexual harassment involved the so-called gauntlet, in which unsuspecting women, many of whom were naval officers themselves, would enter a long narrow hotel corridor only to be physically thrust down a line of male officers on either side. The men would grope, poke, and paw their surrounded victims, often to the point of removing some of their clothes. An officer stationed at the elevator would cry "Decks afoul" for women deemed too unattractive to attack and "Decks awash" for fair game. The authors report that seventy officers were implicated in the scandal, which included allegations of sexual battery and attempted rape, although all charges were ultimately dismissed and cover-up of the misconduct was rampant.

Selection 8 by Linda Bird Francke elaborates on sexual harassment in the military with a host of compelling examples. A female Army recruit's male supervisor grabbed her while she was driving sixty miles per hour on an airfield whose floodlights she had been ordered to negotiate at high speed. A Navy subordinate was intimidated into visiting her captain after hours at his request, in order to sexually excite him by talking dirty to him. "He's a damn captain in the Navy and I'm a measly seaman. What else could I do?" she said. According to Francke, 43 percent of the enlisted women interviewed by Army auditors in 1982 reported that their superiors successfully bartered sex for promotion because the women were convinced they had no other means of getting ahead. Army commanders, who are often the perpetrators of harassment, are still largely responsible for investigating and judging harassment cases; they have no incentive to report harassment by others when commanders receive perks based on problem-free leadership records. However, as the incidents at Tailhook make clear, peer sexual harassment can be just as brutal as a supervisor's, especially when men believe that their place in the gender hierarchy is being threatened. Francke recounts how a female recruit was pinned to the floor by another male recruit (while two other male recruits watched), groped, kissed, and told that she was going to get what she "deserved." During the 1980s, male officers succeeded in ousting hundreds of fellow female officers from the Army with accusations of lesbianism at a time when just being a homosexual was grounds for dismissal. Given a military culture that values unwavering obedience to superior officers, a closing of ranks under fire, and a machismo that regards women as unsuitable for the rigors of military life, Francke argues that the sexual harassment of women in the military is endemic to the institution itself.

Tina Daunt and Anne-Marie O'Conner in Selection 9 document sexual harassment in the Los Angeles County Sheriff's Department, where, like the U.S. military, women are still regarded by many male officers as an unwelcome presence in a man's world. And, like the military, ambitious women are presented with an obstacle course, not a meritocracy, in their pursuit of promotion. Deborah Tannen's discussion of sexualizing women as a means of instilling feelings of vulnerability and humiliation is relevant here: One female police officer was unnerved to find lace panties in her mailbox and a dildo in her patrol car, placed there by officers unwilling to countenance a woman in their professional ranks. Male officers openly referred to sanitary napkins as "manhole covers," and porn foldouts in a supervisor's office were decorated with a photograph of his face pinned to the crotch. Daunt and O'Connor point out that male officers' sexual harassment of the women in their ranks was often not only humiliating but also life-threatening. Male deputies would ignore female deputies' calls for backup in dangerous situations. Inmates threatened one female deputy in charge of the jail with sexual assault after a disgruntled boss told them in her presence, "Us men have to stick together." According to the authors, many of the female deputies who left the sheriff's department were close to mental collapse or in fear for their lives. And when female officers were bold enough to file written complaints, they were either ignored, or, when they were taken seriously, the publicity only made the harassment worse. Police helicopters allegedly buzzed the house of a female deputy who had lodged a formal sexual harassment complaint against her supervisor.

Sexual harassment in a Mitsubishi Motors manufacturing plant in Normal, Illinois, during the 1990s is the subject of Stephen Braun's article in Selection 10. Over an eight-year period, 350 female employees were the alleged victims of hundreds of instances of sexual harassment at Mitsubishi. Men's bathroom walls were covered with crudely drawn nudes of female employees, with the women's names and telephone numbers written alongside cartoon phalli and graphic descriptions of sex acts. Low-level supervisors threatened retaliation against women who refused to perform oral sex. Production-line workers routinely grabbed female workers' breasts, buttocks, and genitals. One assembly line reminiscent of Tailhook was called the "zoo": "[W]orkers regularly hooted like monkeys and hoisted rating scorecards whenever young women passed by their lines." They also subjected women to blasts from air guns used to tighten metal screws and wandered the floor with coffee cups depicting naked women. For years, the women at Mitsubishi suffered in silence, for reasons typical of harassment victims: They did not feel they would be believed; they were too embarrassed to say anything; they feared reprisal if they spoke out. Mitsubishi provided much-needed jobs, educational support, tax revenue, and charitable donations to the city, and many in the community were unwilling to name Mitsubishi as an evil benefactor. In fact, when some women finally did report their mistreatment to Mitsubishi officials, the company allegedly ignored their complaints. (Settlement of the class action lawsuit filed against the company by the Equal Employment Opportunity Commission is the subject of Selection 26.) Despite the Supreme Court's ruling in *Meritor Savings Bank v. Vinson* (1986) that sexual harassment is a form of sex discrimination actionable under Title VII (see Selection 51) and the Court's ruling in *Harris v. Forklift Systems* (1993) that victims of sexual harassment need not demonstrate psychological trauma to successfully sue for damages (see Selection 53), many victims of sexual harassment remain unconvinced that their complaints will be taken seriously.

Selection 11 by Billie Wright Dziech and Linda Weiner examines sexual harassment on college campuses. Dziech and Weiner describe harassing male professors who make sexist or obscene remarks in class, and professors who stare constantly at female students or consistently comment on their appearance in front of other students. Harassing male professors kiss, squeeze, pat, and pinch their female students in private office hours or conferences, repeatedly make requests for dates, or ask to visit students at home alone. The authors argue that female students may "hassle" their male professors with seductive or flirtatious behavior, but female students cannot in principle harass their professors; students have neither the institutional power nor the academic authority required to perpetrate real harassment. It is argued that students, not professors, suffer from the loss of self-esteem, diminished intellectual self-confidence, and fear of retaliation (bad grades, withheld recommendations, and the like) that are constitutive of the harasser's abuse of his academic authority. Students, not professors, feel frightened, guilty, complicit, powerless, and alone when they are harassed by their professors, particularly if they are women of color or women enrolled in traditionally male fields. And students, not professors, must often drop required classes or change schedules, majors, or even schools to avoid further harassment. In this way, campus harassment mirrors the sexual harassment described in the workplaces above, where behavior that a woman is powerless to stop can ruin her career and destroy her self-image. However, readers should ask themselves whether male students may successfully harass their female professors, especially if they are older students, and whether any student with the power to report her male professor for professional misconduct has the power to successfully harass him.

Selection 12 by Myra Sadker and David Sadker suggests that even if elementary, junior high, and high school students may not successfully harass their teachers, students may certainly harass other students. Sexual taunts directed at young girls by boys—such as "Get down on your knees and give me a blow job," or "My balls itch. Come over and scratch them"—are common. Boys snap girls' bras, lift up or pull down their skirts, wear mirrors on their shoes for a less obtrusive look, poke at girls' bodies with pencils, and draw bathroom graffiti disturbingly similar to the Mitsubishi graffiti described above. And like the Mitsubishi assemblers' scorecards and the Tailhook aviators' gauntlet prerequisites, boys stand at the end of cafeteria food lines with grade cards one to ten to evaluate the attractiveness of the girls who pass by. Boys declare, "Grab a Piece of Ass Week" and "skirt flip-up day," and they circulate lists such as "The Twenty Sluttiest Girls in School." Girls are sexually teased on school buses where there is no escape and, unlike most workplace harassment, are harassed by their peers openly and publicly in stairwells, gym classes, and schoolrooms where the humiliation is greatest.

As with university campus harassment, women of color appear to be targeted more often and more harshly than their white counterparts. This is not to say that teacher/student harassment is uncommon. The authors suggest that music teachers, coaches, driver education teachers, and club advisers who spend time with students in private settings are the adults most likely to harass students. Teachers tease girls about their bodies, massage their shoulders, or "accidentally" rub up against their breasts when helping them with an assignment. Most cases are never reported and teachers' licenses seldom revoked because, like military recruits, students are taught to respect academic authority figures, and, like military commanders, schools seldom volunteer to make their personnel problems public. However, Title IX of the Education Amendments of 1972 allows students to sue educational institutions for sexual harassment as a form of sex discrimination, if the institutions receive federal funds, and the Supreme Court has ruled on two school-based sexual harassment cases, albeit with mixed results. *Franklin v. Gwinnett County Public Schools* (1992) allows students to sue school districts for compensatory damages in sexual harassment cases (see Selection 52). However, *Gebser et al. v. Lago Vista Independent School District* (1998) limits the liability for those damages to schools whose officials with the authority to institute corrective measures have actual notice of a teacher's misconduct but are deliberately indifferent to it (see Selection 56). Readers may wish to compare the decision in *Gebser* to the Supreme Court's decision in the workplace sexual harassment case of *Faragher v. City of Boca Raton* (1998). In *Faragher,* the majority held that despite the fact that city officials did not know about the harassment of female lifeguards by the city's lifeguard supervisor, the city was liable for the harassment because the city, by hiring the supervisor, had invested in the supervisor the authority to act on its behalf (see Selection 55).

Selection 13 by Amy Harmon offers an account of e-mail harassment on the campus of the California Institute of Technology. A promising doctoral candidate was expelled in 1995 for allegedly sending his former girlfriend and her new boyfriend harassing e-mail messages detailing his "happy life in bed" with his erstwhile lover. The case is controversial because the expelled student used e-mail without an electronic signature or encryption to identify himself as the sender, so that someone else with his password could have sent the messages without his knowledge. E-mail can be an especially effective form of harassment because multiple messages to the same person can be sent easily and anonymously, and a single message can be distributed to several people simultaneously. Student-generated lists such as "Top 75 reasons why women (bitches) should not have freedom of speech" have encouraged college campuses to consider how to balance their students' freedom of expression and increasing use of the Internet against the harm caused by e-mail harassment.

So-called public harassment is the focus of Jan Buckwald's discussion in Selection 14. She describes her successful confrontation with a group of carpenters who are hooting and whistling at passing female joggers while the carpenters are working on Buckwald's apartment roof. Her experience reflects the commonly held view that women must first perceive themselves as capable of stopping their harassment if they wish to confront their harassers successfully. (Buckwald threatened to have the carpenters removed from the job by requesting to speak to their supervisor.) Some observers consider such hands-on resolutions to be especially important in cases of public harassment because Titles VII and IX do not cover the sexual harassment of women that occurs outside of work or school. However, given the threatening content of so much sexual harassment, readers might consider how safe it may be to confront one's harassers in situations where no one else is readily available to help diffuse the situation.

Selection 15 by Joan Biskupic discusses the Supreme Court's 1998 decision in *Oncale v. Sundowner Offshore Services* that same-sex harassment counts as sex discrimination under Title VII. The decision is significant because same-sex harassment can occur whether the parties are heterosexual or homosexual; men can harass other men and women other women when there is no sexual attraction between them or when no sexual motives underlie the harassment. Thus, the ruling signaled to gay rights groups that Title VII could be interpreted as prohibiting discrimination based on sexual orientation as well as sex (see Selections 18 and 30 for further discussion of this issue). In the Supreme Court case in question, a heterosexual man named Joseph Oncale charged that his straight coworkers on an offshore oil rig sexually harassed him by subjecting him to persistent sexual humiliation and abuse, which allegedly included sexual assault and threats of rape in the company shower. After the company failed to take action to stop the alleged abuse, Oncale field a sexual harassment claim with the Equal Employment Opportunity Commission. (For excerpts from the *Oncale* case, see Selection 54.) Questions remain as to whether Oncale can prove that he was the target of sex discrimination and whether or not Oncale's treatment was more akin to rough hazing than actual harassment.

Given the variety of sexual harassment described in Part II, the reader might also consider the following: If threatening conduct toward a woman is not explicitly sexual (as in the case of buzzing helicopters), should it still be labeled sexual harassment? If no single person is the target of harassment (as in some cases of office pornography) or if a person is offended by conduct directed at someone else (as in some cases of sexual contact), who is discriminated against? In what ways is a teacher's sexual harassment of his student comparable to a supervisor's sexual harassment of his employee? Is the harassment of a homosexual man by a heterosexual man a case of sex discrimination or a case of discrimination based on sexual orientation? Is there a difference? And if the sexual misconduct is not repeated, or occurs only once, is the conduct appropriately labeled "harassment"?

SEXUAL HARASSMENT AND THE LAW

Part III (Sexual Harassment and the Law) begins in Selection 16 with a fact sheet from the Equal Employment Opportunity Commission summarizing the Commission's guidelines for identifying and preventing sexual harassment. Of particular importance is the fact sheet's definition of sexual harassment, which delineates two basic categories of sexual misconduct: what courts have referred to as "quid pro quo" ("this for that") sexual harassment in which sex is made a condition of employment, and so-called hostile environment sexual harassment in which the conduct unreasonably interferes with a person's work performance or creates an intimidating, hostile, or offensive work environment. Critics of the guidelines have argued that words such as "unreasonably" and "offensive" are much too ambiguous to be of any practical value to courts or policymakers, and that someone can be offended by conduct that may be clumsy or unintentional, not harassing. Supporters argue that the guidelines appropriately define sexual harassment in terms of a work environment's offensiveness to the victim precisely because good intentions or clumsiness may still amount to sexual harassment from the victim's point of view (see Selections 27 and 28).

In Selection 17, Susan L. Webb provides a history of the development of sexual harassment law. She recounts how the first federal court cases in the 1970s were not successful in establishing sexual harassment as a form of sex discrimination under Title VII because the courts interpreted sexual harassment as a "personal proclivity, peculiarity or mannerism" as opposed to a class or group prejudice. However, when women successfully showed that there was a clear relationship between their sexual harassment and negative employment consequences such as firing, demotion, or poor performance reviews, the courts ruled women's sexual harassment the result of workplace conditions that applied differently to men and women, thus a violation of Title VII's prohibition of sex discrimination in employment. In 1972, an Equal Employment Opportunity Commission was created and invested with the power to file federal discrimination lawsuits on behalf of alleged victims. The 1980s saw the publication of EEOC guidelines used by courts to identify cases of sexual harassment and a federal court's determination that both quid pro quo and hostile environment sexual harassment are actionable forms of sex discrimination. In 1986, the Supreme Court ruled in *Meritor Savings Bank v. Vinson* that sexual harassment on the job is a form of sex discrimination even if the victim suffers no economic loss, confirming lower courts' determination that a hostile work environment can constitute sexual harassment. The Court also ruled that for sexual harassment to be actionable, it must be sufficiently severe or pervasive to create an abusive working environment (see Selection 51). Federal courts continued to offer their own interpretations of the EEOC guidelines throughout the 1990s, including both the decision in *Robinson v. Jacksonville Shipyards* (1991) that pornography in the workplace can constitute hostile environment sexual harassment and the decision in *Ellison v. Brady* (1991) that sexual harassment should be determined on the basis of what victims of sexual harassment, the vast majority of whom are women, find unreasonable—what has come to be known as the "reasonable woman" standard for determining sexual harassment (see Selection 29). That same year, the first federal class-action sexual harassment suit was filed, allowing women such as the 350 employees at Mitsubishi four years later to put serious financial pressure on their company to resolve the sexual harassment claims made against it. As mentioned previously, the Supreme Court ruled in *Franklin v. Gwinnett County Public Schools* (1992) that harassed students could sue to collect monetary damages under Title IX of the Education Amendments of 1972 (see Selections 48 and 52) and ruled in *Harris v. Forklift Systems, Inc.* (1993) that claimants need not provide evidence of psychological trauma or inability to continue working to prove they were sexually harassed (see Selection 53). Readers may also wish to review excerpts from three 1998 Supreme Court cases on sexual harassment, found in Selections 54, 55, and 56.

William Petrocelli and Barbara Kate Repa offer a brief legal analysis in Selection 18 of the Supreme Court's decision in the alleged sexual harassment case of *Oncale v. Sundowner Offshore Services* (1998) (also see Selections 15 and 54). The authors argue that the Supreme Court's decision in *Oncale* effectively expands the groups protected under Title VII because by ruling that same-sex discrimination is a form of sexual harassment in violation of federal law, the Court has ruled that harassed gay men and lesbians can seek legal redress under Title VII. However, as the authors point out, Title VII, while prohibiting sex discrimination, does not explicitly prohibit discrimination based on sexual orientation. The question of whether and how sex discrimination under Title VII applies to cases in which the harassed person is gay or lesbian continues to puzzle scholars and the public alike (see Selection 30).

In Selection 19, Robert J. Shoop describes the procedures for filing sexual harassment claims with the EEOC and the Office of Civil Rights, the federal bureau responsible for filing federal discrimination lawsuits on behalf of those seeking redress under Title IX of the Education Amendments of 1972 (see Selection 50). Shoop points out that both the EEOC and the Office of Civil Rights may be involved in campus sexual harassment claims: Faculty, nonstudent staff, and students employed by the university may file sexual harassment lawsuits against their schools as employers and against their schools as educational institutions receiving federal funds. This double filing can be especially important in collecting damages because, unlike Title VII, there is no limit placed on Title IX damage awards, which may include awards for pain and suffering, emotional distress, attorney's fees, and tuition refunds, as well as changes in campus sexual harassment policy.

Anita Hill offers in Selection 20 her account of her 1991 interrogation by the Senate Judiciary Committee charged with investigating her allegations of sexual harassment by Supreme Court Justice nominee Clarence Thomas during his tenure as Director of the Equal Employment Opportunity Commission. She reminds her readers that she did not initiate her contact with the Senate, nor was she responsible for the media frenzy and public outcry over her allegations, which were leaked to the press after she submitted to the Committee what she believed would be a confidential statement. She remains convinced that she could not have stopped her harassment by Thomas except by leaving the EEOC because few would have believed that the head of a federal agency responsible for filing sexual harassment lawsuits against alleged perpetrators would be a perpetrator himself. Hill points out that members of the Judiciary Committee refused to recognize that different people respond to sexual harassment in different ways—that an angry response to Thomas's behavior could have made her situation at the office much worse (as Daunt and O'Connor's description of the harassment of female police officers show in Selection 9) or that maintaining contact with Thomas after she left the EEOC was neither a matter of career opportunism nor sexual pursuit of Thomas. Rather, Hill contends that her continued contact with Thomas was a legitimate means of obtaining the kinds of employment records and job recommendations that a competent former employee in search of a new job could expect from her former boss. She reports how her publicized allegations were met with threats of rape, sodomy, and other forms of physical assault. She describes her humiliation at having to answer senators' unnecessarily provocative questions about Thomas's alleged sexual misconduct in front of millions of television viewers, when she had already described the conduct in great detail in her opening statement. Readers may ask to what extent one's political affiliations and cultural background affect one's views about sexual harassment, and whether men must be specially educated about the oppression of women if they are to adjudicate women's sexual harassment cases fairly (see Selections 21 and 29).

In Selection 21, Beverly Grier documents how and why African-American women have differed so markedly in their reactions to Anita Hill's charges of sexual harassment against Clarence Thomas. Grier suggests that black women who did not believe Hill's Senate testimony have internalized the sexist and racist beliefs of the dominant culture in which they live, including the belief that women, particularly black women, are devious, opportunistic, and sexually voracious. Grier speculates that those African-American women who believed that Hill was mistaking trivial sexual banter for sexual harassment may be so immersed in a male culture of violence against women that they are unable to recognize that violence when it appears. However, many of these same African-American women have argued that social issues such as poverty, crime, drugs, police harassment, and racism are much more important to bring to the public's attention than one woman's sexual harassment. One of the most troubling complaints came from African-American women who believed that Hill was being a traitor to her race even if her allegations against Thomas were true. According to this view, Hill should have been supporting a fellow black in his pursuit of a seat on the Supreme Court bench instead of reinforcing on national television white stereotypes of black sexuality and professional incompetence. Not surprisingly, black female supporters of Hill tended to be similar to Hill in age, social class, and education, suggesting to Grier that those who were critical of Hill could not identify with what they considered to be an elitist and overly assimilated black woman. Critics of the "reasonable woman" standard have argued that such divergent views show that there is no one "reasonable woman" to which a reasonableness standard may consistently refer; others have contended that surveys on the pervasiveness of sexual harassment will always be suspect when women have such different views on what counts as sexually harassing conduct (see Selections 29, 32, and 33).

Orlando Patterson argues in Selection 22 that even if we presume that all of Anita Hill's allegations against Clarence Thomas are true, Thomas can still be regarded as a sensitive man who respected his female employees. From Patterson's point of view, if we understand Thomas's behavior from the perspective of his own Southern, black subculture, Thomas's conduct can be considered a "down-home style of courting" that someone from a similar cultural background, like Anita Hill, would have understood. Patterson contends that this explains why Hill never filed a sexual harassment complaint against Thomas and why she kept in contact with him after she left the EEOC. Patterson goes on to argue that if Thomas did lie under oath to the Senate Judiciary Committee, he probably had good reason to do so because he could expect that his conduct would have been misunderstood and unfairly vilified by a white audience. According to Patterson, contrary to feminist naysayers and political cynics, Thomas's Supreme Court nomination should show us how much progress we have made in race relations in the United States. However, if Patterson is right about the progress of race relations in America, readers may wish to ask themselves why Thomas would have felt it necessary to lie under oath about behavior his white audience would not have understood. Moreover, on what basis could Patterson construe the comment, "Who put this public hair on my Coke?" (quoted at the beginning of this Introduction) as a "down-home style of courting"? Such questions raise the larger issue of whether appeals to cultural relativism can excuse conduct that persons from a variety of cultural backgrounds believe is offensive.

In Selection 23, Allan Freedman recounts the allegations of sexual harassment against former Senator Bob Packwood of Oregon, which the Senate Ethics Committee compiled and presented to Packwood while he was still in office in 1995. The Senate rejected Packwood's characterization of himself as nothing more than an "overeager kisser," when testimonies from numerous women combined with Packwood's own diaries implicate Packwood in a persistent pattern of sexual misconduct. Packwood allegedly propositioned women who worked for him and hounded them if they refused. He allegedly fondled women he asked to dance with him and chased a staff assistant around her office desk. He allegedly grabbed aides and campaign workers in parking lots or elevators and stuck his tongue in their mouths. Yet Packwood denied being able to recall any of the conduct of which he was accused, often citing drunkenness, and denied his diaries always reflected an accurate picture of his behavior. However, with evidence that Packwood began altering his diaries upon learning of the allegations against him, the Senate called for Packwood's resignation, to which he agreed later that year. If readers consider Packwood's alleged conduct toward his aides unacceptable, could he have partially redeemed himself if he had volunteered his unaltered diaries to the Ethics Committee and confirmed his victims' testimony?

Selection 24 is an excerpt from the federal court case *Jones v. Clinton* in which Arkansas Judge Susan Webber Wright is asked to determine, not whether Paula Jones's allegations of sexual harassment against President Bill Clinton are true, but rather, if they were true, would they provide sufficient reason for a sexual harassment case against Clinton to go to trial. Jones claimed that Clinton, while governor of Arkansas, made inappropriate sexual advances toward her in his hotel room where she had allegedly been invited to meet him (see the quotation at the beginning of this Introduction). Claiming that she refused these and other sexual overtures by Clinton, Jones testified that she was subjected to hostile and unfair treatment by her boss, whom Clinton had allegedly told her was his "good friend." Jones also contended that when she asked Clinton to make a public apology to her for his conduct, one of Clinton's public relations officers delivered a statement saying that the sexual misconduct described by Jones never occurred. Indeed, Clinton denied ever meeting Jones. Judge Webber Wright dismissed Jones's case, arguing that Jones had shown no compelling evidence that her refusal of Clinton's advances had tangibly affected the terms or conditions of her employment as per Title VII. According to Webber Wright, Jones received all appropriate merit and cost-of-living increases at work, she was given different but no less responsible jobs to perform than before her encounter with Clinton, and any anger her employer may have subsequently directed at her did not result in any negative job evaluations or other job detriment. Moreover, Webber Wright argued that although Clinton's alleged behavior toward Jones was "certainly boorish and offensive," it was not frequent, severe, or threatening enough to satisfy either the pervasiveness or the severity criterion requisite for identifying the conduct as sexual harassment. Given that Webber Wright was judging the merits of the case on the assumption that all of Jones's allegations were true, her disagreement with the reasonableness of Jones's allegations raises yet more questions about whether any one "reasonable woman" standard is possible. Readers may also question whether Webber Wright's controversial interpretation of what counts as illegal sexual misconduct lends credence to the criticism that, as criteria for sexual harassment, "severity" and "pervasiveness" are too vague to be useful no matter what standard of reasonableness is used.

Gloria Steinem argues in Selection 25 that feminists should not desert Clinton despite the number of allegations of sexual harassment lodged against him because, like Webber Wright in the *Jones* case above, Steinem believes Clinton's conduct may have been insensitive but constitutes no cause for legal action. Steinem points out that Clinton made a clumsy and reckless pass at Democratic supporter Kathleen Willey at a point in her life when she was emotionally vulnerable and financially strapped, but Willey pushed him away and it never happened again. According to Steinem, the same description can be given to then-Governor Clinton's pawing of Paula Jones: Clinton's conduct was crude, unwise, and unprofessional but was not sexual harassment because he stopped when she refused his request to "kiss it," and Jones could show no compelling evidence that her job suffered as a result of her refusal. If Clinton lied about these encounters, including lying under oath about his affair with Monica Lewinsky, Steinem claims that Clinton was understandably doing what many American men would have done in the same position: He was trying to keep his private life private. Readers may wish to compare their reactions to these claims to the reactions of readers who wrote to the *New York Times* in which Steinem's article appeared. One writer agrees with Steinem's position that accepting "no" like a gentleman does not constitute harassment. Others were not so sanguine. One reader points out that although Clinton's behavior toward Jones or Willey may not constitute sexual harassment, there is something seriously amiss when a man believes that groping one woman after another until he strikes pay dirt is an acceptable way to behave toward women. Another reader argues that Clinton's behavior is sexual harassment "in any sensible woman's eyes" and is adultery to boot. Still another reader argues in the spirit of Billie Wright Dziech and Linda Weiner that twenty-one-year-old interns such as Monica Lewinsky cannot in principle consent to sex with men who have so much power over their lives and careers.

In Selection 26, Stephen Braun concludes his account of the allegations of sexual harassment at Mitsubishi Motors by describing the $34 million settlement Mitsubishi agreed to pay in 1998 to the 350 female employees who filed an EEOC class action suit against the company. Braun reports that the settlement does not obligate Mitsubishi to admit to any wrongdoing but does require the company to place future policy procedures and complaints concerning sexual harassment under the supervision of an external review board. It was charged that Mitsubishi had intimidated many of its workers to join a company-sponsored protest in front of the Chicago office of the EEOC, and that Mitsubishi officials, who often took their American counterparts to sexually oriented hostess bars in Japan, did not think that sexual harassment would be a serious problem (see Selection 43). Some critics charge that sexual harassment law should remain in the realm of common law torts (see Selection 32). However, the success of federal class action suits such as those against Mitsubishi may weaken this criticism because they put the kind of financial pressure on companies to resolve sexual harassment complaints that private suits often cannot.

Richard Bernstein questions in Selection 27 whether the vigorous campaigns waged on many college campuses to combat sexual harassment do more harm than good. He voices his concerns with reference to the sexual harassment case made in 1992 against J. Donald Silva, English professor at a two-year college affiliate of the University of New Hampshire. Bernstein contends that the university administration has joined a growing trend across the nation to limit academic freedom of expression by fostering a climate of overzealous prosecutions of alleged faculty harassers. Universities accomplish this, Bernstein charges, by aggressively soliciting complaints from students who charge professors with making students feel uncomfortable. Bernstein claims that on campuses with repressive sexual harassment bureaucracies and affirmative action counselors intent on validating students who believe they have been victimized, what a "reasonable student" might consider harassment is biased from the start. According to Bernstein, Silva's allegedly offensive conduct could be construed as inappropriate, even tasteless, but not sexually harassing. (See an example of Silva's alleged sexual harassment at the beginning of this Introduction.) Indeed, Silva claimed his comments were misheard or misrepresented by students in ways that could be construed as sexually harassing when they were not. (For example, Silva says he believed that a vibrator was a massage aid, not a sex aid.) Given Billie Wright Dziech and Linda Weiner's claims about the power that professors have over students, many feminists have argued, contrary to Bernstein, that campuses must adopt student-friendly sexual harassment policies and procedures if students are to feel secure about reporting their harassment. Such policies raise the question of what kinds of evidence schools should require in sexual harassment cases of a professor's word against his students'.

In Selection 28, Mary M. Clark, Chair of the University of New Hampshire Appeals Board that heard the case against Professor Silva, attempts to answer this question. She reports that when Silva heard about his students' complaints, he attempted to defend himself, using angry and intimidating physical gestures, in a restaurant where a group of students had congregated. Several students also reported that Silva would often call them at home to check up on their work, would habitually touch the shoulders of his female students when discussing school assignments (compare the harassment of students by their teachers described by Myra Sadker and David Sadker), and would come unnecessarily close to them during conversations. Such conduct was defended by Silva as a "cultural characteristic" of his Portuguese upbringing that encouraged close physical contact in personal relationships (compare Orlando Patterson's explanation of Clarence Thomas's behavior in terms of Thomas's Southern background). Clark argues that Silva's case did not involve any principle of academic freedom because the comments in question did not express Silva's own intellectual or political ideas, and that the alleged conduct was clearly serious and frequent enough to significantly disturb several students. Indeed, when the case became public, many of Silva's former students wrote to complain of their harassment when he was their professor. According to Clark, at no time did Silva take responsibility for his conduct, saying that any communication problems in his classes were caused by his students' "imperfect knowledge of English usage" and that he never singled out women as targets of his remarks. Clark suggests that conservative critics like Bernstein misrepresent cases like Professor Silva's by focusing on the most obscure or controversial allegations and by intimating (if not claiming) violations of due process without a full accounting of what review boards actually hear (see Selection 27). In September 1994, a New Hampshire appeals court reinstated Silva, deciding that his conduct was constitutionally protected. The question remains as to what students, faculty, and staff can do to make sexual harassment policies and procedures fair to all parties involved.

Kathryn Abrams in Selection 29 critiques the "reasonable woman" standard for adjudicating cases of sexual harassment, first recommended by the court in *Ellison v. Brady* (1991). Abrams notes that the standard was designed, among other things, to delineate more carefully otherwise vague expressions such as "severe" and "pervasive" by identifying what a "reasonable woman" would find harassing. The standard was also introduced to emphasize the importance of identifying sexual harassment based on the point of view of the victims, the vast majority of whom are women. However, Abrams points out that, despite its intent, the standard has come under serious criticism from feminists, who have argued that such a standard reinvigorates the view that women are deserving of special but not equal consideration, thus inhibiting their advancement on equal terms with men in the workplace, and that the standard misleadingly suggests that women of very different cultures and classes have the same views about sexual harassment. In fact, as Susan Webber Wright, Gloria Steinem, and the African-American women described by Beverly Grier show, women may not necessarily be sympathetic to other women's claims of sexual harassment, even if they claim to be feminists. Abrams argues that, given these difficulties, we should return to a "reasonable person" standard that both avoids differentiating reasonable women from reasonable men and proactively informs judges, juries, attorneys, and legislators, with the help of specialists in the field, about the kinds of institutionalized workplace inequities, oppressive sexual stereotypes, and differences among women that can enlighten all persons about women's sexual harassment in the workplace. Readers may wish to ask whether recommending specialists in feminist analyses of *women's* oppression to elaborate a reasonable *person* standard may appear to bias the case in favor of women alleging sexual harassment. Moreover, it remains an open question as to whether men and women already skeptical of feminism who are also the adjudicators of sexual harassment cases (recall Anita Hill's Senate Judiciary Committee) will be swayed by standards of conduct based on it.

In Selection 30, Sandra Levitsky argues that by interpreting sexual harassment as perpetuating gender hierarchies, rather than isolating gender differences, same-sex harassment and bisexual ("equal opportunity") harassment can be appropriately viewed as forms of sex discrimination actionable under Title VII. Levitsky notes that courts asked to decide cases of sexual harassment have typically applied two tests to determine alleged sex discrimination: (1) a "but for" test in which courts ask, "[B]ut for the plaintiff's sex, would the plaintiff have been the object of harassment?" and (2) a comparative test in which courts ask, "Did the harasser treat the plaintiff differently than a similarly situated employee of the opposite sex?" However, Levitsky argues that, based on these two tests, victims of same-sex and bisexual harassment fail to make successful claims of sexual harassment because they cannot show that the harasser harmed the claimant based on the claimant's sex. Rather, the harassment appears to be based on the claimant's sexual orientation, or there is no similarly situated employee of the opposite sex with which to compare the claimant's treatment, or there is no difference in the way the sexes are treated by the harasser. Levitsky contends that in order to capture more actual cases of sexual harassment, we need to ask a very different question, namely, Did the claimant endure "harassment that perpetuated gender stereotypes in the workplace"? This question is grounded in the feminist contention that women's sexual harassment by men constitutes sex discrimination because women are perceived by their male harassers in the workplace as men's domestic and sexual subordinates. According to Levitsky, this dominance analysis can also be applied to same-sex and bisexual harassment cases, thus including them under the umbrella of Title VII's antidiscrimination law; same-sex and bisexual harassers who are motivated by antigay or pro-heterosexual sentiments punish their victims for not being appropriately macho or feminine, and same-sex and bisexual harassers motivated by sexual desire reinforce the idea that being a sexual object is a subordinate status in society. Critics of such an analysis argue that rather than revealing the need for a new test for identifying cases of sexual harassment under Title VII, the failure of traditional tests shows that we should abandon any interpretation of sexual harassment as a form of sex discrimination (see Selections 5 and 32).

CURRENT DEBATES OVER SEXUAL HARASSMENT

Part IV (Current Debates Over Sexual Harassment) offers a broad range of competing views on sexual harassment law and social policy. In Selection 31, James P. Sterba reviews developments in sexual harassment law, hoping to increase our understanding of what is (or, better, what should be) sexual harassment. He then argues that two fundamental beliefs help explain the high incidence of sexual harassment in military and civilian life, respectively: the belief that women do not belong in the military and the belief that while women do belong in civilian life, it is still appropriate to treat them as sexual objects and, hence, as sexually subordinate to men. Lastly, he suggests two positive norms that we need to attend to, in addition to the negative one prohibiting sexual harassment, if we want to better rid society of this practice: (1) a Principle of Androgyny (or Equal Opportunity), which requires that truly desirable traits be equally open to both women and men; and (2) a Principle of Desert, which requires that, when appropriate, we treat people based on their role- or job-related qualifications. Critics of Sterba's account might question whether we must favor a society without prescribed gender roles if we wish to rid ourselves of sexual harassment.

Ellen Frankel Paul asks in Selection 32 what kinds of undesirable behavior women should be legally protected from, and which actions should be morally condemned but not adjudicated. Paul argues that polls that attempt to measure the incidence of sexual harassment must be considered suspect because sexual harassment is "notoriously ill-defined and almost infinitely expandable" to include everything from a neck massage to rape. Some women may find jokes, leers, unwanted requests for dates, and other sexual annoyances at work offensive, but, according to Paul, these annoyances should be suffered in silence, complained of to higher management, or left behind in search of new employment. Paul suggests that it should not be surprising that there is tension in the workplace as women compete for what were once exclusively men's jobs, and she agrees that sexual harassment in the workplace as a result of this tension is a serious matter. However, she claims that we need to make a distinction between being injured and being merely offended, the latter of which can usually be resolved by returning a few "risqué barbs" oneself. In Paul's view, only sexual harassment that is objectively injurious, not subjectively offensive, should have its day in court. Moreover, she contends that, as a type of private injury, sexual harassment should be adjudicated under common law torts, not under federal antidiscrimination law, which she believes unfairly holds companies liable for employees' sexual misconduct.

However, feminists have argued that making sexual harassment a type of illegal sex discrimination compels employers to regard sexual harassment as an institutionalized prejudice against women for which institutions are responsible; in addition to filing under Title VII, private civil actions are still available to victims if they wish to file them. Readers may also wish to ask whether women, especially single mothers, poor women, and women of color, will be able to leave their jobs if they cannot resolve their harassment (see Selection 42); as the Mitsubishi case shows, companies may not be willing to deal fairly and in good faith with employees who decide to stay. Moreover, many women who have experienced sexual harassment would claim that to dispense a few "risqué barbs" to an angry or vindictive harasser is a recipe for disaster (see Selections 7, 8, 9, and 10).

Like Paul, Katie Roiphe in Selection 33 is suspicious of sexual harassment surveys that purport to show the pervasiveness of sexual harassment. Roiphe is particularly critical of feminist researchers who characterize respondents' experience as harassing even when respondents do not perceive their experience this way. Roiphe points out that if sexual harassment is merely equivalent to unwanted sexual behavior, then all women are victims of sexual harassment. Indeed, we all become victims because Roiphe claims that to find sexual attention, people have to give and receive a certain amount of unwanted sexual attention. Roiphe is also extremely disturbed by what she perceives as exaggerated sexual harassment rhetoric on college campuses, where provocative brochures depict imminent crises of sexual assault on vulnerable women by predatory men. Indeed, Roiphe believes such messages institutionalize female weakness in the very ways feminists are supposed to combat. She also contends that sexual harassment paranoia on campuses dampens intellec-

tual exchange between professors and students by making close working relationships between them impossible. Like Richard Bernstein, Roiphe would prefer that campuses write
sexual harassment policies that encourage women to deal with difficult or distasteful aspects of their personal relationships; instead, harassment policies encourage women to file
hostile environment claims whenever they feel uncomfortable. Indeed, Roiphe contends
that it is foolish to expect sex to be either unambiguous or egalitarian when its unpre-
dictability and volatility are part of the eroticism. Feminists critical of Roiphe's assessment
of sexual harassment on college campuses have argued that many women's inability to recognize the wrongness of their harassment or to know what to do about it reveals just how
important feminist surveys, informational brochures, and legal activism have been to identifying and reporting sexual misconduct. So too, given Professor Silva's perception of what
constitutes a close working relationship with his students, feminists have argued that students are legitimately wary of meeting professors in intimate settings.

Libertarian Camille Paglia advocates in Selection 34 that government may limit speech
only when others are harmed by it. However, according to Paglia, erotic art, family photographs, and joking around the office—all of which have been cited as sexual harassment—
fail to meet this test. According to Paglia, while quid pro quo sexual harassment should be
punished, hostile environment harassment is, in essence, what any one woman might be
offended by. As such, it is a capricious and reactionary instantiation of law. Moreover,
Paglia contends that because offendedness is a product of white, middle-class standards of
gentility, using offendedness to ground legal charges will inevitably be class- and culture-
biased. Paglia argues that it is natural for working women to find sexual harassment pervasive because workplaces have always been marked by cutthroat competition and political infighting. Like Ellen Frankel Paul, Paglia recommends developing a thick skin to
survive office politics and successfully move up the ranks. Overbearing sexual harassment
policies in workplaces and on campuses do women a disservice, in Paglia's view, by removing women's responsibility for dealing with the harsh realities of life. Indeed, Paglia
asserts that women's sexual presence and allure are in large part responsible for the workplace disruption that women contest. Paglia believes that feminists should be teaching
women how to use their sexual power to their advantage, instead of victimizing them with
schoolmarmish sexual mores. Feminists critical of Paglia's point of view argue that by making women responsible for men's sexual misconduct, Paglia absolves men of their responsibility to refrain from harassing women. Moreover, if workplaces are as hostile as Paglia
insists, it is an open question whether women should accept this hostility and deal with it.

In Selection 35, Linda LeMoncheck notes that feminists have typically underplayed the
sexual component of sexual harassment and emphasized its power component in order to
argue that sexual harassment expresses and maintains institutionalized male dominance.
However, LeMoncheck claims that when feminists talk about the sexual harassment of
women primarily in terms of power and not sex, the sexual stereotyping of women vital to
understanding this power component remains hidden. Like Catharine MacKinnon, Barbara Gutek, Deborah Tannen, and James P. Sterba, LeMoncheck contends that women and
men in the industrialized West are socialized to regard women primarily in terms of their
sexual availability to men. Thus, according to LeMoncheck, putting a rubber dildo on a
woman's computer keyboard can remind a woman of her sexual vulnerability and subordinate status in a way that a rubber chicken does not. Because masculinity is associated not
just with dominance but with heterosexual dominance, LeMoncheck argues that young
boys looking for special status among their peers will lift up a girl's skirt rather than trash
her locker or steal her bicycle. Moreover, when girls learn that being appropriately feminine is being sexually submissive, they will do little to combat their harassment, complain

about it, or return the harassment in kind. LeMoncheck notes that thinking about women primarily as sexual objects can encourage men to believe that a woman's ostensibly friendly gesture is "asking for it" and that her fashionable clothing is meant to turn him on. Paradoxically, men also sexualize women by *de*sexualizing them, as when Tailhook officers shouted "Decks awash!" LeMoncheck also contends that stereotyping women of color as animalistic or exotic can help explain their particular vulnerability to sexual harassment (see Selection 40), and synonyms for heterosexual sex such as "nailed" and "knocked up" reinforce regarding women as properly violated and abused. Many women do not see themselves as sexually subordinate to men, but they know that many men believe this or wish it were true. LeMoncheck argues that recognizing how sexual stereotypes inform sexual harassment does not turn women into victims as Katie Roiphe and Camille Paglia claim; rather, such recognition encourages women to look for ways to redefine their sexuality in their own terms. Readers may ask whether putting a rubber chicken on a woman's computer keyboard still counts as sexual harassment if doing so communicates to her that women are not welcome in the workplace (see Selection 36). If we want to name this type of behavior sexual harassment, would LeMoncheck's account of sexual stereotypes help elucidate the problem?

In apparent opposition to LeMoncheck, Vicki Schultz argues in Selection 36 that sexual harassment is not about sex but about sexism on the job. Specifically, the sexual harassment of women by men is about men claiming the workplace as a preserve of male competence and authority. For Schultz, as for Sandra Levitsky, the aim of men's sexual harassment of women is to put women in a subordinate place in the gender hierarchy. Schultz argues that emphasizing the "sex" in sexual harassment has ill-served women in courtrooms. Judges have dismissed women's sexual harassment suits on the grounds that the misconduct was rooted in the harasser's sexual attraction for the harassed, not in discrimination against women as per Title VII. Dismissals have also been based on the finding that the conduct was reprehensible but not sexual, and so not a form of *sexual* harassment. However, Schultz argues that by locating the wrong of sexual harassment in the sexist failure to take women seriously as workers, sexual harassment can be seen as an attempt to ensure male dominance in the workplace. Schultz notes that this analysis explains the higher likelihood of men's harassment of women in nontraditional jobs for women. Moreover, the harassment on such jobs typically takes nonsexual forms, such as relegating women to menial tasks, withholding job assignments necessary for promotion, perpetrating outright job sabotage, or threatening physical violence (see Selections 8, 9, and 10). And like Levitsky, Schultz argues that emphasizing the sexist element of sexual harassment also explains why heterosexual men harass other heterosexual men when doing so aims at purging the workplace of men not suitably masculine enough to work alongside other men (see the *Oncale* case in Selection 54). Schultz says that we ought to be able to work in environments that are both free of sex discrimination and open to the kinds of sexual banter, flirtation, and attraction among employees that reduce office stress and encourage collegiality. However, Schultz contends that any hint of sexuality will disappear from the workplace when workers are fearful that the slightest sexual misstep will result in accusations of sexual harassment. Readers may wish to consider whether Schultz's and LeMoncheck's analyses may be combined. For example, how do sexual stereotypes play a role in claiming the workplace as a preserve of male power and authority? Would learning more about how sexual stereotypes affect our behavior toward women and men in the workplace help ease sexual tensions or reduce sexual offense?

In Selection 37, Daphne Patai claims that feminist researchers, public policy advocates, and liberal academics have developed a literature of propaganda on sexual harassment that advances their own political agenda at the expense of truth and justice. Like Katie Roiphe,

Patai argues that the purveyors of this literature, whom Patai dubs the "Sexual Harassment Industry" (or "SHI"), see sexual harassment everywhere, even when its purported victims do not. In this way, the SHI can "prove" that women are the daily victims of men's violence and abuse. According to Patai, this approach encourages women to believe they have been victimized by men, resulting in false accusations of sexual misconduct and gross miscarriages of justice that critics like Patai, Richard Bernstein, and others believe should be exposed to public scrutiny lest the SHI get the upper hand (also see Selection 39). Patai makes her case by focusing on several examples of the "true" victims of sexual harassment as she sees them, namely, men falsely accused of sexual misconduct. Patai recounts accusations of sexual harassment, made by female students against their professors, that purportedly include allegations on the basis of uncorroborated or blatantly false evidence; assumptions of the guilt of the accused before any evidence had been seen or solicited by school administrators; failures by review boards to allow the accused to meet his accusers or to hear formal charges against him; the failure to believe the testimony of the accused despite a vindicating polygraph test and no investigation of the complaints; ruined faculty reputations; crushed professional motivations; and severely tapped finances. All of the above can occur, Patai laments, even when the accused professor is ultimately exonerated of all charges. However, given the differences in Richard Bernstein's and Mary Clark's accounts of the Silva case, how do we assess the accuracy of Patai's reporting? Is Patai susceptible to the charges she makes of the SHI, namely, that her political agenda drives her analysis of sexual harassment in biased and distorting ways? At the very least, does such an agenda make her own arguments no less suspect than feminist accounts?

In 1978, Jeannette Oppedisano was the affirmative action officer at Skidmore College. In Selection 38, Oppedisano argues that sexual harassment will continue unabated unless administrations promote forming campus coalitions that include faculty committed to combating harassment of students, faculty, and staff alike. She makes her case by offering a number of anonymous, diverse first-person accounts of sexual harassment by those who were the victims of it. Her stories include those of a female student whose grades fell for refusing her professor's advances; a female student who was the butt of her male professor's sexist jokes; a female student who was raped by a popular local athlete; a female student who was intimidated by another student's love notes; a male student who was angered by the way his male professor would touch discomfited female students; female professors whose ideas were ignored by the male professors in their department; campus staff who were ogled through a bathroom peephole by the resident janitor; and a secretary who was intimidated by the sexual pranks of her boss. Oppedisano argues that the isolated efforts of a few are insufficient to successfully combat the problem. She recommends that faculty do a variety of things: learn how to identify sexual harassment; recognize its pervasiveness; understand that most victims simply want to end the harassment, not punish their harassers; begin forging direct lines of communication with campus officials in charge of helping students file complaints; and help build coalitions among all segments of the campus community to design collaborative solutions to the problem. Readers may wonder what, if any, incentives administrations should offer faculty to encourage them to tackle such work. (Course reductions? University service credit? Money? Public recognition?) How optimistic should we be that departments notorious for protecting their intramural autonomy will build the kinds of coalitions conducive to collaborative work on sexual harassment policies and procedures?

In agreement with Ellen Frankel Paul, Katie Roiphe, and Camille Paglia, Warren Farrell contends in Selection 39 that legally prohibiting trivial matters such as telling dirty jokes and making sidelong glances means that the definition of sexual harassment has expanded well beyond what is reasonable or appropriate. Indeed, Farrell argues that determinations of hostile environment sexual harassment violate men's constitutional rights to equal protection under the law; according to Farrell, whether or not an environment is hostile depends on a *woman's* account of what is offensive to *her,* even if the man she accuses of harassment does not intend to offend her and no one else considers his conduct offensive. Like Daphne Patai, Farrell claims that the result of this double standard is that women's charges of sexual harassment against men are assumed to be true (often on the basis of no evidence), whereas the accused man is assumed to be guilty unless he can unequivocally demonstrate otherwise (which he often has no opportunity to do). What particularly riles Farrell is that women are not being held accountable for using their sexual wiles and guiles to make headway in the workplace. Indeed, according to Farrell, women's magazines, romance novels, and self-help books actively encourage their readers to engage in the kinds of flirtatious and seductive behavior that sexual discrimination law forbids in men. Farrell contends that such sexual manipulation of men is a classic form of traditional feminine behavior. Therefore, manipulative working women are communicating to men that women are in the workplace only to land a husband. According to Farrell, men are at great risk of being accused of sexual harassment under such conditions because women are encouraging men to respond to them sexually without telling men directly what offends them. As Farrell remarks, "When it works, it's called courtship. When it doesn't work, it's called harassment." Farrell argues that men are made less powerful than women, not more so, by being expected to take the sexual initiative because men must suffer both the anxiety of possible rejection and the humiliation of real rejection. Farrell contends that if more women would simply tell their harassers to stop, they would. From Farrell's point of view, women's sexual empowerment requires women to be more direct with men by taking the sexual initiative and telling men what they want. However, is Farrell correct that the definition of sexual harassment defines offensiveness exclusively from a woman's point of view? (See Selection 16.) Is Farrell correct that most men would stop harassing women if they were told to stop? (See Selections 7, 8, 9, and 10.) And why think that women will be made more powerful by taking the sexual initiative if men are made less powerful by it?

MULTICULTURAL AND INTERNATIONAL ISSUES

Part V (Multicultural and International Issues) speaks directly to the relevance of cultural perspectives in understanding and legislating sexual harassment. Kimberlé Crenshaw argues in Selection 40 that understanding black women's cultural history and their sexual stereotyping by whites is essential to comprehending black women's sexual harassment. Crenshaw points out that forced sexual access to black women was institutionalized under slavery, and that white stereotypes of black women as sexually voracious, indiscriminate, and animalistic have been used to justify their sexual victimization and abuse. According to Crenshaw, these stereotypes contribute to the belief that black women are sexual fair game because a promiscuous woman cannot be sexually violated when she has no chastity (literally, no whiteness) to violate. Crenshaw also notes that when black women are victimized, especially by white men, perpetrators receive lighter sentences and the public hears less about them than when white women are victimized. Moreover, most white feminists, in Crenshaw's view, are unwilling to recognize both the racial and gendered dimensions of black women's sexual harassment. Such cultural blindness can make Anita Hill's decision not to press EEOC charges against Clarence Thomas look like nothing more than a smart career move to avoid a potential glass ceiling. But as Crenshaw and several of the black women in Beverly Grier's discussion point out, many black women refuse to publicly accuse another black man of sexual misconduct because they do not wish to reinforce racist sexual stereotypes of black men. Readers may wish to consider what feminists can do to dismantle the cultural barriers among women that militate against productive collaboration within the women's movement (see Selections 41 and 42).

In Selection 41, Celia Kitzinger echoes Crenshaw's observation that women can suffer multiple forms of discrimination by virtue of their particular cultural backgrounds. Kitzinger notes that most questions about sexual harassment oversimplify women's oppression: Is a black lesbian the victim of sexual harassment because she is black? Or because she is a lesbian? Or because she is a woman? Kitzinger contends that these kinds of questions are misleading because a person's identity is an interrelated combination of factors such as gender *and* race *and* class *and* sexual orientation. According to Kitzinger, thinking about personal identity in this way allows us to see that sexism *and* racism *and* heterosexism may play simultaneous and interrelated roles in one woman's life. Moreover, Kitzinger echoes Beverly Grier's contention that how sexual harassment is understood will be reflected in how a person experiences and prioritizes oppressions. Thus, according to Kitzinger, a black woman's priority to combat racism may prompt her to believe that when a black lesbian is harassed, racism—not sexism or heterosexism—is the appropriate battleground. Moreover, as Kimberlé Crenshaw points out, the way people stereotype others informs their rationales for sexual harassment. Thus, according to Kitzinger, a man may justify his sexual harassment of a lesbian on the grounds that because she is homo*sexual*, she, not he, has introduced sex into the conversation. On the other hand, some men accuse women of being lesbians when women do *not* reciprocate the harasser's sexual attention. Men's harassment of lesbians is further complicated by the fact that an "out" lesbian will not fear public disclosure of her sexual orientation if she were to complain; a closeted lesbian, on the other hand, may have such fears. Indeed, if we accept Lin Farley's definition of sexual harassment as unwanted male sexual attention, Kitzinger notes that lesbians can define all sexualized behavior from men as sexual harassment. In Kitzinger's view, not painting the picture of antilesbian harassment in this way makes it difficult for many straight women to understand why simple flirtation or a request for a date can be offensive to lesbians. Kitzinger argues that the expression "'anti-lesbian' harassment" is useful for identifying the multiple oppressions experienced by lesbians, as long as we remember that the word "lesbian" does not completely circumscribe a woman's identity. Readers might try testing Kitzinger's analysis of sexual harassment against those of Linda LeMoncheck, Vicki Schultz, and James P. Sterba. Is antilesbian harassment best understood as a case of sexual stereotyping? A case of reinforcing gender hierarchies? Is antilesbian harassment perpetuated by not allowing women the opportunity to act in ways that men are allowed to act?

Diana Vellos examines in Selection 42 the sexual harassment of Latina immigrant domestic workers. Vellos notes that undocumented Latina immigrants are especially vulnerable to harassment by their employers because such workers risk both unemployment and deportation if they report their mistreatment. Vellos contends that the United States tolerates the economic and sexual exploitation of undocumented immigrants in the belief that if the work were bad enough, immigrants would simply return home. However, according to Vellos, immigrant domestic workers, unlike factory workers, often live in the homes of their employers in middle-class suburbs where immigrants feel isolated and alone, inhibiting them from challenging sexual misconduct directed toward them. Moreover, given their poor language skills, limited available work, and the need to support their families, many undocumented domestic workers victimized by sexual harassment continue to suffer in silence in the jobs they have. According to Vellos, this silence is reinforced by the fact that a Latina immigrant's culture encourages her to be self-blaming and passive, which militates against her aggressively responding to her harassment. Indeed, if she has learned that it is proper to acquiesce to the sexual demands of men, she may not even recognize sexual harassment as sexual misconduct (see Selection 45). As a result, Latina domestic immigrants' sexual harassment is difficult to document. There are cases in which undocumented workers have filed sexual harassment suits and won. However, as Vellos points out, these cases tend to be marked by special circumstances, as when an undocumented domestic worker has a support network of U.S. citizens to help her bring suit against her private employer, or when a group of undocumented immigrants working as housekeepers in a hotel can bring witnesses on their behalf and validate each other's stories. Vellos contends that protecting Latina domestic workers from exploitation requires new legislation that would facilitate their legal immigration into the United States. In Vellos's view, if immigrants had legal status, this would put pressure on U.S. employers to offer domestic workers fair salaries and benefits. Such status would also give immigrants the confidence to leave exploitive workplaces without fear of deportation and give them the legal standing to combat sexual harassment when it occurs. Readers may ask, What responsibility should be federal government have for the sexual harassment of undocumented immigrants?

In Selection 43, Nicole Gaouette reports on a unique case of alleged quid pro quo sexual harassment in Japan, in which a male American dancer in the touring company of a popular Japanese female singer charged her with threatening to fire him unless he had an affair with her. Gaouette notes that the case marks the first time a woman has been sued for sexual harassment in Japan. (The singer denies all charges.) The timing of the 1998 case was noteworthy in Gaouette's view in light of the fact that the Japanese government recently passed an amendment to an employment law, effective April 1999, which makes employers liable in sexual harassment cases. However, as in the United States, the sexual harassment of men by women is rare. Japanese women report that *sekuhara,* as sexual harassment is known in Japan, is a common occurrence both in their workplaces and outside them. In fact, much of the building of Japanese corporate relationships occurs after hours in bars or clubs where bosses get drunk and harass the female employees they have pressed to join them. However, few Japanese women complain of their mistreatment in a male-dominated culture in which female staff assistants are referred to as "office flowers" and there are few female executives, police officers, or judges with the power to speak on their behalf. Indeed, Japanese business culture discourages personal criticism, especially of an employer by a lower-ranking employee. As a result, any well-publicized complaints of sexual harassment tend to come from U.S.-based American workers in Japanese-owned businesses, prompting most Japanese to think of sexual harassment as largely an American problem (see Selections 10 and 26). Nevertheless, Gaouette reports that, given the government's public support of antiharassment legislation, more women are openly objecting to their mistreatment. Readers may wish to compare the cultural background that informs sexual harassment in Japan with the cultural traditions of India and Mexico, described below.

Ramni Taneja examines in Selection 44 the implications of a 1997 landmark decision by the Supreme Court of India, in which the court ruled that a female social worker allegedly being gang-raped because she was trying to prevent a child marriage violates a woman's fundamental right to work. Taneja notes the radical nature of such a decision in an Indian cultural context in which dowry death, female infanticide, and restrictions on women's education and employment are still common. More radical still, the court included in its decision a set of comprehensive domestic legislative guidelines for identifying and preventing sexual harassment, referring to such international conventions as the

United Nations Convention on the Elimination of all Forms of Discrimination Against Women (see Selection 57). Indeed, the guidelines stipulated by the Indian high court are strikingly similar to the U.S. EEOC guidelines with regard to identifying sexual harassment as a form of sex discrimination (see Selection 49). However, Taneja reports that the Indian Parliament must still enact laws that reflect the court's recommendations, and that women must be encouraged to assert their rights in a culture that teaches female submission to male authority. Nevertheless, Taneja notes that many political liberals in the country believe that the guidelines have made a significant contribution to protecting the rights of working women in India.

In Selection 45, Pia Hilbrert discusses the special difficulties faced by employed professional women in Mexico. Like the "office flowers" of Japanese business culture, Mexican women work in a society in which women are still encouraged and expected to serve men. Women occupy the lowest-paying and least prestigious jobs in Mexico, so that, like the Latina domestic workers in the United States described by Diana Vellos, Mexican working women's vulnerability to sexual harassment and their fear of reprisal for reporting it remain high. Moreover, charm and flattery are cultural insignia of Latin masculinity, making it difficult for Mexican women and men to differentiate between complimenting a woman and harassing her. Even those relatively few women who hold executive positions in Mexico's corporate sector are often regarded as provoking their own harassment and presumed less credible in cases of he said/she said. According to Vellos, Mexican male clients often refuse to work with businesswomen in executive positions or slight them at meetings by presuming they are secretaries of male executives. Indeed, in a culture in which women are supposed to be home with the children while their husbands work hard to support their families, reporting a man's alleged workplace harassment looks like an unprincipled woman's scurrilous attack on a decent man. Hilbrert suggests that as more women in Mexico attain real corporate power and more U.S. companies establish offices in Mexico, management-supported sexual harassment policies will become a more common feature of the workplace. Yet, as Hilbrert points out, in a culture in which male chauvinism is still encouraged, most Mexican citizens will perceive U.S. cases of sexual harassment, particularly the well-publicized and contentious ones, as overblown and unnecessary. Readers may ask, Does the similarity of cultural attitudes toward women in Japan, India, and Mexico bolster the feminist claim that sex discrimination is institutionalized worldwide? Can increasing U.S. economic presence around the globe positively affect entrenched cultural attitudes toward women and work?

Gaby Oré-Aguilar examines in Selection 46 the efforts by international organizations to develop a unified and proactive approach to sexual harassment worldwide. However, as Oré-Aguilar points out, a single global approach to sexual harassment is made difficult by the fact that such organizations as the European Economic Community, the Council of the European Union, the International Labor Organization, and the United Nations, among others, differ in their understanding of what sexual harassment is and how it should be prevented. According to Oré-Aguilar, some organizations understand sexual harassment as an affront to moral decency; others regard sexual harassment as an attack on principles of equality and nondiscrimination, and still others see sexual harassment as one of several forms of violence against women. Each organization then incorporates its preferred approach into its international conventions, treaties, and documents. Oré-Aguilar argues for the international adoption of a gender-based model for understanding sexual harassment because such a model can be used to define sexual harassment as a violation of women's human rights. According to Oré-Aguilar, countries could then be required to incorporate measures against sexual harassment into their domestic human rights legislation, and victims of sexual harassment could seek compensation for damages through both domestic and international agencies. However, even if the international adoption of a gender-based model were successful, the question arises as to how an organization can require compliance by its members when ousting a member nation means it is no longer subject to the organization's rules, and when punishing a member (for example, with economic sanctions) may result in that nation's renouncing its membership. And how should international organizations respond to non–member nations perceived to be committing violations of women's rights?

SELECTED LEGAL DOCUMENTS AND COURT CASES

Part VI (Selected Legal Documents and Court Cases) begins with an excerpt from Title VII of the Civil Rights Act of 1964 prohibiting sex discrimination in the workplace, the civil rights legislation that forms the basis of sexual harassment law (Selection 47). Although many congressmen in the 1960s did not believe that discrimination based on sex was a serious issue, they were under considerable pressure from the Lyndon Johnson administration to improve civil rights legislation as a way of combating racism. Thus, feminists and other political activists were able to take advantage of the antidiscrimination language of Title VII to successfully lobby for the inclusion of sex, as well as race, color, religion, and national origin, as a prohibited basis for unequal treatment. Selection 48 excerpts Title IX of the Education Amendments of 1972, which prohibits sex discrimination in federally assisted educational programs. The amendments' passage was originally stimulated by restrictions on women's participation in school athletics programs. As a form of antidiscrimination law, Title IX has been recognized by the courts as prohibiting sexual harassment in schools receiving federal funds, thus providing the legal umbrella under which sexual harassment of students, faculty, and school staff is covered. Selection 49 excerpts the current Equal Employment Opportunity Commission guidelines regarding the workplace sexual harassment prohibited by Title VII. These guidelines are the primary means by which courts and legislators identify cases of sexual harassment and assess employer liability. In particular, the guidelines specify that in cases of quid pro quo harassment, employers are liable for damages whether or not they knew about the offending conduct; in cases of hostile environment sexual harassment, employers are liable if they could or should have known about the harassment but failed to take steps toward correcting the problem. The Office of Civil Rights (OCR) of the U.S. Department of Education offers its guidance, excerpted in Selection 50, on dealing with the campus sexual harassment prohibited by Title IX. These guidelines include recommendations for identifying the offending conduct, assessing liability, and determining the unwelcomeness, pervasiveness, and severity of the conduct. Because the OCR guidelines on sexual harassment were modeled after those of the EEOC, readers may wish to compare the two with regard to their definitions of sexual harassment and their recommendations for assessing liability. It is worth emphasizing that the EEOC guidelines and the OCR's sexual harassment guidelines are recommendations only, not court decisions or laws in their own right. As a result, legislators, judges, and policymakers continue to disagree over the guidelines' applications in particular cases (see Selections 23 and 56). Selections 51 through 56 highlight a variety of Supreme Court decisions to which several of the previous selections refer, and which are definitive in interpreting sexual harassment law. Selection 57 excerpts a United Nations convention document formally condemning all forms of discrimination against women. The document has been used by countries around the world in their formulation of sexual harassment legislation and social policy (see Selections 44 and 46). An extensive bibliography follows for further reading.

The anthology can be read in several ways. For readers unfamiliar with the topic of sexual harassment, the anthology is organized to offer a comprehensive introduction to the subject by reading the selections in the order given. Readers already familiar with specific aspects of sexual harassment, such as sexual harassment law, may wish to focus on Section IV concerning current philosophical debates on sexual harassment or Section V on multicultural and international issues. Some readers who have kept up with the current debates may be most interested in some of the prevailing Supreme Court decisions concerning sexual harassment in Section VI. Other readers may wish to get a sense of the variety of sexual harassment in Section II and then return to the question of how sexual harassment is to be defined in Section I. Instructors who may wish to use only part of the anthology for their courses will find each section self-contained and informative. In short, the anthology is designed with both the student and scholar, the novice and knower, in mind.

Although some of the selections in the anthology are primarily descriptive of the problem of sexual harassment, many other selections challenge readers to weigh the author's point of view against their own. Indeed, many of the selections have been chosen precisely because they provoke readers to reflect not only on their own beliefs about sexual harassment but also on why they might hold them, and whether any of the authors' conclusions conflict with their own sense of what is right or just. As philosophers by profession, the editors of this anthology believe that all discussions of contemporary moral issues—whether they are about abortion, assisted suicide, capital punishment, or sexual harassment—are discussions that will inevitably raise as many questions as they answer. Nevertheless, the editors firmly believe that the selections from this anthology can provide our readers with the deliberative tools to make reflective and informed decisions about sexual harassment, which can in turn advance the dialogue on sexual harassment in ways beneficial to us all.

PART I

The Nature of Sexual Harassment

1. Sexual Shakedown: The Sexual Harassment of Women on the Job

Lin Farley

For almost two decades our society has been undergoing a changing social awareness about what constitutes acceptable standards of behavior between the sexes. New information by women about the quality of their lives has often been the catalyst for this new consciousness. The sexual harassment of women on-the-job is the most recent illustration of this process. By testifying in their own behalf working women have begun to lay bare the male coercion, often masquerading as sexual initiative and frequently backed by the force of higher rank at work, which has been their daily fare on-the-job. Such male behavior is in sharp violation of ideas of equality, and the neutrality of work. Among the many concerns of this book are the psychological, sociological, ideological, ethical, legal and economic questions which are now being brought to bear in this new controversy, but underlying all of them there is still one central issue. Do women have to acquiesce to sex or sexual behavior from men on-the-job in order to participate in wage-work in our society?

Public exposure of this abuse has been permeated by a notion that the sexual harassment of working women is of only minor concern in comparison with the whole battery of injustices that beset women at work, particularly the lack of equal pay with men. However, there is no aspect of women's deplorable situation at work today, be it economic or otherwise, that has not either been created or maintained by this behavior and the way working women respond to it. This is because patriarchal relations, not capitalism, are at the root of working women's problems.

To begin at the beginning, although it cannot be said often enough, our society is first, last and foremost a patriarchy. Essentially, this means that it is a social system organized according to a principle of male rule and that it is this principle that shapes the matrix of systems such as democracy and capitalism which for the present characterize our particular kind of patriarchy. Throughout successive epochs the patriarchy has maintained itself by generating ideas that legitimize, i.e. make acceptable, the very conditions which make this rule possible. Enter male sexual harassment, which has until recently been a completely acceptable idea—although it is by this fiat that male aggression toward working women has been extensively practised, a practice that has kept working women both individually and collectively locked into a position of economic inferiority. Men accordingly have successfully insured their domination of modern work, hence society, because the patriarchy cannot lose control of its material base. The sexual harassment of working women is an issue of enormous significance. In light of this, underrating the extent and importance of the abuse is probably a result of an historically inadequate analysis of women and work which has continued right up to the present day.

As an example of this, much has been written over the last decade about a feminist success in women's employment; this is largely measured by the increased numbers of women who are working outside the home. However, this is less a result of feminism than it is a consequence of the expansion of the service sector in our increasingly service-oriented economy. In addition, women's overall employment conditions compared to those of men have deteriorated. The head of the department of Economics at American University, Nancy Smith Barrett, in a reference to women's increased labor force participation in the sixties wrote, ". . . the average job status of women relative to men actually declined during the period and the male-female earnings gap widened."[1] This is not surprising. The concentration of working women in a few over-crowded job categories which is the cause of these problems is virtually the same as it was in 1900. Edward Gross has explained this in an "index of segregation." By computing the percentage of women in the labor force who would have to change jobs in order for the occupational distribution of women workers to match that of men, Gross's index showed that female sex segregation was 66.9 in 1900, 68.4 in 1960 and the index had not substantially altered in 1974.[2]

The only major feminist success in recent women's employment, then, is what Barrett went on to describe as "a growing recognition that a problem existed."[3] This is true and this recognition of inequality resulted in three federal mandates to guarantee women equal pay and equal employment opportunity. The enforcement of these three mandates, the Equal Pay Act of 1963, Title VII of the 1964 Civil Rights Act and Executive Order Number Four began in some cases with sweeping court suits to repair damages to female employees and to correct sex discrimination in the future. Affirmative action plans have resulted and these plans in conjunction with what would have to be rather stringent enforcement are now considered the primary hope for women's employment opportunities.

Unfortunately, this strategy ignores the way men have patriarchalized capitalism and as a consequence the optimism is poorly grounded. Unequal pay, lack of promotion and poor opportunities are often only symptoms. Meanwhile, job segregation by sex is to a large degree sustained by male sexual harassment. This abuse is already rolling back the momentum of affirmative action and it will continue to coerce women by the means of severe economic and emotional abuse into over-crowded, sexually-segregated job categories. These occupations are tantamount to a female job ghetto and this is a primary cause of women's low wages. At the same time the abuse also impacts destructively within this ghetto, disrupting female job attachment, promoting female unemployment and inhibiting female solidarity. Until we understand sexual harassment, its historical function, the way it has been used to keep women 'in line' and the way this coercion interacts with women's employment conditions, women will remain an exploited underclass, the female workhorses in a male-managed economy. . . .

How Does It Work?

Sexual harassment is best described as unsolicited nonreciprocal male behavior that asserts a woman's sex role over her function as worker. It can be any or all of the following: staring at, commenting upon, or touching a woman's body; requests for acquiescence in sexual behavior; repeated nonreciprocated propositions for dates; demands for sexual intercourse; and rape. These forms of male behavior frequently rely on superior male status in the culture, sheer numbers, or the threat of higher rank at work to exact compliance or levy penalties for refusal. The variety of penalties include verbal denigration of a woman sexually; noncooperation from male co-workers; negative job evaluations or poor personnel recommendations; refusal of overtime; demotions; injurious transfers and reassignments of shifts, hours, or locations of work; loss of job training; impossible performance standards and outright termination of employment. Sexual harassment also frequently influences many hiring situations, as when companies employ across-the-board policies of hiring only those women who are attractive sex objects regardless of skills, or where there will be an outright demand for some form of sexual behavior which will result in the reward of the job while refusal will result in a nonhire.

Disapproval of sexual harassment tends to focus on demands for sex as a condition of hiring as well as for keeping a job. These are considered serious manifestations of sexual coercion, while generalized staring, commenting, touching, and other forms of male familiarity are regarded as merely annoying and of little consequence. The outright demand for sex appears more serious because the economic penalties for noncompliance are easily discernible and the consequences to both the woman who refuses and the woman who submits against her will are easily imagined. Sexual harassment is nevertheless an act of aggression at any stage of its expression, and in all its forms it contributes to the ultimate goal of keeping women subordinate at work.

Adrienne Rich has written that men maintain the patriarchy in part through "etiquette."[4] Her choice of words in this context is interchangeable with what psychologist Nancy Henley has described as the "micropolitics" of human interactions.[5] A close look at male sexual harassment leaves no doubt the name of the game is dominance. As Erving Goffman has explained in *The Nature of Deference and Demeanor,* superordinates can often be identified by the exercising of familiarities which the subordinate is not allowed to reciprocate. He cites these familiarities as touching, teasing, informal demeanor, using familiar address, and asking for personal information.[6] Further clues to the communication of power between persons have been established by Michael Argyle. These include: bodily contact, physical proximity and position, gestures, posture, nodding or smiling, and silences or interruptions.[7] It is also generally agreed that those who communicate dominance will initiate standing closer, precipitate touching, and interrupt freely.

Eye contact is another dimension important to any micropolitical power analysis. In this realm, according to George Maclay and Humphry Knipe, staring can be characterized as a *threat display.*[8] Henley has also described touching as "one of the closer invasions of one's personal space. . . . It is even more a physical threat than space violation, pointing, or staring, perhaps a vestige of the days when dominance was determined by physical prowess."[9]

In view of this, women's statements about sexual harassment——"He would always stand right on top of me"; "He was always staring at me"; "He'd always manage to rub against me"—are articulations of the way men use these gestures to assert dominance. In her article "The Politics of Touch" Henley says, "Some typical dominant gestures which may evoke submissive ones are staring directly at a person, pointing at a person and touching a person." She also noted that "Corresponding gestures of submission, all of them common to women, include lowering the eyes, shutting up or not even beginning to speak when pointed at, and cuddling to the touch."[10] Women stand up to these male assertions of dominance with extreme difficulty—or at the very least uneasily. They have been socialized to powerlessness—in Henley's words, to "docility and passivity."[11]

It is a matter of sex-role conditioning. The essential nature of women's and men's conditioning has been well documented in the last ten years, but its importance to this discussion warrants a brief restatement. Social psychologists Harriet Connolly and Judith Greenwald explain:

> In our culture the importance of sex-role conditioning cannot be underestimated. In general, boys learn to be independent, to initiate action, to be task-oriented, rational, analytical. In contrast, girls are schooled in empathy, noncompetitiveness, dependency, nurturance, intuitiveness. These standards continue to provide the model for "normal" behavior and exert a powerful demand for conformity throughout adult life.

Female passivity is further encouraged by social confusion. Because men possess the right of sexual initiative, the communication of power and dominance by men is generally discounted as mere sexual interest. Nevertheless, as Henley has explained, "Even those who put forward a sexual explanation for males' touching of females have to admit that there is at least a status overlay: female factory workers, secretaries, students, servants and waitresses are often unwillingly felt or pinched but women of higher status (e.g., 'boss ladies,' 'first ladies,' and 'ladies' in general) aren't."[12]

That sex is hardly the real meaning of much male behavior at work is further indicated by testing the results. A recent study of female response to touching by male co-workers showed that the female respondents were "unattracted and unaroused." Catherine Radecki, a graduate student at the University of Delaware, conducted the study among forty women at three different work-sites. As a result of her research she concluded the "women were somewhat disgusted, unaroused, unexcited, turned off, insulted, not attracted by or disliked the experience of men at work touching them."[13]

Whether it results from unsolicited demands for sex as a condition of working, or from the pressure of unsolicited daily intimidation, sexual harassment is described by Connolly and Greenwald as including the following elements:

> Structurally, both types of actions usually are initiated by someone with power against someone with lesser power, not the other way around. In a word, they are nonreciprocal. The second structural similarity is the element of coercion, that is, it is either stated or implied there will be negative consequences if the woman refuses to acquiesce and/or comply. These actions function to assert superior power. As a result the consequences for the victims are much the same. All sexual harassment is a stressful experience and ego functioning may well be seriously impaired. The victim is violated either physically or psychologically and she experiences a loss of autonomy and control.

Because sexual harassment is an assertion of male power that undermines the autonomy and personhood of female workers, the generalized expressions of dominance must be condemned and eradicated, by both men and women, certainly no less vigorously than specific demands for sex.

Says Henley: "Men should become conscious of their tactual interaction with women especially, and guard against using touch to assert authority . . . women similarly have a responsibility to themselves to refuse to accept tactual assertion of authority—they should remove their hands from the grasp of men who hold them too long and remove men's hands from their person when such a touch is unsolicited and unwanted. . . ."[14]

The patriarchy has perpetuated itself through insuring the subordination of female labor by endlessly maintaining and adapting its systems of hierarchical control. Before capitalism, for example, men controlled the work of women and children in the family. The emergence of capitalism, however, threatened this base of control by instituting a "free" market in labor. Capitalism, writes economist Heidi Hartmann, "threatened to bring all women and children into the labor force and hence to destroy the family and the basis of the power of men over women (i.e., the control over their labor power in the family)."[15]

The critical question remains: if capitalism would have equalized laborers in the marketplace, regardless of sex, why are women still in an inferior position at work today? There are a score of possible answers, but more and more evidence has begun to identify the most important factor as job segregation by sex. Hartmann writes:

> Job segregation . . . is the primary mechanism in capitalist society that maintains the superiority of men over women because it enforces lower wages for women in the labor market. Low wages keep women dependent on men because they encourage women to marry. Married women must perform domestic chores for their husbands. Men benefit, then, from both higher wages and the domestic division of labor. This domestic division of labor, in turn, acts to weaken women's

position in the labor market. Thus, the hierarchical domestic division of labor is perpetuated by the labor market and vice versa.[16]

From the beginning, women entered wage-labor handicapped by the patriarchy that influenced capitalist development. Male dominance was already beginning to express itself in some sex-ordered jobs, with women's work offering lower pay, demanding less skill, and involving less exercise of authority or control. However, male workers soon effectively turned a trend into an ironclad tradition. Hartmann explains:

"Men acted to enforce job segregation in the labor market; they utilized trade union associations and strengthened the domestic division of labor which required women to do housework, child care and related chores."[17]

Modern Male Control of Female Labor

Originally, in England, the rise of capitalism required little adjustment in the prevailing male methods of control, since the early factories utilized a family industrial system. Men could hire their own children for assistants, and whole families were often employed by the same factory for the length of the same day. When technological change made this system obsolete around 1840, male factory workers began to switch their demands of the preceding two decades from continuing the family system to limiting work for children. According to Neil Smelser, the effect of the subsequent child labor laws was that parents began to have difficulty with child care. The remedy then proposed by male workers and a majority of the upper and middle classes was to remove women from the factories.[18] Frederick Engels described the concerns about women workers that readily facilitated the auspiciousness of this remedy; "incapacity as housekeepers, neglect of home and children; indifference, actual dislike to family life . . . the crowding out of men from employment . . . husbands supported by their wives and children."[19]

It is about this period in English history that one finds male workers beginning to drive women out of industry, chiefly by means of trade unions. This prompted Engels to refer to these unions as elite organizations of grown-up men interested solely in their own benefits and not in benefits for workers who happened to be women or children. Hartmann explains:

"That male workers viewed the employment of women as a threat to their jobs is not surprising, given an economic system where competition among workers was characteristic. That women were paid lower wages exacerbated the threat. But why their response was to attempt to exclude women rather than to organize them is explained, not by capitalism, but by patriarchal relations between men and women: men wanted to assure that women would continue to perform the appropriate tasks at home."[20]

Needless to say, the male unions were successful in creating the widespread idea that women belonged at home and men's wages therefore should be increased since they should be paid on a family basis. Because men were never able to force women out of the labor market entirely, however, union policy eventually adapted by evolving a strategy of confining women to women's jobs. This was accomplished by denying them training. In 1891 Sidney Webb, in the Webb–Rathbone–Fawcett–Edgeworth series of articles in the British *Economic Journal* justified women's lower wages on the ground that women rarely did the same grade of work as men, but he also admitted that the male unions were intransigent in permitting women to gain equal skills.[21]

The full effect of this policy crystallized at the end of World War I, when—as is usual in time of war—more women had worked and performed many jobs normally reserved for men. Women consequently expected better employment prospects. Millicent Fawcett wrote in 1918 that equal pay for equal work was now possible. She reasoned that the integration of females throughout the entire work force would demand this equality of pay if men's wages were not to be undercut. The only obstacles in the path of this realization were male unions and social customs, she said, since they both led to an overcrowding in women's jobs—a condition which, of course, deflated women's wages.[22] In 1922, F. Y. Edgeworth formalized Fawcett's observations into an overcrowding model. Job segregation by sex, he said, produces a surplus in the supply of workers in the female sector so that male wages are raised while female wages are lowered. Edgeworth explained: "The pressure of male trade unions appears to be largely responsible for that crowding of women into comparatively few occupations, which is universally recognized as a main factor in the depression of their wages."[23]

We have, then, as early as 1922, a depiction of the effect of male policy in forcing female workers into "women's jobs," as well as a clear indication of the way men adapted their techniques of hierarchical regulation to ensure their continued control of female labor.

American workingmen never entertained the idea of excluding women from the work force totally, since American capitalism frequently turned to female labor power. This is a pattern throughout American economic history that has continued to the present, with the post-World War II expansion of female employment.

In many cases female employment opportunities have been the consequence of a field being abandoned by men who forced women out of more skilled jobs while simultaneously apportioning them occupations of only the most monotonous and dead-end nature. Job segregation then lowered women's wages even in those few skilled occupations which became associated with women. One example is public-school teaching, where wages became notoriously low.[24] Clerical work too offers a good illustration of this process. When the increased demand for these workers first appeared, there simply were not enough males with a high school education equal to the need; but, even more, the subdivision of the tasks and the introduction of machines had changed the job structure. Hartmann writes this "reduced its attractiveness to men—with expansion the jobs became dead-end ones—while for women the opportunities compared favorably with their opportunities elsewhere."[25]

Much of the literature of the late nineteenth century tied this changing sex composition of jobs to technological factors and biological sex differences, but the role of unions and male workers cannot be denied. Edith Abbott indicates the way male workers enforced the sex composition of jobs in an incident that involved mule spinners, a machine traditionally operated by males in the textile industry. According to Abbott, a woman had learned to run "the mule" in Lawrence, Massachusetts, and then she moved to Waltham when "mules" were introduced there. The woman apparently had to leave, however, because (according to a male operative), "The men made unpleasant remarks and it was too hard for her, being the only woman."[26] As Hartmann writes, "Social pressures were powerful mechanisms of enforcement."[27]

American trade union policy also maintained job segregation by turning the British program of exclusion into one of limited participation. The form for this was "protective" legislation for female workers. The policy of the Cigarmakers International Union is a good example of the way this strategy evolved. In 1878, twenty years after the union had publicly stopped excluding females, according to Elizabeth Baker, a Baltimore local wrote Adolf Strasser, the Cigarmakers' president, "We have combatted from its incipiency the movement of the introduction of female labor in any capacity whatever, be it bunch maker, roller or what not."[28] One year later, according to Andrews and Bliss, Strasser himself would say, "We cannot drive the females out of the trade, but we can restrict their daily quota of labor through factory laws: No girl under 18 should be employed more than eight hours per day; all overwork should be prohibited. . . ."[29]

This kind of attitude has been interpreted by many as a justified hostility to unskilled labor rather than as a hostility to women per se but, as Hartmann writes, "Male unions denied women skills while they offered them to young boys.[30] The American unions were as determined in this policy as were their British counterparts. In printing, for example, women had been typesetters from Colonial times; it was a skilled trade that required no heavy work. However, they were eventually driven out by the National Typographical Union, which in 1854 declared it would not "encourage by its act the employment of female compositors."[31] As a result women were forced to learn what they could in nonunion shops or as strikebreakers. In fact, Susan B. Anthony was refused a seat at the annual National Labor Convention of 1869 on the grounds she had encouraged women to serve as scabs. (As Gail Falk has explained, Anthony freely admitted she had so encouraged women compositors. Her actions, she said, were the direct result of union policy because women could learn the trade no other way.)[32]

Male unionists discouraged women in more ways than just union policy. In 1870 the National Typographical Union agreed to charter a woman's local in New York City, but union men would not support the fledgling local and it died before the end of eight years. In the words of Augusta Lewis, its president, "It is the general opinion of female compositors that they are more justly treated by what is termed "rat" foremen, printers, and employers than they are by union men."[33]

The printers' union was no isolated exception in the main-stream of American union attitudes; if anything, this union was a trend-setter. This is evident in Edith Abbott's 1910 statement that "Officers of other trade unions frequently refer to the policy of the printers as an example of the way in which trade union control may be successful in checking or preventing the employment of women."[34] The typographical union, incidentally, backed equal pay for equal work; it was the means by which men protected their own wage scale, since, as Hartmann writes, "Women who had fewer skills could not demand, and expect to receive, equal wages."[35]

As long as barring women could place them in a position to strike-break, the overall male union strategy had to continue its efforts to cripple the competitive market power of female labor. The drive for "protective" legislation began to gather momentum. Eventually it gained wide popular support, and by 1908 the Supreme Court upheld a maximum-hours law for women. This decision was a major victory for male workers. Even though it wasn't long before there was a similar decision about men, this was never followed—as it was in relation to women—by a flurry of state maximum-hours laws. Hartmann explains, "Unions did not support protective legislation for men, although they continued to do so for women. Protective legislation, rather than organization, was the preferred strategy for women."[36] As a result, female competition against men was successfully curtailed and the maintenance of job segregation further assured.

There are many who argue that this particular impact of "protective" legislation is over-rated, since narrow coverage and inadequate enforcement softened its effect. However, this ignores the fact that wherever male unions had a foothold they could now conjure up the specter of the law to deny women opportunities. In many occupations where long hours and night work were essential, as in printing, women were successfully excluded. Hartmann writes, "While the law may have protected women in the 'sweated' trades, women who were beginning to get established in 'men's jobs' were turned back."[37] The devastating impact of the laws on women's overall employment cannot be discounted. As Ann C. Hill has explained, they confirmed women's "alien" status as a worker.[38]

Attacks on this alienation of women from work outside the home are receiving a relatively popular reception at present. This change is the result of two influences occurring back to back. The first is that business has had a big stake in encouraging nonworking segments of the female population to meet the rising demand in the service sector, a traditionally female field. The second is the curtain that still hides the on-going role of male workers in hamstringing female competition and in isolating women inside a female job ghetto. Nearly a century has passed since the results of this male stratagem were first noted, and yet the flawed motto of "equal pay for equal work" has become the renewed rallying cry for improving women's working conditions. Equal work *and* equal pay is more to the point. Even so, this still ignores the importance of male sexual harassment. Its influence on the sex composition of jobs was noted earlier in this chapter. This is a significant aspect of male practice, but it is one that will be dealt with in the present period. Historically, sexual harassment has had an effect that can no longer be countenanced today.

A History of Sexual Harassment

Sexual harassment of working women accompanied the new methods developed to control female labor with the rise of capitalism. The historical record is unofficial, a patchwork pieced together from letters, recorded conversations, interviews, women's writings, and newspaper articles that often mentioned the abuse only incidentally. It is nevertheless clear enough. The practice of sexual harassment throughout much of the nineteenth and early twentieth centuries contributed to the premature deaths of an incalculably large number of working women.

Understanding the full past impact of sexual harassment requires a reminder about the Victorian era. This was the golden age of the double standard in sex relations. All attitudes of public morality weighed hard on women. Elisha Bartlett, M.D., made this patently clear in his 1841 article, "A Vindication of the Character and Condition of the Females Employed in the Lowell Mills. . . ."[39] In this article on conditions of factory morality Bartlett declared: "It is only by maintaining an unsullied and unimpeachable character that a girl can retain her situation in the mill, and when dismissed for any impropriety from one establishment, there is no possibility of her getting a place in any of the others. . . ." It would be hard to find a situation more ripe for exploitation when the mere imputation of bad conduct from any mill authority could literally drive a woman out of town. In addition, the climate of the times made it extremely difficult for a woman accused of sexual wrongdoing to clear herself, since mere accusation tended to smear her reputation irrevocably.

Illustrative of this is the report of a trial in an 1846 issue of the *Voice of Industry,* a magazine of the Lowell Female Labor Reform Association.[40] According to the paper a "lady" who had worked for the Middlesex Corporation under an overseer named Snow "left his employ or was dismissed 'irregularly' . . . and he is charged with having circulated slanderous reports relative to her character to prevent her obtaining work elsewhere." There had been two previous trials. In the first Snow was fined five hundred dollars and costs; in the second the jury could not agree, "though ten were in favor of his conviction." In this, the third trial, the case was decided against the woman.

"It is important," the article concluded, "to break up the infamous conspiracy of the agents in this place to libel the characters of all who are turned out of their employment or leave irregularly that they may deprive them of work in other factories and drive them out of the city."

Subsistence wages contributed to the mortal danger sexual harassment posed for these early working women. Most female wage-earners barely eked out the necessities of life from their weekly earnings. In the face of this economic reality and the prevailing moral code, the sexual advance was disastrous. To refuse invariably resulted in retaliation, which commonly ended in either a decrease in present wages or losing the job altogether, the sure road to starvation. At the same time, to accept was sure damnation; after this marriage was out of the question and future employment was also forbidden. Prostitution was the only remaining option. As a result of widespread sexual harassment, many former working women swelled the ranks of prostitutes into numbers which have never been equaled throughout American history. The phenomenon was much lamented in the press of the time. There was less sighing, however, over the venereal disease that regularly killed these women within two or three years.[41]

Sexual harassment (before the arrival of cheap immigrant labor) was somewhat affected by the periodic push-pull between capitalism and man's patriarchal imperative. The early manufacturers, concerned with attracting and insuring a ready supply of domestic labor, strove to appear above reproach. The Lowell Manufacturing Company in 1836 stated that it would not "continue to employ any person who shall be wanting in proper respect to the females employed by the company."[42] However, with the arrival of cheap foreign labor the abuse became endemic. Manufacturers no longer cared either to make the effort to restrain their managers or even to give the appearance of doing so.

Upton Sinclair's searing exposé *The Jungle* (1905) portrayed the struggle for survival by the Lithuanian peasants Jurgis Rudkus and his wife Ona in Chicago's giant meat-packing industry. The book caused a sensation, although not for the pervasive sexual harassment it unsparingly revealed; this was a given. Sinclair explains that Ona was subject to sexual abuse at her job and that "she would not have stayed a day, but for starvation, and as it was she was never sure that she could stay the next day."

> But there was no place a girl could go in Packing-town, [Sinclair continued] if she was particular about things of this sort; there was no place in it where a prostitute could not get along better than a decent girl. Here was a population, low-class and mostly foreign, hanging always on the verge of starvation, and dependent for its opportunities of life upon the whim of men every bit as brutal and unscrupulous as the old-time slave drivers; under such circumstances immorality was exactly as inevitable, and as prevalent, as it was under the system of chattel slavery. Things that were quite unspeakable went on there in the packing houses all the time, and were taken for granted by everybody; only they did not show, as in the old slavery times, because there was no difference in color between master and slave.[43]

The sexual exploitation described in *The Jungle* was an accurate reflection of a daily reality. It was not a reality of general concern (except to the victims) and it never became a popular cause. But the consequences were a matter of life and death well into the twentieth century. Andrew J. Cawley of the Bronx attests to this in a letter he wrote to the wife of William Sulzer, the governor of New York. It was dated January 5, 1913, and written to Mrs. Sulzer a few days after her husband's inaugural in the hope she would exert influence on the new governor to get Mrs. Cawley out of jail. "I can't understand why the man who wronged her is at liberty," Cawley wrote. "His wife was alive when this happened and my wife says he asked her to come to his office in reference to getting employment in the health department. It was while there that he locked the door and attacked her which was not right. . . ." At other points in the letter Cawley had explained that they had one young daughter, that his wife was pregnant, and that he was unemployed. There is no way to know if the Sulzers intervened.[44]

The Practice Against White Women

In 1887 a remarkable woman journalist, Helen Campbell, investigated the circumstances of working women and published the results in a book titled *Prisoners of Poverty.* About the authenticity of her information Campbell wrote it was "based upon minutest personal research . . . it is a photograph from life; and the various characters, whether employers or employed, were all registered in case corroboration were needed."[45] Although Campbell had never heard the words *sexual harassment,* the practice turned up repeatedly.

When they could, working women sometimes aided one another in the face of such coercion, as exemplified by the story of Rose Haggerty, who was protected in her first work at home by an older woman who would daily pick up each of their sewing bundles, assuming the additional burden of delivering Haggerty's to her. Campbell explained this was so "the agent had no opportunity to follow out what had now and then been his method, and hint to the girl that her pretty face entitled her to concessions that would be best made in a private interview."[46]

This is Campbell's description of the prevailing employment practices: "The swarming crowd of applicants are absolutely at the mercy of the manager or foreman, who, unless there is a sudden pressure of work, makes the selections according to fancy, youth and any gleam of prettiness being unfailing recommendations. There are many firms of which this could not be said with any justice. There are many more in which it is the law, tacitly laid down, but none the less a fact. . . ."[47]

A woman known only as a Mrs. W. is reported saying, "So far I've kept decent; I came of decent folks; but it's no fault of many a man that I've worked for that I can say so still. I've had to leave three places because they wouldn't let me alone, and I stay where I am now because they're quiet respectable people, and no outrageousness. . . ."[48]

"The True Story of Lotte Bauer" follows a young German girl's losing efforts to keep her wages at survival; about midway through this struggle, Campbell wrote:

> by January her ten and twelve hours' work brought her but six dollars instead of the eight or nine she had always earned. The foreman she hated made everything as difficult as possible. Though the bundle came ready from the cutting-room he had managed more than once to slip out some essential piece, and thus lessened her week's wages, no price being paid where a garment was returned unfinished. He had often done this where girls had refused his advances, yet it was impossible to make complaints. The great house on Canal Street left these matters entirely with him and regarded complaint as mere blackmailing. . . .[49]

Aside from manufacturing work, the largest field for women at this time was domestic service, where conditions of sexual harassment were the same if not worse. Campbell recorded the following bitter story from a discussion among sweatshop workers:

> Do you know what come to my girl . . . I put her with a lady that wanted a waitress and said she'd train her well. She'd three boarders in the house, and all gentlemen to look at, and one that's in a bank to-day he did his best to turn her head on the sly, and when he found he couldn't one Sunday when she was alone in the house and none to hear or help, he had his will. The mistress turned her off the hour she heard it, for Nettie went to her when she came home. Such things don't happen unless the girl is to blame, she said. "Never show your shameless face here again." Nettie came home to me kind of dazed, and she stayed dazed till she went to a hospital and a baby was born dead, and she dead herself a week after. It's over an' over that that thing happens . . . I'll warn every girl to keep to herself an' learn a trade, an' not run the risk she'll run if she goes out to service.[50]

Risk or not, many women could only earn money by entering this field. Louisa May Alcott, who wrote *Little Women,* began her writing career with newspaper articles, the theme of one of these early pieces being "How I Went Out to Service." It is a description of sexual harassment by the Reverend Josephus, a thirty-five-year-old bachelor, who first lavished "tender blandishments" and then, when rejected, only the ugliest and dirtiest of work. Alcott quit the post, writing that her heart had "suffered many of the trials that wound deeply yet cannot be told."[51] Whether they could be told or not, the trials of sexual harassment in domestic service were rampant. As a result of her investigations into conditions in this field Campbell wrote:

"Household service has become synonymous with the worst degradation that comes to woman. Women who have been in service, and remained in it contentedly until marriage, unite in saying that things have so changed that only here and there is a young girl safe, and that domestic service is the cover for more licentiousness than can be found in any other trade in which women are at work."[52]

In addition to manufacturing work and domestic service, a working woman of the time might have sought employment in the newer occupations of shop girl and waitress, but if she hoped by these routes to bypass sexual harassment she was bound to be frustrated; the hazards persisted. From one of Campbell's interviews:

"I was at H——'s, for six months, and there you have to ask a man for leave every time it is necessary to go upstairs (to the ladies' room) and half the time he would look and laugh with the other clerks. I'd rather be where there are all women. They're hard on you sometimes, but they don't use foul language and insult you when you can't help yourself."[53]

Campbell commented: "Many sensitive and shrinking girls have brought on severe illnesses arising solely from dread of running this gauntlet."[54]

Waitresses were prey to other hazards. A 1907 issue of *McClure's Magazine* includes "The Diary of An Amateur Waitress" by Maud Younger, who recounted the way a regular waitress advised her to get customers. "Oh, you must jolly your customers along. Sometimes I give him a whack. The boss likes us to be fresh with the customers."[55]

The Practice Against Black Women

The history of sexual harassment toward black working women begins with slavery, when the pattern for exploitative sex with black women first evolved. Gerda Lerner writes in *Black Women in White America:* "Their free availability as sex objects to any white man was enshrined in tradition, upheld by the laws forbidding intermarriage, enforced by terror against black men and women and, though frowned upon by white community opinion, tolerated both in its clandestine and open manifestations."[56] When slavery ended this pattern was perpetuated in both the North and South through sexual harassment of black women on the job.

In a 1912 issue of *The Independent* a black nurse published "More Slavery at the South," in which she wrote of this first-hand:

I remember very well the first and last work place from which I was dismissed. I lost my place because I refused to let the madam's husband kiss me. He must have been accustomed to undue familiarity with his servants, or else he took it as a matter of course, because without any love-making at all, soon after I was installed as cook, he walked up to me, threw his arms around me, and was in the act of kissing me, when I demanded to know what he meant, and shoved him away. I was young then, and newly married, and didn't know then what has been a burden to my mind and heart ever since; that a colored woman's virtue in this part of the country has no protection. I at once went home, and told my husband about it. When my husband went to the man who had insulted me, the man cursed him, and slapped him, and—had him arrested! The police judge fined my husband $25. I was present at the hearing, and testified on oath to the insult offered me.

The white man, of course, denied the charge. The old judge looked up and said: "This court will never take the word of a nigger against the word of a white man."[57]

Conditions in the North were as terrible, only different; there the black woman was excluded from all but the most menial labor and sexually victimized by dishonest employment agencies, agencies that pushed her more and more into odd jobs and "disorderly houses." In a 1905 issue of *Charities and the Commons,* Frances A. Kellor, general director of the Inter-Municipal Committee on Household Research, described the employment-agency traffic in black women workers:

> These green Southern girls are collected in the South by white agents and shipped North, assured that good places exist. They are charged $19.50 for transportation which costs $7; they sign a contract to work one or two months without pay; they agree to send their baggage to the employment agency, which can keep it if they do not pay at the end of sixty days; a runner meets them at the docks and often robs them of their small savings; they are taken to a lodging-house— often the agency—where men and women, colored and white, habitués of disorderly houses, intemperate and good are all lodged together. There is no protection at the docks or at the stations. The new arrival does not meet one person outside of those under the influence of this agent. When a girl without baggage, $20 in debt, and a total stranger in the city, is sent to a disorderly place, upon threats or promises, can she be said to be anything more than a slave?[58]

Kellor, in typical Victorian fashion, begs the real issue. Jane Addams in *A New Conscience and an Ancient Evil* did not. According to Brownlee and Brownlee, she was among the first to show that these "agencies" were "often found to be associated with pimps . . . arranged lodging in a house owned by a pimp, and thereby provided a means to ease young women into prostitution. Facilitating the exploitation was the reluctance of courts to give credit to the testimony of black women when it was given against white men."[59]

Notes

1. Nancy Smith Barrett, "The Economy Ahead of Us," *Women and the American Economy,* edited by Juanita Kreps (Englewood Cliffs, N.J.: Prentice-Hall, 1976) p. 157.
2. Edward Gross, "Plus Can Change . . . ? The Sexual Structure of Occupations over Time," *Social Problems* (Fall 1968) p. 202.
3. Barrett, loc. cit.
4. Adrienne Rich, *Of Woman Born* (New York: Norton, 1976) p. 57.
5. Nancy M. Henley, "Power, Sex and Nonverbal Communication" in *Language and Sex,* edited by Barrie Thorne and Nancy Henley (Massachusetts: Newbury House Publishers, 1975) p. 184.
6. Erving Goffman, "The Nature of Deference and Demeanor," *American Anthropologist,* LVIII, 1956, pp. 473–502.
7. Michael Argyle, *Psychology of Interpersonal Behavior,* (London: Cox and Wyman Ltd., 1967).
8. "Both physical closeness and staring seem to be perceived as warning signals in the confrontation sequences. . . ." George Maclay and Humphry Knipe, *The Dominant Man* (New York: Delacorte, 1972) p. 58.
9. Henley, op. cit., p. 192.
10. Nancy M. Henley, "The Politics of Touch," *Radical Psychology,* edited by Phil Brown (New York: Harper, 1973) p. 423.
11. Henley, *Language and Sex,* p. 184.
12. Ibid., p. 192.
13. Catherine Radecki, "Differences in the Use of Dominance Gestures in an Occupational Setting by Sex and Status," mimeographed, University of Delaware, September 1976.

14. Henley, "The Politics of Touch," pp. 431–432.
15. Heidi Hartmann, "Capitalism, Patriarchy and Job Segregation by Sex," *Signs: Journal of Women in Culture and Society*, Vol. I, No. 3 (Spring 1976), Part 2 pp. 138–139.
16. Ibid.
17. Ibid. p. 153.
18. Neil Smelser, *Social Change and the Industrial Revolution* (Chicago: University of Chicago Press, 1959), chaps. 9–11, cited in Hartmann.
19. Frederick Engels, *The Condition of the Working Class in England in 1844* (London: George Allen & Unwin, 1892) p. 199, cited in Hartmann.
20. Hartmann, op. cit., p. 155.
21. Sidney Webb, "The Alleged Differences in the Wages Paid to Men and Women for Similar Work," *Economic Journal* 1, No.4 (December 1891) pp. 639–658, cited in Hartmann.
22. Millicent G. Fawcett, "Equal Pay for Equal Work," *Economic Journal*, 28, No. 1 (March 1918) pp. 1–6, cited in Hartmann.
23. F. Y. Edgeworth, "Equal Pay to Men and Women for Equal Work," *Economic Journal*, 32, No. 4 (December 1922), p. 439, cited in Hartmann.
24. Hartmann, op. cit. p. 160.
25. Ibid. p. 161.
26. Edith Abbott, *Women in Industry* (New York: Arno Press, 1969) p. 92, cited in Hartmann.
27. Hartmann, op. cit. p. 161.
28. Elizabeth F. Baker, *Technology and Women's Work* (New York: Columbia University Press, 1964) p. 34, cited in Hartmann.
29. John B. Andrews and W. D. P. Bliss, "History of Women in Trade Unions" in *Report on Condition of Woman and Child Wage-Earners in the United States*, Vol. 10, printed by Government Printing Office, 1911, reprinted as *History of Women in Trade Unions* (New York: Arno Press, 1974) p. 69.
30. Hartmann, op. cit. p. 163.
31. Abbott, op. cit. pp. 252–253, cited in Hartmann.
32. Gail Falk, "Women and Unions: A Historical View," mimeographed, Yale Law School, published in shortened form in *Women's Rights Law Reporter*, 1 (Spring 1973) pp. 54–65, cited in Hartmann.
33. Eleanor Flexner, *Century of Struggle* (New York: Atheneum, 1970) p. 136, cited in Hartmann.
34. Abbott, op. cit. p. 260.
35. Hartmann, op. cit. p. 164.
36. Ibid. p. 165.
37. Ibid.
38. Ann C. Hill, "Protective Labor Legislation for Women: Its Origin and Effect," mimeographed, Yale Law School, 1970; published in part in Barbara A. Babcock, Ann E. Freeman, Eleanor H. Norton and Susan C. Ross, *Sex Discrimination and the Law: Causes and Remedies* (Boston: Little, Brown & Company, 1975), cited in Hartmann.
39. Elisha Bartlett, "A Vindication of the Character and Condition of the Females Employed in the Lowell Mills Against the Charges Contained in the Boston *Times* and the Boston *Quarterly Review*," orig. published Lowell, Massachusetts, 1841; reprinted in *Women of Lowell* (New York: Arno Press, 1974) p. 19.
40. *Voice of Industry*, Fitchburg, Massachusetts, September 18, 1846. Cornell University Industrial and Labor Relations Archives.
41. This is largely based on William Wallace Sanger, *History of Prostitution: Its Extent, Causes and Effects throughout the World* (New York: Harper, 1869), an official report to the Board of alms-house governors of New York City; Reginald Wright Kauffman, *The House of Bondage* (New York: Moffat, Yard and Company, 1910), a report of the special Grand Jury appointed in New York in January 1910 to investigate white slave traffic; and Havelock Ellis, *Sex in Relation to Society* (Philadelphia: F. A. Davis Company, 1910).
42. Helen Laura Sumner, "History of Women in Industry in the United States, 1910," in *Report on Condition of Woman and Child Wage-Earners in the United States*, Vol. 9, printed by Government

Printing Office, 1911; reprinted as *History of Women in Industry in the United States* (New York: Arno Press, 1974) p. 98.

43. Upton Sinclair, *The Jungle,* orig. published 1905 (New York: New American Library, 1960) p. 109.

44. William Sulzer papers, 1890–1940. Department of Manuscripts and University Archives. Cornell University.

45. Helen Campbell, *Women Wage-Workers, Their Trades and Their Lives* (Boston: Roberts Brothers, 1887), reprinted as *Prisoners of Poverty* (Westport, Conn.: Greenwood Press, 1970, 1975) preface.

46. Ibid. p. 22.

47. Ibid. p. 35.

48. Ibid. p. 87.

49. Ibid. p. 97.

50. Ibid. pp. 135–136.

51. Louisa M. Alcott, "How I Went Out To Service," *The Independent,* New York, June 4, 1874.

52. Campbell, op. cit. p. 234.

53. Ibid. p. 181.

54. Ibid., loc. cit.

55. Maud Younger, "The Diary of an Amateur Waitress," *McClure's Magazine,* 1907.

56. Gerda Lerner, *Black Women in White America* (New York: Random House, 1973) pp. 149–150.

57. Ibid., pp. 155–156.

58. Frances A. Kellor, "Southern Colored Girls in the North," *Charities and the Commons,* 1905.

59. Mary M. Brownlee and W. Elliott Brownlee, *Women in the American Economy* (New Haven: Yale University Press, 1976) p. 244.

❖ 2. Sexual Harassment of Working Women: A Case of Sex Discrimination

Catharine A. MacKinnon

Intimate violation of women by men is sufficiently pervasive in American society[1] as to be nearly invisible. Contained by internalized and structural forms of power, it has been nearly inaudible. Conjoined with men's control over women's material survival, as in the home or on the job, or over women's learning and educational advancement in school, it has become institutionalized. Women employed in the paid labor force,[2] typically hired "as women," dependent upon their income and lacking job alternatives, are particularly vulnerable to intimate violation in the form of sexual abuse at work. In addition to being victims of the practice, working women have been subject to the social failure to recognize sexual harassment as an abuse at all. Tacitly, it has been both acceptable and taboo; acceptable for men to do, taboo for women to confront, even to themselves. But the systematic silence enforced by employment sanctions is beginning to be broken. The daily impact upon women's economic status and work opportunities, not to mention psychic health and self-esteem, is beginning to be explored, documented, and, increasingly, resisted.

Sexual harassment, most broadly defined, refers to the unwanted imposition of sexual requirements in the context of a relationship of unequal power. Central to the concept is the use of power derived from one social sphere to lever benefits or impose deprivations in another. The major dynamic is best expressed as the reciprocal enforcement of two inequalities. When one is sexual, the other material, the cumulative sanction is particularly potent. American society legitimizes male sexual dominance of women and employer's control of workers, although both forms of dominance have limits and exceptions. Sexual harassment of women in employment is particularly clear when male superiors on the job coercively initiate unwanted sexual advances to women employees; sexual pressures by male co-workers and customers, when condoned or encouraged by employers, might also be included. Lack of reciprocal feeling on the woman's part may be expressed by rejection or show of disinclination. After this, the advances may be repeated or intensified; often employment retaliation ensues. The material coercion behind the advances may remain implicit in the employer's position to apply it. Or it may be explicitly communicated through, for example, firing for sexual noncompliance or retention conditioned upon continued sexual compliance.

Sexual harassment may occur as a single encounter or as a series of incidents at work. It may place a sexual condition upon employment opportunities at a clearly defined threshold, such as hiring, retention, or advancement; or it may occur as a pervasive or continuing condition of the work environment. Extending along a continuum of severity and unwantedness, and depending upon the employment circumstances, examples include

> verbal sexual suggestions or jokes, constant leering or ogling, brushing against your body "accidentally," a friendly pat, squeeze or pinch or arm against you, catching you alone for a quick kiss, the indecent proposition backed by the threat of losing your job, and forced sexual relations.[3]

Complex forms include the persistent innuendo and the continuing threat which is never consummated either sexually or economically. The most straightforward example is "put out or get out." . . .

SEXUAL HARASSMENT AS SEX DISCRIMINATION: AN INEQUALITY ARGUMENT

Practices which express and reinforce the social inequality of women to men are clear cases of sex-based discrimination in the *inequality* approach. Sexual harassment of working women is argued to be employment discrimination based on gender where gender is defined as the social meaning of sexual biology. Women are sexually harassed by men because they are women, that is, because of the social meaning of female sexuality, here, in the employment context. Three kinds of arguments support and illustrate this position: first, the exchange of sex for survival has historically assured women's economic dependence and inferiority as well as sexual availability to men. Second, sexual harassment expresses the male sex-role pattern of coercive sexual initiation toward women, often in vicious and unwanted ways. Third, women's sexuality largely defines women as women in this society, so violations of it are abuses of women as women.

Tradition

Sexual harassment perpetuates the interlocked structure by which women have been kept sexually in thrall to men and at the bottom of the labor market. Two forces of American society converge: men's control over women's sexuality and capital's control over employees' work lives. Women historically have been required to exchange sexual services for material survival, in one form or another. Prostitution and marriage as well as sexual harassment in different ways institutionalize this arrangement.

The impact of these forces, which affect all women, often varies by class. Exclusion of moderately well-off women (that is, women attached to moderately well-off men) from most gainful occupations was often excused by fears that virtuous women would fall victim to sexual predators if they were allowed to work.[4] This exclusion, however, insured their dependence for survival upon bartering attractiveness and sexuality for subsistence, only from different men. Deprived of education and training in marketable skills, excluded from most professions, and disdaining as unsuitable the menial work reserved for their lower-class sisters, such women's adequacy was traditionally measured in large part by sexual allure. As they entered the paid labor force in increasing numbers, the sexual standard they were judged by accompanied them; the class status they held as adjuncts to middle-class men did not. Working-class and poor women did not have the choice between the home and the workplace. And they have always maintained an even more precarious hold on jobs than their male counterparts, with chronically lower wages, and usually without security or the requisites to claim advancement. Because they were women, these factors put them at the mercy of the employer sexually[5] as well as economically. Once in the work force, usually in women's jobs, the class distinctions among women were qualified by their common circumstance, which was sex defined. "Sometimes the employer's son, or the master himself, or the senior stablehand, would have taken them. Men didn't always use brute force, the physical coercion or the threat of it that is the standard definition of rape. Often the threat of dismissal was sufficient."[6]

This point is illustrated in the following excerpt from Olive Pratt Rayner's *The Typewriter Girl* (dated by Margery Davies as late nineteenth century):

> Three clerks (male), in seedy black coats, the eldest with hair the color of a fox's, went on chaffing with one another for two minutes after I closed the door, with ostentatious unconsciousness of my insignificant presence. . . . The youngest, after a while, wheeled around on his high stool and broke out with the chivalry of his class and age, "Well, what's your business?"
>
> My voice trembled a little, but I mustered up courage and spoke. "I have called about your advertisement . . ."
>
> He eyed me up and down. I am slender, and, I will venture to say, if not pretty, at least interesting looking.
>
> "How many words a minute?" he asked after a long pause.
>
> I stretched the truth as far as its elasticity would permit. "Ninety-seven," I answered. . . .
>
> The eldest clerk, with the foxy head, wheeled around, and took his turn to stare. He had hairy hands and large goggle-eyes. . . . I detected an undercurrent of double meaning. . . . I felt disagreeably like Esther in the presence of Ahasuerus—a fat and oily Ahasuerus of fifty. . . . He perused me up and down with his small pig's eyes, as if he were buying a horse, scrutinizing my face, my figure, my hands, my feet. I felt like a Circassian in an Arab slavemarket.[7]

Millett generalizes this observation: "A female is continually obliged to seek survival or advancement through the approval of males as those who hold power. She may do this through appeasement or through the exchange of her sexuality for support and status."[8]

The generality of "women" and "men" must be qualified by recognizing the distinctive effect of race. Racism does not allow black men to share white men's dominance of economic resources. Black women have not tended to be economically dependent upon black men to the degree white women have been upon white men. To the extent black women are employed by white men, as most have been from slavery until the present, the foregoing analysis applies directly to them, intensified, not undercut, by race. There is little indication that this statement by an anonymous black woman in 1912 is significantly outdated.

I remember very well the first and last work place from which I was dismissed. I lost my place because I refused to let the madam's husband kiss me. . . . he took it as a matter of course, because without any love-making at all, soon after I was installed as cook, he walked up to me, threw his arms around me, and was in the act of kissing me, when I demanded to know what he meant, and shoved him away. . . . I believe nearly all white men take, and expect to take, undue liberties with their colored female servants. . . . where the girl is not willing, she has only herself to depend upon for protection. . . . what we need is present help, present sympathy, better wages, better hours, more protection, and a chance to breathe for once while alive as free women.[9]

Moreover, when black women enter the labor market of the dominant society, they succeed to the secondary place of white females (remaining, in addition, under the disabilities of blacks), while black men succeed at least to some of the power of the male role. Indeed, many of the demands of the black civil rights movement in the 1960s centered upon just such a recovery of "manhood."

Similar to the way in which the status of American blacks of both sexes encompasses personal and economic exploitation, sexual harassment deprives women of personhood by relegating them to subservience through jointly exploiting their sexuality and their work. As women begin to achieve the minimum material conditions under which equality with men can concretely be envisioned, and increasingly consider their skills worth a wage and their dignity worth defending, the necessity to exchange sex for support becomes increasingly intolerable. It is a reminder of that image of a deprived reality in which sexuality and attractiveness to men were all a woman had to offer—and she had very little control over either. The history of the role of sexuality in enforcing women's second-class economic status, sketched only very briefly here, makes sexual requirements of work "uniquely disturbing to women."[10]

It is a reminder, a badge or indicia [sic] of the servile status she suffered . . . and which she is now trying to shake off. . . . To make her advancement on the job depend on her sexual performance is to resurrect her former status as man's property or plaything.[11]

But is such status really a thing of the past? The sexual harassment cases and evidence suggest that it is not. Emma Goldman's analysis has no less vitality now than in 1917:

Nowhere is a woman treated according to the merit of her work, but rather as a sex. It is therefore almost inevitable that she should pay for her right to exist, to keep a position in whatever line, with sex favors. Thus it is merely a question of degree whether she sells herself to one man, in or out of marriage, or to many men.[12]

A guarantee against discrimination "because of sex" has little meaning if a major traditional dynamic of enforcement and expression of inferior sex status is allowed to persist untouched. A guarantee of equal access to job training, education, and skills has little substance if a requirement of equality in hiring, promotion, and pay can legally be withheld if a woman refuses to grant sexual favors. A man who is allowed to measure a woman's work by sexual standards cannot be said to employ her on the basis of merit. If a woman must grant sexual consideration to her boss in exchange for employment benefits, her material status still depends upon her sexual performance, and the legal promise of equality for women is an illusion.

Sex Roles

In *Stanton v. Stanton*, the Supreme Court spoke of the "role-typing society has long imposed"[13] on the basis of sex. Congress effectively recognized the unsuitability of sex-based

social role distinctions as they deprive women of economic opportunities in the original enactment and later extension and strengthening of Title VII, the federal contract compliance provisions, and in the Congressional passage of the Equal Pay Act and Equal Rights
Amendment. No difference between the sexes was considered to justify the inferior economic status women were found to occupy throughout the economy, a status which sexual
harassment exploits and promotes.[14] In the vast and growing scholarly literature investigating social role differentiation by sex in America,[15] dominance and aggressiveness are
found to characterize the ideal of "masculinity" in general and in sexual relations. Women's
sex roles define the feminine ideal in general and in sex as submissive, passive, and receptive to male initiative. A major substantive element in the social meaning of masculinity,
what men learn makes them "a man," is sexual conquest of women; in turn, women's femininity is defined in terms of acquiescence to male sexual advances. Social expectations,
backed by a variety of sanctions ranging from rape to job reprisals to guilt manipulation,
enforce these models by which both sexes learn to act out, and thereby become, the sex they
are assigned. The inequality in the description is apparent: women are conditioned to become, and to think of themselves as, the proper subordinates of men, who learn to define
their male identity partly in terms of their prowess in sexually dominating women. Some
men are beginning to consider that this aspect of male identity not only systematically oppresses women, but, as it aggrandizes men's power, restricts their humanity.[16]

Sexual harassment is discrimination "based on sex" within the social meaning of sex, as
the concept is socially incarnated in sex roles. Pervasive and "accepted" as they are, these
rigid roles have no place in the allocation of social and economic resources. If they are allowed to persist in these spheres, economic equality for women is impossible. The "sex
stereotype" comes the closest to capturing the sex role argument in legal form. In the sexual harassment cases, some plaintiffs' attorneys have urged it as a theory for prohibiting
sexual harassment under Title VII. Difficult as it is to criticize one of the few concepts
available, the sex stereotype is ill-suited to the requisite analysis of sexual harassment.

A claim that a practice is discriminatory because it is based upon a sex stereotype is
grounded either upon an argument that the stereotype is not, in general, true (hence practices based upon it are arbitrary), or upon an individual woman's claim to be an exception
or potential exception to what *is* generally true of women. The concept essentially addresses
the use of false images of women in employment. Accordingly, it is useful for attacking sexualized job descriptions and work-related conceptions. It also helps to rebut the misconception that women enjoy sexual harassment, were a kind of "consent" defense to arise. In
a sense, a sex stereotype is present in the male attitude, expressed through sexual harassment, that women are sexual beings whose privacy and integrity can be invaded at will, beings who exist for men's sexual stimulation or gratification. The strength of the argument
is that it allows men to be considered sincere, if wrong, in their treatment of women according to long accepted, if inappropriate, norms. But as an affirmative argument—that is,
that sexual harassment is treatment based on sex because it is treatment based upon a sex
stereotype—the argument is unfortunately incomplete.

The sex stereotype concept locates the overgeneralization, the distortion which is the
substance of the injury of stereotyping, on the level of *image,* when the injury of sexual harassment is both on the level of image and on the level of reality. In the context of employment, sexual harassment is plainly an arbitrary practice. But it is not only or even fundamentally arbitrariness—in the sense of a divergence between a reality and a behavior
purported to be based upon it—that is damaging to women about the practice. To the extent sexual harassment converges with, and mirrors, the accepted social reality of sexual relations, it corresponds to the real social meaning of the sex difference. It does not diverge

from or distort this reality. To the extent sexual harassment reflects real social differences between the sexes, it is not arbitrary. If the social meaning of sexuality is accepted, sexual harassment can be seen as a differentiation in treatment due to the social realities of sex.

That is, it is the social reality of sexual relations, as expressed in sexual harassment, that "normally" and every day sexually oppresses women in order to affirm male sexual identity, as socially defined. This reality of treatment, which is the reference point for the argument of stereotyping that the practice is sex-based, is no false picture or illusion. These social relations themselves are shaped by an arguably false but, nevertheless, socially controlling image of relations between women and men. Thus, sexual harassment forms an integral part of the social stereotyping of all women as sexual objects and each individual grievant is but one example of it. So how does the practice lack a "factual basis"? To what true generalization about women is a sexually harassed woman "an exception"? For a heterosexual male so inclined, it is true, not illusory, that only a woman qualifies as the object of sexual harassment, just as for a white racist only a black qualifies as the object of racial harassment. This is true not because of a stereotype from which an exceptional woman might except herself, but because of the pervasively stereotyped social reality women live in. . . .

Sexuality

Sexual harassment is discrimination "based on sex" in the inequality approach because women are socially defined as women largely in sexual terms. The behaviors to which women are subjected in sexual harassment are behaviors specifically defined and directed toward the characteristics which define women's sexuality: secondary sex characteristics and sex-role behavior. It is no accident that the English language uses the term *sex* ambiguously to refer both to gender status (as in "the female sex") and to the activity of intercourse (as in "to have sex"). The term *sexual* is used in both senses. Further study of the language reveals that references to sexuality have a pejorative connotation for woman as a gender that is not comparable for men.

> Words indicating the station, relationship or occupation of men have remained untainted over the years. Those identifying women have repeatedly suffered the indignity of degeneration, many of them becoming sexually abusive. It is clearly not the women themselves who have coined and used these terms as epithets for each other. One sees today that it is men who describe women in sexual terms and insult them with sexual slurs, and the wealth of derogatory terms for women reveals something of their hostility. . . . [T]he largest category of words designating humans in sexual terms are those for women—especially for loose women. I have located roughly a thousand words and phrases describing women in sexually derogatory ways. There is nothing approaching this multitude for describing men.[17]

As a critical convergence of the physiological, psychological, social, economic, cultural and aesthetic, and political forces, sexuality is overburdened with determinants. Gender itself is largely defined in terms of sexuality in that heterosexuality is closely bound up with the social conceptions of maleness and femaleness.

Woman's sexuality is a major medium through which gender identity and gender status are socially expressed and experienced. An attack upon sexuality is an attack upon womanhood. A deprivation in employment worked through women's sexuality is a deprivation in employment because one is a woman, through one of the closest referents by which women are socially identified as such, by themselves and by men. Only women, and (as is not the case with pregnancy) all women possess female sexuality, the focus, occasion, and vehicle for this form of employment deprivation. Few men would maintain that they would have found a given woman just as ready or appropriate a target for sexual advances if she had been sexually male. Indeed, the close association between sexuality and gender identity makes it hard to imagine that a woman would be sexually the same if male. If any practice could be said to happen to a woman because she is a woman, sexual harassment should be one of the more straightforward examples of it.

Notes

1. Sexism is by no means unique to American culture. This discussion, for purposes of application to American law, focuses upon its forms in this culture.
2. Houseworkers (paid and unpaid) are excluded from this discussion of working women not because I think they do not work, nor because they do not suffer from sexual harassment. Most are not covered by Title VII's limitation to workplaces with fifteen or more employees. For one review of quantitative studies which discuss the contribution of unpaid housework to the Gross National Product, see Juanita Kreps, *Sex in the Marketplace: American Women at Work* (Baltimore: Johns Hopkins University Press, 1971), chap. 2.
3. "Sexual Harassment on the Job: Questions and Answers" (Ithaca, N. Y.: Working Women United Institute, 1975 [mimeograph]).
4. See Mary Bularzik, "Sexual Harassment at the Workplace: Historical Notes," *Radical America,* vol. 12, no. 4 (July-August 1978), at 25–43, especially the discussion at 29–31; Robert Smuts, *Women and Work in America* (New York: Schocken Books, 1971), at 88; Louise A. Tilly, Joan W. Scott, Miriam Cohen, "Women's Work and European Fertility Patterns," *Journal of Interdisciplinary History,* vol. 6, no. 3 (1976), at 463–470.
5. See William Sanger, *A History of Prostitution* (New York: Medical Publishing Co., 1858), repr. in Rosalyn Baxandall, Linda Gordon, and Susan Reverby, *America's Working Women* (New York: Random House, 1976), at 96; Richard B. Morris, *Government and Labor in Early America* (New York: Columbia University Press, 1946), repr. at *id.,* at 26–29.
6. Edward Shorter, "On Writing the History of Rape," *Signs: Journal of Women in Culture and Society,* vol. 3, no. 2 (Winter, 1977), at 475.
7. Bliven, *Wonderful Writing Machine,* at 75–76 (no date given), repr. in Margery Davies, *Woman's Place Is At the Typewriter: The Feminization of the Clerical Labor Force* (pamphlet), at 13, repr. from *Radical America,* vol. 8, no. 4 (July-August 1974).
8. Kate Millett, *Sexual Politics* (New York: Avon, 1969), at 54.
9. Gerda Lerner, *Black Women in White America* (New York: Vintage Books, 1973), at 149–150.
10. Memorandum in Opposition to Defendant Company's Motion to Dismiss Plaintiff's Title VII Claim at 10, *Tomkins v. Public Service Electric & Gas Co.,* 422 F. Supp. 553 (D.N.J. 1976).
11. *Id.,* at 14–15.
12. Emma Goldman, *The Traffic in Women* (New York: Times Change Press, 1970), at 20.
13. 421 U.S. 7, 15 (1975) (*Stanton I*). (Justice Blackmun for the majority).
14. In any argument to extend the coverage of Title VII, the issue of legislative intent requires disposition. No specific evidence of Congressional contemplation of sexual harassment was found. The view is widely held that the term *sex* was included in Title VII as a joke, by a fluke, or in an attempt to overload the legislation. There is evidence that certain members of Congress were less than sincere in their commitment to eliminating sex discrimination when they included the term in the original act. However, first, since the original enactment, courts have taken Congress at its word. The issue is, thus, whether sexual harassment comes within the term *sex,* as interpreted. Second, the appropriateness of understanding the legislative history of Title VII together with that of its amendments in 1972 and the Equal Pay Act is apparent. See *Barnes v. Costle,* 561 F.2d 983, 987 (D.C. Cir. 1977), and the following comments by Bessie Margolin, for 25 years Assistant or Associate General Counsel for the Department of Labor:

    The most illuminating measure of the significance of both the Equal Pay Act and the "sex" amendment requires particular emphasis because the mistaken idea has been circulating that, in contrast to race, color and creed discrimination, there is little or no legislative history or documentation bearing on the legislative intent or objectives of the "sex" amendment to Title VII. Anyone who asserts that the case against sex discrimination has not been documented prior to the inclusion of sex discrimination in Title VII, or that "the legislative history was virtually blank" and "the intent and reach of the amendment were shrouded in doubt" has manifestly overlooked the overwhelmingly impressive documentation presented at the hearings on the Equal Pay bills. This documentation is certainly no less thorough and convincing than the documentation of discrimination against the Negro. The chronology of the enactment of the Equal Pay Act and the Civil Rights Act, and the extensively documented facts and statistics emphasized at the hearings and in the debates on the Equal Pay bills can leave no doubt, I submit, of the direct relevance of this legislative history of the "sex" amendment of Title VII of the Civil Rights Act. . . . It seems fair to say, therefore, that only ignorance or thoughtless oversight of the pertinent legislative background, if not simply "entrenched prejudice" rooted in a psychological downgrading of women generally, can explain the view that the inclusion of sex discrimination in Title VII was no more than a "fluke" not to be taken seriously. . . . Commissioner Graham in his speech to the Personnel Conference of the American Management Association of February 9, 1966, specifically denounced the "fluke" charge and warned against the negative approach implicit in that characterization. He also made clear that the Commission is quite aware of the impressive legislative background underlying the Equal Pay Act and its manifest pertinence to the "sex" amendment of Title VII." (Bessie Margolin, "Equal Pay and Equal Opportunities for Women," N.Y.U., 19th Conference on Labor, 1967, at 297, 301, 306.) Third, Congress has had numerous opportunities to eliminate the term *sex* if it was not serious about its inclusion, but has chosen rather to strengthen and extend the provisions. On the occasion of the 1972 amendments, additional legislative history supports a commitment to ending sex discrimination. For example, Senator Percy said: "Even among the resolution's opponents, there seems to be little question but that tradition and law have worked together to relegate women to an inferior status in our society. In many cases, this has been intentional, based on an archaic precept that women, for physiological or functional reasons, are inferior." 118 Cong. Rec. 9595 (1972). In response to such perceptions, Congress extended coverage to previously exempted federal employees (leaving administration for federal employees to the Civil Service Commission, 42 U.S.C. §2000e-16; see also *Parks v. Dunlop*, 517 F. 2d 785, 787 (5th Cir. 1975), lowered the statutory minimum of number of employees over which coverage extends from 25 to 15 and conferred significant enforcement power on the EEOC. These strengthening, enforcement, and extension provisions would not have been made by a Congress that thought sex discrimination was a joke.

15. There are numerous excellent reviews and collections of sex role research. A classic in the field is Eleanor E. Maccoby, ed., *The Development of Sex Differences* (Stanford, Cal.: Stanford University Press, 1966). A bibliography of research conducted from 1973 to 1974 can be found in *Women's Work and Women's Studies, 1973–74, A Bibliography* (The Barnard College Women's Center, 1975), at 285–302, and a list of bibliographies on the subject at *id.,* 321–322. Recent books on varying levels include Carol Tavris and Carole Offir, *The Longest War: Sex Differences in Perspective* (New York: Harcourt, Brace Jovanovich, 1977); Nancy Reeves, *Womankind: Beyond the Stereotypes* (Chicago: Aldine Publishing Company, 1977); Shirley Weitz, *Sex Roles: Biological, Psychological and Social Foundations* (Oxford University Press, 1977). For a political perspective on sex roles in terms of power, see, *e.g.,* Nancy Hartsock, "Political Change: Two Perspectives on Power," *Quest: A Feminist Quarterly* (Summer 1974), at 10–25. An application to the law is Barbara Kirk Cavanagh, "A Little Dearer than His Horse: Legal Stereotypes and the Feminine Personality," 6 *Harv. C.R.C.L. Rev.* (1970), at 260–287.

16. Jon Snodgrass, ed., *For Men Against Sexism* (Albion, Cal.: Times Change Press, 1977) contains the best essays from this perspective to date. Warren Farrell, *The Liberated Man* (New York: Bantam, 1974) also treats this subject, substantially less well.

17. D. Schulz, "The Semantic Derogation of Women," in Barrie Thorne and Nancy Henley, eds., *Language and Sex: Difference and Dominance* (Rowley, Mass.: Newbury House, Publishers, 1975), at 67, 71.

❖ 3. Understanding Sexual Harassment at Work

Barbara A. Gutek

I. INTRODUCTION

The topic of sexual harassment at work was virtually unstudied until the concern of feminists brought the issue to the attention of the public and researchers. Much of the research on sexual harassment addresses two complementary questions. (1) How do people define sexual harassment? (2) How common is it? Research on these two issues provides useful background information for lawyers and policy makers interested in seeking legal redress for harassment victims, and ultimately in eradicating sexual harassment. . . .

II. THE DISCOVERY OF SEXUAL HARASSMENT

In the mid-1970s, sexuality in the workplace suddenly received considerable attention through the discovery of sexual harassment, which appeared to be relatively widespread and to have long-lasting, harmful effects on a significant number of working women. This "discovery" was somewhat counterintuitive, since some women were believed to benefit from seductive behavior and sexual behaviors at work, gaining unfair advantage and acquiring perks and privileges from their flirtatious and seductive behavior. The first accounts of sexual harassment were journalistic reports and case studies.[1] Soon the topic was catapulted into public awareness through the publication of two important books. Lin Farley's book, *Sexual Shakedown: The Sexual Harassment of Women on the Job,* aimed to bring sexual harassment to public attention, create a household word, and make people aware of harassment as a social problem. Catharine MacKinnon's book, *Sexual Harassment of Working Women,* sought a legal mechanism for handling sexual harassment and compensating its victims. [See Selections 1 and 2.] In a strong and compelling argument, MacKinnon contended that sexual harassment was primarily a problem for women, that it rarely happened to men, and therefore that it should be viewed as a form of sex discrimination. Viewing sexual harassment as a form of sex discrimination would make available to victims the same legal protection available to victims of sex discrimination. In 1980, The Equal Employment Opportunity Commission (EEOC) established guidelines consistent with MacKinnon's position and defined sexual harassment under Title VII of the 1964 Civil Rights Act as a form of unlawful sex-based discrimination. Several states have passed their own increasingly strong laws aimed at eliminating sexual harassment and legal scholars have sought additional avenues to recover damages incurred from sexual harassment. Various public and private agencies as well as the courts have seen a steady if uneven increase in sexual harassment complaints since the early 1980s.

The various guidelines and regulations define sexual harassment broadly. For example, the updated EEOC guidelines state that

> [u]nwelcome sexual advances, requests for sexual favors, and other verbal or physical conduct of a sexual nature constitute sexual harassment when (1) submission to such conduct is made either explicitly or implicitly a term or condition of an individual's employment or academic advancement, (2) submission to or rejection of such conduct by an individual is used as the basis for employment decisions or academic decisions affecting such individual, or (3) such conduct has the

purpose or effect of reasonably interfering with an individual's work or academic performance or creating an intimidating, hostile, or offensive working or academic environment.[2]

Researchers began serious study of sex at work only after Farley's and MacKinnon's books and two compendia of information on sexual harassment[3] were in progress and generally after the EEOC had established guidelines in 1980. Not surprisingly, researchers were heavily influenced by these important developments in policy and law. These developments focused the concerns of researchers on the two specific issues mentioned above: definition of harassment and frequency of occurrence.

III. DEFINING SEXUAL HARASSMENT

The first issue can be succinctly stated: "What constitutes sexual harassment?" For lawyers, the courts, personnel managers, ombudspersons, and others, this is perhaps the most important issue that they must face. If "it" is harassment, it is illegal; otherwise it is not. Researchers, aware of the problems in defining harassment and perhaps eager to contribute to the developments in law and policy, began to supply a spate of studies.

Studies concerned with the definition of sexual harassment come in two types. First are surveys of various populations of people who are asked to tell whether various acts constitute sexual harassment. Second are experimental studies in which students, employees, or managers are asked to rate one or more hypothetical situations in which aspects of the situation are varied along important dimensions. These experimental studies using a hypothetical situation, also known as the "paper people paradigm," come in two variants. In the first variant, subjects are asked to determine whether a particular scenario depicts an instance of sexual harassment. In the second variant, researchers examine the attributions of subjects to understand how subjects' interpretations of a scenario affect their use of the label, sexual harassment.

The strengths of the experimental research design—random assignment to conditions and manipulation of causal variables—allow researchers to make causal statements about what affects how people define sexual harassment. The weakness of the design is that the situation is invariably insufficiently "real": subjects who have limited information and little appreciation of, or experience with, the subject matter may not respond the way people would in a real (rather than hypothetical) situation.

The survey studies show that sexual activity as a requirement of the job is defined as sexual harassment by about eighty-one percent[4] to ninety-eight percent[5] of working adults, and similar results have been reported with students as subjects.[6] Lesser forms of harassment such as sexual touching are not as consistently viewed as sexual harassment. For example, I found that fifty-nine percent of men but eighty-four percent of women asserted that sexual touching at work is sexual harassment.[7] A sizable minority (twenty-two percent of men and thirty-three percent of women) considered sexual comments at work meant to be complimentary to be sexual harassment.[8]

In contrast to the survey studies which often ask respondents to specify which of a set of actions constitutes harassment, in experimental studies, subjects are usually asked to rate how harassing some incident is, on a five-point or seven-point scale. Such a method makes it impossible to say what percentage of people consider any particular act or event harassment and results are usually reported as mean scores (on, say, a three-, five-, or seven-point scale). It should be noted that experimental studies are generally not concerned with the percentage of their subjects, usually students, who consider behavior X to be harassment, but instead address the factors or variables which affect whether or not some specified incident or act is labeled harassment.

The experimental studies show that except for the most outrageous and clearly inappropriate behavior, whether or not an incident is labeled harassment varies with several characteristics of the incident and the people involved. In these studies, the following variables make a difference: (1) the behavior in question, (2) the relationship between harasser and victim, (3) the sex of the harasser, (4) the sex and age of the victim, (5) the sex of the rater, and (6) the occupation of the person doing the rating. Another way of categorizing these factors is shown in Figure 1: characteristics of the behavior, nature of the relationship between the actors, characteristics of the observer/rater, and context factors all affect whether or not a particular act or event is considered sexual harassment.

Figure 1: Factors affecting the definition of sexual harassment

1. *Characteristics of the behavior.* The more physically intrusive and persistent the behavior, the more likely it is to be defined as sexual harassment by an observer.

2. *The nature of the relationship between actors.* The better the two actors know each other (friends, spouses, long-time co-workers) the less likely the behavior will be labeled sexual harassment by an observer.

3. *Characteristics of the observer.* Men and people in authority (e.g., senior faculty, senior managers) are less likely than others to label a behavior sexual harassment.

4. *Context factors.* The greater the inequality (in position, occupation, age), the more likely the behavior will be labeled sexual harassment by an observer. When the "recipient" of the behavior is low status or relatively powerless (female, young, poor), the behavior is more likely to be judged harassment than when the "recipient" is high status or relatively powerful.

The most important factor determining judgment of sexual harassment is the behavior involved. The experimental studies and survey studies yield the same pattern of findings: explicitly sexual behavior and behavior involving implied or explicit threats are more likely to be perceived as harassment than other, less threatening or potentially complimentary behavior. Touching is also more likely to be rated as sexual harassment than comments, looks, or gestures. In addition, Weber-Burdin and Rossi concluded that the initiator's behavior is much more important than the recipient's behavior, although if a female recipient behaved seductively, college student raters may reduce the ratings of harassment.[9]

The relationship between the two people is also important. The situation is considered more serious harassment when the initiator is a supervisor of the recipient rather than an equal or a subordinate or more serious if the person previously declined to date the harasser than if the two people had a prior dating relationship. The incident is more likely to be viewed as sexual harassment when a man is the harasser, a woman is the victim and when the female victim is young.

The person doing the rating makes a difference. The most important characteristic of the rater is gender. When women are doing the rating, they define a wide variety of sexual behaviors at work as sexual harassment, while men tend to rate only the more extreme behaviors as harassment. Similarly, on a scale of Tolerance for Sexual Harassment (TSHI), college men reported more tolerance than women, that is, men objected less than women to sexually harassing behavior. In short, the finding that women apply a broader definition of sexual harassment than men is pervasive and widely-replicated although not universally found. It is worth noting that at least one factor strongly associated with gender, sex role identity, did not make much of a difference in people's judgments of sexual harassment.

Powell, using a student sample, found that sex-role identity generally did not affect the definition of sexual harassment although highly feminine subjects were somewhat more likely than others to label some behaviors sexual harassment and highly masculine male students were somewhat less likely than others to label insulting sexual remarks sexual harassment.[10] In addition, organizational status seems to have an effect. Higher-level managers rating an incident are less likely to see it as serious harassment than middle-level or lower-level managers. In one study, faculty tended to view an incident as less serious than students[11] whereas in another, there were no substantial differences in the ratings of faculty and students.[12]

The experimental studies using an attribution analysis probe an evaluator's thought processes as he or she makes a determination whether or not a particular scenario constitutes harassment. Pryor suggested that people are more likely to judge a man's behavior sexual harassment if his behavior is attributed to his enduring negative intentions toward the target woman.[13] Such negative intentions can either reflect hostility or insensitivity to women. Pryor and Day found that the perspective people take in interpreting a social-sexual encounter affects their judgments of sexual harassment.[14] This may help explain why men and women tend to differ in their judgments of sexual harassment, that is, men may take the man's (usually the initiator's) point of view whereas women are more likely to take the woman's (the victim in many experimental studies) point of view. In support of this view, Konrad and Gutek found that women's greater experience with sexual harassment helps to explain the sex differences in defining sexual harassment.[15] In a similar vein, Kenig and Ryan came to the conclusion that men's and women's perceptions of sexual harassment reflect their own self-interest.[16] It is in men's self-interest to see relatively little sexual harassment because men are most often the offenders whereas it is in women's self-interest to see relatively more sexual harassment because women tend to be the victims in sexual harassment encounters.

Cohen and Gutek's analyses suggest that people may make different attributions depending on whether or not they view the initiator and recipient as friends.[17] More specifically, they found that when student subjects were asked to evaluate an ambiguous, potentially mildly sexually harassing encounter, they tended to assume that the two participants were friends, perhaps dating partners, and that the behavior was welcome and complimentary rather than harassing. Similarly, student subjects were less likely to rate a behavior harassment if they knew that the parties formerly dated and were more likely to rate a behavior harassment if the woman recipient had formerly refused to date the male initiator. In the latter case, subjects may attribute the man's overture to his "enduring negative intentions" toward the woman since her prior refusal of a date presumably eliminates the explanation that he was unsure how she felt about him.

IV. FREQUENCY OF SEXUAL HARASSMENT AT WORK

The other area of research that developed in response to legal and policy development was a documentation of the forms and prevalence of harassment experienced by people. In 1979, MacKinnon wrote: "The unnamed should not be taken for the nonexistent."[18] Thus, providing a label and then a definition for sexual harassment was an important step in developing ways to measure the prevalence of sexual harassment.

The research on frequency of harassment focuses heavily but not exclusively on heterosexual encounters.[19] It is often studied separate from the research on definition and employs a different research design and different subjects. Research aiming to establish rates of harassment in a population must be concerned with drawing a representative sample from a known population in order to generalize results in that population.

The research on prevalence shows a broad range of rates, depending in part on the time frame used. The U.S. Merit Systems Protection Board's study found that forty-two percent of the women respondents reported experiencing sexual harassment on the job within the previous two years.[20] When the study was repeated several years later, the figure remained the same.[21] In a Seattle, Washington study of city employees, more than one-third of all respondents reported sexual harassment in the previous twenty-four months of city employment.[22] Dunwoody-Miller and Gutek found that twenty percent of California state civil service employees reported being sexually harassed at work in the previous five years.[23] Reviewing the results from several different measures of prevalence she used, Gutek suggested that up to fifty-three percent of women had been harassed sometime in their working life.[24] The figures are higher in the military; two-thirds of women surveyed in a 1990 study said they have been sexually harassed.[25]

Other studies using purposive or convenience samples generally show higher rates of harassment. In a study by the Working Women's Institute, seventy percent of the employed women respondents said they had experienced sexual harassment on their jobs.[26] An early study of the readers of *Redbook* magazine found that eighty-eight percent of those mailing in questionnaires had experienced sexual harassment.[27] Schneider reported that more than two-thirds of her matched sample of lesbian and heterosexual working women had experienced unwelcome sexual advances within the previous year.[28]

Because respondents in purposive or convenience samples can either choose whether or not to respond, and participating in the study may require some expenditure of effort, researchers assume that people who have been harassed may be more motivated to participate. Thus, the incidence rates are likely to be somewhat inflated.

Although women of all ages, races, occupations, income levels, and marital statuses experience harassment, research suggests that young and unmarried women are especially vulnerable. Not surprisingly, most women are harassed by men, not by women. In addition, women in nontraditional jobs (e.g., truck driver, neurosurgeon, engineer, roofer) and in nontraditional industries such as the military and mining are more likely to experience harassment than other women. These higher rates are over and above what is expected by their high amount of work contact with men. On the basis of the set of studies done so far, it seems likely that overall, from one-third to one-half of all women have been sexually harassed at sometime in their working lives, although frequency rates in some types of work may be higher.

Sexual harassment at work has also been reported by men in several studies. The U.S. Merit Systems Protection Board's study found fifteen percent of the men to be harassed by males or females at work.[29] On the basis of men's reports of specific behavior, Gutek suggested that up to nine percent of men could have been harassed by women sometime in their working lives.[30] After a careful analysis of men's accounts of harassment, however, Gutek concluded that very few of the reported incidents were sexual harassment as it is legally defined, and some of the incidents may not have even been considered sexual if the same behavior had been initiated by a man or by another woman who was considered a less desirable sexual partner by the man.[31]

V. FREQUENCY OF SEXUAL NONHARASSMENT

Several studies have also examined other kinds of sexual behavior at work, behavior that most people do not consider harassment, including comments or whistles intended to be compliments, quasi-sexual touching such as hugging or an arm around the shoulder, requests for a date or sexual activity often in a joking manner, and sexual jokes or comments that are not directed to a particular person.[32] These other "nonharassing," less serious, and presumably nonproblematic behaviors are considerably more common than harassment. For example, Gutek, found that sixty-one percent of men and sixty-eight percent of women said that they had received at least one sexual comment that was meant to be complimentary sometime in their working lives.[33] In addition, fifty-six percent of men and sixty-seven percent of women reported that they had been the recipient of at least one sexual look or gesture that was intended to be complimentary. About eight out of every ten workers have been recipients of some kind of sexual overture that was intended to be a compliment. Schneider found that fifty-five percent of a sample of heterosexual working women and sixty-seven percent of a sample of lesbian working women reported that within the last year at work, someone had joked with them about their body or appearance.[34] Other studies show similar findings. Dunwoody-Miller and Gutek reported that seventy-six percent of women and fifty-five percent of men indicated that as California state civil service employees, they had received complimentary comments of a sexual nature.[35] Looks and gestures of a sexual nature that were meant as compliments were also common (reported by sixty-seven percent of women and forty-seven percent of men.)

Although men seem rarely to be harassed, the amount of sexual behavior reported by them at work remains substantial. For example, Gutek found that men were more likely than women to say that they were sexually touched by an opposite-sex person on their job.[36] According to Abbey, Davies, and Gottfried and Fasenfest, men are more likely than women to perceive the world in sexual terms.[37] Also, men are more likely than women to mistake friendliness for seduction and find the office is a little too exciting with women around. This seems consistent with the common stimulus-response view that women's presence elicits sexual behavior from men. Reports from men, however, suggest that sex is present in male-dominated workplaces, whether or not women are actually present. This "floating sex" takes the form of posters, jokes, sexual metaphors for work, comments, obscene language, and the like. The relationship seems to be quite straightforward: the more men, the more sexualized the workplace. The fact that much of this sexualization of work is degrading to women as well as sexual is what creates the "hostile" environment that government regulations aim to eliminate.

Taken together, the research on harassment and "nonharassment" shows that sexual behavior is so common at work that one might say that sex permeates work. An equally important conclusion of this body of research is that the legal behavior is considerably more common than the illegal sexual harassment. This finding is not surprising, but it is important; when some people first hear about sexual harassment, they may confuse it with the more common legal behavior at work which they, themselves, have seen and experienced. This confusion of non-threatening legal behavior with sexual harassment can lead some to incorrectly denigrate women's complaints as prudish or overly sensitive.

VI. IMPACTS OF SEXUAL BEHAVIOR AT WORK

Any behavior that is as common as sexual harassment and nonharassment at work is likely to have a wide variety of ramifications, for the individuals involved. So far researchers have concentrated on identifying negative effects of sexual harassment, in order to call attention to harassment as a social and workplace problem. Only scattered attempts, however, have been made toward studying the impacts of other types of sexual behavior at work.

Sexual harassment has a variety of negative consequences for women workers. In addition to the discomfort associated with the sexually harassing experiences and violation of physical privacy, women often find that their careers are interrupted. Up to ten percent of women have quit a job because of sexual harassment. Others fear becoming victims of retaliation if they complain about the harassment, and some are asked to leave. For example, Coles found that among eighty-one cases filed with the California Department of Fair Employment and Housing between 1979 and 1983, almost half of the complainants were fired and another quarter quit out of fear or frustration.[38]

Women may also experience lower productivity, less job satisfaction, reduced self-confidence, and a loss of motivation and commitment to their work and their employer. They may avoid men who are known harassers, even though contact with those men is important for their work. Thus, harassment constrains the potential for forming friendships or work alliances with male workers. Furthermore, women are likely to feel anger and resentment and even exhibit self-blame, which leads to additional stress. Crull and Cohen also stated that, while the implicit/overt types of harassment may not have the same direct repercussions as those of the explicit/overt types, all types of sexual harassment at work create high stress levels and serve as a hidden occupational hazard.[39] Finally, sexual harassment helps to maintain the sex segregation of work when it is used to coerce women out of nontraditional jobs.

Besides affecting their work, sexual harassment affects women's personal lives in the form of physical and emotional illness and disruption of marriage or other relationships with men. For example, Tangri, Burt, and Johnson reported that thirty-three percent of women said their emotional or physical condition became worse,[40] and Gutek found that fifteen percent of women victims of harassment said their health was affected and another fifteen percent said it damaged their relationships with men.[41]

What is even more intriguing is that nonharassing sexual behavior also has negative work-related consequences for women workers, although even they are not always aware of them. For example, Gutek found that the experience of all kinds of sexual behavior, including remarks intended to be complimentary, was associated with lower job satisfaction among women workers.[42] In addition, women reported that they are not flattered, and in fact are insulted, by sexual overtures of all kinds from men. In one study, sixty-two percent of women said they would be insulted by a sexual proposition from a man at work. Another example, the office "affair," can have serious detrimental effects on a woman's credibility as well as her career, especially if the relationship is with a supervisor.

Men seem to suffer virtually no work-related consequences of sexual behavior at work. Less than one percent of men reported that they quit a job because of sexual harassment, and, in the course of discussing sexual incidents, not one man said he lost a job as a consequence of a sexual overture or request from a woman at work.[43] In the same study, sixty-seven percent of men said they would be flattered by sexual overtures from women. In addition, many men view a certain amount of sexual behavior as appropriate to the work setting, and, as noted above, they are less likely to consider any given behavior as sexual harassment. In one study, fifty-one percent of the men who received overtures from women said they themselves were at least somewhat responsible for the incident.[44] That men experience so few work-related consequences of sex at work is especially odd, since they report so much sexual behavior both that is directed at them by women and that seems to float throughout the workplace.

When men do report "consequences," they are personal rather than work-related, and again, they are viewed in a positive manner. Most often, they report dating relationships or affairs that they find enjoyable; for instance, "There was this little blond who had the hots for me" or "I think she liked me. I was young and she was married. She wasn't very happy with her husband."

VII. UNDERSTANDING SEXUAL BEHAVIOR AT WORK

As mentioned earlier, most studies of sexual behavior at work have been in response to the discovery of sexual harassment and policies developed to address harassment. Much of the research is descriptive and diverse, providing interesting information about sexual behavior at work, and useful information for policymakers and lawyers. Some researchers have begun to develop frameworks for studying sexual behavior at work.

One framework sometimes used to study harassment is the power perspective; that is, sexual harassment is an expression of power relationships, and women constitute a threat to men's economic and social standing. Within that perspective, Lipman-Blumen viewed the women's "seductive" behavior as micro-manipulation, as a response to male control of social institutions—including the workplace and the academy—which she labeled macro-manipulation.[45] Other researchers explicitly borrowed from the literature on rape. They contend that sexual harassment is analogous to rape in that power, not sexual drive, is the dominant motivation. They further contend that victims of rape and harassment experience similar effects.[46]

In an attempt to explain their own findings on sexual harassment, Tangri, Burt, and Johnson developed three models: the natural/biological model, the organizational model, and the sociocultural model.[47] The natural/biological model assumes that sexual harassment and other forms of sexual expression at work are simply manifestations of natural attraction between two people. According to Tangri, Burt, and Johnson, one version of this model suggests that because men have a stronger sex drive, they more often initiate sexual overtures at work as well as in other settings.[48] The organizational model assumes that sexual harassment is the result of certain opportunity structures within organizations such as hierarchies. People in higher positions can use their authority (their legitimate power) and their status to coerce lower-status people into accepting a role of sex object or engaging in sexual interactions. The third model, the sociocultural model, "argues that sexual harassment reflects the larger society's differential distribution of power and status between the sexes."[49] Harassment is viewed as a mechanism for maintaining male dominance over women, in work and in society more generally. Male dominance is maintained by patterns of male-female interaction as well as by male domination of economic and political matters. Tangri, Burt, and Johnson's analysis revealed that none of the three models could by itself offer an adequate explanation of their data on sexual harassment.[50] Another model, emphasizing the effects of sex-role expectations in an organizational context, is called sex-role spillover. The following analysis builds on earlier research on this concept.[51]

VIII. SEX-ROLE SPILLOVER

Sex-role spillover denotes the carryover of gender-based expectations into the workplace. Among the characteristics assumed by many to be associated with femaleness (such as passivity, loyalty, emotionality, nurturance) is being a sex object. Women are assumed to be sexual and to elicit sexual overtures from men rather naturally. In a thirty-nation study of sex stereotypes, the characteristics of sexy, affectionate, and attractive were associated with femaleness.[52] This aspect of sex-role spillover, the sex-object aspect, is most relevant to the study of sex at work.

Sex-role spillover occurs when women, more than men in the same work roles, are expected to be sex objects or are expected to project sexuality through their behavior, appearance, or dress. What is equally important is the fact that there is no strongly held comparable belief about men. For example, of the forty-nine items that were associated with maleness in at least nineteen of the twenty-five countries studied by Williams and Best, none was directly or indirectly related to sexuality.[53] While it is generally assumed that men are more sexually active than women and men are the initiators in sexual encounters, the cluster of characteristics that are usually associated with the male personality do not include a sexual component. Rather the stereotype of men revolves around the dimension of competence and activity. It includes the belief that men are rational, analytic, assertive, tough, good at math and science, competitive, and make good leaders. The stereotype of men—the common view of the male personality—is the perfect picture of asexuality. Sex-role spillover, thus, introduces the view of women as sexual beings in the workplace, but it simply reinforces the view of men as organizational beings—"active, work-oriented."[54] It should also be noted that these stereotypes of female characteristics and male characteristics have remained quite stable through the 1970s and into the 1980s.

The spillover of the female sex-role, including the sexual aspect, occurs at work for at least four reasons. First, gender is the most noticeable social characteristic, that is, people immediately notice whether a person is a man or a woman. Second, men may feel more comfortable reacting to women at work in the same manner that they react to other women in their lives, and unless a woman is too young, too old, or too unattractive, that includes viewing her as a potential sexual partner. Third, women may feel comfortable reacting to men in a manner expected by the men, that is, conforming to the men's stereotype. Fourth, characteristics of work and sex roles may facilitate the carryover of sex role into work role. Sex roles remain relatively stable throughout our lives and permeate all domains of life. On the other hand, the work role may change many times and is specific to only one domain of life. Sex roles are also learned much earlier than are work roles, and they entail a wide variety of diffuse skills and abilities. Work roles, on the other hand, call for more specific skills and abilities.

The important point here is that being sexual and being a sex object are aspects of the female sex role that frequently are carried over to the workplace by both men and women. A variety of subtle pressures may encourage women to behave in a sexual manner at work, and this then confirms their supposedly essential sexual nature. Because it is expected, people notice female sexuality, and they believe it is normal, natural, an outgrowth of being female.

Unfortunately, women do not seem to be able to be sex objects and analytical, rational, competitive, and assertive at the same time because femaleness is viewed as "not-maleness,"[55] and it is the men who are viewed as analytic, logical, and assertive. Despite the fact that the model of male and female as polar opposites has been severely criticized on several grounds, a dichotomy is used by researchers and laypersons alike (for example, we speak of the "opposite" sex). This is an important part of sex-role spillover. Not only are the sexual aspects of the female role carried over to work, but also they swamp or overwhelm a view of women as capable, committed workers. This is especially true in an environment where sexual jokes, innuendos, posters, and small-talk are common. A recent study by Mohr and Zanna showed that sex-role traditional men exposed to sexually explicit material behaved in a significantly more sexual and obtrusive manner toward women than men who did not see sexually explicit material.[56] As Kanter noted, a woman's perceived sexuality can "blot out" all other characteristics, particularly in a sexualized work environment.[57] Thus, sex role interferes with and takes precedence over work role.

What is doubly troublesome about this inability to be sexual and a worker at the same time is that women are not the ones who usually choose between the two. A female employee might decide to be a sex object at work, especially if her career or job is not very important to her. More often, however, the working woman chooses not to be a sex object but may be so defined by male colleagues or supervisors anyway, regardless of her own actions. A woman's sexual behavior is noticed and labeled sexual even if it is not intended as such. In order to avoid being cast into the role of sex object, a woman may have to act completely asexual. Then she is subject to the charge of being a "prude," an "old maid," or "frigid," and in her attempt to avoid being a sex object, she is still stereotyped by her sexuality, or more accurately, by her perceived lack of sexuality.

The situation for men is entirely different. Benefiting from the stereotype of men as natural inhabitants of organizations—goal oriented, rational, analytic, competitive, assertive, strong, or, as Deaux puts it, "active, work-oriented"[58]—men may be able to behave in a blatantly sexual manner, seemingly with impunity. Even when a man goes so far as to say that he encourages overtures from women by unzipping his pants at work, he may escape being viewed as sexual or more interested in sex than work by supervisors and colleagues. While the image of women acting in a seductive manner and distracting men from work is viewed as a detriment to the organization, many executives know of men in their employ who are "playboys" and harassers, yet they may not see that these men are a detriment to the organization. Although these men may hire the wrong women for the wrong reasons, make poor use of female human resources in the organization, squander the organization's resources in their quests for new sexual partners, and make elaborate attempts to impress potential sexual partners, all this may escape the notice of employers. In short, men's sexual behavior at work often goes unnoticed. At least two reasons for this can be cited. First, as noted above, there is no strongly recognized sexual component of the male sex role. Thus, men's sexual behavior is neither salient nor noticed. Second, perhaps sexual pursuits and conquests, jokes and innuendos can be subsumed under the stereotype of the organizational man—goal-oriented, rational, competitive, and assertive—which are expected and recognized as male traits. Men may make sexual overtures in an assertive, competitive manner. Likewise, sexual jokes, metaphors, and innuendos may be seen as part of competitive male horseplay. Thus the traits of competitiveness, assertiveness, and goal orientation are noticed, whereas the sexual component is not.

To recapitulate, expectations about male and female behavior that are derived from stereotypes (clusters of beliefs) about men and women spill over, or are carried over, into work roles for a variety of reasons. While the female stereotype has a sexual component (sex object), the male stereotype revolves around competence and achievement. The stereotype declares men to be asexual and women to be sexual. People attend to behavior that is expected, and behavior that is consistent with a stereotype is expected. Beliefs (stereotypes) take precedence over behaviors. Thus, men's sexual behavior is not noticed, and even some men's sexually intended behavior is not interpreted by target women or their employers as such. On the other hand, women's behavior is interpreted as sexual even when it is not intended as such.

Notes

1. Patricia Bernstein, *Sexual Harassment on the Job,* Harper's Bazaar, Aug. 1976, at 33; Karen Lindsey, *Sexual Harassment on the Job,* Ms., Nov. 1977, at 47–51, 74–78; Letti Pogrebin, *Sexual Harassment: The Working Woman,* Ladies Home J., June 1977, at 24; Caryl Rivers, *Sexual Harass-*

ment: The Executive's Alternative to Rape, Mother Jones, June 1978, at 21–22, 24, 28–29; Claire Safran, *What Men do to Women on the Job: A Shocking Look at Sexual Harassment,* Redbook, Nov. 1976, at 149, 217–23.

2. EEOC Guidelines on Discrimination Because of Sex, 29 C.F.R. § 1604.11 (1991).
3. Constance Backhouse & Leah Cohen, The Secret Oppression: Sexual Harassment of Working Women (1978); Sexuality in Organizations: Romantic and Coersive Behaviors at Work (Gail Ann Neugarten & Jay M. Shafritz eds., 1981).
4. Barbara A. Gutek, *Sexuality in the Workplace,* 1 Basic & Applied Soc. Psychol. 255 (1980).
5. Barbara A. Gutek, Sex and the Workplace: Impact of Sexual Behavior and Harassment on Women, Men and Organizations (1985) [hereinafter Sex and the Workplace].
6. S.J. Adams & S.E. Peterson, A Survey of Students' and Professional College Staffs' Experiences with and Definitions of Sexual Harassment (1983) (unpublished Master's thesis, University of New York (Plattsburgh)); Gary N. Powell et al., Sexual Harassment as Defined by Working Women (1981) (paper presented at the annual meeting of the Academy of Management, San Diego, CA).
7. Sex and the Workplace, *supra* note 5, at 40.
8. *Id.* at 43.
9. Eleanor Weber-Burdin & Peter H. Rossi, *Defining Sexual Harassment on Campus: A Replication and Extension,* 38 J. Soc. Issues 111 (1982), at 111. Sometimes there is no behavior to judge. Long-standing sexist terminology, posters or pin-ups, for example, usually cannot be attributed to anyone's behavior. Even the sudden appearance of pornographic material in the workplace often cannot be traced clearly to a particular actor or set of actors. Research subjects have generally not been asked to rate this kind of "behavior."
10. Gary N. Powell, *What Do Tomorrow's Managers Think About Sex Intimacy in the Workplace?* 29 Bus. Horizons 30 (1986).
11. Timothy Reilly et al., *The Factorial Survey: An Approach to Defining Sexual Harassment on Campus,* 38 J. Soc. Issues 99 (1982) [hereinafter *Factorial Survey*], at 99.
12. Louise F. Fitzgerald & Mimi Ormerod, *Perceptions of Sexual Harassment: The Influence of Gender and Academic Context,* 25 Sex Roles 281–94 (1991).
13. John E. Pryor, *Sexual Harassment Proclivities in Men,* 13 Sex Roles 273 (1987).
14. John Pryor & Jeanne Day, *Interpretation of Sexual Harassment: Attributional Analysis,* 18 Sex Roles 405 (1988).
15. Alison M. Konrad & Barbara A. Gutek, *Impact of Work Experiences on Attitudes Towards Sexual Harassment,* 31 Admin. Sci. Q. 422–38 (1986).
16. Sylvia Kenig & John Ryan, *Sex Differences and Levels of Tolerance in Attribution of Blame for Sexual Harassment on a University Campus,* 15 Sex Roles 535 (1986).
17. Aaron Cohen & Barbara A. Gutek, *Dimensions of Perceptions of Social-Sexual Behavior in a Work Setting,* 13 Sex Roles 317, 325–26 (1985).
18. Catharine A. MacKinnon, Sexual Harassment of Working Women: A Case of Sex Discrimination (1979), at 28.
19. *See, e.g.,* U.S. Merit Systems Protection Board, Sexual Harassment in the Federal Workplace: Is It a Problem? (1981) [hereinafter Federal Workplace]; U.S. Merit Systems Protection Board, Sexual Harassment in the Federal Workplace: Is It a Problem?: An Update (1987) [hereinafter U.S. Merit Systems].
20. Federal Workplace, *supra* note 19.
21. U.S. Merit Systems, *supra* note 19.
22. Donna M. Stringer-Moore, Sexual Harassment in the Seattle City Workforce (1982).
23. Vera Dunwoody-Miller & Barbara A. Gutek, S.H.E. Project Report: Sexual Harassment in the State Workforce: Results of a Survey (1985).
24. Sex and the Workplace, *supra* note 5.
25. *See* Women's Legal Defense Fund, Sexual Harassment in the Workplace (1991).
26. Working Women's Institute, Sexual Harassment on the Job: Results of a Preliminary Survey (1975).

27. Safran, *supra* note 1.

28. Beth E. Schneider, *Consciousness about Sexual Harassment Among Heterosexual and Lesbian Women Workers,* 38 J. Soc. Issues 74, 88–91 (1982) [hereinafter *Consciousness*].

29. Sandra S. Tangri et al., *Sexual Harassment at Work: Three Explanatory Models,* 38 J. Soc. Issues 33, 43 (1982), at 43.

30. Sex and the Workplace, *supra* note 5.

31. *See id.; see also* Kathryn Quina, *The Victimization of Women, in* Ivory Power: Sexual Harassment on Campus (Michele A. Paludi ed., 1990) [hereinafter Ivory Power], at 93.

32. Marilynn Brewer, *Further Beyond Nine to Five: An Integration and Future Directions,* 38 J. Soc Issues 149, 156 (1982).

33. Sex and the Workplace, *supra* note 5.

34. *Consciousness, supra* note 28.

35. Dunwoody-Miller & Gutek, *supra* note 23.

36. Sex and the Workplace, *supra* note 5.

37. Margery W. Davies, Women's Place Is at the Typewriter (1982); Antonia Abbey, *Sex Differences in Attribution for Friendly Behavior: Do Males Misperceive Females' Friendliness?,* 42 J. Personality & Soc. Psychol. 830 (1982) [hereinafter *Sex Differences*]; Heidi Gottfried & David Fasenfest, *Gender and Class Formation: Female Clerical Workers,* 16 Rev. Radical Pol. Econ. 89, 96–100 (1984).

38. Frances S. Coles, *Forced to Quit: Sexual Harassment Complaints and Agency Response,* 14 Sex Roles 81, 89 (1986).

39. Peggy Crull & M. Cohen, *Expanding the Definition of Sexual Harassment,* Occupational Health Nursing, Mar. 1984.

40. Tangri, *supra* note 29, at 47.

41. Sex and the Workplace, *supra* note 5.

42. Id.

43. Sex and the Workplace, *supra* note 5.

44. Sex and the Workplace, *supra* note 5.

45. Jean Lipman-Blumen, Gender Roles and Power (1984).

46. Inger Jensen & Barbara A. Gutek, *Attribution and Assignment of Responsibility in Sexual Harassment,* 38 J. Soc. Issues 121, 126–30 (1982); M. Koss, *Changed Lives: The Psychological Impact of Sexual Harassment, in* Ivory Power, *supra* note 31, at 73; Kathryn Quina, *The Victimization of Women, in* Ivory Power, *supra* note 31, at 93.

47. Tangri, *supra* note 29, at 34.

48. *Id.* at 35.

49. *Id.* at 34.

50. *Id.* at 51.

51. Veronica F. Nieva & Barbara A. Gutek, Women and Work: A Psychological Perspective (1981); Sex and the Workplace, *supra* note 5.

52. *See* John E. Williams & Deborah Best, Measuring Sex Stereotypes: A Thirty-Nation Study (1982).

53. *See* Williams & Best, *supra* note 52.

54. Kay Deaux, *Sex and Gender,* 36 Ann. Rev. Psychol. 49 (1985), at 54–65.

55. Kay Deaux & Laurie L. Lewis, *The Structure of Gender Stereotypes: Interrelationships Among Components and Gender Labels,* 46 J. Personality & Soc. Psychol. 991 (1984); H.C. Foushee et al., *Implicit Theories of Masculinity and Femininity: Dualistic or Bipolar?,* 3 Psychol. Women Q. 259 (1979); Brenda Major et al., *A Different Perspective on Androgyny: Evaluations of Masculine and Feminine Personality Characteristics,* 41 J. Personality & Soc. Psychol. 988 (1981).

56. Doug M. Mohr & Mark Zanna, *Treating Women as Sexual Objects: Look to the (Gender Schematic) Male who has Viewed Pornography,* 16 Personality & Soc. Psychol. Bull. 296, 305 (1990).

57. Rosabeth M. Kanter, Men and Women of the Corporation (1977).

58. Kay Deaux, *Sex and Gender,* 36 Ann. Rev. Psychol. 49 (1985).

4. The Definition of Sexual Harassment

Jan Crosthwaite and Graham Priest

I. INTRODUCTION

Sexual harassment is a pervasive feature of the society in which we live. It occurs in both public and private life. It is distinctive both in the role that it plays in social interactions and in its phenomenology for those who experience it. A common response to the subject, particularly amongst men, is to consider it a trivial and unimportant one. This, we think, could not be further from the truth: it is a phenomenon of no little importance, not only to those who experience it, but to our understanding of the nature of the society in which we live. Understanding and combating sexual harassment, both in the workplace and more generally in women's lives, has been a concern for many feminists, and has produced a variety of analyses of the phenomenon ([1], [9], [14], [16], for example). A small number of philosophers, too, have addressed this issue and offered analyses of sexual harassment ([5] and [6], for example). We find none of these analyses of the nature of sexual harassment entirely satisfactory, and aim in this paper to give an account that is, we hope, more adequate.[1]

We will try to achieve this aim by providing a definition of sexual harassment. We are not after what is often called a nominal definition, that is, an analysis of the meaning of the phrase 'sexual harassment'. We are after a real definition of the phenomenon itself. Sexual harassment is a social phenomenon with a particular nature. The nature manifests itself in the causal role that sexual harassment plays in our society. An adequate grasp of this nature provides an explanation of various things whose connection is not immediately apparent, and a fuller understanding of the society in which we function.

An adequate understanding of the nature of sexual harassment must inform actions or policy in this area (practice without theory is blind), but we make no claims that the definition of sexual harassment will have straightforward legislative or regulatory implications. Many definitions of sexual harassment are given with this consequence in mind.[2] But such concerns may lead, for example, to overemphasising features of actions which are easily demonstrable, unlike, say, intentions, because these are easier to deal with in regulations. They have also motivated attempts to locate sexual harassment as a form of sex discrimination, because this would subsume it under already accepted regulations. But this approach restricts consideration of sexual harassment to its occurrence in public areas like the workplace. The risk of such distortions means that practical and policy concerns should not in themselves dictate understanding or theorising.

II. PARADIGM EXAMPLES

In approaching a definition, it helps to have before us some paradigm examples of the thing to be defined. So we shall start with a list of examples of sexual harassment. A diverse range of actions and situations have been identified as sexual harassment, from rape and coercive sexual intercourse through actions which create a 'hostile environment' for women in the workplace. Some of these examples are contentious. In some cases a given action may have significance as sexual harassment only in the context of a pattern of behaviour.[3] However, we think that the most unproblematic examples of sexual harassment fall into the following categories. This list is not intended to be exhaustive, but we do think that it captures the most significant cases in an illuminating way.[4]

1. A position of power or authority may be used to secure sexual access of some sort to a subordinate. This includes such classic examples as an employer, teacher, etc., using either incentives (such as promotion or higher grades) or, more commonly, threats of sanction (such as dismissal or failure) to secure his sexual aims with respect to an employee or student. The threat of sanction is often explicit, but need not be. Victims may feel threatened simply because they know there is an institutional power inequality. (We are using 'institution' here in a conventional and rather narrow sense, to refer to economic, political (in the traditional sense), professional, etc., institutions—such things as businesses, universities, churches, etc., rather than in the wider sense it is sometimes given where any conventional social practice—like marriage or heterosexuality—is regarded as an 'institution'.)

The sexual access involved may be of many kinds, from a sort of voyeurism, through sexual talk and touching, to sexual intercourse. A complaint by a woman in her mid-thirties, H, about her employer, E, gives an indication of the range of behaviour which can be involved.

The behaviour complained of included: a 'peeping tom' incident where E visited H's home late one night; remarks about H's sexual habits and the colour of her underwear; pinning H to the work bench; E asking H if he could have a 'peep' at her; attempts to lift her skirt and to kiss her; E exposing his erect penis and trying to force H to touch him; and discussions of a sexual nature. [15, p. 59]

Such behaviour can occur outside contexts of institutional power, but we would then categorise it differently. The distinguishing characteristic of this first category of examples is the use (indeed, abuse) of institutional power, in some form, for sexual ends.

2. Sexual access can also be sought and taken in contexts where there is no institutional power difference to serve as a source of threat or incentive. Groping, persistent sexual invitations, etc., by fellow workers and fellow students are common examples of this category. At the extreme of this category are acts of rape, including rape through violence or threat of violence. These interactions, like those in category 1, are directed towards some form of sexual access or gratification of the perpetrator. This distinguishes them from examples in the following groups.

3. Sexually harassing behaviour need not be directed towards sexual access or gratification. Its aim may be rather to make the victim aware of the presence of the perpetrator and her vulnerability to his sexual appraisal. Sometimes this awareness is the perpetrator's explicit aim; sometimes it is a corollary of another intention, such as showing oneself to be 'one of the boys'.[5] Leering, wolf-whistles, etc., fall into this category. Rarely does a wolf-whistler expect to obtain sexual favours. There may, but need not be, some sexual gratification from eliciting a response in the victim, but the point is really to force the presence and attention of the harasser on the harasser in a certain way. Ostentatious leering at a woman's breasts is unlikely to be a matter of obtaining sexual pleasure from looking at her breasts; it is better explained as forcing her to be aware of her sexuality as perceived by (some) men and of herself as vulnerable to the sexual predation of men. Sexual harassment of this kind may occur within or outside institutional power relationships.

4. Sexual behaviour may also result unintentionally in a similar response to that in-

tended in examples of group 3. Telling 'dirty' jokes, and displaying sexually explicit pictures, etc., will be examples of this kind in certain contexts. The major difference between this group and the previous group of examples is that the intention of the harasser to have an effect on the harassee may be quite absent. Consider, for example, the case of a woman who reported feeling humiliated every time she came to work and 'saw this picture of a woman with her legs wide open, looking passive and provocative'. She explained that 'I felt it reflected on me, my work status, even my ability to do my job' [14, p. 14]. This response, though understandable and even predictable, need not have been foreseen, let alone intended, in displaying the picture concerned.

Unwelcome or inappropriate compliments on someone's physical appearance might be included in this category, in that while they are usually intended to have an effect on the victim, it need not be one which highlights the presence of the harasser in the way of examples in 3. (Of course, some compliments are offered and function in the same way as wolf-whistles characteristically do, and hence would fall into group 3.) Hadjifotiou cities a complaint by a woman manager which seems to provide an example of sexual harassment of this sort, though without further details the intention behind the comments (and hence categorisation as group 3 or group 4) is unclear.

My boss is incapable of having a meeting or discussion with me without some comment about my sex. There are constant references to the fact that you are a woman, your dress, etc., and remarks such as 'you're looking attractive today' or 'I know you will be able to influence so-and-so by fluttering your eyelashes'. I try to ignore it. [14, p. 14]

So much for the examples. It is clear from these that a range of morally problematic features is exhibited by actions classified as sexual harassment: abuse of power, injustice, failure of respect for the wishes and interests of victims, treating women as sex objects, causing distress or otherwise harming the victim, and creating sexually discriminatory work and study environments. While each of these has provided the focus for some account of sexual harassment, we don't think that any of them captures its real nature.

We are also concerned that, while a definition of sexual harassment should include all the examples above, it should not be so wide as to rule out the possibility of morally acceptable sexual interaction in the variety of situations in which people find themselves, even those where there is an institutional power imbalance. Nor do we think that every form of immoral or unacceptable sexual interaction counts as sexual harassment. Some sorts of sexual interaction might count as unprofessional conduct but not sexual harassment; for example, where a female academic has an affair with an older male graduate student she is supervising. With these points, and the above examples in mind, let us now turn to the question of a definition. We will start by considering an appealing but misleading approach, and then suggest a better one.

III. SEXUAL HARASSMENT IS NOT HARASSMENT THAT IS SEXUAL

An obvious starting place for defining sexual harassment is the surface structure of the term itself, which suggests that sexual harassment is harassment of a sexual nature, as religious harassment and racial harassment are harassment of a religious or racial nature respectively. We will argue, though, that such an approach yields a definition which is both too narrow and too broad. To avoid this suggestion that we think is misleading, we will refer to sexual harassment as SH from now on.

The Shorter Oxford English Dictionary says that to harass is: to trouble or vex by repeated attacks; to worry, distress. But applying this gives too narrow a definition of SH. There are classic examples of SH which do not involve harassment in this sense, such as the following example (of category 1) of SH of a college student by her teacher.

> Well, [in] my freshman year I took a class. I didn't understand all of the readings and by the time the final came around I found myself with an F. So I asked him if I could talk to him about grades in his office. So I went to his office and he gave me a choice—either be with him or take the F. So I met him at his house, and spent three hours with him in his bed . . . I felt dirty but I didn't get the F. He gave me a D. Was it worth it? Yes and no. I felt it was something I had to do to save myself. [8, p. 59]

There is no repeated attack here; nor does the student's further description of her response to this choice fit our usual conception of being troubled or worried. (Though her feeling dirty does indicate a sense of humiliation or degradation.) Hence this is not harassment according to the above definition, but it is still SH.[6]

Any account of SH as a species of the genus harassment is also too broad. To make this clear, it will be useful first to note an ambiguity in the idea of harassing behaviour being *of a sexual nature*. This could mean harassment *by means of sexual behaviour,* or harassment *on the basis of the sex* of the victim. Definitions of SH sometimes run these two aspects together.[7] We think both meanings of 'sexual' are significant, though neither separately nor in combination do they define a category of harassment which is sexual harassment.

Religious and racial harassment are not harassment by religious or racial behaviour (though the latter will include some *racist* behaviour). Rather, the victim is subject to harassment *because of* his/her race or religion. Such parallels suggest that sexual harassment is harassment on the basis of sex.[8] There is some truth to the idea that the sex of the victim is a determining feature of SH, as our analysis will make clear. But not all harassment on the basis of sex is SH, as an example, suggested by Dodds, et al., makes clear. A 'female academic whose male colleagues continually ridicule her ideas and opinions may be the object of sexist harassment' though not thereby of SH [6, p. 114].

Is SH then harassment by means of sexual behaviour? The sexual nature of the behaviour involved is an important component of SH,[9] but not all harassment by means of sexual behaviour is SH. For example, one male might harass another who is modest or prudish by explicitly sexual behaviour towards women in his presence. Or consider a more contentious case. A woman employee wants to court her employer. Over a period of time she persistently asks him to go out with her, gives him gifts, etc., all in a very open and non-threatening way. The employer, we may suppose, does not want to have a sexual relationship with his employee, and comes to find the constant advances embarrassing and annoying. He is harassed, and the harassment is of a sexual nature. But we are inclined not to call this SH, for reasons we will make clear shortly.

We think then that SH is not best understood as harassment of a sexual nature; it is not a species of the genus harassment at all. To that extent, the terminology is unfortunate and misleading. We must look for another definition. Rather than explore other dead ends, we will turn now to the definition we think correct. We will then consider some reasons for preferring this to alternative analyses.

IV. SH AND OPPRESSION

We approach the issue of providing a definition of SH in good traditional form; first we locate its genus, and then its species. SH is a form of behaviour, but of what genus? Our answer is that SH is a form of oppressive behaviour. This, of course, raises the question of what oppression is. Various analyses of oppression have been given, particularly by feminist theorists. (For example, [2], [10], [22], and [24].) What they share, and what for our purposes is sufficient, is that oppression is a relation between social groups which involves one group wielding power which is illegitimate, in some sense, over another group in the society. Oppression is systematic and systemic, though not necessarily intentional. And it involves a limitation of the prospects for self-development, realisation of goals and material success, of members of the oppressed group, often through the psychological impact on these people of the behaviour and structures which sustain the oppression.

The illegitimacy of the exercise of group power or dominance involved in oppression is to be understood in terms of wider notions of political or moral rightness, rather than the narrower conventions of the particular society. Thus, slave-owners oppress slaves, but police do not oppress the general public in a democratic society. (At least, according to liberal political theory they do not. In practice police clearly do play an oppressive role sometimes, e.g., in race relations.) The room for debate about when power is illegitimate captures in part the room for contention about whether a particular group is oppressed.

Next, what species of oppressive behavior is SH? Our answer is, essentially, that SH is a pattern of sexual behavior that constitutes or contributes to the oppression of one gender group by another. ('Constitutes' because SH can itself be an exercise of illegitimate power; and 'contributes to' because SH has a role in creating and maintaining the general situation of men's oppression of women.) This, however, still lacks adequate specificity. For, as SH is normally practised, it constitutes or contributes to oppression in a quite distinctive way. Feminist analyses of oppression have pointed out the role of effects on the psychological states of victims in maintaining oppression.[10] We believe that SH contributes to the maintenance of gender power particularly through its psychological impact on victims. We therefore propose that SH is any form of sexual behaviour by members of a dominant gender group towards members of a subordinate gender group whose typical effect is to cause members of the subordinate group to experience their powerlessness as a member of that group. To say that the effect is typical does not imply, of course, that it is invariable.[11] Nor do we wish to suggest that the experience is one of complete powerlessness; all that is required is that the behaviour be of a kind which promotes in its recipients an awareness of having less power than the harasser, in virtue of their respective genders. This is the definition we will defend in the rest of the paper.

As given, the definition is gender-neutral. In our society, it is men who are the dominant gender group, and so only men who can sexually harass. (This is an important point, and we will return to it later.) But if there were, or could be, a society where the power roles between men and women were reversed, behaviour of the kind we are talking about directed by women against men would constitute SH.[12]

So much for the definition. We think that it has some initial plausibility, but not that it wears the mark of its correctness on its face. In what follows we will discuss the definition and try to show how it makes sense of a number of issues, including the paradigm examples. That it does so provides further evidence of the correctness of the definition.

V. SH AND THE ABUSE OF POWER

The definition we have given locates SH as an abuse of power of a certain kind. Many have seen the issue of power, and the abuse or misuse of power, as central to SH.[13] We think that SH cannot adequately be characterised just as abuse of power for sexual ends, for reasons we will give shortly. But by placing it as we have in the context of the gender power of a group, and, specifically, the procedures that men use (collectively) for disempowering women, the power connection is made clear.

Abuse of power is a feature of the examples we mentioned in category 1. However, it is not this which constitutes their nature as SH. Institutional power may be abused in many ways, and misusing it for sexual ends shares the moral wrongness of any other form of corruption. Some misuses of institutional power for sexual ends will, in addition to being corrupt, be SH and wrong in this further way. But it is possible to misuse power for sexual ends without this being SH. Consider, for example, a club treasurer who uses club funds to take a prospective lover to dinner.

Moreover, focussing on SH as an abuse of power for sexual ends does not satisfactorily account for examples of SH in the other categories we have outlined. Examples such as wolf-whistling make clear that SH can occur in situations where there is no institutional power structure involved, and it is possible, even common, for male employees and students to sexually harass their female peers. Particularly, a definition directly in terms of the abuse of power would exclude category 2 examples, even though they may share all other features of examples in category 1.

One response to this problem might be to generalise the notion of power to include non-institutional power inequalities. Men are characteristically more powerful physically than women, and this difference is often present and carries an implicit threat in situations of SH. A harasser might also have some other non-institutional source of power through which he threatens the harassee—for example, information about her which she does not wish disclosed. However, appeal to a range of possible power inequalities is unsatisfactory. First, no power inequality need be present for SH (other than the background social inequality of the sexes to which our account appeals). Second, even if a satisfactory general account of the exercise of power can be given, it is difficult to give a clear content to the idea of an *abuse* of power outside institutional contexts. We think that the appeal to the socially structured power difference between gender groups, as it functions in our account, best captures the intuitions which have sometimes seen all SH as a function of power inequalities.

VI. THE PHENOMENOLOGY OF SH

The definition also makes sense of what is, emotionally, the dominant feeling that women experience when subjected to SH: one of powerlessness. This has two aspects; one general and one specific. First, the general: being subjected to SH makes women aware of their less powerful position in society in general, in sexual interactions with men particularly, and also in various other contexts such as the workplace. Women are aware that they are subject to sexual harassment as women in a way in which men are not subject to harassment as men. This brings home to women not just the existence of a gender-based power differential, but that it is peculiarly encoded in sexual behaviour.

The second, and specific, aspect of the sense of powerlessness is the common feeling of women subjected to SH of being unable to do anything about the behaviour in question. Typically, what strikes home hardest is not being the object of such behaviour, but being unable to respond effectively. Other than flirtatious playfulness, the appropriate feminine response to sexual solicitation is meant to be a 'polite but firm' rejection. This is unlikely to be effective in stopping the SH behaviour, because feminine 'no-saying' is not to be taken seriously, particularly in the domain of sexual behaviour. Standard sexual stereotypes take sexual predation of women to be a natural expression and prerogative of masculinity. Any aggression or stridency in response is held to be unfeminine, and to diminish a woman's right to respectful treatment. No acceptable response allows the victim of SH to make clear her view that the behaviour is quite unacceptable and often humiliatingly inappropriate. Indeed, to make this clear one would have to address many cultural assumptions embedded in masculine and feminine sex and social roles, including assumptions of male dominance.[14]

To be unable to counter effectively behaviour one finds humiliating is to be further humiliated. Many studies indicate that a frequent response of women to SH is to try and ignore it (and add that this is not effective: the problem does not go away). Another common response is to remove oneself from the situation,[15] often at great personal cost where this is a workplace or educational context. Both attempting to ignore a problem-situation and leaving or withdrawing from it are indications of feeling powerless to respond effectively to the source of one's problems. Examples of category 3 make particularly clear the situation of lacking any effective response.[16] Protest is the only response available to wolf-whistles, and protest is ineffectual because it is precisely the response desired. But it is true of other cases also that what rankles is, typically, not being able to do anything effective about the unacceptable behaviour.

The definition also explains why there is typically a difference between the responses of women and of men subjected to apparently the same kind of sexually harassing behaviour. Again, this is most obvious with respect to cases of category 3. If a man is subjected to wolf-whistles, comments about his sexual attractiveness, etc., his reaction, though possibly mixed with embarrassment, will normally be one of some pleasure. He does not feel any lack of power, and the experience is not an unpleasant one. This is precisely because of the asymmetry in power relations. Similar comments apply to situations like category 2. Sexual advances towards a man typically flatter him [13, p. 97]. And if he really does not want them, he just says so, and that is that. This is not true when the roles are reversed. Such gender differences in experience are explained in our account of SH by the role of power inequalities between the sexes.

VII. CAN WOMEN COMMIT SH?

It is a consequence of the account we offer that, in societies where males are the dominant gender, women cannot commit SH, nor men be victims. This may seem counter-intuitive when both sexes can exhibit the sort of behaviour described in our paradigm examples of SH.

Analyses of SH differ about such gender asymmetry. Some feminist analyses explicitly define SH as something only males can do. For example, Lin Farley says:

> Sexual harassment is best described as unsolicited nonreciprocal male behaviour that asserts a woman's sex role over her function as worker. [9, p. 33]

Philosophical analyses, though, are usually deliberately gender-neutral ([5] and [6] for example). So some further discussion and defence of our position on this issue seem in order.

We think our definition captures genuine and significant gender asymmetries with respect to SH which are often obscured by gender-neutral analyses. As well as the phenomenological differences mentioned above, our account explains, for example, the salient fact that women rarely engage in SH-type behaviour. SH is behaviour of a kind involved in the maintenance of an asymmetric power-structure, and one should therefore expect the dominant to employ it more than the subordinate. But because these gender asymmetries are contingent on particular, society-specific, gender power relations, we avoid the arbitrariness of stipulatively excluding the possibility of women committing SH. It is not an essential feature of SH that women cannot commit it; it is a contingent consequence of gender power relations in our society.

It is easy to think of situations apparently similar to cases of SH, but in which the roles of the sexes are reversed. For example, a woman employer might solicit sexual attention from a male employee under threat of firing him if he does not comply. Or a group of women, out for a night on the town, might harass a man in a restaurant with ribald jokes, sexual gestures and innuendo.[17] While such behaviour is similar in various ways to SH, it is not SH. Crucially, it has a different typical phenomenology and net social effect.

Take the first (employer/employee) case. This is similar to SH of category 1. But even if the man feels powerless in the face of the threat of firing, he is unlikely to feel powerless *in virtue of his gender:* he feels powerless *qua* employee. Moreover, such cases clearly do not have the effect of sustaining gender/power structures—quite the contrary. The fact that the behaviour is not SH does not, of course, mean that it is morally acceptable. It is clearly an abuse of institutional power, as it is when a man does it.

The second sort of example (women out on the town) is more analogous to a case of SH of category 3. But again, the phenomenology is typically different. The man may be annoyed, even to the point of leaving the restaurant; he may even feel embarrassed; but he is unlikely to be reminded of his lack of power *qua* male. And again, such acts are hardly an affirmation of social power, more a subversion of it. This is simply harassment by sexual behaviour, which, as we have already argued, is different.

It might still be asked why the same behaviour should count as SH when done by one sex but not the other. What lurks behind this question is a simple empiricist assumption to the effect that phenomena must be defined in terms of their empirical manifestations. Such empiricism is, in general, quite unsustainable in the social sciences.[18] Empirical manifestations do not float in mid-air: they draw their nature from both the social structure in which they are embedded and the effects they have on this structure. For example, the same utterance could be a request or an order depending simply on the social relationship between the persons involved. There are also familiar cross-cultural examples of very different behaviour having the same empirical manifestation.[19] The point of distinguishing between behaviour of men and women which appears the same is that (as things are) it differs in the much more fundamental ways we have indicated; specifically, in its relation to one of the fundamental structural features of our society: patriarchy. To focus simply on the observable behaviour of SH is to be superficial and miss its essence.[20]

It is, of course, possible for someone to say that they intend to use the term 'sexual harassment' just to mean harassment of a sexual nature. And if someone wishes to do this, we are prepared to yield the term. As we said before, we are not interested in lexicography; we are interested in understanding a certain social phenomenon, the maintenance of a power structure by certain kinds of sexual behaviour. In the last instance, it does not really matter what you call it.

VIII. SH AND HOMOSEXUALITY

But even if it is accepted that women cannot commit SH against men, can't men commit SH against men (and maybe women against women for that matter)? Perhaps the focus of our attention so far has been too heterosexual?

Putative examples of SH of men by men seem to be of three kinds. The first is where someone is abused on the basis of their sexual preference. Thus, for example, a gay man might be the butt of unpleasant jokes, verbal abuse, or physical assault (including some sexual acts—homophobia sometimes expresses itself in such violence). This is simply harassment on the basis of sexual preference; it is no more SH than harassment on the basis of sex (or race, or whatever). The second is where a person simply tries to obtain sexual access to someone of the same sex. If this is any form of harassment, it is harassment by sexual behaviour (and if institutional power inequalities are exploited, it may also be corruption). But as we have already argued, SH and harassment by sexual behaviour are distinct.

The third sort of homosexual behaviour, which would appear to be the clearest counter-example to our definition, is where coercive sexual interactions are part of, and serve to maintain, a power structure. This seems to occur in male prisons and male boarding schools.[21] Within such institutions men belonging to institutionally powerful or dominant groups may sexually exploit men who are members of groups of lower standing. In such cases, sex is actually used as a tool of domination, with the same effects and phenomenological symptoms as in the male/female cases of SH that we have discussed. Sexual acts are both an arena within which, and the means by which, power is announced and affirmed.

These cases then seem to be SH except for the sex of the victim. One response might be to delete 'gender' from the phrase 'gender group' in our definition of SH. Thus, we could define SH as any form of sexual behaviour which one social group uses to keep another oppressed. We are not inclined to this response for the following reasons. First, it raises a problem of the identification and individuation of social groups. People usually belong to more than one social group, in virtue of such things as race, ethnicity, occupation and economic standing, as well as by sex and/or gender. Different groups according to these criteria may be dominant in different contexts or situations. A particular racial group may be subordinate and oppressed within the wider society but dominant through gang structures in a prison environment, for example. Indeed, in some cases it seems that the only thing which might identify those subject to sexual exploitation as a group, and differentiate them from those who dominate, is their subjection to sexual domination.[22]

Second, though sexual violence might function as simply another form of assault used to emphasise dominance, we think that there is more to SH than this. Typically it is experienced as more degrading and dehumanising than other assaults, even where less physically damaging. Moreover, SH may involve only non-violent attempts to secure sexual interaction. How this can serve to assert group dominance needs explanation. The possibility of using sexual activity to assert and maintain group power, arises primarily through the connection to gender. Sexual aggression and predation is masculine; vulnerability to it is feminine. Masculinity is powerful and dominant and femininity is weak and submissive, and not only in the stereotype of heterosexual intercourse, but in other social arenas. Hence, a masculine sexual role casts one as dominant and a feminine sexual role casts one as subordinate.

This connection between sexual activity, gender, and power, is born out by a closer look at the supposed problem cases of sexual harassment of males in the maintenance of male power hierarchies. The gender-stereotyping in such examples is striking. Wooden and Parker comment that 'the targets of [sexual exploitation in prisons] tend to be the young, the good-looking heterosexual, and the known homosexual. These are the persons the assaulter tends *to treat like females*' [23, p. 227, our italics]. They are categorised as female or feminine, and are encouraged or forced to adopt feminised roles and behaviours, both in sexual activity and in other areas like names, dress, mannerisms and domestic tasks.[23] The sexual activity required of them is receiving anal penetration or giving oral or manual stimulation; these are identified with the 'feminine' role in heterosexual sex. Such assaults are often seen as further enhancing the masculinity of the aggressor. Anthony Scacco argues, for example, that rape in prison is 'an act whereby one male (or group of males) seeks testimony to what he considers is an outward validation of his masculinity'.[24] The 'marked' men who succumb to this sexual pressure are tolerated since by conforming to the role of the woman, they protect (and enhance) the masculine image of the man with whom they have sex [23, p. 15]. As Wooden and Parker put it, 'the distinction is between the strong and the weak, the dominant and the dominated, and ultimately between men and women' [23, p. 3].

What we do say in response to the third sort of counter-example, then, is that it is already encompassed in our definition! We say this since we take the word 'gender' seriously. We understand gender to refer to one's categorisation as feminine (a woman) or masculine (a man), and that this categorisation carries with it expectations of both social and sexual behaviour, role, and other characteristics (including physical and psychological characteristics). While gender is normally assigned on the basis of biological sex (maleness or femaleness) and is often thought to be a natural consequence of this, gender and biological sexuality are distinct.[25] The recipients of SH in prisons are gendered feminine, or women, within that micro-society (though not necessarily in the wider society). Hence, this is still gender oppression. This sort of example then turns out to be a striking confirmation of the definition, rather than a counter-example to it. It is, in the proper use of that medieval saying, the exception that proves the rule.

IX. FEMINISM AND SH

Our account coheres well with many feminist concerns about SH, and it explains the significance of SH for feminists. While SH is not a recent phenomenon, theoretical and policy oriented attention to it has arisen along with and out of feminist awareness. The definition we have offered makes it clear both why SH received little analysis or attention prior to the rise of modern feminism, and why feminists should attach the importance they do to what might seem (in some cases at least) rather trivial misdemeanours. SH is of concern to feminists because of its role in sustaining the oppression of women; and it is appreciating this role that allows one to see the connections between such apparently disconnected phenomena as rape and the decoration of workplaces with posters which sexually objectify women.

Many accounts of SH focus on it as a species of unacceptable sexual conduct (while providing different analyses of what makes it unacceptable). These may rightly pick up connections between SH and other sexually problematic behaviour,[26] but without the location in social structures which an account like ours provides, these leave one puzzled as to why SH should be of such concern to feminists. Women, just as much as men, may behave unacceptably, sexually; though it seems men do it more. Neither does the fact that women are more commonly than men the victims of SH suffice to fill this gap. Or, at least, not without this itself being located within a general pattern of discriminatory or oppressive behavior and institutions. (Poverty is disproportionately a problem for blacks, but this doesn't make it a race problem, independently of an analysis which ties the incidence of poverty to other specifically race-based inequalities.)

The role of SH in creating discriminatory workplace and educational environments makes it more understandable why SH should be of specific concern to feminists. However, the arguments for SH being a form of sex discrimination must themselves appeal to the sorts of sex differentiated effects which we think locate SH within the realm of oppression. Moreover, while the discriminatory aspect of SH in the public domain is an important feature, an analysis in terms of this does not capture the uniformities underlying both public and private spheres as does our account of SH in terms of women's oppression. We think that it is obvious that SH occurs in contexts other than the workplace; both public (verbal and physical harassment on the street, for example) and private (men can sexually harass wives and girlfriends as much as employees and co-workers).[27] It is a virtue of our account that it explains and unifies many different areas and kinds of SH.

The definition of SH we are defending is consonant with significant feminist approaches to the analysis of rape. Feminist accounts of rape are concerned to focus on it not as an individual aberration or sexual misconduct, but as slotting into the social framework of women's oppression. Some analyses specifically locate the distinctive wrongness of rape as its role in promoting male social control of women, and most others note that there is such a significant social effect even when they offer a different account of the wrongfulness of individual acts.[28] We see it as an advantage of our account of SH that (i) it shifts the focus on SH from individual wrongdoing or unacceptable sexual interaction to the social patterns within which individual actions occur and which they help to sustain, and (ii) rape emerges as an extreme form of SH.

We have argued that the background social context of power relations between the sexes means that only sexual behaviour by men directed towards women can be SH in our society. But does it also mean that all such behaviour is SH? Obviously, all sexual activity in our society takes place in the social context of gender inequality we have identified as crucial to SH. So won't any heterosexual interaction (or at least any which is male initiated) count as SH? We think not, because we believe that heterosexual interactions (even where male initiated) need not all be of a kind that serves to sustain women's oppression and make them feel powerless. However, we do acknowledge that there are analyses of heterosexual activity according to which all such activity expresses and contributes to the maintenance of male dominance.[29] If one were to accept such an analysis (which we most certainly do not), then all heterosexual activity could turn out to be SH on our account.

One final point in this context. We'd like to return to the question why SH should be called harassment if, as we claim, it is not in fact a species of the genus harassment. We can now give a simple answer.[30] Harassment is a gradual process of wearing down. While some cases of SH, including paradigmatic cases like a boss soliciting sex under threat of firing, may be single and isolated incidents for the individuals concerned, any isolated event of SH fits a much more general pattern of sexual behaviour as used in the disempowerment of women. The process of wearing down applies to women as a group, not necessarily to particular individuals. In that sense, the name 'harassment' is, after all, appropriate.

X. THE EXAMPLES REVISITED

Let us, finally, reiterate some of our central points by way of reviewing our paradigm examples.

Examples of category 3: wolf-whistling, etc., fit the pattern of our definition most obviously. Behaviour of this kind typically impresses on the woman harassed a feeling of impotence, as we have pointed out. Notice that even though the harasser typically intends to have some effect on the harassee, this need not be, and usually is not, that of making her feel powerless.[31] The feeling of powerlessness comes from the recognition that men have, and feel they have, the power to publicly express uninvited sexual appraisals of women. The significant point in classifying behaviour as SH is not the subjective intentions of the harasser, but its objective effect on the harassee, which is partly a reminder of, partly constitutive of, the power asymmetry.

Examples of category 4, jokes, posters, etc., reinforce this point. Since SH is not a matter of the intentions of the harasser, what he thinks is going on, whether or not he intends to offend, etc., are quite irrelevant. This is not to say that everyone who displays explicit sexual material is guilty of SH. Rather, the point is that if this is done in a context where it has the effect in question on women, it is SH. It is then explicable why sexual displays of this sort in the workplace in particular should be taken as SH by women. Highlighting women's sexuality in such a context may both denigrate women's status as workers and assert the dominance of masculine values and interests in the workplace. Hence it affirms and contributes to women's inequality to men in this area of common life.

Examples of category 2 also fit our definition well. Standard discussions of this kind of example tend to stress the taking of sexual liberties. This, though certainly morally objectionable, is not what constitutes SH. The point is, rather, the effect that this has on the harassee, and how this fits into the bigger picture of power relations in society. A woman can take sexual liberties, of course; but as we have already observed, the effect of this on men is typically quite different from the effect of men taking sexual liberties with women.

Finally, similar comments apply to examples of category 1. What makes this kind of example SH is not the attempt to obtain sexual favours. More serious is the effect that this has on people who are already in a vulnerable position (students, employees, etc.). This kind of example is also misleading in a certain way. SH has something to do with an abuse of power, and examples of this kind suggest that it is power of an institutional nature (that of an employer, teacher, etc.). It is not; it is power of a gender nature. What makes it so easy to confuse the two is just the fact that these are, or at least, have been, pretty much coextensive in our society.

XI. CONCLUSION

Life is full of behaviour that is sexual in one way or another. Some of this is unacceptable. With the recognition, brought about by feminism, that much traditionally accepted male sexual behaviour is of this kind, it has become common to lump together much unacceptable sexual behaviour as SH. Though this has a political point, it can be quite misleading; and, in the end, it is harmful. We have located SH by the role it plays in the constitution and preservation of asymmetric gender power relations, i.e., patriarchy. As such, it is a quite specific form of unacceptable sexual behaviour. Lumping it together with other things merely cloaks this, and so cloaks the important political role that it plays in our society. We hope that our account, by cleanly isolating its specificity, produces a clearer understanding of the kind of society in which we live and how it works, and so contributes, if only a little, to changing it.

Notes

1. One of us has written previously on this topic in [5]. While the focus of that earlier paper, on inadequate consideration of the interests of the victim of sexual harassment, rightly emphasises some significant failures in sexual interactions between persons, she now thinks that it does not sufficiently reflect the systemic nature of sexual harassment. This paper develops instead the suggestion in that earlier paper that the real significance of sexual harassment lies in its role in women's oppression.

2. For example, various institutional pamphlets on harassment and sexual harassment need to characterise the phenomenon or behavior they are addressing. And, Dodds, et al., explicitly list being 'useful for policy purposes' as a desideratum of an account of sexual harassment [6, p. 112].

3. In a case which the Human Rights Commission (NZ) took to the Equal Opportunities Tribunal in 1991, a young woman, Mary, had complained that her employer 'hugged her, put his hands on her hips, would lie on the floor to clean the shelves in a way that she would have to step over

him if she wanted to walk past him, and he also 'ogled' her. He was alleged also 'to have made crude jokes, made comments about women's nipples and sharing a double bed . . .' Some of these actions, while clearly components of harassment in this case, might not have been so in a different context (hugging, for example). In describing this case, the HRC comments of 'ogling' that it 'was a subjective perception on the part of Mary so the Tribunal exercised caution in viewing this particular allegation. It viewed the "ogling" in the context of the evidence as a whole' [15, pp. 62–63].

4. In a survey of sexual harassment research [12], James Gruber finds 11 types of sexual harassment. All these types fall into one or other of the categories we outline here. For example, instances of Gruber's type 'sexual bribery' will be either category 1 or 2, and many of the types of sexual harassment Gruber groups as 'remarks' or 'verbal comments' will be of category 3 or 4.

5. Cheryl Benard and Edit Schlaffer report interviewing 60 men, in a range of age groups, who had 'addressed them on the street' [3]. They say that most men found it hard to explain their own behaviour. Some believed firmly that women enjoy receiving such attention, but many had given little thought to how women might feel. 'Only a minority, around 15%, explicitly set out to anger or humiliate their victims. This is the same group that employs graphic commentary and threats' [3, p. 71]. Around 20% would engage in such behaviour only in the company of other men, which 'supports the explanation that the harassment of women is a form of male bonding, of demonstrating solidarity and joint power' [3, p. 72].

6. This example illustrates also the point that neither the recipient's acceptance of a sexual invitation, nor her benefiting from it, remove it from the category of SH.

7. For example, Title IX, 1972 Education Amendments (USA) specifies sexual harassment in terms of both kinds of behaviour, in claiming: 'Sexual harassment consists of verbal or physical conduct of a sexual nature imposed on the basis of sex, by an employee or agent of a recipient that denies, limits, provides different, or conditions the provision of aid, benefits, services or treatment protected under Title IX.' (Cited by Dzeich and Weiner [8, pp. 19–20].)

8. An emphasis on harassment on the basis of sex also tends to support approaches to SH which align it with sex discrimination. We think that SH has connections to sex discrimination; it is often a component of discriminatory environments and practices. But an emphasis on sex discrimination overemphasises the public (particularly employment or education related) occurrences of SH to the exclusion of its private and non-discriminatory occurrences. Catharine MacKinnon's 'inequality' account of discrimination ('that discrimination consists in the systematic disadvantage of social groups . . . that sex discrimination is a system that defines women as inferior from men, that cumulatively disadvantages women for their differences from men, as well as ignores their similarities' [16, p. 116] may avoid this problem. But it comes very close to our own emphasis on the role of SH in women's oppression, and we think that oppression rather than discrimination is the more satisfactory explanatory concept here.

9. While it is not easy to give a general characterization of sexual behaviour, we think that it is clear that behaviour in the examples we mentioned at the beginning is of a sexual nature. Whether behaviour is sexual may depend on the context, and on other behaviour or intentions and attitudes apparent to those involved. Consider the touching of a woman's breast. The context of a medical examination normally removes the sexual nature of such touching, yet other behaviour within such a context may reintroduce this interpretation. While there is room for misunderstanding and subjective difference in response here, we think that for the most part both sexes are well aware of when behaviour is of a sexual nature and when not. It is also appropriate that there should be some areas of uncertainty, as there is room for debate in certain cases as to whether harassment has occurred or not.

10. For example, Bartky suggests that psychological oppression 'can be regarded as the "internalization of intimations of inferiority"' [2, p. 34], and Tormey claims that 'to be oppressed . . . One must be made to have beliefs about oneself, including beliefs about the proper social position for one to occupy, that result in patterns of behaviour which conform to an inferior or subsidiary role' [22, p. 216].

11. Indeed sometimes women who witness or are aware of SH suffered by another woman may feel

both her and their own powerlessness more than she does herself. Gruber refers to this as 'by-stander harassment' [12].

12. It might also be argued that it is possible for there to be distinct and largely independent 'societies' within the larger society, in which women, rather than men, are the gender in power. If this is so, then it is possible that behaviour directed by women against men might constitute SH within such sub-structures.

13. This seems to be strongly emphasised in approaches to SH in universities and colleges. For example, Dzeich and Weiner claim that '"Sexual harassment" implies a misuse of power and role by a faculty member' [8, p. 21]; and that 'There is too much difference in role and status of male faculty and female students to make flirtation or even seduction by students harassment. "Harassment" suggests misuse of power, and students simply do not have enough power to harass' [8, p. 24].

14. The possibility of effective response is in part a function of the availability of complaints procedures and the acceptability of using them. Women are becoming more empowered against SH as there is increasing public recognition not only of the moral unacceptability of sexual exploitation of various kinds, but also of its links to structures of male dominance and discrimination against women. SH may be becoming a less effective tool of oppression, as general awareness of and resistance to gender-based oppression increases. We think that this supports the analysis we are offering of the nature and role of SH.

15. See, for example, [13, pp. 70–73].

16. In 'So Many Choices, So Little Time', Jan Buckwald [20, p. 39] describes the effect of SH from building-site workers, familiar to most women: 'you, yourself have crossed the street probably a jillion times to avoid that scene. You've felt your face burn red in that confounding mix of anger and embarrassment and helplessness. While trying to look as if you didn't even notice them, you, too, have wished for some recourse, some response to their whistles and grunts and gestures and stares.'

17. It is also possible to conceive of a situation in which a man might be harassed by women on the basis of his sex, though not by sexual behaviour. Consider the case of a sole male 'invading' a classically female domain, such as a school for nannies.

18. And in the natural sciences, though we will not stop to argue this here.

19. For example, belching is offensive in Western cultures, but in some other cultures it may be a polite expression of appreciation of food offered.

20. Dodds, et al., offer a behavioral definition of SH. They identify the behaviour concerned in terms of its 'typical' location as associated with certain attitudes in the harasser and producing certain effects in the victim, though they insist that it is the behaviour itself, rather than such attitudes or effects, which identifies an interaction as harassment [6, pp. 119–120]. That is, behaviour of a type usually associated with certain mental states is SH even in the absence of any such states. We agree that the behaviour which constitutes SH needs to be identified more subtly than through its simple overt characteristics. But we disagree about the features which do identify it. Our account locates the behaviour in terms of its locus (causes and effects) in a social structure and divorces it from the intentions and attitudes of perpetrators.

21. The importance of this kind of example was brought home to us by David Armstrong and David Braddon-Mitchell. The same phenomenon does not appear to happen, by and large, in similar women's institutions. Why this might be so is an interesting question, but not one we shall take up here.

22. Power relations and consequent sexual victimisation in prisons may more often be a matter of individual rather than social group power. While the physically powerful may dominate the physically weaker in prisons, it seems odd to describe this in terms of relationships between different social groups. Where group dominance seems clearest is where there is some sense of mutual identification and shared interest, as, for example, where race or gang affiliation provides group identification.

23. This is particularly true of homosexuals who identify as 'feminine'. Wooden and Parker comment that heterosexual victims of sexual assault often do not accept this feminisation [23, p.

108], but add that the demoralising effects of their sexual victimisation may be worse than for effeminate homosexuals also subjected to sexual assault [23, pp. 112–113].

24. Anthony M. Scacco Jr., *Rape in Prison* (Springfield, IL: Charles C. Thomas, 1975) p. 3. (Cited by Russell [18, p. 69].)

25. This is clear from studies of cross-gender identities of the sort reported by John Money and Anke Ehrhardt (*Man & Woman, Boy & Girl: differentiation and dimorphism of gender identity from conception to maturity* (Baltimore: Johns Hopkins University Press, 1972)). The precise delineation of the concepts of sex and gender, like the precise extent of the interconnection of the biological and the social, is of course open to debate. But we think it is clear that there is a distinction here between the biological division of sex and the social dichotomy erected on top of it. We recognise also both that there are social and cultural variations in the articulation of gender divisions and characteristics, and that individuals may not conform to these.

26. For example, accounts of SH in terms of the sexual objectification of women, or failures of respect in sexual interactions, emphasise features which may be common to different kinds of unacceptable sexual behaviour. Swanton, Robinson and Crosthwaite [21] analyse the idea of treating women as sex-objects in similar terms to the account of SH given in Crosthwaite and Swanton [5].

27. The well-known phenomenon of requesting sex as a return for having bought a woman's dinner on a date is, we think appropriately, SH on our account.

28. For example, Brownmiller [4] and Petersen [17], analyse rape as a social device for controlling women, and Shaffer and Frye [19] comment on the macro-level effects of rape (the restriction of women's freedom, specifically through fear), while analysing the wrongness of acts of rape in terms of violations of women's rights of consent.

29. See [11], for example, or Dworkin's analysis of intercourse [7].

30. And in doing so we meet the desiderata Dodds, et al., [6] suggest for any account of sexual harassment, that it 'show the connection between harassment in general and sexual harassment'.

31. Benard and Schlaffer comment that such SH by ordinary 'men in the street' usually declines in the late evening and at night, precisely when it would be most intimidating. In explanation, they suggest that the ordinary 'man in the street' doesn't wish to face the consequences (like cries for help) of inducing real fear of sexual molestation in a woman, and take this as supporting the view that the behaviour is largely symbolic [3, p. 72].

References

1. W. Sandford (ed.), *Fighting Sexual Harassment* (Boston: Alyson Publications and the Alliance Against Sexual Coercion, 1981).

2. S.L. Bartky, 'On Psychological Oppression', *Femininity and Domination: Studies in the Phenomenology of Oppression* (New York: Routledge, 1990).

3. C. Benard and E. Schlaffer, 'The Man in the Street: Why He Harasses', in A.M. Jaggar and P.S. Rothenberg (eds.), *Feminist Frameworks: Alternative Theoretical Accounts of the Relations between Women and Men,* 2nd edn. (New York: McGraw-Hill, 1984).

4. S. Brownmiller, *Against Our Will: Men, Women and Rape* (New York: Penguin, 1976).

5. J. Crosthwaite and C. Swanton, 'On The Nature Of Sexual Harassment' in J. Thompson (ed.), *Women and Philosophy, Australasian Journal of Philosophy,* Supplement to vol. 64 (1986) pp. 91–106.

6. S.M. Dodds, L. Frost, R. Pargetter and E.W. Prior, 'Sexual Harassment', *Social Theory and Practice* 14 (1988) pp. 111–130.

7. A. Dworkin, *Intercourse* (New York: The Free Press, 1987).

8. B.W. Dzeich and L. Weiner, *The Lecherous Professor: Sexual Harassment on Campus* (Boston: Beacon Press, 1984).

9. L. Farley, *Sexual Shakedown: The Sexual Harassment of Women on the Job* (New York: Warner Books, 1980).

10. M. Frye, 'Oppression' in *The Politics of Reality: Essays in Feminist Theory* (Freedom, CA: The Crossing Press, 1983).

11. M. Frye, 'Willful Virgin, or Do You have to be a Lesbian to be a Feminist?' in *Willful Virgin: Essays in Feminism* (Freedom, CA: The Crossing Press, 1992).

12. J.E. Gruber, 'A Typology of Personal and Environmental Sexual Harassment: Research and Policy Implications for the 1990s', *Sex Roles* 26 (1992) pp. 447–464.

13. B.A. Gutek, *Sex and the Workplace* (San Francisco: Jossey-Bass, 1985).

14. N. Hadjifotiou, *Women and Harassment at Work* (London: Pluto Press, 1983).

15. Human Rights Commission, Komihana Tikanga Tangata, *Sexual Harassment in the Workplace* (Auckland: Human Rights Commission, 1991).

16. C. MacKinnon, *Sexual Harassment of Working Women: A Case of Sex Discrimination* (New Haven: Yale University Press, 1979).

17. S.R. Petersen 'Coercion and Rape: The State as a Male Protection Racket' in M. Vetterling-Braggin, F.A. Elliston and J. English (eds.), *Feminism and Philosophy* (Totowa, NJ: Rowman and Littlefield, 1977).

18. D.E.H. Russell, *Sexual Exploitation: Rape, Child Sexual Abuse and Workplace Harassment* (Newbury Park, CA: Sage Publications, 1984).

19. C. Shaffer and M. Frye, 'Rape and Respect', in M. Vetterling-Braggin, F.A. Elliston and J. English (eds.), *Feminism and Philosophy* (Totowa, NJ: Rowman and Littlefield, 1977).

20. A.C. Sumrall and D. Taylor (eds.), *Sexual Harassment: Women Speak Out* (Freedom, CA: The Crossing Press, 1992).

21. C. Swanton, V. Robinson and J. Crosthwaite, 'Treating Women as Sex-Objects', *Journal of Social Philosophy* 20 (1989) pp. 5–20.

22. J.F. Tormey, 'Oppression, Exploitation and Self Sacrifice' in C.C. Gould and M.W. Wartofsky (eds.), *Women and Philosophy: Toward a Theory of Liberation* (New York: Capricorn Books, 1966) pp. 206–221.

23. W.S. Wooden and J. Parker, *Men Behind Bars: Sexual Exploitation in Prison* (New York and London: Plenum Press, 1982).

24. I.M. Young, *Justice and the Politics of Difference* (Princeton, NJ: Princeton University Press, 1990).

· 5. Why the Fight Against Sexual Harassment Is Misguided

Mane Hajdin

The aim of this section is to show that the concept of sexual harassment is not a morally significant concept. The distinctions between sexual harassment and other similar kinds of conduct are not morally significant distinctions. Moreover, there are morally significant distinctions that the concept of sexual harassment hides: even when it is granted that much of the conduct that is classified as sexual harassment is morally wrong, it is difficult to escape the conclusion that different instances of that conduct are wrong on very different grounds. The thesis defended here is thus that classifying an act as an act of sexual harassment, even when it is granted that the act is morally wrong, does not reveal, but obscures, the ground of its wrongness. . . .

Much of sexual harassment involves conduct aimed at establishing sexual relationships that would be adulterous. Also, acts of sexual harassment often belong to a pattern of conduct that involves many short-term sexual relationships that are largely devoid of serious emotional involvement; in other words, it often involves promiscuity.

Most people believe that adultery and promiscuity are, in general, morally wrong (although the details of people's views on these matters differ considerably). It can be a matter of debate whether adultery and promiscuity are really wrong and what precisely it is that makes them wrong,[1] but I do not intend to enter into such debates here. I shall simply assume, for the sake of argument, that the prevailing view that adultery and promiscuity are morally wrong can be justified, in some way or other. If that view can be justified, then it follows that all cases of sexual harassment that involve (attempted) adultery or promiscuity (and there are quite a few of them) are also morally wrong. However, there are also quite a few cases of sexual harassment that involve neither adultery nor promiscuity and, therefore, cannot be wrong on that ground; if they are wrong at all, they are so on some other ground. Thus, although the wrongness of very many cases of sexual harassment can be established by pointing out that they involve adultery or promiscuity, it contributes nothing to proving that sexual harassment as a type of conduct is morally wrong. While there is considerable overlap between sexual harassment and these two types of sexual immorality, there is nothing more than an overlap: in addition to there being quite a few cases of sexual harassment that do not involve either adultery or promiscuity, there are many instances of adulterous and promiscuous conduct that do not constitute sexual harassment. Moreover, the existence and size of the overlap are contingent matters.

Therefore, if what one is bothered by in sexual harassment is the fact that it often involves adultery and promiscuity, then one should focus on the adulterous and promiscuous character of the relevant conduct and dispense with the notion of sexual harassment in thinking about it. One does not need the notion of sexual harassment to express one's moral concerns about adultery and promiscuity, because there already are other notions far better suited for *that* job, namely the notions of adultery and promiscuity.

If one believes that the wrongness of adulterous and promiscuous conduct warrants legal intervention, then one should advocate (re)introduction, or retention and revival, of legal prohibitions of adultery and promiscuity as such. Legal prohibitions of adultery and even of any kind of sex between people who are not married to each other existed in many jurisdictions until the not very distant past, and in some they are still "on the books," although they are practically never enforced. The idea that adultery and promiscuity should be legally prohibited as such may not have a very wide appeal nowadays, but it is a coherent idea. It is, however, incoherent to support the prohibition of sexual harassment on this ground, because that prohibition covers only *some* adulterous and promiscuous conduct, and even that is only contingent. Of course, if one does not believe that the wrongness of adultery and promiscuity is a reason for legal intervention, then it follows straightforwardly that the adulterous and promiscuous character of many instances of sexual harassment cannot be a reason for supporting the law about sexual harassment. Thus, regardless of what one thinks about whether adultery and promiscuity should be legally prohibited, one cannot rationally support the sexual harassment law on the ground of the adulterous and promiscuous character of the conduct involved.

Another way of understanding that point is to remind ourselves that sexual harassment is essentially conduct that occurs within a certain kind of formal framework, such as that of employment. But it is obviously irrelevant to the moral wrongness of, say, adultery, whether it occurs within or outside such a framework. An act of adultery taking place outside any such framework, viewed *as* adultery, is just as wrong as an otherwise similar act taking place within such a framework. The adulterous character of the latter act cannot provide a moral reason for its legal prohibition (or for legal prohibition of attempts at it) without also providing a moral reason for a legal prohibition of the former (and attempts at it).

Now, it is in principle possible for someone to agree that although the adulterous and promiscuous character of sexual harassment does not prove that sexual harassment as such is morally wrong, it may still justify the legal prohibition of sexual harassment, because the prohibition of sexual harassment is likely to be more effective in curtailing such sexual immorality than a straightforward prohibition of promiscuity and adultery. The old-fashioned legal prohibitions of sexual immorality were enforced by the legal system directly, and that, it could be argued, made them cumbersome to operate. The sexual harassment law, on the other hand, curtails such behavior through the employers of the individuals concerned, and the employers are arguably in a much better position to curtail the behavior effectively. Relying on such an argument would, however, be doubly unpopular: not only is support for the idea that sexual immorality such as adultery and promiscuity warrants formal intervention nowadays rather limited, but the argument also runs counter to the idea (which has become widely accepted in recent decades) that employees should enjoy a significant measure of privacy relative to their employers and that employers are allowed to intrude on that privacy only when there is a significant business-related reason for doing so.

Some of my more sophisticated readers will undoubtedly be tempted to say that I am here, in many ways, knocking at an open door because the literature that supports the sexual harassment law and the movement aimed at the eradication of such conduct normally does not rely on the adulterous and promiscuous character of the conduct involved as the ground of its wrongness. It is indeed true that the core of the feminist theorizing about sexual harassment does not use such arguments, but the literature about sexual harassment still often exploits the readers' preexisting attitudes about better-known forms of sexual immorality.

An influential report of early research on sexual harassment, carried out by the Working Women's Institute, for example, took the opportunity to mention that 79 percent of the harassers were married, in a manner that suggested that the fact was relevant to appreciating the seriousness of the problem.[2] A more recent article on sexual harassment quotes "a consultant . . . who specializes in sexual harassment issues," who offers what she calls the "Simple Test" of whether one's behavior is harassing.[3] The first question on that test is "Would you engage in this behavior if your partner or spouse were in the room?" Presenting the prohibition of sexual harassment in this way makes the connection between sexual harassment and adultery crucial, as most people would, of course, not engage in any behavior that is even suggestive of adulterous interests if their regular romantic partners were in the same room. Another question on the "Simple Test" is "Would you be comfortable reading about your behavior in the newspaper?" which presents the notion of sexual harassment as if it were a blanket notion for adultery, promiscuity, and practically every other form of sexual immorality: a person who engages in any such behavior typically would not be comfortable reading about it in the newspaper (not to mention that most people would not be too comfortable reading about their sexual behavior in a newspaper even when there is nothing immoral about it).

In other literature on sexual harassment, one reads that "most of the sex at work . . . does not grow out of a person's interest in establishing a long-term relationship with another employee"[4] and that "faculty Casanovas usually forget to inform the woman that she is only one in a long procession."[5] When interviewed about sexual harassment, a philosophy professor who chaired a committee dealing with such matters at her university said, "Graduate women don't realize, 'You're probably the umpteenth woman this professor had had.'"[6] Such remarks seem to be clearly intended to make people's views about sexual harassment influenced by their views about promiscuity.

Thus, although the connection between sexual harassment and such forms of sexual immorality as promiscuity and adultery is rarely presented as an explicit argument in favor of the sexual harassment law, it may easily, in the minds of many people, end up playing the role of such an argument. This is particularly important in light of the fact that the other arguments in favor of the law may not be fully understood by many people. Many ordinary people may thus be thinking something like the following:

> Some people believe very strongly that the sexual harassment law should exist. I do not quite understand all the reasons that they have for that belief, but I know that the law prohibits conduct, such as adultery and promiscuity, that is bad anyway. Therefore, I see no reason to oppose the law.

The existence of the sexual harassment law is probably as much a result of such quiet nonopposition as it is of direct militant support. Explicitly setting aside the argument that sexual harassment is wrong because it involves adultery and promiscuity is therefore an important first step in thinking about the law critically.

An argument similar to the one discussed above is sometimes made. It relies not on adultery and promiscuity but rather on more subtle forms of sexual immorality that do not have such well-established labels but that one might generally refer to as insensitivity in sexual interactions. Thus, Jan Crosthwaite and Christine Swanton say that

> the central aspect of the wrongness of sexual harassment is this. Behaviour of a sexual nature or motivation in the workplace counts as sexual harassment if and only if there is inadequate consideration of the interests of the person subjected to it.[7]

Now, it is easy to agree that sexual behavior in which "there is inadequate consideration of the interests of the person subjected to it" is morally wrong. But such insensitive conduct seems to be wrong in exactly the same way when it occurs outside a workplace, or any other designated formal framework, as it is when it occurs within it. It is, in the absence of some further argument, unclear why one should be *specially* concerned with insensitivity in sexual matters when it manifests itself within a designated formal framework, as opposed to simply being concerned with such insensitivity in general, regardless of where it manifests itself. It is unclear why insensitivity in sexual interactions should be treated differently depending on the surroundings in which it manifests itself. It is also unclear why insensitivity in sexual matters should receive more attention and be treated differently from insensitivity in other, nonsexual matters. Surely, "inadequate consideration of the interests of the person subjected to" some conduct is a morally bad thing regardless of whether the conduct is of a sexual nature or not. The incidents of nonsexual interaction in which people are insensitive to others, alas, occur every minute, and some of them are quite hurtful. If insensitivity is what one is concerned about, then it seems that one should be equally concerned with insensitivity in all social interactions, regardless of whether they are sexual or nonsexual. Bringing the notion of sexual harassment, with its focus on sexual matters, into one's thinking on these topics, only causes unnecessary confusion.

It is tempting to try to respond to the argument I have just made by saying that although insensitivity is always a bad thing, there is, in fact, a reason for being specially concerned about insensitivity within workplaces, educational institutions, and similar frameworks. It could be said that at such places people are more vulnerable to insensitive conduct of others, more likely to be adversely affected by it, than they are at other places. Being at work, for example, the argument could go, requires people to concentrate on whatever tasks they are expected to accomplish, which makes them feel tense and thus specially sensitive to the insensitive conduct of others.

However, even if thinking about sexual harassment as a form of insensitivity is supplemented in this way, it still does not show that sexual harassment as a type of conduct is wrong. First, the question of why insensitivity in sexual matters should be treated differently from insensitivity in nonsexual matters still remains unanswered. Second, while it is probably true that people are, on the average, significantly more tense and irritable while they are at work or at school than they are elsewhere, that is so only on the average. People often do find themselves under considerable stress and very tense while they are outside any such formal framework. On the other hand, workers in many occupations often enjoy considerable stretches of working time that are relatively free of tension. The difference between the average level of tension within designated formal frameworks and the average level of tension outside them does not justify drawing the *sharp* distinction that thinking in terms of sexual harassment makes between what happens within such frameworks and what happens outside them.

Furthermore, if the wrongness of sexual harassment is to be understood in terms of the insensitivity of its perpetrators, then the argument for its legal regulation becomes exceedingly weak. We do not normally think that the law should be preoccupied with insensitivity in social interactions.[8] The tools of the law are generally thought to be far too blunt for dealing with insensitivities as such, without causing more damage than benefit.

Notes

1. See, for example, Richard Wasserstrom, "Is Adultery Immoral?" and Frederick Elliston, "In Defense of Promiscuity," in *Philosophy and Sex,* ed. Robert Baker and Frederick Elliston (Buffalo: Prometheus Books, 1975), 207–21, 222–43. The Wasserstrom article also appears in several other anthologies.
2. Peggy Crull, "The Impact of Sexual Harassment on the Job: A Profile of the Experiences of Ninety-Two Women," in *Sexuality in Organizations: Romantic and Coercive Behaviors at Work,* ed. Dail Ann Neugarten and Jay M. Shafritz (Oak Park, Ill.: Moore Publishing, 1980), 68.
3. Jill L. Sherer, "Sexually Harassed," *Hospitals and Health Networks* 69, no. 2 (1995): 56.
4. Barbara A. Gutek, *Sex and the Workplace: The Impact of Sexual Behavior on Women, Men, and Organizations* (San Francisco: Jossey-Bass, 1985), 160.
5. Billie Wright Dziech and Linda Weiner, *The Lecherous Professor: Sexual Harassment on Campus,* 2d Edition (Urbana, Ill.: University of Illinois Press, 1990), 76.
6. Ann Levin, "UCSD Alters Sex-Harassment Policy," *Tribune* (San Diego), 26 August 1988.
7. Jan Crosthwaite and Christine Swanton, "On the Nature of Sexual Harassment," *Australasian Journal of Philosophy* 64, supplement (1986): 100 (footnote omitted).
8. Crosthwaite and Swanton seem to acknowledge that their account of sexual harassment does not straightforwardly entail what kind of legal regime we should have for dealing with it. Ibid., 103.

PART II

Varieties of Sexual Harassment

6. What's Sex Got to Do With It?

Deborah Tannen

When the Clarence Thomas [Supreme Court Justice nomination] hearings took place, I was asked to appear on radio and television to talk about the role of language in sexual harassment. I had previously spent the major part of a year appearing on such shows and writing articles on the topic of women's and men's conversational styles and had rarely gotten a negative response. Nearly everyone seemed to appreciate my even-handed approach: Women's and men's styles are equally valid; each has its own logic; problems occur because of the differences in style. But when I made public statements about sexual harassment, I had to say that things were different for women and men. I received several letters of complaint from men who felt I was slighting them. "Men can be sexually harassed too," they accurately protested. Michael Crichton's novel *Disclosure* dramatizes this. But it also shows that, although the situation can occur, its fundamental elements are different from those that underlie harassment of women by men.[1]

Maureen Dowd summarizes the premise of *Disclosure* in a book review:

> Meredith Johnson, the cool, beautiful blonde who is the new boss at Digital Communications in Seattle, summons one of her division managers, Tom Sanders, to her office for their first business meeting.
>
> She has a chilled bottle of chardonnay waiting. Her skirt is riding up her thigh. She kicks off her heels and wiggles her toes. She crosses and uncrosses her legs several times, explaining that she doesn't wear stockings because she likes "the bare feeling." She half parts her full lips and looks dreamily at him through preternaturally long lashes. She tells him that he has "a nice hard tush." She asks for a neck massage.[2]

Dowd comments about the Crichton book, "Here is the novel Hollywood has been waiting for: Sharon Stone as Bob Packwood." But compare her description of the novel's action with a description of Bob Packwood's behavior, according to an account in *The New York Times Magazine*:

> While running for reelection in 1980, Bob Packwood was eager to meet his campaign chairwoman for Lane County, Ore. The Senator invited Gena Hutton to dinner at the motel where he was staying in Eugene for a get-acquainted meeting. Hutton, a 35-year-old divorced mother of two, had brought along pictures of her children and even her cats.
>
> Then it was time to go and Packwood offered to walk her to her car. "As I started to put the key in the car door," Hutton recalls, "he just reeled me around and grabbed me and pulled me close to him." For an instant, she thought he was offering a good-night hug. But then the Senator planted a full kiss on her lips, wriggling his tongue into her mouth. [See Selection 23.][3]

Packwood's behavior toward Hutton was aggressive. He grabbed her, pulled her toward him, and pushed his tongue into her mouth. In contrast, the woman in the Crichton novel, although clearly abusing her power, is seductive: She doesn't begin by lunging at Tom, but by luring him to her. Rather than forcibly pulling him toward her and doing things to him, she invites him to move toward her and do things to her. ("She asks for a neck message.")

Later in Dowd's summary, Meredith is described as physically attacking Tom: "She pushes him onto the couch and pinions him there." But this physical assault comes after the seductive behavior previously described, not out of the blue as in the alleged Packwood example. And if Tom Sanders does not push Meredith Johnson off him, it is not because he is not big and strong enough to fight her off, but because he is unwilling to ruin his career by hitting his boss. Gena Hutton, in contrast, was smaller in stature and weaker in strength than Bob Packwood, as is usually the case when a woman and a man have an encounter. Hutton did not accept Packwood's invitation to enter his motel room, but if she had, and if he had wanted to, he would probably have been physically capable of throwing her down and "pinioning" her, and she would probably have been physically incapable of fighting him off.

Behaviors associated with the sexes in our culture are differently apportioned. Men's sexual behavior is expected to be aggressive, women's seductive. Imagine the scene of the Crichton novel with the genders reversed:

> Tom Sanders, the cool, beautiful blonde who is the new boss at Digital Communications in Seattle, summons one of his division managers, Meredith Johnson, to his office for their first business meeting.
>
> He has a chilled bottle of chardonnay waiting. His trousers are riding up his calves. He kicks off his shoes and wiggles his toes. He crosses and uncrosses his legs several times, explaining that he doesn't wear socks because he likes "the bare feeling." He half parts his full lips and looks dreamily at her through preternaturally long lashes. He tells her that she has "a nice hard tush." He asks for a neck massage.

It would not be surprising if Meredith Johnson, observing Tom Sanders behaving this way, would burst out laughing or determine he had come unhinged. Even the initial description, "cool, beautiful blonde," is incongruous when applied to a man, because it is only with women that physical attractiveness is the key feature, which is why the word "beautiful" has come to be associated with women—except, perhaps, to describe a young man from the perspective of someone who might be drawn to him. A description of a male boss would more likely be in terms of his size and appearance of power. . . .

It is commonly said that sexual harassment is not about sex, but about power. I believe this is true, but the fact that it involves sex is not irrelevant. Rather, sex entails power in our culture. Most important, the corresponding statement is not always true—that sexual harassment necessarily involves the threat of reprisal from one in power toward one in a subordinate position. Although this is undoubtedly a frequent constellation, and perhaps the most frightening, it is not the whole story. Sexual harassment can be experienced at any level of power: It can be encountered among peers, and it is a frequent form of insubordination perpetrated by those of lower rank against those above them in a hierarchy.

Having a high position is not protection from sexual moves that make someone uncomfortable. There is the now well-known case of the state senator from New York who described publicly the many times her male colleagues made her job harder by reminding her she was female. One experience occurred when she needed to get past a man already sitting in his seat, in order to reach her own in the State Senate chamber. He refused to move, so she had to climb over him to get to her seat. Assuming she was wearing a knee-length skirt, one can imagine the compromising position this put her in. As happens with many women, I think, it apparently did not occur to her that she could challenge him by simply refusing to climb over him—sitting in someone else's seat, perhaps, and explaining, if that person arrived, that this colleague would not let her get to her seat. (It probably would not have come to that: He would likely have moved if he saw she would not climb over him.)

Even members of the United States House of Representatives are not immune: In an article about women in the House, Congresswoman Jill Long is quoted as saying that a male colleague "complimented me on my appearance and then said that he was going to chase me around the House floor. Because he was not my boss, I was not intimidated. But I was offended, and I was embarrassed."[4]

These public officials were made uncomfortable by sexual references or behavior on the part of colleagues. Similarly, although a study done in 1993 found that 73% of female residents said they had been sexually harassed primarily by male physicians, many women physicians I interviewed said they experienced as much or more behavior they considered harassment from fellow students, interns, and residents as from their professors.[5] One physician who was the only woman in her medical-school class recalls that the worst offenders were two psychiatric residents. She recalled one in particular:

> I went on rounds with him one day, and he actually said "There's a smell of a woman." And he turned to me and he said, "It's you." He said that women are estrous, and he said, "I thought I could smell a woman." It was—and he was a—it was really foul. It was a very—it was a dirty foul play. It was a curveball. I didn't know what to say. And so I did what all women do when they don't know what to say. I didn't say anything. But I felt humiliated. I was so embarrassed, and I remember feeling immensely anxious. I could feel my heart starting to beat. It was almost as though I'd been found out.

As this physician pointed out when she told me about this and other experiences, men at her own level were able to humiliate her simply by calling attention to her female sexuality.

This seems also to explain why simply leaving pornographic materials in sight can be disturbing—and, yes, intimidating—to women. A woman working on a Ph.D. in linguistics had been asked to share a textbook with another student. Since she had a car and he did not, she offered to deliver the book to him when she was finished with it. When she arrived at his house to hand over the book, she was appalled to find herself surrounded by pornographic magazines. He blithely asked her to sit down, but there was no surface on which she could sit without first handling a magazine that had been left spread open to reveal a woman in a pornographic pose.

Another woman was hired as manager of a department composed entirely of men—some of whom left pornographic pictures of women in places where they knew she would come across them. What is the logic by which leaving pornographic pictures is a form of harassment? These materials were meant to shock and embarrass, to make the woman feel uncomfortable. But how is it different from any other form of hazing that men in subordinate positions might use to test a new boss or "give him a hard time"? It is that pornography, or any reference to sex, reminds the new manager that she is a woman, that they are thinking of her as the object of sexual desire, and, most intimidating, that sex can be used as a format for physical attack. The graduate student who found herself surrounded by pornography in a fellow student's apartment reported that, besides humiliation, what she felt was fear.

More difficult for some to understand is why materials need not be pornographic, but simply explicit, to make women uncomfortable, especially if there is a component of violence. Congresswoman Marjorie Margolies-Mezvinsky describes an experience that took place during her freshman term:

> Last summer, the freshman class was invited to the Motion Picture Association of America for a screening. Because the class is so large, we were invited to come in two groups. The first group saw *In the Line of Fire*. Those of us who went the next night saw Michael Crichton's *Rising Sun*, in which a videotape of a woman being raped is replayed repeatedly.

"It was an appalling choice and all of us felt the same way. We sat there with our colleagues and we were embarrassed," says [Utah Congresswoman] Karen Shepherd, who was particularly disgusted with the movie. . . . "The very next day, we all had to come on the floor and work alongside the men and pretend we don't live in a culture that portrays women in that way. It's very, very difficult," says Karen.[6]

What made the experience so distressing is that it brought to the fore the ways that the women, newly elected to Congress, were different from their male counterparts, and more vulnerable.

FEMALE IS FAULTABLE

Because of this constellation of phenomena—that by reminding a woman she is a woman and therefore seen as sexual, one-down, and (most important) physically vulnerable—being female is in itself "faultable"—a term coined by Erving Goffman to capture the sense in which someone can be embarrassed or made to feel in the wrong because they have a particular characteristic.[7] Although there are situations in which a man may become "faultable" because he is male—say, when the topic turns to sexual harassment or rape and he feels that everyone of his gender is being impugned—a woman can become faultable for being female in any situation at any time. (Comparably, being Jewish or African-American is faultable at any time in our society in a way that being Christian or white is not, although there are situations in which it could be.)

One way that women's sexuality is often called to attention is a subtle matter of fleeting glances. A woman told of interviewing a young man for a job as assistant; the poor fellow was rather nervous, and, among other types of evidence of this, his eyes kept flicking down to her chest. It seems unlikely that this young man did this intentionally, to make her uncomfortable. After all, he was applying for a job, and if he offended her, she would not hire him. The most probable explanation was that it was an involuntary tic, a sign of his own discomfort. Most women recognize the experience of having a man's eyes continually drift to her chest. Although it might be a sign of interest, admiration, or invitation, most women take it as a fleeting but irritating reminder, "You're a woman, and I'm thinking about your sex rather than your brains, your authority, the words you are saying to me."

Although men as well as women can be upset by unwanted sexual advances and uncertain how to deal with them, there is a way that bringing sex to the fore is especially compromising to women. Why are women the ones who are the objects of obscene phone calls? While on a national television call-in show, I received an obscene phone call in which the caller simply made reference to a sexual body part. Why would this be so much less likely to happen to a man in a public position? Why did a visitor to Congresswoman Rosa De-Lauro's office sign her guest book as "Dick Hurtz, 131 Penis Drive"?[8] (Is there a veiled threat of sexual assault in the last name, which was spelled to suggest "hurts"?) Did he do the same in the guest books of congressmen? Reminding him that he is a sexual being does not seem to be regarded as compromising to a man. Quite the contrary, many men regard their sexuality as a form of prowess, not vulnerability. So simply being reminded that he is a sexual being (as distinguished, of course, from sexual behavior that might be considered inappropriate) would be, if anything, enhancing to his image rather than compromising—and that is probably why nobody bothers to bring it up.

Evidence that women's sexuality is regarded as "tainting" is widespread. In a related, though quite different example, a newspaper reported that Graham Leonard, the bishop of London, was distressed when his church decided to ordain women. "Because any bishop's hand would be 'tainted' after placing them on the head of a woman undergoing ordination, he reasoned, the Archbishop of Canterbury could appoint 'flying bishops' to enter the dioceses of dissenting bishops [i.e., those who did not want to ordain women] and do their dirty work for them."[9]

A sense that females can be contaminating made life difficult for the physician I quoted who had been humiliated by a psychiatric resident. Earlier in her training, as the only woman intern at a Catholic teaching hospital, she was not allowed to live in the interns' residence, where the difficult life of a doctor in training was made easier by the ministrations of a live-in housekeeper. As the physician recalled years later:

> And there was a housekeeper there that—that tidied up the rooms . . . and literally took on the mother role. She would make sure that there were snacks there for fellows who were on call, and she was very protective, and absolutely wonderful. She did their laundry, or if they needed to do things—she was marvelous, she was a house mother. Guess what? Not for me, they wouldn't let me stay there. They would not let me stay in that residency.

Even worse, she was not allowed to set foot in the interns' residence:

> The housekeeper said that she would not tolerate me there, and the sense of it was, there was a very clear sense that I would contaminate these men.

It is interesting that the housekeeper did not feel her own presence was tainting, probably because she saw herself as moving in a different realm within the same building, just as women and men in some cultures inhabit the same house but keep to different parts of it. The female resident would have entered "the men's house" in the same realm as the men.

The possibility that a female can be perceived as contaminating is a resource that can be drawn upon to make life more difficult for any woman by anyone, regardless of where they are placed in hierarchical relation to her.

"WHO'S IN CHARGE HERE?"

In the examples I have just given, the relative rank and consequently of power among the participants varies but is fairly clear-cut. Many cases, however, are ambiguous, and the introduction of sexual references or propositions can become moves in the negotiation of power.

What is the distribution of power between a writer and editor? In some ways, editors have power over authors. They decide whether or not to accept a book for publication; they assign tasks to authors and give them deadlines; they tell authors what they must do to their manuscripts to make them acceptable.

In this spirit, the most egregious experience I myself have had occurred with an editor. I was writing my very first book, and the editor insisted I meet him in his hotel room to discuss the draft of my manuscript that I had sent him. I demurred, arranging to meet him in the hotel cafeteria instead. But as we sat in the cafeteria booth discussing the manuscript, he proclaimed that it was impossible to work in the noisy environment, and we should move to his room. Intimidated by his position and unused to raising objections to what sounded like nonnegotiable demands, I followed him to his room. At first we continued discussing my draft, but when we were done, he announced that he had to change, stood up, and began removing his clothes. I sprang for the door but did not walk through it, fearful of offending him. Instead, I stood there with my back to the room and my head buried in my manuscript, keeping him in my peripheral vision so I could bolt if he made a move toward me. He did not. But I did no more work on that book so long as this editor was in place, since it would have required contact with him. I returned to the book when he vacated his position for reasons unrelated to me.

In this scenario from my own life, the editor held the power. I was young and not yet published, and I was eager not to offend the man who kept the gate I wanted to pass through. My book would not be published until he approved it. But the power relations between author and editor seem to be reversed in the following incident. An editor told of an experience in which an author insisted on dropping off his manuscript at her home. When he arrived, he began telling her about the sexual fantasies he had been having since the first time he laid eyes on her. Surprised, I asked if this had happened before, and if her female colleagues ever had similar experiences. She said that sexual advances from authors were not unusual, and that they were troubling. In her words, "It is certainly sexual harassment when an important author makes an uninvited pass at an editor. It's not that they're in a position of authority over you exactly, but they know that they're important to the press and that you will be blamed if they take their business elsewhere."

The relative "importance" of the author is crucial: Unknown authors need to be published more than the presses need to publish them. But presses need established authors with recognizable names, so if these authors leave one house, they can easily get another to publish their work. The "importance" of the authors varied in the two examples.

The doctor-patient relationship is often studied as a classic example of a situation of asymmetrical power: The doctor is in the powerful position, the patient subordinate (although the power balance is complicated in private practice where the patient is paying and can switch doctors). This is reflected in a range of patterns: Doctors typically keep patients waiting, and they wear white coats as symbols of their position while patients wear ordinary clothes or no clothes at all. Commonly, doctors are addressed by title—last name while they address patients by first name. Furthermore, those who have studied conversations between doctors and patients have found that doctors are more likely to interrupt, ask direct-information questions, do more of the talking, change the topic precipitously, and generally control the interaction. But on all these dynamics, women doctors fall somewhat further along the continuum toward what we think of as "powerless" behavior rather than "powerful." According to my own interviews, they are more likely to be addressed by first name by patients. They are also more likely to be interrupted (as sociologist Candace West has shown) and to enlist the patient's agreement before changing topics (according to a study I discussed earlier by linguist Nancy Ainsworth-Vaughn).

In keeping with the image of doctors as the ones in power, and of sexual harassment as flowing from the powerful to the powerless, many surveys have found that a small percentage (but comparatively large numbers) of male doctors, like ministers, judges, therapists, professors and coaches, press sexual advances on women in their charge.[10] Two particularly egregious examples were recounted in full-length books: *Doc* tells the real story of a highly respected physician in Wyoming who systematically raped many of the women who came to him for gynecological appointments. Choosing naïve and sexually innocent Mormon women, he hid behind a cloth and simply inserted his own body part in place of the gynecological instrument. (When the author of this book appeared on a radio talk show, many women listeners called in to tell about their own experiences in which doctors sexually abused them.)

Barbara Noël tells in *You Must Be Dreaming,* a book written with Kathryn Watterson, of her personal experience with Dr. Jules Masserman, a former president of the American Psychiatric Association and co-chair of Psychiatry and Neurology at Northwestern University. Dr. Masserman drugged his patients with sodium amytal, saying the drug would help them overcome resistance to the truth of their problems. One day Noël awakened while undergoing a treatment—and discovered the doctor on top of her, having sex with her.

Eventually, twenty-eight other ex-patients (three were men) came forward with similar stories of having been drugged and subjected to sexual abuse from Dr. Masserman.[11]

The constellation in these examples seems clear: Male physicians are in a position of power, so a small percentage abuse that power by taking sexual advantage of women patients. Yet a recent study published in *The New England Journal of Medicine* found that 77% of women doctors surveyed felt they had been sexually harassed by male patients.[12] In other words, women experience sexual harassment from men over whom they theoretically have power as well as from men who have power over them.

Although the nature of the harassment is far less egregious than in the examples above, the study shows that women physicians are frequently the object of unwanted sexual attention from their patients. The survey of women family physicians in Ontario, Canada, conducted by Susan Phillips (a physician) and Margaret Schneider (a psychologist) found that 321 of the 417 doctors who responded to their questionnaire said they had been sexually harassed by patients. (Some groped them, requested unneeded genital exams, sent sex-related objects and letters, and physically assaulted them.) The doctors reported having minor incidents occur monthly, with the most extreme occurring a few times a year. The study by Phillips and Schneider did not give examples of actual conversations, but sociolinguist Nancy Ainsworth-Vaughn seems to have captured a mild such example on tape.

As part of an ongoing study of doctor-patient conversations, Ainsworth-Vaughn recorded the interactions between twenty-three patients and eight physicians in a private-practice setting, with the agreement of all concerned. One of the twenty-three patients was a man who regularly brought up sexual topics and jokes with a female physician. His ritual greeting had sexual overtones: "So whatta you been doing and who have you been doing it to?" On one occasion, something that occurred in the examination reminded him of the movie *Young Frankenstein,* and he took the opportunity to speak lines from the film: "'Would you like to roll in the hay?' [laughs] 'Oh, great knockers.' Remember that?" This physician told Ainsworth-Vaughn that she was not troubled by this patient's jokes; she regarded them as simply an expression of his personal style. But the nurses in her office found his suggestive remarks offensive. One jokingly told the researcher, "We draw lots to see who will have to put him in [the examining room]." Indeed, most women to whom I showed the examples felt that references to "rolling in the hay" and "knockers" would make them uncomfortable in a professional situation. They felt that the patient was trying to put the doctor down, to counter the power imbalance in the doctor-patient relationship, an interpretation that is supported by the emphasis this patient placed on the need to avoid being intimidated by doctors, when Ainsworth-Vaughn interviewed him.[13] A psychiatry resident at the University of Southern California stated explicitly that she perceives propositions from patients during physical exams to be in this spirit: "They have to put you down to make you lower than them."[14]

Which is it? Is a proposition a sign of affection, of a desire to get closer, or is it a put-down? Is it a put-down when a woman patient propositions a male physician during a physical exam, or lets him know she is romantically interested in him? (It could be considered sexual harassment, whether or not it is deemed a put-down.) Since the same linguistic means are used to create both messages, both interpretations are possible. In fact, the two might go together: Because he likes the doctor, he wants to bring her down to his level so he can get closer to her. It is less likely for the proposition by a female patient toward a male doctor to be taken as a put-down because of the stereotypical constellation of sexual relations in our culture: A man "conquers" a woman, subdues her. This is part of our cultural heritage that lives on in people's consciousness even if it is no longer explicitly subscribed to by everyone. In any case, there is always an actual or potential element of fear present for women in the face of male sexual aggression, which is less likely to be part of men's reaction to women's sexual aggression. In the survey of Canadian women physicians, 26% reported feeling frightened by the sexual behavior of male patients.

The fact that physicians are typically alone in examining rooms with unclothed patients presents an ambiguity that must be resolved by an unspoken agreement on the part of both parties to ignore the potential for sexual relations, just as the audience at a theater must agree not to speak for the period of the performance, since any one of them could disrupt the play by speaking out. This explains why simply bringing up sexual topics can be offensive (like the "knockers" joke): It breaks this unspoken agreement.

Notes

1. Throughout this chapter, I focus on sexual harassment in which the harasser is male and the harassed female. All evidence is that the vast majority of cases fit this constellation. But this is not to imply that women never sexually harass men. I have no doubt that this sometimes occurs, but, as I show here, the dynamics would be extremely different in such cases. I should also mention that those who have told me about personal experiences in which they felt they were sexually harassed by a woman were all women—a situation I do not discuss here because its dynamics, too, are very different from the most common constellation.

2. Maureen Dowd's review of *Disclosure* appeared under the heading "Women Who Harass Too Much" in *The New York Times Book Review*, January 23, 1994, p. 7.

3. The quotation about Bob Packwood comes from "The Trials of Bob Packwood" by Trip Gabriel, *The New York Times Magazine*, August 29, 1993, pp. 30–33, 38–43. The quote is from p. 30.

4. The quotation from Congresswoman Jill Long appears in David Finkel, "Women on the Verge of a Power Breakthrough," *The Washington Post Magazine*, May 10, 1992, pp. 15–19, 30–34. The quote is from p. 15.

5. This finding is attributed by Phillips and Schneider to M. Komaromy, A. B. Bindman, R. J. Haber, and M. A. Sande, "Sexual Harassment in Medical Training," *New England Journal of Medicine* 328(1993):322–26.

6. The quotation from Congresswoman Margolies-Mezvinsky is from her book *A Woman's Place*, p. 47.

7. Goffman introduces the term "faultable" in his essay "Radio Talk," p. 225.

8. That a visitor to Congresswoman Rosa DeLauro's office signed her guest book in this way was reported by David Finkel in "Women on the Verge of a Power Breakthrough," *The Washington Post Magazine*, May 10, 1992, pp. 15–19, 30–34. The quote is from p. 15.

9. "Consecration of Woman Bishop Will Be Anticlimax," by Jack Kapica, *The Toronto Globe and Mail*, December 29, 1993, p. A6.

10. Cases involving these professionals have been much reported in the press. The problem of male coaches and female athletes was brought to my attention by Mariah Burton Nelson's *The Stronger Women Get, the More Men Love Football*.

11. Thirteen people had come forward by the time of the book's publication; the rest spoke up after, according to Ms. Watterson. Five out-of-court settlements had resulted from suits brought by former patients before publication.

12. Susan Phillips and Margaret Schneider, "Sexual Harassment of Female Doctors by Patients."

13. For example, he gave this as a reason for addressing the doctor by first name ("Hi, Sue!"), even though this office had an explicit policy by which staff addressed patients by title—last name. "[W]hen I was younger," he told Ainsworth-Vaughn, "I was intimidated by the people in white coats. But over the years you start to learn . . . and you suddenly realize that yeah, they're no big deal. They're like everybody else, and you make a point of, uh, calling them, speaking to them with their first name. Never call them doctor. Don't let the ego get in there."

14. "Hey Doc, You Got Great Legs!" *Newsweek*, January 31, 1994, p. 54.

7. Tailhook: Scandal Time

Eloise Salholz and Douglas Waller

They may have been officers, but they certainly weren't gentlemen. Navy Lt. Paula Coughlin, 30, saw the group of navy and Marine pilots hanging out in the third-floor corridor of the Las Vegas Hilton, but didn't think twice about heading down the hallway. Then the terror began. It was the 1991 convention of the Tailhook Association, a group of retired and active naval aviators. Coughlin, a helicopter pilot and admiral's aide, hurtled down a gauntlet of groping, poking and pawing officers, who grabbed her breasts and tried to remove her panties. "Help me," she implored a pilot, who then molested her too. "It was the most frightened I've ever been in my life," Coughlin, the daughter of a retired navy aviator, told The Washington Post last week. "I thought, 'I have no control over these guys. I'm going to be gang-raped'."

Even though scores of drunken officers assaulted at least 26 women, 14 of them officers, the navy initially treated Tailhook '91 as little more than a fraternity party that got out of hand. But with Coughlin's decision to speak out last week, the scandal took on a name and a face and finally began to resonate in high places. It had already become clear that senior officers knew behavior at the convention had gotten out of bounds but did nothing to subdue the aviators, and that many of the officers had refused to cooperate after the fact with two separate navy investigations (chart). Since the spring, questions have grown about Navy Secretary H. Lawrence Garrett III's handling of the case and his whereabouts during that infamous weekend. Appalled by Coughlin's account, President Bush summoned Defense Secretary Dick Cheney for a briefing on Friday. Within hours, Garrett tendered his resignation, which Bush—himself a former navy pilot—accepted in a statement conspicuously lacking the usual note of regret.

Garrett took "full responsibility" for the navy's sloppy handling of Tailhook, but he may ultimately have company. *Newsweek* has learned that Adm. Frank Kelso—the navy's top military leader—at one point was also near the hotel corridor where the sexual assaults allegedly occurred. Critics question whether Kelso, who has publicly professed "zero tolerance" for sexual harassment, has done enough to crack down on officers who stonewalled the Naval Investigative Service (NIS). Last week the Senate Armed Services Committee froze 4,500 promotions, retirements and changes of command; chairman Sam Nunn said the ban would come off only after the navy identified and punished the assailants. And the Pentagon ordered the navy to suspend disciplinary proceedings against 70 officers implicated in the affair lest some of the commanders trying the cases turn out to be suspects themselves.

The Tailhook Association—named after the hook that grabs planes when they land on carrier decks—has been meeting annually for more than three decades. Officially, members are there to socialize and learn about advances in aviation technology. Unofficially, in recent years, it's become animal house off the high seas. Strippers and porn films in third-floor "hospitality suites" set the mood last year; liquor flowed from the penis of a papier-mache rhinoceros, flown in from Florida aboard a military plane at the taxpayers' expense. The worst was the gauntlet, present during each of the convention's three nights. A lookout near the elevator would call out, "Decks afoul" for women deemed too unattractive to attack, "Decks awash" for fair game. The NIS reports that one underage girl was shoved down the hall and partially disrobed.

Coughlin says she told both Garrett's personal assistant and her boss, Rear Adm. John Snyder, about the ordeal. She claims Snyder, the only officer thus far removed from his command, dismissed her complaint, saying, "That's what you get when you go to a hotel party with a bunch of drunk aviators." Evidently, the top brass were either deaf and mute—or turning a blind eye. The first NIS report, published in April, made no mention of Garrett's being in the vicinity of the gauntlet corridor; the NIS later disclosed an interview with a Marine captain who claims he saw the navy secretary there. Garrett now acknowledges that he was on a patio adjoining the corridor on Saturday night and that he stepped into a hospitality suite to get a beer; but he has said, through a spokesman, that he saw no "inappropriate or offensive conduct." The navy says Kelso was on the same patio the night before, from 10 to 10:40. Though victims were running the nearby gauntlet that night, a navy spokesman told *Newsweek* that Kelso "did not see or hear of any misconduct or inappropriate behavior." Even by the navy's old-boy standards, the rank-closing in the Tailhook case has been striking. Garrett says he didn't learn about Coughlin's charges for several weeks. The NIS investigators, who conducted some 1,500 interviews among the conventiongoers, faced a conspiracy of silence; they didn't turn up a single aviator or senior officer who would admit that the assaults had taken place. Some officers refused to order their subordinates to be photographed for the purpose of identification. Although at least 70 officers have been implicated, not one has even been identified publicly. Kelso has so far not ordered officers to tell investigators what they know. Garrett grew so frustrated that he finally called upon the Pentagon inspector general to take over the probe.

It won't be easy changing the macho atmosphere of the navy, which has lagged behind the other services in addressing sexual harassment. Recent surveys have shown that almost two thirds of naval women have complained of harassment. (And it's not just the navy's problem: even after the navy cut all ties with Tailhook, one Marine general sent a cable to his commanders asking for nominations for the "Tailhooker of the Year" award.) Yet the seaborne service is making efforts to alter its image, if not its mind-set. Officials say that one leading candidate to replace Garrett is Barbara S. Pope, currently the assistant navy secretary for manpower and reserve affairs. With a woman at the helm, it may be a little harder for boys to be boys.

SEPTEMBER 1991   The Las Vegas Hilton hosts the 35th annual convention of the Tailhook Association for navy and Marine pilots.

OCTOBER 10, 1991   The Naval Investigative Service looks into a complaint by a female aide to Rear Adm. John Snyder who says she was sexually harassed at the convention, forced through a gauntlet of drunken, groping officers. Within a few weeks, the NIS uncovers several more alleged cases of abuse.

NOVEMBER 5, 1991   Snyder is removed from his command for his "apparent failure" to take action on his aide's complaint.

APRIL 30, 1992   Investigation report finds 26 women were assaulted but names just two suspects from 5,000 conventioneers. It blames "closing of ranks" for hindering the inquiry.

JUNE 2, 1992   Navy Secretary H. Lawrence Garrett III broadens the probe, which so far has implicated some 70 officers in the scandal.

JUNE 24, 1992   Lt. Paula Coughlin goes public as the admiral's aide whose complaint launched the investigation.

JUNE 26, 1992   Garrett resigns.

Editor's Note

SEPTEMBER 1992   In response to the Pentagon's investigation of Tailhook '91, which includes an evaluation of the Navy's own internal investigation, three admirals are relieved of their commands. Two are forced to take early retirement.

OCTOBER 1992–MAY 1993   Six senior naval officers are reassigned, three admirals censured, and thirty admirals reprimanded for failing to take appropriate action with regard to the Navy's investigation of Tailhook '91. Defense Secretary Les Aspin refuses to remove Admiral Frank Kelso from his post as Chief of Naval Operations despite strong recommendations to do so from within and outside the military.

FEBRUARY 1994   Admiral Kelso resigns as Chief of Naval Operations.

APRIL 1994   Admiral Kelso retires, without demotion, as a four-star admiral with full pension as per his retirement plan prior to the events at Tailhook '91.

SPRING 1994   All four charges against Tailhook participants (from conduct unbecoming an officer to indecent assault) have been dismissed.

---

8. The Military Culture of Harassment

Linda Bird Francke

. . . The five enlisted women were young, all from the Army base at nearby Fort Meade. They served as ammunition specialists, military policemen and administrative personnel. Three were married.

One had joined the Army for training in law enforcement. Another had followed her brothers and father into the services "because they loved it so much." Another had planned to make the Army her career. But all five of the women were either getting out or had already left. The reason was sexual harassment.

To Private Sarah Tolaro, it was the "several very bad experiences" she'd had in the Army. Beyond the "general outlook on females in the services," beyond being talked to "extremely dirty and nasty," Tolaro most resented "being pushed into a corner by two NCO's and having them expose themselves to me and then laugh."[1]

To Lori Lodinsky, it was the accumulation of being "intimidated" into a relationship with her platoon leader the day she had arrived at Fort Meade, followed by an assault by her supervisor during a night training drive. "He told me to go real fast on the airfield and weave in and out of the lights to test my ability at high speeds in a police sedan," Lodinsky testified. "Then he started grabbing me, while I was going about 60 MPH, all over my body. I screamed. I knocked out a row of lights. . . . That was one of the incidents. There are many more."[2]

According to the women's testimony, virtually every safeguard the Army had established to meld personnel of disparate backgrounds existed only on paper. The Army's required "human relations" training which Specialist Jimi Hernandez had attended in Ger-

many did not follow its syllabus on race relations, gender relations and religious and ethnic differences. Instead, she testified, the twenty men in her discussion group, in which she
was the only woman, focused entirely on sex "as far as women do not belong in the service,
etcetera."[3]

In keeping with the low number of official complaints registered by the services, none
of the women had bothered to report the harassment they had witnessed or experienced,
including the woman who had been forced into a sexual relationship by her platoon leader.
"I was afraid to," said Lori Lodinsky, who subsequently accepted Chapter 5—the inability
to cope with military life—to leave the Army. "He said if I was to tell anyone about this,
I would be in serious trouble."[4]

Neither had Private Tolaro reported the men who had exposed themselves to her nor the
drill sergeant who had told his male troops to hit on female recruits because "women specifically came in the Army for that reason." "Every time I have brought up anything that I
felt was important to me, I have been told 'Do not make waves,'" Tolaro testified. ". . . I
have discovered through my time in the service that if I take it any higher than me, I am
going to come back with 'I'm sure you deserved it anyway,' so, you know, 'just drop it.'"[5]

There it was, every nuance of the harassment issue which would haunt the services and
embarrass the Pentagon for over a decade, recorded in 1980. By any measure, both Congress and the services had enough of a snapshot to start tracking the problem, to collect
data, to survey the captive military population to determine the extent and the ramifica-
tion of sexual harassment and to take the same lead in accomplishing gender integration as
the services had with racial integration. But they didn't.

Instead, the cultural roadblocks to the seriousness of the harassment issue in the Pentagon as well as the corridors of Congress were forecast by the subcommittee's response to the
chilling testimony of Jacqueline Lose, another member of the Military Police, who had
lasted only six months in the Army.

In the most graphic testimony of all, Lose described "several experiences" she'd had with
male peers to the congressional subcommittee. "At one time I was held down in a room by
one man, with two other men in the room present, telling me he was going to give me what
I deserved and I didn't know what I deserved . . . ," she testified. "I had to look to the
others for help, but nobody would give me any. I screamed and yelled, but nobody came."[6]

"Were they aware you were married?" asked Antonio Won Pat, the representative from
Guam, voicing the commonly held perception of married women as inviolate male property and single women as fair sexual game.[7]

"Yes, they were aware," Lose replied.

"But you never succumbed, of course?" Won Pat pressed, as if a screaming woman
pinned to the floor and being molested was still responsible for the outcome of the assault.

"I was held down on the floor and he sat on my chest and held my hands down with his
knees while he was touching me and kissing me," Lose explained. "He eventually let me
go. It was about forty-five minutes he held me down."

But the congressmen still didn't get it. "Did they try to sexually assault you or was it
mainly a feeling maneuver?" asked Congressman Sonny Montgomery, as if anything short
of penetration was acceptable male behavior.[8]

The impossibility of moving sexual harassment up the rung of congressional and service
priorities played out time and again at the 1980 hearing. When one of the servicewomen
testified of her discomfort every afternoon at 4 p.m. when her work supervisor left to watch
the go-go dancers during happy hour at an on-base club, one congressman expressed outrage that the military shift ended so early; another suggested equalizing the situation by
adding male go-go dancers. And to Tolaro's complaint of being talked to "extremely dirty

and nasty," another subcommittee member reminisced almost nostalgically about the "barracks" culture which demanded speaking in "four-letter words."

The solutions to the harassment issue offered by the 1980 congressional subcommittee and by the senior women in the services who also testified would become a familiar mantra in congressional hearing rooms for decades to come. "It is a matter of educating people," concluded Congresswoman Holt. "If they realize the horrible situation, how terrible Mrs. Lose must feel when she has to remember that awful experience . . . then we can overcome it."[9]

The commitment of the chain of command and their congressional overseers to eradicating sexual harassment was the solution to Major General Mary E. Clarke, the last director of the WAC and commander of Fort McClellan, Alabama. "The only way we're going to lick this problem . . . is for all of us to be very concerned about it. It is a leadership problem," said the highest-ranked woman in the Army.[10]

Opening combat jobs to women was the early and constant answer to Congressman Pat Schroeder. "Don't you think you all have a difficult role in being treated seriously unless women are allowed to voluntarily go into all slots?" Schroeder asked the senior women present.[11]

The male members of the House subcommittee remained incapable of seeing harassment as a professional problem, as a management problem, as a serious leadership problem affecting both men and women. Whereas racial harassment would have been seen as an institutional problem demanding swift leadership response, sexual harassment was reduced to a woman's issue and hardly worthy of male attention.

Congressman Montgomery was so determined to make harassment a nonissue that he produced nine other servicewomen representing all four services whom he insisted "had been selected totally at random" from computer lists by the subcommittee's staff.[12] Predictably, not one of Montgomery's witnesses admitted to being sexually harassed.

Where Holt's group objected to coarse and sexual language, Montgomery's group testified they "coped" with it. Where some women felt so intimidated and offended by the prurient behavior of servicemen in mess halls that at one point the Marine Corps had had to designate a separate chow line and eating area for women,[13] Montgomery's women paid no mind. Just as men had been mindlessly harassing women since time began, many women continued just as mindlessly to accept it. "The guys whistle, or, if you are going to eat in the chow hall, you will hear people making comments," a Montgomery airman said nonchalantly at the hearing's inconclusive end. "Most of the harassment is not directed at you per se, it's usually directed simply because you are female."[14]

And so harassment soldiered on. The hierarchical command structure would remain the paradigm for harassment it had always been. Forty-three percent of the enlisted women interviewed by Army auditors in 1982 reported that their superiors bartered sex for favoritism, an offer many young women either fell for or felt they couldn't refuse.[15] The 1990 Defense Department survey of sexual harassment came up with almost the same percentage. Forty-two percent of women experiencing some form of sexual coercion or harassment named their military superiors in the chain of command as the "perpetrators."[16]

Navy company commanders and Army drill sergeants would continue to wield the same power over young recruits they had always wielded. When a man identified himself as a drill sergeant to a recruit celebrating her first twelve hours of liberty after graduating from basic training at Fort Jackson, South Carolina, in 1990 and ordered her to produce the military ID she had left in her motel room, she didn't hesitate. She didn't even doubt his identity in the motel room while he raped and sodomized her. "He kept asking me questions and I kept answering, 'Yes, drill sergeant, no drill sergeant,'" she says. She gave the same explanation later to the Military Police who asked why she hadn't fought back. "He said he was a drill sergeant," she kept repeating.

Senior-subordinate abuse would remain entrenched. A twenty-two-year-old Navy seaman never told her alcoholism counselors at a Navy hospital in Florida about the commodore of her first duty station in 1991 who promised career favors if she would come to his office after hours in civilian clothes and sexually arouse him by talking dirty. "He's a damn captain in the Navy and I'm a measly seaman. What else could I do?" said the young woman at the time. "Every time I said, 'People are talking, this isn't a good idea,' he'd say, 'Don't worry about it, just don't worry about it.'"

The backlash began when the Navy captain was transferred to a new duty station. The seaman, the only woman in her squadron, was shunned by her male colleagues and written up for every infraction they could think of, including her increasing reliance on alcohol. "They didn't want me in the squadron anymore, they didn't want me in that building; they wanted me gone," she says. Because she feared even more retaliation, the seaman didn't dare tell the Navy therapists about her destructive relationship with the captain or her "punishment" by the men in her squadron—the very reasons she'd been sent into treatment. "I'm afraid," she says.

Harassment like the seaman's sexual exploitation was kept silenced by the military's reporting mechanism. The proper procedure was for servicewomen to lodge an "equal opportunity" complaint within their chains of command, the very structure that was often doing the abusing. The improbable equation required the complaint against someone in the chain of command to be evaluated, investigated, judged and adjudicated by that same chain of command. Save for jumping the chain of command and lodging the complaint with the inspector general, servicewomen had no other recourse. Whereas the thousands of civilians employed by the military, many of whom worked side by side with servicewomen, are entitled to bring harassment suits against the military under Title VII of the 1964 Civil Rights Act, their counterparts in uniform could not.[17] "The only person you have to be judge and jury is your commander," says Patricia Gavin, a former Air Force captain.

There was no incentive, however, for military supervisors to address or even to acknowledge harassment problems in their commands. In the highly competitive military structure, promotions and perks are awarded on the basis of *problem-free leadership records*. The mechanism to project seamless perfection depends on denial and deception, even at the company level.

"The officers in the company have people they have to answer to above them," says a former servicewoman. "And they are so worried about answering to those people that they don't want to even admit to themselves that there are any problems, much less try and solve them. They are too afraid somebody is going to find out about them and that puts their career on the line."

Even base commanders were kept in the comforting dark about harassment on their own turf. During Holt's 1980 hearing on sexual harassment, the commander of Fort Meade testified he had first heard about the harassment on his own base from reading the *Baltimore Sun*.[18] In the impetus to paint a rosy picture, harassment complaints were stonewalled at every level, starting at the bottom. "Between a young enlisted woman and the base commander you may have twenty layers of the chain of command that may have been telling her, it is all in your head," says Carolyn Becraft, director of the Women and the Military Project for the Women's Equity Action League in 1992.

Equal opportunity advisors whose job it was to be the vehicle for complaints often contributed to the silence. Save for the Air Force, which offered a permanent career track to equal opportunity advisors, the services treated equal opportunity as temporary, collateral duty. Already pressed by their other responsibilities, personnel assigned to equal opportunity often left the troublesome issues on the lowest rungs of their priority ladders. "They put the regulations in their back pockets, go out to the fleet and forget all about them," says a senior enlisted woman in the Navy.

Even when EO advisors took their roles seriously, they were institutionally handicapped. The advisors were enlisted, giving them little clout in the hierarchy of officers. Moreover, they had no authority to act on equal opportunity complaints, but could only advise their commanders on what action to take. The decision lay entirely in the hands of the commanders, who were more apt to bury the complaint to maintain the appearance of their trouble-free leadership. There was nothing an EO advisor could do without risking his or her career.

"We are taught to be loyal to our boss," says an Army platoon sergeant and EO advisor in 1992. "If we go around him, it's very dangerous. Even as an equal opportunity staff advisor, I can't think of a time I would not be loyal to my boss. I would document any complaint and let him know I was documenting it and how I feel about the situation. But I've been in personnel for seventeen years and I've been to bat for young soldiers who've been discriminated against, who've been assaulted. I know what the command problem is. Hopefully, he'll have a conversion overnight and come in and change his opinion."

The regulatory status of sexual harassment further complicated the reporting process. Harassment was not, and is not, included as a punishable offense under the Uniform Code of Military Justice. Though the UCMJ provides penalties of a bad conduct discharge and one year of imprisonment for dueling (Article 114) and three months of confinement and forfeiture of pay for abusing a public animal (Article 134), there are no such safeguards for abusing women. In the extreme, UCMJ penalties for rape carry the death penalty or life confinement and forced sodomy can put a man or woman away for twenty years, but the subtler forms of harassment are not codified.

To force sexual harassment charges under the UCMJ, servicewomen have to try to link their charges to such recognized offenses as "conduct unbecoming" (Article 133) if the harasser is an officer, or among enlisted, "maltreatment of subordinate" (Article 93), "indecent, insulting or obscene language prejudicial to good order" (Article 134) or "extortion" (Article 127).[19]

The smoke screen made it impossible to track either the number of harassment incidents or their resolutions. Most complaints were resolved at the lowest level, and the punishment meted out, if any, reduced to the nonjudicial Article 15 for minor offenses. "Anecdotal evidence suggests that a slap on the wrist is much more common than severe punishment and that significant redress for victims is unusual," says Nancy Duff Campbell, co-president of the National Women's Law Center in Washington.

Most women didn't bother to report harassment at all. By reporting a problem in what was supposed to be a trouble-free command, she became the problem. She risked being written up by her superiors for the most minor infractions or losing seniority by being moved out of her company to a new company or being shunned by her peers as the Navy seaman had been and Navy Lieutenant Paula Coughlin would be after Tailhook. There were so many ways to backlash women that reporting harassment was just not worth it. In 1984, four years after the Navy established its sexual harassment programs and policies, only twenty-four sexual harassment cases were brought up for hearings, and of those, nine were dismissed as unsubstantiated.[20] In contrast, 31,488 sex discrimination complaints were lodged with the EEOC in 1984, 5,035 of which were for sexual harassment.[21]

The Pentagon's policies made it far easier for men to harass women than for women to defend themselves, especially during the presidency of Ronald Reagan. In 1981, soon after

Reagan and his conservative entourage moved into the White House, the Defense Department tightened its policies against homosexuality to close any loophole from legal challenges in the courts. No longer did individual commanders have discretionary authority to retain or dismiss enlisted homosexuals. The new policy mandated the administrative discharge of "a person, regardless of sex, who engages in, desires to engage in, or intends to engage in homosexual acts."[22] By the time the policy was extended to cover officers in 1985, what can only be described as a decade of terror for women had begun.

Sexual blackmail became the order of the day. Service personnel who resented taking orders from women, who had received bad performance reports from women, who'd had their sexual advances turned down by women, could start the rumor mill rolling by dropping hints of lesbianism. Women's only recourse was to have voluntary or involuntary sex with their potential accusers. "Some women have allowed themselves to be raped by male officers, afraid that the alternative would be a charge of lesbianism," the late Randy Shilts writes in his 1993 book, *Conduct Unbecoming: Gays and Lesbians in the U.S. Military.*[23]

Lesbian-baiting became a military art form. At a joint Army and Air Force base in Kaiserslautern, Germany, in 1984, servicewomen gathering at local bars after work dreaded hearing the theme to the film *Ghostbusters* blasting out of the jukebox. The song signaled the arrival of the "Dyke-busters," a predator posse of servicemen sporting T-shirts bearing the word "dyke" with a slash through it who would press them for sex. If the women reported the "Dyke-busters" for sexual harassment, the odds were their superiors would tell them it was just a joke and to lighten up. But if the women refused to have sex with the men, they could be thrown out of the military. The men "reported those who didn't agree to the military investigative services as dykes," said Michelle Benecke, a former Army officer in Germany, Harvard Law School graduate and advocate for servicewomen.[24]

That some women were homosexual goes without saying. An oft-cited study of 1,456 former service personnel in 1984 indicated that while the proportion of homosexual males seemed to be the same both inside and outside the services, homosexual women were more likely than heterosexual women to have had military service.[25] A former Army officer, herself a lesbian, estimated that as many as 20 to 25 percent of the women in the services in the 80s were lesbians. "Lesbians represented a significant population in the military," she says. "They were nontraditional women with high levels of confidence who would have been stigmatized in the private sector. They fit in better in the military."

The "witch-hunts" for lesbians, however, were way out of proportion. Entire bases were swept in the Army and Air Force, as was virtually every Navy ship in the new Women at Sea program. Twenty-nine of the sixty-one women aboard the USS *Norton Sound,* including all but one of the nine black female crew members, were investigated for lesbianism by the Naval Investigative Service. So were five of the thirteen female crew members aboard the USS *Grapple,* the salvage ship which would help raise the remains of TWA 800 off Long Island in the summer of 1996. "It has become the only accepted way, the only legal way to harass women in the Navy," USS *Grapple* petty officer Mary Beth Harrison explained to Connie Chung in 1991.[26]

No woman was immune, whether homosexual or heterosexual, married, single or a mother. The senior enlisted woman in one Army aviation brigade was called in by her sergeant major for taking the young female troops in the brigade to the NCO club. It didn't "look good," he warned her. People "were talking." But she held her ground. "Why deny these young women the same right to a mentor you had growing up in the military?" she challenged the sergeant major, who subsequently backed down. But the suspicion lingered. "Whenever they see more than one or two women together, they think we're either going to take over or we're lesbians," says the sergeant.

Ironically, the very qualities most admired in men—aggressiveness, strength, athleticism—made women suspect. Rosters for the women's softball teams were ready-made launch points for investigations by the Naval Investigative Service. So was the length of a woman's hair. "Sometimes they will call you, or accuse you of being a lesbian because your hair is short," said a crew member of the USS *Yellowstone*. "Well, we cut our hair short for the cruise because they won't let you have curling irons on the ship and [long hair] is too hard to take care of in the summer when it's hot."[27] . . .

Short of driving women to suicide, charges of lesbianism proved to be the single most effective weapon in driving women out of the services. In 1979 six times as many Army women as Army men were discharged for homosexuality.[28] The lopsided ratios were even greater in the Navy and Marines. Between 1982 and 1987 eight times as many Marine women as men were discharged for homosexuality.[29] In 1989 the discharge rate for women was ten times that for men.[30]

The tragedy of the lesbian witch-hunts is that they had so little to do with lesbians. In the hyperheterosexual military culture, men are far more threatened by male homosexuality than by female homosexuality. Lesbians wouldn't figure at all in the national furor over gays in the military following the 1992 election of Bill Clinton. The passionate debate about overturning the DOD ban against homosexuals would be led by men about men, without a nod to women. Sam Nunn, then chair of the Senate Armed Services Committee, would choose the cramped living quarters on board an all-male submarine as a photo op to illustrate the impossibility of mixing gay and straight men. Ignored would be the racks in berthing areas for women on Navy ships, stacked three deep and separated by only forty inches.

Male homosexuals in the military would turn out to be just as dismissive of female homosexuals. While women veterans would work tirelessly to overturn the military's discriminatory policies toward both servicemen and servicewomen, male advocates would take notice only of themselves. At a 1993 fund-raiser for the Campaign for Military Service in East Hampton, Long Island, not one lesbian veteran was on the invitation list. "The military is a man's world," campaign director Thomas Stoddard would tell me by way of explanation. "Besides, women can't afford a high-ticket event."

Notes

1. *Woman in the Military*, testimony of Pvt. Sarah Tolaro, Feb. 11, 1980, p. 300.
2. Ibid., testimony of Lori Lodinsky, pp. 304–305.
3. Ibid., testimony of Specialist Jimi Hernandez, p. 300.
4. Ibid., testimony of Lodinsky, p. 302.
5. Ibid., testimony of Pvt. Tolaro, p. 304.
6. Ibid., testimony of Jacqueline Lose, p. 302.
7. Ibid., Congressman Antonio Won Pat, p. 302.
8. Ibid., Congressman Sonny Montgomery, p. 303.
9. Ibid., Congresswoman Marjorie Holt, p. 307.
10. Ibid., testimony of Gen. Mary Clarke, p. 337.
11. Ibid., testimony of Congresswoman Patricia Schroeder, p. 339.
12. Ibid., testimony of Congressman Montgomery, p. 343.
13. Ibid., testimony of Brig. Gen. Margaret Brewer, USMC, p. 341.
14. Ibid., testimony of Airman Marilyn Fields, p. 346.
15. U.S. Army Audit Agency, "Enlisted Women in the Army," Report HQ 82-212, April 30, 1982, p. 37.

16. Melanie Martindale, Ph.D., "Sexual Harassment in the Military: 1988," 1988–89 DOD Surveys of Sex Roles, Defense Manpower Data Center, Arlington, VA, September 1990, p. 34.

17. The military's special exception to legal avenues of redress from its members has been reinforced time and again by the courts. In 1953, in *Orloff v. Willoughby*, 345 U.S. 83 (1953), Supreme Court Justice Robert Jackson deemed the military "a specialized community governed by a separate discipline from that of the civilian." The judicial testing of Title VII thirty years later would not penetrate that "specialized community." In 1983 the Supreme Court, in *Chappell et al. v. Wallace et al.*, 462 U.S. 296 (1983), would let stand a lower court ruling that the protections of Title VII did not extend to a group of black sailors trying to sue the Navy for racial discrimination in duty assignments. Military justice was a stand-alone. "The special status of the military has required, the Constitution has contemplated, Congress has created, and this Court has long recognized two systems of justice, to some extent parallel: one for civilians and one for military personnel," Chief Justice Warren Burger wrote in *Chappell v. Wallace*. Cited by Judith Hicks Stiehm in *Arms and the Enlisted Woman* (Philadelphia: Temple University Press, 1989), p. 109, and by Karst in "The Pursuit of Manhood and the Desegregation of the Armed Forces," p. 565, note 247.

18. *Women in the Military*, statement of Col. Thomas E. Fitzpatrick, post commander, Fort Meade, MD, Feb. 11, 1980, p. 318.

19. *DOD Service Academies: More Actions Needed to Eliminate Sexual Harassment*, p. 18. The GAO lists a total of ten articles under the UCMJ to which harassment can be attached, including bribery and graft (Article 134) for servicemen offering rewards for sexual favors and Dereliction of Duty (Article 92) for those engaging in sexual harassment to the detriment of job performance.

20. Jean Ebbert and Marie-Beth Hall, *Crossed Currents: Navy Women from WWI to Tailhook* (Washington, DC/New York: Brassey's [U.S.], 1993), p. 187.

21. Tamar Lewin, "A Case Study of Sexual Harassment and the Law," *New York Times*, Oct. 11, 1991, p. 24.

22. U.S. General Accounting Office, *DOD's Policy on Homosexuality*, GAO/NSIAD-92-98, June 1992, p. 10.

23. Randy Shilts, *Conduct Unbecoming: Gays and Lesbians in the U.S. Military* (New York: St. Martin's, 1993), p. 5.

24. Celia Morris, *Bearing Witness: Sexual Harassment and Beyond—Everywoman's Story* (Boston: Little, Brown, 1994), p. 189.

25. J. Harry, "Homosexual Men and Women Who Served Their Country," *Journal of Homosexuality* 19 (1–2), 1984, p. 117, cited in Theodore R. Sarbin, Ph.D., and Kenneth E. Karois, M.D., Ph.D., "Nonconforming Sexual Orientations and Military Suitability," Deputy Personnel Security Research and Education Center (PERSEREC), Monterey, CA, 1989, p. 23.

26. *Face to Face*, Connie Chung, CBS TV, Nov. 8, 1991.

27. B. D. Clark, "The 'Lesbian' Label to Hold Back Women," *Virginian-Pilot and Ledger-Star*, Sunday, Oct. 21, 1990.

28. Cynthia Enloe, *Does Khaki Become You? The Militarisation of Women's Lives* (Boston: South End, 1983), p. 143.

29. Lynch, "Witch Hunt at Paris Island," *The Progressive*, March 1989, p. 24.

30. Shilts, p. 595.

9. Sex Bias Persists in L.A. County Sheriff's Department

Tina Daunt and Anne-Marie O'Connor

She was a respected, happily married Los Angeles County sheriff's deputy assigned to the jail.

He was her boss. He made advances. She resisted. He tried to get physical, then got hostile. He said he could make her life hell. He licked his lips when she walked by. He called her a "dumb female" in front of the rapists and murderers she guarded and told inmates "us men have to stick together." Prisoners began threatening to sexually assault her. "The brass is on our side," they taunted. Department helicopters buzzed her house.

It was like some creepy Alfred Hitchcock flick. And according to the scenario she described in court records and retirement files, it derailed her career and life.

Her marriage to a fellow deputy crumbled. Her boss—who denies the allegations—was transferred to a station near her home. She left the state. In 1996, the county paid her $750,000 to avoid a jury award its lawyers feared would exceed $3 million.

While attempts to integrate overwhelmingly male police forces have produced examples of fine teamwork between men and women, agencies like the Los Angeles County Sheriff's Department have spawned stories of horrific discrimination, from sexual harassment to male deputies ignoring calls for backup from female deputies in danger. Women who complain say they are railroaded out of their jobs by co-workers while their alleged abusers remain—and sometimes harass other women.

Sheriff Lee Baca, who some lawsuits allege did not deal strongly enough with such behavior in the past, now says his department will have zero tolerance for harassment and respond promptly to resolve complaints. To combat the problem, Baca said he has issued a new set of departmental values that forbid such conduct.

"We want to make sure our supervisors are vigilant in detecting early signs of inappropriate behavior," he said.

Los Angeles County taxpayers have paid more than $2.6 million since mid-1995 in gender-related claims and lawsuits. Last year, the Sheriff's Department paid $661,000 to settle such suits, which amounted to 40% of the county's $1.7 million sexual harassment bill in 1998.

That sum dwarfed the $51,000 the county Fire Department paid for such cases and far outstripped the $450,000 payout by its public works department, the next biggest spot for sexual harassment complaints.

Experts say the Sheriff's Department has been so slow to comply with a federal order to correct the problem that it may be violating the federal Violence Against Women Act.

"The bottom line is they've done nothing," said attorney Dennis Harley, who has been involved in litigation against the department on sexual harassment issues since 1974.

Harley documented one 1998 case in which a supervisor suspected of criminal sexual battery against a female student worker stayed unpunished on the job, while the department "lost contact" with the woman.

Another sergeant who reportedly put his hands down the front of a female officer's pants in 1998 was allowed to stay on the job for a year, during which he dipped into pornographic files stored in the department's computer system and used them to harass other officers, Harley wrote in a report filed in federal court.

But if the department has been tolerant of such behavior, the courts increasingly are not. Juries are more sympathetic to women whose careers were wrecked and personal lives strained by sexual harassment—forcing the county to make big cash payouts to stave off even more expensive jury awards.

The stakes for ending such behavior will only grow, experts say, because gender integration of police forces, like the military, is on the rise.

WOMEN 14% OF FORCE

About 14% of the Sheriff's Department's deputies are women, ranking it 39th nationwide in the percentage of female officers on law enforcement forces, according to the National Center for Women and Policing. About 10% of them are in supervisory positions. Nationwide, Pittsburgh is the police force with the most women—25%—with females comprising 37.5% of the top command.

The Los Angeles Police Department, too, grapples with gender-equality issues—one notorious former clandestine departmental group called itself Men Against Women—and sexual harassment lawsuits. The city attorney's office says LAPD payout figures are not available.

Nationwide studies find that "discrimination and sexual harassment are pervasive in police departments and supervisors and commanders . . . are frequently perpetrators themselves," according to a 1997 report by the National Center for Women and Policing. "A large number of women across the country have been driven from their jobs in law enforcement due to unpunished, unchecked and unrelenting abuse."

In Los Angeles County, however, such abuse is drawing greater scrutiny.

Last week, Harley filed a statement in U.S. District Court charging that the Sheriff's Department has failed to promptly investigate harassment complaints as promised under a 1988 decree imposed by a federal judge. Harley accused the department of perpetuating a hostile work environment, of allowing discriminatory intimidation, ridicule and insults against female deputies to flourish.

"The data demonstrates clear and repeated instances wherein female deputies are the subject of name-calling, disparate treatment and subjective application of rules, all in an effort to cause them to go elsewhere," Harley wrote.

Baca said the department is now making significant strides in dealing with harassment cases. He said eight of the 21 pending cases have been completed and will be heard by a department disciplinary committee within the next few weeks.

In the past, investigators spent up to 18 months scrutinizing the claims. They now hope to complete investigations in two to three months.

Baca acknowledged that there is a "disincentive" for victims to complain because they know some of their co-workers will label them "a pariah."

"The disincentive isn't by department policy," he said. "It's by a culture that is underneath department policy.

"We punish the offender. Then the offender's friends, through inappropriate remarks, attack the person who complained," he said.

The Board of Supervisors, which approves the settlements, has demanded more information on the department's handling of harassment cases. The board acted after *The Times* reported that Baca's proposal to increase the number of female deputies on patrol unleashed a wave of high-profile hostility against women officers two weeks ago.

Supervisors Gloria Molina and Yvonne Brathwaite Burke have called for an investigation into sexism in the department. Molina said many people do not seem aware that slurs against women are as discriminatory as racist slurs.

"People don't realize that this is something that's very, very painful," she said, as well as expensive. Molina said the board will be taking a much closer look to determine, among other things, if taxpayers are repeatedly paying for the same abusive officers over and over again.

"Looking at the settlements, things are getting worse," she said. "The reason these women have won these lawsuits is because you had [department] supervisors who did nothing."

On Monday, the County Claims Board is set to approve $275,000 to settle with former Deputy Jamila Bayati, who took disability retirement from the department in 1995.

Bayati claims her supervisor permitted the worst kind of workplace ambience, allowing deputies to watch a raunchy video at a colleague's workstation. She also alleges that the supervisor's office was decorated with a porn fold-out with his face pasted on it at crotch level. One deputy kept asking Bayati for dates, and when she declined, enlisted her colleagues against her. Male colleagues called sanitary napkins "manhole covers."

Bayati also alleges that her harassment was triggered by her role as a whistle-blower, calling into question the use of force—and subsequent death—of an inmate in 1994.

Female deputies who, like Bayati, file complaints are often hounded out of the department on stress-related disability retirement—often after just a few years of service—because they are exposed to hostile reprisals, according to attorneys. That means the county must pay half their salaries—tax-free—for the rest of their lives.

The total bill for each deputy forced out is well over $1 million.

A few months ago a highly qualified female officer got a coveted assignment, and jealous male colleagues began to discuss her in such graphically sexual terms that a male deputy who sat in on the conversation was loath to repeat what they said.

MORE COMPLAINTS DETAILED

With such cultural barriers, both male and female deputies say it is an illusion to think that even the most qualified female officers can move ahead as quickly as a similarly talented male. For many women deputies, the department is not a meritocracy, but an obstacle course, they say.

Kathy Tinker, a female deputy who won $350,000 in a hostile work environment settlement last year, said she was told she did not score high enough on a 1995 test to qualify for a transfer to the shooting range. She got another officer to show her the test scores, and found she had been passed over for a male officer who scored lower than her.

She took the test to try to transfer out of Field Operations, where for three years, another deputy made snide remarks about her bra size and her clothes in front of everyone else in the office, according to her disability evaluation report.

When she was a trainee at Walnut, she said, lace panties appeared in her mailbox. An officer patted her on the behind. Male deputies on her shift would go off to breakfast together—never inviting her—and ignore her calls for backup, even when she radioed that she had a suspect at gunpoint.

"When I hear about incompetent female officers, I just laugh," she said. "There were plenty of male deputies I worked with who scared me to death."

Carmen Higuchi reported finding a dildo on her patrol car once as her male colleagues stood around and watched for her reaction. While at Century station in 1995, she was treated with hostility on a daily basis, and one deputy told her, "I could do you right here and throw you down the stairs and leave you here," according to her complaint to the department. The county settled her case for $200,000.

Charlotte Landolfi, the deputy who had been assigned to the jail, said her boss sided against her when the inmates—including accused killers and sex offenders at the Pitchess North facility—complained about her. She said he told her women had no place in law enforcement, according to the account in her retirement disability report.

Landolfi worked on the same shift in 1991 as her husband, also a deputy, but she said that did not stop her boss, Lt. Ron Moya, from making constant advances, once even brushing her breast, her account said. She claims that at one point he got hostile, saying, "Us men have to stick together" in front of the prisoners and shaking his finger in her face and yelling: "Just look what you have done! They are going to take care of you!" Later, inmates would tell her: "You're dead, the brass is on our side, and we are going to drag you down and [sexually assault] you," her account said.

Moya, a 30-year veteran, who denies Landolfi's allegations, remained at the jail until he was promoted to watch commander at the Walnut station in March 1994. He has been out of the office since February 1995 on a medical disability leave, he said.

During the investigation, two other female deputies reported that Moya also made advances to them, Moya said—which he denies. Moya said the department let him listen to their tapes. He said both women were "discipline problems."

Moya denied enlisting inmates against Landolfi, though he believes having women guard some male prisoners can fuel tensions.

"You have to understand the clientele we served in the jail are a lot of Latinos, not U.S. Latinos but South Americans," he said. "In their culture, women don't really have a place. It's a macho lifestyle. Women don't really make decisions."

Baca concedes that the department harbors its own cultural problems: "I don't think sexual harassment is rampant in the Sheriff's Department, but I do believe we have a sexism problem."

❖ 10. Mitsubishi Plant Split on How to Define Writing on the Wall

Stephen Braun

Normal, Ill.—The tile-lined walls of the men's bathrooms inside Mitsubishi Motors Corp.'s cavernous auto plant are pristine these days, scrubbed and sanded almost daily by cleaning crews.

Not long ago, those same walls were used as sounding boards for the private impulses of Mitsubishi workers—blank slates darkened day after day with furtive messages left by men seething with racial and sexual anger.

Female and black workers, identified by name, were regularly singled out for epithets and obscenities. Crudely drawn nudes of female co-workers, some stretching 3 feet tall, blossomed on bathroom stalls. Graphic descriptions of sex acts, festooned with cartoon phalli and the phone numbers of women who worked in the plant, ran on like excerpts from pornographic novels. The scrawls sometimes remained for weeks before they were sanded off, only to sprout again, say veteran Mitsubishi workers.

"If you wanted to know what was really on people's minds, all you had to do was look at the walls," said Jeff Woodard, a Mitsubishi employee who is also a union civil rights representative.

Outsiders have had few glimpses of the Mitsubishi plant's bathroom graffiti or the alleged incidents of harassment that female workers and federal Equal Employment Opportunity Commission officials contend grew by the hundreds, triggering the most widespread investigation of sexual harassment in an American workplace.

What happened over the past eight years within the sprawling complex that Mitsubishi built near the twin communities of Normal and Bloomington is as hard to get at as the scrawls that once appeared in the plant's lavatories. The allegations, which have spawned several private lawsuits and a recent massive class-action filing by the EEOC against Mitsubishi, pit workers against each other and the plant's management in convoluted tales that date back years.

The government allegations are starkly drawn: Low-level supervisors threatening retaliation against women who refused to perform oral sex. Scores of incidents in which production line workers grabbed female colleagues' breasts, buttocks and genitals.

FRAT PARTY ATMOSPHERE

Several women who work in the plant elaborated on the government's skeletal details in interviews with The Times, describing some work areas that operated like fraternity parties. In one assembly section, several Mitsubishi workers allege, workers regularly hooted like monkeys and hoisted rating scorecards whenever young women passed by their lines. Other women on the line, workers say, were regularly subjected to blasts from air guns normally used to tighten screws in metal.

Yet the contested nature of the EEOC's case and the legal secrecy that surrounds it—neither factory officials nor female plaintiffs will discuss the lawsuits—have roused widespread suspicion against the government in the towns where Mitsubishi has long been hailed as a generous employer.

Despite the fact that some of the community's own daughters and wives helped launch the federal probe, residents and town leaders have rallied to Mitsubishi's corner. Some, like Bloomington Mayor Jesse Smart, joined 2,000 workers on a recent march against regional EEOC offices in Chicago. Others have deluged local newspapers and political leaders with pro-company mailings.

Many echo the plaint of Gary Shultz, the Mitsubishi plant's general counsel and spokesman, who wonders aloud how allegations of widespread sexual harassment could have been kept secret from the surrounding community for eight years. "It's obvious," Shultz scoffed, answering his own question. "It's not pervasive."

SKEPTICAL RESIDENTS

If sexual harassment was rampant at the plant, many Normal and Bloomington residents reason, they would have known. Of the 4,000 workers at the plant, 700 of whom are women, more than half live in surrounding McClean County.

"The only complaints I ever heard was that they were making too much overtime and they didn't have any time to themselves," said Wayne Johnson, who serves dozens of arriving auto workers each morning at Sooooooooo Convenient, a store a mile from the plant.

The instinctive rush to support Mitsubishi might be expected in a community that has been well-served for its loyalty. Although the area has been bolstered financially by the presence of Illinois State University and national and regional headquarters for State Farm Insurance Co., Mitsubishi's eight-year existence just west of the two towns has produced more than a stable flow of well-paying jobs.

Along College Road, not far from where the plant and its rows of tall smokestacks rear up from the earth like a whitewashed battleship, an entire industrial park has sprung up, filled with factories supplying Mitsubishi with paint, parts and equipment essential for production-line work.

And years of donations to local schools, libraries and charities have lent Mitsubishi an image as community provider. The plant has funded foreign exchanges of college professors and high school students, contributed to medical charities and sent used test cars to be disassembled by area vocational schools.

"We think the company's been unjustly accused," said Normal Mayor Kent Karraker, who politely declined a request by Mitsubishi officials that he join in the anti-EEOC march—but left no doubt where his loyalties lie. "We've never had a single complaint, formal or otherwise. Don't you think word would have gotten out if it was that bad?"

A vocal chorus of male and female auto workers who support the EEOC investigation counters that many at the plant failed to talk openly about problems because they feared losing their jobs—and that harassment would worsen. Mitsubishi workers who offer up details of sexual and racial harassment insist that some victims were reluctant to go public because they were embarrassed by the nature of their complaints—and were forced to go to private lawyers and government investigators with their stories only when it became clear the company was not taking the complaints seriously.

Patricia Benassi, a lawyer representing 29 women in a private lawsuit against Mitsubishi, said that female employees often were cowed by the manner in which company managers responded to their complaints.

"What would happen is that when women would complain, managers would go down to the floor and announce publicly to their coworkers that there had been a complaint and then they would name the complainer," Benassi said. "So, of course, the harassers would only harass them further."

Mitsubishi spokesman Shultz declined to discuss specifics of charges against the company but said it has always responded quickly and toughly to any harassment cases.

Within the plant, workers' knowledge about incidents of harassment depends on their years of service and the shops where they have worked, Mitsubishi workers say. "Things were at their worst two to three years ago" when the first private lawsuits were filed and the EEOC investigation began, said George Walker, a Mitsubishi employee who has filed his own lawsuit alleging racial discrimination in hiring practices. "The newer workers have no idea how bad it was."

THE "ZOO"

And while some smaller departments within the plant, such as the factory's quality-control inspection team, have been known as havens from blatant harassment, other shops were dreaded assignments for some women.

Perhaps the most feared was the final assembly area, known as the "zoo," where young women were regularly taunted and subjected to the air gun blasts, some workers say. Girlie calendars were on open display and men drank from cups decorated with pictures of naked women. Shovels, forklifts, car chassis covers and other equipment were covered and scratched with lewd comments, and insults regularly circulated through the area.

"Young women got it the worst," said one female worker who declined to be named out of fear of retaliation. "There's nothing more humiliating I can think of than to see 60 guys making monkey noises when a woman walks past them. It was awful."

Workers who support the factory tell a different story. Although many acknowledge that some incidents of harassment took place, they say the episodes were hardly pervasive—and offenders were swiftly disciplined. Contrary to EEOC officials who have said that as many as 500 separate allegations were actionable, Shultz said Mitsubishi employee relations officers count only 89 complaints in eight years—and 10 male workers fired for harassment.

Kathleen McLouth, a worker who commutes 140 miles to the plant each day to deliver parts to the line, said she was harassed several years ago by a manager who "talked to me in a menacing way." But when McLouth went to United Auto Workers representatives and to company supervisors to complain, the problem was dealt with promptly, she said.

"My boss gave me his guarantee that would never happen again—and it hasn't," McLouth said.

UNEASE AT UNION

Local UAW leaders declined to comment on the case, but low-level representatives said the union's response to harassment allegations was hampered by the lack of a clear response policy often found at other auto factories. And local UAW officials were reluctant to involve themselves in volatile cases in which both parties belonged to the union.

"It's uncomfortable for the union," said Jeff Woodard, who sits on the UAW's civil rights committee. "Either way, they get burned."

Some female workers who support the company say many of those who have filed lawsuits were super-sensitive to factory life and, in some cases, slackers trying to take advantage of Mitsubishi.

"People here work elbow to elbow, and sure, you're going to get some spicy talk," said Judy Scurlock, who works in the plant's quality-control department. "If they touch you, it's one thing. But if a woman can't take a few words, what I say is, 'Grow up.'"

Still, even in the three weeks that have passed since the EEOC's filing, there have been disquieting incidents inside the plant, hinting that relations between male and female workers are not as unified as the protest march against the EEOC by 2,000 Mitsubishi employees suggested.

Two of the 29 female workers who filed the private lawsuit two years ago have been on temporary stress leave after one received death threats and the other grew fearful after hearing repeated slurs while working on the line.

Hours after the march against the EEOC, one of the plaintiffs, Terry Paz, found a note in her factory locker that read: "Die, bitch! You'll be sorry." Local police are investigating the incident and Shultz has said the company has sent out repeated warnings to employees not to harass any of the 18 workers who filed the suit and still work for Mitsubishi (11 other plaintiffs have left the company).

And union representative Woodard said that on a recent Saturday shift, not long after the EEOC suit was filed, he entered a bathroom stall and saw a few familiar scribbled lines of graffiti—but with a new hint of menace. "If some _____ is responsible for my losing my job, I'm going on a _____ hunt," the message read.

By the next Monday, Woodard said, the threat was gone, erased by cleaning crews.

"The good news," Woodard allowed, "is that they're at least getting rid of it a lot faster."

❖ 11. The Lecherous Professor

Billie Wright Dziech and Linda Weiner

. . . Discussion of sexual harassment usually includes the "yes, but" view: "Yes, but some women invite ogling, touching, or sexual propositions." Every campus has its real or imaginary tales of beautiful coeds who show their professors nude photographs of themselves or promise they will "do anything" for a better grade. Many are second- or third-hand accounts, more fiction than fact. The implication is that the campus is hazardous for male faculty, that men too are victims of sexual harassment. The underlying message, of course, is that men have a right to harass women because women "ask for it."

The "yes, but" notion distorts the issue. There *are* women who flirt with male faculty and women who cause professors discomfort and embarrassment by pursuing them. Some women *do* get crushes on professors; they *do* engage in seduction. But this has nothing to do with sexual harassment of students by professors. These are two separate problems involving very different dynamics, consequences, and resolutions.

One way to distinguish them is to use clearer terminology. A student is more capable of causing "sexual hassle" than she is of sexually harassing. There is too much difference in role and status of male faculty and female students to make flirtation or even seduction by students harassment. "Harassment" suggests misuse of power, and students simply do not have enough power to harass.

Persistent, unwanted attention from a female student can be extremely disruptive to a male professor. It may embarrass, annoy, and anger him; it may cause turmoil in both his private and professional life. But it cannot destroy his self-esteem or endanger his intellectual self-confidence. Hassled professors do not worry about retaliation and punitive treatment; they do not fear bad grades or withheld recommendations from women students. They are not forced to suffer in silence because of fear of peer disapproval. In fact, many men are eager to discuss being sexually hassled. Their talk may be locker room bragging or a self-protective strategy to prevent gossip.

Even in the most extreme cases of sexual hassle, men faculty seldom suffer the complex psychological effects of sexual harassment victims. They may have to endure unpleasant scenes, disturbed domestic relations, and temporary unease, but they have the power to control the problem. They work in an environment they understand. They are at home in academe as students are not and know how to protect themselves and to discourage students causing them discomfort.

Sexual hassle is not an excuse for tolerating or ignoring sexual harassment. Students do not set the tone or the parameters of interactions with professors. They do not have that kind of authority. No behavior, however seductive, from a student ever legitimizes inappropriate, irresponsible behavior by faculty. Sexual hassle does not give college professors the right to violate responsibilities to students or the ethics of their profession.

When defensive faculty are not bemoaning the vulnerability of professors, they are advocating for openness and sexual health in the academic environment. They worry that prohibition of sexual harassment will become zealous and jeopardize positive interaction between the sexes and make all give-and-take between men and women unacceptable.

The dynamics of men and women working together on the campus and elsewhere is not yet truly understood. Until there is more systematic analysis, the most that can be said is that the presence of both men and women lends a certain excitement and energy to work. Sexual give-and-take—the friendly verbal interaction between colleagues, the acknowledged attraction between coworkers, the accepted physical gesturing of male and female—is a healthy behavior in which individuals of various ages and stations choose to engage.

"Choice" is the critical concept. Give-and-take implies mutual choice by people of equal status. The boundaries of the relationship are understood and accepted by both parties. There is no confusion, no doubt, no feeling of coercion or fear. The effects of jokes, comments, and gestures are that both feel good. The humor and affection in sexual give-and-take may be a way to reduce sexual tensions. It may relieve the monotony of routine work. It may even be preliminary courtship, a kind of testing before proceeding with a more serious relationship.

Whatever the intent, sexual give-and-take is based on mutual consent of equals. This is obviously not the case in sexual harassment. Normal sexual give-and-take is not possible in student-teacher relationships because the power imbalance and role disparity are too great. The legal, public, and institutional concern about sexual harassment is a concern about *unhealthy* sexual dynamics, about behaviors that are exploitive, abusive, and psychologically and academically damaging. In fact, if people become more aware of the sexual harassment problem, a healthier sexual environment for both men and women should result. . . .

VULNERABILITY

College women may suffer because of misconceptions about their behaviors and characters, but do they also somehow permit themselves to be sexually harassed? An important factor in understanding women's responses to harassment is the education and socialization of females. For over half a century, studies of female development—from language acquisition to sexual behavior—have emphasized women's docility, passivity, dependency, and avoidance of risk. A twenty-five-year project by Moss and Kagan[1] revealed that passivity patterns in females were remarkably high and that dependent orientations to authority figures continued from adolescence into adulthood. Elizabeth Douvan and Joseph Adelson's *The Adolescent Experience* compared 1,045 boys from ages fourteen to sixteen with 2,005 girls from eleven to eighteen and concluded that dependency is a way of life that increases as females mature.[2]

One of the primary places where females learn to respect authority figures is the school. David Bradford, Alice Sargent, and Melinda Sprague stressed that educational institutions are primary sources of reinforcement for male-female stereotypes:

> A substantial body of research demonstrates that from birth boys and girls are consistently treated differently. The types of games, toys, and books given to boys, as well as the kinds of behavior for which boys are rewarded and punished, teach boys different values, aspirations, and behavioral skills than girls. Boys are supported for being aggressive, assertive, analytical and competitive,

while girls are praised for being helpful, passive, deferential and concerned with interpersonal relationships. Teachers as well as parents support these differences. One example is the research by Serbin (1973), who found that elementary school teachers, both male and female, responded more often to questions raised by boys than girls, and gave the boys longer answers that were richer in content. Girls received more perfunctory answers often accompanied by a pat on the head or arm around the shoulder—as if support and not cognitive content were the important response.[3]

Women's vulnerability to harassers becomes clearer in light of this stereotyping process. The education system, from nursery school through college, reinforces women's dependency and reliance on authority. Women are taught submission, not aggression. They learn that being "good" implies not acting but reacting, not trusting oneself but entrusting oneself to the authorities—parents, clergy, teachers—that promise reward. Forced into a choice between a teacher's wishes and their own, some students do what they have learned to do best—defer, submit, agree. In their own peculiar ways, they once again act out the roles of "good little girls," doing what teacher says is best.

Even Fanny, the classic young temptress in *Dubin's Lives,* shows dependence on authority. Early in the novel, she walks into Dubin's study, throws off her clothes, and waits for him to respond. Later she writes to him of confusion and fears typical of the college-age woman:

> I have ideas about what I ought to be doing but am afraid of the next move. I don't want to get into something I can't get out of if I make the wrong choice. Or into something that won't come to much, and will make me feel, again, that I am up Shit Creek in a leaky rowboat. William, please advise me about my life . . . Could you specifically say what I ought to be thinking about in the way of a job or career, or recommend books that might be helpful? Or give me the names of courses I could take when I get back to New York City? I'd like to be better organized and enjoy my life more . . . I'm afraid of my day-to-day life. A day scares me more than a week or a month. But the truth of it is I want to be responsible, to work my life out decently.[4]

In addition to the burdens imposed by sexual stereotyping, many women confront new and greater pressures upon entering college. College is not a particularly quiescent juncture in anyone's life. Alumni view the experience far differently from those who are living it. For most students, it is a time of uncertainty, pressure, and confusion, a time in which joy is counterbalanced by despair and achievement, by defeat. Students must decide successfully about academic programs, careers, and personal independence and relationships. College is a period of constant trial and judgment by oneself and others, in truth a far more harrowing experience than students care to admit. But for some women, it is particularly trying.

One of the most comprehensive analyses of the psychological differences between men and women is Eleanor Maccoby and Carol Nagy Jacklin's *The Psychology of Sex Differences,*[5] which examines the results of more than 1,400 research studies to probe the myths and facts of gender distinctions. One finding was that women of college age (18 to 22) exhibit less sense of control over their own fates and less confidence in their probable performances on school-related tasks than men of similar age. This was *not* observed in either older or younger women.

It should not surprise anyone that many women feel less self-confidence and control once they reach college. Most academic environments are patterned after male interests and male behaviors. Since the turn of the century, cognitive rationality and the scientific mode of enquiry have dominated higher education. Women, socialized in humanistic and intuitive forms of knowledge, are at a psychological disadvantage in this kind of environment. The institution's emphasis on competition and intellectual aggressiveness runs counter to all that they have been taught.

There may be a link between women's vulnerability to sexual harassment and their diminished confidence and sense of control in academic settings. Because higher education is a male-dominated institution, college women are often treated less seriously. A man who hopes to become a physician is taken at his word. A woman elicits raised eyebrows and questions about her marriage and child-bearing plans. Her intentions meet with scepticism, so she is forced to prove herself and to endure more from faculty.

Nonassertive women are not the only likely victims for sexual harassers. The data are anecdotal, but there are overwhelming similarities in accounts of counselors, ombudsmen, and administrators who deal with the problem daily. Women who are experiencing serious stress are vulnerable, as are women uncertain about academic programs. Women who are loners, without visible friends, seem to be sought out by harassers. One ombudsman commented, "This will sound really crazy, but I think we tend to have more blondes coming to our office. They aren't beautiful or necessarily even pretty and I haven't kept a running count, but I'm almost sure that's the case." Others note that the nontraditional woman student, the individual attending college after some time has elapsed, also seems to be a target for the lecherous professor.

Harassers are influenced by multiple characteristics in women—physical characteristics, economic status, marital status. However, from analysis of stories of sexual harassment collected from college women, two particularly vulnerable groups arise: minority women and females enrolled in traditionally male fields. The reasons they attract harassers are easy to identify.

A racist stereotype of minority women is that they are "easier" and more responsive to sexual advances. For some males, the sexuality of women of a different race reportedly appears mysterious. Either of these conditions could account for what one counselor describes as some harassers' "quick-target" attitude toward minority women. An even more insidious possibility is that the lecherous professor may sense the unease experienced by some minority women entering the academic environment. If the self-esteem of women students in general is on trial during college, then that of minority females is sorely threatened as they seek to establish credibility in institutions that are not only traditionally male but also white-dominated.

Women in nontraditional fields exhibit some of the uncertainty and vulnerability of minority women. Male-dominated disciplines are governed by a fraternity of men with strong credentials who until very recently were unaccustomed to the presence of women in their classrooms. Women entering these fields tend to be high achievers, often academically superior to their male counterparts. Disconcerted by this new situation, some male faculty are openly hostile to such women; others ignore them. At any rate, female students in engineering, architecture, accounting, medicine, law, and a variety of other historically male disciplines report discomfort in their environments.

The sense of being an intruder can have consequences beyond the classroom. Women who feel themselves "outsiders" are especially vulnerable to displays of interest or kindness from instructors. Some faculty prey on the distress of such students for their own ends. One administrator observed, "These women feel like such pariahs that they'll hang onto any shred of human kindness, and a lot of faculty are not beyond taking advantage of that fact."

A story told by a black woman professor of accounting reflects the environmental stress. She recalled her own freshman collegiate days when she was singled out by a faculty member who was very arrogant about his five degrees and his predominantly male profession. She was the only one in class whom he did not address by first name; he preferred calling her, "Miss _____." At the end of the quarter he asked to speak with her after class. She was 17 at the time, and he was a middle-aged married man. She described her shock when he asked her to attend a dance with him: "I just looked him in the face and said, 'You're the wrong age, the wrong color; and if you want to take someone to a dance, it ought to be your wife.'"

ATTEMPTS AT COPING

Whatever her age, appearance, race, or field of study, there is vulnerability in the student's status that makes sexual harassment by teachers a most intimate betrayal of trust. In case after case, students report their initial reactions as disbelief and doubt about the most blatant acts.

College is a time when students question their sexual identities and relationships and evaluate their values and self-images. Most see faculty on the other side of the threshold called maturity, part of the adult world, more parents than peers. Sexual harassment by faculty, even in its most impersonal, generalized forms, injects a note of unexpected, incestuous sexuality that shocks the average woman student.

After shock comes the feeling of powerlessness. College professors are older, more adept verbally, more sophisticated socially, and certainly more knowledgeable about the workings of the college or university. A student at a Midwestern university asked, "Who was going to believe me? I was an undergraduate student and he was a famous professor. It was an unreal situation." A graduate student complained to her college counselor:

> What was it that I did that led him to believe I was interested in him in anything but a professional sense? I am quite outgoing and talkative; could that be interpreted wrongly? I realized how utterly vulnerable I was in a situation like this . . . Everything that happened would be interpreted in his favor, if it ever became public. It would be said that I got my signals wrong, that he was just truly interested in helping me in my career.[6]

Closely related to women's feelings of powerlessness are those of guilt. Student victims report feeling responsible, feeling at fault somehow. Some have an almost childlike fear of having broken some rule they did not know. They wonder what they should have known or done to prevent the harassment. "I keep asking myself what I did to get him started. There were twenty-two other girls in the class. Why did he pick on me?" Michelle Y., a student at a Southern university, asked.

Women recognize early that power and sexuality are equated by society. Some students are unsophisticated and fearful about the possibilities suggested by their sexuality; they may develop conflict about it and, correspondingly, guilt about their intentions and behaviors. They know that in cases of sexual harassment and rape someone always asks, "Did she encourage it?" and "Did she enjoy it?" The questions linger in the minds of even the most innocent and make them impotent to confront the harassment. Too many members of both sexes assume that women say "no" when they really mean "yes," that they secretly savor squeezing, patting, and pinching.

Men are not misunderstood or vulnerable to the same degree. An average woman of fifty would never be expected to whet the sexual appetite of a twenty-year-old male, and he would not be accused of seducing her. But people believe a twenty-year-old female can easily be transported to rapture by the attentions of a fifty-year-old male. After a while, the culturally induced confusion makes some women actually begin to doubt their own motivations. They then discover that their abusers prey on their uncertainties.

Paramount in the minds of many student victims is fear of what will happen if they resist or report the professor's behaviors. Victims often believe that the authority of the professor equals power over their futures—in a sense, their lives. Ambivalent about her academic capabilities, the typical student may be devastated when a professor, the symbol of intellect, treats her as if she has only a body and no mind. Even the best students worry about reprisals by the harasser and his associates. They fear that grades, jobs, careers, and sometimes even their physical safety will be threatened. Kelly H., a pre-med student, observed:

> It's easy for someone else to say I should do something about Dr. _____, but how can I? He was the first person at _____ to take my work seriously. At least I think it's my work that made him notice me. He's the one who's pushing for me to get into med school. If I refuse him, then I ruin my whole life.

Another repeated reaction of women victims is their ambivalence about and sometimes sympathy for the harasser. Women students, especially if they are considering making a formal complaint, worry about the professor's career, marriage, and future. Over and over, they comment, "I don't want anything bad to happen to him." A major source of this guilt is the harasser himself; when confronted by a student, harassers often distract them with discussions of personal and professional costs professors pay. Students may also feel guilty because they are flattered by the professor's interest in them. They may find him physically and socially unattractive, but being the object of attention from an older man can be a heady experience. A student may worry that she is stepping out of her proper place by affecting a faculty life, or she may have a certain amount of gratitude for the interest he has in her. This, as much as compassion, may lead to students' frequent pleas that deans or counselors "make sure he doesn't get in a lot of trouble."

Given this complex set of reactions, victims of harassment respond to their experiences in different ways. The important point to remember about their coping strategies is that because they feel frightened, guilty, complicit, powerless, and alone, most victims usually attempt to deal with harassment, however serious, on their own. The significance is that for every reported incident, there are innumerable others, some even more serious, about which no one ever knows.

A frequent coping tactic is refusal to acknowledge that harassment exists. Some students are either too naive or too self-deluded to admit that sexual exploitation can occur in their relationships with teachers. The students explain their intimate relationships with faculty in idealistic terms. They use hyperbole to describe the professor—he has "given life meaning," he has taught them "what it is to be an adult." They may know the definition of harassment, but what happens to them is "different" or "special."

A woman engaging in this kind of denial would be wounded if anyone suggested that a forty-year-old professor who works in a highly cerebral environment must have interest in something other than the stimulation of her mind. Confronted with her hero's record of previous lechery charges, she would refuse to accept the accusations. This naiveté makes her especially vulnerable to manipulation.

Another coping strategy is to deny the seriousness of the problem. Many students attempt to ignore incidents in the hope that they will not recur. Their optimism usually proves false, since most harassers are encouraged by a student's failure to resist. One professor, enraged that students were disturbed by his sexist remarks in class, contended, "No one has ever complained to me! Obviously, they like what I do and enjoy my humor, or someone would have said something by now. I'm certainly not going to change my whole teaching style on the basis of a few rumors." Ignoring harassment usually produces similar results. The offending individual interprets silence as assent or even encouragement to continue his behavior.

Often women who do acknowledge the seriousness of harassment try to cope through avoidance. They invent appointments, enlist the presence of friends, cut class, or even hide to prevent encounters. Another tactic is "dressing down," trying to appear asexual and unattractive to avoid notice. Each of these maneuvers is a passive-aggressive strategy; the student attempts to control external factors in the environment because she realizes she cannot control the professor.

Avoidance strategies indicate that students are sensitive to the power imbalance. They take friends to meetings with harassers because another person can provide reinforcement. They avoid meetings with harassers by claiming obligations equally important to those imposed by faculty. In both cases, students are trying to convince themselves and to communicate to their professors that powers can be offset.

Dressing down is a form of avoidance that demonstrates women's use of clothing to symbolize self-perceptions. A woman may make herself unattractive to escape the attention of an undesirable male, but dressing down may also be a way of declaring feelings of inferiority and victimization. It can express self-doubt as well as desire to deal with a threatening situation. Making oneself unattractive can be a way of declaring, "I don't feel good about myself. I feel inadequate and incompetent to cope with this problem."

Even when students do try to resist more directly, their intentions are frequently misread or intentionally misunderstood. Women tend to reject romantic overtures from their professors by talking about their boyfriends, expressing reluctance to become involved with faculty, contending that their families or friends would disapprove, or explaining that they lack time for social activities. Barbara H., a senior in an agricultural program, described her experience:

> I kept making up all kinds of excuses to keep from going out with _____. I told him that my mother was sick and I had to work on weekends. The times he called me at home I said I had to study for big tests. I guess he didn't believe me or didn't care because he just kept on calling me and staring at me and talking to me in class. Finally the only thing I could do was drop the course because I knew he was never going to let me alone as long as I was in his class.

Seldom are students willing to resist emphatically. But an adult who is confused enough to make advances toward a student is likely to misinterpret subtle as well as overt expressions of rejections. This was the case with a student who responded to the National Advisory Council:

> I had a class with _____ when I started my doctoral program. He left notes on my papers asking me to come in and see him. I was really impressed—he seemed to take such genuine interest in my program. I asked him to be my chairman. He changed. He began to touch me, my arms and legs, giving me neck rubs, kissing me. I would try and pull away, he'd pull closer. He kept asking to come to my house. He came and brought wine. He began touching me again only going farther. I told him I didn't think a sexual relationship for us was a good idea because he was my chairperson, married, etc. He assured me it was a good idea. I got him to leave without having sex but his pursuits became heavier. He frequently said he wanted to be sure I knew that I didn't have to make love to him to get through the program. (Ha!) Finally when I couldn't take it any longer I tried to politely but firmly tell him no. Once again I was chastized for my "coldness." About three weeks later, out of the blue, he threatened to give me an incomplete in a class. He began to be bitter and sarcastic with me. I confronted him with what I thought was unfair behavior. He told me he was angry because I hadn't been "straight" with him—he said he knew now I didn't want him so why hadn't I told him. It was obvious the man was out of touch. I tried to placate him but keep distance. I have not finished my program so I still have to deal with him. I have married . . . which I have really played up to keep him at a distance. He remains periodically unfair to me, was a complete jerk during my comprehensives, and generally makes life difficult. I stay away from him as much as possible.[7]

"Staying away" is not as simple as it sounds. Staying away means that women are forced to drop courses, to alter schedules, sometimes to change majors or colleges because they feel they have no other recourse. Frequently they transfer to other institutions without admitting their reasons. Worst of all, there are students so unable to withstand harassment and so estranged from the institution that the only solution they discover is leaving school. There is no way to determine the number who eventually adopt this drastic measure. Few colleges have adequate exit interviews of graduates, dropouts, or transfers, so information about sexual harassment is not likely to be collected and assessed by proper authorities. Nevertheless, counselors in a variety of schools state emphatically that the number of women who leave college because of harassment is substantial.

Herein lies the tragedy of sexual harassment on the campus. It is not a minor inconvenience soon to be forgotten by the women compelled to deal with it. Sexual harassment has the power to change lives, and what few inside higher education face is that the costs it exacts from victims are too enormous to estimate. Karen F., a senior, found the price high:

Prof. M. was my adviser and taught several of the required courses in my language major, so I didn't have any choice about taking his courses. He used a lot of obscenities in class—taught us how to say "fuck" five different ways, for instance. And he used to embarrass women in class—I think he liked that. Finally he started flirting with me in class. He'd make comments about my hair or my hands, saying he wanted to touch them. The real trouble came on the trip that summer. There were 20 of us and he was the program coordinator. We got academic credit and a chance to speak the language for real. I borrowed money from my folks to go. Within the first week, he started coming on to me, saying he wanted to make love to me, inviting me to go away with him for a weekend, telling me I was prudish, saying his wife was frigid. I'd try to be nice but I told him I didn't want to do that, that I was engaged. He'd get really emotional and upset and cry and I'd tell him we could be friends. But then it would start all over again. He'd talk to the other students about me. I guess at first I was sorry for him and I didn't want to make trouble. But he kept at me and wouldn't leave me alone. One night he got really drunk and came into my room. My roommates were asleep. He made this big scene, grabbing me all over. I wasn't really frightened, just really embarrassed. After that, I stayed away from him the rest of the trip. I had classes from him the next term, but I thought he'd leave me alone, especially because I got married. But fall quarter he started again, telling me now that I was married I could have an affair. I cut class to avoid him, but I still feel nervous and can't sleep. I want to go to graduate school here—I've been accepted—but I'd have courses from him and I just can't take any more.

Much is heard from educators concerned about the reputations and livelihoods of those accused of harassment, but there is little discussion of the long-term effects it has on the women abused. Sexual harassment obviously has the power to damage careers; women leave colleges every day because they cannot deal with it. It alters their attitudes toward institutions and may have longlasting effects on their perceptions of men and sex. Perhaps most insidious are its influences upon the self-images of those forced to endure it. Higher education has been able to ignore consequences of sexual harassment because the victims' damage and pain are often felt years later, long after women have left the institutional environment and forfeited their claims to its protection.

Notes

1. Howard Moss and Jerome Kagan, *Birth to Maturity* (New York: John Wiley, 1962).
2. Elizabeth Douvan and Joseph Adelson, *The Adolescent Experience* (New York: John Wiley, 1966).
3. David Bradford, Alice Sargent, and Melinda Sprague, "The Executive Man and Woman: The Issue of Sexuality," *Bringing Women into Management,* eds. Francine Gordon and Myra Strober (New York: McGraw-Hill, 1975), p. 18.

4. Bernard Malamud, *Dubin's Lives* (New York: Farrar, Straus & Giroux, 1977), pp. 143–44.
5. Eleanor Maccoby and Carol Nagy Jacklin, *The Psychology of Sex Differences* (Palo Alto: Stanford University Press, 1974), p. 359.
6. Eileen Shapiro, "Some Thoughts on Counseling Women Who Perceive Themselves to Be Victims of Non-Actionable Sex Discrimination: A Survival Guide," in "Sexual Harassment: A Hidden Issue," *On Campus with Women,* Project on the Status and Education of Women (Washington, D.C.: American Association of Colleges, 1978), p. 3.
7. Frank J. Till, *Sexual Harassment: A Report on the Sexual Harassment of Students,* Report of the National Advisory Council on Women's Educational Programs (Washington, D.C., 1980), pp. 26–27.

❖ 12. Failing at Fairness: How Our Schools Cheat Girls

Myra Sadker and David Sadker

. . . In 1992, in Michigan, 1,808 students were interviewed about what it was like to be male or female at school. In elementary school 45 percent of the students said girls and boys were treated differently in school. By high school this number had risen 31 points to 76 percent. Evidently the different treatment had a chilling effect on girls. In elementary school 3 percent of males and 15 percent of females said they wanted to be the opposite sex. By high school the male percentage was the same, but almost one-quarter of the girls said they wished they were the other gender. To learn more about their impressions of the different treatment depending on gender, a difference that became greater as they grew older, we went to talk with students in one of the most elite magnet high schools for mathematics and science in the United States.

"Have you noticed any differences in the ways males and females are treated in this school?" we ask the class of bright, talented students. "Or have you felt any sexism yourself? The question is for males as well as females. Take about ten minutes to describe your experiences, and then we'll talk about them."

Several students begin to write furiously. "Ten minutes," one girl murmurs. "I need days." Others, mainly boys but some girls, stare ahead stone-faced and write nothing. As we walk around the room, we stop by one all-male table. Several boys are slumped at an angle, their legs stretched across the floor and their arms folded.

"Can we help?" we ask.

"I'm thinking," one boy mutters. "I don't have a pencil," says another. We put one on his desk, but he makes no move to pick it up. As we turn to leave, we hear someone whisper, "Just what we need—politically correct BS from liberal Democrats."

"Five more minutes to write," we announce. The hostile male table is still in position—slouched, sprawled, arms folded. But they are the minority and aren't able to set the tone in the room. Most of the students have written something; they look interested and are ready to respond.

A girl sitting toward the front begins to read her statement: "I had a sexist gym teacher last year. He was constantly putting down the girls in my gym class. He would say things like, 'You!' pointing to a girl, 'Get out of the way! Mark actually is trying to make a basket.' He hardly ever called the girls by name, and no matter how hard we tried, he used to say we were lazy."

A white male agrees and adds, "Male gym teachers pick boys to demonstrate things, and they expect more of boys. But P.E. is the only class where I've ever seen anything sexist. I've never experienced any sex discrimination myself."

"I've seen it in computer science and math class," another boy volunteers. "Girls aren't pushed to go to higher levels. It's partly the teacher's fault, but a lot of it is peers. Guys say girls can't do these things, so it discourages them."

Two Hispanic boys are sitting together, and one raises his hand. "Usually boys and girls are treated the same, but some teachers seem to joke more when a girl, usually a blond, does something wrong."

"Yeah," the boy next to him agrees. "Sometimes a male teacher will joke with me or other boys about girls being slow to understand technology. I remember once a teacher made a face behind a girl's back while he explained repeatedly how to do something on a computer."

"I've seen those faces," a serious Asian girl says. "In one of my science classes a certain male teacher made rude remarks about my intelligence. He assaulted me verbally, but there are other science teachers—I've only heard of this, I haven't seen it—who favor girls depending on the length of their skirts."

This comment strikes a chord. Several students begin talking at once:

"I know who you mean. I've heard about him."

"No, it's not true. I had him last year, and he never acted like that."

"Well, my best friend had this particular science teacher last year. She didn't understand the material the entire year, but she wore low-cut blouses and escaped the course with a B."

"A lot of people talk about this," a boy volunteers. "If an attractive girl flirts with a male teacher, he'll let her get away with just about anything."

"Those are just rumors," several students call out.

"It is true! It happened to me," another girl says. "In my chemistry class I felt that if I wore a short skirt or a low-cut blouse—low-cut for a fifteen-year-old—I'd get more attention and help. He massaged girls' shoulders while they were taking tests. Believe me, that massage was anything but relaxing. He looked down their blouses and up their skirts. I heard he had to apologize to one girl."

"I really resent these generalizations," another girl says.

"Once a final grade of mine was rounded up to an A. The overwhelming reaction from other students, especially males, was, 'What did you do? Wear a short skirt?' The teacher gave it to me because he knew I was working hard and had come in for tutoring often—not because I'm a girl. I think those short skirt stories are a put-down of my and other girls' intelligence."

Almost everyone in the room has something to say about science teachers and short skirts. But the discussion is becoming a free-for-all, so we intervene and try to paraphrase: "It sounds as though at least some of you think there is a sexist culture here."

"Yes!" "Definitely!" Several girls from the all-female table begin talking at once. "The worst place is the lounge," Betsy, a slight girl with long brown hair, says. "There's usually a group of guys who start talking and making rude comments about girls. I would never go in there alone."

"What do they say?" we ask.

"They usually say things like, 'Go fetch!'" She snaps her fingers. "Get us something to eat. Go fetch a Coke." She snaps her fingers again. "Come do sexual favors for us." She turns beet red but is determined to make her point.

Several boys object: "That's just some guys. Most of us don't act like that."

One boy, the only African-American male in the class, says, "It's mostly people wearing these jerseys." He points to the shirt he and several other boys are wearing that signify they are athletes. "I think it's tough to be a girl here. I don't get to say what I want around certain people. You have to choose your words carefully if you're a minority. And here girls are like a minority."

Another boy, also wearing an athletic jersey, objects. "I think a lot of this is blown out of proportion and there's a double standard. I had a calendar with girls in bathing suits in my locker. I was called a male chauvinist pig. But girls have calendars of guys, and nobody says anything."

Another boy agrees. "You don't dare say anything anymore. You can't even tell a girl she looks good without her getting upset. Girls are so sensitive, and boys are running scared."

A teacher appears at the door. "Where's my geoscience class? The period ended a few minutes ago. You're supposed to go to your next class."

"Geoscience!" several students groan. "We need to stay here and talk," Betsy protests. "Geoscience is forever. This is going on now."

The class begins to gather their books. A few students exit quickly through the rear door, but most walk up front. A group of girls gathers around us, reluctant to go. There is so much more they want to say. Several boys stand just outside the female circle and listen.

"This guy asked his girlfriend to go fetch a soda," Betsy says. "And she did it. That's what annoyed me most. I asked why. She said, 'He can talk to me that way. He's my boyfriend.'"

"Guys say things but they don't mean them," another girl says. "It's just when they're in a group they show off."

"That's true," another girl says. "I see certain guys that are friends of mine going around pinching girls' behinds. Some girls just laugh, other girls tell them to stop, but no one ever really gets mad. But I know that a lot of the girls do not appreciate the advances. When it happens, I don't do anything because I feel it is ultimately up to the other females to tell them to stop."

"It's just testosterone poisoning. It'll go away when they grow up."

"No, it doesn't. Look at that Tailhook scandal."

"It sure is bad now," a blond girl says. "They say things that make me feel awful."

"What things?" we ask.

Several girls begin talking, clearly upset and angry.

"Get down on your knees and give me a blow job."

"I need sex. Come with me now."

"My balls itch. Come over and scratch them."

"It's a joke, but if you don't brush it off, they'll take you seriously."

"What can you do about the boys who say these things? Is there someone you can go to?"

"Oh, no. We could never tell. They would know it was us. They would make our lives miserable," Betsy says.

The girl standing next to Betsy agrees: "You have to just let it go. Just say, 'Sure,' whatever . . ." She tosses her head as if to show the triviality of the boys' behavior. "But I have a friend who freaked out when those guys said gross things. Now they totally hate her here. She doesn't even want to come to school."

Slowly the students file out, late to geoscience. The last one to leave is a boy from the outer circle. He stands stiffly and awkwardly, looking at us through thick glasses. "I want you to know I would never treat a girl like that. I don't think a lot of boys would. But you have to understand there's a fear of being sexual and a fear of being not sexual. It's a mass of confusion."

As we gather up our books and notes and the essays the students have written, an undergraduate from the university who came with us says, "I didn't know what would happen today, but I never expected this."

"We're shocked, too," we admit. "We expected to talk about textbooks and teaching." As we are about to leave the room, Betsy comes back. She is out of breath, pale, and a little shaken.

"You know that story I told you about the boy who told his girlfriend to fetch and get him things? Well, he heard about what I told you. He and his friends—a group of them—were waiting for me at my next class. They blocked me and said, 'Go fetch, Betsy. Do sexual favors for us, Betsy.' They stood in the hallway in a line in front of me so I couldn't get by."

"That's terrible. What can we do to help?"

"Oh, it doesn't bother me. I just take it as a joke." Betsy manages a faint smile.

"It's not funny, and you look upset."

"Yeah, it kind of hurts. But I can handle it. I have friends who'll help me. Besides, it'll die down. This is Friday. By Monday they'll probably have forgotten all about it. At least I hope so."[1]

In 1980 the Massachusetts State Department of Education conducted the nation's first study of sexual harassment in school. Educators surveyed racially diverse students from urban, suburban, and rural schools across the state. They found that girls experienced sexual harassment in both academic and vocational schools. Ranging from verbal insults to rape, peer harassment was rampant. A 1986 Minnesota survey of predominantly white, middle-class juniors and seniors enrolled in a vocational school found that 33 percent to 60 percent of the girls, but only one out of 130 male students, had experienced sexual harassment.[2] In 1992, conversations with 150 girls and boys in California high and middle schools revealed that almost every student had watched, experienced, or participated in some form of sexual harassment.[3]

"What's happening to you?" the September 1992 issue of *Seventeen* asked its readers. The magazine's survey queried whether secondary school students had been touched, grabbed, pinched, or cornered against their will during the past year and whether they had been subjected to comments, notes, pictures, gestures, jokes, or pressure to do something sexual.[4] According to Nan Stein, director of the Wellesley-based project that analyzed the survey results, thousands of responses poured in from every section of the country and from every racial and ethnic group. She said that letters came in envelopes marked urgent and please read. Typically written on blue-lined notebook paper, they told chilling stories about daily, accepted sexual mistreatment at school: snapping girls' bras, lifting up or pulling down skirts, touching, pinching, poking at girls' bodies with fingers or pencils, comments and jokes about parts of their bodies, bathroom graffiti depicting them in obscene sexual acts. Sometimes the letters described actual physical assault and even rape.

Bernice Sandler, former director of the Project on the Status of Women at the American Association of Colleges, has been investigating the sexual climate in schools for years. Although she began her research in colleges and universities, she is now concerned about what happens in secondary and even elementary schools. "Sexual persecution," she said, "starts at a very early age. In some elementary schools there is skirt flip-up day; in others girls refuse to wear clothes with elastic waistbands because the boys pull down their slacks and skirts. In junior high schools boys tape mirrors to the tops of their shoes so they can look up girls' dresses. Groups of boys in some high schools claim tables near the line where food is purchased. Whenever a female student walks by, they hold up a card with a number on it: one for an unattractive girl and ten for a superstar. In other schools there is 'Grab a Piece of Ass Week' or lists circulate, such as 'The Twenty Sluttiest Girls in School.'"

In 1993 the American Association of University Women published *Hostile Hallways,* a national survey of middle and high school students conducted by Louis Harris and Associates. The conclusion: Harassment is rampant in schools across America, with 81 percent of girls and 76 percent of boys reporting they have been subjected to some form of unwanted sexual behavior. More than two-thirds of students say they have been the target of sexual jokes and gestures, and 11 percent report being asked to do something sexual other than kissing. Sixty-five percent of girls and 42 percent of boys say they have been grabbed, touched, or pinched in a sexual way.

While boys experience unwanted sexual behavior, girls are far more likely to have been harassed repeatedly and at younger ages. Minority girls are especially likely to be targets, with 42 percent of African-Americans and 40 percent of Hispanics reporting sexual harassment by grade six or earlier as compared with 31 percent of white girls. Girls are also far more likely than boys to report feeling embarrassed and upset, self-conscious and scared as a result of the experience. Thirty-three percent of girls and 12 percent of boys were so troubled after being harassed sexually they did not want to talk in class or even go to school.

In a boys' bathroom in Minnesota's Duluth Central High School, vulgar graffiti described sophomore Katy Lyle as having intercourse and oral sex with boys and animals. Anonymous phone calls frequently disturbed Katy's home, and she was tormented by teasing in the school building and on the school bus. When she told the principal, Katy had the feeling he was wondering what she had done to deserve these degrading slurs. Although she had never even had a serious boyfriend, she began to wonder, too. Her behavior changed. She became quiet, withdrawn, and cried often. She dreaded going to school.

When Katy's mother found out what was causing the drastic change in her daughter's behavior, she phoned the school immediately. Eighteen months and fifteen complaints later, the graffiti had not gone away. According to Duluth School District attorney Elizabeth Storaasli, the "graffiti was considered a building maintenance problem at the time." It was only when the Lyles spoke with a representative from the Program for Aid to Victims of Sexual Assault that they realized "building maintenance" was the wrong term. What they were dealing with was sexual harassment. Finally, after a formal complaint was filed with the Minnesota Department of Human Rights, the walls were painted and the ugly words were at last removed. This case was prepared for court and eventually reached a settlement that clarified school sexual harassment policies: Katy was awarded $15,000 for mental anguish, the first time a high school girl received damages for sexual harassment by male students.[5]

Unlike organizations in the workplace, schools rarely distribute and explain their policies to students. And unlike workplace harassment, which is more likely to occur behind closed doors, school harassment is generally in public—in hallways, stairwells, the cafeteria, the gym, on the school bus, and even in classrooms.[6] Part of an escalating climate of inappropriate language, crude behavior, and violence at school, school harassment is also the result of a high school gender gap in attitudes toward sexual coercion. Even more than college males, high school boys are likely to blame the victim for causing rape. These boys believe that "women secretly want to get raped" and "only bad girls get raped."[7] School teachers and administrators rarely intervene because they do not realize the damage done or because they are afraid to confront the perpetrators. So harassment continues, uninterrupted and unchallenged.

While peer-to-peer sexual harassment is most prevalent, occasionally the perpetrators are educators who are supposed to be safeguarding the school.

A high school girl in Maine is the target of daily crude and suggestive remarks by her science teacher. When she complains to her guidance counselor and asks to transfer out of the class, the request is denied. She is told to learn to handle it because it will give her practice in dealing with the real world.

In Indiana teachers watch as a principal makes suggestive remarks to students. He stares directly at the chests of two high school girls. "Are those real," he asks, "or are they Memorex?" When a high school girl asks if she can use this principal's car to transport supplies to another building, as a boy had done the previous day, he responds, "I'll let you use my car, and then you can use me."

In the cafeteria a teacher teases girls about their bodies and their boyfriends. He tickles them and massages their shoulders, sometimes letting his hands brush across their breasts. When they tell the guidance counselor this makes them feel uncomfortable, they are told that the man is just being "friendly" and that the behavior is "harmless."

In Montana a Latin teacher stands by the desk of a high school girl and sways back and forth, rubbing his genitals across her upper arm. Although she complains to the principal, nothing is done and she eventually drops the course. Since there is only one Latin teacher in the high school, she is no longer able to take Latin.[8]

According to Nan Stein, music teachers, coaches, driver education teachers, and extracurricular club advisers, those who spend time with students in private settings, are most likely to become involved in sexual abuse or harassment. These teachers are often extremely popular with students and sometimes are very skilled at identifying cooperative victims. One California teacher started the school year with a self-esteem questionnaire; female students with low scores become candidates for seduction. Of 220,000 teachers in California, 145 lost their licenses between 1985 and 1990 because of sexual misconduct with students. It is difficult to get any clear idea of the number of sexually deviant teachers nationally, however, because most cases never get reported and teaching licenses are rarely revoked.[9]

Proving sexual harassment charges is like walking through a legal mine field, so superintendents and school boards frequently make arrangements for accused teachers or administrators to leave quietly. They ask for a voluntary letter of resignation and offer in return a letter of reference. While this transaction "passes the trash" and rids the school system of trouble, a mobile molester is created, one who takes his teaching credentials and his letters of reference to another unsuspecting school system. This scenario is almost what happened in the case of Andrew Hill, a sports coach and economics teacher at North Gwinnett High School in Gwinnett County, Georgia. But high school student Christine Franklin didn't allow him to leave quietly. Instead she took him to court.

In 1986, when Christine Franklin was a high school sophomore, Hill began to make inappropriate remarks, asking her about her sexual experiences with her boyfriend and whether she would consider having intercourse with an older man. Three different times he interrupted classes she was attending and requested that she be excused; he took her to a private office and forced her to have intercourse. Although other students complained to teachers and the principal about Hill's behavior, the school did not take action. In fact, the school's bandleader tried to talk Christine out of pursuing the matter because of negative publicity. Finally, when Hill resigned with the understanding that all charges against him would be dropped, the school closed its investigation. But Christine persisted and filed for damages in federal court under Title IX, the law which prohibits sex discrimination in schools that receive federal financial assistance. The case eventually reached the Supreme Court. In February 1992 the Court ruled that compensatory damages were available under Title IX, and this decision should significantly enhance the power of this law.[10] [See Selections 48 and 52.]

Girls exhibit the same symptoms as women who are persecuted by sexual harassment: They become withdrawn and fearful, feel intimidated, and may display the physical symptoms of illness. They often transfer out of courses or programs and sometimes drop out of school altogether. But schoolgirls are doubly endangered by harassment. They are at an age of confusion when they are struggling to define their sexual identity. Sexual harassment can stunt and twist their normal development. Without the range of knowledge or experience that comes with maturity, female children are even more powerless and more defenseless than adults. When a student is harassed by peers in public, observers as well as the victim feel threatened and intimidated. All students, those victimized and those who watch, lose faith in grown-ups and in the ability of the school to safeguard and protect them. When the offender is a teacher, counselor, or principal, the betrayal and the trauma are even more devastating.

Notes

1. The classroom scenes in this chapter are based on our discussions with classes of high school students; however, the names of individual students have been changed.
2. Stein, Nan. "It Happens Here, Too: Sexual Harassment in the Schools," *Education Week* (November 27, 1991), p. 37.

3. Conversations with California students reported in Gross, Jane, "Schools, the Newest Arena for Sex-Harassment Cases," *The New York Times* (March 11, 1992), p. B8.
4. LeBlanc, Adrian Nicole. "Harassment in the Hall," *Seventeen* (September 1992), pp. 163–65, 170; quote from p. 163.
5. Researched by Louis Harris and Associates. *Hostile Hallways: The AAUW Survey on Sexual Harassment in America's Schools.* Washington, DC: American Association of University Women, 1993.
6. "What's Happening to You?" *Seventeen,* quote on p. 163.
7. Blumberg, Michelle, and David Lester. "High School and College Students' Attitudes Toward Rape," *Adolescence* 26:103 (Fall 1991), pp. 727–29. Feltey, Kathryn, Julie Ainslie, and Aleta Geib. "Sexual Coercion Attitudes Among High School Students," *Youth and Society* 23:2 (December 1991), pp. 229–50.
8. These incidents have been told to us by teachers and administrators at our workshops. Others were reported in Stein, Nan, "Sexual Harassment in Schools," *School Administrator* (January 1993), pp. 14–21.
9. Le Draoulec, Pascale. "Student Seduction: When Teachers Betray Trust," *The San Diego Union Tribune* (October 25, 1992), pp. A1, A6.
10. Zirkel, Perry. "Damages for Sexual Harassment," *Phi Delta Kappan* 73:10 (June 1992), pp. 812–13.

❖ 13. Caltech Student's Expulsion Over Contents of E-Mail Raises Concerns

Amy Harmon

In a controversial decision that has polarized the Caltech campus, a promising doctoral candidate was expelled last month for allegedly sexually harassing another student—largely via electronic mail.

The unusual action has raised new concerns over the nature of harassment in a digital age, and the credibility of e-mail records at a time when the use of the medium is steeply increasing, both on and off campus.

Jinsong Hu, 26, who spent six months in County Jail before being acquitted by a Los Angeles Superior Court jury in June of stalking, insists that he did not send some of the e-mail in question and that parts of the mail he did send were doctored.

Jiajun Wen, Hu's former girlfriend, also accused him of verbal and written harassment. But the bulk of the evidence examined in court and in the university's disciplinary hearings was electronic mail.

Complaints of e-mail harassment at many of the nation's universities have risen sharply over the last 18 months as students, faculty and staff have gained increased access to electronic communications.

Given the ease and relative anonymity with which e-mail can be sent, university officials worry that it's an especially potent tool for harassment. But at the same time, it's often possible for e-mail to be manipulated or "spoofed"—made to look as though it has been sent by someone else—and thus many schools are treating e-mail evidence with considerable caution.

In the Hu case, for example, one of the apparently harassing e-mail messages that Wen originally told campus authorities had come from Hu was later found to have been a joke sent by a friend of Wen's new boyfriend from Salt Lake City.

"Forging e-mail is notoriously easy," said Gary Jackson, director of academic computing at Massachusetts Institute of Technology. "If you get a piece of ordinary e-mail from me, you have absolutely no way of establishing that I sent it."

The Caltech case comes at a time when policy-makers at the national and state level are wrestling with myriad questions about how to govern cyberspace. A congressional committee is debating several bills that would regulate the distribution of "indecent" material over the Internet—and sexually oriented or harassing e-mail could fit that definition. Connecticut recently passed the nation's first anti-computer harassment law.

But important precedents may well be set on university campuses, where most students get a free Internet account and daily tasks are migrating to cyberspace more quickly than anywhere else. Many schools have wired their residence halls to the global computer network, and students are doing homework on-line and attending "virtual office hours."

Caltech may be the first academic institution to expel a student for harassment primarily based on e-mail records. Hu's appeal to Caltech Vice President Gary Lorden was rejected last month.

Students and faculty at Caltech say the case has divided the campus and especially its close-knit Chinese community.

"E-mail is the bread and butter of an institution like this," said Yuk Yung, a geology professor at Caltech. "But it is very hard to prove that the person whose name is on it indeed sent it, and that it has not been tampered with. Especially here, where these kids all have extraordinary computing ability."

Described by his adviser, chemistry and applied physics professor William Goddard, as a brilliant student who scored the highest of nearly 1 million students taking the Chinese equivalent of the GRE exam, Hu was one year away from finishing his degree.

While a university computer expert testified that she traced the offending e-mail back to Hu's account, Hu's defenders argue that Wen had his password, that others had access to his computer—which was often left logged on—and that e-mail is easily edited once it is received.

"Nobody should be convicted or expelled based on unencrypted e-mail," said Hu's attorney, Anita Brenner, who has written several articles on cyberspace and the law. "Particularly in a campus climate of account sharing, sharing of passwords and mail spoofing."

Because of the difficulties involved in authenticating e-mail—and because the social and legal protocols defining electronic harassment have not yet been fully worked out—many university administrators advise recipients of unwanted e-mail simply to ask the suspected sender to stop. Many schools, including Caltech, also prohibit students from sharing passwords.

Kathleen McMahon, assistant dean of students at UCLA, says e-mail harassment has become prevalent in several forms. Four students were suspended last quarter for planting "e-mail bombs" that disrupted the school's computer system. And there have been several incidents of e-mail threats of violence.

Most common, though, is e-mail harassment stemming from romantic troubles.

"I'm amazed with the amount of sexual harassment among students and the use of e-mail to express it," McMahon said. "When relationships go bad, instead of stalking the student they send 10 e-mail messages saying 'I can't believe you won't go out with me.'"

In cyberspace, where facelessness has often led to extreme forms of expression, from angry "flaming" to amorous confessions, some believe such messages may mean less than they do in other forms. Civil libertarians say that moves to restrict or monitor e-mail may violate the 1st Amendment. And, they note, one can simply not read unwanted e-mail.

But anti-harassment advocates say the scope of the Internet and the capability it provides individuals to publish their opinions widely make it particularly dangerous.

Largely in response to the increased usage, the University of California recently drafted a system wide e-mail policy that critics fear will compromise the privacy of those who use a UC account to log on to the Internet.

Cornell University is grappling with a similar issue this month. University administrators are getting barraged with e-mail from Internet users across the country offended by an e-mail message initially sent among four freshmen titled "Top 75 reasons why women (bitches) should not have freedom of speech."

"I think everybody who got it forwarded it to everybody they knew, and we're receiving a tremendous number of complaints," said Marjorie Hodges, Cornell's legal policy adviser on computer matters. "It's a perfect example of something that might not violate university policies but is indeed offensive and does disrupt university business."

Hodges says individual complaints regarding e-mail harassment doubled last year and the previous year, and she expects the trend to continue as more members of the campus community go on-line.

MIT's Jackson, whose colleagues started calling him "Dear Abby" after he helped resolve a particularly convoluted e-mail triangle across three campuses, says that most cases can be dealt with simply by getting those involved to ask for it to stop. At MIT, where e-mail has long been the main form of communication, the university has implemented a system called "stop it" to handle harassment complaints.

But the borderline between free speech and harassment can be blurry, especially when electronic harassment takes on particularly ugly forms. Last year, a racist message about Asians was posted to a widely read newsgroup on Chinese literature, under the name of an MIT student.

The student denied having sent the message, but she nonetheless became the recipient of hundreds of angry e-mails. Jackson was unable to identify the actual sender.

Further complicating the unfamiliar territory is the assumed authenticity of electronic records.

"There is a tendency for noncomputer experts to believe anything the computer says because the computer says it," said Steve Worona, a computer expert at Cornell. "But that's just not the case."

There are several tools for encrypting messages and stamping e-mail with an electronic signature to verify the sender, but no good way of telling if an unencrypted message is authentic.

At MIT, Jackson handles about 50 harassment complaints a year. "But if there's been an incident and all the woman has in her hand is a piece of harassing e-mail and that is the sole evidence, there's nothing you can do at that point," he said.

The Caltech case involved four pieces of e-mail. The first one Hu allegedly sent to Wen when they broke up in August, 1994. The other three were apparently sent to Bo Yu, her new boyfriend, in January.

Of those, the first described a sexual experience with Wen. "I would like to talk about our happy life in bed and her body which I know so well," the e-mail printout said, according to court records. The next one continued, "If you are beginning to suffer now, tell Jiajun about it. She knows what it means."

Hu maintains he did not send either of them. He says he first learned of messages allegedly being forged from his account when he tried to sign on one day in early January and found that it had been disabled by a campus computer administrator.

Caltech's dean of graduate students, Arden Albee, says that e-mail is no different than any other form of communication, and therefore falls under the university's harassment policy.

"Just like phone calls, it typically turns out that the system keeps many more records of the e-mail messages than most understand," Albee said. "These can be traced if the need arises."

Albee was one of three faculty members on the panel that decided to expel Hu. The university said all disciplinary matters are confidential and declined to explain what records the committee relied on to determine who sent the e-mail.

The court case, in which many students testified on both sides, involved allegations of both verbal and electronic harassment and threats. Hu, who had been held on $150,000 bail, was acquitted after three hours of jury deliberations.

Goddard says the main issue in the university's investigation of Hu was whether he had an alibi for the times when the e-mail message log indicated they were sent. And he did—for two of them. But even then, administration officials noted that he could have written a program to have the computer send the mail while he was no longer at his terminal.

"My own belief is that he didn't send the mail," Goddard said. "And in the worst-case scenario that he did send it, it's not clear to me that it's sexual harassment. It's e-mail."

Goddard has appealed the expulsion to Caltech's provost.

"My personal belief is that the underlying reason they took what I think is a very unreasonable position is that it's the safest thing for Caltech. And that may be true, but on the other hand we're supposed to be here for the students."

14. So Many Choices, So Little Time

Jan Buckwald

Women and harassment. It's a question of choice, isn't it? With so many examples, it's hard to choose just one. Well, here's mine. Not the most insidious, or complex, or even the most disgusting. But it did make me Superwoman for a day. And it is for that reason that I share the story.

It was a normal, sunny day in the city. People going to work (well, it was more normal back then, in 1983) or going for coffee or going out to jog. Some other people—carpenter people—were wandering around on the roof of my apartment building, getting ready to carpent. Me, I was just going out for a run.

Do the carpenters have anything to do with this story, you ask? You needn't ask. You already know the answer. Because you, yourself, have crossed the street probably a jillion times to avoid that scene. You've felt your face burn red in that confounding mix of anger and embarrassment and helplessness. While trying to look as if you didn't even notice them, you, too, have wished for some recourse, some response to their whistles and grunts and gestures and stares. I have, too, only I didn't actually come up with a super good one until that day I went out for a run.

I had tried a few different things before. Staring back doesn't work. Looking critically at the beams and joists only works once in a while; it works while you're facing the crew. (Once you've passed, it's hunting season for them again, and there may be an added backlash against your questioning their ability). Spitting, I find, works more effectively with this type of jerk and the ones who drive by hanging out of their car windows. Something about superimposing the image of a woman spitting onto that of a Playboy bunny just doesn't work for them.

Anyway, the city. I'm just walking down the steps from my apartment when I hear the whistling of carpenters on the roof, whistling and yelling at another jogger (female, of course) running by. She does the usual, used to this treatment from the time she was a teenager. She pretends not to hear, looks straight ahead, and keeps on running. I head the other way, my best plan at the moment being to avoid them altogether. (This does work, but sets something brewing inside.) And something was a-brew as I continued running. When I got back to the building, in my shorts and T-shirt, they saw me. They whistled. They couldn't know what was coming. To them I looked like just another defenseless female. My cape was tucked in and hidden beneath my T-shirt.

My heart had started pounding several moments before, when it started seeping into my consciousness that this time I would have to do my part to save the city for myself and other women who ran. Blood raced through my body. My mouth was dry. But I knew what I had to do. I stopped. I took a deep breath. I looked straight up at one of them and said I wanted to speak to the person in charge.

"He's not here."

"Where is he and when will he be back?" (Can he see me shaking?)

"He's at lunch."

"What's his name?" I pushed.

A shaky voice mumbled his name. (Funny how fragile they become.)

"You give him a message," I said. "You tell him that if there is one more instance of harassment from anyone here, you all are off this job."

Silence.

"You understand what I mean by harassment?" I pursued.

"Yes." Gulp. More silence.

"What? Tell me what I mean!" (Not the loving teacher approach.)

Pause. "You mean that if we harass anyone." (Hidden genius.)

"That means whistling, ogling, yelling, or anything that makes anyone feel uncomfortable."

He nods to signal that he has comprehended.

"What's your name?" (Well, why not, now that I see he's scared? I want him to take this seriously and personally.)

He mumbles a name.

I repeat his name out loud and tell him to make sure everyone gets that message. Things have become unusually quiet. He returns to working on a piece of wood, slowly, quietly, slowly and quietly like everyone else up there on the roof. After getting the company name and number, I leave the quiet carpenters working humbly on the serious roof of my building.

I'll tell you the truth. I didn't know what I could realistically threaten. It wasn't even my building. I hadn't hired them. It was 1983, before harassment had been discovered by the boys on Capitol Hill. But something told me that I would call the mayor if I had to, and she would handle it.

The rest of the truth is that my legs were jelly, but I got them to carry me around the corner, to the stairs, where I grabbed the railing just as my knees buckled beneath me.

For the rest of the week, the carpenters continued to putter around up there. I heard not a peep from any of them. The way I see it, if they can learn to be jerks, then they can learn not to be. Sort of like how I learned a long time ago that I had to put up with it. And then, that day, I learned that, as Superwoman, I didn't. My choice.

15. Court Says Law Covers Same-Sex Harassment

Joan Biskupic

The Supreme Court ruled unanimously yesterday that a federal law against sexual harassment on the job covers misconduct even when the victim and the harasser are the same sex. The decision ensures for the first time that men who are taunted or abused by other men, and women who are harassed by women, can sue for damages.

The justices said in their ground-breaking decision that the law covers homosexual situations, as well as harassment between two people of the same sex when neither person is gay.

"It clearly states that no one should have to suffer sexual harassment when going to work in the morning," said Steven Shapiro, national legal director for the American Civil Liberties Union, "and it shouldn't matter if you are a man or a woman, gay or straight."

Civil rights lawyers had argued that the law should apply beyond opposite-sex behavior, to cases, for example, in which male employees target a co-worker whom they regard as not "manly" enough, or a female supervisor who makes sexual advances toward female underlings. But some employer groups contended that the law—originally aimed at deterring men's discrimination against women—should not be transformed into a general prohibition on workplace misconduct or a code of civility.

Jeffrey C. Londa, representing the Texas Association of Business and Chambers of Commerce, said the decision could raise the number of frivolous filings against employers and have the unintentional effect of encouraging companies to inquire into workers' sexual orientation. He noted the court said same-sex harassment may be inferred if the harasser is homosexual.

Yesterday's case, coming as sexual harassment claims of all types are on the rise nationwide, involved a male Louisiana roustabout on an offshore oil rig who was subjected to sexual humiliation, assault and threats of rape by his boss and co-workers, all men.

The victim, Joseph Oncale, complained to Sundowner Offshore Services, but the company supposedly did nothing and Oncale quit. A federal appeals court threw out his discrimination complaint, ruling that the federal law banning sex bias on the job, known as Title VII of the 1964 Civil Rights Act, applies only to behavior between the sexes.

Reversing that stance of the 5th U.S. Circuit Court of Appeals, the Supreme Court said nothing in the law prohibits a claim of discrimination simply because the victim and offender are both men or both women.

"[M]ale-on-male sexual harassment in the workplace was assuredly not the principal evil Congress was concerned with when it enacted Title VII," Justice Antonin Scalia wrote for the court. "But statutory prohibitions often go beyond the principal concerns of our legislators."

Responding to business's concern about frivolous filings, Scalia emphasized that "common sense" should prevail in all harassment cases. He said courts should not "mistake ordinary socializing in the workplace—such as male-on-male horseplay"—for sexual discrimination.

"The prohibition of harassment on the basis of sex requires neither asexuality nor androgyny in the workplace," he said. "It forbids only behavior so objectively offensive as to alter the conditions of the victim's employment."

The court emphasized that plaintiffs must show that they were targeted because of their sex and left open questions about how easy it will be for someone like Oncale, working in an all-male environment, to prove that the men picked him because he was a man. [See Selection 54.]

Advocates for gay men and lesbians, who had been closely following the case, praised yesterday's decision. "This is important for them because they often experience this form of harassment," said Beatrice Dohrn, legal director of Lambda Legal Defense and Educational Fund.

In a similar vein, Elizabeth Birch, executive director of the Human Rights Campaign, said, "Civil rights law will no longer unfairly exclude same-sex sexual harassment, and this fact will benefit all American workers."

Reaction from business was mixed. Londa, who had submitted a brief supporting Sundowner, said he feared a male subordinate could get fired and then sue, charging that he was in fact sexually harassed by a male supervisor who had simply put his arm around him.

But Ann Elizabeth Reesman, general counsel for the Equal Employment Advisory Council, which represents business interests, noted that the court emphasized that the law still only applies to severe or pervasive misconduct.

Scalia, who tends to narrowly interpret statutes, wrote, "Common sense, and an appropriate sensitivity to social context, will enable courts and juries to distinguish between simple teasing or roughhousing among members of the same sex."

As an example, he said a pro football player who is smacked on the behind by the coach as he heads onto the field likely would not have a case, but the coach's secretary experiencing the same treatment might.

Title VII makes it illegal for an employer to discriminate against any individual because of that person's sex. In 1986, the court said harassment is a type of discrimination [See Selection 51.] But in recent years, as same-sex harassment complaints have risen, courts have been split over whether they are covered by the law.

The U.S. Equal Employment Opportunity Commission reports that sexual harassment claims have doubled since 1991, to 16,000 a year. The agency says 12 percent of those are filed by men. The government does not keep track of the sex of the alleged harassers but experts say that most of those brought by men are against other men.

Yesterday's ruling in Oncale v. Sundowner Offshore Services sends the case back to federal district court to determine whether it meets the terms of federal law: that the victim was singled out because of his or her sex and the harassment was severe and pervasive.

Oncale alleged that the abuse he endured went beyond aggressive horseplay. He said the men grabbed him in the company shower and forced a bar of soap between his buttocks and threatened to rape him.

Sundowner lawyer Harry Reasoner said yesterday that while the men might have been "engaged in a kind of rough hazing," it did not rise to a level of illegal harassment. He also asserted that because all employees were men, Oncale will not be able to show that the mistreatment resulted from the fact that he was a man and would not have occurred had he been a woman.

PART III

Sexual Harassment and the Law

❖ 16. Basic Facts About Sexual Harassment

U.S. Equal Employment Opportunity Commission

Sexual harassment is a form of sex discrimination that violates Title VII of the Civil Rights Act of 1964.

Unwelcome sexual advances, requests for sexual favors, and other verbal or physical conduct of a sexual nature constitutes sexual harassment when submission to or rejection of this conduct explicitly or implicitly affects an individual's employment, unreasonably interferes with an individual's work performance or creates an intimidating, hostile or offensive work environment.

Sexual harassment can occur in a variety of circumstances, including but not limited to the following:

- The victim as well as the harasser may be a woman or a man. The victim does not have to be of the opposite sex.

- The harasser can be the victim's supervisor, an agent of the employer, a supervisor in another area, a co-worker, or a non-employee.

- The victim does not have to be the person harassed but could be anyone affected by the offensive conduct.

- Unlawful sexual harassment may occur without economic injury to or discharge of the victim.

- The harasser's conduct must be unwelcome.

It is helpful for the victim to directly inform the harasser that the conduct is unwelcome and must stop. The victim should use any employer complaint mechanism or grievance system available.

When investigating allegations of sexual harassment, EEOC looks at the whole record: the circumstances, such as the nature of the sexual advances, and the context in which the alleged incidents occurred. A determination on the allegations is made from the facts on a case-by-case basis.

Prevention is the best tool to eliminate sexual harassment in the workplace. Employers are encouraged to take steps necessary to prevent sexual harassment from occurring. They should clearly communicate to employees that sexual harassment will not be tolerated. They can do so by establishing an effective complaint or grievance process and taking immediate and appropriate action when an employee complains.

❖ 17. The History of Sexual Harassment on the Job

Susan L. Webb

Not long ago I was conducting a sexual harassment workshop and we were waiting for everyone to come in and sit down so we could get started. A man in the front row turned to the woman sitting next to him and said loudly and, I thought at the time, jokingly, "What the hell are we doing here? I don't know what the stink's all about. Ten years ago you never heard anything about sexual harassment. Now there's something in the paper every damn day!"

He got no reaction, so he went on. "I wish I could get someone to sexually harass *me*. I've been trying for years to get someone to sexually harass me, and no one will do it." Then he burst out laughing.

The woman he was talking to looked upset and embarrassed, and apparently she didn't believe, know, or care whether or not he was joking. After his second statement, about wanting someone to harass him, she delivered her comeback, telling him in some detail exactly why she thought no one would ever bother to sexually harass him, emphasizing his lack of appeal and other not-so-endearing characteristics. That was the end of their discussion.

Actually, he was right—in the first part of his comments, at least: for the most part, ten years ago most of us hadn't heard much about sexual harassment, and now there is something in the paper almost every day. The truth is it's just a very, very old problem, getting a lot of new attention.

Many people who are facing the issue of sexual harassment for the first time today have little or no knowledge of how we got to this point. A bit of historical background can go a long way in helping us see the overall picture of sexual harassment and understand the intricacies of this complex and troubling problem.

Court records as far back as American colonial times show examples of what we today call sexual harassment. According to Charles Clark in the August 1991 *CQ Researcher,* it was in 1734 that a group of female servants published a notice in the *New York Weekly Journal* that said, "We think it reasonable we should not be beat by our mistresses' husbands, they being too strong and perhaps may do tender women mischief." Strikingly similar examples were reported in Canadian court records (Toronto, 1915) and in Genesis 39 (in which the harasser was female and the victim of harassment was male).

According to Clark, in the 1960s the basis for today's awareness of sexual harassment fell into place:

- Women began entering (and staying in) the work force in large numbers. In 1959 there were 22 million women in the work force, or approximately 33 percent; by 1991 there were 57 million working women, or 45.5 percent of the American work force.
- The 1964 Civil Rights Bill was passed, which broadened the employment-discrimination section, Title VII, to cover sex discrimination. [See Selection 47.]
- The birth control pill, the women's movement, and the sexual revolution began changing society's views of men, women, work, and family.

THE 1970s

"The 1970s ushered in an era of dramatic efforts to curb workplace discrimination of all forms," says Clark. In 1972 Congress passed the Equal Employment Opportunity Act, giving the federal Equal Employment Opportunity Commission (EEOC) an independent general counsel appointed by the president. This counsel was given the authority to bring cease-and-desist orders and to sue in federal court those employers guilty of workplace discrimination. Also in 1972, Congress passed the Education Act Amendments prohibiting sex discrimination at schools and universities that receive any federal funding.

But it was well into the 1970s, actually ten years after the enactment of the Civil Rights Act, when federal courts heard the first cases in which sexual harassment was the primary complaint. In these cases (*Miller* v. *Bank of America, Corne* v. *Bausch & Lomb, Inc., Barnes* v. *Train*) the courts interpreted sexual harassment based on sex as a "personal matter" between the two individuals, and not as actions directed at or affecting groups of people. Thus, these cases were not successful in establishing sexual harassment as a form of sex discrimination.

In the very first case (*Corne* v. *Bausch & Lomb, Inc.*), two female employees resigned because of repeated verbal and physical advances by their supervisor. The district court refused to hold the company liable because the supervisor's conduct served no employer policy and didn't benefit the employer. The court called the supervisor's conduct "a personal proclivity, peculiarity or mannerism."

But in 1976 a case (*Williams* v. *Saxbe*) finally did establish a cause of action for sexual harassment. The court ruled that the behavior in question had only to create an "artificial barrier to employment that was placed before one gender and not the other, even though both genders were similarly situated." Thus, conditions of employment that were applied differently to men and women, such as sexual harassment, were forbidden under Title VII as sex discrimination. This was a major and landmark decision in beginning to address sexual harassment in the workplace.

These early sexual harassment cases involved claims that the plaintiffs had been deprived of tangible job benefits for their failure to succumb to sexual advances (*Tomkins* v. *Public Service Gas & Electric*). The women had to show that there was a clear relationship between the objectionable conduct (the harassment) and the negative employment consequences (being fired or demoted, given distasteful job assignments or poor performance reviews). If they could not show these tangible, negative consequences, then the harassing behavior was seen as isolated sexual misconduct, not a Title VII violation (*Hill* v. *BASF Wyandotte Corp., Neely* v. *American Fidelity Assurance Co., Davis* v. *Bristol Laboratories*).

In 1977 the first charge of sexual harassment of students was brought under Title IX of the 1972 Education Act Amendments. A female undergraduate at Yale University said that her professor offered her an A in his course if she would accept his sexual proposition and that when she refused she got a C. In her suit (*Alexander* v. *Yale University*) she demanded that the lower grade be removed from her record; she was joined in this demand by four other students and a faculty member.

The district court maintained that sexual harassment may constitute sex discrimination under Title IX, stating, "It is perfectly reasonable to maintain that academic advancement conditioned upon submission to sexual demands constitutes sex discrimination in education, just as questions of job retention or promotion tied to sexual demands from supervisors have become increasingly recognized as potential violations of Title VII's ban against sex discrimination in employment."

Her suit was dismissed in 1980 because she had graduated from Yale and in the meantime the university had established a sexual harassment grievance procedure for dealing with complaints. However, the importance of this case is that it served to define sexual harassment in the educational system and bring attention to teacher-student types of harassment.

In addition to the rush of legal activity taking place in the seventies, a number of major studies and surveys were published. Lin Farley's book, *Sexual Shakedown: The Sexual Harassment of Women on the Job* (1978), defined the problem and told story after story of women who experienced harassment at work. Catharine A. MacKinnon wrote *Sexual Harassment of Working Women: A Case of Sex Discrimination* (1979) and argued the legal remedies. [See Selections 1 and 2.] Even anthropologist Margaret Mead contributed, with an article, titled "A Proposal: We Need Taboos on Sex at Work," that is still quoted today.

The 1980s

What seemed to be a quiet start for the 1980s was truly a noisy beginning. In November 1980, during the final days of the Carter Administration, EEOC's Guidelines on Discrimination Because of Sex were formalized by chairman Eleanor Holmes Norton. [See Selection 49.] The Guidelines had been published earlier in the spring of that year and subject to public discussion and debate. In the fall they became official.

It was in the early eighties that the first district court decision allowed for a suit over an "atmosphere of discrimination" (*Brown* v. *City of Guthrie*). While the woman could not show loss of tangible job benefits, she did establish that the harassment created a hostile, offensive, and unbearable work environment. The *Brown* court was the first to cite the EEOC Guidelines on Discrimination Because of Sex, quoting Section A, that sexual harassment is a violation of Title VII when "such conduct has the purpose or effect of substantially interfering with an individual's work performance or creating an intimidating, hostile, or offensive work environment."

Shortly after *Brown*, in *Bundy* v. *Jackson* (1981), the circuit court ruled on the basis of the atmosphere of discrimination, and cited the Guidelines to support its opinion. The court interpreted "terms and conditions of employment" protected by Title VII to mean more than tangible compensation and benefits.

Other courts, however, did not follow the pattern of *Brown* and *Bundy*. In *Hill,* the district court had held that no action under Title VII for sexual harassment was available where the plaintiff did not show that her success and advancement depended on her agreeing to her supervisor's demands. The court observed that Title VII should not be interpreted as reaching into sexual relationships that arise during the course of employment but do not have a "substantial effect" on that employment.

Then, in 1982 and 1983, two federal circuit courts of appeal adopted their own classification scheme for sexual harassment cases, identifying two basic varieties of sexual harassment: (1) "Harassment in which a supervisor demands sexual consideration in exchange for job benefits ('quid pro quo')" and (2) "harassment that creates an offensive environment ('condition of work' or 'hostile environment' harassment)" (*Henson* v. *City of Dundee* and *Katz* v. *Dole*).

Quid pro quo ("this for that") harassment, as defined by the courts, encompasses all situations in which submission to sexually harassing conduct is made a term or condition of employment or in which submission to or rejection of sexually harassing conduct is used as the basis for employment decisions affecting the individual who is the target of such conduct.

In the typical quid pro quo harassment case, an employee (or prospective employee) is approached by an individual with the power to affect the employee's employment future and asked for sexual consideration in return for a job benefit or in order to avoid losing a job benefit.

The *Henson* court stated four elements that a plaintiff must prove to establish a case of quid pro quo sexual harassment:

- He or she belongs to a protected group, i.e., is a male or female.
- He or she was subjected to unwelcome sexual harassment.
- The harassment complained of was based on sex.
- The employee's reaction to harassment complained of affected tangible aspects of the employee's compensation, terms, conditions, or privileges of employment.

Condition of work or hostile environment sexual harassment, as defined by the courts, is roughly equivalent to the third category of sexual harassment listed in the EEOC Guidelines: unwelcome and demeaning sexually related behavior that creates an intimidating, hostile, and offensive work environment. In the *Henson* case, the circuit court reversed the lower court's holding that the plaintiff must show some tangible job detriment in addition to the hostile work environment created by sexual harassment. The court said that although not every instance or condition of work environment harassment gives rise to a Title VII claim, a plaintiff who can prove a number of elements can establish a claim. These elements are similar to those for quid pro quo harassment also outlined by *Henson:*

- The employee belongs to a protected group under Title VII, i.e., is a man or a woman.
- The employee was subjected to unwelcome sexual harassment.
- The harassment complained of was based on sex.
- The harassment complained of affected a term, condition, or privilege of employment.
- The employer knew or should have known of the harassment in question and failed to take prompt remedial action.

The U.S. Supreme Court Decision on Sexual Harassment: *Meritor Savings Bank* v. *Vinson* (1986)

On June 19, 1986, the U.S. Supreme Court ruled that sexual harassment on the job is illegal discrimination even if the victim suffers no economic loss. The Court held that "the language of Title VII is not limited to 'economic' or 'tangible' discrimination" and the law's phrase "terms, conditions or privileges" of employment indicates congressional intent to "strike at the entire spectrum of disparate treatment of men and women," including harassment that creates a hostile work environment.

The Court quoted the *Henson* court, saying, "Sexual harassment which creates a hostile or offensive environment for members of one sex is every bit the arbitrary barrier to sexual equality at the workplace that racial harassment is to racial equality. Surely, a requirement that a man or woman run a gauntlet of sexual abuse in return for the privilege of being allowed to work and make a living can be as demeaning and disconcerting as the harshest of racial epithets."

The Court reiterated that not all workplace behavior that may be defined as harassment can be said to affect terms or conditions of employment. For sexual harassment to be actionable it must be sufficiently severe or pervasive to "alter the conditions of the victim's employment and create an abusive working environment."

The Court's key holdings were:

- Sexual harassment is a form of sex discrimination illegal under Title VII of the 1964 Civil Rights Act.

- Sexual harassment is illegal even if the victim suffered only a hostile work environment and not the loss of economic or tangible job benefits.
- Employers are not automatically liable for sexual harassment by their supervisors.
- Lack of knowledge of the harassment does not automatically relieve the employer of liability for supervisors' harassment.
- The complainant's consent to the behavior does not relieve the employer of liability. The question is not the "voluntariness" of the complainant's participation, but whether her conduct indicated that the behavior was unwelcome.
- The complainant's behavior, such as provocative speech and dress, may be considered in determining whether the complainant found particular sexual advances unwelcome. [See Selection 51.]

Since then, other courts have continued to define and refine the definition of what constitutes sexual harassment. The courts' answers to this question have, for the most part, become somewhat predictable and followed a pattern parallel to that of racial harassment.

While some people believed (or hoped) that the courts would narrow the scope of what they consider discriminatory sexual harassment, this has not been the case. Actually, the opposite has occurred: initial rulings limited the scope of what was defined as harassment, and subsequent rulings broadened the definition.

THE 1990s

In the 1990s the problem of sexual harassment has continued to get widespread attention. On March 19, 1990, the EEOC issued updated Guidelines on sexual harassment, reflecting decisions made by the agency itself as well as by various courts since the first Guidelines were issued in 1980.

A number of studies and surveys have also been conducted and their results published. In September 1990, the Pentagon released the largest military survey ever on sexual harassment, showing that of 20,000 military respondents worldwide, 64 percent of the women and 17 percent of the men said that they had been sexually harassed. In a separate study (1991), the Navy revealed that of the 6,700 they surveyed, 75 percent of the women and 50 percent of the men responding said that sexual harassment occurs within their commands.

In the business world, estimates continue to run from 15 to 40 percent of women and 14 to 15 percent of men who experience sexual harassment. On campuses, the estimates range from 40 to 70 percent of female students experiencing harassment, with most harassment coming from other students.

The number of complaints filed with the EEOC has shown a general upward trend over the years (1986, 4,431; 1987, 5,336; 1988, 5,215; 1989, 5,204; 1990, 6,127; 1991, 6,883; 1992, 10,532; 1993, 11,908; 1994, 14,420; 1995, 15,549). However, these numbers don't reveal much about the problem, because many harassment victims sue privately and don't go through the EEOC at all.

Pinups and Sexual Harassment: *Robinson v. Jacksonville Shipyards*

Already in the nineties, two landmark court decisions have been delivered. In the first (*Robinson* v. *Jacksonville Shipyards,* January 1991), the Sixth U.S. Circuit Court of Appeals in Florida ruled that nude pinups in the workplace can constitute sexual harassment. In this case, a female shipyard welder accused her employer of sexual harassment and won, with the court ruling that posting pictures of nude and partly nude women is a form of sexual harassment.

In other cases, courts have found that pornographic pictures may contribute to an atmosphere of sexual harassment. But *Robinson* is thought to be the first finding that such pictures are sexual harassment in and of themselves.

The federal district court judge in Jacksonville, Florida, Howell Melton, said that the employer, Jacksonville Shipyards, Inc., and two of its employees were directly liable for the harassment, and rejected what he called their "ostrich defense." The company claimed that it had been unaware of many of the women's complaints.

The judge said that the shipyard maintained a boys' club atmosphere with a constant "visual assault on the sensibilities of female workers." The pictures included pinup calendars and close-ups of female genitals posted on the walls. The judge went on to say that the sexualized atmosphere of the workplace had the effect of keeping women out of the shipyard.

The opinion also said, "A pre-existing atmosphere that deters women from entering or continuing in a profession or job is no less destructive to and offensive to workplace equality than a sign declaring 'men only.'" Judge Melton ordered the shipyard to institute a sexual harassment policy written by the National Organization for Women's Legal Defense and Education Fund. NOW, the New York-based women's advocacy group, had brought the case to trial.

The decision found both verbal and visual sexual harassment, and described thirty pornographic pictures displayed at the shipyard. One was of a woman's pubic area with a spatula pressed against it. Some of the pictures came from calendars provided by tool companies and included one of a nude woman bending over with her buttocks and genitals exposed. Another showed a frontal view of a female torso with the words "U.S.D.A. Choice" written on it. The verbal harassment included explicit sexual remarks.

The decision said that when the woman told her co-workers that their behavior was sexual harassment, they took that as a new subject of ridicule and denied that they were harassing her. Two other female employees testified that they were also subjected to sexual harassment, in the form of remarks, pinches, and sexual teasing.

According to the testimony, the female welder complained repeatedly to her supervisors about the pictures. At one meeting when she complained, a supervisor told her that the company had no policy against the pictures and that the men had "constitutional rights" to post them, so he would not order them removed. According to the ruling, the shipyard had no system for recording sexual harassment complaints and supervisors had no instructions to document such complaints.

The judge ordered the shipyard to pay her legal fees but did not order it to pay back pay for time lost from work. The woman said that she had missed workdays because of the strain of the harassment, but the judge said that her estimates of missed days were too vague. Under Title VII, no other damages are available.

In this case, expert-witness testimony about sexual stereotyping was used. Based on the testimony, the judge said that the women were subject to "sex role spillover," whereby women are evaluated by co-workers and supervisors based on the women's sexuality and sexual worth rather than their value as workers.

Alison Wetherfield of the NOW Legal Defense and Education Fund said, "Judge Melton understands how damaging and illegal it is for women workers to be given the message that they are welcome at work only so long as they accept the stereotypical role of sex object. . . . The decision recognizes the impossible position many harassed women are in, in a very sensitive and unusual way."

According to the decision, women are still rare in this shipyard's skilled jobs, with only 6 women among 846 men employed as skilled craft workers in 1986. The company has never employed a woman in a supervisory position such as foreman, leadman, or quarterman.

A year after the suit was filed the company had instituted a sexual harassment policy forbidding employees to make any kind of sexual conduct a condition of employment or to create an intimidating, hostile, or offensive work environment (as per the EEOC Guidelines). The policy was posted on bulletin boards, but the employees received no training in connection with them. The court ruled that the policy had little or no effect on what it said was a sexually hostile work environment and that the company did not adequately communicate the new policy to employees.

The latest policy, ordered by the court, called for the offensive pictures to be removed and for workers to be educated about sexual harassment. It provided for penalties, including warnings, suspensions, and firings, for those who violate the policy.

The Reasonable-Woman Decision: *Ellison* v. *Brady*

Then, on January 23, 1991, a second and more even important landmark ruling was made by the Ninth U.S. Circuit Court of Appeals in San Francisco. This case, *Ellison* v. *Brady,* has serious implications with regard to investigating and resolving complaints. In its ruling, the court established a new legal standard, called the "reasonable woman" standard. This case is especially important to employers, not only because of the expanded definition of sexual harassment, but also because the court indicated that it expects swift and decisive actions in response to harassment in the workplace.

In *Ellison,* the employer's response to the harassment was to repeatedly counsel the harasser, instructing him to leave the woman alone, and to transfer him to a different facility for four months—a response that many employers would characterize as appropriate. In fact, before *Ellison* went to the federal court, the EEOC had held that the employer, the Internal Revenue Service, was not liable because it had taken sufficient steps to remedy the situation.

Nevertheless, the court disagreed. It found fault with the employer's not consulting the victim about the harasser's return to the office, for not reprimanding the man with probation, suspension, or some other type of discipline, and finally for transferring the woman to avoid further conflict, even though she had requested the transfer.

The court also said that in some cases the mere presence of an employee who has harassed a co-worker may create a hostile work environment, so that the only reasonable recourse is to discharge the harasser. The *Ellison* decision suggests that managers take preventive steps to protect themselves, their organizations, and their employees:

- Develop a clear sexual harassment policy statement and grievance procedures, spelling this out in the employee manual.

- Tell employees that harassment is taken from the victim's perspective, so employees should be sensitive to the feelings and viewpoints of their co-workers.

- Treat sexual harassment as a serious employee infraction, taking prompt and remedial action to correct the situation. If harassment continues, the harasser should be disciplined by suspension, demotion, or some other form of concrete punishment.

- Include the victim in determining the appropriate action, at least when consideration is being given to allowing the harasser to work alongside the victim.

- Do not alter the terms or conditions of the victim's employment when responding to the incidents of harassment.

- Consider whether the harasser must be terminated because his or her mere presence creates a hostile work environment for the victim.

- Show that the severity of conduct varies inversely with the frequency of the conduct.

The court also said:

- An understanding of the victim's perspective requires an analysis of the different perspectives of men and women.

- A female employee may state a *prima facie* case of hostile environment sexual harassment by alleging conduct that a reasonable woman would consider sufficiently severe; however, the employer does not have to accommodate the idiosyncrasies of the rare hypersensitive employee.

- The reasonable-woman standard is not static but will change over time as the views of reasonable women change.

- There can be unlawful sexual harassment even when harassers do not realize that their conduct creates a hostile working environment.

In this case, Kerry Ellison, the plaintiff, was an agent for the IRS office in San Mateo, California. Sterling Gray, who worked about twenty feet from her, asked her out for lunch one day in June 1986, and they went out to eat. A few months later Gray asked her out again, for drinks and lunch, and Ellison refused and made it clear that she was not interested. Gray then started to write her love letters.

In an October 1986 note scribbled on a message pad, he wrote, "I cried over you last night and I'm totally drained today." She continued to refuse his advances, which he made in person and in writing, and finally asked a co-worker to tell Gray to leave her alone—all to no avail. A few days later he wrote a three-page, single-spaced letter, saying "I know that you are worth knowing with or without sex. . . ."

Ellison said she was frightened by his attentions and "frantic" about what he might do next. She filed a complaint with her employer, alleging sexual harassment. Gray was counseled, instructed to leave Ellison alone, and eventually transferred to another location. Three months later he was allowed to return to Ellison's office under two conditions: that he complete additional training for a month at another location and that he leave Ellison alone when he returned.

Ellison was not consulted about Gray's transfer or the conditions of his return. When Ellison learned that Gray was returning to her workplace, she requested and received a transfer. Then she filed suit.

The trial court federal judge dismissed the case, applying the "reasonable person" test to the circumstances and ruling that Gray's actions were "isolated and genuinely trivial." The judge ruled that the average adult, regardless of sex, would not have found Ellison's workplace hostile. But the appeals court reversed that decision and threw out the reasonable-person rule. The court ruled that a hostile work environment must be judged from the perspective of the victim—in this case, the "reasonable woman."

The 1991 Civil Rights Act: *Amendments to the 1964 Act*

Prior to 1991, under federal equal employment law, such as Title VII, remedies such as mental suffering or punitive damages were not allowed. The original intent of these laws was to restore the individual to the status he or she would have been had the discrimination (or harassment) not occurred, i.e., to make the individual "whole" again. Such "make-whole" remedies included back pay, reinstatement to the job, granting of a promotion, or attorneys' fees.

However, the federal 1991 Civil Rights Act as enacted allows for expanded remedies for pain and suffering, including compensatory and punitive damages. The 1991 law places caps or limits on the amounts of damages which can be awarded: $50,000 for firms with up to 100 employees, $100,000 for those employing more than 100, and $300,000 for companies with more than 300 employees. Firms with fewer than 15 employees are exempt from the law. The caps apply to cases involving sex discrimination or harassment; no caps on awards exist for discrimination of other protected groups.

Second Supreme Court Sexual Harassment Case:
Title IX of the Education Amendments of 1972

In February, 1992, the U.S. Supreme Court ruled that sexually harassed students may sue to collect monetary damages from their schools and school officials. In this case, which involved sexual harassment of a student, the court said that Congress intended to let students try for monetary damages and compensation when it passed Title IX of the Education Amendments of 1972. The law, referred to as Title IX, bars sexual bias in educational programs receiving federal funding, and thus includes nearly all educational institutions. [See Selections 48 and 52.]

Third Supreme Court Sexual Harassment Case:
Harris v. Forklift Systems, Inc.

In November, 1993, the U.S. Supreme Court ruled unanimously, and with unusual swiftness, in rejecting a lower court test that employees who say they have been sexually harassed in hostile work environment situations, must prove psychological damage to win the suit and collect damages. The Court also said that victims need not show that the harassment left them unable to perform their jobs and continue with their employment.

The justices said that while the plaintiff's emotional reaction to sexual harassment may be relevant, she does not have to show extreme distress or damage. Justice Sandra Day O'Connor, writing for the court said that legal protection "comes into play before the harassing conduct leads to a nervous breakdown." [See Selection 53.]

Sexual Harassment as a Class Action Suit

In early 1992, a U.S. District Court in Minnesota granted women who work for a mining company the right to file a class-action sexual harassment suit. The mining company had argued that sexual harassment claims cannot be made on a class-wide basis. It stated that reactions to profanity, pornography, or other potentially offensive material are highly individualized.

Usually sexual harassment cases are filed by one individual plaintiff, or a small number of individual plaintiffs joined in one suit, or a small number of plaintiffs filing separate suits. For a woman, or several women, to be able to file a sexual harassment suit on behalf of a class of people—all the other women who were in the group subjected to harassment, is indeed a new, interesting, and potentially explosive occurrence. It could greatly expand the number of people entitled to damages and the amount of the total monetary judgment.

It's not necessary that you study this chapter in depth, but it is difficult to fully understand and appreciate the gravity of sexual harassment without some awareness of how the issue came to be what it is today. Even though sexual harassment is a very old problem, it continues to be troubling, complex, and extraordinarily damaging.

SUMMARY

Sexual harassment is not a new problem, but one that goes back thousands of years.

The first sexual harassment cases heard by the courts, in the 1970s, involved only those in which the victim had lost tangible job benefits such as pay, promotions, job assignments, or even the job itself, because of the harassment.

In the fall of 1980 the EEOC issued its Guidelines on Discrimination Because of Sex, saying that sexual harassment is a form of sex discrimination and should be treated the same as other forms of illegal discrimination.

In the early 1980s the first court decision was made that allowed for an "atmosphere of discrimination" whereby an employee was subjected to harassment "interfering with an individual's work performance or creating an intimidating, hostile, or offensive work environment."

In 1982 and 1983 two courts made the distinction between quid pro quo (tangible job benefits) harassment and "hostile environment" harassment.

The first Supreme Court case involving sexual harassment was heard in 1986, and validated what other courts had said in previous rulings about sexual harassment.

In the 1990s more attention has been focused on the problem of sexual harassment, by court rulings about pinups at work and the reasonable-woman standard, and by allegations of harassment against public officials.

---

18. Legal Update

William Petrocelli and Barbara Kate Repa

. . . Perhaps the biggest leap forward in recent years was the U.S. Supreme Court's recent decision in *Oncale v. Sundowner Offshore Services* (1998). In that case, the Court expanded the concept of who is protected under the sexual harassment laws and gave those laws a broader underpinning.

The *Oncale* case involved a straight male who worked on an oil rig and who claimed he was sexually harassed by his supervisors and other members of the crew, all of whom were ostensibly heterosexual as well. The harassment was relatively severe, including allegations of threats and physical assault.

But what made the case so significant was that it clearly answered the question of how and whether gender and sexual orientation play in sexual harassment. The Court was undeterred by the fact that the harassers and harassed worker were of the same gender. It was also unswayed by the fact that the acts of harassment—although sexual in content—were apparently not motivated by sexual desire. The Court instead focused on the conduct and found it to be illegal sexual harassment.

Although maintaining that it had not expanded the law, it seems clear that the Supreme Court did just that. If the Court could find in this situation—as it did unanimously—something that it could characterize as "discrimination because of sex," it seems likely that it would do so in cases in which the sexual component is closer to the forefront in the harasser's motivation. In the future, a person who is harassed because he or she is a gay man or a lesbian is very likely to be covered.

This was a big step forward for the Supreme Court. In ruling that the law's prohibition against sexual harassment "must extend to sexual harassment of any kind that meets the statutory requirements," the Court came close to placing sexual harassment on a legal footing of its own. Earlier cases suggested that the prohibition against sexual harassment was simply a necessary extension of the law against sexual discrimination—a way of preventing a person from accomplishing indirectly, through violent or threatening conduct, what he or she was prohibited from doing directly by discriminating. The opinion in *Oncale* simply recognizes that abusive sexual conduct should not be allowed in the workplace whatever the relationships between those involved. [See Selection 54.]

❖ 19. The Legal Context of Sexual Harassment on Campus

Robert J. Shoop

EQUAL EMPLOYMENT COMMISSION

The U.S. EEOC enforces Title VII[1] and provides oversight and coordination of all federal regulations, practices, and policies affecting equal employment opportunity. EEOC also develops policies, writes regulations, conducts outreach and education efforts, and coordinates all federal issuances affecting equal employment opportunity, and implements approved affirmative employment programs. [See Selection 47 and 49.]

If a person believes that he or she has been discriminated against under the protections of Title VII, he or she may file a charge of discrimination with EEOC. Although the charge can be filed in writing, by phone, or in person, there are strict time frames that must be adhered to. For the Commission to act and to protect the right to file a private lawsuit, charges must be filed with EEOC within 180 days of the alleged discrimination. EEOC's policy is to seek full and effective relief for each and every victim of employment discrimination, whether sought in court or in conciliation agreements before litigation, and to provide remedies designed to correct the discrimination and prevent its recurrence. However, in reality EEOC's caseload is backlogged, and cases can take months or years to be resolved without a lawsuit. If the Commission decides not to litigate a charge, or any time after the expiration of 180 days from the date the original charge was filed, the charging party may request a notice of the right to file a private suit in federal district court. A private suit may be filed within 90 days of receiving a notice of right-to-sue from EEOC.

After a complaint is filed with EEOC, the charging party is interviewed to obtain as much information as possible about the alleged discrimination. If all legal jurisdictional requirements are met, a charge is drafted and the investigative procedure is explained to the charging party. EEOC will then notify the party who is charged with discrimination that a charge has been filed.

EEOC then requests information from the employer that addresses the issues directly affecting the charging party as well as other potentially aggrieved persons. When investigating allegations of sexual harassment, EEOC looks at the whole record: the circumstances, such as the nature of the sexual advances, and the context in which the alleged incidents occurred. A determination on the allegations is made from the facts on a case-by-case basis. Any witnesses who have direct knowledge of the alleged discriminatory act will be interviewed. If the evidence shows there is no reasonable cause to believe discrimination occurred, the charging party and the employer will be notified. At this point or earlier the charging party may elect to bring a private court action.

If the evidence shows there is reasonable cause to believe discrimination occurred, EEOC then attempts to persuade the employer to voluntarily eliminate and remedy the discrimination. Monetary damages may also be available to compensate for future monetary loss, mental anguish, or pain and suffering, and to penalize a respondent who acted with malice or reckless indifference. In addition, the employer may be required to post a notice in the workplace advising employees that it has complied with orders to remedy the discrimination.

Most charges are conciliated or settled, making a court trial unnecessary. EEOC may then file a lawsuit in federal district court on behalf of the charging party.[2] As a result of court action, the Commission's regulations on sexual harassment have been upheld as a lawful regulatory interpretation of Title VII of the Civil Rights Act of 1964. Other court cases have upheld that sexual harassment is a violation of Title IX of the Education Amendments of 1972.

TITLE IX

In the late 1960s and early 1970s, concerned educators and students intensified the struggle against sex bias and discrimination in our nation's schools and universities. At that time Title VII specifically excluded educational institutions from its coverage. Sex discrimination against students was not prohibited by any statutes. An awareness of this exclusion and a commitment to equity resulted in the passage of Title IX of the Education Amendments of 1972. [See Selection 48.] The legislative history of Title IX makes it clear that Congress intended to apply Title VII claims standards to Title IX.

Title IX of the Education Amendments of 1972 prohibits discrimination on the basis of sex in educational programs or activities which receive federal financial assistance. Title IX covers both employees and students and virtually all activities of a university or college. The prohibition covers discrimination in employment of professors and other university personnel as well as discrimination in admissions, financial aid, and access to educational programs and activities. Title IX states: "No person in the United States shall on the basis of sex be excluded from participating in, be denied the benefits of or be subjected to discrimination under any education program or activity receiving federal financial assistance." In general, Title IX is enforced by the U.S. Department of Education. Under Title IX students may sue to collect monetary damages from the school or the school may lose federal funds.

Students at all levels of education are protected by Title IX of the Education Amendments of 1972. Title IX is one of the most sweeping sex discrimination laws ever passed. Although it had little early enforcement, it is now the primary tool that defines equal educational opportunity for women in universities. Under Title IX, sexual harassment is defined as "verbal or physical conduct of a sexual nature, imposed on the basis of sex, by an employee or agent of a recipient that denies, limits, or provides different, or conditions the provision of aid, benefits, services, or treatment protected under Title IX."

The courts look to the principles developed under Title VII when they interpret Title IX. Although Title IX law has evolved slowly, it is clear that sexual harassment is sex discrimination under Title IX. In several recent Title IX cases, the courts have continued to clarify how Title VII standards apply to Title IX claims.[3] The first federal case brought under the auspices of Title IX dealt with quid pro quo, hostile environment, and appropriate grievance procedures. In *Alexander v. Yale,* the plaintiff alleged that she received a low grade because she refused to cooperate sexually with her professor.[4] Although leaving this and the other issues undecided, the Second Circuit confirmed the right to sue for quid pro quo sexual harassment. In two 1986 cases, federal courts allowed claims based solely on the allegation of hostile work environments.[5] In the 1992 case of *Franklin v. Gwinnett County Public Schools,*[6] the U.S. Supreme Court unanimously ruled that institutions could be sued for compensatory damages as a remedy for the intentional violation of Title IX. [See Selection 52.]

OFFICE FOR CIVIL RIGHTS

Title IX is enforced by the Office for Civil Rights (OCR) at the U.S. Department of Education which has issued a regulation detailing the general requirements of Title IX. Currently in the process of creating guidelines for sexual harassment in education institutions, OCR generally interprets Title IX from the perspective of the EEOC guidelines and what the courts have said concerning sexual harassment. [See Selection 50.]

Some additional guidance can be taken from the 1994 OCR document "Investigative Guidance on Racial Incidents and Harassment Against Students,"[7] created to guide investigators in racial harassment incidents. According to Sorenson, this document identifies five factors to consider when assessing the circumstances of harassment. These factors are: severity, pervasiveness, and/or persistence of the conduct; whether the recipient of federal financial assistance had actual or constructive notice; and whether the recipient acted in a reasonable, timely, and effective manner to eliminate the harassment.[8]

According to the Title IX regulation, each institution must provide a grievance procedure for sex discrimination. Title IX's protection against sexual harassment covers prospective students, students and employees of programs that are operated by the university. Thus employees, including student employees, may file under both Title VII and Title IX. Title IX coverage also extends, with a few exceptions, to all programs and activities whether or not they receive direct federal assistance.

Individuals may file a complaint on behalf of themselves and/or on behalf of another aggrieved party. Generally a Title IX complaint must be filed within 180 days from the date of sexual harassment. A person who files with OCR can go directly into court without having to obtain permission from OCR. Both Title VII and Title IX allows states to be sued in federal court for sex discrimination.

OCR can conduct compliance reviews on its own initiative, and it is required to conduct a prompt investigation whenever a complaint is filed. If, after an investigation is conducted, OCR determines that sexual harassment has taken place, it attempts to secure voluntary compliance from the institution. OCR does have the authority to institute proceedings to suspend or terminate federal assistance or bar future assistance but rarely does so. It may also request the U.S. Department of Justice to initiate court action.

Unlike Title VII, there is no limit placed on Title IX awards. In the case of a student complaint, the court may award monetary damages to cover such things as pain and suffering; emotional distress; attorney's fees; and the cost of past, present and future therapy. The court may also require the university to initiate or change its policy and develop training programs. It may also require the university to waive various time limits for degree completion and/or provide tuition refunds.

In the case of an employee complaint, the court may require the university to reinstate or promote the employee, pay back wages, and so on. It may also award monetary damages to cover lost wages, attorney's fees, and therapy.

Notes

1. The popular interpretation of the addition of "sex" to Title VII is that it was the result of a deliberate ploy of foes of the bill to scuttle it. An alternative explanation is that this inclusion is a typical example of "incubated" legislation. For an extensive analysis of the over forty-year process of seeking equal rights for women *see:* Freman, J., "How sex got into Title VII: Persistent opportunism as a maker of public policy." *Law and Inequality: A Journal of Theory and Practice,* Vol. 9, No. 2, March 1991, pp. 163–184.

2. Material regarding EEOC was drawn from EEOC documents that are in the public domain. Information on all EEOC-enforced laws may be obtained by calling toll free on 800-669-EEOC.

3. See *Lipsett v. University of Puerto Rico,* 864 F.2d 881, 897 (1st Cir. 1988); *O'Connor v. Peru State College,* 781 F.2d 632, 642 n. 8 (8th Cir. 1986); *Doe v. Petaluma City Sch. Dist.,* 830 F.Supp. 1560, 1571–72 (N.D. Cal. 1993); and *Nagel v. Avon Bd. of Educ.,* 575 F.Supp. 105, 106 (D. Conn. 1983).

4. 631 F.2d 178 (2d Cir. 1980).

5. See *Moire v. Temple University of Medicine,* 613 F.Supp. 1360 (E.D. Pa. 1985). aff'd 800 F.2d 1136 (3d Cir. 1986) and *Lipsett v. University of Puerto Rico,* 864 Fd 881 (1st Cir. 1988).

6. 112 S.Ct. 1028 (1992).

7. 59 Fed. Reg. 11448 (1984).

8. Sorenson, Gail, Peer sexual harassment: Remedies and guidelines under federal law, 92 E. Law Rep. [1] (Sept. 8, 1994).

❖ 20. Speaking Truth to Power

Anita Hill

. . . One of the first reactions to my [confidential] statement to the [Senate] that I heard was from Arizona Senator Dennis DeConcini, who said the following during a press conference on the afternoon of October 7, a short time after my own press conference [regarding my allegations of sexual harassment by Clarence Thomas] was ended.

> If you're sexually harassed you ought to get mad about it, and you ought to do something about it and you ought to complain, instead of hanging around a long time and then all of a sudden calling up anonymously and say "Oh, I want to complain." I mean, where is the gumption?

Later, more than one person would ask me, "Did you hear what DeConcini said?" Each person who asked seemed more incensed than the last, and none of them seemed to care that DeConcini was a Democrat. As one woman put it, "Here is a man who probably never had to face discrimination in his life telling women how they ought to react to being sexually harassed. 'Where is the gumption' indeed?"

I can't count the number of times since October 1991 that I have been asked, "Why did you wait ten years to raise charges of sexual harassment against Clarence Thomas?" To which I must first say that I wasn't waiting from 1983 to 1991 to raise charges against Clarence Thomas. I was living my life. I was involved in the day-to-day struggles that everyone who lives and works and cares about their families and friends has. I had a full life of which Clarence Thomas was no longer a part. Moreover, the question misconceives what I was attempting to do in disclosing the information. I did not see the response as an effort to get relief or redress for the behavior. I was supplying information about how Thomas conducted himself in his professional role.

Perhaps a different question, and I believe a better question, is "Why didn't you bring charges of sexual harassment immediately after you left the EEOC?" To understand the muteness of my response, one must understand that I wanted most of all for the behavior to stop. That was my chief objective throughout. I found a way to make that happen by removing myself from the situation. Even in hindsight I am convinced that there was no way to stop the harassment decisively except by leaving. What were the precedents? There was a woman in the District of Columbia who sued Department of Corrections officials for harassment she experienced in the late 1970s. She is still attempting to obtain relief for her harm despite the fact that she won her suit years ago. I also recall one of the very first sexual harassment lawsuits ever filed. The woman involved in this case, Paulette Barnes, was an African American suing her supervisor in the Environmental Protection Agency, complaining that he stripped her of all job responsibilities after she rejected his sexual advances, ultimately abolishing her position altogether. I know of a third woman whose career as a doctor was stalled for over ten years because as a resident she complained about a doctor's harassment. I also know of countless women who changed college majors or professional careers and sometimes even relocated to other cities in lieu of confronting their harassers.

These were my options. I assessed the situation and chose not to file a complaint. I had every right to make that choice. And until society is willing to accept the validity of claims of harassment, no matter how privileged or powerful the harasser, it is a choice women will continue to make. I do not believe that in the early 1980s I lived and worked in a society, either in Washington or in Tulsa, that would have supported my right to raise a claim of harassment against the head of the EEOC. And given the state of the law and what occurred in 1991, I do not believe that a complaint would have stopped what was happening. For years I made the choice to remain silent about my experience and to push on in my life. I made that choice, like many other women, because I thought that it was my only choice. Even today most women choose to keep to themselves the slights, innuendos, harassment, and abuse they experience—because they are women. I hear from former students, now young lawyers working with seasoned professionals and struggling to maintain their dignity and their jobs in this kind of ongoing balancing act. I hear from middle-aged and older women who believe that their silence has allowed them to survive both economically and socially. In the world according to Senator DeConcini, all these women are sorely lacking in gumption. Yet they function in a world that encourages them to question their own reaction and to stop being "so sensitive" to the pain of their experiences. That alone takes a lot of gumption.

DeConcini also misrepresented the sequence of events that led to my statement to the Senate. No one contests that my first contact with the Senate came at the initiation of Senate staffers; it was a point I sought to stress at the press conference and one that was not debatable. Therefore, not only did I not make a call to the Senate and say that I wanted to complain, but there was never any anonymity. The Senate staffers called me and thus always had my name and my location. By the time of the hearings they had ample information about my background. Even Senator Simpson, in a rare display of probity on the matter, allowed that at least some Democrats on the committee had my name as early as September 23.

What is more important, DeConcini's remarks reveal that he based his dismissal of my charges more on how he thought a woman should respond to harassment than on whether he believed that Thomas had actually harassed me. At one point in the days preceding the hearing, DeConcini said, "I don't say it didn't happen. I say there is another side." Very often the responsibility for ending discriminatory behavior, in whatever form, is placed on the target of the discrimination, rather than the person who carries it out or those in a position of authority to stop it.

In his comments DeConcini described how a victim of discrimination should feel and act. First that person should "get mad," and then she should "complain." If she does not, according to DeConcini, nobody should care, even when a lifetime appointment to the nation's highest court is at stake. In other words, those who do not react in the way prescribed by DeConcini deserve no attention from those who should be concerned about the problem. In focusing on the target's reaction instead of the behavior of the harasser, DeConcini failed to understand that most harassment victims experience a variety of emotions in the face of harassment; anger is just one of them. And different people deal with harassment in different ways. Some women internalize the anger; others deny it.

Filing a complaint in response to harassment is only one way of "getting mad." As I said, it is one that many harassment victims feel would be fruitless. Only 3 percent of reported harassment incidents end in a formal complaint. DeConcini proposed this reaction as the only valid course in response to harassment, though it is one that few harassment targets ever take.

In addition to revealing real ignorance about the harassment issues, DeConcini's comments reveal a good deal of arrogance. Given the negative reactions to charges of sexual harassment, telling women that they should angrily complain, without any consideration of the effectiveness of the complaint mechanism, is tantamount to telling them that they should subject themselves to further abuse.

DeConcini was not a trial judge responding to a plaintiff attempting to bring a claim in federal court ten years after events occurred. He was a member of a committee reviewing the entire record of a nominee for a lifetime appointment. The committee had spent the last few months reviewing Thomas' life as far back as his childhood in Georgia. No one on the committee prevented Thomas or his supporters from bringing in character evidence dating back nearly forty years. Moreover, the committee had spent hours discussing Thomas' role as assistant secretary of education and chair of the EEOC. Thomas' performance in those capacities and his role as a member of the Reagan administration were chief topics of the first round of the confirmation hearing, during which the committee had also received and discussed evidence of Thomas' improprieties in handling expense and travel reimbursement. There were claims that he was reimbursed by the government for what was essentially personal business relating to his membership on the board of his alma mater, Holy Cross University. No one objected that the material was outdated. Nevertheless, when the topic of his conduct in official positions turned to sexual harassment, DeConcini and many other senators balked at the idea of hearing it.

DeConcini and some of his colleagues apparently had a double standard for receiving information, depending on the nature of the information. The committee seemed willing to exclude "old" information on sexual harassment while considering "old" information on practically anything else. If the Senate is unwilling to view evidence of sexual misconduct with the same openness as it views evidence of other types of improprieties, victims of sexual misconduct, most often women, will face trouble when they attempt to inform Senate committees of such behavior, whether in an information-gathering session for legislative purposes, a confirmation hearing, or a disciplinary proceeding such as the Ethics Committee hearings on harassment allegations against Senator Robert Packwood. The double standard casts harassment as "personal behavior" rather than behavior that reflects on professionalism.

DeConcini's willingness to let harassers and those with the power to end harassment off the hook is not shared by the courts. One issue of litigation in the sexual harassment arena is whether an employer is relieved of liability after taking steps to end discrimination in the workplace. Courts scrutinize the employer's sexual harassment policy to determine if it is adequate and evenhandedly enforced. The courts have concluded that it is not enough for an employer simply to say that sexual harassment is prohibited. The employer must establish a procedure under which targets of such behavior can come forward and state a claim without fear of retaliation, and the procedure must provide for the fair investigation and resolution of the complaint should the complaint prevail. The employer does not relieve himself of responsibility for ridding the workplace of harassment by declaring that the target of the behavior should get angry. Nor does the duty to an aggrieved employee end simply because the employee failed to avail herself of the employer's grievance procedure. The employee may still file a lawsuit.

In his press conference DeConcini essentially claimed that the Senate had no duty to investigate my charges because I had not filed a complaint against Thomas ten years ago. DeConcini should not have been allowed to sidestep his responsibility to me, or more important, to the American public, with such a bold assertion, which ignored one critical fact. The responsibility of the Senate Judiciary Committee to investigate the character and fitness of nominees to the Supreme Court is comprehensive in scope and time. It is by no means limited to formal complaints filed against the nominee, nor to events of two, three, or even ten years past.

During the [Senate confirmation] hearing [of Clarence Thomas for Supreme Court Justice], when Senator DeConcini questioned me, our exchange would prove quite revealing. "And the fact that you admit that, in retrospect, maybe you should have done something, you have concluded that it is all someone else's fault; none of it is your fault." What was supposed to be a question became a statement—an accusation. "Yes," I responded. If he meant that the harassment was not my fault, certainly my answer was yes. And if he was referring to the circumstances that brought me before the public, my answer was still yes. I had no say in how his committee had handled my statement, and certainly no part in the leak to the press. "Is that your frame of mind?" DeConcini's dissatisfaction with my response was obvious in his tone. "That is my frame of mind," I answered. Clearly, DeConcini wanted to blame me for what was happening in 1991 because I failed to file a complaint ten years earlier, but I held firm. The hearing was no more my fault than the harassment itself.

On Monday afternoon a group of women requested a meeting with the Senate majority leader, George J. Mitchell of Maine, to discuss a postponement of the Senate vote on the confirmation. The group included black and white women from academic and political backgrounds. Their objective was to persuade Mitchell to delay the vote and allow time for a thorough investigation. They were asked to wait until the senator was available, and one of them finally had to leave because of a prior commitment. The meeting with Senator Mitchell was perhaps more frustrating because of the long wait that preceded it. "My hands are tied. I can't do anything," Mitchell declared. Despite his perceived power as majority leader, he would take no responsibility for the action the Senate was about to take in voting to confirm Judge Thomas to the Court. The schedule for the vote was set, and according to Mitchell it could not be changed. Yet later when Daniel Patrick Moynihan of New York, the senator in charge of the Senate Calendar, threatened to call a week's recess, Mitchell exerted his authority, reminding his colleague that he, not Moynihan, was the majority leader. Senator Mitchell's inaction opened the door for the Republican senators to go on the offensive.

Unconstrained by any sense of senatorial decorum, Senator Alan Simpson appeared on ABC's *Nightline* that evening. He brought with him telephone logs that Thomas supporters had retrieved from his garage, hoping they would kill my claim. More numerous than the eleven calls I had made to Thomas' office at the EEOC in the ten years since I left my job were the calls and remarks that had been blacked out, removed from any public scrutiny. Yet no one questioned Thomas' selection of what the committee would see. Simpson implied that I had "pursued" Thomas. The campaign that began with DeConcini's "blame the victim" remark continued with Simpson's labeling me the aggressor in my relationship with Thomas. And the anticipation of a second round of the Thomas confirmation hearing, which might have been seen as an opportunity for responsible consideration of my claim, seemed instead to provoke greater irresponsibility among some senators. The press appeared to relish their remarks, calling upon senators from the Judiciary Committee in particular.

When Senator Simpson appeared on *Nightline* on October 7, armed with Clarence Thomas' telephone logs, he raised another question I have been asked countless times since: "Why did you keep in touch with him?" To which I must say that I was not threatened by Thomas as a person. I was threatened by the power he had held over me as an employer. That threat ended when I left his employ. Tellingly, so did the behavior.

By no means were Clarence Thomas and I good friends. I did not invite him to my home during the time we worked together. I spent five weeks in Washington during the summer of 1987 without contacting him or his office. My telephone calls to him had each had a work-related purpose. Some commentators have described them as "opportunistic," suggesting that I was seeking something I had no right to expect, though I had worked for Clarence Thomas for two years and had performed my job conscientiously. When I called upon him or his office for information, or to pass along a legitimate request, I did so on the basis of that performance. Never would I have considered those solicitations opportunism. I received no personal gain. Besides, I had not been the one to behave inappropriately. So why should I later allow his behavior to deprive me of a job benefit I had rightfully earned?

Part of the answer to the complex question of why I stayed in touch has to do with the idea of control. By pretending that my departure from the EEOC was cordial, I denied to myself the significance of the harassment. But by staying in touch subsequently, I regained something I hadn't been able to maintain working for Clarence Thomas: professional decorum.

In 1992 I met a retired man who had gone to fight in World War II and left his young bride, his high school sweetheart, at home. She worked to support herself while he was away. When we met, he appeared to be as in love with her as when they were newlyweds. During the hearing he asked her jokingly whether she had ever been harassed, fully expecting she would say no. To his surprise, she said she had been harassed, in fact by their high school principal for whom she worked while he fought in Europe. But he had revered the principal, now a good friend, and rather than cause tension between the two, she kept quiet. Throughout what they both described as a happy marriage, filled with love and open communication, she had denied her own pain to spare his respect for a man who was his "role model." Paradoxically, I am both consoled and saddened by the fact that so many others do the same. I wonder if something in our training tells us to "forgive and forget" or "let bygones be bygones," or any of the other clichés that allow us to deny our hurt.

In stark contrast to Senator Barbara Mikulski, Senator Simpson was exasperated by the prospect of reconvening the confirmation hearing. In a profoundly crass statement, following his *Nightline* appearance Simpson broadcast his ignorance about sexual harassment and the purpose of the upcoming hearing. The tall Wyoming native, who projects a "cowboy" image despite his gray flannel suit and conservative necktie, warned of the treatment I could expect from the Senate:

> It's a harsh thing, a very sad and harsh thing, and Anita Hill will be sucked right into the—the very thing she wanted to avoid most. She will be injured and destroyed and belittled and hounded and harassed, real harassment, different from the sexual kind, just plain old Washington variety harassment which is pretty unique in itself.

I looked for some sympathy in Senator Simpson's words. I found none. I took his message as an unfriendly warning, something just this side of a threat—an attempt to dissuade me from coming forward.

In distinguishing sexual harassment from "real harassment," Simpson's statement suggests that the former is tolerable, if not excusable—that it is mild or harmless, or at least less harmful than the "real" kind he had apparently experienced or inflicted as part of the politics of Washington, D.C. According to Simpson, being "injured and destroyed and belittled and hounded" is a consequence of "real harassment," not sexual harassment. Perhaps because Senator Simpson never experienced sexual harassment, and is not likely to, he did not perceive it as real, injurious, or destructive. What *was* real to Simpson was "plain old Washington variety harassment." The pity is that Simpson could not extend his understanding of Washington-variety harassment to sexual harassment to see that both have the same basis—abuse of power—and the same aim: self-gain through devastating or demoralizing the target.

Nor did Simpson's personal experience with Washington-variety harassment relieve him of his responsibility to attempt to relate to the experience of the thousands of his constituents who understood well that sexual harassment is real harassment. Although Simpson apologized after the hearing for his choice of words, he could not take back the twin message they sent: that sexual harassment is not real and that complaints about sexual harassment should be met with "real harassment." I will not count the number of times, even before the hearing, that I have been threatened with sodomy, rape, assault, and other forms of sexual and nonsexual violence. Some of the callers have used almost the same words: "Now you will know what real harassment is like."

Senator Alan Cranston of California summed up the danger of Senator Simpson's dismissive assessment of my claims in the debate on the postponement of the hearing:

> I am appalled at statements being made that these are not serious charges because they involve verbal, not physical, abuse. I am appalled at the stunning admissions of a lack of sensitivity to the problem of sexual harassment. What has a majority of this body been saying to all the women who are subjected to sexual harassment? Who have been, are now, or will be subjected to sexual harassment?

Needless to say, Simpson's views on "real harassment" did not suggest that he was approaching the hearing with anything like an open mind. And if there was any doubt on that score, his reference to my claim on the second day of the hearing as "sexual harassment crap" extinguished it. Simpson's statement played over and over in my mind during the next few days. I contemplated the prospect of experiencing "real harassment." The statement became self-fulfilling—almost a call for the Republican senators to sink to the level of Simpson's vision of the proceeding. Simpson set the tone for the hearing and his colleagues followed him. Ironically, their view of "real harassment" Washington style was quite similar to what many women who complain about sexual harassment in the workplace experience as well. . . .

Having settled the quarrel about the rules, and then recovered from my family's disorderly entry, at 11:00 a.m. Senator Biden began his questioning of me. The thirty-minute quizzing period began with general inquiries about my background and professional life. Gradually, the questions became more specific and focused on Thomas' behavior at Education and EEOC.

"Let's go back to the first time that you alleged Judge Thomas indicated he had more than a professional interest in you," Senator Biden approached the subject of harassment in a matter-of-fact way. "Do you recall what the first time was and, with as much precision as you can, what he said to you?"

"It either happened at lunch or it happened in his office when he said to me, very casually, you ought to go out with me sometime . . . ," I recalled.

"Was that the extent of that incident?"

"That was the extent of that incident . . . I declined and, at that incident, I think he may have said something about, you know, he didn't understand why I didn't want to go out with him. . . ."

"Would you describe for the committee how you felt at that time when he asked you out? What was your reaction?" the senator questioned.

To describe what took place was difficult, but the emotional impact of having to recall my feelings about what had happened was monumental. I struggled to keep calm. "Well, my reaction at that time was a little surprised, because I had not indicated to him in any way that I knew of that I was interested in dating him. We had developed a good working relationship. It was cordial and it was very comfortable, so I was surprised that he was interested in something else."

The logistics of making arrangements to travel to Washington, informing and gathering my family, friends, and advisers together, had left me little time to prepare for my testimony. Yet as the questioning began I realized that no amount of preparation could have made it easy to address the kinds of questions that, ultimately, Biden asked. Senator Biden's tone became even more somber.

"Now I must ask you to describe once again, and more fully, the behavior that you have alleged [Thomas] engaged in while your boss which you say went beyond the professional conventions and were unwelcome to you. Now, I know these are difficult to discuss, but you must understand that we have to ask you about the . . ."

Perhaps to ease the impact of the intrusion into my memory, Biden asked the question differently. "Did all of the behavior that you have described to us in your written statement to the committee and your oral statement now and what you have said to the FBI, did all of that behavior take place at work?"

"Yes, it did . . . if you are including a luncheon during the workday to be at work, yes," I responded, thankful for the new approach.

But further probing was inevitable, and in short time the senator asked the question which had to be asked: "Can you tell me what incidents occurred, of the ones you described to us, occurred in his office?"

"Well, I recall specifically that the incident involving the Coke can occurred in his office at the EEOC."

"And what was that incident, again?" Biden asked.

"The incident with regard to the Coke can, that statement?" I said, perhaps hoping to avoid repeating what had so disgusted me at the time, having already described it once in the opening statement.

But Biden would not allow me to avoid the matter. He would not rely on the testimony I had given. "Once again for me, please," he half asked, half insisted.

Gradually, something moved from the pit of my stomach and expanded until it became a tightness in my chest. "The incident involved his getting up from a work table, going to his desk, looking at this can and saying, 'Who put pubic hair on my Coke?'"

At once, I was twenty-five years old again, standing in the middle of Thomas' office. By that time I had had several jobs and worked with many different people, but never before had anyone ever uttered such an absurdly vulgar and juvenile comment to me. Disgusted and shocked, I could only shake my head and leave the office. I heard him laughing as I closed the door.

The lapse was temporary. Biden's next question brought me back to the reality of my present situation. In its way it was equally shocking. "Was anyone else in his office at the time?" Biden asked.

"No."

"Are there any other incidents that occurred in his office?"

"I recall at least one instance in his office at the EEOC where he discussed some pornographic material and he brought up the substance or the content of pornographic material."

Chairman: "Again, it is difficult, but for the record, . . . what was the content of what he said?"

I probed my memory for the details the committee seemed to require. "This was a reference to an individual who had a very large penis and he used the name that he had referred to in the pornographic material—."

Senator Biden: "Do you recall what it was?"

"Yes, I do. The name that was referred to was Long Dong Silver," I recalled.

But these details of what had happened would not satisfy the committee. Senator Biden wanted more. "Can you tell us how you felt at the time?"

I collected myself in order to respond. "I felt embarrassed. I had given him an explanation that I thought it was not good for me, as an employee working directly for him, to go out with him. I thought that he did not take seriously my decision to say 'no,' and that he did not respect my having said 'no' to him." I did not know any better words to explain to someone with power how it felt to be utterly powerless. . . .

"I—the conversations about sex, I was much more embarrassed and humiliated by. The two combined really made me feel sort of helpless in a job situation because I really wanted to do the work that I was doing, I enjoyed that work. But I felt that was being put in jeopardy by the other things that were going on in the office. I was really, really very troubled by it and distressed over it." I strained to define feelings that were so basic that defining words seemed unnecessary. Nevertheless, they were feelings so foreign to the committee members that full explanations were imperative if they were to understand.

"Can you tell the committee what was the most embarrassing of all the incidents that you have alleged?"

In the back of my mind I knew that by reciting the details of my experiences I was simply responding to those who claimed that I had overreacted to Thomas' remarks. Perhaps even Biden himself believed that the behavior which I complained about was inoffensive. Knowing why I was being asked to repeat details of the experience did not make it any easier. Yet I tried to keep the purpose in mind as I struggled to recite more of the behavior.

"I think the one that was the most embarrassing was this discussion of pornography involving women with large breasts and engaged in a variety of sex with different people or animals. That was the thing that embarrassed me the most and made me feel the most humiliated."

"If you can, in his words—not your—in his words, can you tell us what, on that occasion, he said to you?" the senator asked, seeking even more particulars.

Within the first hour of my appearance before the committee I was asked to repeat details of experiences which I had already forced myself to describe first to [Senator] Metzenbaum and staff attorney Jim Brudney, then to the committee in my written statement of September 23, then to the FBI, and finally in my opening statement. Inherent in these demands for repetition was a fundamental hostility to the claim, as though each time what I had said before had been insufficient. "Tell us . . . once again . . . what was the most embarrassing . . . in order for us to determine." The hearing had only begun and I found myself wondering, "How many times . . . how much detail . . . how vulgar did the language have to be and . . . how uncomfortable do I have to feel in order for [them] to comprehend what happened to me?" By the end of the day, I would conclude that no amount of detail would satisfy the committee, though at no point during the day's questioning would I consider withdrawing.

"My time is up," Biden announced just before noon. "By the way, I might state for the record, once again we have agreed that we will go back and forth: half-hour conversation on each side. . . ." I had not been a part of this agreement that in essence the Democrats and Republicans would take turns with me.

"Let me yield to my friend from Pennsylvania, Senator Specter," Biden said, concluding his "turn," as Senator Specter prepared for his thirty-minute "conversation" with me.

Specter began by assuring me that he was simply trying "to find out what happened." But I was well aware of Specter's public statement that he had already concluded that he believed Thomas' denials. I thanked him when he asserted that he did not view the hearing "as an adversarial proceeding," still hoping that he would move beyond his initial reaction to the claim and see that his "duties [ran] . . . to the constitutional government and the Constitution." As an attorney he might have placed the significance of a Supreme Court appointment over the partisanship that had prevailed in the debate over whether or not to hold the hearing. Nevertheless, in short order, any hope that Senator Specter would transcend the political was dashed. He began his questioning with an unmistakably prosecutorial tone. He used a familiar cross-examination tactic—a tactic common in sexual harassment cases. He ridiculed my reaction to Thomas' behavior, suggesting that I was being oversensitive, even to the point of misrepresenting my testimony.

"Professor Hill, I can understand that it is uncomfortable, and I don't want to add to that." But his emulation of concern immediately turned to condescension. "You testified this morning, in response to Senator Biden, that the most embarrassing question involved—this is not too bad—women's large breasts. That is a word we use all the time. That was the most embarrassing aspect of what Judge Thomas had said to you."

"No. The most embarrassing aspect was his description of the acts of these individuals, these women, the acts that those particular people would engage in. It wasn't just the breasts; it was the continuation of his story about what happened in those films with the people with this characteristic, physical characteristic," I responded, trying to control my outrage. Senator Specter had taken this mortifying episode of my life in which my supervisor had described to me acts of bestiality and had deliberately reduced its offending elements to the use of the term "breasts," which, witheringly, he had dismissed as "not too bad." Despite the graphic details I had already described, Senator Specter ignored the numerous sexual references far more contemptible than anything merely anatomical and chose to focus on the innocuous-sounding word "breast," suggesting that I was overreacting. Of course, any woman who has ever been made to feel uncomfortable about the size of her breasts would know that even *this* term could be used to embarrass or demean.

By ignoring the far more contemptible and numerous explicit sexual references, the senator focused attention away from Thomas and his behavior and attempted to render a caricature of me and my standard of the offensiveness. A typical reaction to complaints of harassment, Senator Specter's scoffing portrayed me as the silly prude who can't handle normal adult conversation. But even if the senator had correctly reported my testimony, his portrayal of my experience as "not too bad" would nevertheless be inaccurate. Reference to breasts alone could certainly be demeaning. And a supervisor's constant references to women's breasts or breast size could be more damaging yet. Senator Specter's suggestion that a reference to a woman's breast was not a "bad" thing ignored the fact that the workplace is rarely a place where women go to discuss their own anatomy or the anatomy of other women, particularly when the discussion is of a sexual nature.

21. Making Sense of Our Differences: African American Women on Anita Hill

Beverly Grier

The testimony of Professor Anita Hill before the Senate Judiciary Committee in October 1991 had a profound effect on most African American women. I was particularly struck by their diversity of views about Hill's charge of sexual harassment. In the beginning, I assumed that most African American women felt as I and my closest friends and associates did: painful and dangerous though it may be to air our linen before white America, African American women had been silent for too long about sexist oppression by African American men. However, as the circle of women with whom I discussed Hill's charges widened, I began to realize that most of my sisters saw the issue differently from me. Some of the African American women with whom I talked did not believe Hill was telling the truth. Many others felt that her experience of being sexually harassed by Clarence Thomas was a trivial matter. It certainly was not serious enough to keep a Black man off the Supreme Court. Most were very angry, and many were ashamed that Hill had made her charges public. There was some bitterness about the possibility that the charges might prevent the upward climb of an African American male (and, by extension somehow, the upward climb of the race). As it turned out, only a minority of African American women I encountered warmly embraced and defended Hill, heralding her testimony as the beginning of a new era in African American women's struggle against oppression from within the race.

What accounts for the diversity of views expressed by African American women on Hill's charges? How do we explain the absence of solidarity in our support of Hill? Can our disparate and contradictory views be connected in some way? What does our reaction to the Hill-Thomas controversy say about how we value ourselves and how we struggle as women in a racist, sexist, and classist society?

I will explore these questions using formal and informal discussions among groups of African American women in the Boston area. The women come from a variety of educational backgrounds, from those with high school diplomas to those with law and doctorate degrees. Most of the women are middle- and lower-middle-class, and their ages range from eighteen to eighty. Many are not native to the Boston area but, like me, were born and educated in other parts of the United States. Some are my college students. Though not a cross-section of African American women, these women can tell us a great deal about the anger and confusion generated by the double or even triple oppression of race, class, and gender of African American women. In discussions so heated at times that friendships and civility were strained, the ambiguous and divided identities and loyalties that have marked our outlook and forms of struggle since slavery were painfully apparent.

Unlike African American men and European American women, we have yet to articulate and act upon an identity that is ours in particular. This is because of the complexity of our multiple oppression. Most African American women believe that though we are women, we are Blacks first. We believe that racism is and always has been a more powerful force in our lives than sexism. In the current period in which many European Americans no longer hide their racism and in which African American men are under threat of extinction, this perspective is reinforced. Racial solidarity and struggle along racial lines, the argument goes, must take precedence over "in-house" or "family matters" such as the sexism of our men. We can deal with sexism quite easily, on our own, at a later time. I am sympathetic with this view and have held it for most of my life. However, I am becoming increasingly convinced that our situation as an oppressed people and as oppressed women is far more complex than the "race first" line allows. Just as we tell European American feminists that they must acknowledge race and class privilege as well as gender oppression as forces shaping their lives, African American women must acknowledge gender oppression along with race and class oppression as integral forces shaping our lives.

If Kimberly Rae Harbor were alive today, she would testify to this. She was the young African American woman who was repeatedly raped, stabbed, and bludgeoned to death in a park in Boston on Halloween night in 1991. Her attackers were several teenage African American and Hispanic males. The racial line would have us attribute her murder to the pressures of racism, primarily or even solely. It would have us deny the importance of the widespread anger, hostility, and emotional, physical, and sexual abuse that younger African American males, in particular, direct toward their mothers, sisters, girlfriends, and other females in their lives. Is it merely a coincidence that as racism has become more intense, so has sexism? Is it a coincidence that the 1980s and early 1990s have witnessed an increase in racist attacks and in the incidence of violence against women in all communities? We cannot deny the anger and frustration of young men who have been consigned to the permanent reserve army of the unemployed and who are despised, feared, and imprisoned by European American society. But sexism within our community only serves the larger dominant interests. It deflects anger and energy away from the real sources of oppression toward more accessible and acceptable targets, African American women. We will not be able to overturn race and class oppression until we see that it is intimately connected to gender oppression.

Bell hooks put it well when she wrote about the "devaluation" of African American womanhood by white men, white women, African American men, *and* African American women. Socialized by racism and sexism, African American women have been conditioned to "devalue our femaleness and to regard race as the only relevant label of identification" (1984:1)."[1] As a consequence, we identify more readily with the aspirations and frustrations of Clarence Thomas than with the humiliation and pain of Anita Hill. Cynically, Thomas knew he could play on African American racial sensibilities by calling the hearings a "high-tech lynching" when, in fact, the person who was degraded and "lynched" by the process was Hill. As could have been predicted, African American male and female support for Thomas increased after his speech. In spite of the personal experiences most African American women have had with sexual harassment, exploitation, battering, incest, or rape by African American men, we have been so conditioned to devalue our femaleness that we keep silent and label as traitors to the race women like Hill who dare to speak out.

"SHE'S LYING. I JUST DON'T BELIEVE HER"

Unfortunately, like the privileged white males who sat on the Senate Judiciary Committee, many African American women simply did not believe Hill's story. So deep was the distrust that some African American women, like the fourteen white men, resorted to elaboration and fabrication. Hill had to have had an ulterior motive.

1. She's lying. She was probably in love with Clarence Thomas and was angry he did not return her affections. And then he turned around and married a white woman? I think Hill was trying to pay him back.

2. She's envious. You know Black women have a history of bringing down Black men in this country. We never support our men.

3. Hill allowed herself to be used by the leadership of the Democratic Party and the Civil Rights establishment, yes. But she was working out her own personal agenda with Thomas at the same time.

The actual sequence of events—the refusal of Hill to discuss publicly what had happened to her until she was compelled to do so by the FBI in early September 1991, followed by the leakage of the contents of the interviews—suggests to me that for a number of years, Hill was engaged in protecting the reputation and career of Thomas at the expense of her own self-esteem and that she would have continued to do so had it been her choice. However, knowledge of this sequence of events made no difference to the women who expressed disbelief.

What explains this level of distrust? As already suggested, in a society that is profoundly sexist and racist, African American women too often internalize sexist and racist views of themselves. In patriarchal societies, women and men are taught that women are not to be trusted; they are the source of evil, they always have hidden agendas, they are devious and manipulative, and they will lie to get what they want. Most men buy this, and, unfortunately, so do many women. Racism intensifies the mistrust of African American women. We belong not only to a gender that cannot be trusted but to a race that cannot be trusted as well. As a consequence, we become the least trustworthy of all human beings. With our origins in enslavement, the myths surrounding us are numerous: we are disloyal and unfaithful to our men, devious, opportunistic ("golddiggers" in the current lingo); we are sexually insatiable and promiscuous. These myths were and continue to be functional to our sexual and economic exploitation by both European and African American men and by European American women. At some level, Thomas and every other man who has sexually harassed, raped, and otherwise abused an African American woman have been aware of the double burden on African American women. Since we are not to be trusted, we are not to be believed. Anything can be done to us, and the perpetrator will not be punished.

When African American women condemn rather than support the victims of sexual harassment and abuse, we think we are separating ourselves from such women and thereby protecting ourselves from similar treatment. ("Women who are abused ask for it. Only bad women are treated that way.") In fact, we are paving the way for condemnation and disbelief when it is ourselves or our daughters who are abused. Very often, the women who are most vehement in expressing their disbelief are in a state of denial about the abuse they have suffered. Ashamed of having been victims and of having remained silent about it, they wish to silence those women who remind them of their own pain and humiliation.

"WHAT IS SHE CRYING ABOUT? WHAT HE DID TO HER WAS NOTHING, REALLY. HE DIDN'T RAPE HER"

Many African American women, in particular, do not consider verbal abuse a violation of their rights. Some of the women in the discussion groups and many of my students had a difficult time taking Hill's charges seriously because Thomas did not assault her physically. Her treatment was mild, according to them, even if it did occur in the workplace. She should have been able to handle it. Running the verbal gauntlet of the boys or men on the corner and being "felt up" in grade school are familiar experiences to every African American woman who grew up in the community. For too many African American women, and men, such behavior on the part of African American males is neither improper nor unacceptable. We seem to have a narrower definition than other groups of what constitutes proper and improper African American male behavior. Yet if a white man whistles and calls out to one of us, "I'd like to take you home, baby" or "I sure would like some of that," all of us, male and female alike, would quickly name the behavior. It's racist and sexist at the same time.

Here again, our socialization in a racist and sexist society and the multiple sources of our oppression are the keys to explaining why we accept inappropriate behavior from our men. Sexism within the African American community is so pervasive that it is hegemonic. We do not recognize it or name it when we see it. We reproduce it daily in our responses to it and in the way we raise our boys and girls. Sexism has become part of our "culture." It imbues the way strangers on the street, lovers, and other black men talk to and treat us—curse words, references to body parts, sexually explicit details of what they would like to do to us, the rough physical treatment during lovemaking. To reject the language, the playing around, and the lovemaking approach is to open ourselves up to more abuse: "Who do you think you are?" "You too good?" "You must like women." "You must think you white." We try not to see in such abuse the effort to dominate and control us through humiliation and disrespect. After all, these are brothers, and we face the same racist oppression. When most of us heard Hill describe what Thomas said to her, we instantly knew it was true. It sounded so familiar to us. How many of us have tried to ignore or laugh off this kind of treatment from a friend, schoolmate, coworker, or church member, hoping it would eventually stop? It never does. It often gets worse.

Because Hill continued to work for Thomas and because she "followed" him from the Department of Education to the Equal Employment Opportunity Commission, many Americans, European and African, male and female, found it difficult to believe that Thomas's remarks had offended her. As Hill explained during the hearings and subsequently with a greater sense of the victim's syndrome, she was in a vulnerable position in relation to Thomas. She hoped the behavior would stop. She felt it was her fault. Moreover, how would it look if her immediate supervisor, who was also the head of the department, did not write a letter of recommendation for her for a significant period and place of employment? Cordial relations had to be maintained for a considerable time after Hill's government employment. Thomas knew of his power and abused it.

Even when actual physical assaults occur, many African American men and women (like their European American counterparts) are not likely to believe the alleged rape victim. Witness the reaction on the part of many African American men and women of all ages to the Mike Tyson rape case. None of my African American female students believed Desiree Washington had been raped. Roughed up during foreplay or in the process of having sexual intercourse, perhaps, but not raped. "After all," one African American male student remarked, "what did she think she was going up to his room for? A cup of coffee?" Both Tyson and Thomas needed to assert power and control. Forced sex and explicit language were means to this end.

"HOW COULD SHE GO AGAINST A BLACK MAN HEADED FOR THE SUPREME COURT?"

A majority of the women in one discussion group and many of the older women I talked with felt that Hill had betrayed the race by telling what had happened to her. One of my students shook her head and said, "They [the brothers] will point to Hill and say all we do is tear them down. We never build them up." Though most of the women were aware of Thomas's record at the EEOC, of his anti-Civil Rights agenda, and of the contempt he showed for his sister during the hearings, they still wanted him to be appointed to the Supreme Court. Many argued:

4. He will change, discover his roots, upon being appointed for life. He will have no more political debts to pay.

5. It's better to have a Black conservative on the Court than a white conservative. At least there's some hope with a Black.

6. This is our only chance to maintain an African American presence on the Court. We have to support him, no matter what his views are.

7. The elevation and advancement of one Black man serves all Black people.

Most startling to me was the anger and hostility of many women toward Hill. The complexity of our multiple oppressions is at the root of these feelings. Hill appeared to have chosen her identity as a woman over her identity as an African American. What's more, she did so publicly, for European Americans to see and exploit. She washed our dirty linen before the European American public. She broke the unity of the family and set herself up as the primary obstacle in the way of an African American man's ascent to the Supreme Court. She reinforced European American stereotypes about the sexuality of African American men *and* women.

The unveiling of Black sexual stereotypes caused tremendous pain and embarrassment for African Americans. We know that European Americans are extremely curious about Black sexuality. The hearings provided them with an opportunity to satisfy some of that curiosity. Many of us sensed that most European Americans viewed the testimonies of Hill and Thomas not as a confrontation about gender and power relations but as sexual entertainment. And it was Hill's deeds, not Thomas's, that made the "show" possible. Hill's charges against Thomas reinforced the stereotype of the sexually aggressive Black male. (Meanwhile, the charges and rumors about the Kennedys, George Bush, Bill Clinton, Franklin Delano Roosevelt, Gary Hart, Brock Adams, and so on, were statements simply about individual European American men.) Having failed to paint Hill with the brush of promiscuity, the senators accused her of fantasizing about sex. The next best thing. The point was that African American women, like African American men, are obsessed with sex.

More distressing for an elderly friend of mine were the graphic descriptions Hill was forced to give. My friend was torn. On the one hand, she was angry with the senators because she knew they would never have forced a European American woman to convey such details before the entire American public. On the other hand, my friend was angry with Hill for having gone along with it. She felt humiliated as an African American woman. Hill's testimony reinforced for my friend the slavery-era stereotype that African American women are at ease with everything about sex, including talking about breast sizes, penis sizes, and pubic hairs on Coke cans in front of their elderly parents and on national television. I feel my friend was right to be angry with the senators, Arlen Specter and Ted Kennedy alike. The objective of the Republicans was to demean and humiliate Hill. The Democrats just "got off" on her testimony. I must admit I, too, was annoyed with Hill for giving those European American men and the European American public such satisfaction. I remember yelling out at my TV set, "Tell them you will not repeat what you have already read in your statement just for their vicarious sexual gratification!"

"THAT IS ONE BRAVE SISTER"

For reasons that are not completely clear to me, I found that the African American women who were most supportive of Hill were those whose age, education, and professional experiences most closely resembled hers: lawyers, academics, women working in the nonprofit and European American corporate sectors. At a discussion group consisting of such women, I found my ideological home. By the time this group met (in late October), most of us had discovered that not all our sisters shared our views. So, after affirming and building upon our own perspective, we spent some time talking about why we saw things differently from so many of our sisters. We speculated that perhaps Hill appeared too "white" or too assimilated for the tastes of many working and poverty-level African American women. Perhaps Hill was not like anyone they knew and, therefore, did not seem genuine. To many of these women, Hill has been privileged by an elitist education and profession. How could she possibly complain about a little kidding around by her boss?

What is at work here are increasingly different perspectives among African American women based on our education, class, and daily experiences. Though most of the women in this discussion group were from working-class or poor rural Southern backgrounds, education and income have now positioned us in a different arena of daily struggle in racist and sexist America. Our socialization often diverges from that of our working and poverty-level sisters. As professors in predominantly European American universities, as lawyers in a European American-controlled legal system, or as managers in European American corporations, we are confronted overtly and covertly every day with assaults on our intellectual capacities and our right to be where we are. Often, we are in positions of power and authority over European Americans, or we are in positions that demand at least formal respect from coworkers, subordinates, clients, or students. Many European Americans resent this and work diligently to undermine our self-confidence and boost their own. An African American woman or man who succeeds in this world might appear, like Hill, to be less "Black," but he or she is not. Most of us (and I would wager that Hill is one) have learned to switch our cultural personas depending on the dictates of the situation.

This is also a world in which collegiality is critical to keeping one's job and to advancement. For African American men, this means walking a tight rope with racist coworkers. For African American women, this means getting along with racist and sexist coworkers, some of whom might be Black. I can understand Hill's need to remain collegial with Thomas. Though she is a Yale-trained lawyer, Thomas had the power to make her future job searches a rocky or smooth process. It is not unusual in this arena to ask for letters of recommendation from professors or superiors with whom one has not had contact for ten years or so.

At an earlier meeting of a group of African American women in a town south of Boston, I sensed that many were unsympathetic with (indeed, hostile toward) Hill because they could not identify with her. The women in this group were mostly nonprofessionals (city workers, clerks, homemakers), though some were professionals (teachers, nurses, social workers). They were organized around issues of concern to their community, issues related particularly to African American children. There was such disagreement at this meeting about Hill's charges that my head was spinning. The discussion was called to a halt after about an hour because the women realized they had to continue to work together on issues such as education, drugs, crime, police harassment, and racism. At one level, the decision to move on symbolized that gender issues could wait. At another level, it was clear to everyone that gender issues were too painful, too hot to handle. We were having trouble accepting and processing our differences. Though our ambiguous loyalties and identities were apparent, we did not know what to do with them.

CONCLUSION

These issues will not go away. We will be confronted more frequently in the future with sexual oppression within our community. Sometimes our awareness will go forward through outrage over specific events: the failure of most African American male leaders to speak out on Hill's charges or on the way she was treated by the Senate Judiciary Committee; the lack of response of leaders to the rape and brutalization of a New York African American woman just a few weeks before the European American Central Park jogger was raped, and to the acquittal of five European American St. John's University students for the rape of a Jamaican American female student; the misogyny of rap music; the attention given to the crisis of young African American males compared to the neglect of the crisis of young African American females; the "studding" of our young men who have few positive ways of exercising manhood.

Sometimes our awareness will go forward through slow realizations: the ultraconservative voting record of Thomas on the Supreme Court thus far has caused many African American women and men to pause and think. Perhaps it would have been better had he not been confirmed at all.

Note

1. hooks, bell. *Ain't I a Woman: Black Women and Feminism.* Boston: South End Press, 1984.

22. Race, Gender, and Liberal Fallacies

Orlando Patterson

Clarence Thomas's second round of confirmation hearings was one of the finest moments in the modern history of America's democratic culture, a riveting, civic drama that fully engaged the electorate in an exposure and examination of its most basic fears and contradictions concerning class, race, sex and gender.

But even as it urged us to question some of our basic values and positions, it reconfirmed the strength and suppleness of our system of governance. It also revealed one of its greatest weaknesses: there are serious misperceptions of what is really going on in our society, and lamentable failure in our threadbare, predominantly liberal discourse on it.

Thanks to this drama, we have entered an important new phase in the nation's discourse on gender relations, and it goes well beyond the enhanced realization by men that the complaints of women must be taken seriously. Implicit in these hearings was an overdue questioning of the legalistic, neo-Puritan and elitist model of gender relations promoted by the dominant school of American feminists.

We must face certain stark sociological realities: in our increasingly female, work-centered world, most of our relationships, including intimate ones, are initiated in the workplace; gender relations, especially new ones, are complex and invariably ambiguous; in our heterogeneous society, the perception of what constitutes proper and effective male-female relations varies across gender, class, ethnicity and region; and in keeping with our egalitarian ideals, we take pride in the fact that the WASP boss may legitimately desire or want to marry his or her Puerto Rican aide or chauffeur.

One revealing feature of these hearings is the startling realization that Judge Clarence Thomas might well have said what Prof. Anita Hill alleges and yet be the extraordinarily sensitive man his persuasive female defenders claimed. American feminists have no way of explaining this. They have correctly demanded a rigorously enforced protocol of gender relations in the workplace. But they have also demanded that same intimate bonding that men of power traditionally share, the exclusion from which has kept them below the glass ceiling. There is a serious lacuna in the discourse, for we have failed to ask one fundamental question: how is nonerotic intimacy between men and women possible?

Clarence Thomas emerged in the hearings as one of those rare men who, with one or two exceptions, has achieved both: in general, he rigorously enforced the formal rules of gender relations, and he had an admirable set of intimate, nonerotic relations with his female associates.

And yet, tragically, there is his alleged failing with Professor Hill. How is this possible? While middle-class neo-Puritans ponder this question, the mass of the white working class and nearly all African Americans except their intellectually exhausted leaders have already come up with the answer. He may well have said what he is alleged to have said, but he did so as a man not unreasonably attracted to an aloof woman who is esthetically and socially very similar to himself, who had made no secret of her own deep admiration for him.

With his mainstream cultural guard down, Judge Thomas on several misjudged occasions may have done something completely out of the cultural frame of his white, upper-middle-class work world, but immediately recognizable to Professor Hill and most women of Southern working-class backgrounds, white or black, especially the latter.

Now to most American feminists, and to politicians manipulating the nations' lingering Puritan ideals, an obscenity is always an obscenity, an absolute offense against God and the moral order; to everyone else, including all professional social linguists and qualitative sociologists, an obscene expression whether in Chaucerian Britain or the American South, has to be understood in context. I am convinced that Professor Hill perfectly understood the psycho-cultural context in which Judge Thomas allegedly regaled her with his Rabelaisian humor (possibly as a way of affirming their common origins), which is precisely why she never filed a complaint against him.

Raising the issue 10 years later was unfair and disingenuous: unfair because, while she may well have been offended by his coarseness, there is no evidence that she suffered any emotional or career damage, and the punishment she belatedly sought was in no way commensurate with the offense; and disingenuous because she has lifted a verbal style that carries only minor sanction in one subcultural context and thrown it in the overheated cultural arena of mainstream, neo-Puritan America, where it incurs professional extinction.

If my interpretation is correct, Judge Thomas was justified in denying making the remarks, even if he had in fact made them, not only because the deliberate displacement of his remarks made them something else but on the utilitarian moral grounds that any admission would have immediately incurred a self-destructive and grossly unfair punishment.

The hearings also brought to light the fact that the American public is way ahead of its journalistic and social-science commentators with respect to race relations. The sociological truths are that America, while still flawed in its race relations and its stubborn refusal to institute a rational, universal welfare system, is now the least racist white-majority society in the world; has a better record of legal protection of minorities than any other society, white or black; offers more opportunities to a greater number of black persons than any other society, including all those of Africa; and has gone through a dramatic change in its attitude toward miscegenation over the past 25 years.

Increased reports of racial and gender conflicts are actually indicative of things getting better, not worse, as commentators seem to think, since they reflect the greatly increased number of contacts between blacks and whites, and males and females, in competitive, high-powered situations as the number of Thomases and the many capable, strong-willed women we saw during the hearings rapidly increase.

One great good to come out of the hearings was the revelation to the average white American that, superstar athletes, news anchors and politicians aside, not all African Americans are underclass cocaine junkies and criminals, which is an understandable delusion in any white person whose only knowledge of African Americans comes from the press and television.

Above all, they saw in Judge Thomas and Professor Hill two very complex, highly intelligent persons who knew how to get and use power in the mainstream society, and were role models for black and white people alike.

However, perhaps the most remarkable feature of the hearings is the response of the public. Here again, liberal expectations were at odds with realities. It was thought that racism would be reinforced by these hearings—which is one simple-minded reason given for criticizing them—but in fact what has emerged is not only the indifference of the white public to the racial aspect of the proceedings but the degree to which white men and women have identified their own interests and deepest anxieties with the two African American antagonists. Indeed, the only aspect of these hearings likely to have increased racism was the journalists' shrill and self-fulfilling insistence that the nation is exploding with racism. This is one of those cases where the messengers deserved to be shot.

White men, especially those in power, are not tittering in locker rooms about black men, as the commentators all seem to think; instead, they are deeply worried about the implications for their relations with white women brought out by these hearings, as well they might. And women, white and black, are taking all kinds of positions on the issues raised. Indeed, most of Professor Hill's supporters seem to be middle-class white women.

My own daughter, Barbara, a post-feminist young woman brought up by two feminists who came of age in the 60's, believes along with her friends that Judge Thomas did say those raunchy things, should have been told at once what a "dog" he was and reported to the authorities by Professor Hill if his advances had continued to annoy her. But they cannot see the relevance of Judge Thomas's down-home style of courting to his qualifications for the Supreme Court.

African Americans must now realize that these hearings were perhaps the single most important cultural development for them since the great struggles of the civil rights years. Clarence Thomas and Anita Hill suffered inhuman and undeserved pain, tragic pain, in their public ordeal, and they will never be quite the same again. Nor will we all, for what all African Americans won from their pain, "perfected by this deed," this ritual of inclusion, is the public cultural affirmation of what had already been politically achieved: unambiguous inclusion; unquestioned belonging. The culture of slavery is dead.

The great achievement of these hearings, then, has been, first, to bring us to a greater awareness of the progress in racial and gender relations already achieved by this country. Second, superficial liberal stereotypes of blacks as victims or bootstrap heroes are seen for what they are: a new form of racism that finds it hard to imagine African Americans not as a monolithic group but, as several of the African American panelists on TV correctly informed the nation, a diverse aggregate of perhaps 30 million individuals, with all the class differences, subcultural and regional resources, strength, flaws and ideologies we find in other large populations.

Finally, the hearings have also highlighted the need to go beyond mere legalistic protocol in gender relations at the workplace. If women are to break through the glass ceiling, they must escape the trap of neo-Puritan feminism with its reactionary sacralizaton of women's bodies, and along with men develop at the workplace something that America still conspicuously lacks: a civilized culture of intimate social intercourse between men and women that recognizes, and contains, the frailties of male and female passions. It's not going to be easy, but these extraordinary hearings have pushed us in the right direction.

❖ 23. The Fall of Bob Packwood

Allan Freedman

The evidence is voluminous, 40 pounds and 10,145 pages, a rare glimpse into the private musings of a public man. Buried in the 10 green volumes are details as mundane as dinner plans and as lurid as a tryst with a staffer on an office rug.

The evidence against Sen. Bob Packwood, R-Ore., released by the Senate Ethics Committee on Sept. 7, includes in detail the stories of women who have accused him of sexual misconduct, numerous illustrations of how the senator altered his diaries, and conversations about soliciting employment for his ex-wife from lobbyists.

The bound volumes of evidence and the 174-page report by the committee counsel include page after page illustrating why the panel rejected Packwood's characterization of himself as an "overeager kisser" and instead saw a pattern of abuse of office.

Among the more striking aspects of the compilation is Packwood's unvarnished bravado and the contrasting recollections by the women who have accused him.

In his own mind, Packwood appeared to be a man who had an abundance of confidence in his sexuality, who joked that he was performing his "Christian duty" to have sex with a staff member. His recollections, laid out in a taped diary that the committee obtained under subpoena, tell a tale of sex and power, of having "made love" with 22 aides and expressing passionate feelings for 75 others.

At one point in his diary, he contends that the document would reveal "nothing about being a rejected suitor—only my successful exploits."

Yet to many of the women who told their stories to the Senate Ethics Committee, Packwood cut a sometimes awkward and often threatening figure. In the case of Paige Wagers, a mail clerk who worked for Packwood in 1975–76, the panel concluded that Packwood left a painful and indelible emotional scar.

According to an account verified by the committee, Packwood pinned her, held her hair in one hand, bent her head backwards and kissed her, sticking his tongue into her mouth. In a subsequent incident, he tried to kiss her in the basement of the Capitol.

The committee report concluded that these incidents caused her to be "hurt in every possible way . . . [so] that emotionally she has remained frozen in time."

Packwood told the committee that he did not recall any encounters with Wagers. Packwood cast some doubt on the veracity of his diary, saying in a deposition, "I might relate a conversation that did not take place on a subject that did not take place."

But the committee counsel's report concludes that the diaries were in fact "an attempt by Sen. Packwood to accurately recall events which he witnessed."

The committee found that Packwood selectively altered his diaries, specifically revising sections that might prove damaging.

In the case of sexual misconduct and other allegations, the evidence taken collectively revealed to the committee a clear pattern that, according to the counsel's report, "reflect an abuse of his United States Senate office by Sen. Packwood, and . . . this conduct is of such a nature as to bring discredit upon the Senate."

SEXUAL MISCONDUCT

In its resolution to expel Packwood, the Ethics Committee found "substantial credible evidence" that Packwood may have abused his office by "engaging in a pattern of sexual misconduct between 1969 and 1990."

The résumé of Packwood's accusers ran the gamut from Hill staff to campaign workers. . . .

During an encounter with a Capitol Hill elevator operator in 1977, the report said, Packwood tilted his head to one side and said "kiss"—at which point he grabbed the woman's shoulders, pushed her to the side wall of the elevator and kissed her on the lips.

Packwood told the committee he did not recall the incident, but the committee verified the account.

In another encounter at the elevator operator's house, the report said, Packwood, who was then married, told her that he wanted to make love to her and have her supply information on overheard conversations in the elevator.

The woman escorted Packwood out of her home, but he later banged on the door and telephoned her, repeating his wish to spend the night with her. After this incident, Packwood continued to grab and kiss her in the elevator.

A 1990 incident involved an unnamed staffer who was the press secretary for the minority staff of the Senate Finance Committee.

The woman and several other staff members joined Packwood at the Irish Times, a Capitol Hill bar, to celebrate the passage of the 1990 budget agreement. Toward the end of the evening, the report said, Packwood told the staff member that they needed to find some way to "do this" without letting Elaine Franklin, his chief of staff, know about it.

The staffer told the committee that it then dawned on her that Packwood was under the impression that they were about to initiate an affair. This made her nervous. She followed Packwood back to his office, where Packwood said he had information on labor leaders to show her.

❖ PACKWOOD: THE CHARGES

The Senate Ethics Committee's case against Bob Packwood, R-Ore., was formally outlined in a May 16 resolution adopted unanimously by the six-member panel. Following is a summary of the alleged incidents of possible sexual misconduct that the committee investigated.

- **1990.** In his Washington Senate office, Packwood kissed a staff member on the lips.
- **1985.** In Bend, Ore., Packwood "fondled a campaign worker as they danced." Later, in Eugene, Ore., he grabbed the same worker's face "with his hands, pulled her toward him and kissed her on the mouth, forcing his tongue into her mouth."
- **1981 or 1982.** In his Washington Senate office, Packwood kissed a lobbyist on the mouth.
- **1981.** In a room in the Capitol basement, he grabbed a former staff assistant and kissed her, forcing his tongue into her mouth. While the same woman was on Packwood's staff in 1975, he grabbed her, pinned her against a wall or desk, fondled her and kissed her, forcing his tongue into her mouth.
- **1980 or 1981.** In a Portland, Ore., hotel, Packwood kissed a desk clerk on two separate occasions.
- **1979.** In Washington, he kissed a Senate staff member on the lips.
- **1977.** In a Capitol elevator, he pushed the operator up against the wall, kissed her on the lips, and later "came to this person's home, kissed her and asked her to make love with him."
- **1977.** In an Oregon motel room, Packwood "grabbed a prospective employee by her shoulders, pulled her to him and kissed her."
- **1975.** In his Washington Senate office, he kissed a staff assistant on the mouth.
- **Early 1970s.** In his Portland Senate office, Packwood "chased a staff assistant around a desk."
- **1970.** In a Portland restaurant, Packwood "ran his hand up the leg of a dining room hostess and touched her crotch area."
- **1970.** In his Washington Senate office, Packwood kissed a staff member on the mouth.
- **1969.** In his Washington Senate office, he "made suggestive comments to a prospective employee."
- **1969.** At his home, Packwood "grabbed an employee of another senator who was baby-sitting for him, rubbed her shoulders and back, and kissed her on the mouth. He also put his arm around her and touched her leg as he drove her home."
- **1969.** In his Portland Senate office, he "grabbed a staff worker, stood on her feet, grabbed her hair, forcibly pulled her head back and kissed her on the mouth, forcing his tongue into her mouth. Sen. Packwood also reached under her skirt and grabbed at her undergarments."

Packwood grabbed the staffer by the shoulders with both hands and exclaimed, "God, you're great," and kissed her on the lips. He later told the committee that the staffer was indiscreet, fantasized, lied and was not to be trusted, but he supplied no specifics.

The committee confirmed the incident with a number of witnesses, including Franklin.

"Sen. Packwood himself has not denied that the incident occurred," the committee report said. "He has testified that he was too drunk to remember the details of the evening."

DIARIES ALTERED

The second major violation detailed in the committee expulsion resolution involved Packwood's altering his diaries. The committee found that his conduct reflected on the Senate and possibly "violated federal law" regarding evidence tampering.

The resolution states that sometime between December 1992 and November 1993, Packwood "intentionally altered diary materials that he knew or should have known the committee had sought or would likely seek" as part of its preliminary inquiry, which began Dec. 1, 1992.

Sections of the diaries flagged by the committee range from questions about possible campaign violations to sexual misconduct beyond the scope of the charges by Packwood's accusers.

Regarding possible sexual misconduct, one passage involves an unnamed staffer identified as S-1. In his original tape recordings for June 29, 1993, Packwood reflects on his own concerns about the woman's recollection of their sexual encounter.

Did she tell another staff member that "we had a sexual relationship where I forced myself on her or what?" asked Packwood. "I should have thought to pursue it."

In the altered version, Packwood deleted this reference. That raised questions for the committee about whether there "could have been a nonconsensual aspect to Sen. Packwood's relationship with the staffer."

During questioning by the committee staff, the staffer declined to answer questions about unwanted advances.

The committee report noted that elsewhere in the diary Packwood details a consensual sexual encounter with the same staffer in his office. That entry, for Nov. 21, 1989, has been the subject of lurid news accounts.

While other staffers milled about in an outer office, Packwood had sexual intercourse with the woman, and afterward the two rested for more than an hour in the nude on the senator's office rug.

"She is a sexy thing," wrote Packwood. "Bright eyes and hair and that ability to shift her hips."

At one point, Packwood recalls the woman saying admiringly, "You have no idea the hold you have over people."

❖ 24. *Jones v. Clinton*

U.S. District Court, Arkansas, Western Division

SUSAN WEBBER WRIGHT, District Judge

The plaintiff in this lawsuit, Paula Corbin Jones, seeks civil damages from William Jefferson Clinton, President of the United States, and Danny Ferguson, a former Arkansas State Police Officer, for alleged actions beginning with an incident in a hotel suite in Little Rock, Arkansas. This case was previously before the Supreme Court of the United States to resolve the issue of Presidential immunity but was remanded to this Court following the Supreme Court's determination that there is no constitutional impediment to allowing plaintiff's case to proceed while the President is in office. . . . Following remand, the President filed a motion for judgment on the pleadings and dismissal of the complaint pursuant to Rule 12(c) of the Federal Rules of Civil Procedure. Ferguson joined in the President's motion. By Memorandum Opinion and Order dated August 22, 1997, this Court granted in part and denied in part the President's motion. . . . The Court dismissed plaintiff's defamation claim against the President, dismissed her due process claim for deprivation of a property interest in her State employment, and dismissed her due process claims for deprivation of a liberty interest based on false imprisonment and injury to reputation, but concluded that the remaining claims in plaintiff's complaint stated viable causes of action. Plaintiff subsequently obtained new counsel and filed a motion for leave to file a first amended complaint, which the Court granted, albeit with several qualifications. . . . The matter is now before the Court on motion of both the President and Ferguson for summary judgment pursuant to Rule 56 of the Federal Rules of Civil Procedure. Plaintiff has responded in opposition to these motions, and the President and Ferguson have each filed a reply to plaintiff's response to their motions. For the reasons that follow, the Court finds that the President's and Ferguson's motions for summary judgment should both be and hereby are granted.

I.

This lawsuit is based on an incident that is said to have taken place on the afternoon of May 8, 1991, in a suite at the Excelsior Hotel in Little Rock, Arkansas. President Clinton was Governor of the State of Arkansas at the time, and plaintiff was a State employee with the Arkansas Industrial Development Commission ("AIDC"), having begun her State employment on March 11, 1991. Ferguson was an Arkansas State Police officer assigned to the Governor's security detail.

According to the record, then-Governor Clinton was at the Excelsior Hotel on the day in question delivering a speech at an official conference being sponsored by the AIDC. Plaintiff states that she and another AIDC employee, Pamela Blackard, were working at a registration desk for the AIDC when a man approached the desk and informed her and Blackard that he was Trooper Danny Ferguson, the Governor's bodyguard. She states that Ferguson made small talk with her and Blackard and that they asked him if he had a gun as he was in street clothes and they "wanted to know." Ferguson acknowledged that he did and, after being asked to show the gun to them, left the registration desk to return to the

Governor. The conversation between plaintiff, Blackard, and Ferguson lasted approximately five minutes and consisted of light, friendly banter; there was nothing intimidating, threatening, or coercive about it.

Upon leaving the registration desk, Ferguson apparently had a conversation with the Governor about the possibility of meeting with plaintiff, during which Ferguson states the Governor remarked that plaintiff had "that come-hither look," i.e. "a sort of [sexually] suggestive appearance from the look or dress."[1] He states that "some time later" the Governor asked him to "get him a room, that he was expecting a call from the White House and . . . had several phone calls that he needed to make," and asked him to go to the car and get his briefcase containing the phone messages. Ferguson states that upon obtaining the room, the Governor told him that if plaintiff wanted to meet him, she could "come up."

Plaintiff states that Ferguson later reappeared at the registration desk, delivered a piece of paper to her with a four-digit number written on it, and said that the Governor would like to meet with her in this suite number. She states that she, Blackard, and Ferguson talked about what the Governor could want and that Ferguson stated, among other things, "We do this all the time." Thinking that it was an honor to be asked to meet the Governor and that it might lead to an enhanced employment opportunity, plaintiff states that she agreed to the meeting and that Ferguson escorted her to the floor of the hotel upon which the Governor's suite was located.

Plaintiff states that upon arriving at the suite and announcing herself, the Governor shook her hand, invited her in, and closed the door. She states that a few minutes of small talk ensued, which included the Governor asking her about her job and him mentioning that Dave Harrington, plaintiff's ultimate superior within the AIDC and a Clinton appointee, was his "good friend." Plaintiff states that the Governor then "unexpectedly reached over to [her], took her hand, and pulled her toward him, so that their bodies were close to each other." She states she removed her hand from his and retreated several feet, but that the Governor approached her again and, while saying, "I love the way your hair flows down your back" and "I love your curves," put his hand on her leg, started sliding it toward her pelvic area, and bent down to attempt to kiss her on the neck, all without her consent. Plaintiff states that she exclaimed, "What are you doing?," told the Governor that she was "not that kind of girl," and "escaped" from the Governor's reach "by walking away from him." She states she was extremely upset and confused and, not knowing what to do, attempted to distract the Governor by chatting about his wife. Plaintiff states that she sat down at the end of the sofa nearest the door, but that the Governor approached the sofa where she had taken a seat and, as he sat down, "lowered his trousers and underwear, exposed his penis (which was erect) and told [her] to 'kiss it.'"[2] She states that she was "horrified" by this and that she "jumped up from the couch" and told the Governor that she had to go, saying something to the effect that she had to get back to the registration desk. Plaintiff states that the Governor, "while fondling his penis," said, "Well, I don't want to make you do anything you don't want to do," and then pulled up his pants and said, "If you get in trouble for leaving work, have Dave call me immediately and I'll take care of it." She states that as she left the room (the door of which was not locked), the Governor "detained" her momentarily, "looked sternly" at her, and said, "You are smart. Let's keep this between ourselves." . . .

Plaintiff states that the Governor's advances to her were unwelcome, that she never said or did anything to suggest to the Governor that she was willing to have sex with him, and that during the time they were together in the hotel suite, she resisted his advances although she was "stunned by them and intimidated by who he was." She states that when the Governor referred to Dave Harrington, she "understood that he was telling her that he had control over Mr. Harrington and over her job, and that he was willing to use that power." She states that from that point on, she was "very fearful" that her refusal to submit to the Governor's advances could damage her career and even jeopardize her employment.

Plaintiff states that when she left the hotel suite, she was in shock and upset but tried to maintain her composure. She states she saw Ferguson waiting outside the suite but that he did not escort her back to the registration desk and nothing was said between them. Ferguson states that five or ten minutes after plaintiff exited the suite he joined the Governor for their return to the Governor's Mansion and that the Governor, who was working on some papers that he had spread out on the desk, said, "She came up here, and nothing happened."

Plaintiff states she returned to the registration desk and told Blackard some of what had happened. Blackard states that plaintiff was shaking and embarrassed. Following the Conference, plaintiff states she went to the workplace of a friend, Debra Ballentine, and told her of the incident as well. Ballentine states that plaintiff was upset and crying. Later that same day, plaintiff states she told her sister, Charlotte Corbin Brown, what had happened and, within the next two days, also told her other sister, Lydia Corbin Cathey, of the incident. Brown's observations of plaintiff's demeanor apparently are not included in the record. Cathey, however, states that plaintiff was "bawling" and "squalling," and that she appeared scared, embarrassed, and ashamed.

Ballentine states that she encouraged plaintiff to report the incident to her boss or to the police, but that plaintiff declined, pointing out that her boss was friends with the Governor and that the police were the ones who took her to the hotel suite. Ballentine further states that plaintiff stated she did not want her fiance to know of the incident and that she "just want[ed] this thing to go away." Plaintiff states that what the Governor and Ferguson had said and done made her "afraid" to file charges.

Plaintiff continued to work at AIDC following the alleged incident in the hotel suite. One of her duties was to deliver documents to and from the Office of the Governor, as well as other offices around the Arkansas State Capitol. She states that in June 1991, while performing these duties for the AIDC, she encountered Ferguson who told her that Mrs. Clinton was out of town often and that the Governor wanted her phone number and wanted to see her. Plaintiff states she refused to provide her phone number to Ferguson. She states that Ferguson also asked her how her fiance, Steve, was doing, even though she had never told Ferguson or the Governor his name, and that this "frightened" her. Plaintiff states that she again encountered Ferguson following her return to work from maternity leave and that he said he had "told Bill how good looking you are since you've had the baby." She also states that she was "accosted" by the Governor in the Rotunda of the Arkansas State Capitol when he "draped his arm over her, pulled her close to him and held her tightly to his body," and said to his bodyguard, "Don't we make a beautiful couple: Beauty and the Beast?" Plaintiff additionally states that on an unspecified date, she was waiting in the Governor's outer office on a delivery run when the Governor entered the office, patted her on the shoulder, and in a "friendly fashion" said, "How are you doing, Paula?"

Plaintiff states that she continued to work at AIDC "even though she was in constant fear that [the Governor] would retaliate against her because she had refused to have sex with him." She states this fear prevented her from enjoying her job. Plaintiff states that she was treated "very rudely" by certain superiors in AIDC, including her direct supervisor, Clydine Pennington, and that this "rude treatment" had not happened prior to her encounter with the Governor. She states that after her maternity leave, she was transferred to a position which had much less responsibility and that much of the time she had nothing to do. Plaintiff states that she was not learning anything, that her work could not be fairly evaluated, and that as a result, she could not be fairly considered for advancement and other opportunities. She states that Pennington told her the reason for the transfer was that her prior position had been eliminated, but that she later learned this was untrue, as her former position was being occupied by another employee. Plaintiff states that she repeatedly expressed to Pennington an interest in transferring to particular positions at a higher "grade" which involved more challenging duties, more potential for advancement, and more compensation, but that Pennington always discouraged her from doing so and told her she should not bother to apply for those positions. She goes on to state that her superiors exhibited hostility toward her by moving her work location, refusing to give her meaningful work, watching her constantly, and failing to give her flowers on Secretary's Day in 1992, even though all the other women in the office received flowers.

Plaintiff voluntarily terminated her employment with AIDC on February 20, 1993, in order to move to California with her husband, who had been transferred. She states that in January 1994, while visiting family and friends in Arkansas, she was informed of an article in The American Spectator magazine that she claims referred to her alleged encounter with the Governor at the Excelsior Hotel and incorrectly suggested that she had engaged in sexual relations with the Governor. Plaintiff states that she also encountered Ferguson in a restaurant during this same time and that he indicated he was the source for the article and that he knew she had refused the Governor's alleged advances because, he said, "Clinton told me you wouldn't do anything anyway, Paula."

On February 11, 1994, at an event attended by the media, plaintiff states that she publicly asked President Clinton to acknowledge the incident mentioned in the article in The American Spectator, to state that she had rejected his advances, and to apologize to her, but that the President responded to her request for an apology by having his press spokespersons deliver a statement on his behalf that the incident never happened and that he never met plaintiff. Thereafter, on May 6, 1994, plaintiff filed this lawsuit. . . .

II.

The President moves for summary judgment. . . .

Summary judgment is appropriate when "the pleadings, depositions, answers to interrogatories, and admissions on file, together with the affidavits, if any, show that there is no genuine issue as to any material fact and that the moving party is entitled to a judgment as a matter of law." . . . The nonmoving party may not rest on mere allegations or denials of his pleading, but must "come forward with 'specific facts showing that there is a genuine issue for trial.'"

. . . Plaintiff recognized that courts have separated sexual harassment claims into two categories—*quid pro quo* cases and hostile work environment cases—and represented to this Court that her allegations, as analyzed under Title VII, were sufficient to state claims under both categories. Specifically, plaintiff stated with respect to her *quid pro quo* claim that sexual harassment occurs when, among other things, "rejection of such conduct by an individual is used as the basis for employment decisions," citing as support for this claim Title VII cases and guidelines promulgated by the Equal Employment Opportunity Commission ("EEOC"), and stated with respect to her hostile environment claim, again citing Title VII cases and EEOC guidelines. . . . Several of this Court's discovery rulings in favor of plaintiff were premised on this Court's understanding and plaintiff's representations (in her complaint and elsewhere) that she was asserting workplace harassment as understood in reference to Title VII standards, *i.e.,* that she suffered tangible job detriments for her refusal to submit to Governor Clinton's alleged advances. Based on plaintiff's prior representations and the clear weight of authority, the Court will look to Title VII in addressing plaintiff's *quid pro quo* and hostile work environment sexual harassment claims. . . .

To make a prima facie case of *quid pro quo* sexual harassment, this plaintiff *must* show, among other things, that her refusal to submit to unwelcome sexual advances or requests for sexual favors resulted in a tangible job detriment . . . "[A] supervisor's mere threat or promise of job-related harm or benefits in exchange for sexual favors does not constitute *quid pro quo* harassment. . . ."

Apparently recognizing the infirm ground upon which her assertion of tangible job detriments rests (which will be discussed *infra*), plaintiff *first* argues that a showing of a tangible job detriment is not an essential . . . element of an action for *quid pro quo* sexual harassment under Title VII. The Court rejects this argument as it conflicts with the Eighth Circuit's requirement that a refusal to submit to unwelcome sexual advances or requests for sexual favors resulted in a tangible . . . job detriment, . . . and conflicts with the majority of the other circuits on this point as well, including the recent decisions cited from the Fifth Circuit in *Sanders,* 134 F.3d 331, and the District of Columbia Circuit in *Gary,* 313 U.S. App. D.C. 403, 59 F.3d 1391. . . .

Even without benefit of the settled authority requiring a showing of a tangible job detriment in *quid pro quo* cases, the three cases upon which plaintiff relies in support of her argument, *Nichols v. Frank,* 42 F.3d 503 (9th Cir. 1994), *Karibian v. Columbia Univ.,* 14 F.3d 773 (2nd Cir. 1994), and *Jansen v. Packaging Corp. of America,* 123 F.3d 490 (7th Cir. 1997). . . . *Burlington Indus., Inc. v. Ellerth,* 139 L. Ed. 2d 865, 118 S. Ct. 876 (Jan. 23, 1998), do not obviate the need for a showing of a tangible job detriment under the facts of this case. First, *Nichols* and *Karibian* were "submission" cases in which the victims of sexual harassment submitted to the unwelcome sexual advances. Plaintiff, by contrast, alleges that she *resisted* Governor Clinton's alleged advances and thereby suffered reprisals in her workplace. The court in *Karibian* recognized the distinction between so-called "submission" and "refusal" cases, noting that "in the nature of things, evidence of economic harm will not be available to support the claim of the employee who submits to the supervisor's demands." . . . Both *Nichols* and *Karibian* . . . were addressing the narrow situations before them in which the victim submitted to the demands for sexual favors and do not stand for the proposition that a showing of a tangible job detriment is unnecessary in a *quid pro quo* sexual harassment case where, as here, it is claimed that the alleged advances were resisted.

While it is true that the Seventh Circuit in *Jansen* concluded that a "clear and unambiguous" *quid pro quo* threat that "clearly conditions concrete job benefits or detriments on compliance with sexual demands" can constitute an actionable claim "even if the threat remains unfulfilled," plaintiff acknowledges that no one, including Governor Clinton, ever told her that if she refused to submit to his alleged advances it would have a negative effect on her job, that she had to submit to his alleged advances in order to receive job benefits, or that the Governor would use his relationship with AIDC Director Dave Harrington to penalize her in her job. She merely states that "reading between the lines, she "knew what [the Governor] meant" when he allegedly indicated in the hotel suite that Harrington was his good friend. Be that as it may, the Governor's alleged statements do not in any way constitute a clear threat that clearly conditions concrete job benefits or detriments on compliance with sexual demands. Plaintiff's claim therefore would not survive a *Jansen* analysis, her "reading between the lines" notwithstanding. . . .

Based on the foregoing, the Court finds that a showing of a tangible job detriment is an essential element of plaintiff's *quid pro quo* sexual harassment claim. It is that issue to which the Court now turns.

As evidence of tangible job detriments (or adverse employment action), plaintiff claims the following occurred after she resisted Governor Clinton's alleged advances on May 8, 1991: (1) she was discouraged from applying for more attractive jobs and seeking reclassification at a higher pay grade within the AIDC; (2) her job was changed to one with fewer responsibilities, less attractive duties and less potential for advancement—and the reason given for the change proved to be untrue; (3) she was effectively denied access to grievance procedures that would otherwise have been available to victims of sexual harassment; and (4) she was mistreated in ways having tangible manifestations, such as isolating her physically, making her sit in a location from which she was constantly watched, making her sit at her workstation with no work to do, and singling her out as the only female employee not to be given flowers on Secretary's Day. The Court has carefully reviewed the record in this case and finds nothing in plaintiff's employment records, her own testimony, or the testimony of her supervisors showing that plaintiff's reaction to Governor Clinton's alleged advances affected tangible aspects of her compensation, terms, conditions, or privileges of employment.

Plaintiff's claim that she was discouraged from applying for more attractive jobs and seeking reclassification at a higher pay grade within the AIDC does not demonstrate any "tangible" job detriment as she has not identified a single specific job which she desired or applied for at AIDC but which she had been discouraged from seeking. When asked for such specific information, plaintiff merely testified that the unidentified jobs she sought were "a grade higher" but that her supervisor "would always discourage me and make me believe that I could grow within the administrative services, which in fact I didn't. I got degrade—downgraded." She further states that those "few" times that she would talk to her supervisor and receive discouragement, she "would go ahead and fill out an application maybe or something." There is no record of plaintiff ever applying for another job within AIDC, however, and the record shows that not only was plaintiff's position never downgraded, her position was reclassified upward from a Grade 9 classification to a Grade 11 classification, thereby increasing her annual salary. Indeed, it is undisputed that plaintiff received every merit increase and cost-of-living allowance for which she was eligible during her nearly two-year tenure with the AIDC and consistently received satisfactory job evaluations. Specifically, on July 1, 1991, less than two months after the alleged incident that is the subject of this lawsuit, plaintiff received a cost-of-living increase and her position was reclassified from Grade 9 to Grade 11; on August 28, 1991, plaintiff received a satisfactory job evaluation from her supervisor, Clydine Pennington; and on March 11, 1992, the one-year anniversary of her hire date with AIDC, plaintiff received another satisfactory evaluation from Pennington and Cherry Duckett, Deputy Director of AIDC, which entitled her to a merit raise. In addition, plaintiff was given a satisfactory job review in an evaluation covering the period of March 1992 until her voluntary departure from the AIDC in February 1993. Plaintiff signed this review on February 16, 1993, and would have received another merit increase one month later in accordance with this review had she elected to continue her employment at AIDC.

It is plaintiff's burden to come forward with "specific facts" showing that there is a genuine issue for trial, and the Court finds that her testimony on this point, being of a most general and non-specific nature (and in some cases contradictory to the record), simply does not suffice to create a genuine issue of fact regarding any tangible job detriment as a result of her having allegedly been discouraged from seeking more attractive jobs and reclassification. . . .

Equally without merit is plaintiff's assertion that following her return from maternity leave in September 1992, she suffered a tangible job detriment when her job was changed to one with fewer responsibilities, less attractive duties and less potential for advancement. These matters do not constitute a tangible job detriment as it is undisputed that there was no diminution in plaintiff's salary or change in her job classification following her return from maternity leave and, further, that her last review at AIDC following her return was positive and would have entitled her to another merit increase had she not resigned her position in order to move to California with her husband. Changes in duties or working conditions that cause no materially significant disadvantage, such as diminution in title, salary, or benefits, are insufficient to establish the adverse conduct required to make a prima facie case.

Although plaintiff states that her job title upon returning from maternity leave was no longer that of purchasing assistant and that this change in title impaired her potential for promotion, her job duties prior to taking maternity leave and her job duties upon return-ing to work both involved data input; the difference being that instead of responsibility for data entry of AIDC purchase orders and driving records, she was assigned data entry re-sponsibilities for employment applications. That being so, plaintiff cannot establish a tan-gible job detriment. A transfer that does not involve a demotion in form or substance and involves only minor changes in working conditions, with no reduction in pay or benefits, will not constitute an adverse employment action, "[o]therwise every trivial personnel ac-tion that an irritable . . . employee did not like would form the basis of a discrimination suit." . . . Whether or not the reasons given for the change were untrue, plaintiff's alle-gations describe nothing "more disruptive than a mere inconvenience or an alteration of job responsibilities."

The Court also rejects plaintiff's claim that she was effectively denied access to grievance procedures that would otherwise have been available to victims of sexual harassment. Plaintiff merely states that from her "perspective," it "appeared very unlikely that any good would come from pursuing a grievance," and that "it was natural for her to conclude that invoking the grievance procedure would be futile and perhaps worse." As the Court has previously noted, however, plaintiff acknowledges that she was never threatened with ad-verse employment action if she did not submit to the Governor's alleged advances, but that she was only "read[ing] between the lines." Such subjective perceptions and beliefs re-garding the efficacy of invoking any grievance procedures are nothing more than "specula-tion and conjecture" and do not constitute a tangible job detriment. . . .

Finally, the Court rejects plaintiff's claim that she was subjected to hostile treatment hav-ing tangible effects when she was isolated physically, made to sit in a location from which she was constantly watched, made to sit at her workstation with no work to do, and sin-gled out as the only female employee not to be given flowers on Secretary's Day. Plaintiff may well have perceived hostility and animus on the part of her supervisors, but these per-ceptions are merely conclusory in nature and do not, without more, constitute a tangible job detriment. Absent evidence of some more tangible change in duties or working condi-tions that constitute a material employment disadvantage, which the Court has already de-termined does not exist, general allegations of hostility and personal animus are not suffi-cient to demonstrate any adverse employment action that constitutes the sort of ultimate decision intended to be actionable under Title VII.

Similarly, plaintiff's allegations regarding her work station being moved so that she had to sit directly outside Pennington's office and, at times, not having work to do, describe nothing more than minor or de minimis personnel matters which, again without more, are insufficient to constitute a tangible job detriment or adverse employment action. . . .

Although it is not clear why plaintiff failed to receive flowers on Secretary's Day in 1992, such an omission does not give rise to a federal cause of action in the absence of evidence of some more tangible change in duties or working conditions that constitute a material employment disadvantage.

In sum, the Court finds that a showing of a tangible job detriment or adverse employment action is an essential element of plaintiff's *quid pro quo* sexual harassment claim and that plaintiff has not demonstrated any tangible job detriment or adverse employment action for her refusal to submit to the Governor's alleged advances. The President is therefore entitled to summary judgment on plaintiff's claim of *quid pro quo* sexual harassment.

The Court now turns to plaintiff's hostile work environment claim. Unlike *quid pro quo* sexual harassment, hostile work environment harassment arises when "sexual conduct has the purpose or effect of unreasonably interfering with an individual's work performance or creating an intimidating, hostile, or offensive working environment." To prevail on a hostile work environment cause of action, a plaintiff must establish, among other things, that she was subjected to unwelcome sexual harassment based upon her sex that affected a term, condition, or privilege of employment. The behavior creating the hostile working environment need not be overtly sexual in nature, but it must be "'unwelcome' in the sense that the employee did not solicit or invite it, and the employee regarded the conduct as undesirable or offensive." The harassment must also be sufficiently severe or pervasive "to alter the conditions of employment and create an abusive working environment." . . .

The President essentially argues that aside from the alleged incident at the Excelsior Hotel, plaintiff alleges only two other contacts with him, alleges only a few additional contacts with Ferguson, and contains conclusory claims that plaintiff's supervisors were rude. He argues that taken individually or as a whole, these contacts do not in any way constitute the kind of pervasive, intimidating, abusive conduct that courts require to establish a hostile work environment claim. The Court agrees.

In assessing the hostility of an environment, a court must look to the totality of the circumstances. Circumstances to be considered include "the frequency of the discriminatory conduct; its severity; whether it is physically threatening or humiliating, or a mere offensive utterance; and whether it unreasonably interferes with an employee's work performance." No single factor is determinative, and the court "should not carve the work environment into a series of discrete incidents and then measure the harm occurring in each episode."

First, the Court finds plaintiff's reliance on her assertions of tangible job detriments as establishing a hostile work environment to be misplaced. In its August 22 Memorandum Opinion and Order, the Court noted that although the President's argument for outright dismissal of plaintiff's hostile work environment claim had "some force," further development of the record was nevertheless necessary. The Court based this conclusion in large part on plaintiff's representations that her rejection of the President's alleged advances caused her to suffer adverse employment action, including being transferred to a position that had no responsible duties for which she could be adequately evaluated to earn advancement and failing to receive raises and merit increases. In this regard, the Court determined that the "totality" of the allegations in this case were such that they could be said to have altered the conditions of plaintiff's employment and created an abusive work environment. However, development of the record has now established that plaintiff's allegations of adverse employment action are without merit, with her claim of failing to receive cost of living increases apparently having even been abandoned. Plaintiff received every merit increase and cost-of-living allowance for which she was eligible during her nearly two-year tenure with the AIDC, her job was upgraded from Grade 9 to Grade 11 (thereby increasing her salary), she consistently received satisfactory job evaluations, and her job responsibilities upon her return from maternity leave were not significantly different from prior to her taking leave and did not cause her any materially significant disadvantage. These facts are clearly established by the record and dispel the notion that she was subjected to a hostile work environment.

Plaintiff certainly has not shown under the totality of the circumstances that the alleged incident in the hotel and her additional encounters with Ferguson and the Governor were so severe or pervasive that it created an abusive working environment. She admits that she never missed a day of work following the alleged incident in the hotel, she continued to work at AIDC another nineteen months (leaving only because of her husband's job transfer), she continued to go on a daily basis to the Governor's Office to deliver items and never asked to be relieved of that duty, she never filed a formal complaint or told her supervisors of the incident while at AIDC, and she never consulted a psychiatrist, psychologist, or incurred medical bills as a result of the alleged incident. In addition, plaintiff has not shown how Ferguson's alleged comments, whether considered alone or in conjunction with the other alleged conduct in this case, interfered with her work, and she acknowledges that the Governor's statement about him and her looking like "beauty and the beast" was made "in a light vein" and that his patting her on the shoulder and asking her how she was doing was done in a "friendly fashion."

While the alleged incident in the hotel, if true, was certainly boorish and offensive, the Court has already found that the Governor's alleged conduct does not constitute sexual assault. This is thus not one of those exceptional cases in which a single incident of sexual harassment, such as an assault, was deemed sufficient to state a claim of hostile work environment sexual harassment. . . .

Considering the totality of the circumstances, it simply cannot be said that the conduct to which plaintiff was allegedly subjected was frequent, severe, or physically threatening, and the Court finds that defendants' actions as shown by the record do not constitute the kind of sustained and nontrivial conduct necessary for a claim of hostile work environment. . . .

In sum, the Court finds that the record does not demonstrate conduct that was so severe or pervasive that it can be said to have altered the conditions of plaintiff's employment and created an abusive working environment. Accordingly, the President is entitled to summary judgment on plaintiff's claim of hostile work environment sexual harassment.

III.

For the foregoing reasons, the Court finds that the President's and Ferguson's motions for summary judgment should both be and hereby are granted. There being no remaining issues, the Court will enter judgement dismissing this case.

Notes

1. Ferguson states that plaintiff informed him that she would like to meet the Governor, remarking that she thought the Governor "was good-looking [and] had sexy hair," while plaintiff states that Ferguson asked her if she would like to meet the Governor and that she was "excited" about the possibility.
2. Plaintiff states in her amended complaint that the Governor "asked" her to "kiss it" rather than telling her to do so. She states in her deposition that the Governor's specific words to her were, "Would you kiss it for me?"

25. Feminists and the Clinton Question

Gloria Steinem

If all the sexual allegations now swirling around the White House turn out to be true, President Clinton may be a candidate for sex addiction therapy. But feminists will still have been right to resist pressure by the right wing and the media to call for his resignation or impeachment. The pressure came from another case of the double standard.

For one thing, if the President had behaved with comparable insensitivity toward environmentalists, and at the same time remained their most crucial champion and bulwark against an anti-environmental Congress, would they be expected to desert him? I don't think so. If President Clinton were as vital to preserving freedom of speech as he is to preserving reproductive freedom, would journalists be condemned as "inconsistent" for refusing to suggest he resign? Forget it.

For another, there was and is a difference between the accusations against Mr. Clinton and those against Bob Packwood and Clarence Thomas, between the experiences reported by Kathleen Willey and Anita Hill. [See Selections 20 and 23]. Commentators might stop puzzling over the President's favorable poll ratings, especially among women, if they understood the common-sense guideline to sexual behavior that came out of the women's movement 30 years ago: no means no; yes means yes.

It's the basis of sexual harassment law. It also explains why the media's obsession with sex qua sex is offensive to some, titillating to many and beside the point to almost everybody. Like most feminists, most Americans become concerned about sexual behavior when someone's will has been violated; that is, when "no" hasn't been accepted as an answer.

Let's look at what seem to be the most damaging allegations, those made by Kathleen Willey. Not only was she Mr. Clinton's political supporter, but she is also old enough to be Monica Lewinsky's mother, a better media spokeswoman for herself than Paula Jones, and a survivor of family tragedy, struggling to pay her dead husband's debts.

If any of the other women had tried to sell their stories to a celebrity tell-all book publisher, as Ms. Willey did, you might be even more skeptical about their motives. But with her, you think, "Well, she needs the money."

For the sake of argument here, I'm also believing all the women, at least until we know more. I noticed that CNN polls taken right after Ms. Willey's interview on "60 Minutes" showed that more Americans believed her than President Clinton.

Nonetheless, the President's approval ratings have remained high. Why? The truth is that even if the allegations are true, the President is not guilty of sexual harassment. He is accused of having made a gross, dumb and reckless pass at a supporter during a low point in her life. She [Willey] pushed him away, she said, and it never happened again. In other words, President Clinton took "no" for an answer.

In her original story, Paula Jones essentially said the same thing. She went to then-Governor Clinton's hotel room, where she said he asked her to perform oral sex and even dropped his trousers. She refused, and even she claims that he said something like, "Well, I don't want to make you do anything you don't want to do."

Her lawyers now allege that as a result of the incident Ms. Jones described, she was slighted in her job as a state clerical employee and even suffered long-lasting psychological damage. But there appears to be little evidence to support those accusations. As with the allegations in Ms. Willey's case, Mr. Clinton seems to have made a clumsy sexual pass, then accepted rejection.

This is very different from the cases of Clarence Thomas and Bob Packwood. According to Anita Hill and a number of Mr. Packwood's former employees, the offensive behavior was repeated for years, despite constant "no's." It also occurred in the regular workplace of these women, where it could not be avoided.

The women who worked for Mr. Packwood described a man who groped and lunged at them. Ms. Hill accused Clarence Thomas of regularly and graphically describing sexual practices and pornography. In both cases, the women said they had to go to work every day, never knowing what sexual humiliation would await them—just the kind of "hostile environment" that sexual harassment law was intended to reduce.

As reported, Monica Lewinsky's case illustrates the rest of the equation: [a former White House intern who had a sexual relationship with President Clinton] "Yes means yes." Whatever it was, her relationship with President Clinton has never been called unwelcome, coerced or other than something she sought. The power imbalance between them increased the index of suspicion, but there is no evidence to suggest that Ms. Lewinsky's will was violated: quite the contrary. In fact, her subpoena in the Paula Jones case should have been quashed. Welcome sexual behavior is about as relevant to sexual harassment as borrowing a car is to stealing one.

The real violators of Ms. Lewinsky's will were Linda Tripp, who taped their talks, the F.B.I. agents who questioned her without a lawyer and Kenneth Starr, the independent prosecutor who seems intent on tailoring the former intern's testimony.

What if President Clinton lied under oath about some or all of the above? According to polls, many Americans assume he did. There seems to be sympathy for keeping private sexual behavior private. Perhaps we have a responsibility to make it O.K. for politicians to tell the truth—providing they are respectful of "no means no; yes means yes"—and still be able to enter high office, including the Presidency.

Until then, we will disqualify energy and talent the country needs—as we are doing right now.

Are Feminists Right to Stand by Clinton?

To the Editor:

Gloria Steinem is right: by definition consensual sex cannot be harassment because it is not unwelcome (Op-Ed. March 22). However, there are complications. First, in some circumstances, institutions forbid or discourage even consensual sex—not because it is harassment but because it undermines concerns about fairness to parties not in the relationship.

Yes, as Ms. Steinem explains, there is no harassment when the groping employer takes the employee's "no" seriously and doesn't retaliate or ask the same woman twice. Yet at the same time there is something foul about an employer who can call in his employees one by one, make an advance and take his chances.

Serial groping may not be harassment, but it is a workplace burden that no employee should have to put up with even once.

Carol Sanger
New York, March 22, 1998
The writer is a professor at Columbia Law School.

Amorphous Law

To the Editor:

Gloria Steinem (Op-Ed, March 22) argues that President Clinton's alleged sexual misconduct can be distinguished from the charges against Bob Packwood and Clarence Thomas because "according to Anita Hill and a number of Mr. Packwood's former employees, the offensive behavior was repeated for years, despite constant 'no's.'"

Ms. Steinem is incorrect. Like President Clinton, Senator Packwood knew how to take no for an answer: none of his employees alleged that he repeated his advances after being rebuffed, and only one complaint occurred after 1985.

Moreover, Anita Hill has never alleged that she was the victim of legally actionable harassment.

The Lewinsky affair should remind us that, like President Clinton, Senator Packwood and Justice Thomas were unfairly accused of violating the amorphous law of sexual harassment. It is unfortunate that instead of clarifying the harassment debate, Ms. Steinem adds to the confusion.

Jeffrey Rosen
Washington, March 23, 1998
The writer is an associate law professor, George Washington University.

Defenders of Adultery

To the Editor:

Re Gloria Steinem's defense of President Clinton (Op-Ed, March 22): President Clinton's alleged behavior is harassment in any sensible woman's eyes. And if the allegations of President Clinton's activities are true, he has committed adultery, the ultimate act of dishonor a man can take against his wife.

I thought that feminism was about making men responsible for their behavior. Now it becomes clear that, once again, it's the woman's responsibility to enforce morality in every workplace, home and university across the country. The louts of the world must be breathing a sigh of relief.

Georgette Mosbacher
New York, March 23, 1998

Not 'Consenting'

To the Editor:

Gloria Steinem (Op-Ed, March 22), like many feminists, would like to ignore the obvious: While many adults commit adultery, it is damaging to their relationships and is not the preferred standard of a President who in better times reflected our aspirations, not our failings.

Also, "consenting" emotionally vulnerable 21-year-old interns or mature women in deep financial difficulties are oxymoronic concepts. The "punishment" for unwanted or exploitative advances does not consist solely of denying job opportunities but of the emotional consequences of the act.

Stanley A. Renshon
New York, March 23, 1998
The writer, a psychoanalyst, is a professor of political science at the CUNY Graduate Center.

Accepting Rejection

To the Editor:

Gloria Steinem speaks for many women (Op-Ed, March 22). President Clinton apparently makes passes, often rather clumsy ones. But so do most men. When I was just out of college and working in Washington, I received at least a pass a day, usually from older and often powerful men. They tried, but accepted rejection like gentlemen. Just as Mr. Clinton apparently does. He doesn't seem to take "no" personally.

Patricia Shillingburg
Shelter Island Heights, N.Y.
March 22, 1998

Environment of Respect

To the Editor:

I'm worried by Gloria Steinem's definition of a feminist standard of relations between the sexes (Op-Ed, March 22). I have always believed that we should be trying to create an environment in which people respect each other, regardless of gender. If "no means no" is all that needs to be applied to the first sexual proposition, I don't think that anyone is safe, nor are we any nearer to a social model that assumes respect for women or for men.

James E. Smith
Atlanta, March 22, 1998

❖ 26. Mitsubishi to Pay $34 Million in Sex Harassment Case

Stephen Braun

Chicago—Abandoning a two-year fight against federal charges of widespread sexual harassment at its sprawling central Illinois auto factory, Mitsubishi Motors agreed Thursday to pay hundreds of female employees a total of $34 million—the largest such settlement on record in a corporate case.

The proposed consent decree between Mitsubishi and the U.S. Equal Employment Opportunity Commission came after two months of negotiations shepherded by former federal Judge Abner J. Mikva. U.S. District Judge Joe Billy McDade still must approve the deal—a process that could be worked out in a few weeks, lawyers on both sides said.

The deal also obligates Mitsubishi to place all harassment policies and future complaints by female workers at its 636-acre plant in Normal, Ill., under the supervision of a panel of outside monitors. The three-member team will scrutinize the company for a year and re-port to McDade and the EEOC, said Paul M. Igasaki, the agency's chairman.

Lawyers for the Japanese-owned auto maker deftly avoided a legal admission of guilt. But after months of insisting that harassment cases were rare, the company's stiff payout came as a sign that a good number of the 350 women involved in the case had been wronged.

"Whatever the company did or didn't do wrong, they're acknowledging they have to make changes," Mikva said.

Mitsubishi Executive Vice President Larry Greene, surrounded by company executives during a news conference to announce the settlement, said: "We of course apologize to any employee who has been harassed or retaliated against."

For weeks after the EEOC filed its lawsuit against the company in April 1996, female workers told of enduring a horrific litany of abuses.

Female assembly-line crews told of being fondled, targeted with air guns and taunted as "bitches" and even cruder, sexually explicit names. Phalluses and pornographic drawings were scrawled on bathroom walls. Some women said they were baldly propositioned by male workers, managers and even union officials to provide sexual services.

"The memory is still terrible," one former worker, Pat Jetton, said soon after the case was filed. "The thought of Mitsubishi will always be spoiled for me."

SOME CONTRITION SHOWN BY MITSUBISHI

Despite the shocking nature of the charges, the firm's hard-line denials and the lingering doubts that hundreds of women could have been subjected to systematic abuse for years without any corrective measures from Mitsubishi or their union—the United Auto Work-ers—seemed to undercut the government's case.

Mitsubishi officials showed some contrition Thursday but still preferred to talk about the corrective moves of the coming year instead of what happened in the past. "The settle-ment has occurred, we're here, we want to go forward," Greene said.

But the company's decision to award its female workers the record $34 million lent cre-dence to the charges. The settlement also seemed to bolster speculation by some women's rights groups that harassment is more widespread in the workplace than many corporations are willing to admit.

"The clear lesson is that harassment will cost companies at the end of the day,' said Mar-cia Greenberger, co-president of the National Women's Law Center in Washington.

And despite the compromise nature of the deal, the EEOC's effort to prosecute the case may help it shed an image as a government paper tiger.

Michael D. Karpeles, a Chicago attorney who represents employers in labor disputes, said the settlement "shows the EEOC is serious about remedying what they call systemic discrimination and sexual harassment."

"They will continue to aggressively attack large-scale harassment situations," he added. "The message here for employers is that they should get a serious anti-harassment policy in place, enforce it and train employees about what is and isn't acceptable."

Although the Mitsubishi settlement is apparently the biggest ever in a sexual harass-ment case, a handful of other employment discrimination suits have brought even larger sums. What is believed to be the biggest settlement in an employment dispute was the $250 million won in 1992 by a group of female plaintiffs who accused State Farm of sex-ual discrimination in denying them jobs as sales agents.

On Thursday, one EEOC official suggested that the number of women who could claim awards from Mitsubishi could rise even higher than the 350 cases already documented.

"We expect the number of claimants to be at least 300 and maybe 100 or 200 more," said John C. Hendrickson, a lawyer in the EEOC's Chicago office who headed negotiations with Mitsubishi. Each woman could receive anywhere from a few thousand dollars to up to $300,000, the federal limit for a complainant, Hendrickson said.

Mitsubishi said about 20 workers were fired in 1997 for sexual harassment and several others were disciplined.

"People Are Glad It's Over"

Several former and current Mitsubishi workers who had complained of harassment could not be immediately reached for comment Thursday. But Patricia Benassi, a lawyer who represented 29 women in a civil lawsuit against Mitsubishi, said that many of her clients are "greatly relieved."

"People are glad it's over," Benassi said. "A lot of families in central Illinois had a big stake in that plant. Mitsubishi is one of the biggest employers, and one of the best-paying around. They wanted to believe the company was doing right, but they also wanted to believe their wives and daughters would be treated like human beings."

Benassi's clients, who claimed they were groped and fondled on the job, settled with the company last year. Benassi would not divulge the settlement, but it was reportedly close to $10 million.

George Galland, a Chicago lawyer who worked with Benassi on the case, was named Thursday as one of the three outside monitors who will scrutinize Mitsubishi's sexual harassment policies and complaints. The others are Nancy Kreiter, the head of Women Employed, an anti-harassment group, and Joyce E. Tucker, who headed the EEOC in the George Bush administration.

The monitors are expected to "ensure zero tolerance" of sexual harassment, Igasaki said. The team would serve as "a model to employers to emulate in dealing with the scourge of sexual harassment."

Mitsubishi's willingness to accede to scrutiny from a group of outsiders came in sharp contrast to the stance the company took for much of the past two years.

Just days after the EEOC filed its massive lawsuit against the firm, Mitsubishi packed more than 2,000 employees into 58 buses bound for Chicago, where they marched around the agency's offices, chanting: "Two, four, six, eight, we're here to set the record straight." Months later, some workers confided that the march was orchestrated by the firm—and that some of them had been intimidated into joining the march.

The company hired former Bush administration Secretary of Labor Lynn Martin to overhaul its sexual harassment code and policies. But despite being paid $2 million, Martin did not dwell on Mitsubishi's past abuses. And she played no role in the negotiations leading to the settlement, Mikva said.

Mitsubishi's response should serve as a lesson for other corporations, said Frank Cassell, emeritus professor of engineering and business at Northwestern University, explaining that the company's refusal to acknowledge the extent of the sexual harassment early on clearly hurt it more in the end.

"The real message is that if management wants its directives on sexual harassment obeyed, it has to follow through down through the ranks," Cassell said. The hiring of an outsider like Martin—a government official with little experience in dealing with such cases, he added—"looked a lot like window-dressing. The fact she had nothing to do with the agreement shows exactly that."

Mitsubishi's reluctance to take the government's lawsuit seriously, Cassell said, also exposed the failure of its Japanese-based executives to understand the cultural nuances that should have impelled them to correct harassment at the Normal plant.

"They were micromanaging from Tokyo, and it's pretty clear they didn't have a clue about how to get this problem behind them," Cassell said.

Even Mikva indirectly backed up that sentiment, acknowledging he had heard reports that Japanese Mitsubishi officials may have mistakenly conveyed the impression that sexual harassment might be tolerated by taking their American managers to sexually oriented hostess bars. The nightclubs have long been a part of Japanese business culture.

His words stung a newly appointed team of Japanese Mitsubishi officials who had crowded into a Chicago hotel where the settlement was announced. But the loss of $34 million seemed to bite even harder.

"The money," said Koehi Ikuta, executive vice president of Mitsubishi's American arm, "is not a small amount, I assure you."

· 27. Guilty If Charged

Richard Bernstein

This fall on the campus of the University of New Hampshire there suddenly appeared a set of five dramatically large posters that spelled out the sins against which war would be officially waged. "Sexism has no place at UNH," one poster said. "We seek not only to be a diverse community but a caring one." Below that, in boldface print the poster said: "Tell someone. File a complaint," and it listed telephone numbers by which students and faculty could inform against malefactors in their midst. Other posters of exactly the same format urged students to complain about racism, homophobia, discrimination, and religious persecution.

These evils, of course, have no place at any university, but questions have been raised whether the campaign to combat them fosters a tolerant community at the University of New Hampshire. Last spring at UNH, a clash of opinions took place over a proposal to expand the university's official policy on harassment to include not only sexual behavior but any remarks that created "a degrading, intimidating or hostile environment." I spoke to Chris Burns-DiBiasio, the director of the Affirmative Action Office and the policy's principal author, who argued that the code would result in no overzealous prosecutions. Harassment, she assured me, "must involve a pattern of repetition such that a reasonable student would be offended." "Reasonable student" seems the key term. One case at UNH that has now reached the courts in the form of a lawsuit charging the university with wrongful dismissal shows that aroused students and an administration that encourages people to become informers cannot always be counted on to be reasonable.

The case involves J. Donald Silva, a tenured professor of English who has taught at UNH for thirty years and, as it happens, is also the pastor of the Congregationalist Church on Great Island, a couple of miles from Portsmouth. Silva is fifty-eight years old, the grandfather of four; he has an MA in English from UNH and has published just two articles, both of them about the Portuguese island of Madeira. Until his recent troubles, he was a full-time teacher in the Thompson School of Life Science, a two-year college attached to UNH, most of whose students are preparing for careers in such subjects as animal science, forestry, and horticulture. Silva was part of a tiny humanities faculty at the Thompson School. Every other semester he taught three or four sections of a mandatory course on technical writing, with about twenty-six students in each section.

The sexual harassment charges against him began in one technical writing class early in the spring of 1992 when Silva was trying to explain the concept of "focus" to his students. "Focus is like sex," he said, trying, he told me later, to capture what he perceived to be the students flagging attention. "You zero in on your subject. You seek a target. You move from side to side. You close in on the subject. You bracket the subject and center on it. Focus connects experience and language. You and the subject become one."

A couple of days later, Silva was giving an example of a simile to the same class, and he chose an expression that seems a bit odd coming from the longest-serving pastor in the three-hundred-year history of the Great Island Congregational Church. More than twenty years ago, Silva says, he gave his wife a phonograph record called "How to Belly Dance For Your Husband," a record accompanied by a brochure with the same title, authored by a certain Little Egypt. The brochure contained a line that inspired an example Silva has used in class from time to time, including on February 26, 1992, as an example of a simile: "Belly dancing is like jello on a plate with a vibrator under the plate," he told his students.

Some women students took offense at these two remarks saying such sexual references made them extremely uncomfortable. A few of them went to a class taught by a faculty colleague of Silva's, Jerilee Zezula, the head of the animal science program at the Thompson School, and told her what Silva had said. Zezula, according to her own notes of her meeting with the students, which were later turned over to Silva and his advisers, told them that they had a "legitimate complaint" and asked them "how far they wished to go with this." Within days eight women had filed "To Whom It May Concern" letters describing what they felt was Silva's offensive behavior, sending them to Neil B. Lubow, the university's associate vice-president for academic affairs.

The matter was quickly reported to the university's Sexual Harassment and Rape Prevention Program (SHARPP), a very active and prominent campus advocacy group created in 1988 by the administration whose several duties include receiving complaints of mistreatment from women on campus. On March 3, five days after Silva's second classroom comment, an informal hearing was held in Lubow's office at which Silva was confronted with the evidence of what now was being called sexual harassment, all of which was provided in the letters submitted by the eight female undergraduate students.

I telephoned several of these women, none of whom agreed to talk to me. I spoke to a secretary at the Thompson School, who said that Zezula would not speak to me either. Silva and one of his faculty advisers told me that, in hearings later held on the case, students testified that Zezula encouraged the women's recourse to judicial action against him and that she also solicited complaints about Silva from other students in her own classes, and I wanted to ask her about this. I was also unable to ask the women what actual harm they felt Silva had done them with his classroom comments. I did obtain copies of the women's written complaints, however, which served as the basis for the long prosecution of Silva that was to follow.

One woman, Holly Alverson Woodhouse, who submitted three letters altogether over a period of ten months, said that she felt "degraded" by Silva's "vocabulary and insinuations" in class. "If he wants to make a point that we'll remember, certainly a Professor [sic] of English can find enough vocabulary to draw from without needing to use the visualizations he chooses," she wrote. Another of the women, Rachel Powers, said, "There is a border of what is tasteful and what is unacceptable and offensive. Don since has greatly crossed this border."

Another student, Robyn Ferreira, recounts an argument she had with Silva immediately after his remarks in class, which she termed "very unappropriated [sic] and also very affending [sic]."

> Well then he went back to the bowl of jello and the vibrator and that he knew allot [sic] of people who used it to massage there [sic] muscles and that he was one of them. I told him that he was wacked because there are allot [sic] of other little massages their [sic] that do the same thing.

Some of the women wrote complaints accusing Silva of harassment outside class as well, most of it occurring on what appears to be a single day in the library. Woodhouse, for example, recounts how she was there with Silva and several other students. One of them, Nicole Libbey, talked about getting started on an assignment and said, "I guess I'll jump on a computer before someone else does." Woodhouse reports: "Don Silva smiled and said, 'I'd like to see that.' We all laughed a bit uneasily & wandered off."

Woodhouse goes on to say that later, still in the library, "I was on the floor in the card indexes looking up books. Don Silva stopped, saw me on my hands and knees pulling out a floor level card index. Kate & Nikki heard him say to me, 'You look like you've had a lot of experience on your knees.'" Silva, who does not deny having spoken to Woodhouse, remembers his words as: "You look like you've had a lot of experience doing that."

Two other students, Jamalyn Brown and Denise Kohler, wrote a joint complaint, accusing Silva, apparently, of implying that the two of them had a sexual relationship. According to the students, Silva asked them, "How long have you two been together?" Silva remembers saying. "How long have you two known each other." Yet another letter is from Kimberly Austin. She and a male student overheard Silva administering a spelling test to a third student. "Myself and the male student went into his office and there heard him using sentences with Sexual Slants," Austin writes. "I don't remember the *exact* words. One out of every three sentences had a sexual slant."

Those were the reported actions of Silva, perhaps tasteless or inappropriate ones, in some cases showing a middle-aged man doing nothing more offensive than trying, clumsily, to banter with his students. He seems to have foolishly wanted to appear to be "hip." But from the beginning, the UNH administration chose to see Silva's remarks in exactly the same way that the women students, saw them, as unmistakably sexual in content and as instances of harassment. In March, Brian A. Giles, the dean of the Thompson School, while he did not talk to Silva as part of any investigation he may have made, wrote a letter informing him that his "pattern of sexual remarks in and out of the classroom has created an intimidating, hostile, and offensive academic environment that has substantially interfered with [the students'] educational experience." The proposed punishment involved several requirements, the most important being that Silva undergo a year of "weekly counseling ses-

sions" with a "professional psychotherapist approved by the university." Silva was also required to reimburse the university for $2,000 to cover the cost of setting up an alternative
section of his course to accommodate the students who could no longer study with him. Finally, Silva was required to apologize, in writing, "for creating a hostile and offensive academic environment."

Silva says that he was willing to apologize to the women for any offense he had given
them, but he denied having sexually harassed them. Others at UNH reasoned that even if
Silva had suffered a lapse of judgment in his remarks in class, those lapses had not created
an "offensive learning environment" and should have been protected by Silva's right to academic freedom.

"What you have here," said Chris Balling, a professor of physics who served as an adviser to Silva during his ordeal, "is a professor who probably exercised poor judgment in
searching for a way to grab students' attention. I don't know anyone who doesn't think it
was a mistake, but I don't see how one can construe it as sexual harassment." The classroom
remarks were not directed specifically to the individuals who complained. He said them
each once. He was not warned that these particular students took offense. He was just immediately hit by a formal harassment charge. Yet to harass somebody you have to go at
someone more than once, it has to be individually and you have to know it is offensive and
yet keep on doing it." Certainly, several important details in the sexual harassment charges
suggest a spirit of overzealousness was in the air. For example, the student who was going
to jump on the computer, Nicole Libbey, was not the one who filed a complaint against
Silva and in fact she testified in his behalf at the formal hearing. But Holly Woodhouse,
who overheard Silva's comment to Libbey, reported it as an instance of harassment. As for
Woodhouse's complaint regarding Silva's remark to her when she was on her knees at the
card file, she acknowledges that she was informed of it by two other women. She did not
hear it herself.

So too with Kimberly Austin's report of overhearing Silva's spelling test. The person
who actually took the test did not complain about it. In addition, the male student who
was with Austin at the time, Robert Wardleigh, testified at Silva's hearing later that he
heard nothing with a "sexual slant." Yet, nearly a year later when a formal hearing took
place, all three incidents remained prominent in what was called "findings of fact," the conclusion of the university apparently being that one can be harassed even when the harasser
is talking to somebody else.

Silva, despite this, rejected Giles's reprimand, and thus in June Giles, who still had not
talked to Silva as part of any investigation he conducted, suspended him, a tenured full professor, from teaching. The suspension was short lived because Silva appealed to a faculty
grievance committee, which found in his favor, forcing the university to reinstate him and
to go through the procedure that exists when accusations of sexual harassment are concerned. The procedure had not been used before because all the others accused of harassment accepted what Burns-DiBiasio called an "informal resolution" of the charges against
them. The first step in the procedure involved a formal complaint from seven of the eight
students who originally complained, and who wrote to Lubow in November 1992.

"In light of the seriousness of the initial offense and his behavior since then, we would
like to see Mr. Silva's position and tenure at UNH terminated," the women wrote. "We feel
it is imperative that the University implement mandatory Sexual Harassment/Assault education for all incoming students, not just freshmen, as well as for all faculty."

The main event of the university's procedure is a hearing before a sexual harassment
hearing panel, whose five members, Burns-DiBiasio told me, are chosen and given train-

ing by her. As head of of the Affirmative Action Office, she also led the administration's effort to draft a new, expanded policy on harassment this past spring. Burns-DiBiasio, who emerged as a key figure in Silva's case, is an example of a new type of specialist to be found at many universities. She has never been a member of a university faculty but has made a career in what she calls "equity issues," meaning, she told me, explaining and implementing Title VII and Title IX of the Civil Rights Act, the provisions involving discrimination and harassment. DiBiasio has a master's degree in education from Montana State University, worked on "equity issues" for the Department of Health, Education and Welfare during the Carter administration, and has headed the UNH Affirmative Action Office since its creation in 1989.

Burns-DiBiasio told me that she maintains a "pool of people," proposed to her informally by various campus organizations, from which harassment hearing panels can be chosen. Acting on behalf of the university's president, she then chooses the specific members of each pool and oversees their training, which, she said, involves briefings on recent court cases and the current state of the law governing discrimination.

The panel drawn together to hear Silva's case on February 2, 1993, involved two associate professors, a data analyst, and two undergraduate students. The chairperson was one of the students. The panel met for more than nine hours during which Burns-DiBiasio from time to time talked privately with the five panel members outside the hearing room. I asked her about these private sessions. She acknowledged that they had taken place but said they were over procedural issues. Silva and Silva's adviser, a physics professor emeritus named John E. Mulhern. Jr., who says he had all of twenty-four hours to prepare for the hearing, believe, they told me, that the private meetings showed Burns-DiBiasio had an entirely too cozy relationship with Silva's judges. At the hearing itself, the student complainants were represented by a SHARPP counselor, Jane Stapleton, who led each of them through a lengthy recitation of Silva's offenses. Lubow, Giles, and Zezula testified against Silva, even though none of them had ever actually witnessed anything that Silva was accused of doing.

Five students, including Libbey and Wardleigh, testified on Silva's behalf; another female student, Danielle E. Foley, submitted a sworn statement describing Silva as a "thoughtful lecturer" who "makes a point of speaking with his students in an informal and pleasant manner," and who never "conducted himself in a manner that could in any way be construed as sexually harassing." Nonetheless, the panel's written judgment was that a reasonable female student would find Professor Silva's comments and his behavior to be offensive, intimidating and contributing to a hostile academic environment.

A few weeks later, an appeals board was convened, whose members, three from the faculty and two students, were appointed by the same university administration, including Burns-DiBiasio, that appointed the first panel. (The official policy provides that "appointment to the board will be made with consideration to relevant experience, knowledge of affirmative action and sensitivity to the issue of sexual harassment.") The chairperson of this board was later a supporter of Burns-DiBiasio in the attempt, so far not successful, to promulgate an expanded harassment policy.

This second hearing was an emotional affair, lasting nearly thirteen hours, until about 1:00 AM on March 30. At one point, according to both Silva and Thomas Carnicelli, an English professor who served as his counsel during the appeal, one of the women, Kimberley Austin, who had overheard the questionable spelling test, suddenly got up from the table, lurched toward the door, and fell to the floor. Another young woman supported her and the two of them staggered out of the room together. At another point, Holly Woodhouse said that it's not your ordinary household that has a bowl of jello and a vibrator. Silva, unwisely perhaps, says that he muttered "especially jello" into Carnicelli's ear, his private remark surely the sarcasm of an aggrieved man who felt he was being persecuted and needed to vent his sense of the ridiculousness of the situation. The representative of SHARPP, however, jumped to her feet and accused Silva of having said that every girl ought to have a vibrator. With that, several of the women complainants said they heard the same thing, and so did one of the members of the hearing panel. Carnicelli says that Silva spoke so softly that even he did not hear what Silva said. But the incident made him feel that the impulse to ferret out the sinfulness of every one of Silva's gestures was going to prevail over a commonsensical examination of the evidence.

The appeals panel found against Silva, citing him for "repeated and sustained comments and behavior of a sexual and otherwise intrusive nature [that] had the effect of creating a hostile and intimidating academic environment." The panel imposed a penalty more severe than the one specified in the university's initial reprimand. Not only was Silva required to "begin counseling sessions at his own expense, with a licensed and certified counselor selected by the University"; he was also suspended without pay for "at least one year." His office and even the carrel assigned to him in the library were taken away.

How could so harsh a punishment be meted out for so ambiguous an offense? One possible answer to that question of course is that Silva really did commit sexual harassment and the two panels were correct in their judgment. Since Silva has now filed suit in federal court claiming violations of his First Amendment rights (the case will probably not come to trial until well into 1994), that question may get at least a legal answer. [For the outcome of this case, see Selection 28.]

But it is important to note that throughout all of this, there was not a single charge against Silva of physical contact with students, no motivations to meet women after class, no fixed staring: nobody alleges that there was ever a single private encounter between Silva and any student. In what they call their "findings of fact," the two hearing panels merely accept the women's interpretations of Silva's words and actions as though the mere fact that they felt the way they did was proof of harassment. There was no attempt to deal seriously with any of the underlying issues, particularly whether the two offending remarks made by Silva in class would be so disturbing to a "reasonable woman" that Silva's academic freedom could justifiably be overridden.

The charge that seemed to evoke the most anger was the one in which he talked of belly dancing and of a vibrator under a plate of jello. Well before the formal hearing, Silva told me, he sat down with two of the offended students to discuss the charges against him.

"I don't want you to use the word vibrator in class ever again." Silva quoted one woman as saying to him.

"What's wrong with that word?" Silva asked.

"You know that a vibrator is a sex toy," the woman replied.

"I do?" the astonished Silva told me that he replied. "I thought it was a massager."

I called several people in the UNH administration to try to find out how they justified their handling of the Silva case. Lubow, the associate vice-president for academic affairs, said that I should realize that the law's definition of sexual harassment specified that it could occur with mere words that created a "hostile environment," and that action was not required. However, he said, he could not discuss the Silva case, much as he would like to, because the university policy forbade comment on disciplinary matters. Brian Giles, the dean of the Thompson School, refused to discuss the Silva matter with me at all, referring me to the university's general counsel. This person, Ronald Rodgers, reiterated the university's confidentiality requirement, but he expressed confidence that the university would prevail in the pending legal action. Burns-DiBiasio spoke to me about harassment in general but not about the Silva case in particular. She did say that there were elements of the Silva case that I apparently did not know about, specifically a problem with Silva's behavior in the past, which is what led to the harshness of the penalty levied against him.

Burns-DiBiasio would not say what these earlier misdeeds on Silva's part had been, but Silva himself had already told me that, in 1990, four women had complained against him for telling sexual stories and making racist remarks in class. In a speech class, giving an example of rhythm and cadence in poetry, he had read aloud Vachel Lindsay's "The Congo," which today could certainly be seen as a racist poem. Another time, he made a joking reference to an Ann Landers column about a man who tied his wife to the bed and then knocked himself out playing Batman in an effort to leap to her from atop the dresser. Upbraided by Giles at the time, Silva apologized to the entire class for any offense that he had given. That may have been a mistake so far as his future was concerned, since his decision not to contest the charges was treated as an admission of guilt, which became part of Silva's permanent record. The university then used his record to remove him from the classroom.

And so, the question remains: how could the "reasonable people" of the hearing panels have found Silva's behavior so egregious as to warrant suspension?

Balling and Carnicelli, trying to answer that question, both cite what they call "the climate" at UNH, in which the growing harassment bureaucracy encourages an exaggeration of the sense of aggrievement and victimization on the part, especially, of women. Balling takes a certain perverse pleasure in an example given by Burns-DiBiasio of the kind of statement that would have been proscribed in the draft policy on harassment she favored in the spring. The minutes of one meeting show her saying, "In the classroom, a faculty member repeatedly comments that women are not cut out to be scientists, because they do not have the motivation to succeed as men do." That would be an opinion, Balling argues, a very unpopular one, an incorrect one, but one whose expression should be protected by academic freedom.

In my own visit to the UNH campus, I encountered other instances of the climate affecting matters of sex and sexuality. On bulletin boards all over campus, for example, were posters asking "What Is Rape Culture?" and signed by an organization called Against Rape Culture. I visited a counselor at SHARPP, Michelle LeGault, and asked her about the numbers of women who had come to her organization for help. "We had 130 sexual assault survivors and significant others," LeGault told me, giving figures on the number of women who had used SHARPP's services in the previous year. Among them were seventy-three "sexual assault survivors" and thirty-five "child abuse and incest survivors." I asked if the women given the "survivor" designation were found to have actually been victimized or if they just said they had been victimized.

"If a person thinks she's been victimized," LeGault said, "we're here to validate that experience."

Few on campus are willing to risk being viewed as "soft" on harassment by contending that the atmosphere has become oppressive. When, for example, Silva's lawsuit got publicity in the local press, UNH's president, Dale Nitzschke, took care to publish a reassuring statement in the student newspaper that, while his commitment to free speech remained unwavering, the university "will continue to vigorously enforce its policies" on sexual harassment.

In the spring, the executive committee of the American Association of University Professors at UNH came out against the draft policy on harassment being promoted by Burns-

DiBiasio, arguing that it would violate the First Amendment and academic freedom. This prompted Barbara White, an associate professor of women's studies, to circulate a letter to several campus organizations. It said in part:

> The AAUP, indeed, academia itself, has traditionally been dominated by white heterosexual men and the First Amendment and Academic Freedom (I'll call them FAF) have traditionally protected the rights of white heterosexual men. Most of us are silenced by existing social conditions before we get the power to speak out in any way where FAF might protect us. So forgive us if we don't get all teary-eyed about FAF. Perhaps to you it's as sacrosanct as the flag or the national anthem; to us strict construction of the First Amendment is just another yoke around our necks.

Professor White is coordinator of the women's studies program at UNH, and one wonders how she manages to hold a position of such apparent influence at a tax-supported state institution even as she is silenced by existing social conditions. "Where do any of us who aren't white heterosexual men find relief from the discrimination we continually meet at UNH?" she asks, ignoring the extensive network of boards and organizations that the university has set up to provide relief.

"The meaning of the Silva case." Carnicelli told me, "is not that a bunch of zealots got together and packed the hearing. The meaning to me is that a perfectly decent group of people, because of the climate, or the way they were trained, or something, made this incredibly unjust decision. Even the good people can't see clearly anymore."

Or, as Nicole Libbey, the student supposedly harassed by Silva but who actually testified as a character witness for him during his two hearings, put it: "Those women who made the complaints have gone on to live their own lives, and they haven't been affected by this at all. But they practically ruined a man's life."

❖ 28. The Silva Case at the University of New Hampshire

Mary M. Clark

INTRODUCTION

In spring 1992, eight first-year students brought sexual harassment charges against Professor J. Donald Silva, a professor of writing and communication in the University of New Hampshire's Thompson School, our two-year school of applied science. In accordance with our procedures at the time, the charges were heard in three steps—first, an informal meeting with our associate VP for Academic Affairs (March 1992), which resulted in a formal reprimand and the setting up of alternative writing sections for the complaining students; then, because Professor Silva refused to accept the reprimand, a formal hearing before a five-member hearing board (January 1993) followed by a ruling from the university president, Dale F. Nitzschke, supporting the board's decision; and, finally, a second formal hearing (March 1993) before a five-member "appeals" board.[1] Both boards found, unanimously, that Professor Silva had violated our sexual harassment policy. In accordance with the boards' recommendations, Professor Silva was suspended from his teaching duties for one year without pay and required, as a condition for reinstatement, to undergo counseling.

Rather than pursue the additional grievance procedure that is provided by our collective bargaining agreement, Professor Silva, with the backing of the conservative Washington-based Center for Individual Rights, brought suit against the university in federal court. The suit was filed in fall 1993; a year later, in September 1994, Judge Shane Devine, the presiding judge in the case, handed down an Order of Preliminary Injunction against the university, reinstating Professor Silva. The case was ultimately settled out of court in December 1994, under an agreement that returned Professor Silva permanently to the classroom and awarded him $60,000 in back salary and benefits plus $170,000 in legal fees.

As the chair of the appeals board that heard the case on campus, I have a special perspective on this story. In this article, I will describe the case as I saw it, as well as the aftermath in the courts and in the press, and draw what conclusions I can about the implications of this notorious case for the struggle against sexual harassment on university campuses.

THE CHARGES

Professor Silva was charged with violating a clause in our sexual harassment policy that precluded "verbal or physical conduct of a sexual nature . . . [which] has the purpose or effect of unreasonably interfering with an individual's work performance or creating a hostile or offensive working or academic environment" [11, p. 69]. The specific charges, all from one section of his technical writing course for first-year students, included complaints about sexually suggestive and/or overly personal remarks to students, late-night telephone calls to students' homes, and two offensive anecdotes in class—the "focus" and "belly dancing" analogies that later received so much attention in the press.

The first of the "classroom" complaints centered on a presentation in which Professor Silva had compared focus to sex:

> I will put focus in terms of sex, so you can better understand it. Focus is like sex. You seek a target. You zero in on your subject. You move from side to side. You close in on the subject. You bracket the subject and center on it. Focus connects language and experience. You and the subject become one. [2, p. 71]

The other concerned an incident in which Professor Silva had, as an example of a "working definition," compared belly dancing to a plate of Jell-O with a vibrator under the plate. According to one complainant, he said, "[D]escribe a belly dancer: Take a bowl of Jell-O, stick it on a plate, hold a vibrator underneath it, and watch it jiggle" [10, p. 158]. He concluded the analogy by asking, "How many of you have tried this?" [10, pp. 134, 180].[2]

There were also complaints about out-of-class remarks. In one incident, while a student was "on the ground, on my hands and knees . . . flipping through the pages [of the lowest index card drawer in the library]," Professor Silva remarked, "You look like you've had a lot of experience down there" [10, pp. 169–71]. When another student said she was going to "go jump on the computer before someone else takes it," he allegedly "raised his eyebrows and was very expressive in his facial expressions [and said], 'I'd like to see that' [10, p. 26]. In another incident, Professor Silva asked two female students, in a joking tone, "How long have you two been together?" insinuating, they believed, that they "had a lesbian relationship of some kind" [7, appendix].

Professor Silva did not dispute these accounts of his behavior but argued that a professor has the right to do "as he sees fit, within reasonable limits " [10, p. 21]. His remarks were intended not to offend, he told us, but to instruct. For example, his response to the jump-on-the-computer remark was intended "to point out the imprecise use of English in [the student's] statement" [9, p. 1]. "What I'm doing there is pointing out that [the student] doesn't literally mean that she's going to jump on the computer" [10, p. 309]. His question about how long the two students had "been together" was motivated by a concern that they might be collaborating too closely in their work.[3] However, in these and in other instances, Professor Silva's defense was undermined by his own explanations. For example, with regard to the "computer" remark, he went on to observe that

> [a] number of people laughed about it—I assumed . . . because they were visualizing [the student] . . . literally going over and jumping onto a computer, you know, which is very amusing when you see [her] . . . She's a fairly short woman. She's—I wouldn't say she's heavy set, but—but [waving his hands in the air to indicate the shape of her body] she's not *athletic,* I would say, and it's quite interesting to see . . . [Here Professor Silva was stopped by an objection from a member of the Board.] [10, pp. 309–10]

And his explanation of the "how long have you been together" question seemed to indicate an interest in the students' relationship that went beyond their study habits:

> They were together, they were working library exercises together. They seemed to be enjoying learning together. But I asked, you know, "How long have you two known one another?" because in my experience many of my students have known one another in high school and they make arrangements at the university, and when they come to the university I found out, by asking the questions, that they stay in the same dormitory or they stay in the same room. [10, p. 307]

In response to a complaint that he had offered one student an A in the course when she was not doing A work, Professor Silva stated that

> [i]t may sound strange to many of you, but I have more than once promised a student a grade of "A" for the course, within the first three weeks of the course, because the student . . . is discouraged . . . [and] frustrated, and I want to indicate that I'm willing to go the ultimate in a reward. . . . So that's why I said to her, "Do you need an "A" in this course?" Because it appeared to me that she was quite frustrated by some of those early exercises. [10, p. 311]

When a board member asked, "What do you do if students do not live up to your expectations?" he responded, "I give them the A." "Even if they might not deserve it?" asked the questioner. "I follow through on my promises," he replied [10, p. 412].

Several students complained that Professor Silva has a habit of standing too close in conversation. One described a conversation in which he had backed her into a table:

> He stepped forward and put his shoulder to mine, and I backed up, and he stepped forward again. . . . And again, I backed up. And I was against the table. And he backed into me again, and I end up . . . like this on the table. . . . I'm leaning back like this, you can see it's a strain, and this was how I was on the table trying to remove myself from him. [10, pp. 88–89]

And from another student:

> He made me uncomfortable. The way he was in class, he just—he leaned over people, he got right into their faces. . . . I didn't like that at all. [10, p. 119]

Professor Silva admitted that he has a habit of standing very close but argued that it is the result of his cultural background:

> Half of my family is Luso-American, which means Portuguese-American. I have a tendency to speak with my hands [and] to approach very close to even strangers when I talk to them. It's a

cultural characteristic that I've always had. . . . I get very close, you know, when I talk to people. It is true I see people sometimes back away from me. [10, pp. 315–16]

Later, after the case was over, a senior colleague who had publicly supported Professor Silva told me, privately, that she had been surprised at the strength of her own reaction when he stepped up to her one day while they were alone. She was startled, she said, and told him, "Back off, Don! This is just the sort of thing that's getting you in so much trouble with your students."

Both parties agreed that Professor Silva had collected personal information from the students—their addresses and phone numbers, their favorite color, their favorite movie, their goals in life, and so forth—and asked them to fill out a time chart outlining their activities from seven in the morning until midnight [10, pp. 55–80, 299–305]. When one student objected that she was in bed by nine, he responded, facetiously, that he wanted to know what she *did* in bed and what she dreamed about. The complainants testified, further, that they were reluctant to give Professor Silva their telephone numbers because he makes a practice of calling them at home. Professor Silva agreed that is his practice:

> That's my standard policy. I say to the students the first day, . . . "I'm going to get in touch with you, and if there's any difficulties with learning in this class, or if there's any other personal difficulties, call me any time." . . . I'm very concerned for students. If a student misses class for more than a week, I call the dormitory and talk to her roommate or whoever answers the phone. . . . I have had people say, "I wish you wouldn't call me after nine o'clock at night," and I have honored that, you know, I have honored that [though] sometimes I would have wanted to call. [10, pp. 78–80, 340–41]

There were two hostile confrontations between Professor Silva and his students after they made their complaints. The first occurred in Stacey's, a lounge and restaurant area in the Thompson School:

> The next thing I knew, he was sitting down at our table and leaning towards us. He then asked, "Did I offend you in class today?" If there wasn't a table between Don Silva and I, he would have been on my lap. . . . I told him that, yes, he most certainly did offend me, . . . [that] what he said was unacceptable and rude, . . . [that] I felt very violated, . . . [and that] he had some really poor examples when explaining technical writing.
>
> Don Silva then asked me if I could come up with some better examples. I replied that he was the teacher, not I. And . . . sex toys were inappropriate for a classroom example [in the belly dancing analogy]. . . . Don Silva then started getting mad at me. . . . He said that he didn't say "vibratOR," he said "vibratER," and that people his age use it to massage the neck muscles. I said, "That's not the meaning I know of a vibrator." Don Silva then said he would bring the directions in to show me. I replied by saying it would not be necessary. [He] then started raising his voice [and said] who was I to infringe on his freedom of speech? [He] then turned to the [focus is like sex] remark, saying, "If I used animals instead, would it have made a difference?" [10, pp. 148–50]

On another occasion, Professor Silva stood in the doorway of a small vending machine room, blocking a student's exit, and asked if she could "see the bullet holes" in his chest. The student's academic adviser, Dr. Jerilee Zezula, testified that she had come "into my office very visibly upset, trembling, white as a sheet. . . . she was visibly shaken up by it, and felt she had been singled out" [10, p. 256].

There was factual disagreement about one incident—a visit by one of the complainants and a male classmate to Professor Silva's office:

> When we got to the door it was open. . . . And [Professor Silva] was giving a student a spelling test. . . . And he said . . . "Come on in, sit down." . . . One out of every three examples

had a sexual slant. I remember thinking, "My god, doesn't he have any normal examples?" . . . and I remember part of two different sentences that really struck me as being very offensive. . . . The first example . . . was something about a secretary earning her job on the boss's desk, and it was said [in] a very strange manner. And the second one I remember even better, because he looked me square in the eye, and the [spelling] word I believe was "appropriate," and he said something to the effect—and I'm not saying this is exact words, but this was the content of it—"It may or may not be appropriate for a student to earn her "A" by sleeping with her professor." [10, pp. 82–83]

Professor Silva denied using the examples the complainant had cited and said his examples had no "sexual slant" as he would understand that term:

On the spelling test that I gave I was entertaining a male student, who was an older student, by some of the sentences that I gave him. But I deny completely that I used any examples that could be characterized as having been used with a sexual slant. In fact, I don't quite know as I understand—I know what *I* mean by a sexual slant, but I don't know if it's clear to me what's been said [by the complainant]. [10, p. 314]

The complainant's male companion, who was also present at our hearing, confirmed that Professor Silva had made some "humorous remarks," but he could not recall their content [10, pp. 499–500].[4] This was the only charge on which there was significant factual disagreement.

Four students from the class in question—three female and one male—came to our hearing to testify in Professor Silva's favor. They had found him to be a good teacher, they said, and the atmosphere in his class was not hostile to women, though one of them testified that the belly dancing analogy had caught her "off guard" [10, p. 458]. The board also received written statements from four pro-Silva witnesses, all female, who could not be present at our hearing.

THE BOARD'S DECISION

Professor Silva and his adviser, Professor Carnicelli, argued that the incidents in this case did not constitute sexual harassment or create a hostile environment for women students: the number of incidents was not sufficient to create a "pattern," the individual incidents were not serious and not gender-specific, only a handful of students were offended, there was no hostile intent, and Professor Silva had been given no warning about how the students felt. They went on to argue that our harassment policy was too "vague": "It's very difficult to know what sort of . . . verbal conduct . . . is intended" [10, p. 359]. Finally, they argued, his classroom language was protected by the principle of academic freedom, which gives a teacher the right to do in his class "as he sees fit, within reasonable limits" [10, p. 21].

Our board made its decision as carefully as possible, reasoning more or less as follows: First, we did not consider academic freedom to be at issue, since the complaints involved conversational banter rather than intellectual or political ideas. The two classroom analogies were, in our view, unnecessary and even inimical to Professor Silva's stated educational objectives.[5]

With regard to the issues of pattern, seriousness, and gender specificity, we considered the number of incidents to be fairly large, given that this was a two-credit course that had met for only six weeks prior to the breakup of the class. Furthermore, although the individual incidents were not terribly serious, their sum total had, clearly, disturbed the complainants very much, as shown by their willingness to pursue the case through fourteen emotionally trying months of informal and formal hearings, accompanied by all the standard campus politics. We found Professor Silva's comments to be gender-specific in the sense that many of them would have been particularly disturbing to women. As for the claim that only a few students had been offended, we noted that eight students had filed harassment charges, that seven of them had pursued the case to the end, and that twenty-six out of the seventy-four students in Professor Silva's classes that semester (twenty-three of them female) had requested a transfer to another instructor. (Later, when the case became public, the university received letters from female students of many years past, complaining about Professor Silva's behavior when *they* were in his class.)

We accepted Professor Silva's word that he had not deliberately set out to offend his students, but he had, we thought, shown extraordinarily poor judgment on more than one occasion. We were particularly concerned about his behavior after the complaints were brought to his attention. I have already described the angry confrontation in Stacey's restaurant; Professor Silva's written response to the complaints was no more conciliatory. In answer to a complaint that in another section of the class, he had "urged students to apply themselves before the spring weather arrived and the grass is green and they go off playing sports and to beach parties to get drunk and get laid," he wrote, "While the phrase 'get laid' may be common in usage, the claim that it indicates outright gender hostility is unreasonable. Its use once during six weeks of classes and directed against no individual . . . negates this claim. The claim is ambiguous, unreasonable, and an example of a petty slight of one hypersensitive and unaware of current English usage in American society" [9, p. 2]. The problems in his classes were caused, he suggested, by the students' "imperfect knowledge of English usage in discerning facetious and ironic language. . . . The misunderstanding, misinterpretation, and misconception by these students indicate a need to study the English language and its use to increase their skill" [9, pp. 3–4].

Professors Silva and Carnicelli brought this attitude into our hearing, characterizing the students' complaints as "bizarre . . . [and] utterly unreasonable" [10, p. 22] and attacking them on every point, even when their stories accorded with Professor Silva's own. At no point did Professor Silva accept any responsibility for what had occurred. When asked whether students have a *right* to complain, he suggested that if they do not like what he says in class, they should drop the course. This ignores the fact that the course was required for graduation and that until the alternative sections were set up, there was no other section to which the students could have transferred. We found that Professor Silva's behavior toward his students was inappropriately sexualized and that the cited incidents, taken together, had created a hostile environment for women students, and we imposed, as penalty, a one-year suspension without pay. Professor Silva was also required to attend counseling sessions with a university-approved counselor, with his return to the university contingent upon the counselor's recommendation. We rejected the complainants' request for a formal apology: What is the value of an apology that would, obviously, have been insincere?

We were later criticized by the AAUP investigating team for the severity of the penalty, and especially for the counseling requirement, which they regarded as an attempt to "elicit a confession" and to "compel Professor Silva to agree to certain ideas about sexual harassment" [2, p. 80]. That was not our intention; if we had wanted a "confession," we would not have rejected the students' request for a formal apology. We didn't care what *label* Professor Silva attached to his behavior—we just wanted it to stop. Professor Silva had told us repeatedly that he did not know what sort of behavior he should avoid; we thought a counselor would be able to help with this question, and also, perhaps, suggest some techniques for dealing with student complaints. The penalty was severe, admittedly, but I have not heard good alternative suggestions for a situation like this one, in which a faculty member's conduct is clearly unacceptable and there is no indication of a willingness to change.

After reaching our decision on the charges, but before deciding on the penalty, we were informed by the university's Affirmative Action Officer that Professor Silva had received a previous warning in 1990. We were not told the details of that incident, only that it involved an Ann Landers letter that the students found offensive, a poem (Vachel Lindsay's "The Congo") that they considered racist, other remarks that they considered anti-Semitic, and some insensitive remarks to a deaf student in the class. I was familiar with the Vachel Lindsay poem and agreed that it is racist, but I did not know the contents of the Ann Landers column until I read Professor Silva's own account of it in the newspaper a few months later. The letter was from a couple who, responding to frantic calls for help from their neighbors' apartment, found the wife tied to the bed, naked, and the husband lying unconscious on the floor wearing a Batman suit. The husband had hit his head on the ceiling fan while trying to leap onto the wife from a nearby bureau. According to the newspaper article, Professor Silva had used this example to help his students understand the meaning of "communication": The wife was trying to communicate with the neighbors by screaming, and Ann Landers was trying to communicate with the public. Professor Silva later testified that he "was trying to establish with the students that they must communicate with me and with one another in order to learn—what one of the purposes was of the course was to increase skill in communication" [5, p. 66].[6]

PUBLIC REACTION

The president of our local AAUP chapter, Professor Christopher Balling, had served as one of two faculty advisers to Professor Silva during the informal meeting with Associate VP Lubow in spring 1992, and he continued to take a strong interest in the case. Soon after the appeals board decision, Professor Balling and a colleague, Professor Jack Mulhern, circulated a letter to every member of the faculty giving their version of what had occurred. Because of the requirement of confidentiality, the members of the hearing boards were very limited in what we could say, and Professor Balling's version of the case[7] went, essentially, unchallenged.

A four-page article in the New York Review by New York Times reporter Richard Bernstein (January 1994) [3] initiated a long series of sensational accounts in the press. The title of Bernstein's article, "Guilty If Charged," was taken from the Balling-Mulhern memo, and these two faculty, along with Professor Silva's adviser, Professor Carnicelli, seem to have been Bernstein's primary sources of information. Like them, Bernstein regarded the case as the outcome of a "repressive campus climate" exemplified by wall posters with slogans such as "Sexism (racism, homophobia, religious persecution) has no place at UNH" and a campus campaign against date rape ("Tell someone. File a complaint"). "[A]n administration that encourages people to become informers cannot always be counted on to be reasonable," Bernstein wrote.[8] With prodding from the Center for Individual Rights, the story was subsequently picked up by newspapers throughout this country and abroad, as well as PBS, the Today Show, and Connie Chung.

The press, following Bernstein's lead, treated the case as the outcome of feminist hysteria—a "witch-hunt" on the UNH campus. Claire Kittredge, New Hampshire reporter for the Boston Globe, railed against the "student-led tribunals" that had decided against Professor Silva. Anthony Lewis, in the New York Times, repeated this charge, and advised the student complainants to "grow up." Although transcripts of the appeals board hearing were made available to the public, along with documents outlining the charges against

Professor Silva, the press treated the two classroom examples—the focus and belly-dancing analogies—as the sole content of the university's case. As the story developed, media accounts strayed further and further from the truth. Anthony Lewis claimed, erroneously, that Professor Silva had been suspended from the university as a result of his lawsuit; the events had, in fact, occurred in the opposite order. Linda Seebach, in a *Los Angeles Daily News* column, reduced the number of complainants to one: Professor Silva's comments were neither hostile nor intimidating, she opined, "though at least one person found them offensive."

Anthony Brooks, of WBUR, Boston, made the most serious attempt at balanced coverage; his radio piece of September 1994 included an interview with a male student of Professor Silva's who quoted examples of Professor Silva's classroom language that he had witnessed personally. This interview aired only once, however; by evening, when the piece appeared on New Hampshire Public Radio, that part of the story had been edited out, radically altering the tone of the piece. What the press wanted, clearly, was a story about free speech under attack by hysterical campus feminists; the facts were adjusted, where necessary, to support this view.

JUDGE DEVINE'S RULING

In fall 1993, Professor Silva filed suit in federal court in Concord, New Hampshire, charging that by suspending him from his teaching duties, the university had violated his contract and due process rights, as well as his civil rights and his right to freedom of speech under the first and fourteenth amendments. Because we had made the final decision, the members of the appeals board—three faculty and two students—were named in the suit, along with the university president and the associate VP for Academic Affairs.

In September 1994, Judge Shane Devine, the presiding judge in the case, handed down an Order of Preliminary Injunction reinstating Professor Silva, and denying the university's motion for dismissal of the charges. In his 103-page ruling, Judge Devine found our policy and procedures acceptable [7, pp. 45, 67–68] but decided that they had been applied incorrectly to Professor Silva, who, in his opinion, was not guilty of sexual harassment. Like the press, the judge concentrated on the focus and belly dancing analogies, stating that "but for [these two] classroom statements [Professor Silva] would not have been subject to UNH discipline" [7, p. 55]. These statements were constitutionally protected, in the judge's view, because they "advanced [the] valid educational objective of conveying certain principles related to the subject matter of his course" [7, p. 46] and because they were "directly related to (1) the preservation of academic freedom and (2) the issue of whether speech which is offensive to a particular class of individuals should be tolerated in American schools" [7, p. 54].[9] Our application of the sexual harassment policy to the belly dancing example was erroneous, he ruled, because this example "was not of a sexual nature" [7, pp. 43–44].

On the procedural side, the judge was concerned that the boards' "determination of whether [Professor Silva's] conduct constituted sexual harassment" might have been affected by the previous warning [7, p. 74]. In fact, as I have explained, we were not *told* about the previous warning until after we made our decision, but under the judicial standard he adopted, the judge did not have to inquire about the facts: "In determining whether summary judgment is appropriate, the court construes the evidence and draws all justifiable inferences in the nonmoving party's [that is, Professor Silva's] favor" [7, p. 74]. The judge also expressed concern about two incidents in the appeals board hearing that he saw as evidence of "bias" on the part of one of our student members, Shannon Cannon. Professor Silva, in his legal deposition, accused Ms. Cannon of interrupting the hearing to charge him with making an inappropriate sexual remark in the midst of the proceedings. In fact, it was the students' adviser, not Ms. Cannon, who made this accusation; Shannon, who was seated directly across the table from Professor Silva, then stated (very quietly) that she had also heard the remark. During a subsequent break in the hearing, Professor Silva followed Shannon downstairs and attempted to speak with her. We were greatly astonished that the judge used these incidents against our board rather than against Professor Silva.

Professor Silva's lawsuit was directed not only against the university and university administrators but also against the five members of the appeals board, in our professional and our individual capacities. The judge refused to grant us qualified immunity, ruling that "a reasonable University official [sic] would not have believed his or her actions [in disciplining Professor Silva] were lawful" [7, p. 89]; we were held responsible, subject to damages against our own personal assets for any breaches of Professor Silva's due process rights [7, p. 91].[10]

THE AAUP REPORT

Professor Silva had also taken his complaint to the national AAUP, and in spring 1994, while the lawsuit was still in progress, that body sent an investigating team to our campus. Because the members of our board had been advised by legal counsel that anything we said would be used against us in court, we were not able to tell our side of the story.[11] Thus the investigating committee heard a very incomplete version of the story, and their report on the case, published in the November/December 1994 issue of *Academe,* contained a number of factual errors.[12]

The AAUP view was, in some respects, the opposite of Judge Devine's. The judge had found our policy to be appropriate but rejected its application to Professor Silva, whom he considered to be innocent; the AAUP committee concluded that Professor Silva had been guilty of poor judgment, at least, and possibly of sexual harassment [2, p. 79], but found serious fault with our policy and procedures. They particularly criticized the two hearing boards, on the grounds (1) that the members were appointed rather than elected and not all of them were faculty [2, p. 76],[13] (2) that there was no formal statement of charges before the hearing, making it difficult for Professor Silva to prepare his defense, (3) that the charges were not adequately proved [2, pp. 76–77], and (4) that there was "confusion" in the hearings, particularly in connection with the events surrounding Professor Silva's "remark," described above.[14]

Our board could have answered these criticisms if the AAUP had postponed its investigation until we were able to speak. First, although it is true that the members of the board were appointed rather than elected, each party was given the right to two peremptory challenges and to challenge for cause any member of the hearing panel; Professor Silva chose not to challenge the composition of the boards that heard his case. Second, while it is true that there was no formal statement of the charges against Professor Silva, all parties to the hearing received, in advance, the written complaints of the students and their academic adviser, Professor Jerilee Zezula, along with Professor Silva's own summary of the charges, with his responses [8] [9].[15] Furthermore, in reading through the transcript of our hearing, I can find no instance in which charges or testimony were admitted over the objection of Professor Silva or his adviser.

The AAUP's concern about "burden of proof" was apparently based on Professor Balling's contention that the boards had refused to listen to Professor Silva's explanation of the incidents in question. In fact, as I have explained, there was little or no disagreement about the facts, and our understanding of Professor Silva's motivation was based primarily on his own testimony. I believe we gave him a fair hearing. Professor Silva's adviser, Tom Carnicelli, has stated that "the members of the [appeals board] panel were courteous, pleasant, and even-handed" [4, p. 1]. In his deposition [8, p. 40], Professor Silva concurred. Not everyone will agree with our judgment, but it is hard for me to see how anyone could conclude that it was unfair.

I spent several months trying to persuade the AAUP to allow me to respond to their criticisms of our board and to correct the factual errors in their report, but to no avail. The AAUP's obligation is to the accused faculty member, not to the faculty who serve on the hearing board, wrote Jonathan Knight, AAUP Associate Secretary, and it cannot allow its investigation to be delayed by the fact that the case is in litigation. John D. Lyons, editor of *Academe,* informed me that *Academe* does not publish replies to investigative reports and does not issue corrections of factual errors.[16] Professor Jim Perley, AAUP president, explained, oxymoronically, that it was because of their deep concern for freedom of speech that these members of the association were so unwilling to let me tell my side of the story.

AFTERMATH

Following Judge Devine's decision, the university appealed the case to the 1st U.S. Circuit Court of Appeals in Boston but reached an out-of-court settlement in December 1994, under binding arbitration imposed by the court. Professor Silva returned to the classroom in October 1994, and was given two classes to teach. In an interview with our campus newspaper, he affirmed his right to free speech in the classroom and assured the campus that his "warm, informal" teaching style would remain unchanged. At the end of the semester, five students, all male, reported that his teaching style is "blunt" and that he "swears a lot in class," but they had not been offended. As of this writing, Professor Silva is still teaching in the Thompson School, and, to my knowledge, there have been no further complaints about his behavior toward students.

The university, under threat of AAUP sanctions, has now instituted a new harassment policy that differs from the old in three main respects:

1. Whereas our old policy was directed specifically against *sexual* harassment, the new policy has been broadened to include harassment on the basis of race, color, sex, religion, national origin, disability, or sexual orientation.

2. The new policy contains language protecting comments that are "merely offensive" or "controversial," as well as comments in the classroom that are "germane to the curriculum and part of the exchange of competing ideas."

3. Harassment charges will no longer be heard by hearing boards but will be decided by the dean or director of the accused, in consultation with the university's affirmative action officer. The decision may be "grieved" through established grievance procedures that, in the case of faculty, include a review by an elected faculty board, but this board reviews only the procedural conduct of the case; it makes no decision on the charges.

I was surprised at the change in our hearing procedures: the AAUP report on the Silva case had called for a full "adjudicative hearing" of harassment charges against faculty "before an elected faculty body," but our new policy, which the AAUP has accepted, removes faculty from the process altogether. When I inquired about this, I was told that our local AAUP chapter had been reluctant to give this responsibility to faculty. When a faculty member is judged by a hearing board that contains faculty members, as in the Silva case, it becomes difficult and controversial for the AAUP to side unequivocally with the accused. This dilemma is avoided, under our new procedures, by placing the decision entirely in the hands of administrators. It is hard to know how this will work in practice. The new procedures have an advantage in that they allow decisions to be reached quickly; on the other hand, administrators, being easy targets for criticism, may find it difficult to make tough decisions in controversial cases.

The "hostile environment" clause was another controversial feature of our old policy, but, to my surprise, the new policy retains a hostile environment clause, as follows:

> The requirements of federal and state law determine the definition of harassment. The relevant body of law stipulates that any behavior is considered to be harassing when: (1) submission to or rejection of such behavior by an individual is used as a basis for employment or academic decisions affecting that individual; or (2) submission to such behavior is made either explicitly or implicitly a term or condition of an individual's employment or academic work; or (3) *such behavior unjustly, substantially, unreasonably and/or consistently interferes with an individual's work or academic performance or creates an intimidating environment.* (my emphasis)

The new policy has been in effect for only a short time, and no cases have been brought forward under it. In fact, no harassment complaint has been brought against a faculty member since the Silva case, a situation for which there are competing explanations: Possibly, as a result of the Silva case, faculty are now engaging in "self-censorship," so that incidents of this sort no longer occur. Or, possibly, women on our campus may simply have learned not to complain.

CONCLUSION

If I were asked to hear the case again tomorrow, knowing all that I know now, I would have to reach the same conclusion: Professor Silva's peculiar mixture of sexual innuendo and personal insult still seems to me to constitute sexual harassment. And I am still glad, in spite of everything, that we had the courage to stand up and say that this behavior is not acceptable in the classroom. Furthermore, despite the disappointing outcome of the case, I believe it has had a beneficial effect on our campus.

Nothing, however, could have prepared me for the handling of the case in the media. The university should, certainly, have been more aggressive in presenting its side of the story, but I now realize that journalists carry a natural bias in cases of this sort, because of the battle they themselves must constantly wage for freedom of the press.[17] I also gained a new appreciation of the vulnerability of journalists to propaganda groups like the Center for Individual Rights. Under the pressure of deadlines and the desire to participate in a big story, journalists assume the accuracy of the information they are given in press releases; they do not take the time to check the facts or to explore the real-life complexities of the issues they are covering.

Along with my new cynicism about the press, I have also come to doubt the feasibility of prosecuting harassment on campus. Campuses are too politicized to allow judicial processes to proceed without interference, and, in our present climate, campus hearings will always be retried in the courts and in the press, with damage to all concerned. Nevertheless, even a case that turned out as badly as ours still had some positive outcomes. Our new harassment policy is better than I expected, with its retention of the "hostile environment" clause and procedures that are, in some respects, an improvement over the old. A more important and very surprising development is that on a campus where the administration has always been uniformly male, we have now, suddenly, gained a strong new set of women administrators, as well as new female leadership in the faculty. Unlikely as it may seem, I see this partly as an outcome of the Silva case: in the aftermath of that case, participants from all sides of the debate felt compelled to demonstrate that our campus is not, after all, biased against women. Be that as it may, it is very good news indeed that women are finally gaining some power on our campus; that, more than policies and procedures, may be what finally puts an end to sexual harassment at the University of New Hampshire.

Notes

1. Under our procedures, the appeals board was asked not to review the decision of the hearing board but to hear the case all over again, from the beginning. Thus two independent boards heard the charges start to finish, and both reached the same conclusion.
2. Professor Silva told us that he took this analogy from a record album entitled How to Belly Dance for your Husband, which he had bought his wife for Christmas a number of years before [10, pp. 332–33]. In referring to a "vibrator," he had intended not a sexual device, as the students had assumed, but a neck massager.
3. The students responded, and Professor Silva agreed, that at this early stage of the course, in their library exercises, they were *supposed* to be working collaboratively [10, p. 382].
4. After the hearing was over, we heard additional reports of sexually explicit examples in spelling tests. In a September, 1994 interview with Anthony Brooks of WBUR, Boston, UNH student Dan Adams cited an example Professor Silva had used in *his* class for the word "angle": "The angle of the dangle is equal to the heat of the meat." Many of the students were embarrassed, Adams said.
5. For example, the Jell-O/belly dancing analogy was not, as Silva claimed, an example of a "working definition."
6. A colleague who worked with Professor Silva told me, later, that the "anti-Semitic" complaint concerned a classroom story that Professor Silva had told about a Jewish woman whom he referred to as a Jewish "babe." Several students had walked out.
7. Professor Balling argued that the students had misinterpreted innocent remarks by Professor Silva, and that the hearing boards had refused to listen to Professor Silva's explanations.
8. Bernstein also drew attention to the unorthodox spelling and fractured syntax of the complainants (who were, after all, not regular UNH students but members of our two-year technical college) and to the fact that Professor Silva serves as the part-time minister of a nearby Congregational church.
9. This part of Judge Devine's ruling is particularly difficult to understand, since Professor Silva's classroom remarks had nothing to do with either the preservation of academic freedom *or* the issue of whether speech that is offensive to a particular class of individuals should be tolerated in American schools. The reasoning seems to indicate that offensive remarks, simply by virtue of their offensiveness, are automatically concerned with these issues.
10. The university attorney assured us that, barring "reckless" behavior on our part, we would be "fully indemnified" for any damages that might be awarded.
11. Two members of the appeals board did speak briefly with the investigating committee, but they were not in a position to speak freely.
12. Some of these were (1) that our statement of findings had been written by the university's affirmative action officer (it was not), (2) that we had required Silva to undergo "psychotherapy" (we required "counseling"), (3) that the counselor was to be "selected by the university" (Silva was to choose the counselor from a university-approved list), and (4) that Professor Silva was to pay for the counseling himself, unlike the policy for faculty with alcohol-related problems. (Both substance-abuse counseling and counseling of a more general nature are covered by our health insurance; Silva's insurance was continued during his suspension, at the request of the board.)
13. Our policy, which had been approved by our academic senate, stipulated that, in a dispute between a student and a faculty member, both constituencies should be represented. The hearing

board was made up of two faculty, two students, and one member of the professional staff. The appeals board consisted of three faculty and two students.

14. The procedure we followed to resolve this incident was proposed by Professor Silva's adviser, Professor Carnicelli—namely, that everyone who had heard the remark should be asked to write down what they heard, without consulting one another. Contrary to what Professor Carnicelli was apparently hoping, the written responses were quite consistent, but it was impossible to draw any conclusion from this result, because the alleged remark had been repeated several times out loud, and there was no way to be sure what the witnesses were recollecting. The board therefore decided to disregard the entire incident.

15. The AAUP investigating committee was apparently not aware of his document.

16. Professor Lyons's letter to me included—inadvertently, I assume—a note from Associate Secretary Knight asking Lyons to make no decision about my request until he (Knight) had the opportunity to share certain "information" he had obtained about me. I was unable to find out what this information might be.

17. The situations are, of course, quite different: No one is forced to read a newspaper or listen to a newscast, but students are required to take certain courses, and cannot do their work without attending class and listening to what their professors say.

References

1. AAUP. "Academic Freedom and Sexual Harassment." *Academe* 80.5 (1994): 64–79.
2. ———. "Academic Freedom and Tenure: University of New Hampshire." *Academe* 80.6 (1994) 70–81.
3. Bernstein, Richard. "Guilty If Charged." *New York Review* 13 January 1994.
4. Carnicelli, Thomas. "Letter to the UNH Community," Spring, 1994.
5. *Deposition of J. Donald Silva.* United States District Court for the District of New Hampshire. Civil no. 93-533-SD, 1 June 1994.
6. Lewis, Anthony. "Time to Grow Up." *New York Times* 14 October 1994, A19.
7. Order of Preliminary Injunction: *J. Donald Silva v. The University of New Hampshire et al.* United States District Court for the District of New Hampshire. Civil no. 93-533-SD, 16 September 1994.
8. Silva, J. Donald. "Incidents Cited as Evidence of Sexual Harassment." 15 April 1992.
9. ———. "Refutation of the Alleged Claims against Professor Silva." 15 April 1992.
10. *Transcription of Hearing Audio Recording: Sexual Harassment Hearing in re. Professor Donald Silva.* Prepared by Bragan Reporting Associates, Inc. 29 March 1993.
11. *University System Policy Manual.* Durham: University System of New Hampshire.
12. Zezula, Jerilee. "Statement Regarding the Complaints against Professor Silva." 26 February 1992.

❊ 29. The Reasonable Woman: Sense and Sensibility in Sexual Harassment Law

Kathryn Abrams

Is sexual harassment understood differently by men and women? If so (as seems likely), whose understanding should set the standard for court decisions? These questions, which lawyers have argued about for almost a decade, reached the general public with the Senate testimony of Anita Hill. [See Selection 20.] But the ensuing debate—between partisans of a universal common sense and those who see perceptions of sexual harassment as gender-differentiated—has thus far produced more heat than light. Although the debate has offered a fascinating window on movements within feminist theory, it has rarely yielded sufficient guidance for the judgement of actual cases.

The central challenge of sexual harassment litigation has been to define when harassment becomes sufficiently pervasive to create a "hostile environment." The Supreme Court accepted the idea of hostile-environment sexual harassment in 1986, but its pronouncements on the question of pervasiveness have been frustratingly vague. Sexual harassment violates the law when it is "severe or pervasive [enough] to alter the conditions of plaintiff's employment and create an abusive working environment," or when it "unreasonably interferes with [plaintiff's] work performance and creat[es] a hostile, intimidating or offensive" environment. This proliferation of adjectives has raised more questions than it has answered. Is an "intimidating" or "offensive" environment different from an "abusive" one? Do certain kinds of conduct contribute more to the creation of such environments than others? Compounding these difficulties has been a question of perspective or vantage point in assessing the alleged abuse. Courts are frequently confronted with a plaintiff who argues that certain conduct starkly interferes with her work performance, and a defendant who argues that the same conduct is trivial, episodic, jocular, or nonintrusive. How can judges find an independent ground on which to stand in assessing these allegations?

The first solution offered by the courts was to assess the claims of the plaintiff from the perspective of the "reasonable person." This approach offered several advantages. First, it had the legitimizing pedigree of a long history in the law: courts had assessed the conduct of torts defendants from the standpoint of the "reasonable man" and later the (gender-neutral) "reasonable person" to determine whether they had met the required duty of care toward plaintiffs. Second, the specification of a vantage point distinct from that of the actual plaintiff offered reassurance to employers; it protected them from liability arising from idiosyncratic claims. Finally, the resort to a vantage point ostensibly accessible to any observer held the promise of reducing the growing confusion over the "pervasiveness" standard. In the long tradition of jurists who have sought procedural answers to festering substantive disputes, proponents of the "reasonable person" test appealed to perspective—in this case, a kind of universal common sense—to mitigate controversy over "pervasiveness."

But as feminist advocates soon made clear, the "reasonable person" standard only complicated the controversy. Their challenge to this standard reflected the confluence of two intellectual movements within feminist theory. The first was a tendency toward gender differentiation, characteristic of both cultural and radical feminisms. These movements resisted the gender-neutrality characteristic of equality theories, which had described women as substantially similar to men. Cultural feminists argued that this move understated and undervalued the biological and social ways in which women differed from men. Radical feminists charged that the focus on women's conformity to male norms diverted attention from a system of power relations through which male characteristics become normative. Both groups bridled at the possibility that women's perspectives would be described in terms simultaneously applicable to men.

The second influential movement was the challenge to objectivist accounts of knowledge. Feminist writers assailed the notion of "truth" as something "out there," external to the position of the observer, accessible by certain neutral observational methods. The status of legal norms or social understandings as "true" or "neutral," and the legitimation of certain methods for gaining access to them, are incidents of power, they argued. Resisting such power meant exposing the extent to which understandings of social relations are shaped by social location. And it meant exposing those viewpoints considered to be neutral or true as another example of a partial perspective, distinguished only by the ability of its adherents to make their vision normative.

Resistance also required a challenge to objectivist modes of knowledge production. One important strategy in this effort has been a re-valuation of nondominant ways of knowing about the world. Some scholars, influenced by cultural feminism, have valorized "ways of knowing" they describe as characteristic of women: reasoning from personal experience is one example; choosing contextual reasoning over abstract principle is another. Other scholars, retaining a focus on the power dimension, have claimed an "epistemic advantage" for those at the bottom of reigning hierarchies. The oppressed, in this view, enjoy a double source of knowledge: their experience in a society built around the understandings of the privileged familiarizes them with those perspectives, but gives them a view from a subordinated social location that the privileged lack.

These diverse insights combined to fuel a critique of the "reasonable person" standard. Feminist advocates pointed first to the gendered origins of the standard. The "reasonable person" had its beginnings in the "reasonable man," a fellow who "takes the magazines at home and in the evening pushes the lawn mower in his shirtsleeves." (*Hall v. Brooklands Auto Racing Club,* 1933, quoting "unnamed American author.") As this early twentieth century elaboration reveals, what was being presented as universal common sense was in fact the sense of a particular, socially located person: one whose perspective was shaped by his freedom to relax with his magazines at home, and to enjoy sovereignty over his physical—and familial—domain. Moreover, the assertion of a single valid perspective on sexual harassment belied the gender differentiation that many kinds of research were beginning to reveal. Social scientists like Barbara Gutek pointed to a sharp divergence in the way men and women view sexualized conduct in the workplace. [See Selection 3.] Men were likely to see sexualized words or gestures as flattering, indicative of long-term interest, and not threatening to professional progress; women were likely to associate them with manipulation, exploitation, or threat, and to see them as imperiling their professional prospects. Analyses like that of Catharine MacKinnon offered an explanatory social context for these differences. [See Selection 2.] Women workers' experience of marginality within the workplace, and sexual vulnerability in and outside it, caused them to view the sexual inflection of work relations with a fearfulness unlikely to be shared by their male counterparts. Finally, feminists worried that the "reasonable person" standard might confirm the (largely male) judiciary in its unreflective assurance that it understood the phenomenon of sexual harassment. Judges might view it as authorizing them to decide cases on the basis of their own intuition: the same "common sense" that had marked the administration of the "reasonable person" standard in tort law—and the same "common sense" that had normalized the practice of sexual harassment in the first place.

All of these factors suggested the preferability of a "reasonable woman" standard. This formulation would explicitly challenge notions of a universal perspective. It would characterize the evaluation of harassment, like the experience of harassment itself, as a phenomenon strongly differentiated on the basis of gender. The gender-specific language would place male judges on alert that they could no longer rely on their unexamined intuitions. The "reasonable woman" standard would replace those intuitions with a perspective that promised a radical revision of workplace conditions. Yet beyond the notion that such a perspective would "take harassment seriously"—viewing it neither as a right of the employer, nor as a harmless, if vulgar, form of male amusement—there was little explicit discussion of what insights or sensibilities it entailed.

As the eighties closed, this approach began to be embraced by the federal courts. In a landmark case called *Ellison v. Brady,* the Ninth Circuit Court of Appeals held that sexual harassment should be evaluated from the perspective of the "reasonable woman." In *Ellison* a woman received a series of letters from a colleague she barely knew, describing his love for and continuous surveillance of her. The trial court had shrugged off the behavior as a "pathetic attempt at courtship," but the Court of Appeals disagreed. It stressed the importance of considering the conduct from the standpoint of a "reasonable woman": "a sex-blind reasonable person standard," the court noted, "tends to be male biased and tends to systematically ignore the experiences of women." It held that, viewed from the perspective of a "reasonable woman," receiving "long, passionate, disturbing" letters from a person one barely knew represented sufficiently pervasive and severe harassment to create a hostile environment.

The court recognized the need, in such a context, to elaborate the differences in perspective between men and women. And it took a few steps in that direction, noting that conduct considered unobjectionable by men might be offensive to women, and stating that women's vulnerability to sexual assault gave them a "stronger incentive" to be concerned about sexual behavior in the workplace. But the largely passive stance of the *Ellison* court toward the elaboration of perspectival differences is expressed in its "hope that over time men and women will learn what conduct offends reasonable members of the opposite sex."

Both the strengths and the drawbacks of the *Ellison* opinion were underscored in the revolution catalyzed by Anita Hill. Women's denunciation of senators who failed to "get it" stressed the gendered character of perceptions of sexual harassment, and the need for a gendered standard of evaluation. The "reasonable woman" standard was, in fact, adopted by several additional courts in the wake of the Senate hearings. But the growing concern of even well-intentioned men with the "new rules of engagement" pointed to the need for explicit discussion of the determinants of gender difference in this area. Both men and women sought greater clarity about the ways in which their perceptions of sexual harassment diverged, and the "hope" for mutual understanding expressed by *Ellison* failed to fill the bill.

As the call for a fuller elaboration of women's perspectives continued, the "reasonable woman" standard began to be challenged from an unexpected quarter: the feminist movement itself. There were several sources of this attitudinal sea change. Some feminists worried that unitary images of female difference could be manipulated by hostile forces. Images of women that emphasized care or connection could be used to explain the absence of women from more competitive jobs—a link that was made in the notorious *Sears* litigation. "Women's ways of knowing" could be used to reinforce stereotypes of the intuitive or irrational woman. Others challenged accounts of strong gender differentiation as essentialist and potentially oppressive. A range of "anti-essentialist" feminists, led by lesbians and women of color, argued that unitary depictions of women replicated the false and exclusory universalism of the gender-neutral approach. Some asked whether the divergent social circumstances of women could possibly yield the same knowledge: how could modes of reasoning shaped by the domestic context, for example, apply to women who did not remain in the home or live within conventional families? Others argued that the unity presented in depictions of "women's experience" derived not from homogeneity but from erasure. Comparatively privileged white middle class women—through solipsism or strategic exclusion—had eclipsed the experiences of less privileged subgroups.

These insights made many feminists wary of the gathering momentum behind the "reasonable woman" standard. They worried that the "reasonable woman," like other paradigmatic "women" of feminist theory, would turn out to be white, middle class, and heterosexual. Others asked whether simply living as a woman assured a particular perspective on sexual harassment. The disparagement of sexual harassment claims by female "mavericks" like Judge Maryanne Trump Berry gave some advocates pause. The "reasonable woman" might simply free women judges to resort to *their* intuitions, in ways that were not uniformly promising to female claimants. Moreover, the standard might fail to prompt the desired response from male judges—permitting them to indulge their own, biologized visions of female difference. So there was a growing division among feminist advocates over the "reasonable woman" standard, with some calling for a further elaboration or differentiation of the standard, and others seeking a return to gender neutrality or a rejection of all "reasonableness" criteria.

These differences among feminists were brought to the fore by the Supreme Court's second case on hostile environment sexual harassment: *Harris v. Forklift Systems* (November 9, 1993). [See Selection 53.] That case presented the question of whether plaintiffs must demonstrate "serious psychological injury" in order to win their cases. But the court also agreed to consider whether hostile environment claims should be reviewed under a gendered or gender-neutral standard. Those feminist advocates who filed amicus briefs with the court were frankly divided on the question of the standard: the Employment Law Center and Equal Rights Advocates endorsed a "reasonable woman" standard, while Catharine MacKinnon and the Women's Legal Defense and Education Fund argued that "reasonableness" standards, whether gender-specific or gender-neutral, reinforce stereotypes and distract the court from the primary issue—the conduct of the defendant. The decision, when it came, was anticlimactic. Although the court resoundingly rejected the psychological injury requirement, it resolved the question of standard in less than a sentence, stating that the court should review the plaintiff's claim according to the perspective of the "reasonable person," with no elaboration and no explanation of its decision.

It is hard to know what conclusions to draw from this cryptic affirmation of gender-neutrality. It suggests that a court that has displayed studied disinterest in group-based distinctions is not prepared to embrace a standard that underscores—and perhaps risks instantiating—gender difference. Some subset of male judges will now, no doubt, resort to their own, unschooled intuitions in evaluating sexual harassment cases. But has the court scuttled the entire project of introducing a new, non-dominant sensibility about sexual harassment into adjudication? I see no reason to draw so negative a conclusion. The first goal of the "reasonable woman" standard was to emphasize the gendered character of sexual harassment and prevent resort to a "common sense" that was likely to preserve the status quo. The second goal was to permit access to a distinct set of perspectives that would open the way for a transformation of workplace norms. Though the courts have made only limited progress in fleshing out these perspectives, their elaboration is essential to reshaping the perceptions of judges, and ultimately of those who structure the workplace. This second, and arguably more important, task can still be performed under a "reasonable person" standard.

My own argument begins with the anti-essentialist insight that neither modes of knowing nor particular bodies of knowledge are inextricably linked to biological sex or social gender. There are things that women are more likely to know by virtue of having lived as women. There are practices—such as those involving devaluation or sexualization—to which they are likely to have a heightened sensitivity by virtue of having experienced them, heard about them repeatedly, or seen them applied to other women. But this likelihood cannot be collapsed into inevitability: some women have had few of the experiences that produce such sensitivity; others respond with indifference or denial; women who are aware of discriminatory practices may perceive them in different ways. Just as being female does not guarantee transformative perceptions of sexual conduct in the workplace, being male does not exclude the possibility of having, or developing, them. If perceptions of sexual harassment do not depend solely on biology, life experience, or gender-specific modes of knowing, but rather on varied sources of information regarding women's inequality—if such perceptions, in other words, are a matter not of innate common sense but of informed sensibility—then they can be cultivated in a range of women and men. The "reasonable person" standard, properly elaborated, might be a vehicle for the courts to play a role in this educative process. The reasonableness term, as Martha Chamallas has suggested, could be interpreted to mean not the average person, but the person enlightened concerning the barriers to women's equality in the workplace.

What remains is the uncompleted task of elaborating the determinants of this "reasonable" perspective. What should legal decision makers—and actors in the workplace—know about women, work, and sex that would help them assess claims of sexual harassment in ways that transform the present, often oppressive assumptions of the workplace? I would emphasize four kinds of information that could be offered by expert testimony or by counsel in framing their clients' claims. Some might be included in judges' instructions, when these cases are tried to juries. They reflect the experience not of any paradigmatic woman but of diverse groups of women, in and out of the workplace.

(1) The first kind of information concerns barriers that women have faced, and continue to face, in the workplace. Women are newcomers to many work settings; the work they have traditionally performed has been poorly paid, socially undervalued, and situated on the lower rungs of occupational hierarchies dominated by men. Women's entry into nontraditional jobs has been met with outright hostility, expressed through conduct verging on physical intimidation. Once inside the workplace, women have been met by glass ceilings, by ostensibly neutral criteria that (barely) conceal gender-based judgments, by biologized assumptions about their ability to perform particular jobs.

Even in settings where women have not faced overt barriers, they have been confronted with reminders that workplaces were not designed to meet their needs: persistent demographic disparities, machinery constructed to male needs, failures to accommodate women's disproportionate parental responsibilities. As a result, many women feel that they are marginal participants in the workplace, that their hold on their job or on the respect of their superiors is tenuous and subject to factors not within their control. Sexualized conduct in the workplace may interact with all of these factors, inducing a sense of precariousness or professional threat that it would not necessarily induce in a man.

(2) The second kind of information decision makers require concerns the role of sexualized treatment in thwarting women in the workplace. The meanings assigned to sex by women in this culture are various, and include physical pleasure, emotional connection, and opportunities for self-discovery and self-expression. Yet among the most familiar meanings, themes of intimidation, objectification, and devaluation are readily discernible. High rates of sexual assault by strangers and acquaintances have led many women to feel that their sexuality makes them physically vulnerable. The "myth of the black rapist" has produced a complicated legacy for black women, in which fears about physical security vie with suspicions of racial exploitation. Even in their less overtly threatening guises, sexual depictions of women may be trivializing, suggesting that women find their primary purpose in male attention, titillation or satisfaction.

It is largely these negative cultural themes that echo in sexualized treatment in the workplace. Sexual aggression, including violent forms of sexual assault, has been repeatedly used by employers and fellow employees to resist women's entry into blue-collar and other nontraditional workplaces. A male employer who propositions a female subordinate may be expressing a genuine interest, but it is also possible that he is asserting a combination of sexual and economic power, which reminds the woman of her social inequality. Even where the motivation is more ambiguous, the threatening or devaluative resonance may persist. Sexual epithets and targeted sexual talk, whatever their ostensible purpose, remind women that, despite their advancement to roles not technically defined by sex, they can still be treated as sexual objects or addressed in primarily sexual ways. The broader cultural backdrop to these forms of conduct needs to be made explicit, so that professedly well-intentioned men who defend sexual talk as harmless humor can understand that it may have connotations they do not see.

These elaborations of women's circumstances in many workplaces can, and have, been used to assist in the evaluation of sexual harassment claims. In *Lehmann v. Toys 'R' Us* (July 14, 1993), a New Jersey Supreme Court case decided days before *Harris,* Justice Marie Garibaldi pointed to women's historical marginality in the workplace and their vulnerability to sexualized abuse, to give content to a "reasonable woman's" perspective. These same factors, and those articulated below, could be used to explain a "reasonable person" standard as well.

The second two factors that courts should consider concern not the backdrop to sexual harassment but its consequences.

(3) Sexual harassment can produce a range of effects on the work lives of women. Although *Harris* has ruled out a requirement of psychological harm, many legal fact-finders still believe that harassment does not create a hostile environment unless women are rendered professionally nonfunctional. If a woman is able to drag herself to work and perform some acceptable version of her assigned tasks, decision makers—and employers—assume that the behavior has not reached an actionable level. Yet a statute that promises women an environment "free from discriminatory intimidation, ridicule, and insult" requires that fact-finders look further: there are many ways that sexual harassment can create impediments, even for the woman who continues to do her job. Propositions or touching from an unexpected source can make a woman fear sexual assault; sexual epithets may make her feel that she is being objectified. Both can affect not only her self-esteem but the conditions of her employment: they may impair her concentration or productivity, or undermine her confidence in herself as a worker.

Though sexualized treatment can affect the performance of women workers directly, many of its most far-reaching effects derive from its impact on her colleagues and associates. When a woman is addressed by her supervisor as if her most salient attributes were sexual, this may prevent other workers from viewing her seriously. Such impressions may affect evaluations or considerations for promotion. They may compromise the provision of assistance, training, or staff support, or may prevent her from developing the kinds of collegial relationships that facilitate progress in any employment setting. These varied impediments to job performance may have been what Justice Ginsberg had in mind when she stated, in her *Harris* concurrence, that sexual harassment makes it "harder for women to do their jobs" than it is for men. Judges should be aware of the range of effects that even sexualized talk can produce, in assessing the pervasiveness of alleged harassment.

(4) The final type of information that legal decision makers require is information about the responses of women workers to harassment. Provision of this information is, in a sense, defensive: demonstration of some particular response should not, after *Harris,* be necessary for a plaintiff; but information about the ways that many women respond to harassing behavior may prevent judges from relying on stereotyped expectations about victims' responses. Empirical studies of sexual harassment suggest that fewer than 20 percent of women who believe they have been harassed complain to authorities within the workplace, and even fewer leave their jobs. Most women handle the problem with some combination of levity (where the conduct assumes a jocular tone), conversational management, or avoidance. An individual victim's response to sexual harassment is described by psychologists as a function of many things besides the nature of the conduct. Even exposure to the same kinds of oppressive influences may produce different responses in different women. A woman's personality type and the particular coping mechanisms she uses to respond to adverse circumstances may have a major impact on her reaction. Women with strong support from family and friends may be able to weather harassment with less psychological strain than women who lack such resources. What is known about women workers, and workers more generally, suggests that their visible response to harassing conduct will be an unreliable gauge of the severity or the practical impact of the treatment. Providing fact-finders with this information places the individual victim's response in context, so as to prevent judges from "trying the victim" or neglecting more accurate indications of pervasive harassment they may have before them.

The court's embrace of the "reasonable person" standard is not an unequivocal step forward. It avoids promulgating falsely unifying images of women. But it also fails to jolt judges into recognition that their intuitive perspectives are not the only, or the preferable, vantage point on the claims before them. The challenge confronting feminist advocates is to provide this jolt by other means: not through the jarring, but so far unelaborated, mechanism of a gendered referent, but through illumination of those factors that have shaped women's responses to sexual harassment. If viewed as an invitation to offer concrete information about women's lives, the "reasonable person" standard may yet help legal decision makers to create a less oppressive workplace.

30. Closing the "Bisexual Defense" Loophole in Title VII Sexual Harassment Cases

Sandra Levitsky

In December 1992, Francine Ryczek worked as a student intern for Guest Services, a Washington, D.C.-based company specializing in the culinary arts. During her tenure at Guest Services she worked under the supervision of Chef Catherine O'Brien.[1] Ryczek alleges that early in her tenure, O'Brien expressed having a sexual preference for women. O'Brien went on to inquire into Ryczek's own sexual activities, commenting to and touching Ryczek in ways Ryczek felt were sexual and inappropriate.[2] At one point, O'Brien caught Ryczek alone in an elevator and removed her own shirt in an apparent attempt to elicit a sexual response from Ryczek.[3] Ultimately, Ryczek felt compelled to leave the program due to what she perceived as an environment filled with sexual harassment.[4] Ryczek subsequently sued Guest Services under Title VII of the 1964 Civil Rights Act.[5]

Guest Services moved for summary judgment on Ryczek's claim, arguing Title VII created no cause of action for sexual harassment involving members of the same gender.[6] In an attempt to invoke a Title VII loophole unintentionally created by Judge Spottswood W. Robinson, III in *Barnes v. Costle*,[7] Guest Services argued O'Brien was bisexual.[8] Judge Robinson stated in his now-notorious footnote fifty-five that "[i]n the case of a bisexual superior, the insistence upon sexual favors would not constitute gender discrimination because it would apply to male and female employees alike."[9]

The *Ryczek* facts bring to life a legal debate which for two decades has existed only in the realm of the hypothetical.[10] Courts have acknowledged that under current sexual harassment standards, harassers are liable for sex discrimination only when they treat members of one sex differently than members of the opposite sex.[11] Thus in cases of equal opportunity sexual harassment,[12] in which a person presumably harasses both men and women equally, victims have no Title VII remedy.[13] As Guest Services' arguments in *Ryczek* suggest, many courts also deny a Title VII cause of action to victims of same-sex sexual harassment. Courts do so for the same reason they deny a cause of action to victims of equal opportunity sexual harassment—the harassment was not based on "sex."[14] Such a result seems inappropriate given that victims of equal opportunity and same-sex sexual harassment suffer no less an injury from sexual harassment than victims of opposite-sex sexual harassment. Ryczek found her workplace no less hostile, demeaning or offensive because her harasser was bisexual or homosexual.

This article uses same-sex and equal opportunity sexual harassment cases to illustrate the inadequacies of current sexual harassment standards under Title VII's "because of . . . sex" requirement.[15] It offers an alternative analysis that recognizes inequalities in the workplace exist independently of whether employers treat men differently from women. Part I discusses current and evolving definitions of sexual harassment and their application to same-sex and equal opportunity sexual harassment cases. Part II discusses the courts' use of the "but for" causation test in sexual harassment cases. It argues the test allows for too much judicial discretion in deciding when sexual harassment occurs "because of sex," and this discretion disproportionately affects victims of same-sex and equal opportunity sexual harassment. It then criticizes the use of a comparative standard in sexual harassment cases for not recognizing cases in which discrimination occurs when employers appear to treat men and women similarly. Part II also discusses legislative proposals for resolving the problems faced by victims of same-sex and equal opportunity harassment and argues these proposals fail to address the inadequacies of current sexual harassment standards. Part III then proposes an alternative standard that would eliminate both the "but for" and comparative standards in favor of an analysis holding employers accountable for any harassment that is based on gender or gender stereotypes which perpetuate a gender hierarchy. . . .

I. Evolving Definitions of Sexual Harassment

A. Current Standards for Characterizing Sexual Harassment as Discrimination: The "But For" and Comparative Standards

Title VII does not proscribe all offensive sexual conduct in the workplace, only harassment that a person directs toward a victim because of his or her sex.[16] To determine whether harassment occurs because of the victim's sex, the court applies two tests, one to determine causation and the other to determine whether the harassment was discriminatory.[17] Typically, courts attempt to determine causation by applying a "but for" test modeled after tort law concepts—but for the plaintiff's sex, would the plaintiff have been the object of harassment?[18] The "but for" test requires the plaintiff to demonstrate that because of his or her "sex," the harasser singled out the victim for harassment.[19] Victims of same-sex and equal opportunity sexual harassment have had difficulty meeting this test because judges often conclude that the harasser's "sexual orientation" was the motivation for the harassing conduct rather than the victim's "sex."[20]

In addition to the "but for" test, courts apply a comparative standard to determine whether harassment was discriminatory: Did the harasser treat the plaintiff differently than a similarly situated employee of the opposite sex?[21] Some courts have found the comparative standard problematic for victims of same-sex harassment because there is no similarly situated employee of the opposite sex with which to compare the victim's treatment. Moreover, the harasser is not harming the victim based on the victim's sex, because the harasser and the victim are of the same sex.[22] "[The same-sex harasser] certainly does not despise the entire [sex], nor does he wish to harm its members, since he is a member himself and finds others of the group sexually attractive."[23] Similarly, courts cannot readily apply the comparative standard to cases of equal opportunity sexual harassment. The harasser in such cases does not treat the plaintiff differently than members of the opposite sex—by definition, the harasser harasses both sexes equally. . . .

B. Sex Stereotyping

Recently, some feminist theorists have postulated that discrimination is not only about some individuals treating other individuals differently, but also about creating differences at a societal or institutional level that advantage and disadvantage people in unequal ways. Under this "anti-subordination" theory, sex discrimination occurs in two steps. First it occurs through gender differentiation, creating mutually exclusive gender scripts for males and females. Second, it occurs by rewarding those characteristics[24] associated with being male and penalizing and subordinating those characteristics associated with being female.[25] Sex discrimination thus is the act of perpetuating a sexual hierarchy, a social order in which men and all that is associated with being male rank higher than women and all that is associated with being female.[26]

Sexual harassment under this analysis is seen as a tool for maintaining the gender hierarchy; it is a method of control and punishment for those who deviate from scripted gender norms.[27] Andrea Dworkin writes, for example, that women's domain is the house and men's domain is the public world.[28] When a woman ventures into the wider world, "she is an unwanted alien, at best a guest worker with a short-term visa, a stigmatized immigrant."[29] Outside, she is in "male territory, a hands-on zone; her presence there is taken to be a declaration of availability—for sex and sexual insult."[30]

Feminist legal theorists have hailed the sex stereotyping theory as an effective tool in applying an anti-subordination approach to the problem of sexual harassment.[31] The Supreme Court first recognized the role sex stereotyping plays in sex discrimination in *Price Waterhouse v. Hopkins.*[32] The plaintiff, Ann Hopkins, successfully introduced the theory to the court through the expert testimony of Dr. Susan Fiske, a social scientist specializing in stereotyping.[33] Hopkins alleged Price Waterhouse had violated Title VII by permitting stereotyped ideas of women and appropriate female behavior to play a significant role in the denial of her partnership application.[34] The Supreme Court held Price Waterhouse unlawfully discriminated against Hopkins on the basis of sex by consciously giving credence and effect to the partners' sex-stereotyped comments.[35]

The theory of sex stereotyping draws on a body of research in social psychology that explains stereotyping as a function of the organizational structure of the workplace and discrimination as a function of sex stereotyping.[36] According to Fiske, sex discrimination is not a rare occurrence traceable to the bad intentions of a few people, but a by-product of a workplace that lacks a high percentage of women in powerful positions.[37] When a group is dramatically underrepresented in an organization, employers and coworkers are more likely to perceive the token individuals in terms of their social category.[38] "People expect token individuals to fit preconceived views about the traits of the group, to manifest particular qualities. Tokens are highly visible as people who are different, and they are not often permitted the individuality of their unique, nonstereotypical characteristics."[39] For Fiske, the partners' gender-based characterizations of Hopkins were a predictable response to her status as a token woman who did not conform to traditional feminine standards.[40]

While *Price Waterhouse* was not a sexual harassment case, at least one court has extended the prohibition against sex stereotyping to sexual harassment law.[41] Courts have not, however, been as receptive to attempts to use sex stereotyping theory as a way of portraying same-sex harassment as sex discrimination.[42] In *Dillon v. Frank,*[43] for example, Ernest Dillon alleged his male coworkers had sexually harassed him by taunting him with lewd expressions.[44] At oral argument, Dillon advanced a sex stereotyping argument: his coworkers did not consider him "macho" enough and therefore verbally abused him based on prevailing stereotypes of what behavior is appropriate for men and women.[45] The court rejected the sex stereotyping argument, holding Dillon's coworkers deprived him of a proper work environment not because of his gender, but because of his alleged homosexuality.[46] "These actions, although cruel, are not made illegal by Title VII."[47]

II. ANALYZING THE "BUT FOR" TEST, COMPARATIVE STANDARD, AND LEGISLATIVE SOLUTIONS TO THE PROBLEM OF SAME-SEX AND EQUAL OPPORTUNITY SEXUAL HARASSMENT

A. The "But For" Test as a Discretionary Tool for Discrimination

Victims of both same-sex and equal opportunity sexual harassment face two obstacles to establishing a prima facie case of sexual harassment, both derived from the Title VII requirement that a plaintiff prove harassment occurred "because of" sex. The first obstacle is purely definitional: what behavior constitutes harassment based on sex? While courts typically apply the "but for" standard to determine causation, the absence of any precise definition for "sex" allows judges wide latitude in defining the behavior for which the court may then hold a harasser liable.[48] This discretion negatively affects all victims of sexual harassment, but same-sex harassment strikingly illustrates the consequences of judicial discretion for victims attempting to establish a prima facie case.

Because neither Title VII nor the Supreme Court has clearly defined "sex,"[49] courts are allowed to determine whether harassment occurs because of sex or because of factors which courts have determined lie outside the purview of Title VII, such as sexual orientation.[50] This discretion to invoke a victim's sexual orientation as a reason for dismissing a Title VII cause of action typically comes into play only in same-sex harassment cases. In a "classic" sexual harassment case in which a man sexually harasses a woman, the court typically does not raise the issue of sexual orientation. For example, the court does not reason that a man harasses a woman because he is heterosexual. But when a man harasses another man, most courts hold the harasser sexually harassed the victim not because of the victim's sex, but because of his real or perceived homosexuality.[51] If the court were to look consistently at the sexual orientation of the victim in determining whether harassment occurs because of sex, then the rationale that bars claims based on same-sex harassment would bar all claims of sexual harassment: sexual orientation is equally involved in both.[52]

Those courts that have accepted same-sex sexual harassment claims simply have applied the discretionary "but for" test in the opposite way. They have held sexual harassment by a homosexual supervisor of the same sex is an adverse employment action the subordinate would not have faced but for his or her sex.[53] Courts thus interpret virtually identical behavior as occurring because of sex in some cases and because of sexual orientation in others.[54] In distinguishing unlawful harassment based on sex or gender from lawful harassment based on sexual orientation, courts often conflate the concepts of sex, gender, and sexual orientation on "an ad hoc and strategic basis."[55] "The bottom line of the doctrinal status quo is that courts can and do characterize sex and gender discrimination as sexual orientation discrimination virtually at will."[56]

B. The Comparative Standard—An Ineffective Measure of Discrimination

Victims of same-sex and equal opportunity harassment also face doctrinal difficulties in establishing prima facie cases of sexual harassment. Because Title VII is based on the formal equality doctrine, courts in sexual harassment cases apply the comparative standard[57] to assess whether men and women receive equal treatment in the workplace.[58] Victims of same-sex and equal opportunity sexual harassment illustrate the inadequacies of this characterization of discrimination: discrimination can occur without regard to whether an employer treats a member of the opposite sex differently.

Sex discrimination occurs when one sex is subordinated to the other. A system in which one sex is subordinated to the other presupposes two distinct categories of people.[59] Thus, to preserve a system of discrimination, it becomes important to create and preserve differences between the sexes. When supervisors or coworkers harass an employee based on gender or gender stereotypes, they reinforce the differences that support a system of subordination. Harassment based on gender or gender stereotypes reinforces a system of sex discrimination despite the fact that the harasser does not want to harm a member of his or her own sex or treat a member of the opposite sex differently. A comparative standard thus fails to recognize these cases as sex discrimination.

C. Legislative Solutions to Same-Sex and Equal Opportunity Sexual Harassment

One proposed solution to the problem of same-sex and equal opportunity sexual harassment involves either an amendment to Title VII to include sexual orientation as a protected class,[60] or new federal legislation to prohibit employment discrimination on the basis of sexual orientation.[61] Currently, victims of same-sex and equal opportunity sexual harassment are unable to bring claims under Title VII because courts find the category "sex" too narrow to include these types of harassment. While enactment of anti-discrimination legislation would make it easier for victims of same-sex and equal opportunity sexual harassment to establish a prima facie case of sexual harassment, such legislation fails to address the problems of using the "but for" and comparative standards in sexual harassment law.[62] The "but for" and comparative standards[63] can effectively eliminate, at the judge's discretion, cases of harassment that do not involve women being treated differently from men, but that perpetuate gender stereotypes in ways that maintain systems of gender discrimination.[64]

III. AN ANTI-SUBORDINATION ANALYSIS: MOVING THE FOCUS FROM GENDER EQUALITY TO GENDER DOMINATION

A more effective solution to the problem of same-sex and equal opportunity sexual harassment focuses not on gender equality, but on the persistent domination of one gender by another. Rather than asking whether an employer treats men and women differently, the analysis asks how the perception of difference originates and how it is maintained.[65] Such a dominance analysis would replace both the "but for" and comparative standards with a test which asks whether the victim endured harassment that perpetuated gender stereotypes in the workplace. The dominance analysis attempts to disrupt the system of gender subordination through a three-step process. First, it recognizes the role gender differences play in sexual harassment. Second, it analyzes to whose advantage and disadvantage those differences work. Finally, it holds harassers accountable by imposing Title VII liability for harassment that reinforces gender differences and women's subordinate position in society.

A. The Dominance Analysis

1. Recognizing Gender Differences

The most effective way to subordinate is to make it seem as if the dominance of men and the subordination of women occurs not because of any human decision or custom, but as a result of the natural consequences of biology.[66] One could argue that it appears natural that women act deferentially and passively and men act aggressively and competitively. Thus, it appears only natural that men advance further in their careers and earn more money because they are "naturally" more aggressive and competitive.

Feminists premise the gender domination analysis on the idea that sex discrimination exists predominately because of a rigid gender dichotomy that posits one sex (and its host of associated gender characteristics) as superior to the other.[67] The gender dichotomy works by first defining mutually exclusive scripts for being male and female and then by punishing those who deviate from their appropriate gender scripts.[68] A dominance approach to sex discrimination, then, recognizes that men and women act partly as they have been trained to act.[69] "That we are trained to behave so differently as women and as men, and to behave so differently toward women and toward men, itself contributes mightily to the appearance of extreme natural dimorphism. . . . We do become what we practice being."[70]

If sex roles were biological, there would be no need for coercion, no need for penalties for nonconforming gender behavior.[71] Recognizing gender differences as social constructions provides an important first step toward the recognition of the methods by which society subordinates women.

2. Policing Gender Boundaries

Because employers reward men more frequently than women, "men have a stake in justifying and continuing the status quo."[72] Preserving gender distinctions goes hand in hand with preserving the rewards men derive from these distinctions.[73] Sexual harassment acts in this context both as a penalty for departing from scripted gender norms and as a method of maintaining the gender hierarchy.

In opposite-sex, equal opportunity, and sexual harassment cases in which a homosexual supervisor harasses an employee of the same sex, the harasser makes the victim feel like a sex object. Sex objects are usually women.[74] For a woman, feeling like a sex object reminds her that she is a woman trespassing in a man's world; sexual harassment subordinates women by penalizing them for crossing gender boundaries.[75] Male victims of sexual harassment in these cases are victims of a "system of gender domination whose principle effect is to subordinate women."[76] When a person sexually harasses a man, the harasser both feminizes him and reinforces the idea that those qualities associated with women are subordinate to the qualities associated with men.[77]

The policing of gender boundaries is clearest in anti-gay harassment cases, where supervisors or coworkers harass an employee for exhibiting characteristics of the opposite sex. Anthony Goluszek's coworkers, for example, harassed Goluszek for being "effeminate."[78] Harassment was the penalty for not conforming to their image of male heterosexuality.[79] By policing gender boundaries in this way, Goluszek's coworkers preserved the differences between the sexes as well as the hierarchy which forms the basis of sex discrimination.

B. Sex Stereotyping—The Value of *Price Waterhouse*

Sex stereotyping theory plays an integral role in a dominance analysis of Title VII cases. The Court in *Price Waterhouse* held that Title VII prohibited employment discrimination based on sex stereotyping.[80] "[W]e are beyond the day," wrote Justice Brennan, "when an employer could evaluate employees by assuming or insisting that they matched the stereotype associated with their group. . . ."[81]

Rather than asking, as the comparative analysis does, whether the partners at Price Waterhouse would have selected Ann Hopkins for partner if she were a man,[82] a dominance analysis examines which groups are in dominant and subordinate positions of power at Price Waterhouse and the reinforcing effect of sex stereotyping on those positions. In *Price Waterhouse*, men were overwhelmingly in positions of power.[83] Sex stereotyping reinforced their dominant position in two ways. It created expectations that Hopkins should exhibit stereotypically feminine qualities that employers do not value in workers and then it penalized her for deviating from those expectations. "An employer who objects to aggressiveness in women but whose positions require this trait places women in an intolerable and impermissible Catch 22: out of a job if they behave aggressively and out of a job if they do not."[84] To preserve their dominant positions, the Price Waterhouse partners reinforced the distinctions between men and women and penalized Hopkins for not acting "according to script." After the partnership decision, the gender hierarchy was left intact: the partners were still overwhelmingly male, and Hopkins was still a subordinate.[85]

Stereotypical definitions of gender play a role in all of the various kinds of sexual harassment: opposite sex, same-sex, anti-gay, and equal opportunity harassment. Coworkers and employers punish men and women who do not conform to their "proper" gender roles. Men who express some characteristics of a female gender role, or women who express characteristics of a male gender role, blur lines and merge the distinctions between those that dominate and those that are dominated.[86] Sex stereotyping offers a way of holding people accountable when they use gender role nonconformity as a reason for harassment.

C. Resolving the Inadequacies of the "But For" Test

For victims of "classic" male on female sexual harassment, the dominance analysis would make it far easier for a plaintiff to meet the Title VII "because of . . . sex" requirement.[87] Instead of having to prove gender was the sole reason for the harassment under the "but for" test, a plaintiff would have to show only that gender or gender stereotyping was one reason for the harassment. Under the current "but for" test, judges have the power to infuse their own value judgements about proper gender behaviors into their determinations about whether harassment occurred because of sex or because of "typical" male offensive behavior.[88] Ideas of what constitutes "typical" male and female behavior are precisely the stereotypes this proposal seeks to eliminate. Allowing evidence of gender stereotyping to establish a prima facie case of sexual harassment significantly reduces judicial discretion because all harassment based on sex stereotyping would meet Title VII's "because of . . . sex" requirement.[89]

In the case of same-sex and anti-gay sexual harassment, this analysis similarly eliminates judicial discretion in conflating gender with sexual orientation.[90] In *Dillon v. Frank*,[91] for example, when the court applied the "but for" analysis to a case of same-sex harassment, it concluded Dillon's coworkers did not harass Dillon because he was a male, but because he was a homosexual male.[92] Using a dominance analysis in Dillon's case, a court would first focus on how Dillon's workplace constructs difference.[93] Dillon's coworkers singled him out and judged him because he did not conform to stereotypical gender norms.[94] His coworkers did not perceive him as "macho" enough and verbally and physically abused him for demonstrating real or perceived characteristics of a subordinate sex.[95] Under the dominance analysis, a court should find gender stereotypes were prevalent in Dillon's workplace and the stereotypes stigmatized a member of a subordinate group to the advantage of a dominant group. To deny Dillon a cause of action under these circumstances is to preserve the gender hierarchy in his workplace; to hold his employer accountable for his harassment is to disrupt it.

D. Resolving the Inadequacies of the Comparative Standard

Finally, the dominance analysis moves away from the idea that sex discrimination only occurs when women are treated differently than men. Under existing sexual harassment standards, victims of equal opportunity sexual harassment cannot prove the harassment they endured violated Title VII.[96] Defendants take advantage of this loophole by claiming the harasser was bisexual or that he or she harassed men and women equally.[97] The dominance theory recognizes that when an equal opportunity harasser sexually harasses both men and women, he or she reinforces the idea that being a sex object, a gender stereotype usually associated with women but also transferrable to men, is a subordinate status in society.[98] An equal opportunity harasser, like all people who harass, reinforces the sexual hierarchy by taking advantage of the sex object stereotype. The dominance analysis holds individuals liable for any harassment based on gender or gender stereotypes that reinforces this sexual hierarchy, regardless of the sex or sexual orientation of the victims.

CONCLUSION

The hypothetical case of the equal opportunity harasser, an inconsistency in sexual harassment doctrine that courts have universally acknowledged, has now become a reality. The increasing use of the "bisexual defense" to escape Title VII liability illustrates one of the fundamental inadequacies of the comparative standard in sexual harassment law. It leads one to question how courts can uphold the letter and spirit of Title VII's proscription against discrimination if they cannot, consistent with current sexual harassment doctrines, offer victims of equal opportunity harassment a remedy for the harassment they endure. The rise in same-sex sexual harassment suits has similarly challenged the logic of applying the "but for" test to sexual harassment law. Both same-sex and equal opportunity harassment cases compel the courts to reexamine their use of standards which are not only incapable of redressing the kinds of sex discrimination these victims endure, but are incapable of challenging the roots of sex discrimination common to all instances of sexual harassment. By recognizing that gender stereotypes systematically advantage men and disadvantage women, and by holding employers accountable for behavior that reinforces these gender stereotypes, a dominance analysis seeks to disrupt the gender hierarchy on which sex discrimination is based.

Notes

1. Ryczek v. Guest Servs., Inc. 877 F. Supp. 754, 756 (D.C. Cir. 1977).
2. *Id.*
3. *Id.*
4. *Id.* As a result, Ryczek received a failing grade on one project for the internship, required counseling, and missed several months of school and work. *Id.* at 756–57.
5. *Id.* at 757. Ryzcek also asserted claims for breach of contract, breach of covenant of good faith and fair dealing, negligent supervision, tortious interference with contract, and negligent and intentional infliction of emotional distress. *Id.*
6. *Id.*
7. 561 F,2d 983 (D.C. Cir. 1977).
8. *Ryczek,* 877 F. Supp. at 761.
9. *Id.* (quoting Barnes v. Costle, 561 F.2d 983, 990 n.55 (D.C. Cir. 1977)). While the *Ryczek* court declined to rule on the issue of same-sex or bisexual sexual harassment, it did state in dictum that the D.C. Circuit did not "recognize a Title VII cause of action for sexual harassment when the supervisor [was] bisexual." *Id.* at 761–62.
10. Judge Robinson first raised the issue of the bisexual harasser in Barnes v. Costle, 561 F.2d 983, 990 n.55 (D.C. Cir. 1977).
11. *See* Rabidue v. Osceola Ref. Co., 805 F.2d 611, 620 (6th Cir. 1986) (stating that equal opportunity harassment is not gender discrimination), *cert. denied,* 481 U.S. 1041 (1987); Henson v. City of Dundee, 682 F.2d 897, 904 n.11 (11th Cir. 1982) ("Except in the exceedingly atypical case of a bisexual supervisor, it should be clear that sexual harassment is discrimination based upon sex."); Bundy v. Jackson, 641 F.2d 934, 942 n.7 (D.C. Cir. 1981) ("Only by a *reductio ad absurdum* could we imagine a case of harassment that is not sex discrimination—where a bisexual supervisor harasses men and women alike."); Raney v. District of Columbia, 892 F. Supp. 283, 288 (D.D.C. 1995) (stating that there is no discrimination in cases where a supervisor ha-

rasses both sexes equally); *Ryczek,* 877 F. Supp. at 761 n.6 (noting the language of footnote 55 in *Barnes* suggests that a supervisor is immune from Title VII sexual harassment suits when there is evidence that he or she harassed members of both sexes); *Chiapuzio,* 826 F. Supp. at 1336–37 (stating that current legal doctrines such as burden of proof or causation would require adjustments to adequately address the issue of equal opportunity harassment); *cf.* Corne v. Bausch & Lomb, 390 F. Supp. 161, 163 (D. Ariz. 1975) (stating it would be "ludicrous" to call sexual harassment sex discrimination "because to do so would mean that if the conduct complained of [sexual advances from male supervisor to female employees] was directed equally to males there would be no basis for suit").

12. *See* Ryczek v. Guest Servs., 877 F. Supp. 754, 761 (D.D.C. 1995) for example, the defendants argued O'Brien was bisexual, not that she actually harassed members of both sexes. Also see, *e.g.,* Cabaniss v. Coosa Valley Medical Ctr., No. CV 93-PT-2710-E, 1995 WL 241937, at *26–28 (N.D. Ala. March 20, 1995) (finding defendant harassed both men and women equally). In *Chiapuzio v. BLT Operating Corp.,* the court referred to harassers whose remarks are gender driven and directed at both men and women as "equal opportunity harassers." 826 F. Supp. 1334, 1337 (D. Wyo. 1993). Because victims of both bisexual and equal opportunity sexual harassment face similar obstacles under current sexual harassment doctrine, this Note uses the more general term "equal opportunity harassment" to refer to both.

13. *See, e.g.,* Rabidue v. Osceola Ref. Co., 805 F.2d 611, 620 (6th Cir. 1986) (stating in dicta that victims of equal opportunity harassment have no Title VII cause of action), *cert. denied,* 481 U.S. 1041 (1987).

14. *See* sources cited *infra* note 11 (denying a Title VII cause of action to victims of same-sex sexual harassment).

15. 42 U.S.C. § 2000e-2(a)(1) (1988).

16. 42 U.S.C. § 2000e-2(a)(1).

17. *See* McCoy v. Johnson Controls World Servs., Inc., 878 F. Supp. 229, 232 (S.D. Ga. 1995) (stating that a plaintiff must establish harassment was "based upon sex" by showing that but for the fact of her sex, she would not have been the object of harassment, and that her harasser did not treat male employees in a similar fashion); Valadez v. Uncle Julio's of Illinois, Inc., 895 F. Supp. 1008, 1014 (N.D. Ill. 1995) (stating the "critical issue" as whether the plaintiff was exposed to disadvantageous terms or conditions of employment to which male employees were not exposed); Griffith v. Keystone Steel & Wire, 887 F. Supp. 1133, 1137 (C.D. Ill. 1995) (applying the *McCoy* two part test to a determination of sexual harassment); *see generally* Martha Chamallas, *Listening to Dr. Fiske: The Easy Case of* Price Waterhouse v. Hopkins, 15 vt. L. Rev. 89, 100–04 (1990).

18. *See* Price Waterhouse v. Hopkins, 490 U.S. 228, 262 (1989) (O'Connor, J., concurring) ("[A] substantive violation [of Title VII] only occurs when consideration of an illegitimate criteria is the 'but for' cause of an adverse employment action."); *see also* Henson v. City of Dundee, 682 F.2d 897, 904 (11th Cir. 1982) (stating that to prove a claim for sexual harassment, a plaintiff must show that but for the fact of her sex, she would not have been the object of harassment).

19. In *Price Waterhouse,* the Court stated:

> In determining whether a particular factor was a but-for cause of a given event, we begin by assuming that the factor was present at the time of the event, and then ask whether, even if that factor had been absent, the event nevertheless would have transpired in the same way.

490 U.S. at 240. The Court further explained that the critical inquiry is whether gender was a factor at the moment an employment decision was made.

> When an employer considers sex along with legitimate factors at the time of making an employment decision, the "because of sex" requirement is met. *Id.* at 241.

20. *See infra* notes 49–56 and accompanying text (describing the "but for" standard and its application to same-sex and equal opportunity harassment cases).

21. The EEOC Compliance Manual states: "[T]he crucial inquiry is whether the harasser treats a member or members of one sex differently from members of the other sex." EEOC Compliance Manual (CCH) § 615.2(b)(3) (1993) [hereinafter EEOC Manual]. For courts relying on the EEOC language, see Raney v. District of Columbia, 892 F. Supp. 283, 287 (D.D.C. 1995); Van-

deventer v. Wabash Nat'l Corp., 887 F. Supp. 1178, 1181 (N.D. Ill. 1995); *see also* Harris v. Forklift Sys., Inc., 114 S. Ct. 367, 372 (1993) (Ginsburg, J., concurring) ("The critical issue . . . is whether members of one sex are exposed to disadvantageous terms or conditions of employment to which members of the other sex are not exposed.")

22. *See, e.g.,* Goluszek v. Smith, 697 F. Supp. 1452, 1456 (N.D. Ill. 1988) ("During the times relevant to his claim, Goluszek was a male in a male-dominated environment. In fact, with [one] exception . . . each and every one of the figures in this story was a male. . . . Goluszek may have been harassed 'because' he is a male, but that harassment was not of a kind which created an anti-male environment in the workplace.")

23. Ellen F. Paul, *Sexual Harassment as Sex Discrimination: A Defective Paradigm,* 8 Yale L. & Pol'y Rev. 333, 352 (1990).

24. *See generally* Joyce M. Nielsen, Sex and Gender in Society 16–17 (2d ed. 1990) (discussing types of rewards involved in a system of sex stratification).

25. Sandra L. Bem, The Lenses of Gender 80–81, 233 (1993); *see also* Cynthia Fuchs Epstein, Deceptive Distinctions 9, 14 (1988) (arguing society perpetuates gender inequality by ranking those characteristics associated with men higher than those associated with women); I. Bennett Capers, *Sex(ual Orientation) and Title VII,* 91 Colum. L. Rev. 11 1160–62 (1991) (describing how society constructs and maintains a gender dichotomy); *cf.* Patricia Hill Collins, Black Feminist Thought: Knowledge, Consciousness, and the Politics of Empowerment 70 (1990) (describing the ways in which society posits one-half of dichotomies as superior to others).

26. Epstein, *supra* note 25, at 233.

27. *See* Catharine A. MacKinnon, Feminism Unmodified 107 (1987) (arguing sexual harassment both expresses and reinforces the social inequality of women to men); Stephanie Riger, *Gender Dilemmas in Sexual Harassment Policies and Procedures,* 46 Am. Psychologist 497, 503 (1991) (finding workplaces low in perceived equality are the site of more frequent incidents of harassment and concluding that sexual harassment both reflects and reinforces sexual inequality); *cf.* Anita F. Hill, *Sexual Harassment: The Nature of the Beast,* 65 S. Cal. L. Rev. 1445, 1448 (1992) ("The reality is that [sexual harassment] is used to perpetuate a sense of inequality, to keep women in their place notwithstanding our increasing presence in the workplace.").

28. Andrea Dworkin, *Women in the Public Domain: Sexual Harassment and Date Rape, in* Sexual Harassment: Women Speak Out 1–5 (Amber Coverdale Sumrall & Dena Taylor eds., 1992).

29. *Id.* at 2.

30. *Id.* at 4.

31. *See, e.g.,* Martha Chamallas, *Feminist Constructions of Objectivity: Multiple Perspectives in Sexual and Racial Harassment Litigation,* 1 Tex. J. Women & L. 95, 116 (1992) (comparing sex stereotyping expert Susan Fiske's analysis with current feminist scholarship).

32. 490 U.S. 228, 250–51 (1989). In *Price Waterhouse,* the partners in a national professional accounting firm denied plaintiff Ann Hopkins partnership in the firm. After serving five years in a senior management position, Hopkins received evaluations for partnership that noted she was an aggressive and competent executive. *Id.* at 234. The partners described Hopkins as an "outstanding professional" who had a "deft touch," a "strong character, independence and integrity." *Id.* One client described her as "extremely competent, intelligent," "strong and forthright, very productive, energetic and creative." *Id.* Some partners, however, characterized her aggressiveness as "macho." *Id.* at 235. Several partners criticized her use of profanity, one partner suggesting in response that they objected to her swearing "because it's a lady using foul language." *Id.* Another advised her to take a "course at charm school." *Id.* Finally, in explaining the firm's decision to put Hopkins's candidacy on hold, one partner advised that Hopkins could improve her chances for partnership if she would "walk more femininely, talk more femininely, dress more femininely, wear make-up, have her hair styled and wear jewelry." *Id.*

33. *Id.;* Chamallas, *supra* note 17, at 95 n.36 (discussing the comparative and "but for" standards).

34. *Price Waterhouse,* 490 U.S. at 231–32.

35. *Id.* at 250–52.

36. *See* Chamallas, *supra* note 31, at 114–15 (describing how sex stereotyping research demonstrates the way organizational structure and culture influence individual perceptions).

37. Chamallas, *supra* note 17 at 96. Critical to Fiske's analysis was Hopkins's status as a "token woman" at Price Waterhouse, a phenomenon known in social science research as a "rarity." *Id.*

38. The sex stereotyping theory, a derivative of the theory of sex role spillover, applies only to situations in which a member of a subordinate group is working in an environment predominately made up of members of a dominant group, typically a woman working in a mostly male occupation. Barbara A. Gutek, Sex and the Workplace 132 (1985). In traditionally female jobs, where women are the working majority, the jobs themselves take on aspects of sex roles. *Id.* at 135. "Whereas women in nontraditional jobs are viewed as women in jobs, women in traditionally female jobs are viewed as women, period. The work role is the female sex role. . . ." *Id.* Different female jobs emphasize different aspects of the female gender role. For example, nursing and working with children, the aged, handicapped or poor are all jobs that reflect the nurturing aspect of the female gender role. *Id.*

39. Chamallas, *supra* note 17, at 96–97. Fiske noted that under conditions of rarity, evaluators will scrutinize women more closely than men on "feminine dimensions" such as social skills and personality, and that evaluators will focus less on "masculine" task or performance measures. *Id.* at 98. This means that a token woman's "shortcomings" become highly visible, in addition to being shaped in a gender-coded fashion. *Id.*

40. *Id.* at 98.

41. Robinson v. Jacksonville Shipyards, Inc., 760 F. Supp. 1486 (M.D. Fla. 1991). In *Robinson,* the plaintiff was one of a few women working in a skilled crafts position at the shipyards. Male employees described the worksite as a "boys club" and "more or less a man's world." *Id.* at 1493. Pictures of nude or partially nude women were visible throughout the workplace. The plaintiff used the sex stereotyping theory to provide a framework for placing the sexual behavior of men at shipyards into a larger pattern of gender stereotyping. *See* Chamallas, *supra* note 31, at 111 (describing the use of Fiske's testimony in arguing that sexual harassment is part of a greater form of sex discrimination).

42. *See* Capers, *supra* note 25, at 1176 (noting courts have been reluctant to find discrimination based on sex stereotyping in cases involving sexual orientation).

43. 58 Empl. Prac. Dec. (CCH) ¶ 41,332 at 70,101 (6th Cir. Jan. 15, 1992). Ernest Dillon worked as a mail handler at the Bulk Mail Center in Allen Park, Michigan.

44. During the course of his employment, his coworkers taunted him with expressions like "fag" and "Dillon sucks dicks." *Id.* at 70,102. Graffiti appeared on conveyer belts and loading trucks with the words "Dillon gives head." *Id.* at 70,102–03. When management failed to stop the harassment, Dillon sued in federal court alleging sexual harassment under Title VII. *Id.* at 70,103.

45. *Id.* at 70,105.

46. *Id.* at 70,107.

47. *Id.* The court rejected the application of *Price Waterhouse* because the court could find "no specific evidence of sex-stereotyped remarks." *Id.* at 70,108. Critical to the court's analysis of remarks made to or about Dillon, was the assumption that "sex" in Title VII refers to what is biological, and not to gender: "Because the very concept and definition of the word 'sex' is at issue in this case, [this court] will generally use terms such as 'being male or female' to mean the genetic concept of the sex of a human as transmitted by the sex chromosome of the father." *Id.* at 70,104 n.2. Many courts have interpreted Title VII's "sex" provision to mean either sex or gender.

48. In *Bennett v. Corroon & Black Corp.,* for example, the court found that while certain cartoons displayed in the workplace bearing plaintiff's name "were sexually oriented, crude, deviant and personally offensive," the plaintiff was not entitled to relief under the Louisiana equal employment statute because plaintiff had not shown that the cartoons were labelled with her name merely because of her sex. 517 So. 2d 1245, 1247 (La. Ct. App. 1987), *cert. denied,* 520 So. 2d 425 (La. 1988). "The cartoons in the men's room were labelled with the names of both male and female employees. This fact precludes plaintiff from establishing a case of sexual harassment." *Id.; cf.* Steiner v. Showboat Operating Co., 25 F.3d 1459, 1463–64 (9th Cir. 1994) (finding where supervisor who is abusive to both men and women, but limits gender-specific abuses to females, hostile environment is based on sex), *cert. denied,* 115 S. Ct. 733 (1995).

49. *See* Francisco Valdes, *Queers, Sissies, Dykes, and Tomboys: Deconstructing the Conflation of "Sex," "Gender," and "Sexual Orientation" in Euro-American Law & Society*, 83 Cal. L. Rev. 1, 23 (1995) (noting consequences of having no clear legal definition of "sex").

50. *See* Vandeventer v. Wabash Nat'l Corp., 887 F. Supp. 1178, 1180 (N.D. Ind. 1995) ("People who are harassed because they are homosexual—or are perceived as homosexual—are not protected by Title VII any more than are people who are harassed for having brown eyes."); Dillon v. Frank, 58 Empl. Prac. Dec. (CCH) ¶ 41,332, at 70,104 (6th Cir. Jan. 15, 1990) (holding Title VII does not proscribe discriminatory conduct based on sexual orientation); DeSantis v. Pacific Tel. & Tel. Co., 608 F.2d 327, 331 (9th Cir. 1979) (same); *see also* EEOC Manual, *supra* note 21, ¶ 3101 ("If a male supervisor harasses a male employee because of the employee's homosexuality, then the supervisor's conduct would *not* be sexual harassment since it is based on the employee's sexual preference, not on his gender. Title VII covers charges based on gender but not those based on sexual preference."); *cf.* Harvard Law Review, Sexual Orientation and the Law 69 (1990) (stating no plaintiff has recovered under the theory that sexual orientation discrimination is essentially a form of gender discrimination).

51. *See* Dillon v. Frank, 58 Empl. Prac. Dec. (CCH) ¶ 41,332, at 70,104 (6th Cir. Jan. 15, 1992) (finding plaintiff's coworkers harassed him because they believed he was gay); Carreno v. Local Union No. 226, No. 89-4083-S, 1990 WL 159199, at *3 (D. Kan. Sept. 27, 1990) (finding plaintiff was not harassed because he is a male, but rather because he is a homosexual male); *cf.* Fox v. Sierra Dev. Co., 876 F. Supp. 1169, 1175 (D. Nev. 1995) (finding plaintiffs do not perceive work environment to be hostile to them because they are men, but because they may not be entirely at ease with sexuality in general or homosexuality in particular).

52. *See* Samuel A. Marcosson, *Harassment on the Basis of Sexual Orientation: A Claim of Sex Discrimination Under Title VII*, 81 Geo. L.J. 32 (1992) (discussing sexuality as an element of all sexual harassment claims).

53. *See, e.g.,* EEOC v. Walden Book Co., 885 F. Supp. 1100, 1102 (M.D. Tenn. 1995) (stating same-sex sexual harassment is an adverse employment action that victim would not have faced but for his or her sex); Joyner v. AAA Cooper Transp., 597 F. Supp. 537, 542 (M.D. Ala. 1983) (same), *aff'd* 749 F.2d 732 (11th Cir. 1984); Wright v. Methodist Youth Servs., Inc., 511 F. Supp. 307, 310 (N.D. Ill. 1981) (same).

54. *Compare* Griffith v. Keystone Steel & Wire, 887 F. Supp. 1133, 1135–36 (C.D. Ill. 1995) (holding harassment was actionable where male supervisor subjected male employee to sexually suggestive comments and improper physical sexual contacts) *with* Ashworth v. Roundup Co., 897 F. Supp. 489, 490, 494 (W.D. Wash. 1995) (holding harassment was not actionable where male manager made sexually suggestive comments and improper physical sexual contacts to male employee). In cases involving anti-gay or heterosexual male to male harassment, courts universally interpret the harassment as occurring because of sexual orientation.

55. Valdes, *supra* note 49, at 23.

56. *Id.* at 24.

57. *See supra* note 21 and accompanying text (discussing the comparative standard test generally).

58. *See* Chamallas, *supra* note 17, at 100 (discussing the relationship between the comparative standard and the goal of equal opportunity).

59. *See* Marilyn Frye, The Politics of Reality 31–33 (1983) (describing how society constructs and maintains a gender dichotomy).

60. *See, e.g.,* Marie Elena Peluso, Note, *Tempering Title VII's Straight Arrow Approach: Recognizing and Protecting Gay Victims of Employment Discrimination*, 46 Vand. L. Rev. 1549–60 (1993) (arguing that sexual orientation should stand on equal footing with other classes protected by Title VII because it contains all of the elements that courts require of a suspect class); *cf.* Judith L. Dillon, Note, *A Proposal to Ban Sexual Orientation Discrimination in Private Employment in Vermont*, 15 Vt. L. Rev. 435, 471 (1991) (arguing that because courts are reluctant to grant legal protection to gays and lesbians under Title VII, state and local legislatures must enact anti-discrimination legislation).

61. The 104th Congress has introduced two bills that would prohibit employment discrimination based on sexual orientation. S. 932, 104th Cong. (1995); H.R. 1863, 104th Cong. (1995). The

Senate bill is pending in the Committee on Labor and Human Resources and the House bill is pending in the Committee on Economic and Educational Opportunities.

62. *See supra* notes 57–59 and accompanying text (discussing problems with comparative standard in sexual harassment law).

63. *See supra* notes 16–23 and accompanying text (describing the "but for" and comparative standards).

64. See Mary E. Becker, *Prince Charming: Abstract Equality,* 1987 SUP. CT. REV. 208.

That a harasser could escape liability under Title VII because the harasser harassed men and women equally contradicts the reasoning of the Supreme Court's decision in Loving v. Virginia, 388 U.S. 1 (1967). The *Loving* Court rejected the argument that equal application of a racially discriminatory statute removes the statute from the Fourteenth Amendment's proscriptions. *Id.* at 8. The Court stated that the fact that both races were subject to a discriminatory statute did not take away from the Virginia legislature's racially motivated purpose in designing a statute to maintain white supremacy. *See id.* at 7–8 (rejecting the State's "equal application" theory and finding the State designed the statute to maintain white supremacy). Similarly, if we acknowledge that sexual harassment is part of a system of gender domination, then the fact that an employee harasses both sexes should be irrelevant to a determination that the behavior falls within the purview of Title VII.

Also see the following cases (discussing discrimination on the basis of gender stereotypes as a form of sex discrimination), and supra 24–26:

Ryczek v. Guest Servs., 877 F. Supp. 754, 761–62 (D.D.C. 1995). "In addition to this troubling possibility, the prospect of having litigants debate and juries determine the sexual orientation of Title VII defendants is a rather unpleasant one." *Id.* "One can only speculate as to what would be legally sufficient to submit the issue of a supervisor's bisexuality to the jury. Would the supervisor's sworn statement of his or her bisexuality be adequate? Would the supervisor need to introduce affirmative evidence of his liaisons with members of both sexes?" *Id.* at 762 n.7; *see also* Paul, *supra* note 23, at 351–52 ("The identical offense is sex discrimination under Title VII when perpetrated by a man against a woman, by a man against a man, by a woman against a woman, or by a woman against a man; yet if a bisexual of either sex preys equally upon men *and* women, he—or she—is beyond the reach of Title VII.") Michelle Ridgeway Peirce, *Sexual Harassment and Title VII—A Better Solution,* 30 B.C. L. Rev. 1071, 1096 (1989).

Raney v. District of Columbia, 892 F. Supp. 283, 287 (D.D.C. 1995) (noting defendants argued if any discrimination was committed it was perpetrated by bisexual supervisors, an offense not actionable under Title VII); *see also* Cabaniss v. Coosa Valley Medical Ctr., No. CV 93-PT-2710-E, 1995 WL 241937, at *13 (N.D. Ala. March 20, 1995) (noting defendants' argument that the alleged harasser treated males no differently than females); *Ryczek,* 877 F. Supp. at 761–62 (noting that the parties were arguing over the issue of whether defendant was bisexual or a lesbian); Chiapuzio v. BLT Operating Corp., 826 F. Supp. 1334, 1336 (D. Wyo. 1993) (describing defendant's argument that because he harassed both male and female employees, he did not discriminate against plaintiffs based on gender); *cf.* McCoy v. Johnson Controls World Servs., Inc., 878 F. Supp. 229, 232 (S.D. Ga. 1995) (finding that because defendant had not argued that the plaintiff's harasser also harassed the opposite sex, the defendant was still liable under Title VII); Paul, *supra* note 23, at 351–52 ("[I]f sexual harassment is sexual discrimination under Title VII, why are some perpetrators insulated? A savvy harasser need only note this anomaly and become an equal opportunity harasser.").

Ryczek, 877 F. Supp. at 761–62 (stating that parties were arguing over issue of whether defendant was bisexual or a lesbian).

Cabaniss, 1995 WL 241937 at *13 (noting defendants' argument that the alleged harasser treated males no differently than females); *Chiapuzio,* 826 F. Supp. at 1336 (describing defendant's argument that because the supervisor harassed both male and female employees, he did not discriminate against plaintiffs based on gender).

Raney, 892 F. Supp. at 288 (holding a bisexual supervisor who singles out only one sex for sexual harassment liable under Title VII, but leaving unresolved the issue of equal opportunity harassment); *Ryczek,* 877 F. Supp. at 762 (declining to rule on the issue of whether a person who harasses members of both sexes escapes Title VII liability). *But see Chiapuzio,* 826 F. Supp. at 1337 (rejecting current sexual harassment standards and holding equal harassment of both genders does not escape Title VII liability).

65. *See* Frye, *supra* note 59, at 13–14 (arguing that to analyze barriers to equality one must ask who constructs and maintains the barrier and to whose benefit or detriment it works); Chamallas, *supra* note 17, at 109 (arguing that rather than inquiring whether difference exists, the inquiry should be directed toward the ways in which the perception of difference "originates and is maintained").

66. *See* Frye, *supra* note 59, at 34. According to Frye:

> For efficient subordination, what's wanted is that the structure [gender hierarchy] not appear to be a cultural artifact kept in place by human decision or custom, but that it appear *natural.* . . . It must seem natural that individuals of one category are dominated by individuals of the other and that as groups, the one dominates the other.
>
> *Id.*

67. *See supra* note 64 and accompanying text (discussing gender stratification generally).

68. *See* Bem, *supra* note 25, at 80–81 (describing how society constructs and maintains a gender dichotomy).

69. *See generally* Frye, *supra* note 59, at 23–34 (discussing how social controls influence the way men and women act).

70. *Id.* at 34.

71. *See* Epstein, *supra* note 25 at 10 ("Social groups do not depend on instincts or physiology to enforce social arrangements because they cannot reliably do so."); Frye, *supra* note 59, at 35–36 (discussing social pressure to conform to gender roles).

72. Epstein, *supra* note 25, at 9. "Challenges to a social order do not typically come from those who benefit from its arrangements." *Id.* Epstein also notes that dichotomous categories like male and female (and the host of characteristics associated with each) are "especially effective as an ideological mechanism to preserve advantage." *Id.* at 233.

73. *See* Frye, *supra* note 59, at 13 ("The boundary that sets apart women's sphere is maintained and promoted by men generally for the benefit of men generally.").

74. "One of the ways gender stratification is maintained is by emphasizing sex role expectations. Being a sex object is part of the female sex role. Sexual harassment is a reminder to women of their status as sex objects; even at work, women are sex objects." Gutek, *supra* note 38, at 10. Patricia Hill Collins argues that "domination always involves attempts to objectify the subordinate group." Collins, *supra* note 25, at 69. "As subjects, people have the right to define their own reality, establish their own identities, . . . [but] [a]s objects one's reality is defined by others, one's identity is created by others." *Id.* (quoting Bell Hooks, Talking Back: Thinking Feminist, Thinking Black 42 (1989)).

75. *See supra* note 72 (describing the dichotomous categories of male and female).

76. Chamallas, *supra* note 31, at 129 (discussing the operation of sexism on the male sexual harassment plaintiff).

77. *See supra* notes 24–30 and accompanying text (discussing gender stratification generally).

78. Chamallas, *supra* note 31, at 129; *see also* Kathryn Abrams, *Title VII and the Complex Female Subject,* 92 Mich. L. Rev. 2479, 2516 (1994) (arguing that Goluszek suffered either a form of gender discrimination against women—derision of some of the same qualities that make women targets for sexual harassment—or a form of discrimination against men that disciplines a subset of men for abandoning the qualities associated with men).

79. *See* Chamallas, *supra* note 31, at 127–29 (providing a dominance analysis of the *Goluszek* facts).

80. *See supra* notes 32–40 and accompanying text (discussing the facts and holding of *Price Waterhouse*).

81. Price Waterhouse v. Hopkins, 490 U.S. 228, 251 (1989).

82. *See supra* notes 32–35 and accompanying text (discussing *Price Waterhouse*); *see also* Chamallas,

supra note 17, at 109 ("The comparative question presupposes that a judge can discover whether there are salient differences about the person being judged—besides a difference in gender—that might justify treating her unfavorably.").

83. *See Price Waterhouse*, 490 U.S. at 233 (describing the gender composition at the Price Waterhouse firm).

84. *Id.* at 251.

85. *See supra* notes 32–40 and accompanying text (discussing *Price Waterhouse*).

86. *See supra* notes 74–77 and accompanying text (discussing how sexual harassment penalizes gender deviations for each type of harassment).

87. Title VII of the Civil Rights Act makes it unlawful for an employer "to discriminate against any individual with respect to his compensation, terms, conditions, or privileges of employment, because of such individual's race, color, religion, sex, or national origin," 42 U.S.C. § 2000e-2(a)(1) (1988).

88. *See, e.g.,* Rabidue v. Osceola Ref. Co., 805 F.2d 611, 620 (6th Cir. 1986) (finding no hostile environment created by posters of nude women displayed by plaintiff's male coworkers in their offices and by the repeated sexist obscenities of coworkers), *cert. denied,* 481 U.S. 1041 (1987).

89. *See supra* notes 16–20 and accompanying text (discussing Title VII's "but for" analysis).

90. *See supra* notes 48–56 and accompanying text (discussing the tendency of judges to conflate sex with sexual orientation).

91. 58 Empl. Prac. Dec. (CCH) ¶ 41,322 at 70,101 (6th Cir. Jan. 15, 1992); *see supra* notes 43–47 and accompanying text (discussing the facts and holding of *Dillon*).

92. *See Dillon,* 58 Empl. Prac. Dec. (CCH) at 70,107. The *Dillon* court also noted that in *Price Waterhouse* the Court found sex stereotyping created an "intolerable and impermissible Catch-22" (a woman who acts womanly will not get promoted, and a woman who does not act womanly will not get promoted). *Id.* at 70,108–09 (citing Price Waterhouse v. Hopkins, 490 U.S. 228, 251 (1989)). Dillon, the court argued, did not face such a Catch-22. *Id.* at 70,109. To argue because Dillon was a male, and male characteristics are consistent with those qualities valued in employment, misses the point of the *Price Waterhouse* decision. *Id.* The major focus of Title VII's legislative history, the Court noted in *Price Waterhouse,* is the intent to force employers to "focus on qualifications rather than race, religion, sex or national origin." *Price Waterhouse,* 490 U.S. at 243. When an employee endures harassment motivated in part because of gender—regardless of the employee's actual biological sex—that employee should be able to pursue a Title VII remedy. In *Price Waterhouse,* the Court did not state that a Catch-22 was required for sex-stereotyping to play a role in the court's analysis, only that in Hopkins's case the sex-stereotyping did in fact create such a dilemma. *See id.* at 251.

93. The sex stereotyping theory is useful here because it shows how the structural features of a workplace, demographics, and organization shape individual views about proper gender expectations and behavior. *See supra* notes 36–40 and accompanying text (describing the sex stereotyping theory generally).

94. *See* Marcosson, *supra* note 52, at 26. Marcosson states:
    One would not expect Dillon's coworkers to harass him with, "Dillon sucks dicks," and then quickly add, "But that would be OK if you were a woman." The fact that they harassed him over their belief that he did it, and did not harass any women, makes the distinction between what they found acceptable for one sex and not the other obvious. . . . *Id.*

95. Dillon might have demonstrated certain real effeminate characteristics, but Dillon's coworkers believed that his effeminacy implied homosexuality. *Dillon,* 58 Empl. Prac. Dec. (CCH) at 70,105-07. Much of the abuse Dillon suffered was based on perceived "transgressions" of the male gender script.

96. *See supra* notes 11, 64 and accompanying text (discussing the inability of victims of equal opportunity harassment to establish Title VII claims).

97. *See supra* note 64 and accompanying text (discussing cases in which defendants raise the "bisexual defense").

98. *See supra* notes 74–77 and accompanying text (discussing sexual objectification as a means of policing gender boundaries).

PART IV

Current Debates Over
Sexual Harassment

31. Understanding, Explaining, and Eliminating Sexual Harassment

James P. Sterba

In 1998, the U.S. Supreme Court made four attempts to clarify sexual harassment law (*Oncale v. Sundowner Offshore Services, Inc.; Burlington Industries, Inc. v. Ellerth; Faragher v. City of Boca Raton;* and *Gebser et al v. Lago Vista Independent School District*). In 1998 as well, Judge Susan Webber Wright of the U.S. Court of Appeals for the Eighth Circuit dismissed the sexual harassment case of Paula Corbin Jones against President Clinton on the somewhat controversial grounds that even if Clinton (as Governor of Arkansas) had done all Jones claimed he had done (e.g., summoned her from her convention post to his hotel suite; dropped his pants in front of Jones; asked her to "kiss it"; touched her thigh and tried to kiss her on the neck; and, despite apparently accepting her "no" for an answer, partially and momentarily blocked her exit for enough time to tell her that he knew her boss and that it would be best if the incident were kept between the two of them), Clinton would not have sexually harassed Jones because she could not demonstrate any tangible job detriment or adverse employment action for her refusal to submit to Clinton's alleged advances. Thus, although the flurry of judicial activity in 1998 did increase the scope of sexual harassment law—sitting U.S. Presidents are now liable for sexual harassment suits, as are grade school and high school teachers—unfortunately our understanding of the nature of sexual harassment has yet to achieve a comparable advance. Nor as yet do we have a very good explanation of why sexual harassment occurs as frequently as it does in our society. Accordingly, in Part I of this selection, I will review the developments in sexual harassment law, hoping to increase our understanding of what is (or, better, what should be) sexual harassment. Then, in Part II, I will offer a partial explanation of why sexual harassment happens in both civilian and military life. Lastly, in Part III, I will determine what positive norms, in addition to the negative one that prohibits sexual harassment, we need to focus on in order to make progress toward reducing its frequency.

PART I: UNDERSTANDING SEXUAL HARASSMENT

Sexual harassment was not recognized by U.S. trial courts as an offense until the late 1970s, and it was only affirmed by the U.S. Supreme Court as an offense in the 1980s. The term "sexual harassment" itself was not even coined until the 1970s. So the problem of sexual harassment is one that many people have only recently come to recognize. Obviously, the Senate Judiciary Committee hearings in 1991 on Anita Hill's charge that Clarence Thomas had sexually harassed her,[1] the U.S. Navy's Tailhook scandal in 1992, the Bob Packwood scandal in 1995, and more recently in 1997 Paula Jones's amended sexual harassment suit against President Clinton have all helped heighten people's awareness of this problem. (See Selections 7, 20–24.)

In 1976, a federal district judge, in the first legal case that used the term "sexual harassment," ruled that Diane Williams, a public information specialist at the U.S. Department of Justice who was dismissed after turning down her supervisor's sexual advances, had been harassed "based on sex" within the meaning of Title VII of the Civil Rights Act of

1964. Four years later, the Equal Employment Opportunity Commission (EEOC) issued guidelines finding harassment on the basis of sex to be a violation of Title VII of the Civil Rights Act of 1964 (see Selection 49), labeling sexual harassment as "unwelcome sexual advances, requests for sexual favors, and other verbal or physical conduct of a sexual nature" when such behavior occurred in any of three circumstances:

1. Where submission to such conduct is made either explicitly or implicitly a term or condition of an individual's employment

2. Where submission to or rejection of such conduct by an individual is used as the basis for employment decisions affecting such individual

3. Where such conduct has the purpose or effect of unreasonably interfering with an individual's work performance or creating an intimidating, hostile, or offensive working environment

In 1986, the U.S. Supreme Court, in *Meritor Savings Bank v. Vinson* (see Selection 51), unanimously agreed with the EEOC ruling that there could be two types of sexual harassment: harassment that conditions concrete employment benefits on granting sexual favors (called the quid pro quo type), and harassment that creates a hostile or offensive work environment without affecting economic benefits (the hostile environment type). Nevertheless, the Court made it quite difficult for a plaintiff to establish that either of these types of sexual harassment had occurred. For example, a polite verbal "no" does not suffice to show that sexual advances are unwelcome, and a woman's entire conduct both in and outside the workplace is subject to appraisal determining whether or not she welcomed the advances. For example, in the *Vinson* case, there was "voluminous testimony regarding Vinson's dress and personal fantasies," and in the Senate Judiciary Committee hearings, Anita Hill was not able to prevent intensive examination of her private life, although Clarence Thomas was able to declare key areas of his private life as off-limits, such as his practice of viewing and discussing pornographic films.

The Supreme Court also made it difficult to classify work environments as hostile to women unless the harassment is sufficiently severe or pervasive. Applying the Supreme Court's standard, a lower court, in *Christoforou v. Ryder Truck Rental,* judged a supervisor's actions of fondling a plaintiff's rear end and breasts, propositioning her, and trying to force a kiss at a Christmas party to be "too sporadic and innocuous" to support a finding of a hostile work environment.[2] Similarly, in *Rabidue v. Osceola Refining Co.,* a workplace where pictures of nude and scantily clad women abounded (including one, which hung on a wall for eight years, of a woman with a golf ball on her breasts and a man with his golf club standing over her and yelling "Fore!") and where a coworker, never disciplined despite repeated complaints, routinely referred to women as "whores," "cunts," "pussies," and "tits" was judged by a lower court not to be a sufficiently hostile environment to constitute sexual harassment.[3] Notice, by contrast, that the U.S. Senate Armed Services Committee, in its hearings on homosexuals in the military, regarded an environment in which known homosexuals are simply doing their duty in the military to be too hostile an environment in which to ask male heterosexuals to serve.

Yet why should we accept the Supreme Court's characterization of sexual harassment, especially given its unwelcomeness and pervasiveness requirements?[4] As the Supreme Court interprets sexual harassment, a person's behavior must be unwelcome in a fairly strong sense before it constitutes sexual harassment. But why should a woman have to prove that the offer "If you don't sleep with me, you will be fired" is unwelcome before it constitutes sexual harassment?[5] Isn't such an offer objectively unwelcome? Isn't it just the kind of offer that those in positions of power should not be making to their subordinates, an offer that purports to make their continuing employment conditional upon providing sexual favors? Surely, unless we are dealing with some form of legalized prostitution, and maybe not even then, such offers are objectively unwelcome.[6] Given, then, that such offers are objectively unwelcome, why is there any need to show that they are also subjectively unwelcome before regarding them as violations of Title VII of the Civil Rights Act? The requirement of subjective unwelcomeness is simply a gratuitous obstacle that makes the plaintiff's case far more difficult to prove than it should be.[7]

In addition, if the plaintiff is fired after refusing such an offer, the Supreme Court requires her to prove that the firing occurred because the offer was refused, which is very difficult to do unless one is a perfect employee. Wouldn't it be fairer to require the employer to prove that the plaintiff would have been fired even if she had said "yes" to the offer?[8] Of course, employers could avoid this burden of proof simply by not making any such offers in the first place.[9] But when they do make objectively unwelcome offers, why shouldn't the burden of proof be on them to show that any subsequent firing was clearly unrelated to the plaintiff's refusal of the offer? Fairness is particularly relevant in this context because we are committed to equal opportunity in the workplace, which requires employing women and men on equal terms. Accordingly, we must guard against imposing special burdens on women in the workplace when there are no comparable burdens imposed on men.[10]

The demand for equal opportunity in the workplace also appears to conflict with the Supreme Court's pervasiveness requirement for establishing a hostile environment. Citing a lower court, the Supreme Court contends that, to be actionable, sexual harassment "must be sufficiently severe or pervasive 'to alter the conditions of the [victim's] employment and create an abusive working environment.'"[11] But as this standard has been interpreted by lower courts, the pervasiveness of certain forms of harassment in the workplace has become grounds for tolerating them. In *Rabidue,* the majority argued:

> [I]t cannot seriously be disputed that in some work environments, humor and language are rough hewn and vulgar. Sexual jokes, sexual conversations and girlie magazines abound. Title VII was not meant to or can change this. Title VII is the federal court mainstay in the struggle for equal employment opportunity for the female workers of America. But it is quite different to claim that Title VII was designed to bring about a magical transformation in the social mores of American workers.[12]

The Supreme Court itself seems to sound a similar theme by emphasizing the application of Title VII to only extreme cases of sexual harassment as found in *Vinson.*

However, as the EEOC interprets Title VII, the law has a broader scope. It affords employees the right to work in an environment free from discriminatory intimidation, ridicule, and insult. According to the EEOC, sexual harassment violates Title VII when conduct creates an intimidating, hostile, or offensive environment or when it unreasonably interferes with work performance.[13]

But how are we to determine what unreasonably interferes with work performance? In *Rabidue,* the majority looked to prevailing standards in the workplace to determine what was reasonable or unreasonable. Yet Justice Keith, in dissent, questioned this endorsement of the status quo, arguing that just as a Jewish employee can rightfully demand a change in her working environment if her employer maintains an anti-Semitic workforce and tolerates a workplace in which "kike" jokes, displays of Nazi literature, and anti-Jewish conversation "may abound," surely women can rightfully demand a change in the sexist practices that prevail in their working environments.[14] In *Henson v. Dundee,* the majority also drew an analogy between sexual harassment and racial harassment:

Sexual harassment which creates a hostile or offensive environment for members of one sex is every bit the arbitrary barrier to sexual equality at the workplace that racial harassment is to racial equality. Surely, a requirement that a man or woman run a gauntlet of sexual abuse in return for the privilege of being allowed to work and make a living can be as demeaning and disconcerting as the harshest of racial epithets.[15]

And this passage is also quoted approvingly by the Supreme Court in *Vinson.*

Moved by such arguments, the majority in *Ellison v. Brady* proposed that rather than looking to prevailing standards to determine what is reasonable, we should look to the standard of a reasonable victim or—given that most victims of sexual harassment are women—the standard of a reasonable woman.[16] They contend that this standard may be different from the standard of a reasonable man. For example, what male superiors may think is "harmless social interaction" may be experienced by female subordinates as offensive and threatening.[17]

Nevertheless, if we are concerned to establish equal opportunity in the workplace, there should be no question about what standard of reasonableness to use here. It is not that of a reasonable woman, nor that of a reasonable man for that matter, but the standard of what is reasonable for everyone affected to accept. For equal opportunity is a moral requirement, and moral requirements are those which are reasonable for everyone affected to accept. This assumes that apparent conflicts over what is reasonable to accept—for example, conflicts between the standard of a reasonable woman and that of a reasonable man—are conflicts that can and should be resolved by showing that one of these perspectives is more reasonable than the other, or that some other perspective is more reasonable still. However, at least in the context of sexual harassment, this standard of what is reasonable for everyone affected to accept will accord closely with the standard of a reasonable woman, given that once women's perspectives are adequately taken into account, the contrasting perspective of a reasonable man will be seen as not so reasonable after all.[18]

In its decision in *Harris v. Forklift Systems Inc.* (1993), the Supreme Court took an important step toward a more reasonable stance on sexual harassment. In this case, Teresa Harris worked as a rental manager at Forklift Systems. Charles Hardy, Forklift's president, said to Harris on several occasions, in the presence of other employees, "You're a woman, what do you know?" and "We need a man as the rental manager." Again in front of others, he suggested that the two of them "go to the Holiday Inn to negotiate [Harris's] raise." Hardy occasionally asked Harris and other female employees to get coins from his front pants pockets. On other occasions, he threw objects on the ground in front of Harris and other women and asked them to pick the objects up. He made sexual innuendoes about Harris's and other women's clothing. On one occasion, while Harris was arranging a deal with one of Forklift's customers, Hardy asked her in front of other employees, "What did you do, promise some [sex] Saturday night?" Soon after, Harris quit her job at Forklift.

In this case, the Supreme Court struck down the district court's requirement that in order for sexual harassment to be established, Harris needed to show that Hardy's conduct had "seriously affected her psychological well-being." This was an important decision, but obviously it does not go far enough in specifying a reasonable standard for sexual harassment.

It is also important to recognize here that achieving equal opportunity in the workplace will conflict, to some degree, with freedom of speech. Consider the case of *Robinson v. Jacksonville Shipyards,* in which a U.S. District Court upheld claims of sexual harassment on hostile work environment grounds and issued extensive remedial orders.[19] Plaintiff Lois Robinson was one of a very small number of female skilled craftworkers employed at Shipyards—1 of 6 females out of 832 craftworkers. Her allegations of sexual harassment centered around "the presence in the workplace of pictures of women in various stages of undress and in sexually suggestive or submissive poses, as well as remarks by male employees and supervisors which demean women." Although there was some evidence of several incidents in which the sexually suggestive pictures and comments were directed explicitly at Robinson, most were not.

In analyzing this case, Nadine Strossen, past president of the ACLU, argues that even sexually offensive speech should be protected unless it is explicitly directed at a particular individual or group of individuals.[20] Accordingly, Strossen endorses the ACLU's amicus brief in the *Robinson v. Jacksonville Shipyards* case, which considered the court's ban on the public display of sexually suggestive material without regard to whether the expressive activity was explicitly directed toward any employee as too broad. However, in light of the fact that Jacksonville Shipyards had itself banned all public displays of expressive activity except sexual materials, the amicus brief went on to favor the imposition of a workplace rule that would right the balance and permit the posting of other materials as well—materials critical of such sexual expression, as well as other political and religious or social messages that are currently banned. Such a rule would implement a "more speech" approach in an effort to counter offensive speech.

But would such a rule work? Would it succeed in protecting the basic interests of women, especially their right to equal opportunity in the workplace? It is not clear that it would be effective in male-dominated workplaces such as Jacksonville Shipyards, where women are a tiny minority of the workforce and so are likely to have their voices drowned out in the free market of expression that this rule would permit.

Nor does Strossen's distinction between offensive speech explicitly directed at a particular person or group and offensive speech that is not so directed seem all that useful, given that most sexual harassment is directed at women not because they are Jane Doe or Lois Robinson, but because they are women. So why should we distinguish between sexual harassment that is explicitly directed at a particular woman because she is a woman and sexual harassment that is only directed at a particular woman because it is explicitly directed at all women? Of course, sexually harassing speech can be more or less offensive, and maybe its offensiveness does correlate, to some degree, with the manner in which that harassment is directed at women. Nevertheless, what is crucial here is that the offensiveness of sexually harassing speech becomes unacceptable when it undermines the equal opportunity of women in the workplace—that is, when it imposes special burdens on women in the workplace where there are no comparable burdens on men. It is at this point that justice demands that we impose whatever limitations on sexually harassing speech are needed to secure equal opportunity in the workplace.

Most recently, in *Oncale v. Sundowner Offshore Services, Inc.* (1998), the Supreme Court expanded the scope of sexual harassment to include same-sex sexual harassment even when the harasser is not homosexual. In this case, Joseph Oncale was working for Sundowner Offshore Services on a Chevron U.S.A. oil platform in the Gulf of Mexico. He was employed as a roustabout on an eight-man crew that included John Lyons, Danny Pippen, and Brandon Johnson. Lyons, the crane operator, and Pippen, the driller, had supervisory authority. On several occasions, Oncale was forcibly subjected to sex-related, humiliating actions against him by Lyons, Pippen, and Johnson in the presence of the rest of the crew. On one occasion, the men grabbed him in the company shower and forced a bar of soap between his buttocks and threatened to rape him. When he complained to the company's Safety Compliance Clerk, Valent Hohen, about Lyons's and Pippen's behavior, Hohen told Oncale that he was also being harassed by the two men himself. So Oncale quit, asking that his pink slip reflect that he "voluntarily left due to sexual harassment and verbal abuse."

The Supreme Court, seeking to end conflicting stances taken by lower courts in same-sex sexual harassment cases (some found sexual harassment in cases like Oncale's, others held that same-sex sexual harassment could not be supported by Title VII of the Civil Rights Act, and still others held that same-sex sexual harassment is only actionable when the harasser is homosexual), held in a unanimous decision that nothing in Title VII necessarily bars a claim of discrimination "because of . . . sex" merely because the plaintiff and the defendant (or the person charged with acting on behalf of the defendant) are of the same sex. In these same-sex cases of sexual harassment, as in the more standard different-sex cases, special burdens are imposed on the victims of sexual harassment when there are no comparable burdens imposed on others similarly situated. In Oncale's case, sexual taunts, threats, and abuse were directed at him because his appearance and behavior were judged to be not "masculine" enough by his harassers.

It is also important to see that although sexual harassers are usually either the same-sex or different-sex harassers, they can also be what has been called "equal opportunity sexual harassers," that is, harassers who target both men and women. Moreover, some lower courts have argued that equal opportunity sexual harassment falls outside the scope of the protection of Title VII of the Civil Rights Act because such harassers do not limit their harassment to the members of one sex, and so their victims could not claim that they would not have been harassed "but for their sex." Fortunately, in light of the Oncale decision, it should be possible to reinterpret the "because of . . . sex" restriction of Title VII in such a way that all three forms of sexual harassment are prohibited. This is because what is objectionable about all three forms of sexual harassers is that they engage in degrading and abusive sexual conduct that is chosen on the basis of or "because of" the sex of their victims.

Moreover, sexual harassers—whether they be same-sex, different-sex, or equal opportunity sexual harassers—typically impose special burdens on some when there are no comparable burdens imposed on others who are similarly situated, and this frequently is part of what is wrong with sexual harassment. Yet sexual harassment, understood as engaging in degrading and abusive sexual conduct that is chosen on the basis of the victim's sex, would still be wrong even if it were inflicted on everyone within the harasser's reach. Thus, the comparative harm that frequently results from sexual harassment does not exhaust its offensiveness.

Accordingly, drawing on the foregoing discussion, I offer the following:

A Definition of Sexual Harassment: Sexual harassment is objectively unwelcome sexual advances, requests for sexual favors, and other verbal or physical conduct of a sexual nature that are determined to be both objectionable and actionable by the standard of what is reasonable for everyone affected to accept, and which usually, but not always, imposes a special burden on some individuals when there are no comparable burdens imposed on others who are similarly situated.

Sexual harassment so defined can clearly be of the quid pro quo or the hostile environment type, but given that these two types of sexual harassment share this common definition, their features will tend to overlap in particular cases, such as in the Burlington Industries case recently taken up by the Supreme Court.[21] Moreover, even assuming that Kimberly Ellerth did not suffer any economic detriment from the vice president of Burlington Industries who harassed her and Paula Jones did not suffer economic consequences from then-Governor Clinton, they still could have suffered from sexual harassment according to my definition. It all depends on whether the sexual behavior to which they were allegedly exposed is both objectionable and actionable as determined by the standard of what is reasonable for everyone affected to accept. Of course, when the burdens imposed by sexual harassment are slight, they will presumably not be reasonably judged as legally actionable by everyone affected and so will not properly fall within the scope of the law.

PART II: SEXUAL HARASSMENT IN CIVILIAN AND MILITARY LIFE

As is well known, there is a high incidence of sexual harassment in both civilian and military life. In research conducted by psychologists, 50 percent of women questioned in the civilian workplace said they had been sexually harassed. According to the U.S. Merit Systems Protection Board within the federal government, 56 percent of 8,500 female civilian workers surveyed claimed to have experienced sexual harassment. According to the *National Law Journal,* 64 percent of women in "pink-collar" jobs reported being sexually harassed, and 60 percent of 3,000 women lawyers at 250 top law firms said that they had been harassed at some point in their careers. In a survey by *Working Women* magazine, 60 percent of high-ranking corporate women said they have been harassed; 33 percent more knew of others who had been.[22] Similarly, in a 1995 survey of 90,000 female soldiers, sailors, and fliers, 60 percent of the women said they had been sexually harassed. Only 47 percent of the Army women surveyed said that they believed their leaders were serious about putting a stop to sexual harassment.[23] According to another study, 66 percent of women in the military experienced at least one form of sexual harassment in the past year.[24] Another study found that 50 percent of women at the Naval Academy, 59 percent of women at the Air Force Academy, and 76 percent of women at the Military Academy experienced some form of sexual harassment at least twice a month.[25]

Yet despite the high incidence of sexual harassment in both civilian and military life, at least in the United States, there are some important differences that suggest somewhat different explanations of why sexual harassment is taking place in these contexts. The most important difference of this sort is the still widely expressed belief that women do not belong in the military. For example, 45 percent of first-year midshipmen expressed the view that women did not belong in the military, and 38 percent of fourth-year midshipmen felt the same.[26] The same view can be found among the highest commanders in the U.S. military. For example, Air Force Chief General Merrill McPeak testified before the Senate Armed Services Committee in 1991 that if he had to choose between a qualified woman and a less qualified man to fill a combat role, he would go with the man. "I admit it does not make much sense, but that is the way I feel about it," McPeak responded.[27] Surely, it would be difficult to find a male CEO of a Fortune 500 company who would be willing to publicly express the same feelings as General McPeak about the suitability of employing qualified women.

There are, of course, some parallels in civilian life to this attitude toward women found in the military. For example, probably a significant number of the 863 craftworkers who worked along with the 6 women craftworkers at Jacksonville Shipyards in the case previously cited thought that the women did not belong there either. But what is distinctive about the U.S. military is the degree to which the belief that women do not belong there is still widely and openly held. As another general put it:

> War is a man's work. Biological convergence on the battlefield (women serving in combat) would not only be dissatisfying in terms of what women could do, but it would be an enormous psychological distraction for the male, who wants to think that he's fighting for that woman somewhere behind, not up there in the same foxhole with him. It tramples the male ego. When you get right down to it, you have to protect the manhood of war.[28]

What I am suggesting is that this widely and openly held belief that women do not belong is distinctive of military life and helps explain the prevalence of sexual harassment there.

But what, then, explains the prevalence of sexual harassment in civilian life? Because at present there is no comparable widely and openly held belief that women don't belong in civilian life, or even in the civilian workplace where women now occupy 50 percent of the labor force,[29] there must be another belief that supports the sexual harassment that occurs there. I suggest that it is the belief that although women do belong in civilian life, it is still appropriate to treat them as sexual objects in ways that men are not to be treated, with the consequence that they are sexually subordinate to men. It is this belief, I think, that primarily fuels sexual harassment in civilian life. According to this belief, women are classified as having a lesser status than men and so are open to sexual harassment in ways that men are not. Of course, the belief that it is appropriate to treat women as sexual objects in ways that men are not, such that they are sexually subordinate to men, also functions in the military, but there, I think, sexual harassment is more strongly supported by the belief that women just don't belong in the military.

Obviously, so far I have been seeking to explain the sexual harassment of (ostensibly heterosexual) women by (ostensibly heterosexual) men, which is the dominant form of different-sex sexual harassment. But what about same-sex and equal opportunity sexual harassment? Same-sex and equal opportunity sexual harassment are, I believe, best explained in a way analogous to the way I have sought to explain different-sex sexual harassment. In same-sex sexual harassment, either the harassers believe that their victims do not belong in some social setting, as was true in the *Oncale* case, or they believe their victims do belong but that it is still appropriate to treat them as sexual objects in ways that others (including the harasser) are not to be treated, as is standardly the case when the same-sex harasser is homosexual. Similarly, the same holds true of equal opportunity sexual harassers. Either equal opportunity sexual harassers believe that their particular victims do not belong in some social setting, or they believe that they do belong but that it is still appropriate to treat them as sexual objects in ways that others (including the harasser) are not to be treated.

PART III: THE NEED FOR POSITIVE AS WELL AS NEGATIVE NORMS

Suppose, then, that I am right that the high incidence of different-sex sexual harassment in civilian life is explained by the belief, held by many men and also women, that it is appropriate to treat women as sexual objects, and hence as sexually subordinate to men, and that the high incidence of different-sex sexual harassment in military life is explained by the fact that many men and women hold this same belief, but even more so, by the fact that they also hold the belief that women just don't belong in the military. And suppose further that I am right that same-sex and equal opportunity sexual harassment can be similarly explained. What, then, can be done to rid society of the problem of sexual harassment? Well, obviously sexual harassment law and the moral and legal theory that supports it are an attempt to rid society of this problem. This approach primarily tells men not to harass women and then tries to explain what constitutes sexual harassment. However, this approach is essentially negative. It tells men what not to do, not what to do. Of course, in most moral contexts, it is far easier to come up with negative norms than positive ones— it is easier to tell people what they should not be doing than what they should be doing. Nevertheless, when we can come up with appropriate positive norms, they can be helpful in ways that merely negative ones cannot. So what I am suggesting is that specifying some appropriate positive norms can help us to better rid ourselves of this social problem. Accordingly, I want to propose two positive norms for dealing with the problem of sexual harassment. The first is:

The Principle of Androgyny (or Equal Opportunity) requires that the traits that are truly desirable and distributable in society be equally open to both women and men or, in the case of virtues, equally expected of both women and men, other things being equal.

Why this principle? Well, we all know that when we think stereotypically about men and women in our society, we come up with different lists of desirable traits and undesirable traits such as the following:

Men	*Women*
Independent	**Dependent**
Competitive	Cooperative
Aggressive, assertive	Nurturant, caring
Unemotional, stoic, detached	Emotional
Active, **violent**	**Passive**, nonviolent
Unconcerned with appearances	**Concerned with appearances (vain)**
Dominant	**Submissive**, self-effacing
Decisive	**Indecisive**
Seen as subject	Seen as object (of beauty or sexual attraction)
Sloppy	Neat
Sexually active	**Slut or nun**
Reasonable, rational, logical	Intuitive, **illogical**
Protective	In need of protection
Insensitive	Sensitive

And if we assume that the traits in bold are obviously undesirable ones, then in addition to having quite different stereotypical traits associated with men and women in our society, we will also have more undesirable traits on the women's list than on the men's list. Such lists clearly reflect the gender roles and traits that boys and girls, men and women, are socialized into in society. In the past, the desirable gender traits stereotypically associated with men were thought to characterize mental health.[30] More recently, these same traits have been used to describe the successful corporate executive.[31] Accordingly, distinctive gender roles and traits have been used in these ways to favor men over women, and heterosexuals over homosexuals. Nevertheless, there is good reason to think that the only morally defensible attitude we could take toward these gender roles and traits is expressed by the Principle of Androgyny (or Equal Opportunity). This is because for any stereotypical masculine role or trait that is desirable and distributable in society, we can always ask: Why shouldn't women who have the capability be able to fulfill that role or acquire that trait as well? And similarly, for any stereotypical feminine role or trait that is desirable and distributable in society, we can ask: Why shouldn't men who have the capability be able to fulfill that role or acquire that trait as well? And surely the answer to both of these questions is: There is no reason at all why both women and men shouldn't be able fulfill those roles and acquire those traits. This means that the Principle of Androgyny (or Equal Opportunity) is the only norm that is morally defensible in this regard. It opposes enforced gender roles and traits in favor of requiring that the traits that are truly desirable and distributable in society be equally open to both women and men or, in the case of virtues, equally expected of both women and men, other things being equal.[32]

So characterized, the Principle of Androgyny (or Equal Opportunity) represents neither a revolt against so-called feminine virtues and traits nor their exaltation over so-called masculine virtues and traits.[33] This is because it does not view women's liberation as simply the freeing of women from the confines of traditional roles, which makes it possible for them to develop in ways heretofore reserved for men. Nor does it view women's liberation as simply the reevaluation and glorification of so-called feminine activities such as housekeeping or mothering or so-called feminine modes of thinking as reflected in an ethic of caring. The first perspective ignores or devalues genuine virtues and desirable traits traditionally associated with women while the second ignores or devalues genuine virtues and desirable traits traditionally associated with men. In contrast, the Principle of Androgyny (or Equal Opportunity) seeks a broader-based norm for both women and men that combines virtues and desirable traits traditionally associated with women with virtues and desirable traits traditionally associated with men. For this reason, the Principle of Androgyny (or Equal Opportunity) is a common norm for both men (andro-) and women (-gyne).

So the Principle of Androgyny (or Equal Opportunity), by undermining enforced gender roles and traits, will also be undermining those very social structures that give rise to the problem of sexual harassment. Discrimination "because of . . . sex" will be much rarer when there is very little, possibly nothing at all, that is desirable and distributable that stereotypically characterizes men over women or homosexuals over heterosexuals. When people will have the chance to develop themselves in accord with their natural abilities and their free choices rather than socially imposed gender roles and traits, there will arise too many in-group differences and too many between-group similarities either with respect to women and men or with respect to homosexuals and heterosexuals to support anything like the existing practice of sexual harassment. The success of androgyny (or equal opportunity) will thus undercut the very possibility of sexual harassment.

The second positive norm I wish to propose is:

The Principle of Desert requires that we treat and evaluate people on the basis of their proper role- or job-related qualifications and excellences when this is appropriate or required.

Ideally, this principle would pick up where the Principle of Androgyny (or Equal Opportunity) left off. If we had been successful in following the Principle of Androgyny (or Equal Opportunity), then we would have been successful in developing ourselves on the basis of our natural abilities and free choices, and thus we would have had the chance to acquire the proper role- and job-related qualifications and excellences that accord with our natural abilities and free choices. Yet whether or not the Principle of Androgyny (or Equal Opportunity) has been followed, the Principle of Desert still requires that we treat and evaluate people on the basis of their proper role- or job-related qualifications and excellences when this is appropriate or required.

Now if women in the military were treated and evaluated according to this norm, it would surely undermine the belief that they do not belong there and thus drastically reduce the sexual harassment to which that belief gives rise. What most people do not realize is that the opening up of the military to women was not embarked upon as an effort to achieve social equality. Rather the U.S. Defense Department turned to women in order to save the all-volunteer force.[34] The women drawn to military service were smarter and better educated than the men. For example, according to one study, over 90 percent of women recruited had high school diplomas, compared to 63 percent of the men, and women also scored ten points higher on service exams.[35] In addition, proportionately more female than male cadets have been selected as Rhodes and Marshall scholars, and proportionately more women entering West Point have been National Honor Society members and high school valedictorians and salutatorians in all but two years since integration in 1976.[36] As one Defense Department report put it, "The trade off in today's recruiting market is between a high quality female and a low quality male."[37]

Of course, women have less upper body strength, but 32 percent of women have met or exceeded the minimum male test scores, and 78 percent of women have qualified for "very heavy" military jobs after six months of weight lifting, jogging with 75-pound backpacks, and performing squats with 100-pound barrels on their shoulders.[38] Women's physiology also makes them more tolerant of G-forces than men and so more suitable as fighter pilots, one of the most prestigious jobs in the military.[39] Interestingly, in 1961 NASA invited women civilian pilots to join the race for space against the Russians, and the women began testing out extraordinarily well. One woman, who held several world records in flying, had beaten John Glenn on the stress tests, bicycle analysis tests, and lung power tests, and Wally Schirra on vertigo, while setting a record in the bicycle endurance and isolation tests; she lasted ten hours and thirty minutes before hallucinating. But then, without explanation, NASA canceled any further women's tests, and later in 1961, as Linda Bird Francke puts it, "Male astronauts rocketed into our history books."[40]

Of course, women are subject to pregnancy and motherhood, but statistically these have not been much of a problem in the military.[41] In fact, men suffer a higher absentee rate because of disciplinary problems and substance abuse.[42] So when women's strengths and weaknesses are taken into account compared to those of men, women turn out to be highly qualified for many combat and noncombat roles within the military and, in fact, qualified for many more combat roles than those in which they are allowed to serve. Accordingly, attending to women's proper role- or job-related qualifications should undermine the belief that they do not belong in the military and significantly reduce the sexual harassment to which that belief gives rise.

Similarly, attending to women's proper role- or job-related qualifications in civilian life should undermine the belief that it is appropriate to treat women as sexual objects in ways that men are not treated, such that they are sexually subordinate to men, as well as significantly reduce the sexual harassment to which that belief gives rise. In fact, it will simply not be possible for men to treat and evaluate women on the basis of their proper role- or job-related qualifications and excellences when this is appropriate or required and at the same time treat women as sexual objects and, hence, as sexually subordinate to men. Nevertheless, treating and evaluating women on the basis of their proper role- or job-related qualifications and excellences when this is appropriate or required will sometimes require a certain degree of creative imagination. For example, Lani Guinier points out that New York City once used a height requirement favoring tall men to select for police officers. When standards changed and more women became police officers, it became apparent that often they were actually better at keeping the peace than their male counterparts in some situations. For example, in New York City housing projects, black and Puerto Rican women police officers chose to mentor rather than confront teenage boys, thereby offering them respect, and the young men, grateful for the attention from adults, reciprocated by checking their own behavior. And women of all colors have been found to be better at defusing domestic violence situations.[43] Furthermore, when the Los Angeles Police Department wanted to do something about the problem of police abuse, the Christopher Commission report told the city to hire more women. The commission found that women were not reluctant to use force, but that they were not nearly as likely to be involved in the use of excessive force. The women were also more communicative and more skillful at deescalating potentially violent situations. The report concluded that current approaches to policing underemphasize communication skills, sensitivity to cultural differences, and courteousness.[44] What this shows is that it is not always easy to determine what the proper role- or job-related qualifications are, but assuming that these can be determined, treating and evaluating women on the basis of them when this is appropriate or required should help to undermine the belief that it is appropriate to treat women as sexual objects and, hence, as sexually subordinate to men and also should significantly reduce the sexual harassment to which that belief gives rise.

In the case of homosexuals, because of their ability to pass (which enables them to hide their status as homosexuals), they already have been able to demonstrate their ability to perform well in all sorts of social roles and jobs from which they would be excluded if they were openly homosexual. With respect to homosexuals, therefore, the Principle of Desert demands that they be given what they deserve, that is, that they be treated and evaluated according to their proper role- or job-related qualifications and excellences.

Now it is sometimes argued that discrimination can be justified against homosexuals because they engage in forms of sexual intercourse that are not open to procreation. But heterosexuals also engage in those same forms of sexual intercourse, and they are not similarly discriminated against. In fact, in the United States heterosexuals who can reproduce are allowed to marry other heterosexuals who are sterile with the blessings of both church and state, even though the relationships they form are no different from homosexual relationships with respect to their openness to procreation.[45] Correctly applying the Principle of Desert, therefore, should put an end to this discrimination against homosexuals.

Of course, more can and should be said about how we should apply the Principle of Desert to treat and evaluate people on the basis of their proper role- or job-related qualifications and excellences when this is appropriate or required, but hopefully I have said enough to indicate how endorsing both this principle and the Principle of Androgyny (or Equal Opportunity) will, in fact, help to undermine the existing practice of sexual harassment.

In sum, what I have tried to do in this selection is, first, provide:

A Definition of Sexual Harassment: Sexual harassment is objectively unwelcome sexual advances, requests for sexual favors, and other verbal or physical conduct of a sexual nature that are determined to be both objectionable and actionable by the standard of what is reasonable for everyone affected to accept, and which usually, but not always, imposes a special burden on some individuals when there are no comparable burdens imposed on others who are similarly situated.

Second, I have tried to show how two fundamental beliefs help explain the high incidence of sexual harassment in military and civilian life, respectively: the belief women do not belong in the military and the belief that while women do belong in civilian life, it is still appropriate to treat them as sexual objects and, hence, as sexually subordinate to men. Third, I have suggested two positive norms we need to attend to, in addition to the negative one prohibiting sexual harassment, if we want to better rid society of this practice. Those norms are:

The Principle of Androgyny (or Equal Opportunity) requires that the traits that are truly desirable and distributable in society be equally open to both women and men or, in the case of virtues, equally expected of both women and men, other things being equal.

The Principle of Desert requires that we treat and evaluate people on the basis of their proper role- or job-related qualifications and excellences when this is appropriate or required.[46]

Clearly, sexual harassment is a very difficult and troubling problem in our society, but dealing with it also provides us with an opportunity to individually and collectively rethink the roles of men and women in our society, which is one of the most important moral tasks we face.

Notes

1. In 1991 in response to the hearings of the Senate Judiciary Committee, Congress amended the Civil Rights Act to allow victims to claim monetary damages in cases involving all kinds of in-

tentional discrimination, including sexual harassment. As a result, the financial stakes in harassment cases rose dramatically. *South Bend Tribune,* April 6, 1998.

2. *Christoforou v. Ryder Truck Rental,* 668 F.Supp. 294 (S.D.N.Y. 1987).
3. *Rabidue v. Osceola Refining Co.,* 805 F.2d 611, 620 (6th Cir. 1986).
4. In a recent study (see Selection 3), Barbara A. Gutek determined that a number of factors influence whether people tend to classify certain behavior as sexual harassment. They are:
   1. How intrusive and persistent the behavior (The more physically intrusive and persistent the behavior is, the more likely that it will be defined as sexual harassment.)
   2. The nature of relationship between the actors (The better the actors know each other, the less likely the behavior will be labeled sexual harassment.)
   3. The characteristics of the observer (Men and people in authority are less likely to label behavior as sexual harassment.)
   4. The inequality in the relationship (The greater the inequality is, the more likely the behavior will be labeled sexual harassment.)
5. Obviously most offers of this sort will be more subtle, but if they are going to serve their purpose, their message must still be relatively easy to discern.
6. Even where there is legalized prostitution, such offers may still be objectively unwelcome because women would have wanted and could have reasonably expected a fairer array of occupations open to them.
7. There is an analogous requirement of subjective consent in the law concerning rape that is similarly indefensible. See Susan Estrich, "Sex at Work," *Stanford Law Review,* vol. 43 (1991), pp. 813–861.
8. Nor should one be concerned that this suggestion would undercut an appropriate presumption of innocence. This is because the presumption of innocence is weaker for civil cases than for criminal cases. Thus, in a civil law sexual harassment case, the making of an objectively unwanted sexual offer and then firing the person who refused that offer should be sufficient grounds for removing that presumption.
9. Or they could simply not fire those to whom they make the offers.
10. Barbara Gutek contends that sexual harassment is caused by the fact that women are stereotypically identified as sexual objects in ways that men are not. She notes that women are stereotypically characterized as sexy, affectionate, and attractive, whereas men are stereotypically characterized as competent and active. These stereotypes, Gutek claims, spill over into the workplace, making it difficult for women to be perceived as fellow workers rather than sex objects, and it is these perceptions that foster sexual harassment (see Selection 3). It would seem, therefore, that eliminating the problem of sexual harassment from our society will require breaking down these stereotypes. See my *Justice for Here and Now* (New York: Cambridge University Press, 1998), Chapter 4.
11. *Meritor Savings Bank v. Vinson.*
12. *Rabidue v. Osceola Refining Co.,* 805 F.2d 611, 620 (6th Cir. 1986).
13. See Selection 47.
14. *Rabidue v. Osceola Refining Co.,* 805 F.2d 611, 620 (6th Cir. 1986).
15. *Henson v. Dundee,* 682 F.2d 897, 904 (11th Cir. 1982).
16. *Ellison v. Brady,* 924 F.2d 872 (9th Cir. 1991).
17. As one of Gutek's studies shows, reasonable men and reasonable women can disagree over what constitutes sexual harassment in the workplace. In this study, 67.2 percent of men as compared to 16.8 percent of women would be flattered if asked to have sex; 15 percent of the men and 62.8 percent of the women said they would be insulted by such an offer. See Selection 3.
18. Of course, men in particular will have to make a considerable effort to arrive at this most reasonable perspective, and it certainly will not be easy for them to attain it.
19. *Robinson v. Jacksonville Shipyards,* 760 F.Supp. 1486 (M.D. Fla. 1991).
20. Nadine Strossen, "Regulating Workplace Sexual Harassment and Upholding the First Amendment—Avoiding a Collision," *Villanova Law Review,* vol. 37 (1992), pp. 211–228.
21. It does seem reasonable to grant, however, that there is a stronger presumption of employee liability with respect to quid pro quo sexual harassment than hostile environment sexual harass-

ment if only because a company is normally presumed to be more responsible for those who occupy positions of power within it.

22. Cherly Gomez-Preston, *When No Means No* (New York: Carol Publishing Co., 1993), pp.
35–36. Ellen Bravo and Ellen Cassedy, *The 9-5 Guide to Combating Sexual Harassment* (New York:
John Wiley and Sons, 1992), pp. 4–5. The problem is international as well as national. A three-
year study of women in Estonia, Finland, Sweden, and the Soviet Union showed that nearly 50
percent of all working women experience sexual harassment. A survey released in 1991 by the
Santama Group to consider sexual harassment at work showed that about 70 percent of Japanese women say they have experienced some type of sexual harassment on the job. See Susan
Webb, *Step Forward* (New York: Master Media, 1997), pp. xiv, xvii.

23. *New York Times,* November 11, 1996, and February 4, 1997.

24. Linda Bird Francke, *Ground Zero* (New York: Simon and Schuster, 1997), p. 157.

25. Ibid., p. 191.

26. Ibid., p. 187.

27. Ibid., p. 232.

28. Marysia Zalewski and Jane Parpart, *The "Man" Question in International Relations* (Boulder, CO:
Westview, 1998), p. 1.

29. *Time,* March 23, 1998, p. 49.

30. Beverly Walker, "Psychology and Feminism—If You Can't Beat Them, Join Them," in *Men's
Studies Modified,* edited by Dale Spender (Oxford: Pergamon Press, 1981), pp. 112–114.

31. Debra Renee Kaufman, "Professional Women: How Real Are the Recent Gains?" in *Feminist
Philosophies,* 2nd ed., edited by Janet A. Kourany, James P. Sterba, and Rosemarie Tong (Upper
Saddle River, NJ: Prentice-Hall, 1999), pp. 189–202.

32. To distinguish traits of character that are virtues from those that are just desirable traits, we
could define the class of virtues as those desirable and distributable traits that can be reasonably
expected of both women and men. Admittedly, this is a restrictive use of the term "virtue." In
normal usage, the term "virtue" is almost synonymous with the term "desirable trait." But there
is good reason to focus on those desirable traits that can be justifiably inculcated in both women
and men, and so for our purposes let us refer to this class of desirable traits as virtues.

33. For a valuable discussion and critique of these two viewpoints, see Iris Young, "Humanism, Gy-
nocentrism and Feminist Politics," *Women's Studies International Forum,* vol. 8 (1985), pp.
173–183.

34. Francke, *Ground Zero,* p. 16.

35. Ibid.

36. Ibid., p. 198.

37. Ibid., p. 16.

38. Ibid., p. 248.

39. Ibid., p. 236.

40. Ibid., p. 226.

41. Ibid., p. 18.

42. Ibid., p. 16.

43. Lani Guinier, *Becoming Gentlemen* (Boston: Beacon, 1997), pp. 18–19.

44. *Report of the Independent Commission of the Los Angeles Police Department* (Christopher Commission,
1991).

45. John Corvino, *Same Sex* (Lanham, MD: Rowman and Littlefield, 1997), p. 6.

46. These two norms, of course, are not the only positive norms that are relevant to sexual harassment cases, although they are probably the most important ones. Other norms would provide
guidance as to how romantic overtures should be made so as to avoid sexual harassment.

32. Bared Buttocks and Federal Cases

Ellen Frankel Paul

Women in American society are victims of sexual harassment in alarming proportions. Sexual harassment is an inevitable corollary to class exploitation; as capitalists exploit workers, so do males in positions of authority exploit their female subordinates. Male professors, supervisors, and apartment managers in ever increasing numbers take advantage of the financial dependence and vulnerability of women to extract sexual concessions.

VALID ASSERTIONS?

These are the assertions that commonly begin discussions of sexual harassment. For reasons that will be adumbrated below, dissent from the prevailing view is long overdue. Three recent episodes will serve to frame this disagreement.

Valerie Craig, an employee of Y & Y Snacks, Inc., joined several co-workers and her supervisor for drinks after work one day in July of 1978. Her supervisor drove her home and proposed that they become more intimately acquainted. She refused his invitation for sexual relations, whereupon he said that he would "get even" with her. Ten days after the incident she was fired from her job. She soon filed a complaint of sexual harassment with the Equal Employment Opportunity Commission (EEOC), and the case wound its way through the courts. Craig prevailed, the company was held liable for damages, and she received back pay, reinstatement, and an order prohibiting Y & Y from taking reprisals against her in the future.

Carol Zabowicz, one of only two female forklift operators in a West Bend Co. warehouse, charged that her co-workers over a four year period from 1978–1982 sexually harassed her by such acts as: asking her whether she was wearing a bra; two of the men exposing their buttocks between ten and twenty times; a male co-worker grabbing his crotch and making obscene suggestions or growling; subjecting her to offensive and abusive language; and exhibiting obscene drawings with her initials on them. Zabowicz began to show symptoms of physical and psychological stress, necessitating several medical leaves, and she filed a sexual harassment complaint with the EEOC. The district court judge remarked that "the sustained, malicious, and brutal harassment meted out . . . was more than merely unreasonable; it was malevolent and outrageous." The company knew of the harassment and took corrective action only after the employee filed a complaint with the EEOC. The company was, therefore, held liable, and Zabowicz was awarded back pay for the period of her medical absence, and a judgment that her rights were violated under the Civil Rights Act of 1964.

On September 17, 1990, Lisa Olson, a sports reporter for the *Boston Herald*, charged five football players of the just-defeated New England Patriots with sexual harassment for making sexually suggestive and offensive remarks to her when she entered their locker room to conduct a post-game interview. The incident amounted to nothing short of "mind rape," according to Olson. After vociferous lamentations in the media, the National Football League fined the team and its players $25,000 each. The National Organization [for] Women called for a boycott of Remington electric shavers because the owner of the company, Victor Kiam, also owns the Patriots and who allegedly displayed insufficient sensitivity at the time when the episode occurred.

245

UTOPIAN TREATMENT FOR WOMEN

All these incidents are indisputably disturbing. In an ideal world—one needless to say far different from the one that we inhabit or are ever likely to inhabit—women would not be subjected to such treatment in the course of their work. Women, and men as well, would be accorded respect by co-workers and supervisors, their feelings would be taken into account, and their dignity would be left intact. For women to expect reverential treatment in the workplace is utopian, yet they should not have to tolerate outrageous, offensive sexual overtures and threats as they go about earning a living.

One question that needs to be pondered is: What kinds of undesired sexual behavior should women be protected against by law? That is, what kind of actions are deemed so outrageous and violate a woman's rights to such extent that the law should intervene, and what actions should be considered inconveniences of life, to be morally condemned but not adjudicated? A subsidiary question concerns the type of legal remedy appropriate for the wrongs that do require redress. Before directly addressing these questions, it might be useful to diffuse some of the hyperbole adhering to the sexual harassment issue.

HARASSMENT SURVEYS

Surveys are one source of this hyperbole. If their results are accepted at face value, they lead to the conclusion that women are disproportionately victims of legions of sexual harassers. A poll by the Albuquerque *Tribune* found that nearly 80 percent of the respondents reported that they or someone they knew had been victims of sexual harassment. The Merit Systems Protection Board determined that 42 percent of the women (and 14 percent of men) working for the federal government had experienced some form of unwanted sexual attention between 1985 and 1987, with unwanted "sexual teasing" identified as the most prevalent form. A Defense Department survey found that 64 percent of women in the military (and 17 percent of the men) suffered "uninvited and unwanted sexual attention" within the previous year. The United Methodist Church established that 77 percent of its clergywomen experienced incidents of sexual harassment, with 41 percent of these naming a pastor or colleague as the perpetrator, and 31 percent mentioning church social functions as the setting.

A few caveats concerning polls in general, and these sorts of polls in particular, are worth considering. Pollsters looking for a particular social ill tend to find it, usually in gargantuan proportions. (What fate would lie in store for a pollster who concluded that child abuse, or wife beating, or mistreatment of the elderly had dwindled to the point of negligibility!) Sexual harassment is a notoriously ill-defined and almost infinitely expandable concept, including everything from rape to unwelcome neck massaging, discomfiture upon witnessing sexual overtures directed at others, yelling at and blowing smoke in the ears of female subordinates, and displays of pornographic pictures in the workplace. Defining sexual harassment, as the United Methodists did, as "any sexually related behavior that is unwelcome, offensive or which fails to respect the rights of others," the concept is broad enough to include everything from "unsolicited suggestive looks or leers [or] pressures for dates" to "actual sexual assaults or rapes." Categorizing everything from rape to "looks" as sexual harassment makes us all victims, a state of affairs satisfying to radical feminists, but not very useful for distinguishing serious injuries from the merely trivial.

Yet, even if the surveys exaggerate the extent of sexual harassment, however defined, what they do reflect is a great deal of tension between the sexes. As women in ever increasing numbers entered the workplace in the last two decades, as the women's movement challenged alleged male hegemony and exploitation with ever greater intemperance, and as women entered previously all-male preserves from the board rooms to the coal pits, it is lamentable, but should not be surprising, that this tension sometimes takes sexual form. Not that sexual harassment on the job, in the university, and in other settings is a trivial or insignificant matter, but a sense of proportion needs to be restored and, even more importantly, distinctions need to be made. In other words, sexual harassment must be de-ideologized. Statements that paint nearly all women as victims and all men and their patriarchal, capitalist system as perpetrators, are ideological fantasy. Ideology blurs the distinction between being injured—being a genuine victim—and merely being offended. An example is this statement by Catharine A. MacKinnon, a law professor and feminist activist:

> Sexual harassment perpetuates the interlocked structure by which women have been kept sexually in thrall to men and at the bottom of the labor market. Two forces of American society converge: men's control over women's sexuality and capital's control over employees' work lives. Women historically have been required to exchange sexual services for material survival, in one form or another. Prostitution and marriage as well as sexual harassment in different ways institutionalize this arrangement.

Such hyperbole needs to be diffused and distinctions need to be drawn. Rape, a non-consensual invasion of a person's body, is a crime clear and simple. It is a violation of the right to the physical integrity of the body (the right of life, as John Locke or Thomas Jefferson would have put it). Criminal law should and does prohibit rape. Whether it is useful to call rape "sexual harassment" is doubtful, for it makes the latter concept overly broad while trivializing the former.

EXTORTION OF SEXUAL FAVORS

Intimidation in the workplace of the kind that befell Valerie Craig—that is, extortion of sexual favors by a supervisor from a subordinate by threatening to penalize, fire, or fail to reward—is what the courts term *quid pro quo* sexual harassment. Since the mid-1970s, the federal courts have treated this type of sexual harassment as a form of sex discrimination in employment proscribed under Title VII of the Civil Rights Act of 1964. A plaintiff who prevails against an employer may receive such equitable remedies as reinstatement and back pay, and the court can order the company to prepare and disseminate a policy against sexual harassment. Current law places principal liability on the company, not the harassing supervisor, even when higher management is unaware of the harassment and, thus, cannot take any steps to prevent it.

Quid pro quo sexual harassment is morally objectionable and analogous to extortion: The harasser extorts property (i.e., use of the woman's body) through the leverage of fear for her job. The victim of such behavior should have legal recourse, but serious reservations can be held about rectifying these injustices through the blunt instrument of Title VII. In egregious cases the victim is left less than whole (for back pay will not compensate her for ancillary losses), and no prospect for punitive damages are offered to deter would-be harassers. Even more distressing about Title VII is the fact that the primary target of litigation is not the actual harasser, but rather the employer. This places a double burden on a company. The employer is swindled by the supervisor because he spent his time pursuing sexual gratification and thereby impairing the efficiency of the workplace by mismanaging his subordinates, and the employer must endure lengthy and expensive litigation, pay damages, and suffer loss to its reputation. It would be fairer to both the company and the victim to treat sexual harassment as a tort—that is, as a private wrong or injury for which the court can assess damages. Employers should be held vicariously liable only when they know of an employee's behavior and do not try to redress it.

DEFINING HARASSMENT IS DIFFICULT

As for the workplace harassment endured by Carol Zabowicz—the bared buttocks, obscene portraits, etc.—that too should be legally redressable. Presently, such incidents also fall under the umbrella of Title VII, and are termed hostile environment sexual harassment, a category accepted later than *quid pro quo* and with some judicial reluctance. The main problem with this category is that it has proven too elastic: cases have reached the courts based on everything from off-color jokes to unwanted, persistent sexual advances by co-workers. A new tort of sexual harassment would handle these cases better. Only instances above a certain threshold of egregiousness or outrageousness would be actionable. In other words, the behavior that the plaintiff found offensive would also have to be offensive to the proverbial "reasonable man" of the tort law. That is, the behavior would have to be objectively injurious rather than merely subjectively offensive. The defendant would be the actual harasser, not the company, unless it knew about the problem and failed to act. Victims of scatological jokes, leers, unwanted offers of dates, and other sexual annoyances would no longer have their day in court.

A distinction must be restored between morally offensive behavior and behavior that causes serious harm. Only the latter should fall under the jurisdiction of criminal or tort law. Do we really want legislators and judges delving into our most intimate private lives, deciding when a look is a leer, and when a leer is a Civil Rights Act offense? Do we really want courts deciding, as one recently did, whether a school principal's disparaging remarks about a female school district administrator was sexual harassment and, hence, a breach of Title VII, or merely the act of a spurned and vengeful lover? Do we want judges settling disputes such as the one that arose at a car dealership after a female employee turned down a male co-worker's offer of a date and his colleagues retaliated by calling her offensive names and embarrassing her in front of customers? Or another case in which a female shipyard worker complained of an "offensive working environment" because of the prevalence of pornographic material on the docks? Do we want the state to prevent or compensate us for any behavior that someone might find offensive? Should people have a legally enforceable right not to be offended by others? At some point, the price for such protection is the loss of both liberty and privacy rights.

NO PERFECT WORKING ENVIRONMENT EXISTS

Workplaces are breeding grounds of envy, personal grudges, infatuation, and jilted loves, and beneath a fairly high threshold of outrageousness, these travails should be either suffered in silence, complained of to higher management, or left behind as one seeks other employment. No one, female or male, can expect to enjoy a working environment that is perfectly stress-free, or to be treated always and by everyone with kindness and respect. To the extent that sympathetic judges have encouraged women to seek monetary compensation for slights and annoyances, they have not done them a great service. Women need to develop a thick skin in order to survive and prosper in the workforce. It is patronizing to think that they need to be recompensed by male judges for seeing a few pornographic pictures on a wall. By their efforts to extend sexual harassment charges to even the most trivial behavior, the radical feminists send a message that women are not resilient enough to ignore the run-of-the-mill, churlish provocation from male co-workers. It is difficult to imagine a suit by a longshoreman complaining of mental stress due to the display of nude male centerfolds by female co-workers. Women cannot expect to have it both ways: equality where convenient, but special dispensations when the going gets rough. Equality has its price and that price may include unwelcome sexual advances, irritating and even intimidating sexual jests, and lewd and obnoxious colleagues.

Egregious acts—sexual harassment per se—must be legally redressable. Lesser but not trivial offenses, whether at the workplace or in other more social settings, should be considered moral lapses for which the offending party receives opprobrium, disciplinary warnings, or penalties, depending on the setting and the severity. Trivial offenses, dirty jokes, sexual overtures, and sexual innuendoes do make many women feel intensely discomfited, but, unless they become outrageous through persistence or content, these too should be taken as part of life's annoyances. The perpetrators should be either endured, ignored, rebuked, or avoided, as circumstances and personal inclination dictate. Whether Lisa Olson's experience in the locker room of the Boston Patriots falls into the second or third category is debatable. The media circus triggered by the incident was certainly out of proportion to the event.

As the presence of women on road gangs, construction crews, and oil rigs becomes a fact of life, the animosities and tensions of this transition period are likely to abate gradually. Meanwhile, women should "lighten up," and even dispense a few risqué barbs of their own, a sure way of taking the fun out of it for offensive male boors.

---

33. Reckless Eyeballing: Sexual Harassment on Campus

Katie Roiphe

For generations, women have talked and written and theorized about their problems with men. But theories about patriarchy tumble from abstraction when you wake up next to it in the morning. Denouncing male oppression clashes with wanting him anyhow. From playgrounds to consciousness-raising groups, from suffragette marches to prochoice marches, women have been talking their way through this contradiction for a long time.

Sometimes my younger sister and I go out for coffee and talk about our relationships. We analyze everything: why he acts that way, how unfair this is, how we shouldn't be waiting for his call, and how we have better things to do with our time anyway. How men are always like that, and we are always like this, and our conversation goes on, endless, pleasurable, interesting, over many refills, until we go home and wait for their calls.

Heterosexual desire inevitably raises conflicts for the passionate feminist, and it's not an issue easily evaded. Sooner or later feminism has to address "the man question." But this is more than just a practical question of procreation, more than the well-worn translation of personal into political. It's also a question for the abstract, the ideological, the furthest reaches of the feminist imagination.

Charlotte Perkins Gilman, a prominent feminist writing at the turn of the century, found a fictional solution to the conflict between sex and feminism in her utopian novel, *Herland.* Her solution is simple: there is no sexual desire. Even after the male anthropologists arrive with their worldly lusts, the women of Herland remain unruffled. Everything runs smoothly and rationally in Herland, and through the entire course of the book none of the women harbors any sexual feelings, toward men or toward each other. They magically reproduce by parthenogenesis, and motherhood is their driving passion.

Gilman erases whatever problems arise from sexual involvements with men in her happy, if sterile, vision of clean streets, clean hearts, clean minds. In her sociological work, *Women and Economics,* Gilman applies the same device—obliterating the source of conflict—to another site of struggle. She conceives of houses without kitchens as the solution to women's household drudgery. The problem is that most people want kitchens, and most people want sex.

Many of today's feminists, in their focus on sexual harassment, share Gilman's sexual politics. In their videos, literature, and workshops, these feminists are creating their own utopian visions of human sexuality. They imagine a world where all expressions of sexual appreciation are appreciated. They imagine a totally symmetrical universe, where people aren't silly, rude, awkward, excessive, or confused. And if they are, they are violating the rules and are subject to disciplinary proceedings.

A Princeton pamphlet declares that "sexual harassment is unwanted sexual attention that makes a person feel uncomfortable or causes problems in school or at work, or in social settings."[1] The word "uncomfortable" echoes through all the literature on sexual harassment. The feminists concerned with this issue, then, propose the right to be comfortable as a feminist principle.

The difficulty with these rules is that, although it may infringe on the right to comfort, unwanted sexual attention is part of nature. To find wanted sexual attention, you have to give and receive a certain amount of unwanted sexual attention. Clearly, the truth is that if no one was ever allowed to risk offering unsolicited sexual attention, we would all be solitary creatures.

The category of sexual harassment, according to current campus definitions, is not confined to relationships involving power inequity. Echoing many other common definitions of sexual harassment, Princeton's pamphlet warns that "sexual harassment can occur between two people regardless of whether or not one has power over the other."[2] The weight of this definition of sexual harassment, then, falls on gender instead of status.[3]

In current definitions of sexual harassment, there is an implication that gender is so important that it eclipses all other forms of power. The driving idea behind these rules is that gender itself is a sufficient source of power to constitute sexual harassment. Catharine MacKinnon, an early theorist of sexual harassment, writes that "situations of co-equal power—among co-workers or students or teachers—are difficult to see as examples of sexual harassment unless you have a notion of male power. [See Selection 2.] I think we lie to women when we call it not power when a woman is come on to by a man who is not her employer, not her teacher."[4] With this description, MacKinnon extends the province of male power beyond that of tangible social power. She proposes using the words "sexual harassment" as a way to name what she sees as a fundamental social and political inequity between men and women. Following in this line of thought, Elizabeth Grauerholz, a sociology professor, conducted a study about instances of male students harassing their female professors, a phenomenon she calls "contrapower harassment."[5]

Recently, at the University of Michigan, a female teaching assistant almost brought a male student up on charges of sexual harassment. She was offended by an example he used in a paper about polls—a few sentences about "Dave Stud" entertaining ladies in his apartment when he receives a call from a pollster—and she showed the paper to the professor of the class. He apparently encouraged her to see the offending example as an instance of sexual harassment. She decided not to press charges, although she warned the student that the next time anything else like this happened, in writing or in person, she would not hesitate. The student wisely dropped the course. To understand how this student's paragraph about Dave Stud might sexually harass his teacher, when he has much more to lose than she does, one must recognize the deeply sexist assumptions about male-female relations behind the teaching assistant's charge.

The idea that a male student can sexually harass a female professor, overturning social and institutional hierarchy, solely on the basis of some primal or socially conditioned male power over women is insulting. The mere fact of being a man doesn't give the male student so much power that he can plow through social hierarchies, grabbing what he wants, intimidating all the cowering female faculty in his path. The assumption that female students or faculty must be protected from the sexual harassment of male peers or inferiors promotes the regrettable idea that men are natively more powerful than women.

Even if you argue, as many do, that *in this society* men are simply much more powerful than women, this is still a dangerous train of thought. It carries us someplace we don't want to be. Rules and laws based on the premise that all women need protection from all men, because they are so much weaker, serve only to reinforce the image of women as powerless.

Our female professors and high-ranking executives, our congresswomen and editors, are every bit as strong as their male counterparts. They have earned their position of authority. To declare that their authority is vulnerable to a dirty joke from someone of inferior status just because that person happens to be a man is to undermine their position. Female authority is not (and should not be seen as) so fragile that it shatters at the first sign of male sexuality. Any rules saying otherwise strip women, in the public eye, of their hard-earned authority.

Since common definitions of sexual harassment include harassment between peers, the emphasis is not on external power structures, but on inner landscapes. The boundaries are subjective, the maps subject to mood. According to the Equal Employment Opportunity Commission's definition, any conduct may be deemed sexual harassment if it "has the purpose or effect of unreasonably interfering with an individual's work or academic performance or creating an intimidating, hostile or offensive working or academic environment." The hostility or offensiveness of a working environment is naturally hard to measure by objective standards. Such vague categorization opens the issue up to the individual psyche.

The clarity of the definition of sexual harassment as a "hostile work environment" depends on a universal code of conduct, a shared idea of acceptable behavior that we just don't have. Something that makes one person feel uncomfortable may make another person feel great. At Princeton, counselors reportedly tell students, If you feel sexually harassed then chances are you were. At the university's Terrace Club, the refuge of fashionable, left-leaning, black-clad undergraduates, there is a sign supporting this view. It is downstairs, on a post next to the counter where the beer is served, often partially obscured by students talking, cigarettes in hand: "What constitutes sexual harassment or intimidating, hostile or offensive environment is to be defined by the person harassed and his/her own feelings of being threatened or compromised." This relatively common definition of sexual harassment crosses the line between being supportive and obliterating the idea of external reality.

The categories become especially complicated and slippery when sexual harassment enters the realm of the subconscious. The Princeton guide explains that "sexual harassment may result from a conscious or unconscious action, and can be subtle or blatant." Once we move into the area of the subtle and unconscious, we are no longer talking about a professor systematically exploiting power for sex. We are no longer talking about Hey, baby, sleep with me or I'll fail you. To hold people responsible for their subtle, unconscious actions is to legislate thought, an ominous, not to mention difficult, prospect.

The idea of sexual harassment—and clearly when you are talking about the subtle and unconscious, you are talking about an idea—provides a blank canvas on which students can express all of the insecurities, fears, and confusions about the relative sexual freedom of the college experience. Sexual harassment is everywhere: it crops up in dinner conversations and advertisements on television, all over women's magazines and editorial pages. No one can claim that Anita Hill is an unsung heroine. [See Selections 20 and 21.] It makes sense that teenagers get caught up in the Anita Hill fury; they are particularly susceptible to feeling uncomfortable about sexuality, and sexual harassment offers an ideology that explains "uncomfortable" in political terms. The idea of sexual harassment displaces adolescent uneasiness onto the environment, onto professors, onto older men.

The heightened awareness of the potential for sexual encroachment creates an atmosphere of suspicion and distrust between faculty and students. Many professors follow an unwritten rule: never close the door to your office when you and a female student are inside. One professor told a male teaching assistant I know that closing the door to his office with a student inside is an invitation to charges of sexual harassment. If keeping the door open is not enough to ward off the perception or reality of sexual harassment, the authors of *The Lecherous Professor,* [See Selection 11] an early book of essays about sexual harassment, warn faculty that "if a situation is potentially threatening, a colleague can always be asked to sit in on student-teacher conferences."[6] Although these policies may reduce the likelihood of sexual harassment charges, they also increase the amount of sexual tension between students and professors. The open door or the extra faculty member only draws attention to the potential for a sexual dynamic between professor and student. They promote the idea that professors are more interested in bodies than minds.

The inflamed rhetoric against harassment implies that all women are potential victims and all men are potential harassers. "Men in the Academy," an essay in the book *Ivory Power,* vilifies the male academic so effectively that the author is forced to acknowledge that "nonetheless, not all male professors harass female students."[7] That this need even be said is evidence that this perspective is spiraling out of control.

The irony is that these open doors, and all that they symbolize, threaten to create barriers between faculty and students. In the present hypersensitive environment, caution and better judgment can lead professors to keep female students at a distance. It may be easier not to pursue friendships with female students than to risk charges of sexual harassment and misunderstood intentions. The rhetoric surrounding sexual harassment encourages a return to formal relations between faculty and students.

The university, with its emphasis on intellectual exchange, on the passionate pursuit of knowledge, with its strange hours and unworldly citizens, is theoretically an ideal space for close friendships. The flexible hours combined with the intensity of the academic world would appear to be fertile ground for connections, arguments over coffee. Recently, reading a biography of the poet John Berryman, who was also a professor at Princeton in the forties, I was struck by stories about his students crowding into his house late into the night to talk about poetry. These days, an informal invitation to a professor's house till all hours would be a breach of propriety. As the authors of *The Lecherous Professor* warn, "Contacts outside of class deserve thought. Student-teacher conferences should be held in appropriate settings."[8]

In combating sexual harassment, feminists must necessarily distrust the intimacy of the academic environment. They must necessarily distrust a male professor having lunch with a female student. In *Ivory Power,* this is offered as a male professor's typical attitude: "In a classroom setting it is entirely appropriate that personal and professional lives be separated. However[,] undergraduates doing [honors] research and graduate students [are] becoming junior colleagues; a close personal relationship is to be encouraged."[9] In the eyes of the author, this is an outrageous position, one that precipitates sexual harassment. That this professor's harmless comment is so seditious, that it is used as an illustration of dangerous attitudes among male faculty members, indicates the vehemence of the feminist desire for separation between professors and students.

Feminists concerned with sexual harassment must fight for an immutable hierarchy, for interactions so cleansed of personal interest there can be no possibility of borders crossed. Although this approach to education may reduce the number of harmful connections between teachers and students, it may also reduce the number of meaningful connections. The problem with the chasm solution to faculty-student relations is that for graduate students, and even for undergraduates, connections with professors are intellectually as well as professionally important.

In an early survey of sexual harassment, a law student at Berkeley wrote that in response to fears of sexual harassment charges, "the male law school teachers ignore female students . . . this means that we are afforded [fewer] academic opportunities than male students."[10] Many male professors have confirmed that they feel more uncomfortable with female students than with male students, because of all the attention given to sexual harassment. They may not "ignore" their female students, but they keep them at arm's length. They feel freer to forge friendships with male students.

The overstringent attention given to sexual harassment on campuses breeds suspicion; it creates an environment where imaginations run wild, charges can seem to materialize out of thin air, and both faculty and students worry about a friendly lunch. The repercussions for the academic community, let alone the confused freshman, can be many and serious.

In an excessive effort to purge the university of sexual corruption, many institutions have violated the rights of the professors involved by neglecting to follow standard procedures. Since sexual harassment is a relatively recent priority, "standard procedures" are themselves new, shrouded, and shaky. Charges of sexual harassment are uncharted territory, and fairness is not necessarily the compass.

In a recent case a tenured professor at a prominent university was dismissed in a unilateral administrative action, without a faculty hearing, legal counsel, or the calling of witnesses in his defense. Some professors have been suspended indefinitely without a sense of when or what would end the suspension. As an official of the American Association of College Professors framed the problem, "There tends to be publicizing of names at too early a stage, and trigger-quick action to suspend without suggestion of immediate harm."[11]

The American Association of College Professors has issued a statement about such overzealous enforcement of sexual harassment policy, explaining that "sexual harassment—which committee A certainly does not condone—is not somehow so different from other kinds of sanctionable misconduct as to permit the institution to render judgement and to penalize without having afforded due process."[12] This statement emphasizes the danger in looking at sexual harassment as an issue somehow more pressing, more serious, more important, than other disciplinary problems. The reason due process is thrown to the wind is that the pressure is so great, and the issue regarded as so delicate and mysterious, that administrations are overcompensating. They feel that if they deal with the issue swiftly, they are being responsive.

In *The Lecherous Professor,* authors Billie Wright Dziech and Linda Weiner explain why feminists are not concerned with due process:

> Let a single 110-pound nineteen-year-old muster the courage to complain about being fondled or threatened by a Shakespeare professor, and Latin professors, geographers, physicists, architects, engineers, and lawyers are likely to rediscover the bonds that unite them. They will as a chorus mouth platitudes about loyalty to the institution, academic freedom and due process. They will suddenly remember the lyrics to the alma mater.[13]

For Dziech and Weiner, academic freedom and due process are simply more platitudes generated by the old-boy network. They dismiss any concern about fairness with their image of the ranks of male professionals united against the slim victim. Sexual harassment has assumed such grand proportions in the minds of these feminists that they are not concerned with the machinations of the disciplinary system, however Kafkaesque. To many feminists, like Dziech and Weiner, who are interested in cleansing the university of harassers, a few casualties of justice along the way seem like a small price to pay.

The university has become so saturated with the idea of sexual harassment that it has begun to affect minute levels of communication. Like "date rape," the phrase "sexual harassment" is frequently used, and it does not apply only to extremes of human behavior. Suddenly everyday experience is filtered through the strict lens of a new sexual politics. Under fierce political scrutiny, behavior that once seemed neutral or natural enough now takes on ominous meanings. You may not even realize that you are a survivor of sexual harassment.

A student tells me that she first experienced sexual harassment when she came to college. She was at a crowded party, leaning against a wall, and a big jock came up to her, placed his hands at either side of her head, and pretended to lean against her, saying, So, baby, when are we going out? All right, he didn't touch me, she says, but he invaded my space. He had no right to do that.

She has carried this first instance of sexual harassment around in her head for six years. It is the beginning of a long list. A serious feminist now, an inhabitant of the official feminist house on campus, she recognizes this experience for what it was. She knows there is no way to punish the anonymous offender or everyone would be behind bars, but she thinks the solution is education. Like many feminists, she argues that discipline is clumsy, bureaucracy lumbering, and there is no hope for perfect justice in the university. She is more concerned with getting the message across, delineating acceptable behaviors to faculty and students alike, than in beheading professors. She subscribes to a sort of zookeeper school of feminism—training the beasts to behave within "acceptable" parameters.

Many foreigners think that concern with sexual harassment is as American as baseball, New England Puritans, and apple pie. Many feminists in other countries look on our preoccupation with sexual harassment as another sign of the self-indulgence and repression in American society. Veronique Neiertz, France's secretary of state for women's rights, has said that in the United States "the slightest wink can be misinterpreted." Her ministry's commonsense advice to women who feel harassed by co-workers is to respond with "a good slap in the face."[14]

Once sexual harassment includes someone glancing down your shirt, the meaning of the phrase has been stretched beyond recognition. The rules about unwanted sexual attention begin to seem more like etiquette than rules. Of course it would be nicer if people didn't brush against other people in a way that makes them uncomfortable. It would also be nicer if bankers didn't bang their briefcases into people on the subway at rush hour. But not nice is a different thing than against the rules, or the law. It is a different thing than oppressing women. Etiquette and politics aren't synonyms.

Susan Teres of SHARE said, at the 1992 Take Back the Night march, that 88 percent of Princeton's female students had experienced some form of sexual harassment on campus. Catharine MacKinnon writes that "only 7.8% of women in the United States are not sexually assaulted or harassed in their lifetimes."[15] No wonder. Once you cast the net so wide as to include everyone's everyday experience, identifying sexual harassment becomes a way of interpreting the sexual texture of daily life, instead of isolating individual events. Sensitivity to sexual harassment becomes a way of seeing the world, rather than a way of targeting specific contemptible behaviors. In an essay attempting to profile the quintessential sexual harasser, two feminists warn in conclusion (and in all seriousness) that "the harasser is similar, perhaps disturbingly so, to the 'average man.'"[16]

As one peruses guidelines on sexual harassment, it's clear where the average man comes in. Like most common definitions, Princeton's definition of sexual harassment includes "leering and ogling, whistling, sexual innuendo, and other suggestive or offensive or derogatory comments, humor and jokes about sex."[17] MacKinnon's statistic includes obscene phone calls. These definitions of sexual harassment sterilize the environment. They propose classrooms that are cleaner than Sesame Street and Mr. Rogers's neighborhood. Like the rhetoric about date rape, this extreme inclusiveness forces women into old roles. What message are we sending if we say We can't work if you tell dirty jokes, it upsets us, it offends us? With this severe a conception of sexual harassment, sex itself gets pushed into a dark, seamy, male domain. If we can't look at his dirty pictures because his dirty pictures upset us, it doesn't mean they vanish. It means he looks at them with a new sense of their power, their underground, forbidden, male-only value.

Instead of learning that men have no right to do these terrible things to us, we should be learning to deal with individuals with strength and confidence. If someone bothers us, we should be able to put him in his place without crying into our pillow or screaming for help or counseling. If someone stares at us, or talks dirty, or charges neutral conversation with sexual innuendo, we should not be pushed to the verge of a nervous breakdown. In an American College Health Association pamphlet, "unwanted sexual comments, jokes or gestures" are characterized as "a form of sexual assault."[18] Feminists drafting sexual harassment guidelines seem to have forgotten childhood's words of wisdom: sticks and stones may break my bones, but names will never harm me.

Someone I knew in college had an admirable flair for putting offenders in their place. Once, when she was playing pinball in Tommy's Lunch, the coffee shop across from Adams House, a teenage boy came up to her and grabbed her breast. She calmly went to the counter and ordered a glass of milk and then walked over and poured it over his head. She would intimidate obscene phone callers with the line "Listen, honey, I was blow job queen of my high school," and they would inevitably hang up. Most of us probably have less creative ways of handling "sexual harassment," but we should at least be able to handle petty instances like ogling, leering, and sexual innuendo on the personal level.

I would even go so far as to say that people have the right to leer at whomever they want to leer at. By offering protection to the woman against the leer, the movement against sexual harassment is curtailing her personal power. This protection implies the need to be protected. It paints her as defenseless against even the most trivial of male attentions. This protection assumes that she never ogles, leers, or makes sexual innuendos herself.

Interpreting leers and leer-type behavior as a violation is a choice. My mother tells me about the time she was walking down the street in the sixties, when skirts were short, with my older sister, who was then three. A construction worker made a comment to my mother, and my three-year-old sister leaned out of her carriage and said, "Hey, mister, leave my mother alone." My mother, never the conventional sort of feminist, told my sister that the construction worker wasn't hurting her, he was giving her a compliment.

Although my mother's reaction may not be everyone's, this is a parable about individual responses. There is a spectrum of reactions to something like a leer. Some may be flattered, others distressed; some won't notice, and still others, according to some feminist literature, will be enraged and incapacitated. In its propaganda the movement against sexual harassment places absolute value on the leer. According to its rules, whatever that construction worker said to my mother was violating, harmful, and demeaning. According to its rules, my three-year-old sister was right. By rallying institutional authority behind its point of view, by distributing these pamphlets that say leering always makes women feel violated, this movement propels women backward to a time when sexual attention was universally thought to offend. They are saying, as Catharine MacKinnon neatly summarizes it, that "all women live in sexual objectification the way fish live in water."[19] But I think it depends on where you learned to swim.

History offers an example of another time when looks could be crimes, but today feminists don't talk much about what happened to black men accused of "reckless eyeballing," that is, directing sexual glances at white women. Black men were lynched for a previous incarnation of "sexual harassment." As late as 1955, a black man was lynched for whistling at a white woman.[20] Beneath the Jim Crow law about reckless eyeballing was the assumption that white women were the property of white men, and a look too hard or too long in their direction was a flouting of white power. Reckless eyeballing was a symbolic violation of white women's virtue. That virtue, that division between white women and black men, was important to the southern hierarchy. While of course lynchings and Jim Crow are not the current danger, it's important to remember that protecting women against the stray male gaze has not always served a social good. We should learn the lessons: looks can't kill, and we are nobody's property.

All of this is not to suggest that abuses of power are not wrong. They are. Any professor who trades grades for sex and uses this power as a forceful tool of seduction deserves to face charges. The same would be true if he traded grades for a thousand dollars. I'm not opposed to stamping out corruption; I only think it's important to look before you stamp. Rules about harassment should be less vague, and inclusive. They should sharply target serious offenses and abuses of power rather than environments that are "uncomfortable," rather than a stray professor looking down a shirt. The university's rules should not be based on the idea of female students who are pure and naive, who don't harbor sexualities of their own, who don't seduce, or who can't defend themselves against the nonconditional sexual interests of male faculty and students.

Although sexual harassment can be a real and serious problem, like any other abuse of power, there is a difference between handling individual instances and conducting rigorous, large-scale education campaigns and media blitzes about the problem. Organizations like Princeton's SHARE and Harvard's RESPONSE advertise their way of looking at experience to the incoming students. They put up posters and give out pamphlets, they have workshops and counselors and peer counselors and hot lines. A serious concern about substantive abuses of power is one thing, but transforming discussions of sexual harassment into the latest craze is another. Alarmist propaganda warning about the sexual dangers lurking in the freshman's future is not going to help anyone understand anything any better.

David Mamet's play "Oleanna" dramatizes the consequences of sexual harassment propaganda. A young professor rambles—the self-assured, self-involved rambling of status—and a student listens resentfully. At one point she gets upset, and he puts his arm around her, which she interprets as a sexual advance. He tells her he "likes her" when she asks why he is bothering to help her. The play hinges on the way in which she twists his words and actions to fit into her own puzzled ideological context.

Between the first and second acts, she reports the professor to the tenure committee.

Feminism transforms the thick, timid student with an aversion to big words into a full-fledged, jargon-toting, rapid-fire radical. She comes into his office armed with accusations of his classist, sexist, elitist behavior. She thinks he belittles her lack of "privilege." She refers to her feminist group as "My group" and declares that she is acting not as an individual but on behalf of her group. As she gets up to leave, he grabs her by the shoulders to force her to hear him out. This gesture later evolves into her charge of attempted rape. She gives him a list of books, including his own, and agrees to recant her charges if he agrees never to teach them again. He refuses.

Mamet's play is not just a story about words twisted, and the strange origins of false charges, about the uneasy power dynamics between teacher and student. It is not just about two people in the same room at the same time experiencing two wildly different versions of the same event. Mamet gets at the deeper issues always there beneath the he-said-she-said debate that cycles endlessly, fruitlessly on. His play is also an allegory. The student represents a certain kind of no-apologies, no-nuances, no-jokes, it's-our-turn-now feminism. The exchange between the well-meaning, if self-obsessed, professor and the student puffed large with her sense of her own victimization becomes a parable about the political confrontations erupting within universities.

In the final scene the young woman rightfully declares the struggle as one over power. She rightfully notes that the professor hates her because she has power over him. After overhearing many phone calls to his wife, she tells him, victory in her voice, not to call his wife "baby." This drives him over the edge. He has lost everything, his job, his new house, and now she is telling him what to call his own wife. The play seems to accelerate; the action moves fast and hard. He hits her, throws her to the ground, calls her "you little cunt." The tension rattling between them for so long, back and forth in terse, edgy words, bursts into physical action.

In the midst of the violent skirmish, Mamet's message rises above the play's more obvious gritty realism. The student's charges are seen as what they are: a self-fulfilling prophecy. The professor has turned into what she always thought he was. The last words of the play are hers, from her position on the ground: "Yes, that's right, that's right." Feminists, Mamet warns, will conjure up the sexist beast if they push far enough. By seizing power through dogma, by desiring to purge the university of certain books with the "wrong" values, this brand of feminism ensures a fierce response. In pitting women against men, "her" group against "his" group, the student sets up a struggle for power in which there are no winners. She ends up insulted, assaulted, on the ground, the victim she never was, and he ends up the abusive, ugly man he never was.

Mamet is telling us that the so-called male establishment, sensitive as it is, will not sit back and let its books be banned. It will not accept the accusations without a fight. The girl's group necessarily creates, feeds, and—to use her word—empowers its opposition. This is a movement, Mamet warns, that really will change higher education, but not in the way it seeks to. It will force the university's old guard to defend itself, its jobs, and its books against the timid, inarticulate, even dull student who has risen to power on the crest of the multiculturalist wave.

The transformation of the student that Mamet describes has a more prosaic pace in real life. But the pamphlets about sexual harassment do offer sample cases that translate what seem like everyday occurrences into the language of outrage and political indignation. "Maria is one of two women in a precept [Princeton's word for class]. When her preceptor talks to her about a paper he gets closer than she considers necessary. Lately he has been touching her to get her attention, and has brushed against her several times. She feels very tense and this is affecting her work."[21]

Maybe her preceptor is thinking about her sexually and maybe he isn't. Maybe he's near-sighted and that's why he's leaning close to read her papers. Maybe that's just the way he is. In the present environment, this mild set of behaviors constitutes an offense. She can report him. She can seek counseling for this traumatic experience.

Here's another one involving peers: "Marlene and Bill live on the same floor of the dorm. Bill recently approached her and asked her out. She politely declined. Since then, every time Bill sees Marlene he comments on her appearance. Last night Bill walked into her room uninvited. She asked him to leave. He persisted, telling her that she must be hung up about sex, or unliberated, and finally left. Marlene is nervous, depressed, angry. She is afraid to continue living in the dormitory."[22]

Bill is not the picture of maturity, but what's really strange about this exemplum is Marlene's reaction. Maybe from Bill's perspective he likes her. He's nervous around girls and finally got up the courage to ask her to go to a party with him. He told her she looked good in her new suede miniskirt. That didn't help. In his awkwardness, he made a stupid joke about the sexual revolution. He thought it would make her laugh. It didn't—instead she thought it was sexual harassment.

But of course the worry here is not Bill. Bill will be fine. The worry is these distraught women. What's going to happen to this hypothetical Maria and this hypothetical Marlene when they walk through Central Park, when they go to buy a slice of pizza, when they go to the movies, when they go to parties? The streets are full of perilous compliments. Such sensitive souls (and their sensitive bodies) are not going to get along well in our difficult world. If organizations like SHARE and RESPONSE foster and nurture this kind of perspective, their hothouse flowers are going to wilt in the light of postcollege day.

These somber pamphlets don't have much practical value, but they do send messages, they do promote their perspective. Their authors are interpreting everyday experience. They are giving names to nebulous human interchange. If the name we are given is sexual harassment, then that name will affect that experience and how we think about that experience.

As feminists interested in the issue themselves argue, "Many have difficulty recognizing their experience as victimization. It is helpful to use the words that fit the experience, validating the depths of the survivor's feelings and allowing her to feel her experience was serious."[23] In other words, these feminists recognize that if you don't tell the victim that she's a victim, she may sail through the experience without fully grasping the gravity of her humiliation. She may get through without all that trauma and counseling. Buried within this description of helping students overcome the problem of "recognizing their experience as victimization" is the nagging concern that the problem may pass unnoticed, may dissolve without political scrutiny. To create awareness is sometimes to create a problem.

Education about sexual harassment is not confined to the space of freshman week. As sexual harassment is absorbed into public discussion, it enters grade schools as easily as colleges. An article in New York magazine documents the trickle-down effect: "After her first week at a reputable private school in Manhattan, 8-year-old Alexandra didn't want to go back. A 9-year-old boy had been harassing her: 'He said he wanted to hump me.' She wasn't sure what 'hump' meant."[24]

The article describes what happened when Alexandra discovered the name for her traumatic experience. She was listening to Anita Hill's testimony on the radio when she suddenly exclaimed: "'That's what happened to me! He didn't touch me, but his words upset me!'" The article concludes that "Alexandra's first lesson in sexual harassment may not be her last, but thanks to her parents, who listened to her, believed her and supported her, she'll at least be better prepared to deal with sexual abuse than the women and men of

Anita Hill's generation."[25] As Alexandra grows up, will she be better able to deal with sexual abuse, or will she just see it everywhere she looks? Will she blur the line between childish teasing and sexual abuse for the rest of her life? The prospect of a maturing generation of Alexandras, sensitized from childhood to the issue of sexual harassment, is not necessarily desirable from the feminist point of view. As Joan Didion wrote in the sixties, certain segments of the women's movement can breed "women too sensitive for the difficulties of adult life, women unequipped for reality, and grasping at the movement as a rationale for denying that reality."[26]

Responding to sexual harassment in its most expansive definition purges the environment of the difficult, the uncomfortable, and the even mildly distasteful. Feminists concerned with sexual harassment reproduce their own version of Charlotte Perkins Gilman's *Herland,* based on the absence of messy sexual desire. Although it takes some imaginative leaps to get there, their version of Herland is a land without dirty jokes, leers, and other instances of "unwanted sexual attention." Whether or not visions of a universe free from "sexual harassment" are practical, the question becomes whether they're even desirable.

Mary Koss, author of the *Ms.* magazine survey of rape, writes that "experiencing sexual harassment transforms women into victims and changes their lives."[27] Koss sees this transformation into victimhood as something caused by sexual harassment, an external event. In Koss's paradigm, after the student has been harassed, her confidence is perilously shaken, her ability to function and trust men disrupted forever. She sees the "lecherous professor" as the agent of transformation. She does not see that it is her entire conceptual framework—her kind of rhetoric, her kind of interpretation—that transforms perfectly stable women into hysterical, sobbing victims. If there is any transforming to be done, it is to transform everyday experience back into everyday experience.

Notes

1. "What You Should Know About Sexual Harassment." Princeton, N.J.: SHARE.
2. Ibid.
3. A standard definition given by a book about sexual harassment affirms that "harassment can also occur when no such formal [power] differential exists, if the behavior is unwanted by or offensive to the woman." Michele A. Paludi, ed., *Ivory Power: Sexual Harassment on Campus* (Albany: State University of New York Press, 1990), 38.
4. Catharine MacKinnon, *Feminism Unmodified* (Cambridge: Harvard University Press, 1987), 89.
5. *Chronicle of Higher Education,* 24 April 1991.
6. Billie Wright Dziech and Linda Weiner, *The Lecherous Professor: Sexual Harassment on Campus* (Chicago: University of Illinois Press, 1990), 180.
7. Sue Rosenberg Zalk, "Men in the Academy," in Paludi, 143.
8. Dziech and Weiner, 180.
9. Paludi, 122.
10. "Sexual Harassment: A Hidden Issue." Washington, D.C.: Project on the Status and Education of Women, 1978.
11. *Chronicle of Higher Education,* 10 July 1991.
12. "Due Process in Sexual Harassment Complaints," *Academe* 77 September–October 1991).
13. Dziech and Weiner, 49.
14. *New York Times,* 3 May 1992.
15. MacKinnon, *Toward a Feminist Theory of the State* (Cambridge: Harvard University Press, 1989), 127.
16. Louise Fitzgerald and Lauren Weitzman, "Men Who Harass: Speculation and Data," in Paludi, 139.
17. Princeton, N.J.: SHARE.

18. "Acquaintance Rape." Rockville, Md.: ACHA, 1992.
19. MacKinnon, *Toward a Feminist Theory of the State, 149.*
20. Jacquelyn Dowd Hall, "'The Mind That Burns in Each Body': Women, Rape and Racial Violence," in Christine Stansell, Ann Snitow, and Sharon Thompson, eds., *Powers of Desire: The Politics of Sexuality* (New York: Monthly Review Press, 1983), 329.
21. Princeton, N.J.: SHARE.
22. Ibid.
23. Kathryn Quina, "The Victimizations of Women," in Paludi, ed., 99.
24. *New York,* 16 November 1992.
25. Ibid.
26. Joan Didion, *The White Album* (New York: Farrar, Straus and Giroux, 1979), 116.
27. Mary Koss, "Changed Lives: The Psychological Impact of Sexual Harassment," in Paludi, ed., 73.

❖ 34. No Law in the Arena

Camille Paglia

. . . I categorically reject current feminist cant that insists that the power differential of boss/worker or teacher/student makes the lesser party helpless to resist the hand on the knee, the bear hug, the sloppy kiss, or the off-color joke. Servility to authority to win favor is an old story; it was probably business-as-usual in Babylon. Objective research would likely show that the incidence of sycophancy by subordinates far exceeds that of coercion by bosses. That a woman, whether or not she has dependent children, has no choice but to submit without protest to a degrading situation is absurd. Women, as much as men, have the obligation to maintain their human dignity, without recourse to *a posteriori* tribunals (much less those a decade later, as with wily Anita Hill). It is an hour-by-hour, month-by-month, year-by-year process. Literally from the first moment of arrival at a job or in any social situation, a person is being tested and must set the tone by his or her responses. My entire Italian-immigrant extended family, in its transition over fifty years from blue-collar to white-collar work, has followed that policy of forthrightness and self-respect. Lack of money does not excuse groveling.

The *quid pro quo* ruse—where a sex act is demanded for a promotion or job security—is the most grievous of sexual harassment offenses and should be suitably punished, but one wonders just how common so clumsily blatant a proposition is these days. I suspect some men just try for what they can get, and a few unprepared, overly trusting women fall for it. We cannot expect government to make up for ancient lapses in child rearing. The "hostile workplace" clause, on the other hand, which has become an integral part of sexual harassment policy and has even, to my regret, passed review by the Supreme Court, seems to me reactionary and totalitarian. Mere offensiveness, which is open to subjective interpretation, is not harassment. The problem with the "hostile workplace" concept is that it is culturally parochial: it imposes a genteel white lady's standard of decorum on everyone, and when blindly applied by management, it imperialistically exports white middle-class manners, appropriate to an office, into the vigorously physical and more realistic working-class realm. The mincing minuets and sexual etiquette of the scribal class of paperpushers make no sense outside their carpeted cubicles of fluorescent light.

The folly of this nomenclature is that *every* workplace is hostile, as any man who has worked his way up the cutthroat corporate ladder will testify. Teamwork requires cooperation, but companies without internal and external competition remain stagnant. Innovation and leadership require strategies of opposition and outstripping, however one wants to disguise it. The "transformative feminism" of thinkers like Suzanne Gordon (whose progressive politics I respect), which imagines a pleasant, stress-free work environment where the lion lies down with the lamb, is unreachably utopian. Once again, aggression is not being confronted here. For every winner, there are a hundred losers. The workplace is the pagan arena, where head-on crashes are the rule.

It is outrageous that the "hostile workplace" clause is now routinely applied to coarse or ribald language, as when in 1993 a *Boston Globe* writer jokingly called another male staffer "pussywhipped" and was reported by a female employee and fined by his editor. Nude images are also affected by this clause, as when laborers are puritanically forbidden to post risqué calendars or tape *Playboy* pictures to their lockers or even, as in Los Angeles firehouses, to read *Playboy* at work. A graduate student at the University of Nebraska was forced to remove a photo of his bikini-clad wife from his desk, when two female fellow students complained to the chairman that they felt sexually harassed by it. This used to be called "paranoia." Why are snippy neurotics running our lives?

In a highly publicized incident, a dowdy English instructor pressured Penn State administrators to take down a print of Goya's *Naked Maja* from her classroom in an arts building, where it had hung unmolested for decades. She complained that the students were looking at it instead of her (I can't imagine why). The situation has gotten so out of hand that, in 1993, in one of the first British cases, a plumber was fired for continuing to use the traditional term "ball-cock" for the toilet flotation unit, instead of the new politically correct term, sanitized of sexual suggestiveness. This is insane. We are back to the Victorian era, when table legs had to be draped lest they put the thought of ladies' legs into someone's dirty mind.

My libertarian position is that, in a democracy, words must not be policed. Whatever good some people feel may be gained by restrictions on speech, it is enormously outweighed by the damage done to any society where expression is restricted. History shows that all attempts to limit words end by stifling thought. I am a Sixties free speech militant. As part of our rebellion, we middle-class girls flung around the raunchiest four-letter words we could find: we were trying to shatter the code of gentility, delicacy, and prudery that had imprisoned respectable women since the rise of the bourgeoisie after the industrial revolution. Pictures too are protected expression: I define images as pagan speech.

There are very few instances where speech properly falls under government scrutiny, and those involve either fraudulent representations in business contracts or disturbances of the peace, such as shouting "fire" in a crowded theater or disrupting residential neighborhoods or campuses by noisy late-night reveling. In the latter, if offensive epithets are used, it is not the content of the words that is punishable but the fact that anything at all is shouted at that hour. Epithets and stereotypes are not fraudulent in a commercial sense; they are crudely distorted or parodistic versions of a substratum of historical truth or perception, which no one, however well-meaning, has a right to erase.

I question the concept of "fighting words," except when an arresting officer or judge weighing sentencing considers whether a brawl that led to injury was provoked by an insult—which could be aspersions on one's beauty, taste, character, or virility as easily as on one's race or ethnicity. Attitudes are not changed by forbidding their expression; on the contrary, forcing social resentments underground simply increases the power of conservative ideologues or fascist extremists to speak for the silenced. Campus speech codes, that folly of the navel-gazing left, have increased the appeal of the right. Ideas must confront ideas. When hurt feelings and bruised egos are more important than the unfettered life of the mind, the universities have committed suicide.

Sexual harassment guidelines, if overdone, will end by harming women more than helping them. In the rough play of the arena, women must make their own way. If someone offends you by speech, you must learn to defend yourself by speech. The answer cannot be to beg for outside help to curtail your opponent's free movement. The message conveyed by such attitudes is that women are too weak to win by men's rules and must be awarded a procedural advantage before they even climb into the ring. Teasing and taunting have always been intrinsic to the hazing rituals of male bonding. The elaborate shouting matches and satirical putdowns of African tribal life can still be heard in American pop music ("You been whupped with the ugly stick!"—uproarious laughter) and among drag queens, where it's called "throwing shade." Middle-class white women have got to get over their superiority complex and learn to talk trash with the rest of the human race.

A sex-free workplace is neither possible nor desirable. Many people meet their spouses at work, just as students may marry their professors. After the mannish John Molloy dress-for-success look of the Seventies, when women first moved massively into fast-track careers, the more glamourous Eighties professional style allowed women to recover their femininity while still being taken seriously on the job. But we must face the fact that women's formal dress is inherently more erotic than men's. There is a subliminally arousing sensuality to perfume, lipstick, nail lacquer, vivid colors, silky fabrics, delicate jewelry, and high-heeled pumps. Exposed legs, which early Neanderthal feminists saw as a symbol of subordination (more exposed flesh = less power), are in the Nineties beginning to be understood as a visible incarnation of women's sexual power.

For all the feminist jabber about women being victimized by fashion, it is men who most suffer from conventions of dress. Every day, a woman can choose from an army of personae, femme to butch, and can cut or curl her hair or adorn herself with a staggering variety of artistic aids. But despite the Sixties experiments in peacock dress, no man can rise in the corporate world today, outside the entertainment industry, with long hair or makeup or purple velvet suits. Men's aesthetic impulses have been stifled since the industrial revolution. Beautiful, fragile clothing is historically an aristocratic prerogative, signifying freedom from manual labor. The contemporary clothing debate echoes the seventeenth-century standoff between Cavaliers and Puritans, those earnest workaholics whose sober black dress as our "Pilgrim Fathers" is foisted on us yearly in Thanksgiving iconography.

In the modern workplace, men are drones, and women are queen bees. Men's corporate costume, with its fore-and-aft jacket flaps, conceals their sexuality. Woman's eroticized dress inescapably makes her the center of visual interest, whether people are conscious of it or not. Most women, as well as most men, straight or gay, instantly appraise whether a woman has "good legs" or a big bosom, not because these attributes diminish her or reduce her to "meat" (another feminist canard) but because they unjustifiably add to her power in ways that may destabilize the workplace. Woman's sexuality *is* disruptive of the dully mechanical workaday world, in which efficiency means uniformity. The problems of woman's entrance into the career system spring from more than male chauvinism. She brings nature into the social realm, which may be too small to contain it.

One reason I favor reasonable sexual harassment guidelines is that they alert women to the erotic energies they inspire. But the matter is not asymmetrical, with virtuous women dutifully going about their tasks when—horrors!—jets of inky male lust spurt in their direction. (Cf. Hitchcock's Marnie madly bolting for the ladies room when red ink spots her sleeve.) I protest the recent creation, as if by dragon's teeth, of a master class of sexual harassment commissars, the cadres of specialists and consultants with their vested economic interest in this field. Like the campus kangaroo courts (the date-rape and speech-code grievance committees, with their haphazard roosters), the sexual harassment inquisitors are poorly trained for what they are doing. The dreary worldview of professional bureaucrats is untouched by Rabelais, Swift, Fielding, Wilde, or Shaw. How has the society that invented rock and roll ended up in the grip of these schoolmarmish monitors of sexual mores?

Class values have been seriously neglected in feminism, which takes a simplistic designer-Marxist view of the proletarian-as-victim. When they do not docilely act like victims, laborers are treated like heathen. For example, construction workers are demonized for their lunchtime diversion of staring, leering, whistling, and catcalling at passing female office workers, some of whom—lawyers and executives—regard themselves as very mighty indeed and far too lofty for such treatment. One side of me finds these spectacles annoying and sometimes enraging; the other cheers the workers on, for they are among the last remaining masculine men of action in a world where even soldiering has become computerized. We should applaud anything that challenges and explodes bourgeois decorum in our overregimented nine-to-five world. There is likewise a class issue in the prohibiting of nude centerfolds on lockers, since the pictorials of men's magazines correspond, in my view, to museum prints of nude paintings and sculpture that middle-class men can generally collect and display without interference.

When pressed to excess, sexual harassment rules will inevitably frustrate women's aspirations in another area: breaking through the so-called "glass ceiling," the invisible barrier that allegedly stalls women at middle management positions and keeps them out of corporate boardrooms and top executive suites. Feminists blame the "glass ceiling" on gender discrimination and the "old boy" network. But many people, male and female, have difficulty forging a persona of leadership, which may require talents different from the people-oriented and clerical skills of middle managers.

When they are encouraged to overrely on the threat of sexual harassment claims, women are being institutionally deprived of development of precisely the hard-nosed, thick-skinned tactics they need to reach the upper echelons. It is not just a particular job but treacherous office politics that ambitious future executives must master. Hostility and harassment of all kinds lie before you. Men set traps for each other, as well as for women. A mirage of cordial fog covers the snakepits. Breaking into a group requires staking out one's territory, which among humans and other animals means fierce skirmishes and border disputes. Women must find their own place in the pecking order, for which open aggression is sometimes necessary. You must bare your own fangs and not someone else's, if you want to be leader of the pack.

Paradoxically, conservative women like Margaret Thatcher have found it easier to reach the highest post in their countries. Liberal women achieved political prominence in America under the early Clinton presidency because the status of domestic social issues rises in periods of peace. If we are ever to have a woman president, she must, like Thatcher, demonstrate her readiness and ability to command the military. Congresswoman Patricia Schroeder, for example, one of the beaming Betty Crockers who drive crabby Sixties feminists like me crazy, has not shown, despite her long experience on the Armed Services Committee, any of the qualities of reserved authority necessary to win the confidence and respect of the troops, whom, in an emergency, the president must lead. This constitutional obligation was self-destructively neglected by Bill Clinton himself, whose strong mother made him sensitive to women's concerns but whose lack of a positive father figure made him indifferent to military matters until it was too late (the mishandling of the controversy over gays in the military being one result). . . .

Ancient Roman matrons, with their fidelity to clan and state, had more *gravitas* than today's women politicians and professionals. We need to rethink and reappropriate the old personae of grande dame and dragon lady for new use today. Hanging on the walls of the Seven Sisters, the elite women's colleges of the Northeast, are stunning portraits of the early presidents and faculty, whose air of distinction recalls a period in feminism when women accepted, and were determined to match, the highest levels of male achievement. I call them the "battle-ax maiden ladies," and they remain my inspiration.

Another of my role models is St. Teresa of Avila (*not* that tender teen, St. Therese of Lisieux, cradling her dainty roses). Obscure until her flaming forties, Teresa fought with the bishops and singlehandedly reformed the Spanish convents. She was an irascible, hands-on mystic. My American patron saint is Annie Oakley, the real-life sharpshooter known around the world from her tours with Buffalo Bill's Wild West Show. This great home-grown persona demonstrates that the best argument for women in combat is combative women.

My prescription for women entering the war zone of the professions: study football. It is a classic textbook of the strategies and controlled aggression of the ever-hostile workplace. A chapter in the second volume of *Sexual Personae* analyzes the pagan motifs of football, which is not only my favorite sport but my only real religion. Indeed, I credit my success in attacking the academic and feminist establishment to a lifetime mania for football, which provides intricate patterns of offense and defense, as well as impetus for hard hits and my trademark open-field tackling. Women who want to remake the future should look for guidance not to substitute parent figures but to the brash assertions of pagan sport.

⁖ 35. The Power of Sexual Stereotypes and the Sexiness of Power

Linda LeMoncheck

. . . I wish to offer a characterization of sexual harassment that embraces the tensions among competing feminist perspectives in order to further discussion concerning sexual harassment and inform future debate among feminists and nonfeminists. This tactic requires that I retain the political medium within which sexual harassment is understood in its larger cultural and organizational context but nuance the gendered message to negotiate the competing feminist perspectives enumerated in this volume. . . .

When feminists say that sexual harassment is about power, and not about sex, feminists tend to underplay how the *sexualization of women* in the context of harassment informs and elucidates the dominance and control of women. In the absence of a discussion of the ways in which cultural beliefs shared by both women and men fuse gender, sexuality, and power, feminists make men the predators in the game of gender politics but fail to include gender in an assessment of sexual politics. When beliefs such as "Power is sexy" and "Sex is all about power" are understood as part of the social construction of sexual harassment, complaints that sexual harassment is invasive or violative are not the complaints of moralizing prudes who would remove all sex from public discussion. Such complaints become reflections of the ways in which the sexual stereotypes associated with women and men of various cultural backgrounds encourage the specifically *sexual* harassment of women by men. A *sexually* harassed woman does not find a rubber chicken on her computer keyboard; she finds a rubber dildo. A red painted voodoo doll, or even a Barbie doll, is not what a sexually harassed woman sees hanging from her overhead projector; she sees a red painted tampon. She might gladly lend her boss her new golf clubs for a first chance at a cover story but not lend him her body. These distinctions are important in a culture where men can use sex as an instrument of power over, and control of, women. This is accomplished by taking advantage of pervasive and often contradictory sexual stereotypes that circumscribe women's and men's behavioral expectations in contemporary Western culture: Men chase and women retreat; men dominate and women submit. Sex turns men into "studs" and women into "whores" (who cannot get enough). Women are the proper and unconditional sexual objects of men's use and abuse. Women who do not ultimately accept men's sexual advances are sexual neurotics (frigid, lesbian, paranoid). Sex is pleasurable, playful, and fun, but women have to be talked into "feeling okay" about liking it.

Boys' sexual objectification of girls is reinforced by such stereotypes and confirms in boys' minds their own sense of sexual dominance. Boys who grab at, stalk, tease, and pull down the pants of teenage girls just discovering a sexual identity are communicating to such girls that their sexuality is accessible to boys without regard to what the girls want. Such conduct reinforces girls' lack of entitlement in the classroom, where intellect is divorced from sex, and confirms their belief that girls' sexuality must be gate-guarded from men's uncontrollable urges.[1]

When a female aviator at the 1991 Tailhook Convention in Las Vegas voiced her support for women flying combat missions, Navy men accused the aviator of having sex with senior officers on carrier assignments. This type of accusation is specifically designed to humiliate and marginalize ambitious working women by painting them as salacious seductresses who cannot get to the top without sleeping their way up there. The ad feminam harassment by the Tailhook conventioneers thus served to delegitimize the aviator's position on women in combat. At the same time, the sexual "gauntlets" in which women's clothes were literally torn from their bodies before they could walk down a convention hotel hallway were regarded as "spontaneous" fun and "no big deal" by several of the men involved. Women deemed sexually unattractive were rated aloud with a "wave off" that would leave them untouched yet humiliated, a paradoxical form of the sexualization of women through their desexualization, with degrading effects no less painful than those suffered by their groped colleagues.[2] [See Selection 7.]

Faculty women who have supported female students' sexual harassment claims have also become topics of sexual discussion as a way of dismissing their agendas. Like the Tailhook men's denunciations of the female flyer, questioning female faculty's sexual propriety is designed to delegitimize women's support of claims that men do not wish to acknowledge (Is she having a lesbian affair with her student? What are her relations with men? How provocatively does *she* dress?). I find it additionally frustrating that I have been dubbed "one of the guys" by several of my heterosexual male friends, who mean it as a compliment for being accessible, good-natured, and nonthreatening; yet this communicates to me that if they sexualized me, they could not treat me as one of them, that is, as a professional and moral equal.

Indeed, complaints of sexual harassment may arise simply from the introduction of sexuality into an otherwise asexual environment, as a graduate student does when he places a photo of his bikini-clad wife on a desk shared by other female graduate students.[3] I suggest that these women complain of being sexually harassed, because they feel their intellectual professionalism has been delegitimized in the service of their cultural image as sexual objects. A photo of the graduate student's wife playing with their children on the beach would not have this same effect; while women also suffer from a stereotype as domestic and reproductive subordinates, their domestic responsibilities may complicate, but do not eviscerate, their professional status the way their sexual stereotype does. These graduate women are no moralizing prudes, nor are they believers in the predatory "nature" of their male office mate. These are women who, like the women at Tailhook, live with a culture-specific, socially constructed gender identity the content of whose sexual stereotype assumes women's accessibility and subordination to men.

To say that women can "choose" to ignore such stereotypes by "choosing" not to believe their content is too facile, since it is not a matter of what these particular women believe. What matters here is that these stereotypes provide recognizable sexual standards by which other women and men will measure and formulate their own attitudes and behavior. The female aviator's position on women in combat was effectively delegitimized, not because she "allowed" herself to be humiliated by the other conventioneers, but because the cultural milieu in which their comments were addressed provided an ideological framework for her harassment. So too, the women who feel harassed by the bikini photo may not think of themselves as unconditionally sexually available to men, but they know that men other than the one who displayed the photo, particularly other male students who may come by for office hours, either believe this or would like to believe this, if given permission. Indeed, campus undergraduates may find the photo less harassing than their graduate or employed counterparts because they see their environment as legitimate grounds for "checking out" the sexually available "goods."[4]

Power can be sexy to those at the bottom looking up, as when social climbing women associate men's wealth and professional status with men's sexual attraction. Conversely, vulnerability may be sexy to those at the top looking down. John Bargh and Paula Raymond suggest that men's institutionalized authority automatically and nonconsciously triggers thinking in terms of sex toward those women whom they harass.[5] Indeed, feminists have argued that it is a woman's economic vulnerability that makes her easy prey for sexually harassing men who can threaten loss of her job for reporting or complaining about harassment. When she smiles in deference to his position in the organizational hierarchy, he may understand her friendliness as approval of his sexual flirtation or advances. This understanding is exacerbated by specifically sexual myths about women, which assert that women really do want men's sexual attentions but that feminine propriety (recall the "slut" stereotype) precludes women from being forthcoming about it. Such myths also make it easy for men accused of sexual harassment to turn the tables and say that women provoked their own harassment by dating several men at the office, telling dirty jokes, wearing "provocative" clothing (and woe be it to the woman who doesn't!), or simply flirting—which, as noted above, can translate into nothing more than acting with appropriate helpfulness and congeniality. Indeed, a male harasser's organizational power may make him think of himself as sexy, if only because he believes that women will find him attractive in virtue of it.

I would add to this analysis, however, that much of men's sexual harassment of female peers or coworkers is motivated not by women's vulnerability but by their apparent power to threaten men by their presence, as intellectual or workplace competitors. This does not always include a perception of the threatening and raw sexual power that Camille Paglia says women have at their disposal, although it does involve a sexualization of women. [See Selection 34.] Many harassers, whether in positions of organizational power or not, harass particular women because men perceive them as *not* sexually desirable or available when men think they ought to be—this is the complaint of many elderly women, gay women, or women whom men unilaterally decide to "wave off," and smart young girls with no sexual maturity at all are the objects of genital touching by boys who would rather compete in ways that put them "on top."

I would further suggest that much harassment of women is based on men's presumption of women's sexual accessibility to them, undergirded by the sexual stereotype of women as "fair game," and not solely, or even primarily, on the organizational authority to which Bargh and Raymond refer. African American women may be particularly vulnerable to this presumption by white men whose stereotype of black women as voracious sexual animals may make them eager to try sex out "with a black chick."[6] Thus, when feminists say that sexual harassment is about power, not about sex, they lose the complex *sexual* politics, played out in gender expectations across cultural lines, that organizational politics can hide. Indeed, because sexualizing women in a public context can degrade women by telling women what they are "really good for" and can humiliate women by publicizing what so-called good girls are supposed to keep private, men who wish to "put women in their place" will have an especially useful tool in *sexual* harassment. This humiliation is particularly painful when a woman's sexuality is reexposed in the courtroom or in front of a board of policy administrators.

Moreover, men may threaten women by sexual harassment, because women are vulnerable to sexual violence by men in ways that men as a class are not; thus, women are disproportionately victims of sexual assault. Women who have sex with men are "knocked up," "nailed," or "strapped," and this is supposed to be when women are having fun! Men in positions of power may also manipulate those whom they feel are their own to do with as they wish. If they deem women to be sexual objects, the manipulation will be in the form of sexual coercion, bribery, E-mail stalking, or other forms of hostile environment sexual harassment against which women may feel helpless once the incidents have occurred. In sexual harassment, to remind a woman of her sexuality is to remind her of her vulnerability to whatever a man wants to "dish out."[7]

Starting from grade school, many boys see sexual harassment as a rite of passage to manhood, which shows them to be sexually aggressive, provocative, daring, "macho." If masculinity is associated not simply with dominance but with heterosexual dominance, it will not be enough to trash a girl's locker; a boy must lift up her skirt, make kissing noises at her, or trash her locker with pinup photos. If men are more likely to *sexually* harass women than women are to harass men (remember the rubber dildo and not the rubber chicken), it is because of the way many men are taught to think about their (hetero)sexuality, namely, as a vehicle for expressing power and authority over women. Even young women use female sexual epithets like "bitch" and "ho'" in an attempt to harass boys who irritate them, a sorry commentary on their own status as women.[8]

However, women are much less notorious and successful than men at peer harassment precisely because women are not well socialized to think of men, nor men to think of themselves, as women's sexual objects. Indeed, women's heterosexual initiative must be culturally repressed, if men are to define the terms and conditions of the encounter and so reap the rewards of their own sexual initiative. At the same time, this gender role-playing encourages women's view that "men only think with their dicks."[9] Catharine MacKinnon observes of this discrepancy, "[W]omen are defined as gender female by sexual accessibility to men. . . . Sexual harassment makes of women's sexuality a badge of female servitude." Indeed, for MacKinnon, unless we isolate the *sexual* in sexual harassment, thus locating the *sexism* of the sexual stereotype of women, we will not identify the *gender* inequality that is prohibited by law.[10] [See Selection 2.] By contrast, gender stereotypes that associate masculinity with heterosexuality inform men's actions with the presumption of sexual access to women and of gender status when that access occurs. This presumption explains why some men will not identify women's leers, sexual gestures, crude jokes, *Playgirl* calendars, or persistent requests for dates as anything more than a reaffirmation of men's sexual desirability as men. It also explains the fact that when men do feel harassed, more men than women will see themselves as capable of fighting back with treatment in kind, direct confrontation, reports to authorities, or lawsuits, wondering why women will not do the same.

When a woman charges sexual harassment due to favoritism resulting from a coworker's sexual relationship with her boss, what is being charged is that a woman's sexual relationship has conferred an unfair power advantage to her. If feminists talk about examples of sexual harassment such as this one and those detailed above in terms of power and not sex, we lose the ways in which women's sexuality is invested with both the power of seduction and the powerlessness of sexual objectification. On the other hand, if we talk about sexual harassment in terms of sex but not power, women are blamed for men's sexual faux pas in that women are accused of being conniving seductresses who would delude others into thinking they are sexual innocents. My strategy is to talk in terms of the sexual stereotypes that inform the cultural context of sexual harassment, in order to understand the complex relations between gender, sexuality, and power that circumscribe harassing conduct. Submerging the sexual element for fear of "privatizing" and "normalizing" the harassment means that we lose these important relationships. Sexual harassment is about sex because it is about how sexuality can empower some and disempower others; the sexual harassment of women by men is the relegation of women as a class to an inferior status by sexualizing women.

However, this is not to say that sexualizing women always reduces them to subordinates of men. Clearly, women have as much to gain in pleasure and creativity by being sexual subjects as they have to lose by being sexual objects; and both women and men will measure themselves against sexual stereotypes that will affect individuals of different cultural backgrounds and personalities in different ways. To say that men participate in and maintain cultural institutions that oppress women as a class is not the same as saying that every man is a harasser, sexual abuser, or rapist, or even that all men dominate all women. Indeed, since a small minority of men, who repeatedly harass women, seem to constitute the majority of offenders, the sexual stereotypes described here must be understood as circumscribing social behavior under conditions that reinforce and facilitate, but do not dictate or determine, the sexual harassment of women. Thus, I am not, in Katie Roiphe's words, putting an "absolute value on the leer"[11] [See Selection 33]; rather, I am talking about the various possibilities and the potentialities for sexual violation within a framework of socialized gender expectations, so that I may broaden and deepen the discourse on sexual harassment. Re-situating the *sex* in *sexual* harassment can then serve the purpose of negotiating the tensions between feminists who favor a gendered analysis and feminists concerned about an antimale, antisex, and victimizing bias in that analysis, while recognizing the legitimacy of gender politics in discussions of sexual harassment.

Notes

1. See Peggy Orenstein, *SchoolGirls: Young Women, Self-Esteem, and the Confidence Gap* (New York: Doubleday, 1994), 117.
2. Office of the Inspector General, *The Tailhook Report: The Official Inquiry into the Events of Tailhook '91* (New York: St. Martin's Press, 1993), 17, 45, 50.
3. For critical commentary on this case, see Christina Hoff Sommers, *Who Stole Feminism? How Women Have Betrayed Women* (New York: Simon & Schuster, 1994), 271; Camille Paglia, "No Law in the Arena: A Pagan Theory of Sexuality," in *Vamps and Tramps: New Essays* (New York: Vintage Books, 1994), 50.
4. Barbara A. Gutek, "How Subjective is Sexual Harassment? An Examination of Rater Effects," *Basic and Applied Social Psychology* 17 (1995): 459.
5. John Bargh and Paula Raymond, "The Naïve Misuse of Power: Non-conscious Sources of Sexual Harassment," *Journal of Social Issues* 51 (1995): 85–96.
6. For court cases in which white men's sexual harassment of black women complicates the issue of discrimination, see Judy Trent Ellis, "Sexual Harassment and Race: A Legal Analysis of Discrimination," *Journal of Legislation* 8, no. 1 (1981), 41–44.
7. See Deborah Tannen, *Talking from 9 to 5: Women and Men in the Workplace: Language, Sex and Power* (New York: Avon Books, 1994), 257–60; also see Linda LeMoncheck, *Dehumanizing Women: Treating Persons as Sex Objects* (Lanham, Md.: Rowman & Littlefield, 1985), 87–90.
8. See Orenstein, *SchoolGirls,* 150.
9. See LeMoncheck, *Dehumanizing Women,* 89–90, 92–94. For further discussion of the relationship between sexual self-image and identity, see E. Person, "Sexuality as the Mainstay of Identity," in *Women: Sex and Sexuality,* ed. Catherine R. Stimpson and Elaine S. Person (Chicago: University of Chicago Press, 1980).
10. Catharine A. MacKinnon, *Sexual Harassment of Working Women: A Case of Sex Discrimination* (New Haven: Yale University Press, 1979), 182, 189; also see 178–92, 219–20.
11. Katie Roiphe, *The Morning After: Sex, Fear, and Feminism on Campus* (Boston: Little, Brown, 1993), 102.

36. Sex Is the Least of It: Let's Focus Harassment Law on Work, Not Sex

Vicki Schultz

The Clarence Thomas hearings, the Tailhook incident, the Gene McKinney trial,[1] the Clinton scandals [see Selections 7, 20, and 25]—if these events spring to mind when you hear the words "sexual harassment," you are not alone. That such images of powerful men making sexual come-ons toward female subordinates should be the defining ones simply proves the power of the popular perception that harassment is first and foremost about sex. It's easy to see why: The media, the courts and some feminists have emphasized this to the exclusion of all else. But the real issue isn't sex, it's sexism on the job. The fact is, most harassment isn't about satisfying sexual desires. It's about protecting work—especially the most favored lines of work—as preserves of male competence and authority.

This term the Supreme Court heard three cases involving sex harassment in the workplace. Along with media coverage of current events, the Court's decisions will shape our understanding of this issue into the next century, for all these controversies raise the same fundamental question: Does sex harassment require a special body of law having to do with sexual relations, or should it be treated just like any other form of workplace discrimination?

If the Court decides that harassment is primarily a problem of sexual relations, it will be following the same misguided path some courts have taken since they first accepted that such behavior falls under the prohibitions of Title VII of the Civil Rights Act, the major federal statute forbidding sex discrimination in employment. Early decisions outlawed what is known as quid pro quo harassment—typically, a situation where a supervisor penalizes a subordinate who refuses to grant sexual favors. It was crucial for the courts to acknowledge that sexual advances and other interactions *can* be used in the service of discrimination. Yet their reasoning spelled trouble. The courts said harassment was sex bias because the advances were rooted in a sexual attraction that the harasser felt for a woman but would not have felt for another man. By locating the problem in the sexual character of the advances rather than in the workplace dynamics of which they were a part—for instance, the paternalistic prerogative of a male boss to punish an employee on the job for daring to step out of her "place" as a woman—the decisions threatened to equate sex harassment with sexual pursuits. From there it was a short step to the proposition that sex in the workplace, or at least sexual interactions between men and women in unequal jobs, is inherently suspect.

Yet the problem we should be addressing isn't sex, it's the sexist failure to take women seriously as workers. Sex harassment is a means for men to claim work as masculine turf. By driving women away or branding them inferior, men can insure the sex segregation of the work force. We know that women who work in jobs traditionally held by men are more likely than other women to experience hostility and harassment at work. Much of the harassment they experience isn't "sexual" in content or design. Even where sexually explicit harassment occurs, it is typically part of a broader pattern of conduct intended to reinforce gender difference and to claim work as a domain of masculine mastery. As one experienced electrician put it in Molly Martin's *Hard-Hatted Women,* "[We] . . . face another pervasive and sinister kind of harassment which is gender-based, but may have nothing to do with sex. It is harassment aimed at us simply because we are women in a 'man's' job, and its function is to discourage us from staying in our trades."

This harassment can take a variety of forms, most of which involve undermining a woman on the job. In one case, male electricians stopped working rather than submit to the authority of a female subforeman. In another, Philadelphia policemen welcomed their new female colleagues by stealing their case files and lacing their uniforms with lime that burned their skin. Even more commonly, men withhold the training and assignments women need to learn to do the job well, or relegate them to menial duties that signal they are incompetent to perform the simplest tasks. Work sabotage is all too common.

Nor is this a purely blue-collar phenomenon. About one-third of female physicians recently surveyed said they had experienced sexual harassment, but almost half said they'd been subjected to harassment that had no sexual or physical component but was related simply to their being female in a traditionally male field. In one 1988 court case, a group of male surgical residents went so far as to falsify a patient's medical records to make it appear as though their female colleague had made an error.

Men do, of course, resort to sexualized forms of harassment. Sexual overtures may intimidate a woman or label her incompetent in settings where female sexuality is considered incompatible with professionalism. In one 1993 Supreme Court case, a company president suggested that a female manager must have had sex with a client to land an important account. Whether or not the harassment assumes a sexual form, however, what unites all these actions is that they create occupational environments that define womanhood as the opposite of what it takes to be a good worker.

From this starting point, it becomes clear that the popular view of harassment is both too narrow and too broad. Too narrow, because the focus on rooting out unwanted sexual activity has allowed us to feel good about protecting women from sexual abuse while leading us to overlook equally pernicious forms of gender-based mistreatment. Too broad, because the emphasis on sexual conduct has encouraged some companies to ban all forms of sexual interaction, even when these do not threaten women's equality on the job.

How has the law become too narrow? The picture of harassment-as-sex that developed out of the quid pro quo cases has overwhelmed the conception of the hostile work environment, leading most courts to exonerate seriously sexist misconduct if it does not resemble a sexual come-on. In *Turley v. Union Carbide Corp.*, a court dismissed the harassment claim of a woman whose foreman "pick[ed] on [her] all the time" and treated her worse than the men. Citing Catharine MacKinnon's definition of sexual harassment as "the unwanted imposition of sexual requirements in the context of a relationship of unequal power," the court concluded that the case did not involve actionable harassment because "the foreman did not demand sexual relations, he did not touch her or make sexual jokes."

By the same reasoning, in *Reynolds v. Atlantic City Convention Center*, the court ruled against a female electrical subforeman, Reynolds, whose men refused to work for her, made obscene gestures and stood around laughing while she unloaded heavy boxes. Not long before, the union's business agent had proclaimed, "[Now] is not the time, the place or the year, [nor] will it ever be the year for a woman foreman." When the Miss America pageant came to town, an exhibitor asked that Reynolds be removed from the floor—apparently, the incongruity between the beauty contestants and the tradeswoman was too much to take—and Reynolds's boss replaced and eventually fired her. Yet the court concluded that none of this amounted to a hostile work environment: The obscene gestures that the court considered "sexual" were too trivial, and the rest of the conduct wasn't sufficiently sexual to characterize as gender-based.

These are not isolated occurrences. I recently surveyed hundreds of Title VII hostile work environment cases and found that the courts' disregard of nonsexual forms of harassment is an overwhelming trend. This definitely works against women in male-dominated job settings, but it has also hurt women in traditionally female jobs, who share the experience of harassment that denigrates their competence or intelligence as workers. They are often subjected to sexist forms of authority, humiliation and abuse—objectified not only as sexual commodities but as creatures too stupid or worthless to deserve respect, fit only to be controlled by others ("stupid women who have kids," "too fat to clean rooms," "dumb females who [can't] read or write").

Just as our obsession with sexual misconduct obscures many debilitating forms of harassment facing women, it also leads us to overlook some pernicious harassment confronting men on the job. If the legal cases provide any indication, the most common form of harassment men experience is not, as the film *Disclosure* suggests, a proposition from a female boss. It is, instead, hostility from male co-workers seeking to denigrate or drive away men who threaten the work's masculine image. If a job is to confer manliness, it must be held by those who project the desired sense of manhood. It isn't only women who can detract from that image. In some work settings, men are threatened by the presence of any man perceived to be gay—for homosexuality is often seen as gender deviance—or any other man perceived to lack the manly competence considered suitable for those who hold the job. The case logs are filled with harassment against men who are not married, men who are not attractive to women, men who are seen as weak or slow, men who are openly supportive of women, men who wear earrings and even young men or boys. Some men have taunted and tormented, battered and beaten other men in the name of purging the brotherhood of wimps and fags—not suitable to stand alongside them as workers.

We have been slow to name this problem sex-based harassment because it doesn't fit our top-down, male-female, sexual come-on image of harassment. In *Goluszek v. Smith,* the court ruled against an electronic maintenance mechanic who was disparaged and driven out by his fellow workers. They mocked him for not having a wife, saying a man had to be married to be a machinist. They used gender-based images to assault his competence, saying that if he couldn't fix a machine they'd send in his "daddy"—the supervisor—to do it. They drove jeeps at him and threatened to knock him off his ladder, and when he filed a grievance, his supervisor wrote him up for carelessness and eventually fired him. Not only did the court dismiss Goluszek's claim, the judge simply couldn't conceive that what happened to him was sexual harassment. "The 'sexual harassment' that is actionable under Title VII 'is the exploitation of a powerful position to impose sexual demands or pressures on an unwilling but less powerful person,'" the judge wrote. Perhaps lower courts will adopt a broader view now that the Supreme Court has ruled, in the recent *Oncale v. Sundowner Offshore Services* decision, that male-on-male harassment may be actionable even when it is not sexual in design. [See Selections 54.]

Meanwhile, the traditional overemphasis on sex can lead to a repressive impulse to eliminate all hints of sexual expression from the workplace, however benign. Instead of envisioning harassment law as a tool to promote women's equality as workers, the popular understanding of harassment encourages courts and companies to "protect" women's sexual sensibilities. In *Fair v. Guiding Eyes for the Blind,* a heterosexual woman who was the associate director of a nonprofit organization claimed her gay male supervisor had created an offensive environment by making gossipy conversation and political remarks involving homosexuality. It is disturbing that current law inspired such a claim, even though the court correctly ruled that the supervisor's conduct was not sexual harassment.

Other men haven't fared so well. In *Pierce v. Commonwealth Life Insurance Co.,* a manager was disciplined for participating in an exchange of sexually explicit cards with a female office administrator. One of the cards Pierce had sent read, "Sex is a misdemeanor. De more I miss, de meanor I get." After thirty years with the company, he was summarily demoted and transferred to another office, with his pay slashed and his personal belongings dumped at a roadside Hardee's. True, Pierce was a manager and he was responsible for enforcing the company's harassment policy. Still, the reasoning that led to his ouster is unsound—and dangerous. According to his superiors, he might as well have been a "murderer, rapist or child molester; that wouldn't be any worse [than what he had done]." This sort of thing gives feminism a bad name. If companies want to fire men like Pierce, let them do it without the pretense of protecting women from sexual abuse.

Equally alarming are reports that, in the name of preventing sexual harassment, some companies are adopting policies that prohibit a man and woman from traveling or staying at the same hotel together on business, or prevent a male supervisor from giving a performance evaluation to a female underling behind closed doors without a lawyer present. One firm has declared that its construction workers can't even look at a woman for more than five seconds. With such work rules, who will want to hire women? How will women obtain the training they need if their male bosses and colleagues can't interact with them as equals?

It's a mistake to try to outlaw sexual interaction in the workplace. The old Taylorist project of purging organizations of all sexual and other emotional dynamics was deeply flawed. Sexuality is part of the human experience, and so long as organizations still employ people rather than robots, it will continue to flourish in one form or another. And sexuality is not simply a tool of gender domination; it is also a potential source of empowerment and even pleasure for women on the job. Indeed, some research suggests that where men and women work as equals in integrated settings, sex harassment isn't a problem. Sexual talk and joking continues, but it isn't experienced as harassment. It's not impossible to imagine sexual banter as a form of playfulness, even solidarity, in a work world that is increasingly competitive and stressful.

Once we realize that the problem isn't sex but sexism, we can re-establish our concept of harassment on firmer ground. Title VII was never meant to police sexuality. It was meant to provide people the chance to pursue their life's work on equal terms—free of pressure to conform to prescribed notions of how women and men are supposed to behave in their work roles. Properly conceived, quid pro quo harassment is a form of discrimination because it involves men exercising the power to punish women, as workers, who have the temerity to say no, as women. Firing women who won't have sex on the job is no different from firing black women who refuse to perform cleaning work, or female technicians who refuse to do clerical work, that isn't part of their job descriptions.

So, too, hostile-work-environment harassment isn't about sexual relations; it's about how work relations engender inequality. The legal concept was created in the context of early race discrimination cases, when judges recognized that Jim Crow systems could be kept alive not just through company acts (such as hiring and firing) but also through company atmospheres that made African-American workers feel different and inferior. That discriminatory environments are sometimes created by "sexual" conduct is not the point. Sex should be treated just like anything else in the workplace: Where it furthers sex discrimination, it should go. Where it doesn't, it's not the business of our civil rights laws.

It's too easy to allow corporate America to get away with banning sexual interaction without forcing it to attend to the larger structures of workplace gender discrimination in which both sexual and not-so-sexual forms of harassment flourish. Let's revitalize our understanding of harassment to demand a world in which all women and even the least powerful men can work together as equals in whatever endeavors their hearts and minds desire.

Editor's Note

1. McKinney was found not guilty of 18 of 19 of the charges brought against him but found guilty of one charge, that of obstructing justice, for which he was demoted to master sergeant but allowed to retire with pay commensurate with his highest rank.

❖ 37. Heterophobia

Daphne Patai

> As long as the focus remains upon sex (and gender) rather than upon what it is about a given sort of behavior that makes it wrong, the invitation to extremism in implementing the [sexual harassment] regulations will remain. From unjust roots the fruits of injustice will always grow.
>
> —*FERREL M. CHRISTENSEN, "'Sexual Harassment' Must Be Eliminated"*

Stories of predatory professors and boorish employers are staples of the SHI literature, in which anecdotal evidence abounds.[1] But when it comes to false charges, frivolous accusations, and an abandonment of due process, the SHI grows silent. And no wonder. Countertales—alternative narratives that do not conform to SHI stereotypes of heroes and villains—would destabilize the industry's presumptive authority. For the dispassionate consideration of such countercases flushes sexual harassment from the dark corners of despicable outrages and exposes it to the light of observation, in which conflicts between human beings turn out to be common and the truth about these conflicts is always complex, usually ambiguous, and rarely easy to judge.

In the discourse of sexual harassment, I have argued, training in victimhood plays a distinctive role. I can think of no other areas in life in which putative sufferers require so much help in order to recognize the damage supposedly inflicted on them and have come to depend on such careful instruction in how to script the accounts of their victimhood. Article after article produced by SHI writers insists—and this in itself should arouse our suspicion—that people need to learn how to identify the injuries they suffer. A recent example was provided by a professor from California State University at Chico, who sent the following query to the Women's Studies E-Mail List:

> The sexual harassment committee at my university has decided to survey faculty, staff and students about their experiences of sexual harassment. We need a survey that will allow us to identify problematic behaviors, even if the respondent does not recognize the behavior as a form of sexual harassment. We are in the process of compiling surveys used by other colleges and universities to provide us with ideas. Where might I find surveys? If you have a sample of one used at your institution, we would most appreciate having a copy.[2]

Clearly, most of us cannot be counted on to understand that every tacky little episode of sexual (or gender) innuendo may really be a grave example of victimization.

A more moderate vocabulary, in which "victims" did not swiftly pass into "survivors," might suggest that too much is being made of tactless remarks, tasteless jokes, and witless insinuations. But even to speak of tact, taste, or wit is to evoke the pre-SHI consciousness in which women had not yet been turned into perpetual victims. And it is precisely the function of the SHI to oversee this process of transformation.

But what about the other "victims," those against whom charges are brought falsely, motivated perhaps by personal resentment, anger, envy, or frustrated infatuation? The SHI pretends that wrongful accusations happen so infrequently as not to matter. In fact, national figures concerning counterfeit charges are hard to come by because, while sexual harassment accusations receive much attention in local and national newspapers when they are first made, exoneration, when it occurs, is likely to be noted only briefly and obscurely. Furthermore, universities tend to prefer the least expensive path to resolution of sexual harassment cases, and this often means settling out of court, usually by paying off the complainant, regardless of the merits of the charges. Such settlements are frequently shrouded in secrecy; all the outside world knows about them is that charges were withdrawn in exchange for undisclosed sums of money. The alleged harasser's name is never explicitly cleared.

Except for the work of a very few critics, in the vast literature about sexual harassment little has been written from the point of view of those "alleged harassers" whose lives have been brought to virtual standstills by false or merely trivial accusations. This is an omission crying out for redress. In the present chapter, I will focus on several cases that provide vivid glimpses of personal misadventures in the sort of environment the SHI has helped create on university campuses. The costs—it should become clear—are not only personal. They are also social and educational.

"Women Don't Lie"

There is a suspicious circularity to the shape of some sexual harassment cases. They begin and end with the worldview promoted by the Sexual Harassment Industry. Once one is caught in this vicious circle, escape is difficult. Professor Ramdas Lamb's experience of escalating charges of sexual harassment is a frightening example of this pattern.

Born in 1945 to an Italian-German family living in California, Lamb spent eight years in India (1969–77), becoming a Hindu monk and adopting the first name "Ramdas." Upon returning to this country, he married and attended graduate school, receiving his Ph.D. in religious studies from the University of California at Santa Barbara. In the fall of 1991, he took a position as an assistant professor of religion at the University of Hawaii at Manoa. One of his tasks there was to serve as undergraduate adviser for religion majors. In this job he was remarkably successful, doubling the number of majors in just two years. His students (many of whom later testified for him) described him as an immensely popular, enthusiastic, and unusually accessible teacher, one who kept his office door open and allowed his students to come and go virtually as they pleased. He had a following—a group of students who often hung out at his office, discussing issues raised in class, and generally drawing on his wide experience and genial personality.

Trouble began in his second year of full-time teaching when he offered a new course, one he realized would, by its very subject, be controversial. Entitled "Religion, Politics, and Society," it focused on contemporary social issues such as homelessness, gay marriage, animal rights, abortion, and AIDS. In February 1993, Lamb asked his class to read several articles on rape and sexual harassment from the textbook he had chosen for the course. One of these articles sparked a discussion among the students (two-thirds of whom were women) about false allegations of rape. One student said she could see both sides of the issue. She had herself been raped but had also seen her brother falsely accused when he broke off his engagement. Another young woman in the class, Tania Mortensen, who worked as a peer educator for a group called CORE (Creating Options for a Rape-Free Environment), vehemently denied that women ever lie about rape. Women must be believed, she insisted. She stated that data showed that a mere 3 percent of rape charges are false.[3]

Two other students, Michelle Gretzinger and Bonita Rai, supported this view. Gretzinger, who the previous semester had told various friends and professors that she had herself been raped in 1989, was evidently upset by challenges offered by other students to Mortensen's views and spent much of the class close to tears.

Professor Lamb knew Gretzinger well. She was a straight-A student who had decided to major in religion after meeting him. He had urged her to become an honors student, had written letters of recommendation for her, had lent her books, and had allowed her, along with others, to use his computer. As tension rose in his class, Lamb tried to mediate according to the ground rules that—so several of his students later testified—he had laid down at the beginning of the semester: Everyone was to be allowed to have his or her say; everyone's views were to be treated with respect; if a discussion was one-sided, Lamb would play the devil's advocate and introduce contrary points of view. As Wanda Dicks later testified, Lamb tried to get his students to understand the other person's point of view; he did not try to convert them.[4] Another student who, as a Christian Fundamentalist, did not share Professor Lamb's beliefs, also testified to Lamb's open-mindedness.[5]

However, for the first time in his teaching experience, Ramdas Lamb found the class getting out of his control that day. Tania Mortensen dominated the class, did most of the talking, adamantly denied that more than one view of women's truthfulness about rape was possible, and generally seemed to intimidate the other students.

Out of that day's conflict issued an extraordinary drama. First, Ramdas Lamb found himself accused of sexual harassment by the three distraught students (Mortensen, Gretzinger, and Rai) who had argued that "women don't lie." They claimed that Lamb had created a "hostile environment" by challenging their position and characterizing them as "man haters."

It is fascinating to see intellectual controversy about a social problem itself become grounds for sexual harassment charges. As famous a figure as Alan M. Dershowitz came close to facing charges over precisely the same issue. Dershowitz considers the notion of hostile-environment sexual harassment a threat to both freedom of speech and equal protection (since it sets offenses to women apart from all other offenses). He recounts how a group of feminists in his criminal-law class at Harvard, objecting to his discussion of false allegations of rape, threatened to file hostile-environment charges against him. "Despite the fact that the vast majority of students wanted to hear all sides of the important issues surrounding the law of rape," Dershowitz states, "a small minority tried to use the law of sexual harassment as a tool of censorship." The significance of this does not escape him: "[T]he fact that it is even thinkable at a major university that controversial teaching techniques might constitute hostile-environment sexual harassment demonstrates the dangers of this expandable concept."[6] Still, in Dershowitz's case the feminist students eventually decided against bringing charges.

Ramdas Lamb wasn't so lucky. When the original accusations began to crumble, Michelle Gretzinger, who by all accounts had until then shown a special, and apparently personal, interest in Professor Lamb, escalated her charges—initially merely hinting at some sexual relationship between herself and Lamb; later, when pressed, accusing him of repeated rape. The offense was "serial rape" and "mentor rape," as her lawyer was to call it in court.

Reading through the two thousand or so pages of legal transcripts generated by this case, I noticed a distinct pattern emerging of how Gretzinger proceeded in her accusations against Lamb. First she tried to keep the charges vague, so that initially it was not even clear what precisely was being alleged—perhaps merely some suspicion of sexual misconduct to complement the hostile-environment charges she and her two classmates were pursuing. She repeatedly testified that there had been no specific mention of any rapes in the first few months of the investigation because, she said, she had assumed that the charges the three students had already filed would be "enough."

When the initial charges proved flimsy, Gretzinger began to allege that Lamb had sexually assaulted her during the preceding semester, identifying to different acquaintances different locations for the assaults, of which she had given no sign at the time. She variously claimed they had occurred in Lamb's office, in his home, and in her apartment. When forced to come up with specifics (months after her initial charges, even though university regulations expressly required that complaints when first filed were to be accompanied by precise details), Gretzinger asserted that Lamb had raped her between ten and sixteen times in her own apartment after driving her home from his once-a-week class. These rapes, she claimed, had taken place between early September and early October 1992.

Unfortunately for Gretzinger's case, when pushed to come up with concrete dates, she named some that proved to be impossible. In the time frame she mentioned, there were not enough class days, Lamb's lawyer demonstrated in court, to accommodate her charges.

Professor Lamb, for his part, categorically denied having had sexual relations of any sort with her and testified that he had never set foot in her apartment. Furthermore, Gretzinger's own actions throughout the period in which the rapes were supposed to have occurred made the story of rape unconvincing. She had failed to indicate to her husband or to anyone else that repeated assaults were taking place; she had continued to demonstrate enthusiasm for Lamb, his courses, and the extracurricular activities in which he was involved; she had signed up for an elective course with Lamb the following semester—all of which was attested to by many other students. This pattern of behavior was part of the challenge faced by the sexual harassment specialists when they came to Gretzinger's aid.

Confronted by irrefutable testimony of Lamb's innocence—testimony that left the plaintiff's case a shambles—Gretzinger's attorney fell back upon the very claims with which the entire drama had gotten underway: What motive could the plaintiff possibly have for making up such a tale? Why would she expose herself to the humiliation and pain of admitting to being the victim of rape? In short: Women do not lie. The lawyer's closing examination of Gretzinger before the jury in no way addressed the many problems with Gretzinger's testimony. Instead, he merely had Gretzinger confirm one last time (without citing specifics) that she had indeed been raped. Stressing the "painful, humiliating experience" Gretzinger was willing to relive by going to court, and the damage this indignity inflicted on her reputation, he claimed that his client's motivation was nothing more than to prevent other women from coming to the same harm to which she had been subjected.[7] Winding up, he asserted, "There is no motive to lie."[8]

However, this effort failed to persuade the jury to overlook the abundant evidence that Gretzinger had fabricated the charges. Plausible as it is to hold that in some past periods or in other countries the very charge of rape has been so self-vilifying that few women would willingly make it unless it was in fact true, hardly the situation in America in the 1990s, Gretzinger's lawyer's invocation of a prefeminist image of women's disadvantage in legal battles over rape thus proved unconvincing.

The Ramdas Lamb case is a particularly interesting one because of what it reveals about the inner workings of the Sexual Harassment Industry. Here is a professor of religion so profeminist that in class he referred to God as "she," a teacher whom many students described as always treating women with respect and encouraging their work in every way. None of these traits, however, carried any weight once the SHI involved itself in the case. What should have been dismissed at once as an instance of a few angry and vindictive students whose feminist beliefs had been challenged by a professor exercising his right of free speech quickly spun out of control. As Lamb points out, Gretzinger, while constantly alleging her powerlessness, managed, on the basis of mere accusations with no evidence at all, to turn his life upside down very easily—a good illustration of the increasing lag between rhetoric and reality: Victimhood is claimed while the very opposite is demonstrated.

Gretzinger's depositions reveal how thoroughly she knew the typical sexual harassment script. She stressed her vulnerability and "indebtedness" to Lamb, and for this latter case to be made she had to interpret his typical professorial gestures of kindness and helpfulness as instances of "grooming" (or, as some texts call it, "priming") her.[9] Fortunately for Lamb, many of his other students had witnessed Gretzinger's behavior—that she had phoned him, had sought him out, was always hanging around his office, and so on, all of which she denied under oath. Instead, she turned it all around, sounding well versed in the "how to make a case" literature, whose script she followed in every particular, above all in her psychological portrait of herself as a victim of an unscrupulous professor, whose path toward sexual assault she outlined with care.

All the charges made about Ramdas Lamb's behavior in class were refuted by other students, but to Susan Hippensteele, the university's "student advocate," and to Mie Watanabe, its EEO/affirmative action officer, whose handling of the matter also violated university procedures, they were self-evidently true.[10] Hippensteele suggested reading materials to teach the plaintiffs about sexual harassment injuries and how to be on the lookout for them. In that duplication of functions that often characterizes the SHI's involvement with local cases, she also served as adviser to a student group called SHarP (Sexual Harassment Prevention), in which Michelle Gretzinger participated after making her allegations.[11]

Testifying on behalf of the "victim" was Michele Paludi, the same sexual harassment expert whose *Ivory Power: Sexual Harassment on Campus* was one of the books suggested to the complainant by Hippensteele. What did Paludi know about the case? She had read only the supposed victim's account, not the masses of other testimony produced. But she could affirm that the charges were entirely plausible, her judgment being based on her general familiarity with student victims and predatory professors.

Professor Ramdas Lamb's three-and-a-half-year battle to prove his innocence—which is precisely what he had to do—is thus a scary example of the kind of reality the Sexual Harassment Industry has brought upon us.[12] That his case was an administrative outrage was plain as early as 1994—before claims and counterclaims were filed in federal court—when a labor arbitrator brought in by the faculty union examined the evidence and, in deciding in Lamb's favor, meticulously dissected the many abuses of due process that had characterized the university's handling of the case from the beginning. These abuses, the arbitrator made clear, resulted from the zealotry of the university's feminist sexual harassment officers. Nonetheless, the university settled with Gretzinger in 1995 for $175,000, citing inordinate delays in dealing with her case, but offered Lamb no recompense for suffering not only the same delays but also mistreatment by university officials. . . . Gretzinger lost her federal suit against Lamb.

But legal vindication is hardly enough to compensate the real victim in this case. In early 1998, this is what Lamb wrote about the repercussions of his experience:

> I still avoid interacting with women I don't know and trust. I rarely feel good about going to school. I still avoid meeting female students in my office, unless I know someone else will be there. I definitely treat my female students differently now than I do my male students.
>
> The case has had clear ramifications within the university, too. A lot of professors are being very careful with what they say. Several have told me they now avoid becoming advisors for female grad students. There have been policy changes, but that really doesn't mean a thing. In my

case, nearly every administrator who dealt with me simply ignored the policy, from Hippensteele to the dean of the law school.[13]

In June 1998, Lamb was awarded tenure. But he failed in his attempt to save colleagues from an ordeal similar to his. In May 1998, the U.S. Court of Appeals for the 9th Circuit rejected his appeal of a district court's ruling that granted qualified immunity to the individual University of Hawaii officials who participated in the flawed sexual harassment investigation against him. These officials, the court declared, were entitled to qualified immunity; they were, in fact, obligated to investigate the sexual harassment charge. What the Court of Appeals declined to define were the "precise contours of the protection the First Amendment provides the classroom speech of college professors." The same Court of Appeals, however, upheld the federal jury's verdict against Gretzinger.

Finally, Lamb can put this entire episode behind him. But its effects linger: "I don't think I will ever feel the way I did prior to these accusations," he has said. "There are those at the university who still treat me as guilty even though every investigation has found me innocent."[14]

More recently still, Lamb has written: "I used to love to teach. Not any more. I used to love to interact with students and stimulate them to think critically. Not any more. I used to believe that university campuses promoted free speech and the truth. Not any more. I used to believe students when they would tell me things. Not any more."[15]

ACADEMIC FREEDOM BITES THE DUST

If Ramdas Lamb's experience has disturbing implications for the state of academic freedom, another recent case raises even greater alarm in its demonstration of how charges of "sexual harassment" can serve academic inquisitors as an all-purpose warrant for intervention.[16] Ferrel Christensen has warned that the notion of "sexual harassment" has become "the greatest violation of freedom of speech to emerge in decades."[17] How true this is can readily be seen by the following example.

Eddie Vega was an instructor of writing at the SUNY Maritime College in 1993–94.[18] A Cuban by background (his father was imprisoned by Castro), Vega, a poet and novelist who has an M.F.A. in writing from Columbia University, was, according to colleagues, a very courteous and decorous man who worked hard to help his students develop the ability to express themselves in writing. His first year at Maritime had been a great success. His contract had been renewed for a second year, and he was looking forward not only to continued teaching but also to a position he had been offered as assistant dean of freshmen.

In July 1994, Vega was giving a summer course in writing. On July 21, he conducted a "clustering" exercise with his students, in order to stimulate their ideas and vocabularies. A woman in the class suggested "sex" as a topic for the session, which Vega expanded to "sex/relationships." Once the process of free association got underway, he wrote on the board the words and concepts the students came up with. Some of these were four-letter words, and Vega, out of discretion but still wanting to leave the students free to brainstorm, abbreviated them on the board.

Several weeks later, Vega was called into the president's office and shown a student's notebook that contained the X-rated words. He agreed that these words had been generated in his class. With this admission, he was accused of sexual harassment and fired on the spot. Of special significance here is the fact that Vega was not even asked what had occasioned these words, whether he had encouraged the students to use them in their compositions (he had not), and whether he had advised them about appropriate language (he had). His teaching career at Maritime was over; the promised administrative job disappeared. One of Vega's departmental colleagues, a specialist in Lawrence Durrell, wondered whether it was possible even to teach literature in such a climate.

What concerns me in the context of this book is that Vega was not charged with being an incompetent teacher, or with any other dereliction that, because he was an untenured faculty member, an "at-will" employee, might have led to his firing. Instead, Vega was accused of "sexual harassment," the catchall label that, in the minds of many administrators, would appear to obviate the need for due process, not to mention fairness. Vega is now representing himself in a federal suit against his former employer. In response to my asking him why other academics should care about his case, he wrote:

> Your thoughtful question, it seemed to me, sought a principled response, not one grounded in legal theory or case law. Your question, differently worded, was in fact the first and only question Judge Cote put to me during our teleconference in November of last year, "Mr. Vega, what is your case about?"
>
> I was surprised by the question, by its simplicity. I had a yellow pad by the phone with all kinds of legal citations and cleverly worded phrases that I had scribbled in preparation for the conference. I had anticipated questions and arguments. I was going to respond with the measured and commanding tone of an appellate court judge or a Yale law professor. . . .
>
> But she asked instead: "Mr. Vega, what is your case about?"
>
> In a flash the four or five theories of recovery that I had outlined in my complaint, the academic freedom, the free speech, the defamation, all of it vanished in a moment of telephonic silence. I stopped thinking and began talking: "Your honor, I was fired from my humanities teaching job because I was accused of violating the college's sexual harassment policy. This was done without ever affording me a hearing, although I tried many times to get that hearing. I was fired because I allowed students to discuss sex in the classroom during a writing exercise. This was in violation of my free speech and due process rights guaranteed by the First and Fourteenth Amendments to the Constitution. And that's what this case is about."
>
> It all comes down to that. Everything else is legal fluff. Had I spent five hours thinking about what the case is ultimately about rather than the 5 seconds I had, I would still not have given a more honest or to the point answer.
>
> It answers your question, too. The sexual harassment policy was there because it was required by federal law. College administrators are using the weight of this federal law, Title IX, to deny even tenured faculty due process rights. If I can show in Federal Court that even an at-will teacher has due process rights under the U.S. Constitution, if not directly under Title IX, when accused of violating a federally mandated sexual harassment policy, it will restate the primacy of due process rights of the accused, the tenured and non-tenured, at public and private colleges. What happens in the Southern District of New York is carefully monitored by other districts.[19]

Vega's suit in state court, by contrast, is a straightforward defamation case, he says, and of limited interest to him. But federal court is a very different matter: "There we are talking about the most fundamental rights we have as classroom teachers and as citizens in a free and open democracy."

And what effect did this experience have on Professor Vega's teaching? In his new job in Florida, he still uses the same writing exercise, but now he allows only preselected topics and endures students' predictable complaints about their dullness. But even with a safe subject such as "The Right to a Public Education," Professor Vega reports, sex can somehow intrude itself.

> For example, one student, in the nursing program, pointed out the need for adequate sex education and the distribution of condoms at the high school level. Some other students, sensing that the topic had gotten interesting, joined in with similar thoughts. I stopped them there; and here

I think I violated their academic freedom and violated the integrity of the exercise (that thoughts should roam freely as one brainstorms the topic). I told them I thought we'd gathered enough material as a class and that we would continue the exercise working in small groups. They followed my instructions without ever realizing that I had deprived them and myself of free speech.[20]

An interesting comparison might be made between Professor Vega's experience and that of Joanne Marrow, who "showed slides of female genitalia and discussed female masturbation in her psychology class" at California State University at Sacramento. A male student filed a sexual harassment complaint against Marrow, but the school ruled that though the material may have been unwelcome or offensive to the student, it was not sufficiently pervasive or severe to create "an intimidating, hostile or offensive learning environment."[21] As Heinz-Joachim Klatt observes, "It is unimaginable that complainants today would be taken seriously who feel sexually harassed by the ways, for example, feminist instructors lecture in Women's Studies courses."[22]

At my own university, an instructive case occurred in May 1998. John Palmer, a sixty-five-year-old professor about to retire from the biology department at UMass-Amherst, had, for some years, taught a large lecture course called "Biology and Social Issues," a course that, as the catalog description made clear, was designed to be provocative. On April 30, 1998, during a discussion of abortion, a student objected from the floor to Palmer's assertion that from the point of view of biology, life begins at conception. Another student, who worked at the Everywoman's Center, complained to the center's director, Carol Wallace, "on behalf of a group of women" enrolled in the class. She alleged that Professor Palmer had used inappropriate language and had drawn demeaning sketches of female anatomy to illustrate his lectures. Wallace made no attempt to corroborate the truth of these allegations or their meaning. Rather, she at once wrote to Professor Palmer's dean, "Clearly such behavior constitutes sexual harassment, defined as 'conduct having the purpose or effect of unreasonably interfering with an individual's work performance or creating an intimidating, hostile or offensive working or academic environment.'"[23]

What had Professor Palmer actually said? As he had done for the preceding six years, he had explained that from a biological perspective, the zygote is the first stage of human life. And he had pointed out that various methods exist for killing that life by preventing the embryo from becoming embedded in the uterine wall, where it could develop into a fetus. Such methods, he noted, include IUDs and morning-after pills (RU 486), which are designed to induce an abortion.[24] He stressed that science had no answer to the moral questions raised by this issue but that religions had developed a variety of positions on the subject. These statements were enough, Professor Palmer later wrote, to "set off one woman in the class."

[She] jumped up and asked something about why I did not mention the role of women. She was so worked up that she had great trouble speaking and made little sense. Attempting to calm her I suggested she come to my office sometime where we could discuss her concerns. She paid no attention, feeling her agenda—whatever it was—was more important than class material. That is when the class turned on her and loudly told her to leave. She did stomp out, but first turned to the class and called them "a bunch of idiots."[25]

The case then went to the Ombuds Office, whose head, philosophy professor Robert Ackermann, wrote to Palmer that he was going to meet with nine complaining students, who clearly expected some sanctions to be imposed on Professor Palmer. The students had already gone to the Equal Opportunity and Diversity Office but had not yet filed a formal complaint there. The ombudsman was attempting to avoid including anyone from EO &

D at his meeting, since if any such staff member were present and the "magic words" were uttered, a formal complaint of sexual harassment would have to be made and the university would be forced to respond.

By the time the students met with the ombudsman on May 8, 1998, they had learned of Professor Palmer's impending retirement, and this seemed to dampen the prospects for a formal complaint. Instead, the ombudsman wrote a lengthy letter to the chair of the biology department, outlining the charges. This letter is notable for the easy assumptions it makes about the direct consequences of any such charges. Professor Palmer's class, the ombudsman stated, had produced "an absolutely unprecedented negative response in this office"—a rather startling claim if one considers that only 9 students out of a class of 660 had complained and that some 2000 others had heard the same lecture over the preceding half dozen years. To Professor Ackermann, however, this "unprecedented" response required immediate action. His list of the students' complaints covered just about everything in the course—from Professor Palmer's lecturing style to his presentation of information and his syllabus—all of this based upon what the 9 students had reported in their meeting with the ombudsman, and all of it unsubstantiated. Nonetheless, the ombudsman did not hesitate to suggest to the chair that he might in the future wish to take "steps" in appointing faculty to teach this course, and might urge them to take special care to distinguish "fact" from "opinion" when lecturing.[26]

As another colleague commented, upon hearing of this case, it seems to show that the "reasonable person" criterion doesn't hold sway. By jumping to the conclusion that Professor Palmer's class had created a "hostile environment" for nine students, the Everywoman's Center must have assumed that the vast majority of students in the class (including four women who wrote warm letters of support for Professor Palmer) were "unreasonable."[27] As it turned out, Palmer was not given the opportunity to face his accusers. He does not even know the names of six of them.

One can only guess at Professor Palmer's feelings upon receiving such a parting gift from his university at the end of his teaching career. Perhaps it was counterbalanced by the standing ovation his six-hundred-odd students gave him at the last class of the semester, a day after the campus newspaper did a front-page story on the allegations. But what if he had not been on the point of retirement? Perhaps he would then have found himself in a position similar to that of Leroy Young, a tenured professor at Plymouth State College in New Hampshire.

WHY BOTHER INVESTIGATING?

Since his appointment as head of graphic design in the art department in 1988, Leroy Young, a man now in his midfifties who describes himself as looking like Sean Connery's shorter, ugly brother, had built up a highly successful program. He had received much commendation for his efforts, and he thought he was doing good work in a good place. But all this changed abruptly at the beginning of the 1993–94 academic year when he was ordered to appear in the office of his dean. There, he was presented with a handwritten paper accusing him of sexually harassing one of his senior students, Jennifer Otten.

"You must be one of those touching, southern men," an administrator who was present said to him. Otten's charges were that Young had complimented her on her new blazer, had taken her to lunch "against her will," had made sexual innuendos to her at a party, had asked her for a kiss, had hugged her and put his hand on her shoulder, and had (at her request) provided a critique of Madonna's book *Sex.* But of these allegations Young was informed only in general terms. None of the specifics—about which he was to learn only later—were cited, and he was given no opportunity to tell his version of events. Instead, Young says, he had the sense that the real purpose of the meeting was to make him see the error of his ways. Times had changed, he was told, as a result of the Thomas-Hill hearings. "We're going to reeducate you, boy," his dean said to him.

Young denied having committed any impropriety. His initial reaction to the charges was that they must be based on misunderstanding, lack of communication, and misinterpretation. "I have no problem with an apology for misinterpretations, but I will not accept 'guilt' as a consequence of this situation," he wrote early on. If that concession did not suffice—and clearly it did not—he was prepared to fight.

Meanwhile, however, another student of Young's had come forward with more accusations of sexual impropriety. Before she could withdraw her charges (which she did a month later), at a formal hearing Young was found to be in violation of the college's sexual harassment policy and was placed on administrative leave. Though his salary continued, he could not teach and was barred from appearing on campus. He immediately appealed, and the college Sexual Harassment Appeals Board, concluding that there was no evidence to support the charges, eventually ruled, in February 1994, that Young should be reinstated.

By then, a third student who had graduated, Tracy Schneider, had come forward to allege acts of sexual impropriety that were said to have occurred three years earlier. She was not in fact eligible to file complaints against an institution in which she was no longer enrolled. At this point, the case took a different turn. The three young women, having engaged a legal firm that advertised its expertise in prosecuting sexual misconduct ("an emotional burden that can last a lifetime," the firm's ads proclaimed) by offering free seminars for prospective clients, proceeded to sue Young for five hundred thousand dollars in damages. They threatened to sue the college as well. In light of these new developments, Young's "administrative leave" was not rescinded, despite the recommendation of the Appeals Board. No formal charges had ever been filed; no proper investigation of the charges had taken place; indeed, Young was given to understand that the college administrators saw no need for such an investigation.

As often happens in such cases, Young's accusers had formerly been his admirers. Young says, "[From all three of them] I have received inscribed books, photos, invitations to lunch, art work, etc. I was even invited to lunch once and then it was canceled when I said my wife would attend also."[28] The complainants' lawyer asked college officials to meet with the third accusing student, Tracy Schneider, at his office, where they heard her describe various incidents of Young "groping," exposing himself, and trying to take off her blouse. Young responded with the results of a polygraph test (taken at the suggestion of his lawyer), which showed him to be truthful in his denial of each of Schneider's charges. But the college president, Donald Wharton, no doubt frightened by the threat of a sexual harassment suit against the college, declared that Schneider was to be believed and Young was not. Thus, in March 1994, Young was summarily fired for "deliberate and flagrant neglect of duty and moral delinquency of a grave order." The dismissal was effective immediately. As issued to the press, this notice of dismissal was accompanied by a specification of Schneider's accusations, which the president declared he had, on the basis of his own assessment, judged to be "well-founded."[29]

A local newspaper immediately understood the significance of this step and printed an editorial asking "Is Due Process Dead at PSC?" This is how the paper described the sequence of events: "[A]t the moment of his vindication on one set of similar allegations brought earlier, Young was summarily fired on the basis of the college president's own 'investigation' of separate charges brought by Tracy Schneider, a former student."[30] The prevalent attitude among the college's administrations seems to have been, "Why would she say these things if they weren't true?"

No formal hearing on Schneider's charges had been held; no investigation had taken place, President Wharton having acted entirely on his own authority. Young had not been shown any evidence against him. He had not been allowed to call witnesses. It took more than a year longer before Young was finally granted a hearing at which he was able to face his accuser and her "witnesses" (they witnessed only the accusations, Young explains).[31] Two years after his dismissal, a faculty panel found that the president of the college had acted inappropriately in unilaterally firing Young. But at the same time, the panel split over the merits of the charges against Young, finding, three to two, that cause for dismissal existed. Thus, without further procedures, he was fired again, immediately after having been reinstated.[32]

The moral Leroy Young draws from his experience is discouraging:

If I ever teach again, I . . . would censor everything I say or do. To listen to all of the discussion [on this e-mail list] about philosophy of relationships, etc., is interesting, but I cannot let myself participate. I will tell no one of any opinions about sexuality, opinions about pornography, or relate any personal experiences that I have ever had. Any of this could be used as ammunition against me. So I have been effectively censored.[33]

Ramdas Lamb faced far more serious charges and met with less dire consequences. Perhaps because the charges against Young weren't as implausible as "serial rape," his innocence was harder to prove—despite the polygraph test supporting him.

Having discovered that Young had no money, the three women dropped their suit against him. Tracy Schneider then sued the college in state court for negligence in not firing Young sooner. Because the college had not investigated her allegations, it lacked evidence with which to dispute her claims of negligence. As a result, Schneider was awarded $115,000. In a final touch of irony, the college's counsel asked Professor Young if he would be willing to appear as a witness for the college in its appeal of the award to Schneider.

Young's own suit against the college is pending, but as he comments, "[N]o one will win." He has already turned down the college's offer of $80,000, and still hopes for complete vindication. Meanwhile, he cannot find another teaching position. His wife and chief supporter, Tatum Young (a former member of the National Organization for Women), left her job as a special education teacher when they both decided to move back to North Carolina. They live on a small income while awaiting trial in their suit against the college.[34]

Recently, Leroy Young described his state of mind:

In today's paper I saw an advertisement from a local college for adjunct positions in art. My excitement lasted but a few seconds. If I applied it would be just a matter of time before someone at the school [comes across] last year's libelous article in the *Chronicle of Higher Education*,[35] or remembers something someone had told them, or refers to an article in the local papers about the "accused Professor Young." Even if this doesn't happen, there is always, "have you ever been dismissed from a position and if so why?" How much longer will it be before the accusers must bear responsibility? My accusers dropped [their suit], but nothing happened to them. Why don't you sue them? I am told. With what? Lawyers must be paid. So I will continue to go into my studio and try and work and try not to spend the entire day playing solitaire so I don't have to think.

Does anyone out there still believe that this is all coincidence? Does anyone still believe that all of this hysteria is not being fueled? A friend of mine, a retired professor from a prestigious university, told me recently, as I recounted my experience, that if he had not himself been accused of harassment he would have only listened to me with a grain of salt. Somehow, some way, what is happening all across the country must be communicated to all involved.[36]

Notes

1. [Editor's note] Daphne Patai says that she focuses on the activities of reformers of sexual harassment policy, which she labels the "Sexual Harassment Industry" (SHI), because she believes that from the point of view of feminist ideology it appears as the great success story of contemporary feminism. See *Heterophobia* (Lanham, MD.: Rowman & Littlefield, 1998), p. 4.

2. Jo Trigilio, Department of Philosophy, California State University, Chico, e-mail message to wmst-1@umdd.umd.edu, February 19, 1998.

3. See Cathy Young, *Ceasefire: Beyond the Gender Wars* (New York: Free Press, 1999), chapter 6, for a far more realistic assessment of the problem of false allegations. Susan Sarnoff, whose early work was as a victim advocate and who is the author of *Paying for Crime: The Policies and Possibilities of Crime Victim Reimbursement* (Westport, CT: Praeger, 1996), wrote to me that when her dissertation demonstrated "that sexual assault victims receive 76% of the funds meant for all crime victims, I was shunned, black-listed and worse" (e-mail message to author, August 23, 1997). In a recent article, "Measuring the Iceberg," *Women's Freedom Network Newsletter* (Fall 1997), Sarnoff explains why it is likely that false reports of rape have increased in recent years: "The myth of unreported rape, then, is the myth of the submerged part of the iceberg that victim advocates want us to believe is enormous and ever-growing." Sarnoff also notes that victim advocates "refuse to recognize the improvements they themselves have effected." She discusses the important negative consequences of the myth of unreported rape such as scaring women, deflecting attention and services from high-risk women, perpetuating the myth that "all men are potential rapists," and false accusations and convictions. She says, "While some researchers argue that false reports may make up more than 40% of all rape reports, only the most fanatical ideologues insist that the number falls below 8%."

4. Testimony of Wanda Dicks, *Arbitration between Ramdas Lamb and Board of Regents of the University of Hawaii,* before Arbitrator Thomas E. Angelo, Honolulu, Hawaii, April 5, 1994, vol. 3, p. 383.

5. Testimony of Tim Tidwell, *Lamb Arbitration,* April 5, 1994, vol. 3, pp. 371–73. Many other students gave similar testimony. A contentious issue arose from the fact that Mie Watanabe, the investigating officer who went into action once sexual harassment charges had been filed, had made no effort to interview those students who supported Lamb. A few of them had taken the initiative and spoken to Watanabe; they later criticized her written summaries as misrepresentations of their views.

6. Alan M. Dershowitz, "Justice" at http://www.vix.com/pub/men/harass/dershowitz.html.

7. Closing argument of Clayton Ikei, *Gretzinger v. Ramdas Lamb,* United States District Court for the District of Hawaii, Civil No. 94-00864BMK, August 22, 1996, vol. 13, p. 137.

8. Closing argument of Ikei, p. 144.

9. "Grooming" is a particularly noxious term by which fear of niceness is being spread throughout the academy. It has been used for decades in the literature relating to sexual offenders and has evidently been borrowed, because of its nefarious associations, by the SHI.

10. George Tanabe, the chair of Lamb's department, in his testimony before Arbitrator Thomas E. Angelo, described a training session conducted by Hippensteele for the departmental faculty in the wake of the allegations against Lamb, in which it was made clear that "whether or not something proper or improper was taking place [was] totally in the minds and the understandings of the student. If they so perceived a problem, there was a problem." *Lamb Arbitration,* February 17, 1994, vol. 2, p. 223. Hippensteele also told faculty that, they were right to feel "severely limited in what we could say and do without fear of being charged with harassment or discrimination," since the student's "perception would indicate the presence of a problem" (p. 224). She also explained "grooming" in such a way that, Tanabe testified, a woman student in the room "complained that we were discriminating against women, because we were being reluctant about being nice to female students. . . . And so either way, whether we're being nice or whether we were not being nice, we were discriminating against [them]" (p. 228). Tanabe

also testified to the contradictory position in which he, as chair, found himself: "My problem is that any action I took assumed that the complaints were legitimate, and this is an assumption that I have to make prior to any investigation to determine whether or not the complaints are legitimate. And so I found myself in the difficult position of having to take some kind of action, and I cannot, and I still cannot, make the distinction between what might be called legitimate actions before an investigation is carried out and corrective or punitive or disciplinary action" (p. 221).

11. Deposition of Susan Hippensteele, *Gretzinger v. University of Hawaii Professional Assembly and Ramdas Lamb,* U.S. District Court for the District of Hawaii, Civil No. 90-00684 ACK, May 3, 1995, vol. 3, p. 326.

12. See K. L. Billingsley's article on the case, "A Lamb to the Slaughter?" *Heterodoxy 5,* no. 1 (January–February 1997): 1.

13. Ramdas Lamb, e-mail message to author, January 9, 1998.

14. See David E. Rovella, "When Free Speech and Sex Harassment Clash," *National Law Journal,* May 11, 1998, p. A21; *Gretzinger v. University of Hawaii Professional Assembly and Ramdas Lamb,* U.S. District Court for the District of Hawaii, No. 97-15123, D.C. No. CV-94-00684 BMK, May 6, 1998; Craig Gima, "UH Professor Wins Appeal By Accuser," *Honolulu Star-Bulletin,* July 9, 1998, p. A4.

15. Ramdas Lamb, e-mail message to asc-1@csulb.edu, June 2, 1998.

16. Heinz-Joachim Klatt, "Sexual Harassment Policies as All-Purpose Tools to Settle Conflicts," *Sexuality and Culture* 1 (1997): 45–69.

17. Ferrel M. Christensen, *Sexual Harassment Must Be Eliminated,* General Issues Education Foundation Occasional Papers Series, no. 3 (Alberta: General Issues Education Foundation, 1994), p. 27. Hans Bader writes, more generally, that "[h]arassment law is on a collision course with the First Amendment" because harassment claims are often based on speech—jokes, political statements, religious proselytizing, or art on the topics of race, religion, or sex—that is said to create a "hostile or offensive work environment." "Free Speech Trumps Title VII Suits," *National Law Journal,* November 24, 1997. On page A19, Bader discusses several suits in which First Amendment rights won out in the end.

18. Information on the Vega case comes from official documents sent to me by Professor Vega.

19. Eddie Vega, e-mail message to author, May 27, 1998.

20. Eddie Vega, e-mail message to author, May 27, 1998.

21. See *About Women on Campus* 4, no. 4 (Fall 1995): 7.

22. Klatt, "Sexual Harassment Policies as All-Purpose Tools to Settle Conflicts," p. 62. In 1991, Klatt was himself charged with sexual harassment by two students who took offense at his calling another student in his class by the nickname "Lucky Lucy." What followed was, he writes, "worthy of Kafka." Months later, he was called before a one-man tribunal, was not allowed to hear the testimony of witnesses or to cross-examine them, and was told a final judgment would be made without further input from him and without the possibility of an appeal. Two years later, he was exonerated (pp. 63–64).

23. Letter from C. S. Wallace to Linda L. Slakey, May 1, 1998 (copy provided by Professor Palmer). Wallace was also co-chair of the committee promoting the Vision 2000 proposal.

24. Evidently some of the students felt that describing RU 486 as inducing abortion was a prejudicial view of it, and thus an "opinion," not a "fact." Yet a study by radical feminist scholar Janice G. Raymond (also on the faculty at UMass-Amherst), coauthored with Renate Klein and Lynette J. Dumble, *RU 486: Misconceptions, Myths, and Morals* (Cambridge, MA: Institute on Women and Technology, 1991), states as its opening line, "Initial euphoria greeted the arrival of RU 486, the new chemical abortifacient" (p. 1). This work deplores the dangers RU 486 poses to women's health. One can easily envision a situation in which while some of Professor Palmer's students object to his antipathetic labeling of RU 486 as an abortifacient, others object to his failure to denounce the drug as a threat to women's health; both sides could then charge him with "hostile environment" harassment.

25. Letter from John Palmer to Robert Ackermann, Ombudsman, May 1, 1998.

26. Letter from Robert Ackermann to Christopher Woodcock, Chair, Biology Department, May 11, 1998.

27. One of these letters of support stated:

> I was saddened and upset to read that your style of teaching is coming under attack. I have found your straight-forward style [of] teaching very beneficial. It is my opinion that these students who have attacked you are far too sensitive and unwilling to hear anything that is not told to them exactly the way they want to hear it. I have found them to be obnoxious and disruptive in class, often addressing issues that are not relevant to the real message of the lecture.

Another student, identifying herself as "pro-choice," wrote that she "did not see the same things the other nine students did," and offered to gather up pro-Palmer forces to take to the Ombuds Office. Letters dated May 13, 1998 (copies provided to me by Professor Palmer).

28. Leroy Young, letter to author, August 2, 1995.

29. News release from Plymouth State College President Donald P. Wharton, March 28, 1994.

30. Jim Finnegan, "'What Happened with Leroy?'" *Union Leader,* April 29, 1994.

31. Leroy Young, e-mail communication, July 25, 1997.

32. See Denise K. Magner, "College Reinstates Controversial Professor, Then Fires Him Once Again," *Chronicle of Higher Education,* February 9, 1996, p. A20.

33. Leroy Young, introducing himself to asc-1@csulb.edu, July 7, 1995.

34. Tatum Young, personal communication with author, March 16, 1998.

35. Denise Magner's article "College Reinstates Controversial Professor, Then Fires Him Once Again," quoted Tracy Schneider's lawyer, Susanna G. Robinson, as declaring that the university should have stepped in because "[t]his guy has a history of doing this," a statement Leroy Young says is an outright lie.

36. Leroy Young, e-mail message to author, March 1998.

❖ 38. Academics' Shame: Our Failure to Confront Sexual Harassment

Jeannette Oppedisano

In 1978 I accepted the position of affirmative action officer for a university that had two thousand employees and five thousand students—predominantly white male. The president was a man truly committed to developing an educational environment that was free of harassing behavior of all kinds, particularly sexual harassment. He knew that what I was hired to do was not wanted by most people; his direction for my work was that I was to be a "gentle needle." We put the necessary policies and procedures in place with significant input from faculty, administrators, and students; I conducted extensive training programs for all the constituencies; visited departments to answer questions; and thoroughly investigated allegations. These were the ingredients cited for success in such efforts: commitment from the top, input from organizational members, clear and accessible procedures, and action. Yet, we failed. There were many reasons: the president's premature death five years after my arrival, the succession of other presidents, the burnout of those committed to the cause, and, in hindsight, the apathy of faculty.

HISTORICAL RIGHTS TO A NONDISCRIMINATORY ENVIRONMENT

Today we understand that sexual harassment is a type of sex discrimination as interpreted by the courts. We are protected from sexual discrimination under the Civil Rights Act of 1964, although the category was included in that legislation only as a ploy by a Southern senator attempting to defeat the proposed legislation—luckily a futile attempt! The next related governmental action which was even more directly pertinent to faculty and students was the passing of the Education Amendments Act of 1972, stimulated by restrictions on females in athletic programs. The goal of the act was to eliminate sex discrimination in federally assisted educational programs, and to protect those who worked in the organizations that provided these programs. It wasn't until 1980, however, that we got formal guidelines on just what constitutes sexual harassment. These came from the Equal Employment Opportunity Commission (EEOC) under the leadership of Eleanor Holmes Norton. The definition has changed little since then (though I've modified it to include the educational environment language):

> Sexual harassment is a violation of Section 703 of Title VII of the Civil Rights Act of 1964, as amended, and Title IX of the Education Amendments Act of 1972. Unwelcome advances, requests for sexual favors, and other verbal or physical conduct of a sexual nature constitute sexual harassment when (1) submission to such conduct is made either explicitly or implicitly a term or condition of an individual's employment/admission, professional/academic advancement, salary/financial aid, evaluations/grades, tenure/graduation, etc., (2) submission to or rejection of such conduct by an individual is used as the basis for employment/academic decisions affecting such individuals, or (3) such conduct has the purpose or effect of substantially interfering with an individual's work/scholastic performance or creating an intimidating, hostile, or offensive working/learning environment.

Such behavior robs the victim of the opportunity to realize her/his full potential as an employee or student. It is illegal, unprofessional, and unethical behavior. So why do we faculty remain silent?

PLAYING IT SAFE

Certainly we academics cannot be accused of not researching the subject. Adams et al. (1983), Barak et al. (1992), Benson and Thomson (1982), Brooks and Perot (1991), Cammaert (1985), Fitzgerald et al. (1988a, 1988b), Gervasio and Ruckdeschel (1992), Grauerholz (1989), Konrad and Gutek (1986), Mazur and Percival (1989), McKinney (1990), Rabinowitz (1990), Reilly et al. (1986), and Rubin and Borgers (1990) are just a very few scholars who have done so. This research usually elicits a legitimate academic critique, such as that of Lengnick-Hall (1995, 841):

> Seven major methodological problems were found to be prevalent in the research: (a) a disturbing lack of attention to construct validity issues, (b) a weak theoretical development, (c) an overuse of cross-sectional or static approaches for studying a dynamic phenomenon, (d) an almost complete reliance on convenience samples for survey research and college student samples for experimental research, (e) an almost complete reliance on "paper people" or descriptive stimuli, (f) little or no attention paid to the potential reactivity of measures and methods used, and (g) monomethod bias (using the same instruments for measuring both independent and dependent variables).

Reality, Not Perception

It's been six years since I've had formal administrative responsibility for investigations of sexual harassment allegations. During that time I've been a PhD student and faculty member. The stories kept coming; the pain was still evident, especially when I covered the subject of sexual harassment in my Organizational Behavior and Human Resource Management courses. For over twenty-five years to which I can give direct testimony, little has changed in the sexual harassment experiences of many of those who come to educational institutions of higher learning. I *still* hear the same issues from students, faculty, and staff that I heard many years ago. Sexual harassment is *still* perpetrated by those at all levels of the organization—from members of the board of trustees and large donors to faculty and janitors—and the targets are *still* students, faculty, and other employees. It is *still* a behavior perpetrated mostly by men but also by women, and the victims *still* are mostly women but also men. I naively thought that once I left administration and became a faculty member, I'd see just how much teachers/researchers really care about such issues and how often they speak out to try to make changes. I got quite a disappointment. I *still* see most faculty preferring the position of "head in the sand" rather than taking the personal and professional risk involved in becoming advocates for the right of each of us to work and learn in an harassment-free environment. We stay safely ensconced in our rhetoric and rubric, using these devices to distance ourselves from real involvement, from the pain that is right before our eyes if we chose to see. Maybe it's time for us once again to hear the victim's voices; maybe then we'll renew an activism for changing the educational environment that we declare is our domain.

Victims' Voices

Perpetrators, those who impose sexually harassing behaviors on others, come in all sizes, shapes, colors, ages, and positions. So do their victims.

Faculty Perpetrators

I don't want to go to his office anymore but I don't know how to get around it. He leans toward me and touches my leg and tries to hug me when I leave. I have an A in the course and I'm afraid that if I avoid him or stay away, my grade will go down.

He won't call on the female students in class. It's a waste of time to raise your hand, so eventually you just don't bother. I made it a point to get him to allow me to talk but now I'm the "butt" of his attention. . . . Either way the females in class get the message [that] what we have to say is just not valued.

My _____ professor's been calling me at night, asking me out. I have a boyfriend and made sure he knew it, but that didn't stop him. I'm an A student but I'm finding it hard to study for this course and to pay attention in class; when he calls on me or looks at me, I get flustered, so lately I've just been keeping my eyes down wishing I could disappear.

He was the chair of the department. He said he had some papers for me that he left back at his apartment. As soon as I got in the door, he had me pinned against the wall and was all over me. I managed to get out but avoided meeting with him alone. I finished the course with a grade lower than I deserved, and decided to pursue a different graduate program.

I was his grad assistant. He was always checking out my body, trying to hug me. He caught me in the copying room, said that he liked what I was wearing, and then tried to kiss me. . . . He's been bothering the secretaries, too, and I hear there's a freshman who's uncomfortable going into his office. He can't hurt me now that I'm finished, but I don't want anyone else to suffer the way I did.

It's my job . . . trying to bring in money for the college, but some of the male faculty members who make presentations to businesses and alums think it's party time. Recently, Professor _____ came to my hotel room and pushed his way in. . . . It's not the first time he's tried, just the first time I wasn't strong enough to hold the door. . . . He didn't rape me but he was all over me. . . . Somehow I got the physical strength to get him out. . . . He was so drunk.

I'm a PhD student teaching in _____ [Central European country]. Faculty come here from my [home] campus. . . . They do and say things to me here that they know they'd never get away with back home on campus.

I can't believe it! This is a national conference on ethics and I still have to put up with sexist comments and behavior in the sessions—even from presenters. What does it take to make them wake up? How many decades!

She's the basketball coach. . . . When she grabs our behinds, it's sexual. I'm a lesbian but I'm not interested in her; I have a partner. . . . But she keeps asking me and this other player out, . . . and when she's not happy with you, you don't get to play as long.

He comes up behind me when I'm at the computer working on our joint research. He "massages" my shoulders and squeezes them. I don't know what to do. I'm on a student visa. . . . I've seen him do it to the secretaries in the department, too. They seem to not mind. . . . I don't know. . . . He's the chair of the department.

I may be a male student but that doesn't mean I don't mind how he treats the women in class. He calls them "sweetie" or "dear" and gets really close to them. . . . Some sort of flirt back [but] others are uncomfortable. I'm angry and frustrated but I don't know what to do. He's a professor but I wish I could just deck him! I've heard he's been this way for years and the department won't do anything about it. They can't say they don't know. . . . He puts his arm around females in front of other professors!

There are just a few female faculty in our department. . . . When we try to make suggestions, we're ignored or our ideas are scoffed at. Sometimes, later on, a male will make the same point or suggestions, and they're accepted. . . . even praised. I wonder why we bother to try, but it's a "Catch 22." . . . If you don't participate, they'll get you on your evaluations; if you do, they discount you. And the language system they use is all male. When we try to use inclusive language, their nonverbals scream volumes.

Student Perpetrators

Since this academic year started I've been getting harassing phone calls starting at about four in the morning. . . . He talks about masturbation or breathes into the phone; I've asked Security for help; they told me it's probably a friend of mine.

We had been dating for a little while; he kept getting more and more abusive. Then one night he threw me through a glass door. The administration didn't want to get involved because the "incident" happened at a local bar. . . . But I keep running into him on campus. . . . He makes sure of that . . . I'm thinking of dropping out or transferring.

He walked me home from the frat party. I was a freshman and he was an upperclassman. When we got to my dorm, he asked if he could use my bathroom because he had been drinking a lot. . . . How could I say no when he had just done me a favor escorting me home. . . . As soon as we got into my room, he threw me on the bed and raped me.

Some of the students say some awful things about Professor _____ because she's a lesbian. I'm so afraid they'll find out about me.

I've been receiving suggestive pictures on my computer. I'm afraid it might be someone I know and that they'll get kicked out of school if I go to the administration.

How can you feel safe on a campus when somebody goes around painting "fags and queers not welcome here" on the windows and doors?

I was just a stupid little freshman from a really small town. . . . He was an important jock—known all over campus. He made me feel important and wonderful that he could care for me! So we got intimate—not the way I was raised, but I thought I loved him. One night right after we had sex, he got up and the next thing I knew, one of his "buddies" was in bed with me. I looked at _____ in shock and asked him what was going on. He said awful things, . . . called me a tramp and a whore. I felt so dirty, I just let it happen. . . . I'm so ashamed I want to die.

Someone's been putting notes on the door to my room in the dorm. They're like little "love" notes except that I'm beginning to get scared.

I told him it was over but he won't leave me alone. He shows up wherever I am, . . . in hallways where I'm taking classes, in the lunch area when I'm eating, at the computer lab, at the local bars. . . . I feel like I'm being stalked and by someone I thought I used to love!

I thought being a faculty member with a PhD, being bright, you name it, would somehow protect me from sexual harassment, but I went to my first class—an intro engineering course—and the guys in the class started whistling at me and catcalling. . . . The couple of females in the class seemed to shrink down in their seats. . . . I just walked out.

Administrative or Staff Perpetrators

It was my first year at college. He was my boss and I did regular office work. He was always making comments about how pretty I was and how much he liked what I was wearing or how I smelled. Then he asked me to join him on a skiing weekend. I was shocked so at first I didn't say anything; then he mentioned that he knew how much I enjoyed working for him, . . . so I knew my job was on the line.

He was a vice president of the college! And I needed my job. . . . Before, he just made comments about women's breasts or their shapes. . . . I didn't like it but what could a secretary do? . . . But then, at the office picnic, he put an ice cube down my blouse. . . . There were people there who saw him do it, but no one did or said anything. . . . So I just quit.

I went to use the ladies locker room and found a man in there looking at the girls. . . . And then we heard that one of the janitors had been watching us in the toilets through a peephole he made in the wall of the bathroom.

For readers who serve or have served in some affirmative action/diversity capacity on a campus, these stories probably sound all too familiar. That's just the problem. Sexual harassment cannot be eradicated by the isolated actions of the dedicated few. It will take a concerted campaign waged by faculty before such cultural reshaping can occur. But where are our voices?

ACTION ADVOCACY

How dare I lay the responsibility at our feet? After all, our job is to teach, do research, and perform service; there's certainly no shortage of work to do. But I dare because our students cannot be open to what we want to teach them if they are angry or fearful, our colleagues cannot be full participants in university life if they are angry or fearful. I dare because we are the *only* members of the organization who have the likelihood of secure, long-term participation and who therefore have a vested interest in the climate that we create and the organizational power to produce such a positive change. Students are only with us on the average of four years; administrators of all levels can be fired; staff have no real voice in most institutions. And wasn't that one of the reasons why tenure was established—to enable faculty to speak out on issues without fear of retaliation?

But is speaking out on the issue all it would take? No, I'm afraid not. Though these suggestions are certainly not new, here's a starter list:

1. Become knowledgeable about what does and does not constitute sexual harassment and the reality of that behavior in educational institutions. There are many excellent resources; my recommendations include *The Lecherous Professor: Sexual Harassment on Campus* (Dziech and Weiner 1984), *Sexual Harassment: A Report on the Sexual Harassment of Students* (Till 1980), and *Ivory Power: Sexual Harassment on Campus* (Paludi 1990).

2. Take off the blinders. As Dziech and Weiner note, "In most academic departments, there are too many shared students, too close an environment, too much discussion, too small a space for complete invisibility or confusion about who is a genuine offender" (1984, 179). In all of the cases I've investigated involving faculty (in one year alone there were ten such cases) others in the department knew that "something" was going on: "It's none of my business"; "I don't have the time for that stuff. . . . They'll just have to find out how to handle it for themselves"; "That's just the way he is and everybody knows it."

3. Introduce yourself to the official professionals on campus who are charged to assist students; ask them what they do and how they do it. Get a sense of your own comfort level with them. Are they straightforward? Would you go to them with a problem? Ask students to whom they turn when they have or perceive a problem. What avenues are open to faculty? Would you use them? If not, what needs to be changed?

4. Learn how to be a good listener. And ask your interlocutor, What would you like to see happen? The people with whom I have had such a discussion about sexual harassment responded that they just wanted it to stop and not have anyone else go through it or feel the way they felt. Most administrators and faculty fear lawsuits; most victims just want relief.

5. Build coalitions with those who really care—faculty, students, administrators—and design strategies for correcting the problem. Coalitions are critical for a number of reasons: because the variety of voices can help create synergy, keep the goal clear, and the actions on target; because these voices can help keep our personal perspectives clearly focused; and because the old adage is true—there *is* safety in numbers. I'm no longer so naive as to think that your work will be welcomed by all. And remember that just because someone has official responsibility for affirmative action, diversity, or multiculturalism does not assure a campus body that the person is (1) committed to the cause, (2) knowledgeable about rights and responsibilities, or (3) trained to deal with the complexities of victimization. This leads me to the next point.

Always be cognizant of the fact that you are not the victim's counselor.

That's a whole other realm of expertise. What you are is an ombudsperson and advocate—someone who cares enough to take the necessary risks to create a better place for the people who choose to come to your campus (including yourself); someone who will walk with the victim through the process to correction and healing; someone who will be wise enough to know the limits of her/his self, energy, and spirit.

RECOMMENDATIONS FOR FUTURE RESEARCH

Actual organizational investigation files are highly confidential. But there is a gold mine of longitudinal information in the minds of current and former affirmative action/equal opportunity/human resource administrators. Some may even have kept journals at home—just as many of us advise employees and students to do. This data would be on real, not "paper" or lab-created situations. For those complaints that were pursued through the internal and/or external judicial process, there might even be findings of probable or no probable cause to the allegations. Since the data could be aggregated and the organizations disguised, confidentiality could be assured. Those of us who are interested in the reality and scope of sexual harassment on college and university campuses would then have a much clearer, more accurate picture of the problem. Do we care? Do we care enough?

References

Adams, J., et al. 1983. "Sexual Harassment of University Students." *Journal of College Student Personnel* 24: 484–90.

Barak, A., et al. 1992. "Individual Difference Correlates of the Experience of Sexual Harassment among Female University Students." *Journal of Applied Social Psychology* 22: 17–37.

Benson, D., and G. Thomson, 1982. "Sexual Harassment on a University Campus: The Confluence of Authority Relations, Sexual Interest and Gender Stratification." *Social Problems* 29.3: 236–51.

Brooks, L., and A. R. Perot, 1991. "Reporting Sexual Harassment: Exploring a Predictive Model." *Psychology of Women Quarterly* 15: 31–47.

Cammaert, L. 1985. "How Widespread Is Sexual Harassment on Campus?" *International Journal of Women's Studies* 8: 388–97.

"Discrimination because of Sex under Title VII of the Civil Rights Act of 1964, as Amended; Adoption of Final Interpretive Guidelines." 1980. *Federal Register,* 10 November: 74676–77.

Dziech, B. W., and L. Weiner. 1984. *The Lecherous Professor: Sexual Harassment on Campus.* Boston: Beacon.

Equal Employment Opportunity Commission. 1980. "Guidelines on Discrimination because of Sex, Sexual Harassment." *Code of Federal Regulations.* 1604.11.

———. 1988b. "The Incidence and Dimensions of Sexual Harassment in Academia and the Workplace." *Journal of Vocational Behavior* 32: 152–75.

Fitzgerald, L., et al. 1988a. "Academic Harassment: Sex and Denial in Academic Garb." *Psychology of Women Quarterly* 12: 329–40.

Franklin, P., et al. 1981. *Sexual and Gender Harassment in the Academy.* New York: Modern Language Association of America.

Gervasio, A. H., and K. Ruckdeschel. 1992. "College Students' Judgments of Verbal Sexual Harassment." *Journal of Applied Social Psychology* 22: 190–211.

Grauerholz, E., 1989. "Sexual Harassment of Women Professors by Students: Exploring the Dynamics of Power, Authority, and Gender in a University Setting." *Sex Roles* 21: 789–801.

Konrad, A. M., and B. A. Gutek. 1986. "Impact of Work Experiences on Attitudes toward Sexual Harassment." *Administrative Science Quarterly* 31: 422–38.

Lengnick-Hall, M. 1995. "Sexual Harassment Research: A Methodological Critique." *Personnel Psychology* 48: 841–64.

Mazur, D., and E. Percival. 1989. "Students' Experiences of Sexual Harassment at a Small University." *Sex Roles* 13: 21–32.

McKinney, K. 1990. "Sexual Harassment of University Faculty by Colleagues and Students." *Sex Roles* 23: 421–38.

McKinney, K., et al. 1988. "Graduate Students' Experiences with and Responses to Sexual Harassment: A Research Note." *Journal of Interpersonal Violence* 3: 319–25.

Paludi, M. 1990. *Ivory Power: Sexual Harassment on Campus.* Albany: SUNY.

Rabinowitz, V. 1990. "Coping with Sexual Harassment." Paludi 1990. 103–18.

Reilly, M. E., et al. 1986. "Sexual Harassment of University Students." *Sex Roles* 15: 333–58.

Rubin, L. J., and S. B. Borgers. 1990. "Sexual Harassment in Universities during the 1980s." *Sex Roles* 23: 397–411.

Till, F. 1980. *Sexual Harassment: A Report on the Sexual Harassment of Students.* Washington, DC: National Advisory Council on Women's Educational Programs.

❖ 39. The Myth of Male Power

Warren Farrell

WHY SEXUAL HARASSMENT LEGISLATION FEELS UNFAIR TO MEN

ITEM. 1991.   The University of Toronto finds a chemical engineering professor guilty of sexual harassment for "prolonged" staring at a female student at the university swimming pool.[1] He was guilty of creating a hostile environment for her.

ITEM. 1991–92.   Graffiti in a high school men's room which the school neglected to remove resulted in the school being accused of sexual harassment and paying $15,000 for "mental anguish" to the girl mentioned in the graffiti.[2]

ITEM. 1992.   Six-year-old Cheltzie claimed the boys on her bus used nasty language and teased her. So her mom filed a sexual harassment lawsuit on Cheltzie's behalf. The school superintendent responded, "In the future, we're going to have to consider language 'sexual harassment' rather than a cause for discipline."[3]

In the 1960s, the term "sexual harassment" was unheard of. As women who were divorced in the '60s and '70s began to receive income from the workplace, they began to demand the protection from the workplace that they once had in the homeplace. Almost overnight, workplace rules changed.

Previously, few men even thought of using a lawsuit to protect themselves from an offensive joke. A Polish man who heard a Polish joke was expected to laugh, not sue. But men did have ways of defending themselves. If a colleague was offensive, they avoided him. If he couldn't be trusted, they gave him a bad reputation. If a boss was authoritarian or overloaded them with work, some became passive-aggressive—saying "yes, sir" and doing half the job; others worked overtime; others took the boss aside and talked with him; others complained in a written evaluation. And if nothing worked, they applied for a transfer or got another job.

Men never thought of suing the mouth that fed them. Why not? The mouth that fed them also fed their families. The fights that men fought almost all helped them better feed their families—either via higher salaries and workers' compensation when they were alive or via insurance or widows' benefits when they were dead. In essence, he fought for what protected his family more than for what protected him.

In the early 1970s, we began to hear of sexual harassment, but it most often meant a woman being told that if she didn't have sex with the boss, she'd lose her job. Most everyone agreed that was harassment. Harassment soon came to include a boss promising a quicker-than-earned promotion in exchange for sex. Almost all *men* were *opposed to* this because it was mostly men who lost the work favor and whose sexual favors were worth nothing. But because most men felt it was in the *company's* interest to *fire* a boss who exploited the company for personal pleasure, they didn't feel the necessity for government interference.

While men went about their business, so to speak, the federal government expanded the legal definition of sexual harassment to anything *a woman defined* as a "hostile work environment."[4] Men were oblivious until the Clarence Thomas hearings pulled their heads out of the sand: they saw that the definition of harassment had expanded to include *discussing* pornography, telling a dirty joke, calling an employee "honey," or taking a longer look at a shorter skirt.

Does the federal government actually make a dirty joke potentially illegal? Yes.[5] And a look? Yes. And calling an employee "honey"? Yes. *All* these things are illegal *if a woman* decides she doesn't like it, and if a man committed the "offense."

Aren't these guidelines gender neutral? Sometimes, yes; often, no. For example, the sexual harassment guidelines mandate employers to consider it their "affirmative duty" to *"eliminate"* behavior that *women* consider "hostile" or "intimidating"—behavior such as "unwanted sexual advances"[6] or dirty jokes. The Department of Labor's guidelines are explained in a publication entitled "A Working *Woman's* Guide to Her Job Rights" (emphasis added) not "A Worker's Guide to Job Rights."[7] Practically speaking, any man who sued a woman for discussing pornography or for asking him out (à la Hill-Thomas) would be laughed out of the company before the ink on the lawsuit dried.

Who defines "hostile environment"? The woman. *Not even the man's intent makes a legal difference.* In all other criminal behavior, intent makes all the difference. Even in homicide. **Sexual harassment legislation in its present form makes all men unequal to all woman.** It is in blatant violation of the Fourteenth Amendment's guarantee of equal protection *without* regard of sex. Thus the political will to protect only women prevails over the constitutional mandate to protect both sexes equally.

Suppose it is her word against his? When the guidelines of the Equal Employment Opportunity Commission (EEOC) were first formed, a "bare assertion" of sexual harassment—a woman's word against a man's—could not lead to conviction without factual support. Ironically, when Clarence Thomas was chairman of that commission, he was responsible for *reversing* that decision—**now, if it's her word against his, a "bare assertion" of sexual harassment can stand without factual support!**[8] Clarence Thomas now knows why it is important for lawmakers to have to live by the laws they create.

But it's worse than that: a woman doesn't even have to tell the man that he's bothering her. She can now complain *to a girlfriend at work.* The EEOC's decision number 84-1 allows complaining to a girlfriend at work to be "sufficient to support a finding of harassment."[9] That used to be called gossip. Now it's called evidence.

All this led to the filing of 50,000 sexual harassment lawsuits between 1980 and 1990 alone,[10] scaring about three quarters of America's major companies into developing programs designed to fulfill the EEOC guidelines. **In one decade, women had gotten more protection against offensive jokes in the workplace than men had gotten in centuries against being killed in the workplace.** As women entered the workplace and government became a substitute husband, many men felt it was becoming more profitable to be a victim than an entrepreneur; that this was creating a shift in the nation's work ethic: from a nation of entrepreneurs to a nation of victims.

"Your Lips Tell Me 'No, No,' But There's 'Yes, Yes' in Your Eyes": The Politics of Indirect Initiatives

Believe it or not, this is still not the core of what bothers most men. What is? First, men still see women playing *their* old sexual games. And second, men do not see sexual harassment legislation requiring women to take responsibility for their games. For example, the magazine read by the largest number of single working women—*Cosmopolitan*—instructs women on how to take indirect initiatives *at work* to which men *unconsciously* respond.[11] What if the wrong man responds? Other articles tell her how to file a sexual harassment lawsuit should these indirect initiatives elicit direct initiatives from the wrong man![12]

Here are a few indirect initiatives *Cosmopolitan* tells women to take *in the workplace*:[13]

- "As you pass his desk, drop a pile of papers or a purse, then stoop down to gather them up. He'll help. Lean close to him, put your hand on his shoulder to steady your balance. . . ."

- "If you have good legs, wear a very tight, short skirt and very high heels. Bend over with your back to a man (to pick something up or look in a file drawer, etc.). . . ." "Brush up against somebody in the elevator. . . ."

- "Say something slightly inappropriate during a business lunch or dinner, such as, 'You look great in blue.' This should be done while you are talking about something else—for example, 'I was working on the Apex campaign, and did you know you look great in blue?'"

The power of the woman's indirect initiative is that it puts neither her ego nor her career on the line. For example, *Cosmopolitan* advises "*immediately* after you meet him—within seconds—touch him in some way, even if it's just to pick off imaginary lint."[14] Now, if he responds by asking her out but later calls off the relationship, *he's* subject to a harassment suit. (He "initiated.") Once in court, few men would feel comfortable telling a judge, "Your Honor, I asked her out because of the way she picked imaginary lint off my jacket."

What happens if he misses the lint hint? *Cosmopolitan* advises: "Look down at his crotch . . . with a playful look or smile."[15] And if he misses the crotch cue? She can "wear gorgeous red underwear, and show it 'accidentally'—your blouse is open a bit, so a man gets a peek of red lace bra. . . . You cross your legs and your skirt rides up. . . ."

It doesn't stop with *Cosmopolitan*. As women's workforce participation increased, Harlequin Romances discovered a formula that appealed to the working woman. It involves a successful man pursuing a working woman, the working woman resisting, *the man overcoming her resistance,* and her being "swept away." It was the age-old formula—he: pursue, persist; she: attract, resist. But now it was also the definition of sexual harassment.

Were women buying this formula less? Hardly. *The average woman who reads romance novels now reads twenty books per month,* about twice as many as in 1983.[16] And the Harlequin Romance working-woman formula transformed Harlequin from a company on the verge of bankruptcy in the early 1970s to a company that now accounts for 80 percent of the romance market.[17] And the romance market itself has soared—now accounting for 46 percent of all United States mass market paperback sales.[18]

Being "swept away" is her fantasy, not his. He is as much victim as perpetrator. A feeling reinforced when he sees a woman reading books called *Love at Work: Using Your Job to Find a Mate*,[19] with the author's list of the top ten high-powered professions among men and, under each profession, the ten best jobs a woman can get to "target your man."[20]

What's the Big Deal With a Miniskirt?

Many women ask, "What's the big deal with a miniskirt, perfume, and a little flirting in the workplace?" It would not be a big deal for most men if no one were making a big deal of the man's response.

It is a big deal, though, for the woman—if her goal is to be treated seriously at work. Here's why. Her *in*direct initiatives signal to the man her tendency to avoid direct responsibility. *In*direct initiatives signal to him that he is dealing with a woman who is traditional. And traditionally, **indirect initiatives were designed to lead to marriage and the end of her involvement in the workplace. So the miniskirt, perfume, and flirting unconsciously tell the man that this woman wants an end to her involvement in the workplace**—or, at least, an end to her involvement by obligation. If you were a boss who had to choose between promoting someone who had the option to work versus someone with the obligation to work (e.g., to support a spouse and three children), whom would you take more seriously?

None of this female behavior is any more inherently wrong than the male form of direct initiative taking. In almost all cultures throughout human history, women's *in*direct initiatives were their way of signaling their desire for men to take *direct* initiatives. A flirtation was an invitation. In some cultures, lipstick was a woman's way of signaling her willingness to perform fellatio. In the South Sea islands, a fresh flower in a woman's hair signaled availability. The purpose of the flower, lipstick, or the miniskirt is to put the signal out strongly enough to stimulate *every* man's interest. It is only when she has every man's interest that she has real choice—the choice of the "best" men.

What has been the historical importance of her barriers—her "no, noes"? It was her way of selecting a man who could handle life's rejections and survive, who cared enough for her to take risks, and who would assume total responsibility should anything go awry. In a sense, **sexual harassment lawsuits are just the latest version of the female selection process**—allowing her to select for men who care enough for her to put their career at risk; who have enough finesse to initiate without becoming a jerk and enough guts to initiate despite a potential lawsuit. During this process, she gets a sense of his trustworthiness, his commitment, his ability to overcome barriers, the way he handles rejection. It allows her to select for men who will perform, who will assume total responsibility. The more things change . . .

In the past, though, the process of his overcoming her barriers was called "courtship." Now it is called *either* "courtship" *or* "sexual harassment." Here's how gray the boundary is. . . .

When It Works, It's Called Courtship; When It Doesn't, It's Called Harassment

When I ask women in my audiences who had entered the workplace when single and later gotten married to "raise your hand if you married a man you met at work (or through a workplace contact—a client, or someone to whom you were a client)," almost two thirds raised their hands.[21] Another 15 percent of these women lived with or had a long relationship with a man they met while on the job, but never married him. Now here's the dilemma.

The majority of the men these working women married were above them at work; additionally, almost all of these men took the first initiative. **Sexual initiatives by men toward women below them at work is the most frequent definition of sexual harassment. When it works, it's called courtship. When it doesn't work, it's called harassment.**

Isn't it harassment only when he persists? Not legally. For some women, any initiative—even one—could make her feel uncomfortable and therefore create a hostile environment. And that is all she needs to have her lawsuit upheld.

Many women acknowledge being married to men to whom they had at first said "no." By today's standards, they are married to sexual harassers; but some of these women are glad these men pursued.

SHOULD COWORKERS BE LOVERS?

Women especially say it is important to get to know someone before having sex with them. The workplace gives a woman the opportunity to observe a man—how he handles people above him and below him, his competence, his temper, his ethics, values, habits. For most women, it works a lot better than bars. Overall, 35 million Americans report some kind of "social-sexual" experience on their jobs *each week.*[22] More than 80 percent of all workers say they've had such an experience on their job.[23] When it works, we call it a wedding and the woman's picture is in the paper; when it doesn't, we call it a lawsuit and the man's picture is in the paper.

WHY DO MEN TELL DIRTY JOKES?

First, both sexes tell dirty jokes. Even as the mostly male Congress had passed legislation to allow dirty jokes to constitute a "hostile environment," female members of Congress were circulating male-bashing humor.[24] Example? "What's the difference between government bonds and men?" "Bonds mature." This was permitted. But had the men asked, "What's the difference between government bonds and women?" and answered, "Bonds are worth more when they mature," they could be sued. Similarly, the women were joking, "Why is it a good thing there are female astronauts?" and answering, "So someone will ask directions if the crew gets lost in space." Apparently the male congressmen were afraid to ask, "Who answered when the female astronaut asked for directions?"

Although both sexes have their own styles of humor, we often heard during the Thomas-Hill confrontation that dirty jokes were the way male bosses exert their power over women. Hardly. Men share dirty jokes with peers, buddies, and *with anyone with whom they feel comfortable.* A dirty joke is often a male boss's unconscious way of getting his staff to not take him so seriously and therefore *not* be intimated; his way of creating an atmosphere of *easier* feedback, of getting his staff to bond. Men get confused when women say they feel left out when they're not included, then sue when they are included!

Ironically, at the same time millions of dollars are being spent learning about the health benefits of humor, we are spending millions of dollars to censor a form of humor.[25] Like "clean" jokes, dirty jokes that produce laughter stimulate our system with oxygen. "Dirty" jokes are really no dirtier than clean jokes—they just play to our hypocrisy: the hypocrisy that makes us call sex "dirty" and then go out and have sex with someone we love.

When a man is attracted to a woman, being expected to take the sexual initiative

does not increase his power, it increases his paralysis. The possibility of a lawsuit just intensifies the paralysis. Ironically, the more dangerous the waters, the more joking serves as a way of testing the waters: if she laughs, maybe she's interested; if she looks disgusted, maybe she's not. He would feel much more powerful if *she* took responsibility for testing the waters.

Sexual-harassment consultants are now encouraging women to keep private journal notes about hostile-environment behavior such as dirty jokes. Most bosses don't think their employees are intimidated by dirty jokes, but if they are, would like to be told privately rather than discover a woman has kept journal notes and complained to girlfriends on office time, and is now suing them. If a woman is offended, he would like her to tell him, not sue him. . . .

Some Solutions?

If a woman feels sexually harassed, encourage her to tell the man *directly*. How do I know this will work? Well, when two feminists compiled the sexual harassment stories of 100 women, **every single man who was told by a woman directly that she felt his behavior was harassing her stopped immediately.**[26] All of the men apologized, some brought in flowers. When women do not understand men's vulnerability, they miss the degree to which men want to please women, not anger women. Thus the authors who compiled these hundred stories never noticed how each of the men who was informed immediately stopped!

Second, give both sexes an understanding of the other sex's best intent. How, for example, both sexes are doing what we are doing because that was functional for millions of years (men: pursue, persist; women: attract, resist), but how it is no longer functional in an age of equality.

Third, socialize both sexes to share responsibility for taking sexual initiatives. Without shared responsibility, sexual harassment legislation will be just another hoop through which men at work must jump to prove themselves worthy of loving women at work.

Fourth, the adult feminist—as opposed to the adolescent feminist—will encourage women to share the expectation of risking the first kiss on the lips, the first caress on the genitals. Only the adolescent feminist fails to place as much emphasis on resocializing women to take direct initiatives and resorts instead to encouraging women to sue the men who do it badly and marry the men who do it right (*if* they are the right men initiating it at the right moment). The adult feminist is willing to exchange the power of *in*direct initiative taking for the responsibility of direct initiative taking. She is willing to exchange victim power for adulthood.

Fifth, instead of articulating sexual harassment via the perspectives of the women's movement, raise the level of discussion to sexual *contact* via the perspective of a gender transition movement.

All forms of sexual contact at work and at school are best dealt with by the institution's improving communication rather than the government's mandating legislation. The potential damage to the institution gives the institution an incentive to correct it. This is not a perfect solution. It is only more perfect than having government legislation of sexual nuance with its potential for annihilating anyone we dislike via a false accusation.

Conclusion

Sexual harassment is a perfect metaphor for some of the most important challenges of the twenty-first century: the challenge to our genetic heritage of protecting women; the challenge to the stereotype of innocent woman/guilty man; the challenge to keep our work-place flexible and fluid rather than petrified and paralyzed; the challenge to respond to sex-ual nuance more with communication and less with legislation—understanding that com-munication at least responds to nuance with nuance, while legislation responds to nuance with rigidity. When we respond to the nuance of the male-female dance with the rigidity of Stage I regulations, we are going backward, not forward.

If we desire to protect *people* from being hurt, we also have to make laws against love. And against marriage. And automobiles. And gossip. If we desire to protect men from hurt, we would have to outlaw women's sexual rejection of men. Most of us, though, would rather live in a country in which we are free to make our mistakes rather than in one in which we are subject to litigation for each mistake we make.

Early feminists sensed this: they were strong *opponents* of protective legislation. They knew that as long as the princess was protected from the pea, women would be deprived of equality. The modern-day woman's "pea under the mattress" is the rough spots in the workplace. When today's feminists are proponents of protective legislation, they oppose equality.

Sexual harassment legislation is sexist because it makes only the man responsible for the male role in the sexual dance. It protects the woman who is sexual without protecting coworkers from a woman who would use her sexuality for unearned advancement; nor does it protect the company from this woman. Ultimately, it ignores women's role and therefore ignores women. Except as victim.

Notes

1. John Leo, "A Milestone in Sexual Harassment," *US News & World Report*, January 27, 1992. The chemical engineering professor's name is Richard Hummel; the student is Beverly Torfason.
2. Jane Gross, "Schools Are Newest Arenas for Sex-Harassment Issues," *The New York Times*, Education section, March 11, 1992, p. B-8. The high school was Duluth Central High School in Minnesota.
3. Scripps-Howard News Service, "Second-Grader Files Sex Harass Lawsuit," *North County Blade-Citizen* (San Diego), September 30, 1992.
4. Gretchen Morgenson, "Watch That Leer, Stifle That Joke," *Forbes*, May 15, 1989, pp. 69–72.
5. U.S. Department of Labor, "A Working Woman's Guide to Her Job Rights," leaflet no. 55, June 1988.
6. Ibid.
7. Ibid.
8. Clarence Thomas gave his signed approval to these modifications on October 25, 1988. The modifications are explained in a footnote on page 12 of the sexual harassment guidelines of 1988. Cited in Richard Pollak, "Presumed Innocent?" *The Nation*, vol. 253, no. 16, November 11, 1991, pp. 573 and 593. In an interview on April 6, 1992, the EEOC verified that what I said in the text is still accurate under the guidelines as revised in 1990.
9. Pollak, ibid., p. 593.
10. Morgenson, op. cit.
11. "How to Make an Impact on a Man," featured in special section "How to Attract Men Like Crazy," *Cosmopolitan*, February 1989, p. 177. See discussion of women's magazines in *Why Men Are the Way They Are* (New York: Berkley, 1988), pp. 18–23.
12. Ronnie Snadroff, "Sexual Harassment in the Fortune 500," *Working Woman*, December 1988.
13. *Cosmopolitan*, op. cit.
14. Ibid.
15. Ibid.

16. *Forbes* reports that the romance novel buyer spent an average of $1,200 in 1991. Since the price of the average romance novel was about $5 in 1991, an average of approximately 240 books a year, or 20 books per month, were purchased. For women who also read their friends' books, the number of books they read is more than 20 per month; for women who do not do this but buy some hardcovers, the figure is less than 20 per month. See Dana Wechsler Linden and Matt Rees, "I'm hungry. But not for food," *Forbes,* July 6, 1992, pp. 70–75. The 1983 figure comes from an interview on February 18, 1985, with John Markert, independent researcher and author of "Romancing the Reader: A Demographic Profile," *Romantic Times,* no. 18, September 1984 (based on his doctoral dissertation).

17. Ibid.

18. Ibid.

19. There are chapters called "Using Your Job to Meet Men," but no chapters called "Using Your Job to Meet Women." See Margaret Kent and Robert Feinschreiber, *Love at Work: Using Your Job to Find a Mate* (New York: Warner Books, 1988).

20. Ibid., p. 54.

21. I asked this of about 2,000 U.S. and Canadian women between the ages of 25 and 80, from all walks of life, from 1989 to 1992.

22. See James Martin and Sheila Murphy. "The Romantically Charged '80s Office," *Los Angeles Times,* September 11, 1988.

23. Barbara A. Gutek, *Sex and the Workplace* (San Francisco: Jossey-Bass, 1985), p. ix.

24. "Just Desserts," Periscope section, *Newsweek,* August 10, 1992, p. 4.

25. Sexual harassment legislation does much more than censor a form of humor, but it is also doing that.

26. Amber Coverdale Sumrall and Dena Taylor, *Sexual Harassment: Women Speak Out* (Freedom, Calif.: The Crossing Press, 1992).

PART V

Multicultural and International Issues

40. Race, Sexual Harassment, and the Limitations of the Feminist Paradigm

Kimberlé Crenshaw

. . . Rape and other sexual abuses in the work context, now termed sexual harassment, have been a condition of black women's work life for centuries. Forced sexual access to black women was of course institutionalized in slavery and was central to its reproduction. During the period when the domination of white women was justified and reinforced by the nineteenth-century separate-spheres ideology, the few privileges of separate spheres were not available to black women at all. Instead, the subordination of African-American women recognized few boundaries between public and private life. Rape and other sexual abuses were justified by myths that black women were sexually voracious, that they were sexually indiscriminate, and that they readily copulated with animals, most frequently imagined to be apes and monkeys. Indeed, their very anatomy was objectified. Patricia Hill Collins notes that the abuse and mutilation that these myths inspired are memorialized to this day in a Paris museum where the buttocks and genitalia of Sara Bartmann, the so-called Hottentot Venus, remain on display.[1]

The stereotypes and myths that justified the sexual abuse of black women in slavery continue to be played out in current society. They are apparent in the experiences of women who are abused on their jobs and in the experiences of black women elsewhere in society. For example, in many of the sexual-harassment cases involving African-American women, the incidents they report often represent a merging of racist myths with the victims' vulnerability as women. Black female plaintiffs tell stories of insults and slurs that often go to the core of black women's sexual construction. While black women share with white women the experience of being objectified as "cunts" "beavers," or "pieces," for them those insults are many times prefaced with "black" or "nigger" or "jungle." Perhaps this racialization of sexual harassment explains why black women are disproportionately represented in sexual-harassment cases. Racism may well provide the clarity to see that sexual harassment is neither a flattering gesture nor a misguided social overture but an act of intentional discrimination that is insulting, threatening, and debilitating.

Pervasive myths and stereotypes about black women not only shape the kinds of harassment that black women experience but also influence whether black women's stories are likely to be believed. Historically, a black woman's word was not taken as truth; our own legal system once drew a connection—as a matter of law—between lack of chastity and lack of veracity. In other words, a woman who was likely to have sex could not be trusted to tell the truth. Because black women were not expected to be chaste, they were likewise considered less likely to tell the truth. Thus, judges were known to instruct juries to take a black woman's word with a grain of salt. One judge admonished jurors not to apply the ordinary presumption of chastity to black women, for if they were to do so, they "would be blinding themselves to actual conditions."[2] In 1971 a judge was quoted as saying, "Within the Negro community, you really have to redefine rape. You never know about them." Lest it be believed that such doubts have been banished to the past, a very recent study of jurors in rape trials revealed that black women's integrity is still very deeply questioned by many people in society. One juror, explaining why a black rape victim was discredited by the jury, stated, "You can't believe everything they say. They're known to exaggerate the truth."[3]

Even where the facts of our stories are believed, myths and stereotypes about black women also influence whether the insult and injury we have experienced is relevant or important. One study concluded, for example, that men who assault black women are the least likely to receive jail time; when they do, the average sentence given to black women's assailants is two years; the average for white women's assailants is ten years. Again, attitudes of jurors seem to reflect a common belief that black women are different from white women and that sexual aggression directed toward them is less objectionable. In a case involving the rape of a black preteen, one juror argued for acquittal on the grounds that a girl her age from "that neighborhood . . . probably wasn't a virgin anyway."

These responses are not exceptional, as illustrated by the societal response to the victimization of Carol Stuart, the Boston woman whose husband murdered her and then fingered a black male. It would strain credibility to say that the Boston police would have undertaken a door-to-door search of any community had Carol Stuart and her fetus been black, or, on a similar note, that Donald Trump would have taken out a full-page ad in the New York Times calling for the reinstatement of the death penalty had that investment banker raped in Central Park been a black service worker. Surely the black woman who was gang-raped during that same week, whose pelvis and ankles were shattered when she was thrown down an elevator shaft and left to die, along with the twenty-eight other women who were raped that week and received no outpouring of public concern, would find it impossible to deny that society views the victimization of some women as being less important than that of others.

Black women experience much of the sexual aggression that the feminist movement has articulated but in a form that represents simultaneously their subordinate racial status. While the fallen-woman imagery that white feminists identify does represent much of black women's experience of gender domination, given their race, black women have in a sense always been within the fallen-woman category. For black women the issue is not the precariousness of holding on to the protection that the madonna image provides or the manner in which the madonna image works to regulate and thereby constrain black women's sexuality. Instead, it is the denial of the presumption of "madonna-hood" that shapes responses to black women's sexual victimization.

White feminists have been reluctant to incorporate race into their narratives about gender, sex, and power. Their unwillingness to speak to the race-specific dimensions of black women's sexual disempowerment was compounded by their simultaneous failure to understand the ways that race may have contributed to Anita Hill's silence. Their attempt to explain why she remained silent spoke primarily to her career interests. Yet the other reasons why many black women have been reluctant to reveal experiences of sexual abuse—particularly by African-American men—remained unexamined. In fact, many black women fear that their stories might be used to reinforce stereotypes of black men as sexually threatening. Others who may not share this particular concern may nevertheless remain silent fearing ostracism from those who do. Black women face these kinds of dilemmas throughout their lives; efforts to tell these stories may have shaped perceptions of Anita Hill differently among black women, perhaps providing some impetus for breaking through the race-versus-gender dichotomy. Content to rest their case on a raceless tale of gender subordination, white feminists missed an opportunity to span the chasm between feminism and antiracism. Indeed, feminists actually helped maintain the chasm by endorsing the framing of the event as a race versus a gender issue. In the absence of narratives linking race and gender, the prevailing narrative structures continued to organize the Hill and Thomas controversy as either a story about the harassment of a white woman or a story of the harassment of a black man. Identification by race or gender seemed to be an either/or proposition, and when it is experienced in that manner, black people, both men and women, have traditionally chosen race solidarity.

Notes

1. Patricia Hill Collins, "The Sexual Politics of Black Womanhood," *Black Feminist Thought: Knowledge, Consciousness, and the Politics of Empowerment* (New York: Unwin Hyman, 1990), p. 168.
2. See Jennifer Wriggins, "Race, Racism and the Law," 6 *Harvard Women's Law Journal* 103 (1983).
3. See Gary LaFree, *Rape and Criminal Justice: The Social Construction of Sexual Assault* (Belmont, Calif.: Wadsworth Publishing, 1991).

41. Anti-Lesbian Harassment

Celia Kitzinger

TAKING A DEFINITIONAL STAND

It is possible to argue that all forms of harassment done to a lesbian are 'anti-lesbian' harassment, because they are directed against a lesbian, who is and continues to be a lesbian while being harassed. This argument would insist that it is not possible (or not politically desirable) to differentiate between those occasions when a lesbian is harassed as a lesbian, and those occasions when she is harassed as whatever else she is—and when is she ever other than a lesbian?

The counter-argument points to forms of oppression other than anti-lesbianism (including those bundled together as part of the definition of 'hate crime': racism, anti-semitism, religious prejudice—and, we might add, classism, disableism and ageism). Sometimes such oppressions are more salient in causing a lesbian's harassment than is her lesbianism. Lesbians who share other oppressions report confusion as to how accurately to label their experience: 'When working in a white environment it's racism anyway. If they get to know that I'm a lesbian then I can't tell if it's anti-lesbianism or racism.'[1] It is the focus on the motives and intentions of the harassers that leads to these uncertainties and difficulties: do they hate you because you're black, or because you're lesbian? The answer (probably both) is ultimately unknowable. They may not tell you; they may be lying; or they may deceive themselves. In any event, it should not be necessary to rely on the oppressor's testimony to define what happened. An alternative is to shift the focus from the intentions of the harasser to the identity (or identities) of the person being harassed.

We are harassed as whole people: we don't ever stop being all of whom we are. When anti-semitic comments are made because of my surname, being lesbian may not be irrelevant: I have retained my 'maiden' name and my heterosexual sister, who took her husband's non-Jewish name, is not subjected to such comments. My friend who is subjected to racist taunts as she walks through a hostile neighbourhood late at night is certainly harassed because she is black, but the opportunity for the harassment arises as she returns home late at night from a lesbian bar. We do not experience our oppression as fragmented according to discrete identity categories, nor should we have to label what happens to us as though it could be neatly categorised into mutually exclusive or competing oppressions.

The notion of anti-lesbianism which is separate and clearly distinguishable from any other form of oppression can only be a 'prototypical' white, middle-class, able-bodied, gentile concept of what anti-lesbianism is and how it works. *All* lesbians suffer from anti-lesbianism, although the form it takes varies depending on the race/ethnicity, class, age and disability status of the lesbian at whom it is directed. For example, the same man who, drawing on racial and class stereotypes of British women, taunts a middle-class white lesbian with frigidity or sexual inexperience, may assume that a working-class black lesbian is sexually promiscuous, has extensive experience of sex with men, and is continually ready and willing for sexual encounters. The black woman's experience is not anti-lesbianism *plus* racism, but anti-lesbianism *structured by* racism, or racism *structured by* anti-lesbianism. The emphasis she chooses to give this may depend on her audience and her intentions: with black heterosexual women, it may be necessary to speak of the former in order that they notice her oppression *as a lesbian;* with white lesbians, it may be necessary to speak of the latter, in order that they notice her oppression *as a black woman.* (If, on the other hand, she wants emotional support and empathetic understanding, she may choose to emphasise the oppression she shares with her audience.) The question 'Was it anti-lesbianism, or was it racism?' sets up a false dichotomy. There is no 'prototypical' lesbian, harassed 'purely' for her lesbianism, against which all other lesbians' oppression can be compared in order to determine the extent to which their victimisation can be said to be 'additional' to hers. Oppressions are not additive, but interactive.

Although on particular occasions and in specific contexts we may wish to insist on the primacy of one oppression or another, there is much to be gained by starting from the assumption that any incident of harassment, discrimination or oppression is directed at the whole person and can appropriately be labelled anti-lesbian *and* racist *and* disableist *and . . .* whatever other aspects of our identity are routinely under attack. *Every* harassing incident directed against a black lesbian is both racist *and* anti-lesbian; *every* harassing incident directed against a disabled lesbian is both disableist *and* anti-lesbian. We don't have to pit oppression one against another. Rather, by labelling what happens to us as inclusively as possible, we enable a shift of focus from the confusion of either/or to the awareness of both (or all) and how they interact.

(HOMOSEXUAL) WOMAN *OR* (FEMALE) HOMOSEXUAL

Definitions of 'hate crimes' do not include crimes motivated by woman-hatred. Rape, sexual harassment and other forms of sexual assault on women do not qualify as hate-motivated crimes unless the perpetrator can be shown to have attacked some aspect of the victim's identity other than her gender (such as her race, religion or sexual orientation). All lesbians are women[2] and share many aspects of women's general oppression under heteropatriarchy. Yet the need to describe something as a 'hate crime' or as an anti-gay assault requires that we dislocate our experience as 'women' from our experience as 'homosexuals'.

In much social science research, as in policy documents, anti-lesbian harassment must be classified as either 'sexism' (harassment of lesbian-as-woman) or as 'anti-gay' (harassment of lesbian-as-homosexual). Such conceptual divisions suggest that lesbians are harassed *either* because we are women *or* because we are homosexuals, and that any specific case of harassment properly belongs to one category or the other. Were we harassed as women (who happen to be lesbian, a fact which may or may not have been known or suspected by the assailant); or were we harassed as homosexuals (who happen to be female)? While lesbians differ in class, race, ethnicity, age and disability status, we share a common oppression as women. The attempt to 'separate out' one form of oppression from another breaks down completely when confronting the extent to which harassment is 'really' anti-lesbian versus anti-woman. Because all lesbians are women, the overlap of oppression is complete.

By ignoring the fact that one is always a lesbian (even when being harassed as a woman) and always a woman (even when being harassed as a gay person), it is indeed possible to classify *some* incidents as either 'anti-woman' or 'anti-gay'—by focusing on the presumed motives of the harasser. When, for example, in conversation with a male colleague, I bent down to retrieve my appointment diary from my bag on the floor, and another male lecturer known only to my colleague called in passing, 'Hi Pete! I see you've got a woman on her knees! That's the way to keep them!', the incident seems to be 'anti-woman': my lesbianism (if he knew about it) was irrelevant to him—what I symbolised was a generic female. When, on another occasion, after applying for a job for which I was not shortlisted, a member of the selection committee told me that the head of department had flatly refused to consider an 'out' researcher on lesbian and gay issues, saying that 'it would make a laughing stock of the department', it seems not unreasonable to assume that he might have ridiculed a gay male researcher of homosexuality in the same way—in other words, that this is an 'anti-gay' incident. But many other incidents defy such classification. Is it 'sexism' or 'anti-lesbianism' which led a male colleague, walking with me, an 'out' lesbian, through a deserted wooded area of the campus towards the computing centre, to ask me whether I had a partner, adding that he had 'always wanted to go to bed with two lesbians'?

Lesbianism is perceived by many men primarily in terms of sex.[3] Pornographic depictions of pseudo-lesbian activity are commonplace.[4] Lesbians are portrayed as sex objects for men, who perform on each other the necessary 'foreplay' as preparation for the entry of the male and his penis. Consequently, many lesbians are sexually harassed not because they are women, but because they are lesbians.[5] Some forms of sexual harassment are specific to 'out' lesbians—men sometimes act on the assumption that we share a 'male gaze' when looking at women, and that we can be 'one of the boys' in enjoying pornographic pin-ups or ogling passing females; many lesbians find this humiliating and offensive.[6] Rape, too, may be directed not at a 'woman' but at a lesbian: all we need is a good fuck, or the right man. According to researchers of anti-lesbian violence, 'rapists often verbalise the view that lesbians are "open targets" and deserve punishment because they are not under the protection of a man'.[7] Anti-lesbian rape may also involve attempts by the rapist to degrade lesbian sexuality—one lesbian couple were forced at gunpoint to engage in sexual behaviour together, then raped.[8]

Men sometimes seem genuinely surprised to find—having taken pornography as literal truth—that they have offended us with their sexual incursions. One man who attempted to kiss me shortly after I told him I was a lesbian (as part of an academic discussion about our current research projects) was baffled by my outrage, clearly believing that in coming out as lesbian I had 'introduced sex into the conversation': that it was I, not he, who had opened up the topic of sex for public discussion, I who had started the 'salacious' exchange, I who had demonstrated a 'sexually liberated', 'swinging' attitude to sexuality—an attitude to which he was merely responding in kind. Where I understand the words 'I am a lesbian' to mean a statement of political choice, social identity, and personal commitment, as well as (in this context) having implications for the doing of research, he had understood my words as a sexual invitation. 'Coming out' is often perceived as 'coming on', or as 'playing hard to get'. In coming out as lesbians we're 'asking for it'. We 'bring upon ourselves' whatever forms of harassment are subsequently directed at us. We could, after all, have stayed in the closet.

The pressure to pass as heterosexual is itself an indication of oppression, and one which sets the scene for other forms of harassment—including, for the closeted lesbian, the threat of disclosure. Sexual harassment emphasises heterosexual norms of intimacy and behaviour, reminding the lesbian of her own 'outsider' status. For lesbians attempting to 'pass as straight', sexual harassment may have to be endured if they are not to run the risk of being accused of lesbianism. The indivisibility of oppression is apparent in that many lesbians find that what starts as (apparently) a clear case of 'anti-woman' harassment escalates to anti-lesbianism when they signal their unavailability:

> One respondent illustrated this pattern in her analysis of an incident that began with a man asking to see her breast as she walked by him on the street. She ignored the comment and walked on. He continued the harassment by saying 'Dyke'. She concluded, 'so the worst kind of woman that he can imagine, a woman that won't respond to him at all, must be a lesbian. Otherwise I would've been flattered that he wanted to see my breast.'[9]

Although both heterosexual and lesbian women are subjected to this sort of harassment, anti-lesbian insults carry a particular threat for lesbians: women confident in their heterosexual status may be able to ignore or challenge such insults, but for closeted lesbians there is the danger of being 'outed'.

Even if a woman is 'out' as a lesbian in her workplace, she may be engaged in a personal PR campaign in which she sets out to demonstrate the falsity of the stereotypes. Many lesbians, for example, are keen to show by their own behaviour that lesbians are not ugly man-haters, and may set out to dress in a way which men are likely to find attractive, to engage in a friendly manner with men, to demonstrate that they *could* catch a man if they wanted one—that their lesbianism isn't *faute de mieux*.[10] Lesbians engaged in this course of action sometimes find themselves less clear than heterosexuals as to what constitutes 'sexual harassment' and may be forced to tolerate considerably *more* harassment than do many heterosexual women.

The old-fashioned definition of a lesbian as a woman who chooses to engage sexually with women, and not with men,[11] means that for lesbians *all* sexual advances from men are unwanted, unreciprocated and unsolicited. In so far as 'sexual harassment' is defined as 'unreciprocated, unsolicited, unwanted male behaviour which has as its aim the reduction of a woman to a sex object',[12] lesbians can define *all* sexualised behaviour from men as 'sexual harassment'. The term 'sexual harassment' relies upon a distinction between desired and reciprocated heterosexual interaction and unwanted heterosexual interaction. Since as lesbians we want *none* of it, *all* of it can be labelled 'sexual harassment'. Typically, however, lesbians are not comfortable with this relabelling strategy, understanding that for heterosexual women distinctions between 'flirtation' and 'harassment' are important (albeit difficult to make clearly).[13] As lesbians, we are expected to see ourselves as a special 'minority' group who cannot expect our definitions, expectations and preferences to be understood or found acceptable by the heterosexual world.[14]

We are sexually harassed *because we are visible as lesbians* (and therefore a pornographic turn-on or a challenge) or we are sexually harassed *because we are not visible as lesbians,* assumed to be heterosexual or attempting to pass as heterosexual and therefore 'fair game'. The non-additive nature of lesbian oppression is clearly indicated in instances of sexual harassment. Our oppression as lesbians is not the same as the oppression of generic (presumed heterosexual) women, plus that of generic (assumed male) homosexuals.

SEEKING HELP, CHOOSING ALLIES, FIGHTING BACK

In this chapter I have argued, firstly, that we are oppressed or harassed as 'whole people' and, secondly, that our oppression is specific to the 'whole people' that we are. This means that the label 'anti-lesbian harassment' is often not sufficient to describe our experience, because it singles out only one part of our identities. Equally, however, 'anti-lesbian harassment' is necessary as a term which describes a specific form of discrimination which cannot be deduced from adding the experience of being a 'woman' to the experience of being a 'gay person'.

Problems of definition always arise in the construction of any social problem, and 'anti-lesbianism' is no exception. The definitions we apply to our experiences play an important role in determining our understanding of what is going on, and the range of possible reactions. Definitions have implications for action. If we dismiss the catcalls, the sexual innuendo, the anti-lesbian jokes as 'just part of life', refusing to label them as 'harassment', we are unlikely to complain or to seek remedies. If we label them *only* 'anti-lesbian harassment', we may be losing other dimensions of these assaults—their attack on racial, class, age, or disability characteristics.[15] If we label them *only* 'racist' or 'sexist' (for example) we lose sight of the intersection of race, sex and so on in constructing our lesbianism; and, conversely, of the role of our lesbianism in constructing our racialised and gender-specific identities. We need to pay close attention to all aspects of our oppression, and to develop clearer understandings of their interrelationship, if we are to fight back effectively.

The term 'anti-lesbian harassment' has drawbacks. It focuses attention on only one aspect of the whole experience. Harassment in general tends to be constructed as something which can be sliced up into 'pure' exemplars of different oppressions—such that one can identify incidents which are 'purely' racial harassment, 'purely' sexual harassment and so on. The fiction that there is anti-lesbian harassment which is 'purely' anti-lesbianism (uncontaminated by issues of race, class, sex and so forth) actively prevents some lesbians from seeking help. Workers at various of the organisations that have been set up to help lesbian and gay crime victims[16] typically find that lesbians and people of colour are underrepresented in their client populations. A former coordinator of one such group, Community United Against Violence, explains: 'Women who are victimized often are not sure whether it was an anti-lesbian or anti-woman attack. The issue of women not going to Community United Against Violence is directly related to making that distinction.'[17] The current program coordinator makes a parallel point in relation to people of colour:

> The majority of people of color who report to us say that they find it difficult to separate the anti-gay or anti-lesbian element of the attack from the elements that are racial. The incidents seem to be motivated by both for a lot of people.[18]

In terms of seeking help, then—and 'help' in this context refers not only to the provision of emotional or psychological support but also to information about the legal options open to victims of 'hate crimes'—insistence on a 'purist' definition of anti-lesbian harassment is counterproductive. It makes it *less* likely that lesbians (especially black lesbians or those with disabilities) will feel able to use the services on offer.[19]

But it would be a mistake to react by abandoning any notion of the specificity of 'anti-lesbianism'. It would be easy to shrug in bewilderment at the dizzy array of overlapping and multiple oppression, and to resort to the use of 'harassment' as an undifferentiated category. 'I was harassed', you could say—leaving unspecified the particular nature of that experience. However, there are good political reasons for retaining, and for further developing, the notion of 'anti-lesbian harassment'. Firstly, it names an oppressed group and hence renders us (and our oppression) visible to those who might prefer not to see. Apparently inclusive language ('Everyone should be free from harassment of any kind') cannot achieve this. Just as the creators of the US Declaration of Independence somehow overlooked the fact that the inalienable rights and freedoms it purportedly guaranteed to all US citizens were denied to over half the population (women and slaves), so there is always the danger that oppressed groups will be excluded from rights and protections unless they are specifically included by name. A concrete illustration of the power of naming for lesbians and gay men comes from the extension, in May 1988, of Penn State University's policy defining sexual harassment of students specifically to include harassment based on sexual orientation:

> This was a change with practical consequences. Before this, without a mention of lesbians or gay men existing on campus and with no extension of policies about harassment to them, a R[esident] A[ssistant] could dismiss, instead of report, the ubiquitous 'fag' or 'dyke' joke. Following the change, the same joke became 'sexual harassment' and was covered by university sanctions . . . The most important consequence of the amendment to the harassment policy was the long-overdue acknowledgement of the invisible minority, if only in terms of its need for protection from abuse . . . Discussion about 'sexual orientation' now could become routine, and more and more academic and administrative leaders needed to use the 'L and G words'. The silence was broken. More words followed, and quickly. There was now a context in which the words could be said, and in which they had to be heard.[20]

One important reason for insisting on 'anti-lesbianism' as a conceptual category, then, is to signal our existence and our resistance.

A second key reason for wanting to retain the concept of 'anti-lesbian harassment' relates to the exigencies that structure the social movements and communities from which we would hope for social or political support. The practical reality is that, in many instances, to insist on our 'wholeness', to draw attention to our multiple oppression, is to court disaster. 'Secondary victimisation'[21] is the term used by social scientists to designate the experience of further harassment occurring in the place where you have gone for help. When I tell a friend about an anti-lesbian experience and she retorts, 'Well, you shouldn't have been so blatant', that's secondary victimisation. When a lesbian takes her lover, cut and bruised after an attack on the street, to the hospital, and the medical staff separate the two women, phone parents or ex-husbands and refuse to impart information except to 'next of kin', that's secondary victimisation. Lesbians who, for whatever reasons, do not have access to lesbian organisations and communities, and who turn for help to other groups, are very likely to encounter secondary victimisation in the form of further anti-lesbianism.

Of course, many lesbians encounter secondary victimisation *within* lesbian groups as well. Lesbians with disabilities have written of the ableism of the women's and lesbian movements (as well as describing the sexism and anti-lesbianism of the disability movements).[22] Black lesbians have challenged the racism they are forced to confront in feminist and lesbian groups (as well as speaking out against the sexism and heterosexism of their black communities).[23] Jewish women have written of anti-semitism from lesbians and feminists (and of anti-lesbianism from Jewish sources),[24] while working-class lesbians describe the classism of lesbians and feminists (as well as the anti-lesbianism of their working-class communities).[25] The concept of 'racism' is crucially important for a black lesbian in a white lesbian group; so, too, the concept of 'anti-lesbianism' is crucial for her in a group of black heterosexual women.

Ironically it is precisely because of the indivisibility of oppression that we must insist on identifying each oppression individually. Unless lesbian groups are forced to recognise and deal with anti-semitism, racism, classism, disableism and the like, lesbians who seek help from such groups will experience secondary victimisation from women who conceptualise 'anti-lesbianism' from a purely white, gentile, able-bodied, middle-class perspective. Similarly, unless the communities and movements concerned with other oppression are forced to recognise their own anti-lesbianism, lesbians within those groups will be subject to secondary victimisation in parallel fashion. The only way of making *all* our communities safe for *all* lesbians is by drawing attention to anti-lesbianism in all its forms. We need the category 'anti-lesbian harassment' as a practical political tool in working towards this end.

Notes

1. Cited in Nina Taylor (ed.), *All in a Day's Work: A Report on Anti-lesbian Discrimination in Employment and Unemployment in London* (London: Lesbian Employment Rights, 1986), p. 25.
2. In order not to hold up the argument here, and for the sake of clarity of exposition, I'm deliberately overlooking some French feminists' arguments that lesbians are *not* women: cf. Monique Wittig, 'The Straight Mind', in Sarah Lucia Hoagland and Julia Penelope (eds), *For Lesbians Only: A Separatist Anthology* (London: Onlywomen, 1988).
3. Many heterosexual women, too, conceptualise lesbianism as primarily a sexual activity. This sexualised view of lesbians leads to harassment from heterosexual women, for example:
   [My secretary] used to come into my room because we did a lot of dictation and stuff, but when she closed the door behind her to keep the noise out and then came out later, all the others would be nudging her and making gestures. They'd say things like, 'Aren't you brave going in there and having the door locked. Did she make a pass at you then?'
   In Taylor, *All in a Day's Work*.
4. Jenny Kitzinger and Celia Kitzinger, 'Doing It: Representations of Lesbian Sex', in Gabriele Griffin (ed.), *Popular/izing Lesbian Texts* (London: Pluto, 1993).
5. This is a very common experience. Other similar examples are cited in Taylor, *All in a Day's Work*.
6. I have been offered pornography by men who expected me to join with them in admiring the images, and shown photographs of a yachting holiday with a bikini-clad girlfriend by a man who, as I lingered over one of the snaps, commented jocularly, 'You are meant to be looking at the boat, not the woman.'
7. Linda Garnets, Gregory Herek and Barrie Levy, 'Violence and Victimization of Lesbians and Gay Men: Mental Health Consequences', in Gregory Herek and Kevin Berrill (eds), *Hate Crimes: Confronting Violence against Lesbians and Gay Men* (London: Sage, 1992), p. 213.
8. Garnets, Herek and Levy, 'Violence and Victimization of Lesbian: and Gay Men: Mental Health Consequences'.
9. Beatrice von Schulthess, 'Violence in the Streets: Anti-Lesbian Assault and Harassment in San Francisco', in Herek and Berrill, *Hate Crimes*.
10. Ironically, concern about 'appropriate' gender role behaviour may be exacerbated for lesbians who are 'out'—'There's this stereotype that all lesbians are big tough butch women in trousers and crew cuts,' said a librarian whose colleagues know she is lesbian, 'so I make a special effort to do my hair nicely, and wear quite feminine clothing, skirts and make-up, just to sort of say, "look, we're not all like that".' This is explored further in Celia Kitzinger, 'Lesbian and Gay Men in the Workplace' in Marilyn Davidson and Jill Earnshaw (eds), *Vulnerable Workers: Psychosocial and Legal Issues* (London: Wiley, 1991).
11. Definitions are never simply descriptive, and always rely on an implicit politics. This is the definition of 'lesbian' I choose, as a radical lesbian feminist, to signal my political allegiances. Liberals, humanitarians and non-radical feminists have offered a range of other definitions ('anyone who says she is', 'someone who *prefers* sex with women to sex with men', 'someone who primarily chooses sex with women, but may also have sex with men from time to time', and so on). See Celia Kitzinger, *The Social Construction of Lesbianism* (London: Sage, 1987) for a discussion and critique of liberal humanistic definitions of lesbianism; and Celia Kitzinger and Rachel Perkins, 'Watching Our Language' (Chapter 2), *Changing Our Minds: Lesbian Feminism and Psy-*

chology (London: Onlywomen and New York: New York University Press, 1993) for a discussion and critique of non-radical feminist psychological definitions of lesbianism. My use of the term 'old-fashioned' to characterise the radical feminist definition reflects the extent to which Queer Theory presents itself as the newest and most chic perspective on these issues. According to Queer Theory, the radical challenge to normative definitions of sex and gender comes not from lesbianism per se but from 'fucking with gender'—that is, by doing 'sex' (whether with women or with men) in such a way as to expose the fundamental unnaturalness of conventional definitions of 'male' and 'female'. Attempts to do this include portrayals of lesbians with penises, the celebration of sado-masochism, bisexuality, transvestism and transsexuality, and the reclamation of butch/femme roles. For more information on Queer Theory, see Cherry Smyth, *Lesbians Talk Queer Notions* (London: Scarlet, 1992). For a critique of Queer Theory, see Celia Kitzinger and Sue Wilkinson, 'Virgins and Queers', *Gender & Society* special issue on sexuality (1994).

12. Lisa Tuttle, *Encyclopaedia of Feminism* (London: Arrow, 1986).
13. Nicola Gavey, 'Technologies and Effects of Heterosexual Coercion', in Sue Wilkinson and Celia Kitzinger (eds), *Heterosexuality: A 'Feminism & Psychology' Reader,* (London: Sage, 1993) for a discussion of *women's* difficulties in telling the difference between sexual intercourse and rape; and Lloyd Vogelman, *The Sexual Face of Violence* (Johannesburg: Ravan, 1990) for a discussion of *men's* difficulties in telling the difference between sexual intercourse and rape.
14. See G. Green, M. Barnard, R. Barbour and J. Kitzinger, 'Who Wears the Trousers? Sexual Harassment in Research Settings', *Women's Studies International Forum* 16 (6) (1993), pp. 627–37.
15. White people have races and ethnicities too. Exploration of the role of 'whiteness' in constructing lesbian (or *any*) identities is minimal. I have not discussed 'whiteness' in this chapter because the chapter focuses on oppressed identities. See, however, Peggy McIntosh, 'White Privilege and Male Privilege: A Personal Account of Coming to See Correspondences through Work in Women's Studies', in Margaret Anderson and Patricia Hill Collins (eds), *Race, Class, and Gender: An Anthology* (Belmont, Calif.: Wadsworth, 1992), pp. 70–81; Deborah Jones, 'Looking in My Own Back Yard: The Search for White Feminist Theories of Racism for Aotearoa', in Rosemary Du Plessis (ed.), *Feminist Voices: Women's Studies Texts for Aotearoa/New Zealand* (Oxford: Oxford University Press, 1992); Helen (charles), 'Whiteness—The Relevance of Politically Colouring the "Non"', in Hilary Hinds, Ann Phoenix and Jackie Stacey (eds), *Working Out: New Directions for Women's Studies,* (London: Falmer, 1992); Marilyn Frye, 'White Woman Feminist', in Marilyn Frye, *Willful Virgin: Essays in Feminism* (Freedom, Calif.: Crossing Press, 1992); Ruth Frankenberg, *White Woman, Race Matters: The Social Construction of Whiteness* (London: Routledge, and Minneapolis: University of Minnesota Press, 1993).
16. New York City, San Francisco and Boston all have such groups. See Herek and Berrill, *Hate Crimes.*
17. Lester Olmstead-Rose in 'The Community Response to Violence in San Francisco: An Interview with Wenny Kussuma, Lester Olmstead-Rose, and Jill Tregor', in *Hate Crimes.*
18. Jill Tregor, in 'The Community Response to Violence in San Francisco: An Interview with Wenny Kussuma, Lester Olmstead-Rose, and Jill Tregor', in Herek and Berrill, *Hate Crimes.*
19. Community United Against Violence is concerned about this problem, is actively engaged in outreach work to lesbians of all races and now has a multiracial, multiethnic staff, including people of all races, backgrounds, classes and ages, and people with disabilities.
20. Anthony D'Augelli, 'Lesbians and Gay Men on Campus: Visibility, Empowerment, and Educational Leadership', *Peabody Journal of Education* 66 (3) (1989), pp. 124–41.
21. See, for example, Herek and Berrill, *Hate Crimes.* The term 'victim' has been the subject of some debate within feminism because it is seen as emphasising women's powerlessness rather than our resistance. The term 'survivors' (often used within a psychological framework) is a currently popular alternative. It is important to recognise, however, that some women do *not* 'survive' assaults upon them (they end up dead), and also that no woman is ever responsible for her victimhood. A (presumably unintended) negative effect of the vogue for 'survivorhood' has been an increasing tendency to blame women for being 'victims' rather than 'survivors' (see, for example, the New Age literature critiqued in Sue Wilkinson and Celia Kitzinger, '"Whose Breast

Is It, Anyway?": A Feminist Consideration of Advice and "Treatment" for Breast Cancer', *Women's Studies International Forum,* 16 [2] [1993], pp. 229–38). An extended discussion of the use of the terms 'victim' and 'survivor' in the context of power and powerlessness can be found in Kitzinger and Perkins, *Changing Our Minds,* pp. 39–48.

22. See, for example, Kirsten Hearn, 'Oi! What about Us?' in Bob Cant and Susan Hemmings (eds), *Radical Records: Thirty Years of Lesbian and Gay History* (London: Routledge, 1988); M. Sorella, 'Lies, Lies and More Lies', *Sinister Wisdom,* 35 (1988), pp. 58–71.

23. See, for example, Cheryl Clarke, 'The Failure to Transform: Homophobia in the Black Community', in Barbara Smith (ed.), *Home Girls: A Black Feminist Anthology* (New York: Kitchen Table Women of Color Press, 1983).

24. For example, Evelyn Torton Beck, *Nice Jewish Girls: A Lesbian Anthology* (Watertown, Mass.: Persephone, 1982); Merril Mushroom, 'Merrill Mushroom is a Jew', *Common Lives, Lesbian Lives: A Lesbian Quarterly* 7 (1983), pp. 78–85.

25. See the special issue of *Lesbian Ethics* on class and classism (Spring, 1991, 4 [2]) and the special issue of *Sinister Wisdom* on lesbians and class (Winter 1991, 45).

---

42. Immigrant Latina Domestic Workers and Sexual Harassment

Diana Vellos

I. SEXUAL AND ECONOMIC EXPLOITATION OF UNDOCUMENTED DOMESTIC WORKERS

Undocumented Latina domestic workers are faced with low wages and hostile working conditions. These women are vulnerable. "Employers can, and do, exploit undocumented workers by paying them substandard or illegally low wages and blocking their attempts . . . to improve conditions in the workplace."[1] Undocumented Latina workers are especially vulnerable to sexual harassment.[2] Suzanne Goldberg describes a possible work environment in which an undocumented Latina domestic would be placed.

> Pia, a thirty-five year old woman from El Salvador, has lived and worked in California for the last few years. She speaks minimal English and does not have a green card or other documentation allowing her to remain legally in the United States. She has family in El Salvador and some cousins and other relatives living and working (as household workers and day laborers) in the vicinity. She lives with a young white professional couple and their three small children. She earns low wages ($80 per week) and has no Social Security, workers' compensation, or unemployment coverage. She has Sunday off each week, although the employers will occasionally ask her to work when they have another engagement that day . . . She would like to obtain legal documentation, then find other work and arrange for her family to immigrate. She has never been physically or sexually assaulted by the father of the children she cares for, but he and his friends have alarmed her with their sexual suggestion.[3]

In the hypothetical that Goldberg creates, Pia does not experience a sexual assault, but is concerned about the sexual suggestions that her employer makes. Goldberg goes on to describe that Pia "fears sexual exploitation by her male employer and his friends, having heard stories ranging from requests for stripteases to actual rape."[4] In Goldberg's scenario, none of Pia's colleagues reported to the police their stories of abuse.[5]

Even though Pia's story is hypothetical, it is very useful in gaining an understanding of the fears and sexual exploitation undocumented domestic workers face. Unfortunately, there are not many reported cases of sexual abuse experienced by undocumented workers, mainly because undocumented workers depend upon their employers for their livelihood.[6] Consequently, they feel vulnerable to their employers' demands and fear being deported back to their native land.[7]

Goldberg notes that Pia experienced economic necessity, which also can trap women into exploitative positions.[8]

> Pia feels she cannot financially afford to be jobless, even for a few weeks. Also, although she has occasionally tried to find a better paying job which would offer more security and benefits, she has not succeeded either for lack of documentation or, she senses, because of generalized discrimination by employers against foreigners.[9]

Understanding the concept of economic necessity is vital to understanding the issues facing undocumented domestic workers.[10] Many cannot afford the luxury of quitting their current jobs to find better employment.[11] Even though there are networking systems in the domestic service field, undocumented workers are at a disadvantage because of their lack of documentation.[12] Undocumented domestics make employment decisions which reflect their concerns about immigration status, language ability, sexism, racism, poverty, family, and other factors that shape their lives.[13] Many times this balancing of concerns results in women feeling compelled to remain in abusive environments.

Why, then, do undocumented immigrant women go into domestic service if they are paid low wages and fear sexual advances? Many undocumented domestics feel their risk of entrapment by the INS [Immigration and Naturalization Service] is considerably lower in a private home than it is in a public place such as a factory.[14] In addition, the wages and working conditions would not necessarily be better for an undocumented female worker in a public place of employment. Undocumented immigrant women often work in conditions far worse than, and for wages that are below, those offered to immigrant men or non-immigrants.[15]

Exploitation of undocumented domestic workers is accepted by our society. Society expects undocumented workers to accept the least desirable jobs for the least amount of pay. They are expected to put up with abusive working environments and no benefits. The mentality seems to be, if the aliens do not like it, they can leave. According to INS official James Smith, "It's human nature—the abuse and exploitation."[16]

Mary Romero also recounts an incident she witnessed with an undocumented domestic worker and the sexual remarks she encountered:

> I was shocked at my colleague's treatment of the sixteen-year-old domestic whom I will call Juanita. Only recently hired, Juanita was still adjusting to her new environment. She was extremely shy, and her timidity was made even worse by constant flirting from her employer. As far as I could see, every attempt Juanita made to converse was met with teasing so that the conversation could never evolve into a serious discussion. Her employer's sexist, paternalistic banter effectively silenced the domestic, kept her constantly on guard, and made it impossible for her to feel comfortable at work.[17]

Romero describes how Juanita's employer would attempt to break the tension in diffi-cult situations with flirtatious and sexist remarks to Juanita.[18] In the situation Romero re-counts, there is no mention of a sexual assault, but the sexual remarks commonly made cre-ated an uncomfortable working environment for Juanita. Because of the lack of reporting among undocumented workers, it is hard to analyze any statistical data.

II. Case Law Addressing Sexual Harassment of Undocumented Women

There are several cases in which undocumented workers who were sexually harassed brought suit and won. One of the first such cases brought, *United States v. Davila,*[19] in-volved two undocumented women who were sexually assaulted by two border patrol offi-cers.[20] The officers stopped an automobile containing two United States Army privates and two Mexican women.[21] The car entered the country illegally.[22] The border patrol officers kept the two women in their custody and "exacted a price for their liberty."[23] That price was sexual intercourse.[24] The private, who was engaged to one of the Mexican women, filed charges with the INS after he discovered what had happened.[25] Both officers were charged with sexually abusing the two Mexican women and with conspiring to deprive the women of their liberty by coercing sexual favors from them.[26] The border patrol officers were found guilty of the charges.[27] The Fifth Circuit Court found a high degree of corroboration in the testimony of the soldiers and the women surrounding the stop and the sexual assault.[28] This degree of corroboration was more than sufficient to allow a reasonable jury to identify the defendants as the perpetrators.[29]

There are two interesting aspects about this case. First, this case deals with border pa-trol officers. This triggers the protections embodied in the idea of "under color of any law.[30] The officers not only violated the law by coercing sexual intercourse from the undocu-mented women, but they used their positions as governmental officials to do so.[31] This is obviously distinguishable from a situation where an employer coerces sexual acts from an undocumented domestic. In the first situation, the wrongful use of a governmental posi-tion is an issue, whereas in the second situation there is no such issue. The second inter-esting point about this case is that one of the women's fiancé was the person who filed the claim with the INS.[32] He was a private in the military and a United States citizen.[33] One of the likely reasons this case went to litigation is that the women had a support network of United States citizen contacts to help them bring suit. Most undocumented domestic workers do not have such support networks.[34] Many times undocumented domestics feel isolated and are uninformed about their rights under United States law.[35]

Mary Romero discusses this feeling of isolation experienced by many undocumented workers in domestic service.[36] Romero notes how Juanita, the undocumented worker whom she met while staying at a colleague's house, experienced this alienating feeling.[37] "Juanita lowered her head and in a sad, quiet voice told me how isolated and lonely she felt in this middle-class suburb literally within sight of Juarez."[38] Romero explains that Juanita's isolation and loneliness were in response to the norms and values surrounding do-mestic service.[39] Many domestics experience isolation even though they work in large households.[40] Live-in Latina immigrant domestics are separated from family and friends, living with employers who consider them to be invisible. Undocumented Latina domestic workers experience culture shock and language barriers.[41] All of these factors create a feel-ing of isolation, which can and does inhibit many undocumented domestics from chal-lenging exploitative work environments.[42]

EEOC v. Hacienda Hotel[43] raises other interesting issues surrounding undocumented women workers and sexual harassment. Hacienda Hotel is a case in which the EEOC alleged that the hotel general manager, executive housekeeper, and chief of engineering engaged in unlawful employment practices against female housekeeping department employees.[44] The unlawful employment practices included sexually harassing women, terminating them when they became pregnant, failing to accommodate their religious beliefs, and retaliating against them for opposing Hacienda's discriminatory practices.[45] The suit involved five current and former Hacienda maids, all but one of whom were undocumented workers.[46]

When some of the women became pregnant, comments such as "that's what you get for sleeping without your underwear," "stupid women who have kids," "dog," "whore," and "slut" were made by the managing staff of the hotel.[47] Other comments such as "women get pregnant because they like to suck men's dicks" were also made to pregnant workers.[48] These women workers were also terminated due to their pregnancies, after being informed that they were too fat to clean rooms.[49] On many occasions, the chief of engineering threatened to have workers fired if they did not submit to his sexual advances.[50] The chief of engineering also made sexually harassing comments to the women domestics at the hotel.[51] Mercedes Flores, one of the immigrant domestics who brought suit, stated that the chief of engineering regularly offered her money and an apartment to live in if she would "give him [her] body".[52] He also assured her that she would never be fired if she would have sex with him.[53]

The Ninth Circuit Court found that Hacienda's practice of terminating pregnant employees violated Title VII and that the hotel was liable for sexual harassment by its supervisors.[54] This factual situation is different from that experienced by undocumented live-in workers who work in private homes. The women in the Hacienda Hotel had each other for support and corroboration.[55] The stories of each of the women strengthened the story of each individual woman. Domestics working in private homes do not have other people to validate or strengthen their stories, and are isolated from other individuals who would be willing and able to attest to their exploitation.[56] Typically, it is the undocumented domestic worker's word against their employer, who usually appears to be an upstanding member of society.[57]

Harassment of immigrant women is common.[58] One District Attorney's office and a community group in a Northern California town concluded, based on their investigation in a local case of sexual abuse, that such episodes happen quite often.[59] For instance, Maria de Jesus Ramos Hernandez,[60] who traveled from Mexico to the United States to work for a chiropractor, in order to raise money for an operation to cure her daughter's birth defect.[61] Almost immediately, her employer began to sexually abuse her.[62] She did not immediately report the attacks or run away because she was alone and isolated, with no place to go. She felt she "could not deny him pleasure . . . because of what he paid her."[63] Ramos Hernandez did not immediately report the abuse for many reasons.[64] She was afraid that the doctor would kill her (and no one would even notice she was missing); she had no money, identification, or knowledge of English; she did not think that the police would believe her word against that of a doctor; and she felt that she would be blamed.[65]

Ramos Hernandez's story is similar in many ways to the abuse that other immigrant women face working in the home. Her story helps explain why undocumented women are unable to take action to end the harassment they experience. To respond aggressively to the harassment, they must confront their learned cultural values, including self-blame and passivity. Their inability to understand the situation is further complicated because their cultures have different views of sexuality, which may not include the concept of sexual harassment.[66]

Maria Ontiveros noted that the race and gender of immigrant women shape and enhance the harasser's actions.[67] Harassers choose these women because they lack power relative to other workers, and because they are often perceived as passive and unable to complain.[68] Racism and sexism blend together in the mind of the harasser, so that comments made and actions taken against the immigrant women workers embody unique characteristics of their racially stereotyped sexuality.[69] In many ways undocumented working women are targets of discriminatory harassment because of their race. . . .[70]

III. RECOMMENDATIONS

A wide variety of suggestions have arisen from the dilemma of undocumented domestics. Many of these solutions are for the ease and peace of mind of the employer. The domestic becomes somehow invisible in the discussion. It seems that an employer-centered approach to this problem would only perpetuate the discrimination and isolation that undocumented domestics experience. Solutions which focus on the needs and concerns of the exploitable domestic have to be at the center of the discussion in order for the exploitation to be addressed.

Many scholars in this field suggest that there be a liberal immigration policy which would allow immigrant domestics to work legally.[71] There are two guiding objectives: first, to facilitate workers' coverage under relevant employment laws, and second, to minimize the decrease in job supply while enforcing the financial obligations of those who can afford to pay them.[72] Another goal is to reduce the vulnerability and exploitability of immigrant women, particularly those who lack legal paperwork or residence documentation.[73]

One proposal which liberalizes immigration law would exclude household workers under the IRCA [Immigration Reform and Control Act of 1986] thereby permitting employers to hire such workers legally.[74] Under this type of proposal, employers would be required to pay taxes for undocumented domestic workers.[75] This type of proposal has both positive and negative effects for an undocumented domestic worker.

On the positive side, the undocumented domestic worker no longer fears being fired for lack of documentation. The domestic worker will probably have a greater sense of security and will almost entirely overcome her increased difficulty in requesting changes in employment conditions. On the negative side, sexual harassment practices are not stopped in any significant way under this type of proposal. An undocumented domestic will not receive any of the benefits given to documented workers under this proposal.[76] Benefits such as social security, unemployment, and disability will not apply to undocumented workers until the IRCA is changed.[77] Due to this, employers may not be willing to give undocumented domestics raises or vacation time because they feel that they are already paying taxes on the domestics' behalf.[78] It is important to note that a law designed to help women must do more than provide special immigration benefits, it must also guarantee increased wages and benefits for those engaged in work traditionally performed by women.[79]

Another possibility is for household workers to organize.[80] Household workers confront a daunting challenge in the very idea of organizing for change by seeking "rights, privileges, and protections associated with the workplace in a sphere governed by personal and familial values."[81] Domestic workers have a generalized distrust of professional women's and feminist organizations' efforts of assistance.[82] There is also a widespread mistrust of lawyers which impedes organizational efforts by outsiders.[83] Because of these ideological conceptions, workers' organizations are more of an historical phenomenon than a reality.[84]

Scholars such as M. Isabel Medina suggest that a more effective method of preventing abuse of undocumented workers is to more strictly enforce existing labor laws,[85] such as the Occupational Safety and Health Act,[86] the Fair Labor Standards Act,[87] social security laws, unemployment insurance laws, the Age Discrimination in Employment Act,[88] and Title VII.[89] It is contended that stricter enforcement of these laws would "reduce the incentive for employers to hire undocumented workers and to protect against their exploitation."[90] Enforcement of these laws, especially Title VII, would be problematic for undocumented domestics. Title VII is effective only in establishments with twenty-five or more employees.[91] Undocumented domestic workers often do not work in an establishment where there are twenty-five workers because they work in a home. Title VII, which protects against sexual harassment, therefore does not protect most undocumented domestics. It is apparent that undocumented workers are not adequately protected under current laws. New legislation needs to be implemented which would empower and protect undocumented domestic workers who are the most vulnerable to economic and sexual exploitation.

Obviously, undocumented workers are at risk for abuse. One solution to prevent the abuse is to facilitate and streamline the legal immigration of domestic workers. This would ensure that immigrant workers who are hired would receive competitive salaries and fair treatment because they would no longer be "indentured" to the employer who sponsored them for legalization, and would be free to seek better employment if they choose.[92] This proposal would enable undocumented domestics to work legally, and to have the mobility to leave exploitative work environments.

IV. CONCLUSION

The situation which undocumented domestics face is complex because issues of racism, sexism, classism and nationalism are all involved. Undocumented domestics are extremely vulnerable to exploitation both sexually and economically. The current immigration system must be changed so that undocumented domestic workers will have opportunities to work without the fear of deportation and abuse. The services they provide are in grave demand.[93] Accordingly, the women who give these services should be given the dignity they deserve to work and live.

Immigration laws must be changed so that undocumented domestic workers have viable legal options for immigration which do not trap or coerce them into exploitative jobs. These workers need mobility so that they have the opportunity to leave exploitative work environments. If the focus is switched from the needs of the employers to the needs of the exploited worker, issues such as sexual harassment can be properly addressed.

Notes

1. Peter Margulies, *Stranger and Afraid: Undocumented Workers and Federal Employment Law,* 38 DePaul L. Rev. 553, 554 (1989).
2. Suzanne Goldberg, *In Pursuit of Workplace Rights: Household Workers and a Conflict of Laws,* 3 Yale J.L. & Feminism 63, 85 (1990).
3. Goldberg, *supra* note 2, at 63.
4. Goldberg, *supra* note 2, at 63.
5. Goldberg, *supra* note 2, at 82.
6. Goldberg, *supra* note 2, at 82.
7. Goldberg, *supra* note 2, at 82.
8. Goldberg, *supra* note 2, at 82.
9. Goldberg, *supra* note 2, at 81 (commenting that Pia also fears her employers might fire her to hire another woman with legal residential status).
10. Goldberg, *supra* note 2, at 81.

11. Goldberg, *supra* note 2, at 81.

12. Goldberg, *supra* note 2, at 81 (adding that Pia may also be at a disadvantage because of generalized discrimination by employers against foreigners).

13. Goldberg, *supra* note 2, at 82.

14. Goldberg, *supra* note 2, at 81 (stating "Pia" felt safer working in a private residence than in a public place).

15. Maria L. Ontiveros, *To Help Those Most in Need: Undocumented Workers' Rights and Remedies Under Title VII*, 20 N.Y.U. Rev. L. & Soc. Change 607, 618 (1993–1994). *See* Leo L. Lam, Comment, *Designer Duty: Extending Liability to Manufacturers for Violations of Labor Standards in Garment Industry Sweatshops* 141 U. Pa. L. Rev. 623 (1992) (explaining that the garment industry is a labor-intensive industry which is home to small sewing factories that operate under substandard working conditions). The typical garment worker is usually a Latina or an Asian female immigrant who moved to a big city in the United States in search of economic opportunity. These garment laborers work in sweatshops, which regularly violate both wage or child labor and safety or health laws. *Id.* Shop owners often pay their workers, a majority of whom are women, less than half of the federal minimum wage. *Id.* at 633.

16. Quintanilla & Copeland, *Mexican Maids: El Paso's Worst-Kept Secret, in Special Report: The Border,* El Paso Herald Post, Summer 1983, at 84.

17. Mary Romero, *Maid in the USA* 7 (1992), at 2. Many women expressed embarrassment at being identified by their work as housekeepers or cleaning ladies. Some women chose to keep that part of their lives somewhat secretive.

18. Romero, *supra* note 17, at 3 (explaining that the employer felt he was aiding Mexican women from Juarez by helping them cross the border and employing them in his home).

19. 704 F.2d 749 (5th Cir. 1983).

20. *Id.* at 751.

21. *Id.*

22. *Id.*

23. *Id.*

24. *Davila,* 704 F.2d at 751 (stating the incident occurred at an apartment owned by Davila, one of the defendants).

25. *Id.* (stating one of the Mexican women, Alicia Ortiz, told her fiancé, Warren Palmer, about the incident, and he filed a claim).

26. *Id.*

27. *Id.*

28. *Id.* at 751–52 (stating that the Mexican women were able to identify the outside of the apartment where they were taken and where the incident occurred. The apartment was leased to Davila, and the women described the interior of the apartment with accurate detail and without having to enter it again. This description was corroborated by defendant Davila's wife, who was out of town on the date of the incident).

29. *Id.* at 752.

30. *See* 18 U.S.C. § 242 (stating "whoever, under color of any law, statute, ordinance, regulation, or custom, willfully subjects any person in any State, Territory, Commonwealth, Possession, or District to the deprivation of any rights, privileges, or immunities secured or protected by the Constitution or laws of the United States" shall be guilty of an offense against the United States).

31. *Davila,* 704 F.2d at 751.

32. *Id.*

33. *Id.*

34. Romero, *supra* note 17, at 6.

35. Romero, *supra* note 17, at 92.

36. Romero, *supra* note 17, at 4.

37. Romero, *supra* note 17, at 3.

38. Romero, *supra* note 17, at 3.

39. Romero, *supra* note 17, at 3.

40. Romero, *supra* note 17, at 3.
41. Romero, *supra* note 17, at 4 (stating that communication between immigrant domestics and their employers was impossible due to social isolation and language barriers).
42. Romero, *supra* note 17, at 4.
43. 881 F.2d 1504 (9th Cir. 1989).
44. *Id.* at 1507.
45. *Id.*
46. *Id.*
47. *Id.* Theodora Castro, one of the women involved in the case, was subjected to such remarks from both the executive housekeeper and the chief of engineering.
48. *Hacienda Hotel,* 881 F.2d at 1508 (noting that Flora Villalobos had this comment directed at her during her pregnancy).
49. *Id.* (stating that Leticia Cardona was informed during her seventh month of pregnancy that she was too fat to clean rooms and was terminated even though she was willing and able to work and had a note from her doctor indicating she would be able to continue her duties until two or three weeks before her estimated delivery date).
50. *Id.* at 1508.
51. *Id.* (stating that the chief of engineering commented that Villalobos had "such a fine ass. It's a nice ass to stick a nice dick into. How many dicks have you eaten?").
52. *Hacienda Hotel,* 881 F.2d at 1508.
53. *Id.*
54. *Id.* at 1519.
55. *Id.* at 1508.
56. Romero, *supra* note 17, at 3–4.
57. *See* Doreen Carvajal, *For Immigrant Maids, Not a Job But Servitude,* N.Y. Times, Feb. 25, 1996, at A1 (reporting the story of Erelkina Flores, who sued an employer after the employer accused her of stealing four hundred dollars, and subjected her to a strip search); *see also* Romero, *supra* note 17, at 4 (stating that hiring immigrant domestics was viewed as charity by American middle class persons).
58. Suzanne Espinoza, *Remembering the Pain: Female Immigrants Tell of Abuse,* S.F. Chron., Mar. 9, 1993, at A11, A12 (noting the frequency of human rights violations against immigrant women in the United States and reporting on the seven-hour conference held to call attention to the problem).
59. Carla Marinucci, *Despair Drove Her to Come Forward,* S.F. Examiner, Jan. 10, 1993, at A11.
60. *Id.*
61. *Id.* (Maria's one-year-old daughter had pyloric stenosis, which caused constant vomiting and kept her from properly digesting food, resulting in a weight of only twelve pounds).
62. *Id.* (stating her employer was violent and warned her that resistance would "get her sent to Tijuana, " where she would be gang raped by men).
63. *Id.*
64. Marinucci, *supra* note 59, at A11.
65. Marinucci, *supra* note 59, at A11.
66. Marinucci, *supra* note 59, at A11.
67. Ontiveros, *supra* note 15, at 612.
68. *Id.*
69. *Id.* at 818–19. For example, harassment aimed against African American women has incorporated images of slavery, degradation, sexual availability, and natural lasciviousness. Asian American women have been portrayed by their harassers as exotic, submissive, and naturally erotic. Latinas have been perceived as naturally sexual and available. *Id.* n. 103.
70. *Id.*
71. *See* Ontiveros, *supra* note 15, at 608–12 (arguing that the current structure of labor and immigration laws do not allow undocumented workers remedies against employers who exploit them); *but see* Margulies, *supra* note 1, at 555 (arguing that granting undocumented workers ac-

cess to comprehensive remedies for violations of employment law would reduce demand for such workers).

72. Goldberg, *supra* note 2, at 78.
73. Goldberg, *supra* note 2, at 93–94.
74. Goldberg, *supra* note 2, at 79.
75. Goldberg, *supra* note 2, at 79.
76. Goldberg, *supra* note 2, at 79.
77. Goldberg, *supra* note 2, at 79.
78. Goldberg, *supra* note 2, at 75.
79. Nancy Ann Root & Sharyn A. Tejani, *Undocumented: The Roles of Women in Immigration Law,* 83 GEO. L.J. 614–15 (1994).
80. Goldberg, *supra* note 2, at 75.
81. Goldberg, *supra* note 2, at 75.
82. Chaney & Castro, *A New Field for Research and Action,* in Muchachas No More 4 (1989).
83. Gerald Lopez, *The Work We Know So Little About,* 42 Stan. L. Rev. 1, 5 (1989) (arguing that this distrust is particularly prevalent among women of color.) "Instead of using law and lawyers, most low income women of color apparently often deal with oppressive circumstances through their own stock of informal strategies." *Id.* at 8.
84. Goldberg, *supra* note 2, at 75.
85. *See* Medina, note 90, at 173 (arguing that such a policy would shift the burden from employee to employer and reduce employer discrimination).
86. 29 U.S.C. § 651 (1994).
87. 29 U.S.C. § 201 (1994).
88. 29 U.S.C. § 621 (1994).
89. 42 U.S.C. § 2000(e) (1994). Under Title VII, traditional remedies designed for documented workers might not apply to undocumented workers because of a poor fit between the legal doctrine and their status. Undocumented workers cannot be reinstated because they cannot legally work here. Additionally, backpay and front pay generally have been limited to people available to work. Undocumented workers may be considered *de jure* unavailable. Nonetheless, it is clear that the purposes underlying Title VII remedies apply equally to undocumented workers and in most cases do not undermine IRCA. For this to happen, however, the current doctrine must be liberally construed or additional remedies must be created. *See* Ontiveros, *supra* note 15, at 608.
90. M. Isabel Medina, "In Search of Quality Childcare: Closing the Immigration Gate to Childcare Workers," 8 *Geo. Immigra. L.J.,* 173 (1994).
91. 42 U.S.C. § 2000(e) (1994). *See also* Margulies, *supra* note 1, at 577.
92. Goldberg, *supra* note 2, at 174.
93. Medina, *supra* note 90, at 197 (stating that United States Department of Labor statistics indicate that the U.S. market has a shortage of domestic childcare providers); *see also* David McGree, *Reopening Liberty's Arms: Steps Toward Open Immigration,* 4 Kan. J.L. & Pub. Pol'y 127, 128 (1994) (reporting that about one and a half million households hire immigrants as nannies or housekeepers).

❖ 43. Japan Abuzz Over Sexual Harassment

Nicole Gaouette

This story is about a powerful boss, a star-struck junior employee, sexual-harassment allegations, and a media frenzy that would put feeding sharks to shame. Sound familiar? Wait.

The boss is Seiko Matsuda, also known as Japan's Madonna. She's a pop singer with a big smile and a knack for managing the media.

The employee is Christopher Conte, a chiseled American dancer who toured with Ms. Matsuda for years and now claims she sexually harassed him.

Reports in the more sensational press have people tittering, but activists are taking the suit seriously: They're hoping the case will raise awareness about sexual harassment. Given the timing, they actually have a shot.

The Labor Ministry has just unveiled a campaign to highlight a significant change in Japan's approach to the issue: an amendment that makes firms liable in sexual harassment cases as of April 1999. "It's the first law that actually addresses sexual harassment," says Junichiro Numazaki, a professor at Tohoku University in Sendai and an antisexual-harassment activist.

Currently, firms are simply urged to discourage harassment. But the government's amendment of a 1986 employment law last June changed all that. Mr. Numazaki has reservations about the new measure's clarity, but he's upbeat. "This is an improvement," he says.

The Matsuda suit marks the first time a woman has been sued for sexual harassment in Japan. (Activists joke that it's likely to be the last, since so few women wield power here.) Despite its unusual nature, many hope the case will show sexual harassment can be countered.

Sixty percent of women say *sekuhara,* as sexual harassment is known, happens in their office, recent government figures show. While women experience harassment though, few see it as an act they can fight legally.

First-Hand Experience

Yukiko Takiguchi, a talkative homemaker who used to work as a flight attendant for a Japanese airline, says she dealt with pilots who perused "Playboy"-like magazines and a manager who made "disgusting and shocking" comments about her body.

It made her furious, but she did nothing. "I was worried about my job." she says.

Japanese corporate culture also makes it hard to act. It discourages any kind of personal criticism, and lower-ranked employees are never supposed to complain about a superior.

Today, with the Matsuda case and articles about the government's *sekuhara* campaign. Ms. Takiguchi is thinking differently. "I've become much more aware of the issue," she says. "[Now] I would talk to a woman manager in the office. Or I would say to [my manager], 'People call this sexual harassment, sir. You should watch what you say.'"

Awareness of *sekuhara* as a crime is low compared with the US. Indeed, visitors might see aspects of Japanese working life as conducive to harassment. Working women (most of whom are in low-status clerical positions) are often referred to as "office flowers." Most of the sports newspapers that men read feature large photos of nude models. And evening office outings can be difficult to manage, women say.

AFTER-HOURS HARASSMENT

A lot of work in Japan gets done after 5 p.m., when people go to bars or restaurants to forge the personal ties essential to doing business here. Most of that relationship-building involves copious amounts of alcohol. (This practice is such a part of business life that there's slang for it: "*nomu-nication*," *nomu* is the verb "to drink.") A cultural understanding that almost anything done while drunk is permissible provides a way out for those who misbehave.

The work evenings are one of the areas activists worry about, as the law doesn't discuss these situations. "They're out of the office, [but] the environment is no different for a secretary," says Numazaki. "How can she refuse once her boss starts doing something weird?"

The central challenge, activists say, is education. "People still aren't sure of what the word [*sekuhara*] means," says Tokyo lawyer Asako Shirato, who runs a sexual-harassment hot line.

Into this void danced Mr. Conte, whose unusual $3 million lawsuit, filed in March, is heightening awareness of the underlying dynamic of *sekuhara:* the power a superior wields over an employee. A New York native who uses the stage name Alan Reed, Conte came to Japan in the early 1990s to perform at Tokyo Disneyland. He then toured with Matsuda from 1992 to 1997. They reportedly had an intimate relationship during those years, though Conte now argues she threatened to fire him if he didn't comply with her demands.

Neither he nor Matsuda would comment on the case, but in a just-published book, "Backstage of [sic] Seiko Matsuda," Conte outlines his grievance. The slim volume, written in Japanese, is filled with copies of her love letters and photos of the two hugging and smiling. Underneath, the captions generally begin "Can you believe this is a woman who would . . ." and go on to detail some aspect of the alleged harassment.

NOT JUST A US PROBLEM

Despite or maybe because of the Matsuda case, there's still a strong sense that harassment is more of an American problem. Until now, the most well-known *sekuhara* conflict here was a 1996 suit filed against Mitsubishi Motors Corp. by female workers in Illinois. That suit recently headed into settlement negotiations.

One American insurance company offers Japanese businessmen posted in the US special insurance against *sekuhara* claims. For the past few years, Keidanren, a group representing Japan's largest companies, has offered biannual sexual harassment seminars for US-bound businessmen. But Keidanren offers no training on the issue as a domestic problem. "Until two or three years ago, we never heard of sexual harassment in Japan," says Keidanren spokeswoman Tomoko Hasegawa.

The government aims to remedy that. The Labor Ministry has just released a pamphlet that defines sexual harassment and gives examples of potentially offensive behavior, including the display of nude photos.

Despite the progress, there are cynics. Yoko Matsumura's law office occasionally sees women who would like to take action but shrink at facing the legal system. "There aren't enough women police officers and judges," she explains.

MOST JAPANESE WOMEN KNOW HARASSMENT

Japan's Ministry of Labor conducted its first surveys on sexual harassment last summer. It questioned 2,254 companies across the country. Employees from 35 percent of the firms responded. The ministry also sent a separate survey to government bureaus. Here's what it found:

- 60 percent of Japanese women say they have witnessed sexual harassment at the office.
- 20 percent of female government workers and 1 percent of male government workers report having been sexually harassed.
- 6.2 percent of female government employees say they have been sexually assaulted or almost assaulted by male colleagues or other bureaucrats.
- 56 percent of women who have been harassed ignore it, 35 percent complained to their harasser, and 18 percent spoke to colleagues.
- 31 percent of women said they would use a sexual harassment consulting service at the office if it existed.
- More than 90 percent of firms say they need to do something about sexual harassment, but only 5.5 percent have done so.
- When asked about the sexual harassment of their firm, 37 percent of companies admitted it could happen, 31 percent said it "never" takes place, and 32 percent said they didn't know.

Source: Ministry of Labor, 1997.

On top of that, there is a cultural bias against those who bring lawsuits in general as it disrupts Japan's highly prized social harmony. "People get bullied or pointed at by others [for bringing them]," says Numazaki.

That helps explain why the country has seen only some 100 sexual-harassment suits, mostly in recent years.

"Americans would probably be surprised at how low the number is," says Mizuho Fukushima. Japan's leading female lawyer. "But I think, 'Finally, it's got this far.'"

44. Sexual Harassment of Working Women in India

Ramni Taneja

DISCRIMINATION AGAINST WOMEN

An editorial appearing on 2 June 1997 in the English language newspaper in India *The Times of India,* contained the following stark comments: 'Discrimination against women from cradle to grave has become so much a part of the social fabric [of India] that the frightening figures published each year documenting the missing 40 to 50 million girls who would be expected to be alive has ceased to shock. The survivors fare little better. An apathetic society and a callous government have turned a blind eye to the mounting atrocities against women—the latest figures reveal that there is one rape every 54 minutes, a molestation every 26 minutes, a dowry death every two hours and an act of cruelty every 33 minutes . . .' A writer, Praful Bidwai, writing in the 5 June 1997 issue of the same newspaper, mentions certain other shocking aspects of the position of Indian women in India: 'Indian women suffer systematic discrimination at every stage: female foeticide, nutritional deprivation in infancy, reduced access to food and schooling in adolescence. Unequal employment opportunities as adults, and reduced access to healthcare at all ages. Discrimination threatens women's very survival. Although women are hardier than men, India's sex ratio has declined from 972 in 1901 to 927, putting 50 million in the "missing" category.' Conscious of these alarming statistics, the Government of India has, on 2 October 1997, launched a scheme called 'the Girl Child Scheme', which is aimed at transforming the social perception of girls from 'curses and liabilities' to sought-after family members, especially among the very poor who live below the poverty line.

LANDMARK VERDICT

Against this background, it is heartening that the highest court in India, the Supreme Court of India, has on 13 August 1997 (just two days before India's 50th anniversary of independence), delivered a landmark verdict, protecting the position of working women and formulating certain guidelines and norms to ensure the prevention of sexual harassment of working women in India. This judgment, entitled *Vishaka and others v State of Rajasthan and others,* reported in 1997 AIR SCW 3043 has been given by a three judge bench, comprising the Chief Justice of India, ie Mr Justice S Verma, Mrs Justice Sujata V Manohar and Mr Justice B N Kirpal. As the court has explained in the preliminary paragraphs of the judgment, the immediate cause for the filing of this writ petition is an incident of alleged brutal rape of a social worker, Bhanwari Devi, in a village of Rajasthan. One of the counsel appearing for the petitioners in the case, Ms Meenakshi Arora, has clarified to this writer that the social worker was gang-raped because she tried to prevent a child marriage. In the eloquent words of the court: 'The incident reveals the hazards to which a working woman may be exposed and the depravity to which sexual harassment can degenerate; and the urgency for safeguards by an alternative mechanism in the absence of legislative measures.' The court notes that this petition was filed as a class action by certain social activists and NGOs (non-governmental organisations) with the aim of focusing attention towards this societal aberration, and assisting in finding suitable methods for realisation of the true concept of 'gender equality'.

The court categorically observes that each such incident results in a violation of the fundamental rights of 'Gender Equality' and the 'Right to Life and Liberty'. In the court's opinion, it is a clear violation of the rights under Articles 14,[1] 15[2] and 21[3] of the Constitution of India. The court further explains that one of the logical consequences of such an incident is also the violation of the victim's fundamental right under Article 19(1) (g) 'to practise any profession or to carry out any occupation, trade or business'. Such violations, therefore attract the remedy under Article 32[4] of the Constitution of India for the enforcement of these fundamental rights of women. The court has clarified that the fundamental right to carry on any occupation, trade or profession depends on the availability of a 'safe' working environment. The court has emphasised that 'when, however, instances of sexual harassment resulting in violation of fundamental rights of women workers under Articles 14, 19 and 21 are brought before us for redress under Article 32, all effective redress requires that some guidelines should be laid down for the protection of these rights to fill the legislative vacuum'.

Interestingly, the Supreme Court of India has relied upon international conventions and norms in this case, while formulating the norms and guidelines, including the *Convention on the Elimination of All Forms of Discrimination Against Women*. [See Selection 57.] The court notes: 'In the absence of domestic law occupying the field, to formulate effective measures to check the evil of sexual harassment of working women at all work places, the contents of International Conventions and norms are significant for the purpose of interpretation of the guarantee of gender equality, right to work with human dignity in Articles 14, 15, 19(1) (g) and 21 of the Constitution [of India] and the safeguards against sexual harassment implicit therein . . . This is implicit from Article 51 (c) of the Constitution [of India] and the enabling power of the Parliament to enact laws for implementing the International Conventions and norms by virtue of Article 253 read with Entry 14 of the Union List in [the] Seventh Schedule of the Constitution [of India].' The court has clarified that 'the meaning and content of the fundamental rights guaranteed in the Constitution of India are of sufficient amplitude to encompass all the facets of gender equality including prevention of sexual harassment or abuse.' In exercise of the power available to it under Article 32 of the Constitution of India for the enforcement of fundamental rights, the court emphasises that the guidelines stipulated in its judgment are to be treated as the law declared by it under Article 141[5] of the Constitution of India.

GUIDELINES

Some of the relevant Guidelines set out by the court in its judgment are summarised below. Sexual harassment has been defined in Guideline 2 entitled 'Definitions', in the following terms: 'Sexual harassment includes such unwelcome sexually determined behaviour (whether directly or by implication) as: (a) physical contact and advances; (b) a demand or request for sexual favours; (c) sexually coloured remarks; (d) showing pornography; (e) any other unwelcome physical, verbal, or non-verbal conduct of [a] sexual nature. Where any of these acts is committed in circumstances whereunder the victim of such conduct has a reasonable apprehension that in relation to the victim's employment or work whether she is drawing salary, or honorarium or voluntary, whether in Government, public or private enterprise such conduct can be humiliating and may constitute a health and safety problem.'

Guideline 1 stipulates that it shall be the duty of the employer or other responsible persons in work places or other institutions to prevent or deter the commission of acts of sexual harassment and to provide the procedures for the resolution, settlement or prosecution of acts of sexual harassment by taking all steps required. Guideline 3 enumerates the various preventive steps which are required to be taken by all employers whether in the public sector or the private sector. These include the following: the express prohibition of sexual harassment should be notified, published and circulated in appropriate ways; the Rules/Regulations of Government and Public Sector bodies relating to conduct and discipline should include Rules/Regulations prohibiting sexual harassment and provide for appropriate penalties in such rules against the offender; as regards private employers, steps should be take to include the aforesaid prohibitions in the standing orders under the Industrial Employment (Standing Orders) Act, 1946; appropriate work conditions should be provided in respect of work, leisure, health and hygiene to further ensure that there is no hostile environment towards women at work places and no employee woman should have reasonable grounds to believe that she is disadvantaged in connection with her employment.

According to Guideline 4, the court has clarified that where such conduct amounts to a specific offence under the Indian Penal Code or under any other law, the employer shall initiate appropriate action in accordance with law by making a complaint to the appropriate authority. In particular it should ensure that victims or witnesses are not victimised or discriminated against while dealing with complaints of sexual harassment. The victims of sexual harassment should have the option to seek transfer of the perpetrator or their own transfer. Significantly, Guidelines 6 and 7 respectively stipulate the creation of a Complaint Mechanism and a Complaints Committee. Whether or not such conduct constitutes an offence under law or a breach of the service rules, an appropriate complaint mechanism should be created in the employer's organisation for redress of the complaint made by the victim (Guideline 6). Under Guideline 7, the complaints mechanism should be adequate to provide, where necessary, a Complaints Committee, a special counsellor or other support service, including the maintenance of confidentiality. The Complaints Committee envisaged under Guideline 7 should be headed by a woman and not less than half its members should be women. Further, to prevent the possibility of any undue pressure or influence from senior levels, such a Complaints Committee should involve a third party, who may be either an NGO (Non-Governmental Organisation) or another body who is familiar with the issue of sexual harassment.

Guideline 10 recognises the possibility of third party harassment. It states that where sexual harassment occurs as a result of an act or omission by any third party or outsider, the employer and person in charge will take all steps necessary and reasonable to assist the affected person in terms of support and preventive action. Under Guideline 11, the court has requested the Central and State Governments to consider adopting suitable measures including legislation to ensure that these Guidelines are also observed by employers in the private sector. The court has also ruled that the directions contained in this judgment will be binding and enforceable in law until suitable legislation is enacted to occupy the field.

CONCLUSION

This judgment has generated much debate and discussion in India. Most women activists, while welcoming the judgment, concur that there may be difficulties in the implementation of the Guidelines. Counsel Meenakshi Arora feels that the Guidelines are excellent and that it is now the responsibility of women to seek enforcement of their rights.

While one Indian news magazine[6] describes this judgment as 'A Paper-Knife to Slay the Demon', there is no doubt that the Supreme Court of India has made a significant contribution to the law of gender equality and, in particular, has promoted the protection of the rights of working women in India. It is hoped that the Indian Parliament will soon enact appropriate laws reflecting the Guidelines.

Notes

1. Article 14 of the Constitution of India states: 'The State shall not deny to any person equality before the law or the equal protection of the laws within the territory of India.'
2. Article 15(1) of the Constitution of India states: 'The State shall not discriminate against any citizen on grounds only of religion, race, caste, sex, place of birth or any of them'. Article 15 (3) of the Constitution of India states: 'Nothing in this Article shall prevent the State from making any special provision for women and children'.
3. Article 21 of the Constitution of India states: 'No person shall be deprived of his life or personal liberty except according to procedure established by law.'
4. Article 32 of the Constitution of India states *inter alia* that the right to move the Supreme Court by appropriate proceedings for the enforcement of the rights conferred by this Part [Part III—Fundamental Rights] is guaranteed; the Supreme Court shall have power to issue directions or orders or writs, including writs in the nature of *habeas corpus, mandamus, prohibition, quo warranto* and *certiorari,* whichever may be appropriate, for the enforcement of any of the rights conferred by this Part [Part III—Fundamental Rights].
5. Article 141 of the Constitution of India states 'The law declared by the Supreme Court shall be binding on all courts within the territory of India'.
6. *Outlook,* pages 114–115, 1 September 1997, A *Paper-Knife to Slay the Demon* by Soma Wadhwa.

An Update on Indian Case Law, June 21, 2000

In a recent judgment delivered by the Supreme Court of India, i.e. *Apparel Export Promotion Council vs. A.K. Chopra,* [(1999) I Law Reports of India 13], this court, which is the highest court of appeal in India, reiterated the principles laid down in the *Vishaka* case and amplified them further.

The facts were as follows: The respondent, a private secretary to the Chairman of the appellant company was alleged to have tried to molest a woman employee (Miss X) of the appellant company. The respondent had tried to molest her by making objectionable sexual advances. On complaint, he was suspended and a charge sheet was served on him. The enquiry officer concluded that the respondent had acted against moral sanctions and that his acts did not withstand the test of decency and modesty. The High Court disposed of the writ petition filed by the respondent stating that only an attempt to molest had taken place and directed that the respondent be reinstated in service but that he would not be entitled to receive any back wages. The High Court agreed that the respondent had only tried to molest and that he had not actually molested Miss X and that he had not managed to make the slightest physical contact with Miss X and went on to hold that such an act of the respondent was not a sufficient ground for his dismissal from service. The appellant company appealed.

Allowing the appeal, the Supreme Court of India observed as follows at pages 25 and 26 of the judgment:

The observations made by the High Court to the effect that since the respondent did not 'actually molest' Miss X but only 'tried to molest' her, and therefore, his removal from service was not warranted rebel against realism and lose their sanctity and credibility. In the instant case, the behaviour of respondent did not cease to be outrageous for want of an actual assault or touch by the superior officer. In a case involving charge of sexual harassment or attempt to sexually molest, the courts are required to examine the broader probabilities of a case and not get swayed by insignificant discrepancies or narrow technicalities or dictionary meaning of the expression 'molestation'. They must examine the entire material to determine the genuineness of the complaint. The statement of the victim must be appreciated in the background of the entire case. Where the evidence of the victim inspires confidence, as is the position in the instant case, the courts are obliged to rely on it. Such cases are required to be dealt with great sensitivity. Sympathy in such cases in favour of the superior officer is wholly misplaced and mercy has no relevance. The High Court overlooked the ground realities and ignored the fact that the conduct of the respondent against his junior female employee, Miss X, was wholly against moral sanctions, decency and was offensive to her modesty. Reduction of punishment in a case like this is bound to have [a] demoralizing effect on the women employees and is a retrograde step. There was no justification for the High Court to interfere with the punishment imposed by the departmental authorities. The act of the respondent was unbecoming of good conduct and behaviour expected from a superior officer and undoubtedly amounted to sexual harassment of Miss X and the punishment imposed by the appellant, was, thus, commensurate with the gravity of his objectionable behaviour and did not warrant any interference by the High Court in exercise of its power of judicial review.

The Supreme Court of India referred to international conventions and emphasized that the Indian courts should be vigilant concerning the message given in these conventions. In the eloquent words of the court, at page 25:

The message of international instruments such as the *Convention on the Elimination of All Forms of Discrimination against Women 1979* ["CEDAW"] and the *Beijing Declaration* which directs all state parties to take appropriate measures to prevent discrimination of all forms against women besides taking steps to protect the honour and dignity of women is loud and clear. *The International Covenant on Economic, Social and Cultural Rights* contains several provisions especially important for women. Article 7 recognizes her right to fair conditions of work and reflects that women shall not be subjected to sexual harassment at the place of work which may vitiate [the] working environment. These international instruments cast an obligation on the Indian State to gender sensitize its laws and the courts are under an obligation to see that the message of the international instruments is not allowed to be drowned.

❖ 45. Shameful Silence: Professional Women in Mexico Are Talking More Than Ever About Sex Harassment

Pia Hilbrert

- While 40 percent of Mexican women over age 15 have gone through more than the required six years of primary education, fewer than one in five finishes primary school. And 15 percent of the female population still show no education.
- More Mexican women are working today than 20 years ago, but they represent less than 20 percent of the total female population over age 12 and not even half the percentage of today's male workers. There are three times more men working or actively looking for a job.
- More than half of all working women are office workers (clerks, secretaries, receptionists), in shopkeeping and sales, housekeepers or teachers.
- Most unemployed women are housewives (75.9 percent), while their male counterparts are students (58.6 percent).

(Source: INEGI, La mujer en Mexico 1993 Edition)

There is probably no working woman who hasn't experienced sex discrimination or harassment at one time or another. Its forms—and a woman's recourses against it—can vary according to her level of education, position in the office and the type of organization she works for.

Generally, cases are more frequently reported in lower-level positions, among labourers, clerical workers and secretaries—an overwhelming majority of three-quarters of all economically active females, or more than 4 million women.

Generally, sex harassment is less obvious in higher positions and more direct among lower-level jobs, says Araceli Ruiz Vivanco, head of the Asociacion de Empresarias, A.C., an organization of women entrepreneurs and executives.

And, generally, it is less frequent in the private sector and more frequent in the government sector, Ruiz adds.

Ruiz, president of her own legal-translations business, knows about harassment and discrimination firsthand. Today, she handles it with humor and "telling [men] off in a very nice and diplomatic way." But for others, the task isn't so easy.

CULTURE SHOCKING

When talking about sexual harassment, it is difficult in a Latin culture such as Mexico's to establish the limits of where Latin charm and the complimenting of women stops and where actual harassment starts. Most women agree Mexico's culture can make it more difficult to establish clear limits for sexual harassment than in other cultures. It is a culture where women are still, to a large extent, accustomed to serving men. "Although Mexican men say that they are used to working with women, the truth is that it still causes men inner conflicts," says Rosa Maria Vazquez, director of operations for Keystone Cross Cultural Consultants.

Vazquez's company advises foreign executives, male and female, on how to adjust to the Mexican work environment and culture. She says that relocation here can be an unpleasant surprise for some of her female clients. They find that even if they hold the same position and status in a company, they are not considered equal by co-workers. One woman, for example, went into a meeting with nine fellow male workers and was asked to take the notes.

Maria Victoria Llamas, a former TV talk-show host who frequently dealt with sex-discrimination issues on the air, says Mexican TV and radio don't help. As far as executive positions and decision-making posts are concerned, 90 percent in the media are held by men—easily helping to propagate traditional female stereotypes and prejudices. And the U.S. has little enlightening effect on the industry, she says.

"The main influence U.S. television has in Mexico is in commercials, fashion, music and consumption of Coca-Cola," Llamas says.

MUM'S THE WORD

The response of a Mexican man to his female U.S. co-worker who complains of sex harassment can go to extremes; she could get either no respect or more respect than a fellow Mexican would get. It ultimately seems to depend on her attitude, status and the importance of her position.

When sex harassment and discrimination occur, women generally are afraid to speak up and denounce it because it is hard to prove, and it is typically their word against a man's. The usual male argument is "she provoked it." The usual female response is to feel shame. While younger women today are better informed of the issues and discuss them more openly, many women still blame themselves for all kinds of abuses. They remain socially isolated, afraid of reprisals. They think that if they report a case of sexual harassment or abuse, they will be treated as the instigators and the men as the victims.

"They do not want their families, father, brother or husbands to know because they are afraid that they will be considered guilty of having [brought on] the situation in the first place," explains Marisa Jordan, a co-ordinator for the Asociacion Mexicana de Mujeres del IMEF, a 25-year-old women's association that is one of Mexico's largest with 160 members, mostly secretaries. "It is not female apathy: it is an irrational fear of others knowing about what happened."

MORE PROBLEMS

The problem of sexual harassment and discrimination has always been around; it is just that working women in Mexico are becoming more conscious of it as they slowly entrench themselves in the office hierarchy. One of the problems is that women hold so few higher-level positions where complaints can be taken to.

Maria Teresa Avila is president of Secretarias Ejecutivas de Mexico, A.C., an association of executive secretaries established in 1960. While she says there have been few reported cases on sexual harassment, she readily cites examples of lower-level bosses who have used intimidation to threaten secretaries with their jobs if they don't do what they want them to do. Rather than risk public embarrassment, the secretaries may turn to the next highest person for support. Usually, that is a man.

Several in-house studies conducted by a female professional in a Mexican company high-

WHAT WE FOUND: TOO FEW JOBS, TOO LITTLE PAY

To get an idea of how Mexican working women are faring, AmCham [American Chamber of Commerce] conducted its own survey of female applicants from January to August 1994. The sample population is based on job openings promoted by the employment office; the analysis was done according to area of work, position, age, education level and income.

SURVEY RESULTS

- While there is a large number of women in the job market, opportunities for them are still scarce in all areas and levels of work.
- There is more demand for women in administrative jobs than in technical ones. Women are most frequently requested for:

  1. Secretarial Work
  2. Commercial/Sales/Marketing/Advertising
  3. Accounting/Finance
  4. Management
  5. Human Resources
  6. Production/Manufacturing
  7. Computer Systems
  8. High-Level Posts
  9. Other (translators and interpreters, English teachers, service personnel and general assistants)

- Salary gaps exist between men and women even in positions where job responsibilities are the same. In some management posts, women earn from US$600 to US$1,200 (at least) less a month than men for no reason related to their skill level. This, of course, depends on a company's policies. The most frequently used arguments justifying salary differences are that men, when interviewed, by comparison are more free to travel and can devote more time to the job.
- For secretaries, while the official requested age-range from companies is 18 to 45 years, the average of those getting job is between 20 and 30. In positions that require a university-level education, the average age ranges from 23 to 35 years. For assistant positions, it's 23 to 28. For coordination and middle-management positions, the average is 25 to 34; for upper-management levels, the average is 30 to 35.
- There are women working in upper-management positions aged 45 or older, but if they were forced to change jobs, they would not have much opportunity in finding another job, unlike men, the survey showed.

lights these problems. The firm's secretaries—especially the younger ones—were predominantly the victims of sexual harassment, and most of the time it was the boss harassing the secretary.

The head of the survey told Business Mexico that while most of the secretaries agreed sexual harassment was a problem, only one of the women did something about it. When her boss started harassing her, she confronted him. Despite her confrontation, he contin-ued to harass her, and she finally requested a transfer. When the other women were asked why they didn't do something about their situations, they all said that it would be useless because no one would believe them or support them. Many also said speaking up would make matters worse, and they were not willing to take the risk.

WHO'S A HELP

Such attitudes may change as women attain real power in the office. Maria Elena Juarez, a partner of one of Mexico's top executive-search firms, Amrop International, says that hav-ing U.S. companies in Mexico has helped; some have their own internal policies prohibit-ing sex harassment and discrimination of employees. Companies such as IBM, DuPont and Procter & Gamble also favor the hiring of women directors, she says. And although dis-crimination becomes evident when clients specifically ask for male executives, more and more of the firms are requiring female employees in areas such as control, communications, marketing and computer systems.

But these companies still represent less than 10 percent of all Juarez deals with. Some multinational firms would like to include women in executive positions but feel that the environment is still hostile.

WHO'S NOT

Compounding the problem is that a woman's opinion is often not taken as seriously or is underestimated by male co-workers.

"A woman is not considered equal or given equal treatment on the job because of the underlying assumption that she will get married and have children, and once a mother, will neglect her work," says Sarah Martinez de Graue, former co-host of the TV program "A Quien Corresponda" ("To Whom It May Concern").

"In some cases, women are not included in meetings, or meetings are scheduled outside the office with the excuse of it not being appropriate for women to attend because of bad language used or alcohol consumed."

One of the most obvious forms of sex discrimination is the unequal compensation for equal work, position, responsibilities, performance, experience and education.

In the '60s, recalls a female partner at a Mexico City law firm, discrimination was bla-tant; low pay, less participation in meetings with clients, smaller office space, no secretaries and poor assignments were the norm for women there. While things are certainly improv-ing, the attorney says, hurdles remain. One example is the subtle preference and insistence of clients—both national and foreign—of speaking to a man instead of a woman when re-quiring legal services.

WOMEN ON WOMEN

Meanwhile, some women believe other women can bring problems on themselves, or at least don't help matters.

Tony Allegretti, whose first job was in a family business in the U.S., has been working in Mexico since 1989. Now president of Trade Management Services in Mexico City, she says she has never been a victim of sex harassment or discrimination. Many times, how women expect to be treated and what they convey, either overtly or covertly, influences the actual treatment they get, Allegretti says. That's not to say men haven't made comments to her. But she says it is the woman who sets the tone of the relationship.

As for U.S. sex-discrimination laws, Allegretti says they have created a paranoia among males in higher positions within U.S. organizations.

"They have to be extremely careful with female employees and female co-workers. They have become supersensitive to these issues," says Allegretti. "Mexico, on the other hand, is not even close to that."

Anthea Levy, head of the Professionals in Mexico Association (PRIMA), a support group for executive women based in Mexico, agrees that there is paranoia in the U.S. A slightly chauvinistic comment can readily be interpreted as sexual harassment, she says.

When some women were asked about the most publicized U.S. cases on sexual harassment, most felt they went overboard.

"From the Mexican perspective, I feel they exaggerate," admits Ruiz. "I ask myself if there is no way of avoiding things from getting to such extremes."

❖ 46. The Regulation of Sexual Harassment in International Treaties and Documents

Gaby Oré-Aguilar

Both regional and international bodies have proffered definitions of sexual harassment. For example, the European Economic Community defines sexual harassment in a somewhat broad manner. Accordingly, sexual harassment includes all verbal or physical conduct of a sexual nature that the actor knows or should know is offensive to the employee.[1] Such conduct is considered illegal when: a) the rejection or acceptance of such conduct is used or invoked as a threat regarding a decision that affects the employee's employment or work conditions, or; b) such conduct prejudices the victim's work environment.[2] In March 1997, the Council of the European Union initiated the second phase of a consultation process with social interlocutors to establish a preventative common system regulating such incidents in the workplace.[3] Some of the issues submitted to consultation include the definition of sexual harassment, measures to be adopted to prevent sexual harassment, and the responsibility of employers to implement such measures.[4]

In the United States, the Equal Employment Opportunity Commission ("EEOC") guidelines establish that unwanted sexual advances, demands for sexual favors, and other verbal or physical conduct of a sexual nature constitute sexual harassment.[5] Within its definition, though, the EEOC has created two subcategories. First, *quid pro quo* sexual harassment is when submission to sexual conduct becomes a condition of employment, or when submission to or rejection of such conduct affects decisions at the workplace.[6] Second, *hostile work environment* sexual harassment may apply if such conduct has the objective or the effect of interfering unreasonably with the employee's work performance or creating an intimidating, hostile, or offensive work environment.[7]

International human rights organizations have also tried to formulate a definition of sexual harassment. For example, in the 1988 Meeting of Experts, the International Labour Organization ("ILO") established that the action must assume certain characteristics to constitute sexual harassment.[8] First, the employee must perceive the action as a condition of continued or secured employment.[9] In addition, the incident must influence decisions affecting the employee, undermine the employee's professional performance, or humiliate, insult, or intimidate the employee.[10]

The United Nation's Commission on Human Rights, in its Preliminary Special Report on Violence against Women, states that to fight sexual harassment, a proper definition of what constitutes sexual harassment must be established.[11] The Report emphasizes that actions that fall within this category are very diverse, ranging from actions that may be considered "normal" within a particular social context, to actions that are legally categorized as sexual crimes.[12] As a result, the Report states cultural factors are critical in determining a definition of sexual harassment.[13]

The issue of sexual harassment is complicated not only by different definitions but by varying conceptual models. These models are contained in both the regional laws and international treatises and embody different perspectives on sexual harassment. The first model, the *cultural values model,* treats sexual harassment as an attack against social and cultural values such as decency, modesty, and good morals.[14] This model is evidenced in antiquated regional laws which define harassment as "offensive gallantry," a "malicious" or "dishonest" act that attacks the dignity and integrity of the employee.[15] Such an approach reflects the underlying humanistic and paternalistic vision that characterizes the labor legislation of the early nineteenth century. Although this model is reflected in the domestic laws of some countries, it is not reflected in international standards.

In contrast, the other two models are represented in both international and regional capacities. First, the *anti-discrimination model* calls for laws that penalize sexual harassment as an attack against the principles of equality and nondiscrimination.[16] The second model, the *gender-based violence model,* considers sexual harassment one of several forms of violence against women. This model, although less represented, promises to be a useful tool in eradicating sexual harassment. In reviewing the regional laws and international instruments, the following section will further illustrate the impact of these conceptual models.

INTERNATIONAL EFFORTS

International treaties and documents have attempted to provide a complementary safeguard to regional laws that are oftentimes inadequate. This section briefly analyzes regulatory models based on treaties adopted by the universal and regional systems of human rights protection, including the treaties adopted by the ILO. The international approaches, for the most part, embody either the anti-discrimination model or the gender-based violence model.

The ILO Discrimination (Employment and Occupation) Convention[17] ("Discrimination Convention") has created a conceptual framework based on equal, non-discriminatory treatment in the workplace without specifically addressing the issue of sex discrimination.[18] In 1979, the Convention for the Elimination of All Forms of Discrimination Against Women ("CEDAW")[19] likewise contributed to the effort, offering a broad understanding of the problem of sex discrimination by addressing discrimination in all facets of women's lives. CEDAW explicitly defined sexual harassment as a violation of the principle of equality in the workplace, noting: "discrimination against women . . . constitutes an obstacle to the full realization of the potentialities of women."[20] Thus, in effect, the resolution demands equality-promoting policies, including measures specifically aimed at eradicating sexual harassment.

Although many Latin American governments have created a standard of protection in the workplace by adopting the terms of the Discrimination Convention, CEDAW provisions are proving to be more effective. First, the local rules of domestic procedure often preclude seeking redress under both the regional employment laws and the Discrimination Convention provisions. Second, the Discrimination Convention provisions only apply to the workplace while the CEDAW provisions afford protection to women against discriminatory acts within and outside the workplace.[21] CEDAW provisions also have the power to expand protection in countries like Argentina, whose law only governs public sector employees. To illustrate, an employee in the private sector could invoke the Law of Employment Contracts which protects the physical and psychological integrity of employees[22] via the provisions of CEDAW,[23] which have constitutional status in Argentina.[24] This could serve as a strategic alternative to Argentina's lack of specific legislation dealing with sexual harassment in the private sector.

Thus, while the CEDAW has contributed much to the development of the antidiscrimination model, it also has been involved in the development of the *gender-based violence model*. This model became the center of international attention when the international women's movement demanded that women's human rights, including the right to be free from gender-based violence, be considered an integral and indivisible part of those fundamental human rights recognized by the universal system. In 1993, the World Conference on Human Rights[25] ("Vienna Conference") declared for the first time that "[g]ender-based violence and all forms of sexual harassment and exploitation" constitute attacks against the dignity of the individual and must be eliminated.[26] Only a few months thereafter, the General Assembly of the United Nations echoed the international consensus manifested at the Vienna Conference by adopting the *Declaration on the Elimination of Violence Against Women*[27] ("Declaration"), articulating existing standards for combating gender-based violence in the form of sexual harassment in the workplace and the educational system.[28] The Declaration supports a broad conception of violence which "implies the right to inquire against all forms of action which disempower women because of the fear of violence, whether the fear is instilled by the State, actors in the community, or members of the family."[29]

Amidst this movement, CEDAW became particularly instrumental in advancing the gender-based violence model. In 1992, the Committee on the Elimination of Discrimination Against Women[30] ("Committee") established that gender-based violence—violence resulting in physical, mental, or sexual harm, the threat to commit such acts, and other coercive acts that deprive women of their freedom—is discrimination as described in article 1 of CEDAW.[31] On this basis, the Committee recommended that national governments report on the status of sexual harassment under the norms of CEDAW, and revise their laws and policies accordingly.[32] This initiative by the Committee created the possibility of developing legislation and other mechanisms to penalize sexual harassment in the spheres within CEDAW's reach. In doing so, the Committee successfully created an instrument that regulates gender-based violence as an act of discrimination.

In addition to the efforts of the United Nations, the Inter-American Convention to Prevent, Penalize, and Eradicate Violence Against Women ("Convention of Belem do Para"), which was adopted by the Organization of American States ("OAS") in 1994, has made significant strides against sexual harassment as a gender-based act of violence.[33] The Convention of Belem do Para requires member-states to adopt effective measures to prevent, penalize, and eliminate violence against women. More specifically, it includes examples of "sexual harassment in the workplace, as well as in educational establishments, health facilities, or any other place . . . that is perpetrated or condoned by the State and its agents regardless of where it occurs."[34]

In addition to the substantive provisions on sexual harassment, the Convention of Belem Do Para provides procedural mechanisms to carry out its provisions. Primarily, it provides that any person, group, or nongovernmental organization associated with any member-state of the OAS may lodge petitions against a member-state that fails to fulfill its duties under the established norms.[35] Thus, the Convention of Belem Do Para is the most advanced regional tool in preventing violence against women because it is the only international human rights treaty that specifically requires the States to eliminate sexual harassment in the public and private sphere.[36] . . .

FUTURE STRATEGIES

Sexual harassment acts as a permanent warning to women that their gender, and oftentimes their socio-economic background, makes them vulnerable to harassment and other forms of sexual violence. In all of its forms, sexual harassment is a demonstration of power on the part of the aggressor aimed at subordinating the victim, thereby violating her human rights. Sexual harassment is also linked to social understandings of sexuality based on gender-based sexual stereotypes in which women are seen as engaging in behavior that "provokes" harassment or violence, while men who respond to such provocation by harassing women are excused because they must "fulfill their sexual role" or face scrutiny about their virility.[37]

In light of these findings, how should the law address the issue of sexual harassment? Should it be considered an act of gender discrimination or as a mode of sexual and gender-based violence? As already discussed, as countries and international human rights organizations adopt one or the other approach, different procedures, outcomes, and remedies result with varying degrees of success.

Because sexual harassment often constitutes a kind of "preliminary phase" of sexual assault,[38] the gender-based violence model holds the most promise. It provides a useful framework because it successfully portrays sexual harassment as a violation of women's human rights. This approach encourages the development of effective strategies in two ways. First, it legitimizes the incorporation of measures against sexual harassment into the domestic human rights legislation of each country. Second, it allows victims of sexual harassment to seek compensation for damages using domestic and international mechanisms of protection.

Latin American countries and international organizations must adopt effective and comprehensive measures to counteract the harm that results from sexual harassment.[39] Evidence shows that in countries that penalize sexual harassment by specific laws or human rights legislation, complaints are more frequent[40] and damages include compensatory damages.[41] In some cases, compensation for sexual harassment under such specific statutes does not exclude other means of compensating for damages provided by domestic law.[42] Thus, both regional laws and international instruments can work in concert to provide a comprehensive system of protection. In this respect, the gender-based violence model offers an effective solution because it protects against sexual harassment in the spheres of public and private life outside the workplace without affecting the validity of anti-discriminatory laws in the workplace.

Within the Inter-American system of human rights and in Latin America in general, the Convention of Belem do Para is the only tool that specifically addresses the problem of sexual harassment in terms of gender-based violence. These norms must be respected in those countries that ratify it. As of the date of publication of this article, twenty-five member-states of the OAS have signed the Convention,[43] and almost all of them have ratified it.[44]

Progress may also come in the form of model legislation that has been proposed for countries belonging to the Caribbean Community and Common Market ("CARICOM"). The proposed legislation regulating sexual harassment in the workplace and educational establishments would include provisions for monetary compensation,[45] including compensation for emotional distress.[46] It also proposes the creation of a special tribunal to settle cases of sexual harassment.[47]

Notes

1. Resolution of 29 May 1990, 1990 O.J. (C 157) (regarding the protection of the dignity of women and men in the workplace).
2. *Id.*
3. 1997-3 E.C. Bull., no. 1.3.157, at 58.
4. *Id.*
5. Equal Employment Opportunity Commission, 29 C.F.R. § 1604.11 (1996).
6. *Id.*
7. *Id.*
8. *Equality in Employment and Occupation: General Survey of the Reports on the Discrimination (Employment and Occupation) Convention (No. 111) and Recommendation (No. 111), 1958,* International Labour Conference, Committee of Experts on the Application of Conventions and Recommendations, 75th Sess., rep. III, pt. 4B, para. 45 (1988).
9. *Id.*
10. *Id.*
11. *Preliminary Report Submitted by the Special Rapporteur on Violence Against Women, its Cause and Consequences, Ms. Radhika Coomaraswamy, in accordance with Commission on Human Rights Resolution 1994/45,* U.N. ESCOR, Comm'n on H.R., 50th Sess., Agenda Item 11(a), para. 190, U.N. Doc. E/CN.4/1995/42 (1994) [*hereinafter Preliminary Report on Violence Against Women*].
12. *Id.*
13. *Id.*
14. The Penal Code of Uruguay, for example, considers "offensive gallantry" as a crime and penalizes it with a fine and/or a prison sentence. In India, the Penal Code penalizes the act of insulting a woman's modesty through words, gestures, or actions. Similarly, the Metropolitan Council of Delhi penalizes "malicious annoyance," defined as written or spoken words, signs or visible representations or gestures, the act of reciting or singing indecent words in a public place, or acts or poetry or songs, carried out by a man in order to upset or offend a woman. *See Preliminary Report on Violence Against Women, supra* note 11, para. 193.
15. Texto Unico Ordenado de la Ley Fomento del Empleo [United Text of the Employment Promotion Law] art. 63 (Peru's Civil Law).
16. *See, e.g., supra* notes 5–7 and accompanying text (describing the EEOC guidelines which provide the classic example of anti-discrimination law).
17. *Discrimination (Employment and Occupation) Convention, adopted* June 15, 1960, ILO, 42d Sess., 4th Agenda Item (1958), II ILO, International Labour Conventions and Recommendations 1952–1976, at 176 (1996).
18. *Id.*
19. G.A. Res. 34/180, U.N. GAOR, 34th Sess., Agenda Item 75, U.N. Doc. A/RES/34/180 (1979).
20. *Id.* para. 5.
21. *Id.* art. 1.
22. Ley de Contrato de Trabajo [Law of Employment Contracts] (Astrea ed., 1981).

23. G.A. Res. 34/180, *supra* note 19, art. 81, 172.
24. Const. Arg. art. 75(22).
25. *Report of the World Conference on Human Rights,* U.N. GAOR, U.N. Doc. A/Conf. 157/24 (1993).
26. *Id.* pt. III. 18.
27. G.A. Res. 48/104, U.N. GAOR, 48th Sess., Agenda Item 111, U.N. Doc. A/RES/48/104 (1994).
28. *Id.*
29. See *Preliminary Report on Violence Against Women, supra* note 11, para. 98 (reviewing the progress of the Declaration on the Elimination of Violence Against Women).
30. The Committee on the Elimination of Discrimination Against Women was created pursuant to article 17 of CEDAW. *See* G.A. Res. 34/180, *supra* note 19, art. 17. Its purpose is to "consider[] the progress made in the implementation of the present Convention." *Id.*
31. See *General Recommendation No. 19 (11th Session, 1992): Violence Against Women,* U.N. CEDAW, 11th Sess., Agenda Item 7, para. 8, U.N. Doc. CEDAW/C/1992/L.1/Add.15(1992) ("Gender-based violence which impairs or nullifies the enjoyment by women of human rights and fundamental freedoms under general international law or under specific human rights conventions is discrimination within the meaning of article 1 of the Convention."").
32. *Id.* pt. II.
33. *Inter-American Convention on the Prevention, Punishment and Eradication of Violence Against Women: Convention of Belem do Para, adopted* June 9, 1994, G.A. OAS, Inter-American Comm'n of Women, 24th Sess. [hereinafter *Convention of Belem do Para*].
34. *Id.* art. 2(b)–(c).
35. As stated:

> Any person or group of persons, or any nongovernmental entity legally recognized in one or more member states of the Organization, may lodge petitions with the Inter-American Commission on Human Rights containing denunciations or complaints of violations of Article 7 of this Convention by a State Party, and the Commission shall consider such claims in accordance with the norms and procedures established by the American Convention on Human Rights and the Statutes and Regulations of the Inter-American Commission on Human Rights for lodging and considering petitions.
>
> *Id.* art. 12.

36. *Id.* art. 2, 7, 12.
37. Interviews of Peruvian men convicted of rape reveal that the offenders do not consider as crimes non-violent sexual aggression, such as "abuse or illicit pressure by an individual in a position of authority or superiority." On the contrary, the rapists constructed "discourses of exoneration" that denigrated their victims as human beings and sought to explain the crime based on the actions of the victims. *See* Abraham Siles Vallejos, *Apuntes Sobre lo Hallado* [Notes on the Findings], *in* Yo Actuaba Como Varon Solamente . . . [I was Just Acting Like a Man] 170, 172–73 (Rafael León & Marga Stahr eds., 1995).
38. A Federal Bureau of Investigation study of repeat offenders revealed that crimes of sexual harassment, such as voyeurism, obscene phone calls, or exhibitionism, are often precursors to more violent crimes. *See* Mary Becker et al., Cases and Materials on Feminist Jurisprudence: Taking Women Seriously 203 n.6 (1994) (citing *The Serial Rapist: His Characteristics and Victims,* FBI L. Enforcement Bull., Feb. 1989, at 18, 21).
39. *Preliminary Report on Violence Against Women, supra* note 11, para. 190 (revealing that sexual harassment in the workplace and beyond is a growing problem with serious and alarming consequences for women).
40. For example, in Canada:

> the system of specific human rights statues which is also seen at the state level in the U.S., avoids the difficulties inherent in the British system because the violation of a right labeled a "human right" emphasizes the egregious nature of harassing conduct. While the level of compensation seems relatively modest, the Canadian response seems to have been to increase the seriousness of the tort, allowing the victim to attain psychological vindication by being able to show that the harasser has infringed her or his human rights. This may explain why sexual

harassment litigation seems more frequent in Canada than in Britain, even though the damages awarded in such litigation are broadly comparable.

Joseph Kelly & Bob Watt, *Damages in Sex Harassment Cases: A Comparative Study of American, Canadian and British Law,* 16 N.Y.L. Sch. J. Int'l & Comp. L. 79, 133 (1996) (footnote omitted).

41. *Id.* at 89 n.70.

42. *Id.* at 89.

43. OAS, Inter-American Commission on Human Rights, Documentos Basicos en Materia de Derechos Humanos en el Sisterna Interamericano [Basic Documents Pertaining to Human Rights in the Inter-American System] 160 (1997).

44. *Id.*

45. Protection Against Sexual Harassment Act para. 16.-(1) (Model legislation proposed by CARICOM secretariat).

46. *Id.* para. 16.-(2).

47. *Id.* para. 6.-(1) (providing two options—either the establishment or the appointment of a tribunal).

PART VI

Selected Legal Documents
and Court Cases

SEC. 2000E-2. [*SECTION 703*]
UNLAWFUL EMPLOYMENT PRACTICES

(a) It shall be an unlawful employment practice for an employer—

(1) to fail or refuse to hire or to discharge any individual, or otherwise to discriminate against any individual with respect to his compensation, terms, conditions, or privileges of employment, because of such individual's race, color, religion, sex, or national origin; or

(2) to limit, segregate, or classify his employees or applicants for employment in any way which would deprive or tend to deprive any individual of employment opportunities or otherwise adversely affect his status as an employee, because of such individual's race, color, religion, sex, or national origin.

(b) It shall be an unlawful employment practice for an employment agency to fail or refuse to refer for employment, or otherwise to discriminate against, any individual because of his race, color, religion, sex, or national origin, or to classify or refer for employment any individual on the basis of his race, color, religion, sex, or national origin.

(c) It shall be an unlawful employment practice for a labor organization—

(1) to exclude or to expel from its membership, or otherwise to discriminate against, any individual because of his race, color, religion, sex, or national origin;

(2) to limit, segregate, or classify its membership or applicants for membership, or to classify or fail or refuse to refer for employment any individual, in any way which would deprive or tend to deprive any individual of employment opportunities, or would limit such employment opportunities or otherwise adversely affect his status as an employee or as an applicant for employment, because of such individual's race, color, religion, sex, or national origin; or

(3) to cause or attempt to cause an employer to discriminate against an individual in violation of this section.

(d) It shall be an unlawful employment practice for any employer, labor organization, or joint labor-management committee controlling apprenticeship or other training or re-training, including on-the-job training programs, to discriminate against any individual because of his race, color, religion, sex, or national origin in admission to, or employment in, any program established to provide apprenticeship or other training.

(e) Notwithstanding any other provision of this subchapter, (1) it shall not be an unlawful employment practice for an employer to hire and employ employees, for an employment agency to classify, or refer for employment any individual, for a labor organization to classify its membership or to classify or refer for employment any individual, or for an employer, labor organization, or joint labor-management committee controlling apprenticeship or other training or retraining programs to admit or employ any individual in any such program, on the basis of his religion, sex, or national origin in those certain instances where religion, sex, or national origin is a bona fide occupational qualification reasonably necessary to the normal operation of that particular business or enterprise, and (2) it shall not be an unlawful employment practice for a school, college, university, or other educational institution or institution of learning to hire and employ employees of a particular religion if such school, college, university, or other educational institution or institution of learning is, in whole or in substantial part, owned, supported, controlled, or managed by a particular religion or by a particular religious corporation, association, or society, or if the curriculum of such school, college, university, or other educational institution or institution of learning is directed toward the propagation of a particular religion.

(f) As used in this subchapter, the phrase "unlawful employment practice" shall not be deemed to include any action or measure taken by an employer, labor organization, joint labor-management committee, or employment agency with respect to an individual who is a member of the Communist Party of the United States or of any other organization required to register as a Communist-action or Communist-front organization by final order of the Subversive Activities Control Board pursuant to the Subversive Activities Control Act of 1950 [*50 U.S.C. 781 et. seq.*].

(g) Notwithstanding any other provision of this subchapter, it shall not be an unlawful employment practice for an employer to fail or refuse to hire and employ any individual for any position, for an employer to discharge any individual from any position, or for an employment agency to fail or refuse to refer any individual for employment in any position, or for a labor organization to fail or refuse to refer any individual for employment in any position, if—

   (1) the occupancy of such position, or access to the premises in or upon which any part of the duties of such position is performed or is to be performed, is subject to any requirement imposed in the interest of the national security of the United States under any security program in effect pursuant to or administered under any statute of the United States or any Executive order of the President; and

   (2) such individual has not fulfilled or has ceased to fulfill that requirement.

(h) Notwithstanding any other provision of this subchapter, it shall not be an unlawful employment practice for an employer to apply different standards of compensation, or different terms, conditions, or privileges of employment pursuant to a bona fide seniority or merit system, or a system which measures earnings by quantity or quality of production or to employees who work in different locations, provided that such differences are not the result of an intention to discriminate because of race, color, religion, sex, or national origin, nor shall it be an unlawful employment practice for an employer to give and to act upon the results of any professionally developed ability test provided that such test, its administration or action upon the results is not designed, intended or used to discriminate because of race, color, religion, sex or national origin. It shall not be an unlawful employment practice under this subchapter for any employer to differentiate upon the basis of sex in determining the amount of the wages or compensation paid or to be paid to employees of such employer if such differentiation is authorized by the provisions of section 206(d) of title 29 [*section 6 (d) of the Fair Labor Standards Act of 1938, as amended*].

(i) Nothing contained in this subchapter shall apply to any business or enterprise on or near an Indian reservation with respect to any publicly announced employment practice of such business or enterprise under which a preferential treatment is given to any individual because he is an Indian living on or near a reservation.

(j) Nothing contained in this subchapter shall be interpreted to require any employer, employment agency, labor organization, or joint labor-management committee subject to this subchapter to grant preferential treatment to any individual or to any group because of the race, color, religion, sex, or national origin of such individual or group on account of an imbalance which may exist with respect to the total number or percentage of persons of any race, color, religion, sex, or national origin employed by any employer, referred or classified for employment by any employment agency or labor organization, admitted to membership or classified by any labor organization, or admitted to, or employed in, any apprenticeship or other training program, in comparison with the total number or percentage of persons of such race, color, religion, sex, or national origin in any community, State, section, or other area, or in the available work force in any community, State, section, or other area.

(k) (1) (A) An unlawful employment practice based on disparate impact is established under this title only if—

(i) a complaining party demonstrates that a respondent uses a particular employment practice that causes a disparate impact on the basis of race, color, religion, sex, or national origin and the respondent fails to demonstrate that the challenged practice is job related for the position in question and consistent with business necessity; or

(ii) the complaining party makes the demonstration described in subparagraph (C) with respect to an alternative employment practice and the respondent refuses to adopt such alternative employment practice.

(B) (i) With respect to demonstrating that a particular employment practice causes a disparate impact as described in subparagraph (A) (i), the complaining party shall demonstrate that each particular challenged employment practice causes a disparate impact, except that if the complaining party can demonstrate to the court that the elements of a respondent's decisionmaking process are not capable of separation for analysis, the decisionmaking process may be analyzed as one employment practice.

(ii) If the respondent demonstrates that a specific employment practice does not cause the disparate impact, the respondent shall not be required to demonstrate that such practice is required by business necessity.

(C) The demonstration referred to by subparagraph (A) (ii) shall be in accordance with the law as it existed on June 4, 1989, with respect to the concept of "alternative employment practice".

(2) A demonstration that an employment practice is required by business necessity may not be used as a defense against a claim of intentional discrimination under this title.

(3) Notwithstanding any other provision of this title, a rule barring the employment of an individual who currently and knowingly uses or possesses a controlled substance, as defined in schedules I and II of section 102 (6) of the Controlled Substances Act (21 U.S.C. 802 (6)), other than the use or possession of a drug taken under the supervision of a licensed health care professional, or any other use or possession authorized by the Controlled Substances Act {21 U.S.C 801 et seq.} or any other provision of Federal law, shall be considered an unlawful employment practice under this title only if such rule is adopted or applied with an intent to discriminate because of race, color, religion, sex, or national origin.

(l) It shall be an unlawful employment practice for a respondent, in connection with the selection or referral of applicants or candidates for employment or promotion, to adjust the scores of, use different cutoff scores for, or otherwise alter the results of, employment related tests on the basis of race, color, religion, sex, or national origin.

(m) Except as otherwise provided in this title, an unlawful employment practice is established when the complaining party demonstrates that race, color, religion, sex, or national origin was a motivating factor for any employment practice, even though other factors also motivated the practice.

(n) (1) (A) Notwithstanding any other provision of law, and except as provided in paragraph (2), an employment practice that implements and is within the scope of a litigated or consent judgment or order that resolves a claim of employment discrimination under the Constitution or Federal civil rights laws may not be challenged under the circumstances described in subparagraph (B).

(B) A practice described in subparagraph (A) may not be challenged in a claim under the Constitution or Federal civil rights laws—

    (i) by a person who, prior to the entry of the judgment or order described in subparagraph (A), had—

        (I) actual notice of the proposed judgment or order sufficient to apprise such person that such judgment or order might adversely affect the interests and legal rights of such person and that an opportunity was available to present objections to such judgment or order by a future date certain; and

        (II) a reasonable opportunity to present objections to such judgment or order; or

    (ii) by a person whose interests were adequately represented by another person who had previously challenged the judgment or order on the same legal grounds and with a similar factual situation, unless there has been an intervening change in law or fact.

(2) Nothing in this subsection shall be construed to—

    (A) alter the standards for intervention under rule 24 of the Federal Rules of Civil Procedure or apply to the rights of parties who have successfully intervened pursuant to such rule in the proceeding in which the parties intervened;

    (B) apply to the rights of parties to the action in which a litigated or consent judgment or order was entered, or of members of a class represented or sought to be represented in such action, or of members of a group on whose behalf relief was sought in such action by the Federal Government;

    (C) prevent challenges to a litigated or consent judgment or order on the ground that such judgment or order was obtained through collusion or fraud, or is transparently invalid or was entered by a court lacking subject matter jurisdiction; or

    (D) authorize or permit the denial to any person of the due process of law required by the Constitution.

(3) Any action not precluded under this subsection that challenges an employment consent judgment or order described in paragraph (1) shall be brought in the court, and if possible before the judge, that entered such judgment or order. Nothing in this subsection shall preclude a transfer of such action pursuant to section 1404 of title 28, United States Code.

48. Title IX of the Education Amendments of 1972

US Code: Title 20, Sec. 1681

(a) Prohibition against discrimination; exceptions

No person in the United States shall, on the basis of sex, be excluded from participation in, be denied the benefits of, or be subjected to discrimination under any education program or activity receiving Federal financial assistance, except that:

(1) Classes of educational institutions subject to prohibition in regard to admissions to educational institutions, this section shall apply only to institutions of vocational education, professional education, and graduate higher education, and to public institutions of undergraduate higher education;

(2) Educational institutions commencing planned change in admissions in regard to admissions to educational institutions, this section shall not apply (A) for one year from June 23, 1972, nor for six years after June 23, 1972, in the case of an educational institution which has begun the process of changing from being an institution which admits only students of one sex to being an institution which admits students of both sexes, but only if it is carrying out a plan for such a change which is approved by the Secretary of Education or (B) for seven years from the date an educational institution begins the process of changing from being an institution which admits only students of only one sex to being an institution which admits students of both sexes, but only if it is carrying out a plan for such a change which is approved by the Secretary of Education, whichever is the later;

(3) Educational institutions of religious organizations with contrary religious tenets

this section shall not apply to an educational institution which is controlled by a religious organization if the application of this subsection would not be consistent with the religious tenets of such organization;

(4) Educational institutions training individuals for military services or merchant marine

this section shall not apply to an educational institution whose primary purpose is the training of individuals for the military services of the United States, or the merchant marine;

(5) Public educational institutions with traditional and continuing admissions policy

in regard to admissions this section shall not apply to any public institution of undergraduate higher education which is an institution that traditionally and continually from its establishment has had a policy of admitting only students of one sex;

(6) Social fraternities or sororities; voluntary youth service organizations

this section shall not apply to membership practices—

(A) of a social fraternity or social sorority which is exempt from taxation under section 501(a) of title 26, the active membership of which consists primarily of students in attendance at an institution of higher education, or

(B) of the Young Men's Christian Association, Young Women's Christian Association, Girl Scouts, Boy Scouts, Camp Fire Girls, and voluntary youth service organizations which are so exempt, the membership of which has traditionally been limited to persons of one sex and principally to persons of less than nineteen years of age;

(7) Boy or Girl conferences

this section shall not apply to—

(A) any program or activity of the American Legion undertaken in connection with the organization or operation of any Boys State conference, Boys Nation conference, Girls State conference, or Girls Nation conference; or

(B) any program or activity of any secondary school or educational institution specifically for—

    (i) the promotion of any Boys State conference, Boys Nation conference, Girls State conference, or Girls Nation conference; or

    (ii) the selection of students to attend any such conference;

(8) Father-son or mother-daughter activities at educational institutions

this section shall not preclude father-son or mother-daughter activities at an educational institution, but if such activities are provided for students of one sex, opportunities for reasonably comparable activities shall be provided for students of the other sex; and

(9) Institution of higher education scholarship awards in "beauty" pageants

this section shall not apply with respect to any scholarship or other financial assistance awarded by an institution of higher education to any individual because such individual has received such award in any pageant in which the attainment of such award is based upon a combination of factors related to the personal appearance, poise, and talent of such individual and in which participation is limited to individuals of one sex only, so long as such pageant is in compliance with other nondiscrimination provisions of Federal law.

(b) Preferential or disparate treatment because of imbalance in participation or receipt of Federal benefits; statistical evidence of imbalance

Nothing contained in subsection (a) of this section shall be interpreted to require any educational institution to grant preferential or disparate treatment to the members of one sex on account of an imbalance which may exist with respect to the total number or percentage of persons of that sex participating in or receiving the benefits of any federally supported program or activity, in comparison with the total number or percentage of persons of that sex in any community, State, section, or other area: Provided, That this subsection shall not be construed to prevent the consideration in any hearing or proceeding under this chapter of statistical evidence tending to show that such an imbalance exists with respect to the participation in, or receipt of the benefits of, any such program or activity by the members of one sex.

(c) "Educational institution" defined

For purposes of this chapter an educational institution means any public or private preschool, elementary, or secondary school, or any institution of vocational, professional, or higher education, except that in the case of an educational institution composed of more than one school, college, or department which are administratively separate units, such term means each such school, college, or department.

49. Guidelines on Discrimination Because of Sex: Sexual Harassment

Equal Employment Opportunity Commission

CODE OF FEDERAL REGULATIONS: TITLE 29, SEC. 1604.11

(a) Harassment on the basis of sex is a violation of section 703 of title VII. Unwelcome sexual advances, requests for sexual favors, and other verbal or physical conduct of a sexual nature constitute sexual harassment when (1) submission to such conduct is made either explicitly or implicitly a term or condition of an individual's employment, (2) submission to or rejection of such conduct by an individual is used as the basis for employment decisions affecting such individual, or (3) such conduct has the purpose or effect of unreasonably interfering with an individual's work performance or creating an intimidating, hostile, or offensive working environment.

(b) In determining whether alleged conduct constitutes sexual harassment, the Commission will look at the record as a whole and at the totality of the circumstances, such as the nature of the sexual advances and the context in which the alleged incidents occurred. The determination of the legality of a particular action will be made from the facts, on a case by case basis.

(c) Applying general title VII principles, an employer, employment agency, joint apprenticeship committee or labor organization (hereinafter collectively referred to as "employer") is responsible for its acts and those of its agents and supervisory employees with respect to sexual harassment regardless of whether the specific acts complained of were authorized or even forbidden by the employer and regardless of whether the employer knew or should have known of their occurrence. The Commission will examine the circumstances of the particular employment relationship and the job functions performed by the individual in determining whether an individual acts in either a supervisory or agency capacity.

(d) With respect to conduct between fellow employees, an employer is responsible for acts of sexual harassment in the workplace where the employer (or its agents or supervisory employees) knows or should have known of the conduct, unless it can show that it took immediate and appropriate corrective action.

(e) An employer may also be responsible for the acts of non-employees, with respect to sexual harassment of employees in the workplace, where the employer (or its agents or supervisory employees) knows or should have known of the conduct and fails to take immediate and appropriate corrective action. In reviewing these cases the Commission will consider the extent of the employer's control and any other legal responsibility which the employer may have with respect to the conduct of such non-employees.

(f) Prevention is the best tool for the elimination of sexual harassment. An employer should take all steps necessary to prevent sexual harassment from occurring, such as affirmatively raising the subject, expressing strong disapproval, developing appropriate sanctions, informing employees of their right to raise and how to raise the issue of harassment under title VII, and developing methods to sensitize all concerned.

(g) Other related practices: Where employment opportunities or benefits are granted because of an individual's submission to the employer's sexual advances or requests for sexual favors, the employer may be held liable for unlawful sex discrimination against other persons who were qualified for but denied that employment opportunity or benefit.

❖ 50. U.S. Department of Education Office of Civil Rights, Sexual Harassment Guidance

INTRODUCTION

Under Title IX of the Education Amendments of 1972 (Title IX) and its implementing regulations, no individual may be discriminated against on the basis of sex in any education program or activity receiving Federal financial assistance. Sexual harassment of students is a form of prohibited sex discrimination under the circumstances described in the Guidance. The following types of conduct constitute sexual harassment:

> Quid Pro Quo Harassment—A school employee explicitly or implicitly conditions a student's participation in an education program or activity or bases an educational decision on the student's submission to unwelcome sexual advances, requests for sexual favors, or other verbal, nonverbal, or physical conduct of a sexual nature. Quid pro quo harassment is equally unlawful whether the student resists and suffers the threatened harm or submits and thus avoids the threatened harm. Hostile Environment Sexual Harassment—Sexually harassing conduct (which can include unwelcome sexual advances, requests for sexual favors, and other verbal, nonverbal, or physical conduct of a sexual nature) by an employee, by another student, or by a third party that is sufficiently severe, persistent, or pervasive to limit a student's ability to participate in or benefit from an education program or activity, or to create a hostile or abusive educational environment.

Schools are required by the Title IX regulations to have grievance procedures through which students can complain of alleged sex discrimination, including sexual harassment. As outlined in this guidance, grievance procedures also provide schools with an excellent mechanism to be used in their efforts to prevent sexual harassment before it occurs.

Finally, if the alleged harassment involves issues of speech or expression, a school's obligations may be affected by the application of First Amendment principles.

These and other issues are discussed in more detail in the following paragraphs.

APPLICABILITY OF TITLE IX

Title IX applies to all public and private educational institutions that receive Federal funds, including elementary and secondary schools, school districts, proprietary schools, colleges, and universities. The Guidance uses the term "schools" to refer to all those institutions. The "education program or activity" of a school includes all of the school's operations. This means that Title IX protects students in connection with all of the academic, educational, extra-curricular, athletic, and other programs of the school, whether they take place in the facilities of the school, on a school bus, at a class or training program sponsored by the school at another location, or elsewhere.

It is important to recognize that Title IX's prohibition of sexual harassment does not extend to legitimate nonsexual touching or other nonsexual conduct. For example, a high school athletic coach hugging a student who made a goal or a kindergarten teacher's consoling hug for a child with a skinned knee will not be considered sexual harassment. Similarly, one student's demonstration of a sports maneuver or technique requiring contact with another student will not be considered sexual harassment. However, in some circumstances, nonsexual conduct may take on sexual connotations and may rise to the level of sexual harassment. For example, a teacher's repeatedly hugging and putting his or her arms around students under inappropriate circumstances could create a hostile environment.

Title IX protects any "person" from sex discrimination; accordingly both male and female students are protected from sexual harassment engaged in by a school's employees, other students, or third parties. Moreover, Title IX prohibits sexual harassment regardless of the sex of the harasser, i.e., even if the harasser and the person being harassed are members of the same sex. An example would be a campaign of sexually explicit graffiti directed at a particular girl by other girls.

Although Title IX does not prohibit discrimination on the basis of sexual orientation, sexual harassment directed at gay or lesbian students may constitute sexual harassment prohibited by Title IX. For example, if students heckle another student with comments based on the student's sexual orientation (e.g., "gay students are not welcome at this table in the cafeteria"), but their actions or language do not involve sexual conduct, their actions would not be sexual harassment covered by Title IX. On the other hand, harassing conduct of a sexual nature directed toward gay or lesbian students (e.g., if a male student or a group of male students target a lesbian student for physical sexual advances) may create a sexually hostile environment and, therefore, may be prohibited by Title IX. It should be noted that some State and local laws may prohibit discrimination on the basis of sexual orientation. Also, under certain circumstances, courts may permit redress for harassment on the basis of sexual orientation under other Federal legal authority.

It is also important to recognize that gender-based harassment, which may include acts of verbal, nonverbal, or physical aggression, intimidation, or hostility based on sex, but not involving conduct of a sexual nature, may be a form of sex discrimination that violates Title IX if it is sufficiently severe, persistent, or pervasive and directed at individuals because of their sex. For example, the repeated sabotaging of female graduate students' laboratory experiments by male students in the class could be the basis of a violation of Title IX. Although a comprehensive discussion of gender-based harassment is beyond the scope of this Guidance, in assessing all related circumstances to determine whether a hostile environment exists, incidents of gender-based harassment combined with incidents of sexual harassment could create a hostile environment, even if neither the gender-based harassment alone nor the sexual harassment alone would be sufficient to do so.

LIABILITY OF A SCHOOL FOR SEXUAL HARASSMENT
Liability of a School for Sexual Harassment by Its Employees

A school's liability for sexual harassment by its employees is determined by application of agency principles, i.e., by principles governing the delegation of authority to or authorization of another person to act on one's behalf.

Accordingly, a school will always be liable for even one instance of quid pro quo harassment by a school employee in a position of authority, such as a teacher or administrator, whether or not it knew, should have known, or approved of the harassment at issue. Under agency principles, if a teacher or other employee uses the authority he or she is given (e.g., to assign grades) to force a student to submit to sexual demands, the employee "stands in the shoes" of the school and the school will be responsible for the use of its authority by the employee or agent.

A school will also be liable for hostile environment sexual harassment by its employees, i.e., for harassment that is sufficiently severe, persistent, or pervasive to limit a student's ability to participate in or benefit from the education program or to create a hostile or abusive educational environment if the employee—(1) acted with apparent authority (i.e., because of the school's conduct, the employee reasonably appears to be acting on behalf of the school, whether or not the employee acted with authority); or (2) was aided in carrying out the sexual harassment of students by his or her position of authority with the institution. For example, a school will be liable if a teacher abuses his or her delegated authority over a student to create a hostile environment, such as if the teacher implicitly threatens to fail a student unless the student responds to his or her sexual advances, even though the teacher fails to carry out the threat.

As this example illustrates, in many cases the line between quid pro quo and hostile environment discrimination will be blurred, and the employee's conduct may constitute both types of harassment. However, what is important is that the school is liable for that conduct under application of agency principles, regardless of whether it is labeled as quid pro quo or hostile environment harassment.

Whether other employees, such as a janitor or cafeteria worker, are in positions of authority in relation to students—or whether it would be reasonable for the student to believe the employees are, even if the employees are not (i.e., apparent authority)—will depend on factors such as the authority actually given to the employee (e.g., in some elementary schools, a cafeteria worker may have authority to impose discipline) and the age of the student. For example, in some cases the younger a student is, the more likely it is that he or she will consider any adult employee to be in a position of authority.

Even in situations not involving (i) quid pro quo harassment, (ii) creation of a hostile environment through an employee's apparent authority, or (iii) creation of a hostile environment in which the employee is aided in carrying out the sexual harassment by his or her position of authority, a school will be liable for sexual harassment of its students by its employees under the same standards applicable to peer and third party hostile environment sexual harassment, as discussed in the next section. That is, if the school fails to take immediate and appropriate steps to remedy known harassment, then the school will be liable under Title IX. It is important to emphasize that under this standard of liability the school can avoid violating Title IX if it takes immediate and appropriate action upon notice of the harassment.

Liability of a School for Peer or Third Party Harassment

In contrast to the variety of situations in which a school may be liable for sexual harassment by its employees, a school will be liable under Title IX if its students sexually harass other students if (i) a hostile environment exists in the school's programs or activities, (ii) the school knows or should have known of the harassment, and (iii) the school fails to take immediate and appropriate corrective action. (Each of these factors is discussed in detail in subsequent sections of the Guidance.) Under these circumstances, a school's failure to respond to the existence of a hostile environment within its own programs or activities permits an atmosphere of sexual discrimination to permeate the educational program and results in discrimination prohibited by Title IX. Conversely, if, upon notice of hostile environment harassment, a school takes immediate and appropriate steps to remedy the hostile environment, the school has avoided violating Title IX. Thus, Title IX does not make a school responsible for the actions of harassing students, but rather for its own discrimination in failing to remedy it once the school has notice.

Sexually harassing conduct of third parties, who are not themselves employees or students at the school (e.g., a visiting speaker or members of a visiting athletic club) can also cause a sexually hostile environment in school programs or activities. For the same reason that a school will be liable under Title IX for a hostile environment caused by its students, a school will be liable if third parties sexually harass its students if (i) a hostile environment exists in the school's programs or activities, (ii) the school knows or should have known of the harassment, and (iii) the school fails to take immediate and appropriate corrective action. However, the type of appropriate steps the school should take will differ depending on the level of control the school has over the third party harasser. This issue is discussed in "Recipient's Response."

Effect of Grievance Procedures on Liability

Schools are required by the Title IX regulations to adopt and publish grievance procedures providing for prompt and equitable resolution of sex discrimination complaints, including complaints of sexual harassment, and to disseminate a policy against sex discrimination. (These issues are discussed in the section on "Prompt and Equitable Grievance Procedures.") These procedures provide a school with a mechanism for discovering sexual harassment as early as possible and for effectively correcting problems, as required by Title IX. By having a strong policy against sex discrimination and accessible, effective, and fairly applied grievance procedures, a school is telling its students that it does not tolerate sexual harassment and that students can report it without fear of adverse consequences.

Accordingly, in the absence of effective policies and grievance procedures, if the alleged harassment was sufficiently severe, persistent, or pervasive to create a hostile environment, a school will be in violation of Title IX because of the existence of a hostile environment, even if the school was not aware of the harassment and thus failed to remedy it. This is because, without a policy and procedure, a student does not know either of the school's interest in preventing this form of discrimination or how to report harassment so that it can be remedied. Moreover, under the agency principles previously discussed, a school's failure to implement effective policies and procedures against discrimination may create apparent authority for school employees to harass students.

OCR Case Resolution

If OCR is asked to investigate or otherwise resolve incidents of sexual harassment of students, including incidents caused by employees, other students, or third parties, OCR will consider whether—(1) the school has a policy prohibiting sex discrimination under Title IX and effective Title IX grievance procedures; (2) the school appropriately investigated or otherwise responded to allegations of sexual harassment; and (3) the school has taken immediate and appropriate corrective action responsive to quid pro quo or hostile environment harassment. (Issues related to appropriate investigative and corrective actions are discussed in detail in the section on "Recipient's Response.") If the school has taken each of these steps, OCR will consider the case against the school resolved and take no further action other than monitoring compliance with any agreement between the school and OCR. This is true in cases in which the school was in violation of Title IX, as well as those in which there has been no violation of Title IX.

WELCOMENESS

In order to be actionable as harassment, sexual conduct must be unwelcome. Conduct is unwelcome if the student did not request or invite it and "regarded the conduct as undesirable or offensive." Acquiescence in the conduct or the failure to complain does not always mean that the conduct was welcome. For example, a student may decide not to resist sexual advances of another student or may not file a complaint out of fear. In addition, a student may not object to a pattern of sexually demeaning comments directed at him or her by a group of students out of a concern that objections might cause the harassers to make more comments. The fact that a student may have accepted the conduct does not mean that he or she welcomed it. Also, the fact that a student willingly participated in conduct on one occasion does not prevent him or her from indicating that the same conduct has become unwelcome on a subsequent occasion. On the other hand, if a student actively participates in sexual banter and discussions and gives no indication that he or she objects, then the evidence generally will not support a conclusion that the conduct was unwelcome.

If younger children are involved, it may be necessary to determine the degree to which they are able to recognize that certain sexual conduct is conduct to which they can or should reasonably object and the degree to which they can articulate an objection. Accordingly, OCR will consider the age of the student, the nature of the conduct involved, and other relevant factors in determining whether a student had the capacity to welcome sexual conduct.

Schools should be particularly concerned about the issue of welcomeness if the harasser is in a position of authority. For instance, because students may be encouraged to believe that a teacher has absolute authority over the operation of his or her classroom, a student may not object to a teacher's sexually harassing comments during class; however, this does not necessarily mean that the conduct was welcome. Instead, the student may believe that any objections would be ineffective in stopping the harassment or may fear that by making objections he or she will be singled out for harassing comments or other retaliation.

In addition, OCR must consider particular issues of welcomeness if the alleged harassment relates to alleged "consensual" sexual relationships between a school's adult employees and its students. If elementary students are involved, welcomeness will not be an issue: OCR will never view sexual conduct between an adult school employee and an elementary school student as consensual. In cases involving secondary students, there will be a strong presumption that sexual conduct between an adult school employee and a student is not consensual. In cases involving older secondary students, subject to the presumption, OCR will consider a number of factors in determining whether a school employee's sexual advances or other sexual conduct could be considered welcome. In addition, OCR will consider these factors in all cases involving postsecondary students in making those determinations. The factors include:

> The nature of the conduct and the relationship of the school employee to the student, including the degree of influence (which could, at least in part, be affected by the student's age), authority, or control the employee has over the student.

> Whether the student was legally or practically unable to consent to the sexual conduct in ques-

tion. For example, a student's age could affect his or her ability to do so. Similarly, certain types of disabilities could affect a student's ability to do so.

If there is a dispute about whether harassment occurred or whether it was welcome—in a case in which it is appropriate to consider whether the conduct could be welcome—determinations should be made based on the totality of the circumstances. The following types of information may be helpful in resolving the dispute:

- Statements by any witnesses to the alleged incident.

- Evidence about the relative credibility of the allegedly harassed student and the alleged harasser. For example, the level of detail and consistency of each person's account should be compared in an attempt to determine who is telling the truth. Another way to assess credibility is to see if corroborative evidence is lacking where it should logically exist. However, the absence of witnesses may indicate only the unwillingness of others to step forward, perhaps due to fear of the harasser or a desire not to get involved.

- Evidence that the alleged harasser has been found to have harassed others may support the credibility of the student claiming the harassment; conversely, the student's claim will be weakened if he or she has been found to have made false allegations against other individuals.

- Evidence of the allegedly harassed student's reaction or behavior after the alleged harassment. For example, were there witnesses who saw the student immediately after the alleged incident who say that the student appeared to be upset? However, it is important to note that some students may respond to harassment in ways that do not manifest themselves right away, but may surface several days or weeks after the harassment. For example, a student may initially show no signs of having been harassed, but several weeks after the harassment, there may be significant changes in the student's behavior, including difficulty concentrating on academic work, symptoms of depression, and a desire to avoid certain individuals and places at school.

- Evidence about whether the student claiming harassment filed a complaint or took other action to protest the conduct soon after the alleged incident occurred. However, failure to immediately complain may merely reflect a fear of retaliation or a fear that the complainant may not be believed rather than that the alleged harassment did not occur.

- Other contemporaneous evidence. For example, did the student claiming harassment write about the conduct, and his or her reaction to it, soon after it occurred (e.g., in a diary or letter)? Did the student tell others (friends, parents) about the conduct (and his or her reaction to it) soon after it occurred?

SEVERE, PERSISTENT, OR PERVASIVE

Hostile environment sexual harassment of a student or students by other students, employees, or third parties is created if conduct of a sexual nature is sufficiently severe, persistent, or pervasive to limit a student's ability to participate in or benefit from the education program or to create a hostile or abusive educational environment. Thus, conduct that is sufficiently severe, but not persistent or pervasive, can result in hostile environment sexual harassment.

In deciding whether conduct is sufficiently severe, persistent, or pervasive, the conduct should be considered from both a subjective and objective perspective. In making this determination, all relevant circumstances should be considered:

- The degree to which the conduct affected one or more students' education. For a hostile environment to exist, the conduct must have limited the ability of a student to participate in or benefit from his or her education or altered the conditions of the student's educational environment.

  . . Many hostile environment cases involve tangible or obvious injuries. For example, a student's grades may go down or the student may be forced to withdraw from school because of the harassing behavior. A student may also suffer physical injuries and mental or emotional distress.

  . . However, a hostile environment may exist even if there is no tangible injury to the student. For example, a student may have been able to keep up his or her grades and continue to attend school even though it was more difficult for him or her to do so because of the harassing behavior. A student may be able to remain on a sports team, despite feeling humiliated or angered by harassment that creates a hostile environment. Harassing conduct in these examples alters the student's educational environment on the basis of sex.

  . . A hostile environment can occur even if the harassment is not targeted specifically at the individual complainant. For example, if a student or group of students regularly directs sexual comments toward a particular student, a hostile environment may be created not only for the targeted student, but also for others who witness the conduct. Similarly, if a middle school teacher directs sexual comments toward a particular student, a hostile environment may be created for the targeted student and for the students who witness the conduct.

- The type, frequency, and duration of the conduct. In most cases, a hostile environment will exist if there is a pattern or practice of harassment or if the harassment is sustained and nontrivial. For instance, if a young woman is taunted by one or more young men about her breasts or genital area or both, OCR may find that a hostile environment has been created, particularly if the conduct has gone on for some time, takes place throughout the school, or if the taunts are made by a number of students. The more severe the conduct, the less the need to show a repetitive series of incidents; this is particularly true if the harassment is physical. For instance, if the conduct is more severe, e.g., attempts to grab a female student's breasts, genital area, or buttocks, it need not be as persistent or pervasive in order to create a hostile environment. Indeed, a single or isolated incident of sexual harassment may, if sufficiently severe, create a hostile environment. On the other hand, conduct that is not severe, persistent, or pervasive will not create a hostile environment; e.g., a comment by one student to another student that she has a nice figure. Indeed, depending on the circumstances, this may not even be conduct of a sexual nature. Similarly, because students date one another, a request for a date or a gift of flowers, even if unwelcome, would not create a hostile environment. However, there may be circumstances in which repeated, unwelcome requests for dates or similar conduct could create a hostile environment. For example, a person may request dates in an intimidating or threatening manner.

- The identity of and relationship between the alleged harasser and the subject or subjects of the harassment. A factor to be considered, especially in cases involving allegations of sexual harassment of a student by a school employee, is the identity of and relationship between the alleged harasser and the subject or subjects of the harassment. For example, due to the power that a professor or teacher has over a student, sexually based conduct by that person toward a student is more likely to create a hostile environment than similar conduct by another student.

• The number of individuals involved. Sexual harassment may be committed by an individual or a group. In some cases, verbal comments or other conduct from one person might not be sufficient to create a hostile environment, but could be if done by a group. Similarly, while harassment can be directed toward an individual or a group, the effect of the conduct toward a group may vary, depending on the type of conduct and the context. For certain types of conduct, there may be "safety in numbers." For example, following an individual student and making sexual taunts to him or her may be very intimidating to that student but, in certain circumstances, less so to a group of students. On the other hand, persistent unwelcome sexual conduct still may create a hostile environment if directed toward a group.

• The age and sex of the alleged harasser and the subject or subjects of the harassment. For example, in the case of younger students, sexually harassing conduct is more likely to be intimidating if coming from an older student.

• The size of the school, location of the incidents, and context in which they occurred. Depending on the circumstances of a particular case, fewer incidents may have a greater effect at a small college than at a large university campus. Harassing conduct occurring on a school bus may be more intimidating than similar conduct on a school playground because the restricted area makes it impossible for the students to avoid their harassers. Harassing conduct in a personal or secluded area such as a dormitory room or residence hall can also have a greater effect (e.g., be seen as more threatening) than would similar conduct in a more public area. On the other hand, harassing conduct in a public place may be more humiliating. Each incident must be judged individually.

• Other incidents at the school. A series of instances at the school, not involving the same students, could—taken together—create a hostile environment, even if each by itself would not be sufficient.

• Incidents of gender-based, but non-sexual, harassment. Acts of verbal, nonverbal, or physical aggression, intimidation, or hostility based on sex, but not involving sexual activity or language, can be combined with incidents of sexual harassment to determine if the incidents of sexual harassment are sufficiently severe, persistent, or pervasive to create a sexually hostile environment.

NOTICE

A school will be in violation of Title IX if the school "has notice" of a sexually hostile environment and fails to take immediate and appropriate corrective action. A school has notice if it actually "knew, or in the exercise of reasonable care, should have known" about the harassment. In addition, as long as an agent or responsible employee of the school received notice, the school has notice.

A school can receive notice in many different ways. A student may have filed a grievance or complained to a teacher about fellow students sexually harassing him or her. A student, parent, or other individual may have contacted other appropriate personnel, such as a principal, campus security, bus driver, teacher, an affirmative action officer, or staff in the office of student affairs. An agent or responsible employee of the school may have witnessed the harassment. The school may receive notice in an indirect manner, from sources such as a member of the school staff, a member of the educational or local community, or the media. The school also may have received notice from flyers about the incident or incidents posted around the school.

Constructive notice exists if the school "should have" known about the harassment—if the school would have found out about the harassment through a "reasonably diligent inquiry." For example, if a school knows of some incidents of harassment, there may be situations in which it will be charged with notice of others—if the known incidents should have triggered an investigation that would have led to a discovery of the additional incidents. In other cases, the pervasiveness of the harassment may be enough to conclude that the school should have known of the hostile environment—if the harassment is widespread, openly practiced, or well-known to students and staff (such as sexual harassment occurring in hallways, graffiti in public areas, or harassment occurring during recess under a teacher's supervision).

In addition, if a school otherwise has actual or constructive notice of a hostile environment and fails to take immediate and appropriate corrective action, a school has violated Title IX even if the student fails to use the school's existing grievance procedures. . . .

FIRST AMENDMENT

In cases of alleged harassment, the protections of the First Amendment must be considered if issues of speech or expression are involved. Free speech rights apply in the classroom (e.g., classroom lectures and discussions) and in all other education programs and activities of public schools (e.g., public meetings and speakers on campus; campus debates, school plays and other cultural events; and student newspapers, journals and other publications). In addition, First Amendment rights apply to the speech of students and teachers.

Title IX is intended to protect students from sex discrimination, not to regulate the content of speech. OCR recognizes that the offensiveness of particular expression as perceived by some students, standing alone, is not a legally sufficient basis to establish a sexually hostile environment under Title IX. In order to establish a violation of Title IX, the harassment must be sufficiently severe, persistent, or pervasive to limit a student's ability to participate in or benefit from the education program or to create a hostile or abusive educational environment.

Moreover, in regulating the conduct of its students and its faculty to prevent or redress discrimination prohibited by Title IX (e.g., in responding to harassment that is sufficiently severe, persistent, or pervasive as to create a hostile environment), a school must formulate, interpret, and apply its rules so as to protect academic freedom and free speech rights. For instance, while the First Amendment may prohibit a school from restricting the right of students to express opinions about one sex that may be considered derogatory, the school can take steps to denounce those opinions and ensure that competing views are heard. The age of the students involved and the location or forum may affect how the school can respond consistent with the First Amendment. As an example of the application of free speech rights to allegations of sexual harassment, consider the following:

Example 1: In a college level creative writing class, a professor's required reading list includes excerpts from literary classics that contain descriptions of explicit sexual conduct, including scenes that depict women in submissive and demeaning roles. The professor also assigns students to write their own materials, which are read in class. Some of the student essays contain sexually derogatory themes about women. Several female students complain to the Dean of Students that the materials and related classroom discussion have created a sexually hostile environment for women in the class. What must the school do in response?

Answer: Academic discourse in this example is protected by the First Amendment even if it is offensive to individuals. Thus, Title IX would not require the school to discipline the professor or to censor the reading list or related class discussion.

Example 2: A group of male students repeatedly targets a female student for harassment during the bus ride home from school, including making explicit sexual comments about her body, passing around drawings that depict her engaging in sexual conduct, and, on several occasions, attempting to follow her home off the bus. The female student and her parents complain to the principal that the male students' conduct has created a hostile environment for girls on the bus and that they fear for their daughter's safety. What must the school do in response?

Answer: Threatening and intimidating actions targeted at a particular student or group of students, even though they contain elements of speech, are not protected by the First Amendment. The school must take reasonable and appropriate actions against the students, including disciplinary action if necessary, to remedy the hostile environment and prevent future harassment.

---

51. U.S. Supreme Court, *Meritor Savings Bank v. Vinson* (1986)

REHNQUIST, J., delivered the opinion of the Court, in which BURGER, C. J., and WHITE, POWELL, STEVENS, and O'CONNOR, JJ., joined. STEVENS, J., filed a concurring opinion. MARSHALL, J., filed an opinion concurring in the judgment, in which BRENNAN, BLACKMUN, and STEVENS, JJ., joined. . . .

This case presents important questions concerning claims of workplace "sexual harassment" brought under Title VII of the Civil Rights Act of 1964.

I

In 1974, respondent Mechelle Vinson met Sidney Taylor, a vice president of what is now petitioner Meritor Savings Bank (bank) and manager of one of its branch offices. When respondent asked whether she might obtain employment at the bank, Taylor gave her an application, which she completed and returned the next day; later that same day Taylor called her to say that she had been hired. With Taylor as her supervisor, respondent started as a teller-trainee, and thereafter was promoted to teller, head teller, and assistant branch manager. She worked at the same branch for four years, and it is undisputed that her advancement there was based on merit alone. In September 1978, respondent notified Taylor that she was taking sick leave for an indefinite period. On November 1, 1978, the bank discharged her for excessive use of that leave.

Respondent brought this action against Taylor and the bank, claiming that during her four years at the bank she had "constantly been subjected to sexual harassment" by Taylor in violation of Title VII. She sought injunctive relief, compensatory and punitive damages against Taylor and the bank, and attorney's fees.

At the 11-day bench trial, the parties presented conflicting testimony about Taylor's behavior during respondent's employment. Respondent testified that during her probationary period as a teller-trainee, Taylor treated her in a fatherly way and made no sexual advances. Shortly thereafter, however, he invited her out to dinner and, during the course of the meal, suggested that they go to a motel to have sexual relations. At first she refused, but out of what she described as fear of losing her job she eventually agreed. According to respondent, Taylor thereafter made repeated demands upon her for sexual favors, usually at the branch, both during and after business hours; she estimated that over the next several years she had intercourse with him some 40 or 50 times. In addition, respondent testified that Taylor fondled her in front of other employees, followed her into the women's restroom when she went there alone, exposed himself to her, and even forcibly raped her on several occasions. These activities ceased after 1977, respondent stated, when she started going with a steady boyfriend. . . .

Taylor denied respondent's allegations of sexual activity, testifying that he never fondled her, never made suggestive remarks to her, never engaged in sexual intercourse with her, and never asked her to do so. He contended instead that respondent made her accusations in response to a business-related dispute. The bank also denied respondent's allegations and asserted that any sexual harassment by Taylor was unknown to the bank and engaged in without its consent or approval.

The District Court denied relief, but did not resolve the conflicting testimony about the existence of a sexual relationship between respondent and Taylor. It found instead that

> "[i]f [respondent] and Taylor did engage in an intimate or sexual relationship during the time of [respondent's] employment with [the bank], that relationship was a voluntary one having nothing to do with her continued employment at [the bank] or her advancement or promotions at that institution."

The court ultimately found that respondent "was not the victim of sexual harassment and was not the victim of sexual discrimination" while employed at the bank.

Although it concluded that respondent had not proved a violation of Title VII, the District Court nevertheless went on to address the bank's liability. After noting the bank's express policy against discrimination, and finding that neither respondent nor any other employee had ever lodged a complaint about sexual harassment by Taylor, the court ultimately concluded that "the bank was without notice and cannot be held liable for the alleged actions of Taylor."

The Court of Appeals for the District of Columbia Circuit reversed. Relying on its earlier holding in Bundy v. Jackson, decided after the trial in this case, the court stated that a violation of Title VII may be predicated on either of two types of sexual harassment: harassment that involves the conditioning of concrete employment benefits on sexual favors, and harassment that, while not affecting economic benefits, creates a hostile or offensive working environment. The court drew additional support for this position from the Equal Employment Opportunity Commission's Guidelines on Discrimination Because of Sex, which set out these two types of sexual harassment claims. Believing that "Vinson's grievance was clearly of the [hostile environment] type," and that the District Court had not considered whether a violation of this type had occurred, the court concluded that a remand was necessary.

The court further concluded that the District Court's finding that any sexual relationship between respondent and Taylor "was a voluntary one" did not obviate the need for a remand. "[U]ncertain as to precisely what the [district] court meant" by this finding, the Court of Appeals held that if the evidence otherwise showed that "Taylor made Vinson's toleration of sexual harassment a condition of her employment," her voluntariness "had no materiality whatsoever." The court then surmised that the District Court's finding of voluntariness might have been based on "the voluminous testimony regarding respondent's dress and personal fantasies," testimony that the Court of Appeals believed "had no place in this litigation."

As to the bank's liability, the Court of Appeals held that an employer is absolutely liable for sexual harassment practiced by supervisory personnel, whether or not the employer knew or should have known about the misconduct. The court relied chiefly on Title VII's definition of "employer" to include "any agent of such a person," 42 U.S.C. 2000e(b), as well as on the EEOC Guidelines. The court held that a supervisor is an "agent" of his employer for Title VII purposes, even if he lacks authority to hire, fire, or promote, since "the mere existence—or even the appearance—of a significant degree of influence in vital job decisions gives any supervisor the opportunity to impose on employees."

II

. . . Respondent argues, and the Court of Appeals held, that unwelcome sexual advances that create an offensive or hostile working environment violate Title VII. Without question, when a supervisor sexually harasses a subordinate because of the subordinate's sex, that supervisor "discriminate[s]" on the basis of sex. Petitioner apparently does not challenge this proposition. It contends instead that in prohibiting discrimination with respect to "compensation, terms, conditions, or privileges" of employment, Congress was concerned with what petitioner describes as "tangible loss" of "an economic character," not "purely psychological aspects of the workplace environment."

We reject petitioner's view. First, the language of Title VII is not limited to "economic" or "tangible" discrimination. The phrase "terms, conditions, or privileges of employment" evinces a congressional intent "'to strike at the entire spectrum of disparate treatment of men and women'" in employment. Los Angeles Dept. of Water and Power v. Manhart, (1978). Petitioner has pointed to nothing in the Act to suggest that Congress contemplated the limitation urged here.

Second, in 1980 the EEOC issued Guidelines specifying that "sexual harassment," as there defined, is a form of sex discrimination prohibited by Title VII. As an "administrative interpretation of the Act by the enforcing agency," Griggs v. Duke Power Co., (1971), these Guidelines, "'while not controlling upon the courts by reason of their authority, do constitute a body of experience and informed judgment to which courts and litigants may properly resort for guidance,'" General Electric Co. v. Gilbert (1976). The EEOC Guidelines fully support the view that harassment leading to noneconomic injury can violate Title VII. . . .

Since the Guidelines were issued, courts have uniformly held, and we agree, that a plaintiff may establish a violation of Title VII by proving that discrimination based on sex has created a hostile or abusive work environment.

. . . The question remains, however, whether the District Court's ultimate finding that respondent "was not the victim of sexual harassment," effectively disposed of respondent's claim. The Court of Appeals recognized, we think correctly, that this ultimate finding was likely based on one or both of two erroneous views of the law. First, the District Court apparently believed that a claim for sexual harassment will not lie absent an economic effect on the complainant's employment . . .

Second, the District Court's conclusion that no actionable harassment occurred might have rested on its earlier "finding" that "[i]f [respondent] and Taylor did engage in an intimate or sexual relationship . . . , that relationship was a voluntary one." But the fact that sex-related conduct was "voluntary," in the sense that the complainant was not forced to participate against her will, is not a defense to a sexual harassment suit brought under Title VII. The gravamen of any sexual harassment claim is that the alleged sexual advances were "unwelcome." While the question whether particular conduct was indeed unwelcome presents difficult problems of proof and turns largely on credibility determinations committed to the trier of fact, the District Court in this case erroneously focused on the "voluntariness" of respondent's participation in the claimed sexual episodes. The correct inquiry is whether respondent by her conduct indicated that the alleged sexual advances were unwelcome, not whether her actual participation in sexual intercourse was voluntary.

Petitioner contends that even if this case must be remanded to the District Court, the Court of Appeals erred in one of the terms of its remand. Specifically, the Court of Appeals stated that testimony about respondent's "dress and personal fantasies," which the District Court apparently admitted into evidence, "had no place in this litigation." The apparent ground for this conclusion was that respondent's voluntariness in submitting to Taylor's advances was immaterial to her sexual harassment claim. While "voluntariness" in the sense of consent is not a defense to such a claim, it does not follow that a complainant's sexually provocative speech or dress is irrelevant as a matter of law in determining whether he or she found particular sexual advances unwelcome. To the contrary, such evidence is obviously relevant. The EEOC Guidelines emphasize that the trier of fact must determine the existence of sexual harassment in light of "the record as a whole" and "the totality of circumstances, such as the nature of the sexual advances and the context in which the alleged incidents occurred." Respondent's claim that any marginal relevance of the evidence in question was outweighed by the potential for unfair prejudice is the sort of argument properly addressed to the District Court. In this case the District Court concluded that the evidence should be admitted, and the Court of Appeals' contrary conclusion was based upon the erroneous, categorical view that testimony about provocative dress and publicly expressed sexual fantasies "had no place in this litigation." While the District Court must carefully weigh the applicable considerations in deciding whether to admit evidence of this kind, there is no per se rule against its admissibility.

Although the District Court concluded that respondent had not proved a violation of Title VII, it nevertheless went on to consider the question of the bank's liability. Finding that "the bank was without notice" of Taylor's alleged conduct, and that notice to Taylor was not the equivalent of notice to the bank, the court concluded that the bank therefore could not be held liable for Taylor's alleged actions. The Court of Appeals took the opposite view, holding that an employer is strictly liable for a hostile environment created by a supervisor's sexual advances, even though the employer neither knew nor reasonably could have known of the alleged misconduct. The court held that a supervisor, whether or not he possesses the authority to hire, fire, or promote, is necessarily an "agent" of his employer for all Title VII purposes, since "even the appearance" of such authority may enable him to impose himself on his subordinates. . . .

This debate over the appropriate standard for employer liability has a rather abstract quality about it given the state of the record in this case. We do not know at this stage whether Taylor made any sexual advances toward respondent at all, let alone whether those advances were unwelcome, whether they were sufficiently pervasive to constitute a condition of employment, or whether they were "so pervasive and so long continuing . . . that the employer must have become conscious of [them]."

We therefore decline the parties' invitation to issue a definitive rule on employer liability, but we do agree with the EEOC that Congress wanted courts to look to agency principles for guidance in this area. While such common-law principles may not be transferable in all their particulars to Title VII, Congress' decision to define "employer" to include any "agent" of an employer, surely evinces an intent to place some limits on the acts of employees for which employers under Title VII are to be held responsible. For this reason, we hold that the Court of Appeals erred in concluding that employers are always automatically liable for sexual harassment by their supervisors. For the same reason, absence of notice to an employer does not necessarily insulate that employer from liability.

Finally, we reject petitioner's view that the mere existence of a grievance procedure and a policy against discrimination, coupled with respondent's failure to invoke that procedure, must insulate petitioner from liability. While those facts are plainly relevant, the situation before us demonstrates why they are not necessarily dispositive. Petitioner's general nondiscrimination policy did not address sexual harassment in particular, and thus did not alert employees to their employer's interest in correcting that form of discrimination. Moreover, the bank's grievance procedure apparently required an employee to complain first to her supervisor, in this case Taylor. Since Taylor was the alleged perpetrator, it is not altogether surprising that respondent failed to invoke the procedure and report her grievance to him. Petitioner's contention that respondent's failure should insulate it from liability might be substantially stronger if its procedures were better calculated to encourage victims of harassment to come forward.

In sum, we hold that a claim of "hostile environment" sex discrimination is actionable under Title VII, that the District Court's findings were insufficient to dispose of respondent's hostile environment claim, and that the District Court did not err in admitting testimony about respondent's sexually provocative speech and dress. As to employer liability, we conclude that the Court of Appeals was wrong to entirely disregard agency principles and impose absolute liability on employers for the acts of their supervisors, regardless of the circumstances of a particular case.

Accordingly, the judgment of the Court of Appeals reversing the judgment of the District Court is affirmed, and the case is remanded for further proceedings consistent with this opinion.

52. U.S. Supreme Court, *Franklin v. Gwinnett County Public Schools* (1992)

WHITE, J., delivered the opinion of the Court, in which BLACKMUN, STEVENS, O'CONNOR, KENNEDY, and SOUTER, JJ., joined. SCALIA, J., filed an opinion concurring in the judgment, in which REHNQUIST, C.J., and THOMAS, J., joined. . . .

I

Petitioner Christine Franklin was a student at North Gwinnett High School in Gwinnett County, Georgia, between September, 1985, and August, 1989. Respondent Gwinnett County School District operates the high school and receives federal funds. According to the complaint filed on December 29, 1988, in the United States District Court for the Northern District of Georgia, Franklin was subjected to continual sexual harassment beginning in the autumn of her tenth grade year (1986) from Andrew Hill, a sports coach and teacher employed by the district. Among other allegations, Franklin avers that Hill engaged her in sexually-oriented conversations in which he asked about her sexual experiences with her boyfriend and whether she would consider having sexual intercourse with an older man; that Hill forcibly kissed her on the mouth in the school parking lot; that he telephoned her at her home and asked if she would meet him socially; and that, on three occasions in her junior year, Hill interrupted a class, requested that the teacher excuse Franklin, and took her to a private office where he subjected her to coercive intercourse. The complaint further alleges that, though they became aware of and investigated Hill's sexual harassment of Franklin and other female students, teachers and administrators took no action to halt it, and discouraged Franklin from pressing charges against Hill. On April 14, 1988, Hill resigned on the condition that all matters pending against him be dropped. The school thereupon closed its investigation. . . .

II

In Cannon v. University of Chicago, (1979), the Court held that Title IX is enforceable through an implied right of action.[1] We have no occasion here to reconsider that decision. Rather, in this case we must decide what remedies are available in a suit brought pursuant to this implied right. As we have often stated, the question of what remedies are available under a statute that provides a private right of action is "analytically distinct" from the issue of whether such a right exists in the first place. Davis v. Passman, (1979). Thus, although we examine the text and history of a statute to determine whether Congress intended to create a right of action, we presume the availability of all appropriate remedies unless Congress has expressly indicated otherwise. This principle has deep roots in our jurisprudence.

"[W]here legal rights have been invaded, and a federal statute provides for a general right to sue for such invasion, federal courts may use any available remedy to make good the wrong done."

Bell v. Hood (1946). The Court explained this longstanding rule as jurisdictional, and upheld the exercise of the federal courts' power to award appropriate relief so long as a cause of action existed under the Constitution or laws of the United States.

The Bell Court's reliance on this rule was hardly revolutionary. From the earliest years of the Republic, the Court has recognized the power of the judiciary to award appropriate remedies to redress injuries actionable in federal court, although it did not always distinguish clearly between a right to bring suit and a remedy available under such a right. In Marbury v. Madison, (1803), for example, Chief Justice Marshall observed that our government "has been emphatically termed a government of laws, and not of men. It will certainly cease to deserve this high appellation if the laws furnish no remedy for the violation of a vested legal right." This principle originated in the English common law, and Blackstone described it as a "general and indisputable rule that, where there is a legal right, there is also a legal remedy, by suit or action at law, whenever that right is invaded." W. Blackstone, Commentaries (1783).

In Kendall v. United States, (1838), the Court applied these principles to an Act of Congress that accorded a right of action in mail carriers to sue for adjustment and settlement of certain claims for extra services but which did not specify the precise remedy available to the carriers. After surveying possible remedies, which included an action against the postmaster general for monetary damages, the Court held that the carriers were entitled to a writ of mandamus compelling payment under the terms of the statute.[2] "It cannot be denied but that congress had the power to command that act to be done," the Court stated, "and the power to enforce the performance of the act must rest somewhere, or it will present a case which has often been said to involve a monstrous absurdity in a well organized government, that there should be no remedy, although a clear and undeniable right should be shown to exist. And if the remedy cannot be applied by the circuit court of this district, it exists nowhere."

The Court relied upon this traditional presumption again after passage of the Federal Safety Appliance Act of 1893. In Texas & Pacific R. Co. v. Rigsby, (1916), the Court first had to determine whether the Act supported an implied right of action. After answering that question in the affirmative, the Court then upheld a claim for monetary damages: "A disregard of the command of the statute is a wrongful act, and where it results in damage to one of the class for whose especial benefit the statute was enacted, the right to recover the damages from the party in default is implied, according to a doctrine of the common law. . . ." The foundation upon which the Bell v. Hood Court articulated this traditional presumption, therefore, was well settled. . . .

III

We now address whether Congress intended to limit application of this general principle in the enforcement of Title IX. Because the cause of action was inferred by the Court in Cannon, the usual recourse to statutory text and legislative history in the period prior to that decision necessarily will not enlighten our analysis. Respondents and the United States fundamentally misunderstand the nature of the inquiry, therefore, by needlessly dedicating large portions of their briefs to discussions of how the text and legislative intent behind Title IX are "silent" on the issue of available remedies. Since the Court in Cannon concluded that this statute supported no express right of action, it is hardly surprising that Congress also said nothing about the applicable remedies for an implied right of action.

During the period prior to the decision in Cannon, the inquiry, in any event, is not "'basically a matter of statutory construction,'" as the United States asserts. Brief for United States as Amicus Curiae 8 (quoting Transamerica Mortgage Advisors, Inc. v. Lewis, (1979)). Rather, in determining Congress's intent to limit application of the traditional presumption in favor of all appropriate relief, we evaluate the state of the law when the legislature passed Title IX. In the years before and after Congress enacted this statute, the Court "follow[ed] a common law tradition [and] regarded the denial of a remedy as the exception, rather than the rule." As we outlined in Part II, this has been the prevailing presumption in our federal courts since at least the early nineteenth century. In Cannon, the majority upheld an implied right of action in part because, in the decade immediately preceding enactment of Title IX in 1972, this Court had found implied rights of action in six cases. In three of those cases, the Court had approved a damages remedy. Wholly apart from the wisdom of the Cannon holding, therefore, the same contextual approach used to justify an implied right of action more than amply demonstrates the lack of any legislative intent to abandon the traditional presumption in favor of all available remedies.

In the years after the announcement of Cannon, on the other hand, a more traditional method of statutory analysis is possible, because Congress was legislating with full cognizance of that decision. Our reading of the two amendments to Title IX enacted after Cannon leads us to conclude that Congress did not intend to limit the remedies available in a suit brought under Title IX. In the Civil Rights Remedies Equalization Amendment of 1986, Congress abrogated the States' Eleventh Amendment immunity under Title IX, Title VI, 504 of the Rehabilitation Act of 1973, and the Age Discrimination Act of 1975. This statute cannot be read except as a validation of Cannon's holding. A subsection of the 1986 law provides that, in a suit against a State, "remedies (including remedies both at law and in equity) are available for such a violation to the same extent as such remedies are available for such a violation in the suit against any public or private entity other than a State." While it is true that this saving clause says nothing about the nature of those other available remedies, absent any contrary indication in the text or history of the statute, we presume Congress enacted this statute with the prevailing traditional rule in mind.

In addition to the Civil Rights Remedies Equalization Amendment of 1986, Congress also enacted the Civil Rights Restoration Act of 1987. Without in any way altering the existing rights of action and the corresponding remedies permissible under Title IX, Title VI, 504 of the Rehabilitation Act, and the Age Discrimination Act, Congress broadened the coverage of these antidiscrimination provisions in this legislation. In seeking to correct what it considered to be an unacceptable decision on our part in Grove City College v. Bell, (1984), Congress made no effort to restrict the right of action recognized in Cannon and ratified in the 1986 Act or to alter the traditional presumption in favor of any appropriate relief for violation of a federal right. We cannot say, therefore, that Congress has limited the remedies available to a complainant in a suit brought under Title IX. . . .

In sum, we conclude that a damages remedy is available for an action brought to enforce Title IX. The judgment of the Court of Appeals, therefore, is reversed, and the case is remanded for further proceedings consistent with this opinion.

So ordered. . . .

JUSTICE SCALIA, with whom THE CHIEF JUSTICE and JUSTICE THOMAS join, concurring in the judgment.

The substantive right at issue here is one that Congress did not expressly create, but that this Court found to be "implied." See Cannon v. University of Chicago, (1979). Quite obviously, the search for what was Congress's remedial intent as to a right whose very existence Congress did not expressly acknowledge is unlikely to succeed; it is "hardly surprising," as the Court says, that the usual sources yield no explicit answer.

The Court finds an implicit answer, however, in the legislators' presumptive awareness of our practice of using "any available remedy" to redress violations of legal rights. Bell v. Hood (1946). This strikes me as question-begging. We can plausibly assume acquiescence in our Bell v. Hood presumption when the legislature says nothing about remedy in expressly creating a private right of action; perhaps even when it says nothing about remedy in creating a private right of action by clear textual implication; but not, I think, when it says nothing about remedy in a statute in which the courts divine a private right of action on the basis of "contextual" evidence such as that in Cannon, which charged Congress with knowledge of a court of appeals' creation of a cause of action under a similarly worded statute. Whatever one thinks of the validity of the last approach, it surely rests on attributed, rather than actual, congressional knowledge. It does not demonstrate an explicit legislative decision to create a cause of action, and so could not be expected to be accompanied by a legislative decision to alter the application of Bell v. Hood. Given the nature of Cannon and some of our earlier "implied right of action" cases, what the Court's analytical construct comes down to is this: unless Congress expressly legislates a more limited remedial policy with respect to rights of action it does not know it is creating, it intends the full gamut of remedies to be applied.

In my view, when rights of action are judicially "implied," categorical limitations upon their remedial scope may be judicially implied as well. Although we have abandoned the expansive rights-creating approach exemplified by Cannon, and perhaps ought to abandon the notion of implied causes of action entirely, causes of action that came into existence under the ancien regime should be limited by the same logic that gave them birth. To require, with respect to a right that is not consciously and intentionally created, that any limitation of remedies must be express is to provide, in effect, that the most questionable of private rights will also be the most expansively remediable. As the United States puts it, "[w]hatever the merits of "implying" rights of action may be, there is no justification for treating [congressional] silence as the equivalent of the broadest imaginable grant of remedial authority." Brief for United States as Amicus Curiae 12–13.

I nonetheless agree with the Court's disposition of this case. Because of legislation enacted subsequent to Cannon, it is too late in the day to address whether a judicially implied exclusion of damages under Title IX would be appropriate. The Civil Rights Remedies Equalization Amendment of 1986 must be read, in my view, not only "as a validation of Cannon's holding," but also as an implicit acknowledgment that damages are available. I therefore concur in the judgment.

Editor's Notes

1. An implied right of action is an implied right to bring a specific case to court.
2. A writ of mandamus is an order issued by a superior court to compel a lower court or a government officer to perform.

❖ 53. U.S. Supreme Court,
Harris v. Forklift Systems, Inc. (1993)

O'CONNOR, J., delivered the opinion for a unanimous Court. SCALIA, J., and GINS-BURG, J., filed concurring opinions.

In this case, we consider the definition of a discriminatorily "abusive work environment" (also known as a "hostile work environment") under Title VII of the Civil Rights Act of 1964.

I

Teresa Harris worked as a manager at Forklift Systems, Inc., an equipment rental company, from April, 1985, until October, 1987. Charles Hardy was Forklift's president.

The Magistrate found that, throughout Harris' time at Forklift, Hardy often insulted her because of her gender and often made her the target of unwanted sexual innuendos. Hardy told Harris on several occasions, in the presence of other employees, "You're a woman, what do you know" and "We need a man as the rental manager"; at least once, he told her she was "a dumb ass woman." Again in front of others, he suggested that the two of them "go to the Holiday Inn to negotiate [Harris'] raise." Hardy occasionally asked Harris and other female employees to get coins from his front pants pocket. He threw objects on the ground in front of Harris and other women, and asked them to pick the objects up. He made sexual innuendos about Harris' and other women's clothing.

In mid-August, 1987, Harris complained to Hardy about his conduct. Hardy said he was surprised that Harris was offended, claimed he was only joking, and apologized. He also promised he would stop, and, based on this assurance Harris stayed on the job. But in early September, Hardy began anew: While Harris was arranging a deal with one of Forklift's customers, he asked her, again in front of other employees, "What did you do, promise the guy . . . some [sex] Saturday night?" On October 1, Harris collected her paycheck and quit.

Harris then sued Forklift, claiming that Hardy's conduct had created an abusive work environment for her because of her gender. The United States District Court for the Middle District of Tennessee, adopting the report and recommendation of the Magistrate, found this to be "a close case," but held that Hardy's conduct did not create an abusive environment. The court found that some of Hardy's comments "offended [Harris], and would offend the reasonable woman," but that they were not "so severe as to be expected to seriously affect [Harris'] psychological wellbeing. A reasonable woman manager under like circumstances would have been offended by Hardy, but his conduct would not have risen to the level of interfering with that person's work performance.

"Neither do I believe that [Harris] was subjectively so offended that she suffered injury. . . . Although Hardy may at times have genuinely offended [Harris], I do not believe that he created a working environment so poisoned as to be intimidating or abusive to [Harris]."

II

Title VII of the Civil Rights Act of 1964 makes it "an unlawful employment practice for an employer . . . to discriminate against any individual with respect to his compensation, terms, conditions, or privileges of employment, because of such individual's race, color, religion, sex, or national origin." As we made clear in Meritor Savings Bank v. Vinson, (1986), this language "is not limited to "economic" or "tangible" discrimination. The phrase "terms, conditions, or privileges of employment" evinces a congressional intent "to strike at the entire spectrum of disparate treatment of men and women in employment," which includes requiring people to work in a discriminatorily hostile or abusive environment. When the workplace is permeated with "discriminatory intimidation, ridicule, and insult," that is "sufficiently severe or pervasive to alter the conditions of the victim's employment and create an abusive working environment," Title VII is violated.

This standard, which we reaffirm today, takes a middle path between making actionable any conduct that is merely offensive and requiring the conduct to cause a tangible psychological injury. As we pointed out in Meritor, "mere utterance of an . . . epithet which engenders offensive feelings in a employee," does not sufficiently affect the conditions of employment to implicate Title VII. Conduct that is not severe or pervasive enough to create an objectively hostile or abusive work environment—an environment that a reasonable person would find hostile or abusive—is beyond Title VII's purview. Likewise, if the victim does not subjectively perceive the environment to be abusive, the conduct has not actually altered the conditions of the victim's employment, and there is no Title VII violation.

But Title VII comes into play before the harassing conduct leads to a nervous breakdown. A discriminatorily abusive work environment, even one that does not seriously affect employees' psychological wellbeing, can and often will detract from employees' job performance, discourage employees from remaining on the job, or keep them from advancing in their careers. Moreover, even without regard to these tangible effects, the very fact that the discriminatory conduct was so severe or pervasive that it created a work environment abusive to employees because of their race, gender, religion, or national origin offends Title VII's broad rule of workplace equality. The appalling conduct alleged in Meritor, and the reference in that case to environments "'so heavily polluted with discrimination as to destroy completely the emotional and psychological stability of minority group workers,'" merely present some especially egregious examples of harassment. They do not mark the boundary of what is actionable.

We therefore believe the District Court erred in relying on whether the conduct "seriously affect[ed] plaintiff's psychological wellbeing" or led her to "suffe[r] injury." Such an inquiry may needlessly focus the factfinder's attention on concrete psychological harm, an element Title VII does not require. Certainly Title VII bars conduct that would seriously affect a reasonable person's psychological wellbeing, but the statute is not limited to such conduct. So long as the environment would reasonably be perceived, and is perceived, as hostile or abusive, there is no need for it also to be psychologically injurious.

This is not, and by its nature cannot be, a mathematically precise test. We need not answer today all the potential questions it raises, nor specifically address the EEOC's new regulations on this subject. But we can say that whether an environment is "hostile" or "abusive" can be determined only by looking at all the circumstances. These may include the frequency of the discriminatory conduct; its severity; whether it is physically threatening or humiliating, or a mere offensive utterance; and whether it unreasonably interferes with an employee's work performance. The effect on the employee's psychological wellbeing is, of course, relevant to determining whether the plaintiff actually found the environment abusive. But, while psychological harm, like any other relevant factor, may be taken into account, no single factor is required.

III

Forklift, while conceding that a requirement that the conduct seriously affect psychological wellbeing is unfounded, argues that the District Court nonetheless correctly applied the Meritor standard. We disagree. Though the District Court did conclude that the work environment was not "intimidating or abusive to [Harris]," it did so only after finding that the conduct was not "so severe as to be expected to seriously affect plaintiff's psychological well-being," and that Harris was not "subjectively so offended that she suffered injury." The District Court's application of these incorrect standards may well have influenced its ultimate conclusion, especially given that the court found this to be a "close case."

We therefore reverse the judgment of the Court of Appeals, and remand the case for further proceedings consistent with this opinion.

JUSTICE SCALIA, concurring.

Meritor Savings Bank v. Vinson, (1986), held that Title VII prohibits sexual harassment that takes the form of a hostile work environment. The Court stated that sexual harassment is actionable if it is "sufficiently severe or pervasive 'to alter the conditions of [the victim's] employment and create an abusive work environment.'" Today's opinion elaborates that the challenged conduct must be severe or pervasive enough "to create an objectively hostile or abusive work environment—an environment that a reasonable person would find hostile or abusive."

"Abusive" (or "hostile," which in this context I take to mean the same thing) does not seem to me a very clear standard—and I do not think clarity is at all increased by adding the adverb "objectively" or by appealing to a "reasonable person's" notion of what the vague word means. Today's opinion does list a number of factors that contribute to abusiveness, but since it neither says how much of each is necessary (an impossible task) nor identifies any single factor as determinative, it thereby adds little certitude. As a practical matter, today's holding lets virtually unguided juries decide whether sex-related conduct engaged in (or permitted by) an employer is egregious enough to warrant an award of damages. One might say that what constitutes "negligence" (a traditional jury question) is not much more clear and certain than what constitutes "abusiveness." Perhaps so. But the class of plaintiffs seeking to recover for negligence is limited to those who have suffered harm, whereas, under this statute "abusiveness" is to be the test of whether legal harm has been suffered, opening more expansive vistas of litigation.

Be that as it may, I know of no alternative to the course the Court today has taken. One of the factors mentioned in the Court's nonexhaustive list—whether the conduct unreasonably interferes with an employee's work performance—would, if it were made an absolute test, provide greater guidance to juries and employers. But I see no basis for such a limitation in the language of the statute. Accepting Meritor's interpretation of the term "conditions of employment" as the law, the test is not whether work has been impaired, but whether working conditions have been discriminatorily altered. I know of no test more faithful to the inherently vague statutory language than the one the Court today adopts. For these reasons, I join the opinion of the Court.

JUSTICE GINSBURG, concurring.

Today the Court reaffirms the holding of Meritor Savings Bank v. Vinson, (1986): "[A] plaintiff may establish a violation of Title VII by proving that discrimination based on sex has created a hostile or abusive work environment." The critical issue, Title VII's text indicates, is whether members of one sex are exposed to disadvantageous terms or conditions of employment to which members of the other sex are not exposed. As the Equal Employment Opportunity Commission emphasized, the adjudicator's inquiry should center, dominantly, on whether the discriminatory conduct has unreasonably interfered with the plaintiff's work performance. To show such interference, "the plaintiff need not prove that his or her tangible productivity has declined as a result of the harassment." It suffices to prove that a reasonable person subjected to the discriminatory conduct would find, as the plaintiff did, that the harassment so altered working conditions as to "ma[k]e it more difficult to do the job."

The Court's opinion, which I join, seems to me in harmony with the view expressed in this concurring statement.

---

54. U.S. Supreme Court,
Oncale v. Sundowner Offshore Services, Inc. (1998)

SCALIA, J., delivered the opinion for a unanimous Court. THOMAS, J., filed a concurring opinion.

This case presents the question whether workplace harassment can violate Title VII's prohibition against "discriminat[ion] . . . because of . . . sex," when the harasser and the harassed employee are of the same sex.

I

. . . In late October 1991, [Joseph] Oncale was working for respondent Sundowner Offshore Services on a Chevron U.S.A., Inc., oil platform in the Gulf of Mexico. He was employed as a roustabout on an eight-man crew which included respondents John Lyons, Danny Pippen, and Brandon Johnson. Lyons, the crane operator, and Pippen, the driller, had supervisory authority. On several occasions, Oncale was forcibly subjected to sex related, humiliating actions against him by Lyons, Pippen and Johnson in the presence of the rest of the crew. Pippen and Lyons also physically assaulted Oncale in a sexual manner, and Lyons threatened him with rape.

Oncale's complaints to supervisory personnel produced no remedial action; in fact, the company's Safety Compliance Clerk, Valent Hohen, told Oncale that Lyons and Pippen "picked [on] him all the time too," and called him a name suggesting homosexuality. On-cale eventually quit, asking that his pink slip reflect that he "voluntarily left due to sexual harassment and verbal abuse." When asked at his deposition why he left Sundowner, On-cale stated "I felt that if I didn't leave my job, that I would be raped or forced to have sex."

Oncale filed a complaint against Sundowner in the United States District Court for the Eastern District of Louisiana, alleging that he was discriminated against in his employ-ment because of his sex. Relying on the Fifth Circuit's decision in Garcia v. Elf Atochem North America (1994), the district court held that "Mr. Oncale, a male, has no cause of ac-tion under Title VII for harassment by male co-workers." On appeal, a panel of the Fifth Circuit concluded that Garcia was binding Circuit precedent, and affirmed.

II

Title VII of the Civil Rights Act of 1964 provides, in relevant part, that "[i]t shall be an un-lawful employment practice for an employer . . . to discriminate against any individual with respect to his compensation, terms, conditions, or privileges of employment, because of such individual's race, color, religion, sex, or national origin." We have held that this not only covers "terms" and "conditions" in the narrow contractual sense, but "evinces a con-gressional intent to strike at the entire spectrum of disparate treatment of men and women in employment." "When the workplace is permeated with discriminatory intimidation, ridicule, and insult that is sufficiently severe or pervasive to alter the conditions of the vic-tim's employment and create an abusive working environment, Title VII is violated."

Title VII's prohibition of discrimination "because of . . . sex" protects men as well as women, and in the related context of racial discrimination in the workplace we have re-jected any conclusive presumption that an employer will not discriminate against mem-bers of his own race. "Because of the many facets of human motivation, it would be unwise to presume as a matter of law that human beings of one definable group will not discrim-inate against other members of that group." In Johnson v. Transportation Agency, Santa Clara Cty., (1987), a male employee claimed that his employer discriminated against him because of his sex when it preferred a female employee for promotion. Although we ulti-mately rejected the claim on other grounds, we did not consider it significant that the su-pervisor who made that decision was also a man. If our precedents leave any doubt on the question, we hold today that nothing in Title VII necessarily bars a claim of discrimina-tion "because of . . . sex" merely because the plaintiff and the defendant (or the person charged with acting on behalf of the defendant) are of the same sex. Courts have had little trouble with that principle in cases like Johnson, where an employee claims to have been passed over for a job or promotion. But when the issue arises in the context of a "hostile en-vironment" sexual harassment claim, the state and federal courts have taken a bewildering variety of stances. Some, like the Fifth Circuit in this case, have held that same-sex sexual harassment claims are never cognizable under Title VII. Other decisions say that such claims are actionable only if the plaintiff can prove that the harasser is homosexual (and thus presumably motivated by sexual desire). Still others suggest that workplace harass-ment that is sexual in content is always actionable, regardless of the harasser's sex, sexual orientation, or motivations.

We see no justification in the statutory language or our precedents for a categorical rule excluding same-sex harassment claims from the coverage of Title VII. As some courts have observed, male-on-male sexual harassment in the workplace was assuredly not the princi-pal evil Congress was concerned with when it enacted Title VII. But statutory prohibitions often go beyond the principal evil to cover reasonably comparable evils, and it is ultimately the provisions of our laws rather than the principal concerns of our legislators by which we are governed. Title VII prohibits "discriminat [ion] . . . because of . . . sex" in the "terms" or "conditions" of employment. Our holding that this includes sexual harassment must extend to sexual harassment of any kind that meets the statutory requirements.

Respondents and their amici contend that recognizing liability for same-sex harassment will transform Title VII into a general civility code for the American workplace. But that risk is no greater for same-sex than for opposite-sex harassment, and is adequately met by careful attention to the requirements of the statute. Title VII does not prohibit all verbal or physical harassment in the workplace; it is directed only at "discriminat[ion] . . . because of . . . sex." We have never held that workplace harassment, even harassment between men and women, is automatically discrimination because of sex merely because the words used have sexual content or connotations. "The critical issue, Title VII's text indicates, is whether members of one sex are exposed to disadvantageous terms or conditions of employment to which members of the other sex are not exposed."

Courts and juries have found the inference of discrimination easy to draw in most male-female sexual harassment situations, because the challenged conduct typically involves explicit or implicit proposals of sexual activity; it is reasonable to assume those proposals would not have been made to someone of the same sex. The same chain of inference would be available to a plaintiff alleging same-sex harassment, if there were credible evidence that the harasser was homosexual. But harassing conduct need not be motivated by sexual desire to support an inference of discrimination on the basis of sex. A trier of fact might reasonably find such discrimination, for example, if a female victim is harassed in such sex-specific and derogatory terms by another woman as to make it clear that the harasser is motivated by general hostility to the presence of women in the workplace. A same-sex harassment plaintiff may also, of course, offer direct comparative evidence about how the alleged harasser treated members of both sexes in a mixed-sex workplace. Whatever evidentiary route the plaintiff chooses to follow, he or she must always prove that the conduct at issue was not merely tinged with offensive sexual connotations, but actually constituted "discrimina[tion] . . . because of . . . sex."

And there is another requirement that prevents Title VII from expanding into a general civility code: As we emphasized in Meritor and Harris, the statute does not reach genuine but innocuous differences in the ways men and women routinely interact with members of the same sex and of the opposite sex. The prohibition of harassment on the basis of sex requires neither asexuality nor androgyny in the workplace; it forbids only behavior so objectively offensive as to alter the "conditions" of the victim's employment. "Conduct that is not severe or pervasive enough to create an objectively hostile or abusive work environment—an environment that a reasonable person would find hostile or abusive—is beyond Title VII's purview." We have always regarded that requirement as crucial, and as sufficient to ensure that courts and juries do not mistake ordinary socializing in the workplace—such as male-on-male horseplay or intersexual flirtation—for discriminatory "conditions of employment."

We have emphasized, moreover, that the objective severity of harassment should be judged from the perspective of a reasonable person in the plaintiff's position, considering "all the circumstances." In same-sex (as in all) harassment cases, that inquiry requires careful consideration of the social context in which particular behavior occurs and is experienced by its target. A professional football player's working environment is not severely or pervasively abusive, for example, if the coach smacks him on the buttocks as he heads onto the field, even if the same behavior would reasonably be experienced as abusive by the coach's secretary (male or female) back at the office. The real social impact of workplace behavior often depends on a constellation of surrounding circumstances, expectations, and relationships which are not fully captured by a simple recitation of the words used or the physical acts performed. Common sense, and an appropriate sensitivity to social context, will enable courts and juries to distinguish between simple teasing or roughhousing among members of the same sex, and conduct which a reasonable person in the plaintiff's position would find severely hostile or abusive.

III

Because we conclude that sex discrimination consisting of same-sex sexual harassment is actionable under Title VII, the judgment of the Court of Appeals for the Fifth Circuit is reversed, and the case is remanded for further proceedings consistent with this opinion.

JUSTICE THOMAS, concurring.

I concur because the Court stresses that in every sexual harassment case, the plaintiff must plead and ultimately prove Title VII's statutory requirement that there be discrimination "because of . . . sex."

❖ 55. U.S. Supreme Court,
Faragher v. City of Boca Raton (1998)

SOUTER, J., delivered the opinion of the Court, in which REHNQUIST, C. J., and STEVENS, O'CONNOR, KENNEDY, GINSBURG, and BREYER, JJ., joined. THOMAS, J., filed a dissenting opinion, in which SCALIA, J., joined.

This case calls for identification of the circumstances under which an employer may be held liable under Title VII of the Civil Rights Act of 1964, for the acts of a supervisory employee whose sexual harassment of subordinates has created a hostile work environment amounting to employment discrimination. We hold that an employer is vicariously liable for actionable discrimination caused by a supervisor, but subject to an affirmative defense looking to the reasonableness of the employer's conduct as well as that of a plaintiff victim.[1]

I

Between 1985 and 1990, while attending college, petitioner Beth Ann Faragher worked part time and during the summers as an ocean lifeguard for the Marine Safety Section of the Parks and Recreation Department of respondent, the City of Boca Raton, Florida (City). During this period, Faragher's immediate supervisors were Bill Terry, David Silverman, and Robert Gordon. In June 1990, Faragher resigned.

In 1992, Faragher brought an action against Terry, Silverman, and the City, asserting claims under Title VII and Florida law. So far as it concerns the Title VII claim, the complaint alleged that Terry and Silverman created a "sexually hostile atmosphere" at the beach by repeatedly subjecting Faragher and other female lifeguards to "uninvited and offensive touching," by making lewd remarks, and by speaking of women in offensive terms. The complaint contained specific allegations that Terry once said that he would never promote a woman to the rank of lieutenant, and that Silverman had said to Faragher, "Date me or clean the toilets for a year." Asserting that Terry and Silverman were agents of the City, and that their conduct amounted to discrimination in the "terms, conditions, and privileges" of her employment, Faragher sought a judgment against the City for nominal damages, costs, and attorney's fees.

Following a bench trial, the United States District Court for the Southern District of Florida found that throughout Faragher's employment with the City, Terry served as Chief of the Marine Safety Division, with authority to hire new lifeguards (subject to the approval of higher management), to supervise all aspects of the lifeguards' work assignments, to engage in counseling, to deliver oral reprimands, and to make a record of any such discipline. Silverman was a Marine Safety lieutenant from 1985 until June 1989, when he became a captain. Gordon began the employment period as a lieutenant and at some point was promoted to the position of training captain. In these positions, Silverman and Gordon were responsible for making the lifeguards' daily assignments, and for supervising their work and fitness training.

The lifeguards and supervisors were stationed at the city beach and worked out of the Marine Safety Headquarters, a small one-story building containing an office, a meeting room, and a single, unisex locker room with a shower. Their work routine was structured in a "paramilitary configuration," with a clear chain of command. Lifeguards reported to lieutenants and captains, who reported to Terry. He was supervised by the Recreation Superintendent, who in turn reported to a Director of Parks and Recreation, answerable to the City Manager. The lifeguards had no significant contact with higher city officials like the Recreation Superintendent.

In February 1986, the City adopted a sexual harassment policy, which it stated in a memorandum from the City Manager addressed to all employees. In May 1990, the City revised the policy and reissued a statement of it. Although the City may actually have circulated the memos and statements to some employees, it completely failed to disseminate its policy among employees of the Marine Safety Section, with the result that Terry, Silverman, Gordon, and many lifeguards were unaware of it.

From time to time over the course of Faragher's tenure at the Marine Safety Section, between 4 and 6 of the 40 to 50 lifeguards were women. During that 5-year period, Terry repeatedly touched the bodies of female employees without invitation, would put his arm around Faragher, with his hand on her buttocks, and once made contact with another female lifeguard in a motion of sexual simulation. He made crudely demeaning references to women generally, and once commented disparagingly on Faragher's shape. During a job interview with a woman he hired as a lifeguard, Terry said that the female lifeguards had sex with their male counterparts and asked whether she would do the same.

Silverman behaved in similar ways. He once tackled Faragher and remarked that, but for a physical characteristic he found unattractive, he would readily have had sexual relations with her. Another time, he pantomimed an act of oral sex. Within earshot of the female lifeguards, Silverman made frequent, vulgar references to women and sexual matters, commented on the bodies of female lifeguards and beachgoers, and at least twice told female lifeguards that he would like to engage in sex with them.

Faragher did not complain to higher management about Terry or Silverman. Although she spoke of their behavior to Gordon, she did not regard these discussions as formal complaints to a supervisor but as conversations with a person she held in high esteem. Other female lifeguards had similarly informal talks with Gordon, but because Gordon did not feel that it was his place to do so, he did not report these complaints to Terry, his own supervisor, or to any other city official. Gordon responded to the complaints of one lifeguard by saying that "the City just [doesn't] care."

In April 1990, however, two months before Faragher's resignation, Nancy Ewanchew, a former lifeguard, wrote to Richard Bender, the City's Personnel Director, complaining that Terry and Silverman had harassed her and other female lifeguards. Following investigation of this complaint, the City found that Terry and Silverman had behaved improperly, reprimanded them, and required them to choose between a suspension without pay or the forfeiture of annual leave.

On the basis of these findings, the District Court concluded that the conduct of Terry and Silverman was discriminatory harassment sufficiently serious to alter the conditions of Faragher's employment and constitute an abusive working environment. The District Court then ruled that there were three justifications for holding the City liable for the harassment of its supervisory employees. First, the court noted that the harassment was pervasive enough to support an inference that the City had "knowledge, or constructive knowledge" of it. Next, it ruled that the City was liable under traditional agency principles because Terry and Silverman were acting as its agents when they committed the harassing acts. Finally, the court observed that Gordon's knowledge of the harassment, combined with his inaction, "provides a further basis for imputing liability on [sic] the City." The District Court then awarded Faragher one dollar in nominal damages on her Title VII claim.

A panel of the Court of Appeals for the Eleventh Circuit reversed the judgment against the City. Although the panel had "no trouble concluding that Terry's and Silverman's conduct . . . was severe and pervasive enough to create an objectively abusive work environment," it overturned the District Court's conclusion that the City was liable. The panel ruled that Terry and Silverman were not acting within the scope of their employment when they engaged in the harassment, that they were not aided in their actions by the agency relationship, and that the City had no constructive knowledge of the harassment by virtue of its pervasiveness or Gordon's actual knowledge.

In a 7-to-5 decision, the full Court of Appeals adopted the panel's conclusion. Relying on our decision in *Meritor Savings Bank, FSB v. Vinson* (1986), and on the Restatement (Second) of Agency § 219 (1957) (hereafter Restatement), the court held that "an employer may be indirectly liable for hostile environment sexual harassment by a superior: (1) if the harassment occurs within the scope of the superior's employment; (2) if the employer assigns performance of a nondelegable duty to a supervisor and an employee is injured because of the supervisor's failure to carry out that duty; or (3) if there is an agency relationship which aids the supervisor's ability or opportunity to harass his subordinate."

Applying these principles, the court rejected Faragher's Title VII claim against the City. First, invoking standard agency language to classify the harassment by each supervisor as a "frolic" unrelated to his authorized tasks, the court found that in harassing Faragher, Terry and Silverman were acting outside of the scope of their employment and solely to further their own personal ends. Next, the court determined that the supervisors' agency relationship with the City did not assist them in perpetrating their harassment. Though noting that "a supervisor is always aided in accomplishing hostile environment sexual harassment by the existence of the agency relationship with his employer because his responsibilities include close proximity to and regular contact with the victim," the court held that traditional agency law does not employ so broad a concept of aid as a predicate of employer liability, but requires something more than a mere combination of agency relationship and improper conduct by the agent. Because neither Terry nor Silverman threatened to fire or demote Faragher, the court concluded that their agency relationship did not facilitate their harassment.

The court also affirmed the panel's ruling that the City lacked constructive knowledge of the supervisors' harassment. The court read the District Court's opinion to rest on an erroneous legal conclusion that any harassment pervasive enough to create a hostile environment must *a fortiori* also suffice to charge the employer with constructive knowledge. Rejecting this approach, the court reviewed the record and found no adequate factual basis to conclude that the harassment was so pervasive that the City should have known of it, relying on the facts that the harassment occurred intermittently, over a long period of time, and at a remote location. In footnotes, the court also rejected the arguments that the City should be deemed to have known of the harassment through Gordon, or charged with constructive knowledge because of its failure to disseminate its sexual harassment policy among the lifeguards.

Since our decision in *Meritor,* Courts of Appeals have struggled to derive manageable standards to govern employer liability for hostile environment harassment perpetrated by supervisory employees. While following our admonition to find guidance in the common law of agency, as embodied in the Restatement, the Courts of Appeals have adopted different approaches. We granted certiorari to address the divergence, and now reverse the judgment of the Eleventh Circuit and remand for entry of judgment in Faragher's favor.

II

Under Title VII of the Civil Rights Act of 1964, "it shall be an unlawful employment practice for an employer . . . to fail or refuse to hire or to discharge any individual, or otherwise to discriminate against any individual with respect to his compensation, terms, conditions, or privileges of employment, because of such individual's race, color, religion, sex, or national origin." We have repeatedly made clear that although the statute mentions specific employment decisions with immediate consequences, the scope of the prohibition '"is not limited to "economic" or "tangible" discrimination,"' and that it covers more than "'terms' and 'conditions' in the narrow contractual sense." Thus, in *Meritor* we held that sexual harassment so "severe or pervasive" as to "'alter the conditions of [the victim's] employment and create an abusive working environment'" violates Title VII.

In thus holding that environmental claims are covered by the statute, we drew upon earlier cases recognizing liability for discriminatory harassment based on race and national origin, just as we have also followed the lead of such cases in attempting to define the severity of the offensive conditions necessary to constitute actionable sex discrimination under the statute. . . .

In the instances in which there is a genuine question about the employer's responsibility for harmful conduct he did not in fact authorize, a holding that the conduct falls within the scope of employment ultimately expresses a conclusion not of fact but of law. As one eminent authority has observed, the "highly indefinite phrase" is "devoid of meaning in itself" and is "obviously no more than a bare formula to cover the unordered and unauthorized acts of the servant for which it is found to be expedient to charge the master with liability, as well as to exclude other acts for which it is not." Older cases, for example, treated smoking by an employee during working hours as an act outside the scope of employment, but more recently courts have generally held smoking on the job to fall within the scope. It is not that employers formerly did not authorize smoking but have now begun to do so, or that employees previously smoked for their own purposes but now do so to serve the employer. We simply understand smoking differently now and have revised the old judgments about what ought to be done about it. . . .

The rationale for placing harassment within the scope of supervisory authority would be the fairness of requiring the employer to bear the burden of foreseeable social behavior, and the same rationale would apply when the behavior was that of co-employees. The employer generally benefits just as obviously from the work of common employees as from the work of supervisors; they simply have different jobs to do, all aimed at the success of the enterprise. As between an innocent employer and an innocent employee, if we use scope of employment reasoning to require the employer to bear the cost of an actionably hostile workplace created by one class of employees (*i.e.*, supervisors), it could appear just as appropriate to do the same when the environment was created by another class (*i.e.*, co-workers).

The answer to this argument might well be to point out that the scope of supervisory employment may be treated separately by recognizing that supervisors have special authority enhancing their capacity to harass, and that the employer can guard against their misbehavior more easily because their numbers are by definition fewer than the numbers of regular employees. But this answer happens to implicate an entirely separate category of agency law (to be considered in the next section), which imposes vicarious liability on employers for tortious acts committed by use of particular authority conferred as an element of an employee's agency relationship with the employer. Since the virtue of categorical clarity is obvious, it is better to reject reliance on misuse of supervisory authority (without more) as irrelevant to scope-of-employment analysis. . . .

We therefore agree with Faragher that in implementing Title VII it makes sense to hold an employer vicariously liable for some tortious conduct of a supervisor made possible by abuse of his supervisory authority, and that the aided-by-agency-relation principle embodied in § 219(2)(d) of the Restatement provides an appropriate starting point for determining liability for the kind of harassment presented here. Several courts, indeed, have noted what Faragher has argued, that there is a sense in which a harassing supervisor is always assisted in his misconduct by the supervisory relationship. The agency relationship affords contact with an employee subjected to a supervisor's sexual harassment, and the victim may well be reluctant to accept the risks of blowing the whistle on a superior. When a person with supervisory authority discriminates in the terms and conditions of subordinates' employment, his actions necessarily draw upon his superior position over the people who report to him, or those under them, whereas an employee generally cannot check a supervisor's abusive conduct the same way that she might deal with abuse from a co-worker. When a fellow employee harasses, the victim can walk away or tell the offender where to go, but it may be difficult to offer such responses to a supervisor, whose "power to supervise—[which may be] to hire and fire, and to set work schedules and pay rates—does not disappear . . . when he chooses to harass through insults and offensive gestures rather than directly with threats of firing or promises of promotion." Recognition of employer liability when discriminatory misuse of supervisory authority alters the terms and conditions of a victim's employment is underscored by the fact that the employer has a greater opportunity to guard against misconduct by supervisors than by common workers; employers have greater opportunity and incentive to screen them, train them, and monitor their performance.

In sum, there are good reasons for vicarious liability for misuse of supervisory authority. That rationale must, however, satisfy one more condition. We are not entitled to recognize this theory under Title VII unless we can square it with *Meritor's* holding that an employer is not "automatically" liable for harassment by a supervisor who creates the requisite degree of discrimination, and there is obviously some tension between that holding and the position that a supervisor's misconduct aided by supervisory authority subjects the employer to liability vicariously; if the "aid" may be the unspoken suggestion of retaliation by misuse of supervisory authority, the risk of automatic liability is high. To counter it, we think there are two basic alternatives, one being to require proof of some affirmative invocation of that authority by the harassing supervisor, the other to recognize an affirmative defense to liability in some circumstances, even when a supervisor has created the actionable environment.

There is certainly some authority for requiring active or affirmative, as distinct from passive or implicit, misuse of supervisory authority before liability may be imputed. That is the way some courts have viewed the familiar cases holding the employer liable for discriminatory employment action with tangible consequences, like firing and demotion.

But neat examples illustrating the line between the affirmative and merely implicit uses of power are not easy to come by in considering management behavior. Supervisors do not make speeches threatening sanctions whenever they make requests in the legitimate exercise of managerial authority, and yet every subordinate employee knows the sanctions exist; this is the reason that courts have consistently held that acts of supervisors have greater power to alter the environment than acts of co-employees generally. How far from the course of ostensible supervisory behavior would a company officer have to step before his orders would not reasonably be seen as actively using authority? Judgment calls would often be close, the results would often seem disparate even if not demonstrably contradictory, and the temptation to litigate would be hard to resist. We think plaintiffs and defendants alike would be poorly served by an active-use rule.

The other basic alternative to automatic liability would avoid this particular temptation to litigate, but allow an employer to show as an affirmative defense to liability that the employer had exercised reasonable care to avoid harassment and to eliminate it when it might occur, and that the complaining employee had failed to act with like reasonable care to take advantage of the employer's safeguards and otherwise to prevent harm that could have been avoided. This composite defense would, we think, implement the statute sensibly, for reasons that are not hard to fathom. . . .

In order to accommodate the principle of vicarious liability for harm caused by misuse of supervisory authority, as well as Title VII's equally basic policies of encouraging forethought by employers and saving action by objecting employees, we adopt the following holding in this case and in *Burlington Industries, Inc. v. Ellerth,* also decided today. An employer is subject to vicarious liability to a victimized employee for an actionable hostile environment created by a supervisor with immediate (or successively higher) authority over the employee. When no tangible employment action is taken, a defending employer may raise an affirmative defense to liability or damages, subject to proof by a preponderance of the evidence. The defense comprises two necessary elements: (a) that the employer exercised reasonable care to prevent and correct promptly any sexually harassing behavior, and (b) that the plaintiff employee unreasonably failed to take advantage of any preventive or corrective opportunities provided by the employer or to avoid harm otherwise. While proof that an employer had promulgated an antiharassment policy with complaint procedure is not necessary in every instance as a matter of law, the need for a stated policy suitable to the employment circumstances may appropriately be addressed in any case when litigating the first element of the defense. And while proof that an employee failed to fulfill the corresponding obligation of reasonable care to avoid harm is not limited to showing an unreasonable failure to use any complaint procedure provided by the employer, a demonstration of such failure will normally suffice to satisfy the employer's burden under the second element of the defense. No affirmative defense is available, however, when the supervisor's harassment culminates in a tangible employment action, such as discharge, demotion, or undesirable reassignment.

Applying these rules here, we believe that the judgment of the Court of Appeals must be reversed. The District Court found that the degree of hostility in the work environment rose to the actionable level and was attributable to Silverman and Terry. It is undisputed that these supervisors "were granted virtually unchecked authority" over their subordinates, "directly controlling and supervising all aspects of [Faragher's] day-to-day activities." It is also clear that Faragher and her colleagues were "completely isolated from the City's higher management." The City did not seek review of these findings.

While the City would have an opportunity to raise an affirmative defense if there were any serious prospect of its presenting one, it appears from the record that any such avenue is closed. The District Court found that the City had entirely failed to disseminate its policy against sexual harassment among the beach employees and that its officials made no attempt to keep track of the conduct of supervisors like Terry bypassed in registering complaints. Under such circumstances, we hold as a matter of law that the City could not be found to have exercised reasonable care to prevent the supervisors' harassing conduct. Unlike the employer of a small workforce, who might expect that sufficient care to prevent tortious behavior could be exercised informally, those responsible for city operations could not reasonably have thought that precautions against hostile environments in any one of many departments in far-flung locations could be effective without communicating some formal policy against harassment, with a sensible complaint procedure. . . .

The judgment of the Court of Appeals for the Eleventh Circuit is reversed, and the case is remanded for reinstatement of the judgment of the District Court.

It is so ordered.

Editor's Note

1. Vicarious liability is the imposition of liability on one person for the actionable conduct of another, based solely on the relationship between the two persons.

56. U.S. Supreme Court, *Gebser et al. v. Lago Vista Independent School District* (1998)

O'CONNOR, J., delivered the opinion of the Court, in which REHNQUIST, C. J., and SCALIA, KENNEDY, and THOMAS, JJ., joined. STEVENS, J., filed a dissenting opinion, in which SOUTER, GINSBURG, and BREYER, JJ., joined. GINSBURG, J., filed a dissenting opinion, in which SOUTER and BREYER, JJ., joined.

The question in this case is when a school district may be held liable in damages in an implied right of action under Title IX of the Education Amendments of 1972, for the sexual harassment of a student by one of the district's teachers. We conclude that damages may not be recovered in those circumstances unless an official of the school district who at a minimum has authority to institute corrective measures on the district's behalf has actual notice of, and is deliberately indifferent to, the teacher's misconduct.

I

In the spring of 1991, when petitioner Alida Star Gebser was an eighth-grade student at a middle school in respondent Lago Vista Independent School District (Lago Vista), she joined a high school book discussion group led by Frank Waldrop, a teacher at Lago Vista's high school. Lago Vista received federal funds at all pertinent times. During the book discussion sessions, Waldrop often made sexually suggestive comments to the students. Gebser entered high school in the fall and was assigned to classes taught by Waldrop in both semesters. Waldrop continued to make inappropriate remarks to the students, and he began to direct more of his suggestive comments toward Gebser, including during the substantial amount of time that the two were alone in his classroom. He initiated sexual contact with Gebser in the spring, when, while visiting her home ostensibly to give her a book, he kissed and fondled her. The two had sexual intercourse on a number of occasions during the remainder of the school year. Their relationship continued through the summer and into the following school year, and they often had intercourse during class time, although never on school property.

Gebser did not report the relationship to school officials, testifying that while she realized Waldrop's conduct was improper, she was uncertain how to react and she wanted to continue having him as a teacher. In October 1992, the parents of two other students complained to the high school principal about Waldrop's comments in class. The principal arranged a meeting, at which, according to the principal, Waldrop indicated that he did not believe he had made offensive remarks but apologized to the parents and said it would not happen again. The principal also advised Waldrop to be careful about his classroom comments and told the school guidance counselor about the meeting, but he did not report the parents' complaint to Lago Vista's superintendent, who was the district's Title IX coordinator. A couple of months later, in January 1993, a police officer discovered Waldrop and Gebser engaging in sexual intercourse and arrested Waldrop. Lago Vista terminated his employment, and subsequently, the Texas Education Agency revoked his teaching license. During this time, the district had not promulgated or distributed an official grievance procedure for lodging sexual harassment complaints; nor had it issued a formal anti-harassment policy. . . .

Gebser and her mother filed suit against Lago Vista and Waldrop in state court in November 1993, raising claims against the school district under Title IX, and state negligence law, and claims against Waldrop primarily under state law. They sought compensatory and punitive damages from both defendants. After the case was removed, the United States District Court for the Western District of Texas granted summary judgment in favor of Lago Vista on all claims, and remanded the allegations against Waldrop to state court. In rejecting the Title IX claim against the school district, the court reasoned that the statute "was enacted to counter policies of discrimination . . . in federally funded education programs," and that "[o]nly if school administrators have some type of notice of the gender discrimination and fail to respond in good faith can the discrimination be interpreted as a policy of the school district." Here, the court determined, the parents' complaint to the principal concerning Waldrop's comments in class was the only one Lago Vista had received about Waldrop, and that evidence was inadequate to raise a genuine issue on whether the school district had actual or constructive notice that Waldrop was involved in a sexual relationship with a student. Petitioners appealed only on the Title IX claim. The Court of Appeals for the Fifth Circuit affirmed, . . .

II

Title IX provides in pertinent part that, "[n]o person . . . shall, on the basis of sex, be excluded from participation in, be denied the benefits of, or be subjected to discrimination under any education program or activity receiving Federal financial assistance." The express statutory means of enforcement is administrative: The statute directs federal agencies who distribute education funding to establish requirements to effectuate the nondiscrimination mandate, and permits the agencies to enforce those requirements through "any . . . means authorized by law," including ultimately the termination of federal funding. . . .

Petitioners, joined by the United States as amicus curiae, would invoke standards used by the Courts of Appeals in Title VII cases involving a supervisor's sexual harassment of an employee in the workplace . . .

Specifically, they advance two possible standards under which Lago Vista would be liable for Waldrop's conduct. First, relying on a 1997 "Policy Guidance" issued by the Department of Education, they would hold a school district liable in damages under Title IX where a teacher is "'aided in carrying out the sexual harassment of students by his or her position of authority with the institution,'" irrespective of whether school district officials had any knowledge of the harassment and irrespective of their response upon becoming aware. That rule is an expression of respondeat superior liability, i.e., vicarious or imputed liability, under which recovery in damages against a school district would generally follow whenever a teacher's authority over a student facilitates the harassment. Second, petitioners and the United States submit that a school district should at a minimum be liable for damages based on a theory of constructive notice, i.e., where the district knew or "should have known" about harassment but failed to uncover and eliminate it. Both standards would allow a damages recovery in a broader range of situations than the rule adopted by the Court of Appeals, which hinges on actual knowledge by a school official with authority to end the harassment. . . .

In this case, petitioners seek not just to establish a Title IX violation but to recover damages based on theories of respondeat superior and constructive notice. It is that aspect of their action, in our view, which is most critical to resolving the case. Unlike Title IX, Title VII contains an express cause of action, and specifically provides for relief in the form of monetary damages. Congress therefore has directly addressed the subject of damages relief under Title VII and has set out the particular situations in which damages are available as well as the maximum amounts recoverable. With respect to Title IX, however, the private right of action is judicially implied, and there is thus no legislative expression of the scope of available remedies, including when it is appropriate to award monetary damages. . . .

III

Because the private right of action under Title IX is judicially implied, we have a measure of latitude to shape a sensible remedial scheme that best comports with the statute. That endeavor inherently entails a degree of speculation, since it addresses an issue on which Congress has not specifically spoken. To guide the analysis, we generally examine the relevant statute to ensure that we do not fashion the parameters of an implied right in a manner at odds with the statutory structure and purpose.

Those considerations, we think, are pertinent not only to the scope of the implied right, but also to the scope of the available remedies. . . .

We conclude that it would "frustrate the purposes" of Title IX to permit a damages recovery against a school district for a teacher's sexual harassment of a student based on principles of respondeat superior or constructive notice, i.e., without actual notice to a school district official. Because Congress did not expressly create a private right of action under Title IX, the statutory text does not shed light on Congress' intent with respect to the scope of available remedies. . . .

As a general matter, it does not appear that Congress contemplated unlimited recovery in damages against a funding recipient where the recipient is unaware of discrimination in its programs. When Title IX was enacted in 1972, the principal civil rights statutes containing an express right of action did not provide for recovery of monetary damages at all, instead allowing only injunctive and equitable relief. It was not until 1991 that Congress made damages available under Title VII, and even then, Congress carefully limited the amount recoverable in any individual case, calibrating the maximum recovery to the size of the employer. Adopting petitioners' position would amount, then, to allowing unlimited recovery of damages under Title IX where Congress has not spoken on the subject of either the right or the remedy, and in the face of evidence that when Congress expressly considered both in Title VII it restricted the amount of damages available.

Congress enacted Title IX in 1972 with two principal objectives in mind: "to avoid the use of federal resources to support discriminatory practices" and "to provide individual citizens effective protection against those practices." The statute was modeled after Title VI of the Civil Rights Act of 1964, which is parallel to Title IX except that it prohibits race discrimination, not sex discrimination, and applies in all programs receiving federal funds, not only in education programs. The two statutes operate in the same manner, conditioning an offer of federal funding on a promise by the recipient not to discriminate, in what amounts essentially to a contract between the Government and the recipient of funds.

That contractual framework distinguishes Title IX from Title VII, which is framed in terms not of a condition but of an outright prohibition. Title VII applies to all employers without regard to federal funding and aims broadly to "eradicat[e] discrimination throughout the economy." Title VII, moreover, seeks to "make persons whole for injuries suffered through past discrimination." Thus, whereas Title VII aims centrally to compensate victims of discrimination, Title IX focuses more on "protecting" individuals from discriminatory practices carried out by recipients of federal funds. That might explain why, when the Court first recognized the implied right under Title IX in *Cannon* [*v. University of Chicago* (1979)], the opinion referred to injunctive or equitable relief in a private action, but not to a damages remedy.

Title IX's contractual nature has implications for our construction of the scope of available remedies. When Congress attaches conditions to the award of federal funds under its spending power, as it has in Title IX and Title VI, we examine closely the propriety of private actions holding the recipient liable in monetary damages for noncompliance with the condition. Our central concern in that regard is with ensuring "that the receiving entity of federal funds [has] notice that it will be liable for a monetary award." . . . If a school district's liability for a teacher's sexual harassment rests on principles of constructive notice or respondeat superior, it will likewise be the case that the recipient of funds was unaware of the discrimination. It is sensible to assume that Congress did not envision a recipient's liability in damages in that situation.

Most significantly, Title IX contains important clues that Congress did not intend to allow recovery in damages where liability rests solely on principles of vicarious liability or constructive notice. Title IX's express means of enforcement by administrative agencies operates on an assumption of actual notice to officials of the funding recipient. The statute entitles agencies who disburse education funding to enforce their rules implementing the nondiscrimination mandate through proceedings to suspend or terminate funding or through "other means authorized by law." Significantly, however, an agency may not initiate enforcement proceedings until it "has advised the appropriate person or persons of the failure to comply with the requirement and has determined that compliance cannot be secured by voluntary means." The administrative regulations implement that obligation, requiring resolution of compliance issues "by informal means whenever possible," and prohibiting commencement of enforcement proceedings until the agency has determined that voluntary compliance is unobtainable and "the recipient . . . has been notified of its failure to comply and of the action to be taken to effect compliance."

In the event of a violation, a funding recipient may be required to take "such remedial action as [is] deem[ed] necessary to overcome the effects of [the] discrimination." While agencies have conditioned continued funding on providing equitable relief to the victim, the regulations do not appear to contemplate a condition ordering payment of monetary damages, and there is no indication that payment of damages has been demanded as a condition of finding a recipient to be in compliance with the statute.

Presumably, a central purpose of requiring notice of the violation "to the appropriate person" and an opportunity for voluntary compliance before administrative enforcement proceedings can commence is to avoid diverting education funding from beneficial uses where a recipient was unaware of discrimination in its programs and is willing to institute prompt corrective measures. The scope of private damages relief proposed by petitioners is at odds with that basic objective. When a teacher's sexual harassment is imputed to a school district or when a school district is deemed to have "constructively" known of the teacher's harassment, by assumption the district had no actual knowledge of the teacher's conduct. Nor, of course, did the district have an opportunity to take action to end the harassment or to limit further harassment.

It would be unsound, we think, for a statute's express system of enforcement to require notice to the recipient and an opportunity to come into voluntary compliance while a judicially implied system of enforcement permits substantial liability without regard to the recipient's knowledge or its corrective actions upon receiving notice. Moreover, an award of damages in a particular case might well exceed a recipient's level of federal funding. Where a statute's express enforcement scheme hinges its most severe sanction on notice and unsuccessful efforts to obtain compliance, we cannot attribute to Congress the intention to have implied an enforcement scheme that allows imposition of greater liability without comparable conditions.

IV

Because the express remedial scheme under Title IX is predicated upon notice to an "appropriate person" and an opportunity to rectify any violation, we conclude, in the absence of further direction from Congress, that the implied damages remedy should be fashioned along the same lines. An "appropriate person" is, at a minimum, an official of the recipient entity with authority to take corrective action to end the discrimination. Consequently, in cases like this one that do not involve official policy of the recipient entity, we hold that a damages remedy will not lie under Title IX unless an official who at a minimum has authority to address the alleged discrimination and to institute corrective measures on the recipient's behalf has actual knowledge of discrimination in the recipient's programs and fails adequately to respond.

We think, moreover, that the response must amount to deliberate indifference to discrimination. The administrative enforcement scheme presupposes that an official who is advised of a Title IX violation refuses to take action to bring the recipient into compliance. The premise, in other words, is an official decision by the recipient not to remedy the violation. That framework finds a rough parallel in the standard of deliberate indifference. . . .

Applying the framework to this case is fairly straightforward, as petitioners do not contend they can prevail under an actual notice standard. The only official alleged to have had information about Waldrop's misconduct is the high school principal. That information, however, consisted of a complaint from parents of other students charging only that Waldrop had made inappropriate comments during class, which was plainly insufficient to alert the principal to the possibility that Waldrop was involved in a sexual relationship with a student. Lago Vista, moreover, terminated Waldrop's employment upon learning of his relationship with Gebser. . . .

Petitioners focus primarily on Lago Vista's asserted failure to promulgate and publicize an effective policy and grievance procedure of sexual harassment claims. They point to Department of Education regulations requiring each funding recipient to "adopt and publish grievance procedures providing for prompt and equitable resolution" of discrimination complaints, and to notify students and others "that it does not discriminate on the basis of sex in the educational programs or activities which it operates." Lago Vista's alleged failure to comply with the regulations, however, does not establish the requisite actual notice and deliberate indifference. And in any event, the failure to promulgate a grievance procedure does not itself constitute "discrimination" under Title IX. Of course, the Department of Education could enforce the requirement administratively: Agencies generally have authority to promulgate and enforce requirements that effectuate the statute's nondiscrimination mandate, even if those requirements do not purport to represent a definition of discrimination under the statute. We have never held, however, that the implied private right of action under Title IX allows recovery in damages for violation of those sorts of administrative requirements.

V

The number of reported cases involving sexual harassment of students in schools confirms that harassment unfortunately is an all too common aspect of the educational experience. No one questions that a student suffers extraordinary harm when subjected to sexual harassment and abuse by a teacher, and that the teacher's conduct is reprehensible and undermines the basic purposes of the educational system. The issue in this case, however, is whether the independent misconduct of a teacher is attributable to the school district that employs him under a specific federal statute designed primarily to prevent recipients of federal financial assistance from using the funds in a discriminatory manner. Our decision does not affect any right of recovery that an individual may have against a school district as a matter of state law or against the teacher in his individual capacity under state law. Until Congress speaks directly on the subject, however, we will not hold a school district liable in damages under Title IX for a teacher's sexual harassment of a student absent actual notice and deliberate indifference. We therefore affirm the judgment of the Court of Appeals. . . .

JUSTICE STEVENS, with whom JUSTICE SOUTER, JUSTICE GINSBURG, and JUSTICE BREYER join, dissenting.

The question that the petition for certiorari asks us to address is whether the Lago Vista Independent School District (respondent) is liable in damages for a violation of Title IX of the Education Amendments of 1972. The Court provides us with a negative answer to that question because respondent did not have actual notice of, and was not deliberately indifferent to, the odious misconduct of one of its teachers. As a basis for its decision, the majority relies heavily on the notion that because the private cause of action under Title IX is "judicially implied," the Court has "a measure of latitude" to use its own judgment in shaping a remedial scheme. This assertion of lawmaking authority is not faithful either to our precedents or to our duty to interpret, rather than to revise, congressional commands. Moreover, the majority's policy judgment about the appropriate remedy in this case thwarts the purposes of Title IX.

I

. . . As long as the intent of Congress is clear, an implicit command has the same legal force as one that is explicit. The fact that a statute does not authorize a particular remedy "in so many words is no more significant than the fact that it does not in terms authorize execution to issue on a judgment recovered under [the statute]." Deckert v. Independence Shares Corp., (1940). . . .

II

We have already noted that the text of Title IX should be accorded "'a sweep as broad as its language.'" North Haven Bd. of Ed. v. Bell, (1982) (quoting United States v. Price, (1966)). That sweep is broad indeed. "No person . . . shall, on the basis of sex, . . . be subjected to discrimination under any education program or activity receiving Federal financial assistance. . . ." The use of passive verbs in Title IX, focusing on the victim of the discrimination rather than the particular wrongdoer, gives this statute broader coverage than Title VII.

Moreover, because respondent assumed the statutory duty set out in Title IX as part of its consideration for the receipt of federal funds, that duty constitutes an affirmative undertaking that is more significant than a mere promise to obey the law. . . .

During her freshman and sophomore years of high school, petitioner Alida Star Gebser was repeatedly subjected to sexual abuse by her teacher, Frank Waldrop, whom she had met in the eighth grade when she joined his high school book discussion group. Waldrop's conduct was surely intentional and it occurred during, and as a part of, a curriculum activity in which he wielded authority over Gebser that had been delegated to him by respondent. Moreover, it is undisputed that the activity was subsidized, in part, with federal moneys.

The Court nevertheless holds that the law does not provide a damages remedy for the Title IX violation alleged in this case because no official of the school district with "authority to institute corrective measures on the district's behalf" had actual notice of Waldrop's misconduct. That holding is at odds with settled principles of agency law, under which the district is responsible for Waldrop's misconduct because "he was aided in accomplishing the tort by the existence of the agency relation." Restatement (Second) of Agency, (1957).

This case presents a paradigmatic example of a tort that was made possible, that was effected, and that was repeated over a prolonged period because of the powerful influence that Waldrop had over Gebser by reason of the authority that his employer, the school district, had delegated to him. As a secondary school teacher, Waldrop exercised even greater authority and control over his students than employers and supervisors exercise over their employees. His gross misuse of that authority allowed him to abuse his young student's trust.

Reliance on the principle set out in §219(2)(b) of the Restatement comports with the relevant agency's interpretation of Title IX. The United States Department of Education, through its Office for Civil Rights, recently issued a policy "Guidance" stating that a school district is liable under Title IX if one of its teachers "was aided in carrying out the sexual harassment of students by his or her position of authority with the institution." As the agency charged with administering and enforcing Title IX, the Department of Education has a special interest in ensuring that federal funds are not used in contravention of Title IX's mandate. It is therefore significant that the Department's interpretation of the statute wholly supports the conclusion that respondent is liable in damages for Waldrop's sexual abuse of his student, which was made possible only by Waldrop's affirmative misuse of his authority as her teacher.

The reason why the common law imposes liability on the principal in such circumstances is the same as the reason why Congress included the prohibition against discrimination on the basis of sex in Title IX: to induce school boards to adopt and enforce practices that will minimize the danger that vulnerable students will be exposed to such odious behavior. The rule that the Court has crafted creates the opposite incentive. As long as school boards can insulate themselves from knowledge about this sort of conduct, they can claim immunity from damages liability.

Indeed, the rule that the Court adopts would preclude a damages remedy even if every teacher at the school knew about the harassment but did not have "authority to institute corrective measures on the district's behalf." It is not my function to determine whether this newly fashioned rule is wiser than the established common-law rule. It is proper, however, to suggest that the Court bears the burden of justifying its rather dramatic departure from settled law, and to explain why its opinion fails to shoulder that burden.

III

. . . The majority takes the position that a school district that accepts federal funds under Title IX should not be held liable in damages for an intentional violation of that statute if the district itself "was unaware of the discrimination." The Court reasons that because administrative proceedings to terminate funding cannot be commenced until after the grant recipient has received notice of its noncompliance and the agency determines that voluntary compliance is not possible, there should be no damages liability unless the grant recipient has actual notice of the violation (and thus an opportunity to end the harassment).

The fact that Congress has specified a particular administrative procedure to be followed when a subsidy is to be terminated, however, does not illuminate the question of what the victim of discrimination on the basis of sex must prove in order to recover damages in an implied private right of action. . . .

The majority's inappropriate reliance on Title IX's administrative enforcement scheme to limit the availability of a damages remedy leads the Court to require not only actual knowledge on the part of "an official who at a minimum has authority to address the alleged discrimination and to institute corrective measures on the recipient's behalf," but also that official's "refuse[al] to take action," or "deliberate indifference" toward the harassment.

Presumably, few Title IX plaintiffs who have been victims of intentional discrimination will be able to recover damages under this exceedingly high standard. The Court fails to recognize that its holding will virtually "render inutile causes of action authorized by Congress through a decision that no remedy is available."

IV

. . . A theme that seems to underlie the Court's opinion is a concern that holding a school district liable in damages might deprive it of the benefit of the federal subsidy, that the damages remedy is somehow more onerous than a possible termination of the federal grant. It is possible, of course, that in some cases the recoverable damages, in either a Title IX action or a state law tort action, would exceed the amount of a federal grant.

That is surely not relevant to the question whether the school district or the injured student should bear the risk of harm, a risk against which the district, but not the student, can insure. It is not clear to me why the well-settled rules of law that impose responsibility on the principal for the misconduct of its agents should not apply in this case. As a matter of policy, the Court ranks protection of the school district's purse above the protection of immature high school students that those rules would provide. Because those students are members of the class for whose special benefit Congress enacted Title IX, that policy choice is not faithful to the intent of the policymaking branch of our Government.

I respectfully dissent.

57. United Nations Convention on the Elimination of All Forms of Discrimination Against Women (1981)

The States Parties to the Present Convention

Noting that the Charter of the United Nations reaffirms faith in fundamental human rights, in the dignity and worth of the human person and in the equal rights of men and women,

Noting that the Universal Declaration of Human Rights affirms the principle of the inadmissibility of discrimination and proclaims that all human beings are born free and equal in dignity and rights and that everyone is entitled to all the rights and freedoms set forth therein, without distinction of any kind, including distinction based on sex,

Noting that the States Parties to the International Covenants on Human Rights have the obligation to ensure the equal rights of men and women to enjoy all economic, social, cultural, civil and political rights,

Considering the international conventions concluded under the auspices of the United Nations and the specialized agencies promoting equality of rights of men and women,

Noting also the resolutions, declarations and recommendations adopted by the United Nations and the specialized agencies promoting equality of rights of men and women,

Concerned, however, that despite these various instruments extensive discrimination against women continues to exist,

Recalling that discrimination against women violates the principles of equality of rights and respect for human dignity, is an obstacle to the participation of women, on equal terms with men, in the political, social, economic and cultural life of their countries, hampers the growth of the prosperity of society and the family and makes more difficult the full development of the potentialities of women in the service of their countries and of humanity,

Concerned that in situations of poverty women have the least access to food, health, education, training and opportunities for employment and other needs,

Convinced that the establishment of the new international economic order based on equity and justice will contribute significantly towards the promotion of equality between men and women,

Emphasizing that the eradication of apartheid, all forms of racism, racial discrimination, colonialism, neo-colonialism, aggression, foreign occupation and domination and interference in the internal affairs of States is essential to the full enjoyment of the rights of men and women,

Affirming that the strengthening of international peace and security, the relaxation of international tension, mutual co-operation among all States irrespective of their social and economic systems, general and complete disarmament, in particular nuclear disarmament under strict and effective international control, the affirmation of the principles of justice, equality and mutual benefit in relations among countries and the realization of the right of peoples under alien and colonial domination and foreign occupation to self-determination and independence, as well as respect for national sovereignty and territorial integrity, will promote social progress and development and as a consequence will contribute to the attainment of full equality between men and women,

Convinced that the full and complete development of a country, the welfare of the world and the cause of peace require the maximum participation of women on equal terms with men in all fields,

Bearing in mind the great contribution of women to the welfare of the family and to the development of society, so far not fully recognized, the social significance of maternity and the role of both parents in the family and in the upbringing of children, and aware that the role of women in procreation should not be a basis for discrimination but that the upbringing of children requires a sharing of responsibility between men and women and society as a whole,

Aware that a change in the traditional role of men as well as the role of women in society and in the family is needed to achieve full equality between men and women,

Determined to implement the principles set forth in the Declaration on the Elimination of Discrimination against Women and, for that purpose, to adopt the measures required for the elimination of such discrimination in all its forms and manifestations,

Have agreed on the following:

PART I

Article I

For the purposes of the present Convention, the term "discrimination against women" shall mean any distinction, exclusion or restriction made on the basis of sex which has the effect or purpose of impairing or nullifying the recognition, enjoyment or exercise by women, irrespective of their marital status, on a basis of equality of men and women, of human rights and fundamental freedoms in the political, economic, social, cultural, civil or any other field.

Article 2

States Parties condemn discrimination against women in all its forms, agree to pursue by all appropriate means and without delay a policy of eliminating discrimination against women and, to this end, undertake:

(a) To embody the principle of the equality of men and women in their national constitutions or other appropriate legislation if not yet incorporated therein and to ensure, through law and other appropriate means, the practical realization of this principle;

(b) To adopt appropriate legislative and other measures, including sanctions where appropriate, prohibiting all discrimination against women;

(c) To establish legal protection of the rights of women on an equal basis with men and to ensure through competent national tribunals and other public institutions the effective protection of women against any act of discrimination;

(d) To refrain from engaging in any act or practice of discrimination against women and to ensure that public authorities and institutions shall act in conformity with this obligation;

(e) To take all appropriate measures to eliminate discrimination against women by any person, organization or enterprise;

(f) To take all appropriate measures, including legislation, to modify or abolish existing laws, regulations, customs and practices which constitute discrimination against women;

(g) To repeal all national penal provisions which constitute discrimination against women.

Article 3

States Parties shall take in all fields, in particular in the political, social, economic and cultural fields, all appropriate measures, including legislation, to ensure the full development and advancement of women, for the purpose of guaranteeing them the exercise and enjoyment of human rights and fundamental freedoms on a basis of equality with men.

Article 4

1. Adoption by States Parties of temporary special measures aimed at accelerating de facto equality between men and women shall not be considered discrimination as defined in the present Convention, but shall in no way entail as a consequence the maintenance of unequal or separate standards; these measures shall be discontinued when the objectives of equality of opportunity and treatment have been achieved.

2. Adoption by States Parties of special measures, including those measures contained in the present Convention, aimed at protecting maternity shall not be considered discriminatory.

Article 5

States Parties shall take all appropriate measures:

(a) To modify the social and cultural patterns of conduct of men and women, with a view to achieving the elimination of prejudices and customary and all other practices which are based on the idea of the inferiority or the superiority of either of the sexes or on stereotyped roles for men and women;

(b) To ensure that family education includes a proper understanding of maternity as a social function and the recognition of the common responsibility of men and women in the upbringing and development of their children, it being understood that the interest of the children is the primordial consideration in all cases.

Article 6

States Parties shall take all appropriate measures, including legislation, to suppress all forms of traffic in women and exploitation of prostitution of women.

PART II

Article 7

States Parties shall take all appropriate measures to eliminate discrimination against women in the political and public life of the country and, in particular, shall ensure to women, on equal terms with men, the right:

(a) To vote in all elections and public referenda and to be eligible for election to all publicly elected bodies;

(b) To participate in the formulation of government policy and the implementation
thereof and to hold public office and perform all public functions at all levels of government;

(c) To participate in non-governmental organizations and associations concerned with
the public and political life of the country.

Article 8

States Parties shall take all appropriate measures to ensure to women, on equal terms with
men and without any discrimination, the opportunity to represent their Governments at
the international level and to participate in the work of international organizations.

Article 9

1. States Parties shall grant women equal rights with men to acquire, change or retain
their nationality. They shall ensure in particular that neither marriage to an alien nor
change of nationality by the husband during marriage shall automatically change the
nationality of the wife, render her stateless or force upon her the nationality of the husband.

2. States Parties shall grant women equal rights with men with respect to the nationality of their children.

PART III

Article 10

States Parties shall take all appropriate measures to eliminate discrimination against
women in order to ensure to them equal rights with men in the field of education and in
particular to ensure, on a basis of equality of men and women:

(a) The same conditions for career and vocational guidance, for access to studies and for
the achievement of diplomas in educational establishments of all categories in rural
as well as in urban areas; this equality shall be ensured in pre-school, general, technical, professional and higher technical education, as well as in all types of vocational
training;

(b) Access to the same curricula, the same examinations, teaching staff with qualifications of the same standard and school premises and equipment of the same quality;

(c) The elimination of any stereotyped concept of the roles of men and women at all levels and in all forms of education by encouraging coeducation and other types of education which will help to achieve this aim and, in particular, by the revision of textbooks and school programmes and the adaptation of teaching methods;

(d) The same opportunities to benefit from scholarships and other study grants;

(e) The same opportunities for access to programmes of continuing education, including adult and functional literacy programmes, particularly those aimed at reducing, at the earliest possible time, any gap in education existing between men and women;

(f) The reduction of female student drop-out rates and the organization of programmes for girls and women who have left school prematurely;

(g) The same opportunities to participate actively in sports and physical education;

(h) Access to specific educational information to help to ensure the health and well-being of families, including information and advice on family planning.

Article 11

1. States Parties shall take all appropriate measures to eliminate discrimination against women in the field of employment in order to ensure, on a basis of equality of men and women, the same rights, in particular:

(a) The right to work as an inalienable right of all human beings;

(b) The right to the same employment opportunities, including the application of the same criteria for selection in matters of employment;

(c) The right to free choice of profession and employment, the right to promotion, job security and all benefits and conditions of service and the right to receive vocational training and retraining, including apprenticeships, advanced vocational training and recurrent training;

(d) The right to equal remuneration, including benefits, and to equal treatment in respect of work of equal value, as well as equality of treatment in the evaluation of the quality of work;

(e) The right to social security, particularly in cases of retirement, unemployment, sickness, invalidity and old age and other incapacity to work, as well as the right to paid leave;

(f) The right to protection of health and to safety in working conditions, including the safeguarding of the function of reproduction.

2. In order to prevent discrimination against women on the grounds of marriage or maternity and to ensure their effective right to work, States Parties shall take appropriate measures:

(a) To prohibit, subject to the imposition of sanctions, dismissal on the grounds of pregnancy or of maternity leave and discrimination in dismissals on the basis of marital status;

(b) To introduce maternity leave with pay or with comparable social benefits without loss of former employment, seniority or social allowances;

(c) To encourage the provision of the necessary supporting social services to enable parents to combine family obligations with work responsibilities and participation in public life, in particular through promoting the establishment and development of a network of child-care facilities;

(d) To provide special protection to women during pregnancy in types of work proved to be harmful to them.

3. Protective legislation relating to matters covered in this article shall be reviewed pe-

riodically in the light of scientific and technological knowledge and shall be revised, repealed or extended as necessary.

Article 12

1. States Parties shall take all appropriate measures to eliminate discrimination against women in the field of health care in order to ensure, on a basis of equality of men and women, access to health care services, including those related to family planning.

2. Notwithstanding the provisions of paragraph I of this article, States Parties shall ensure to women appropriate services in connection with pregnancy, confinement and the post-natal period, granting free services where necessary, as well as adequate nutrition during pregnancy and lactation.

Article 13

States Parties shall take all appropriate measures to eliminate discrimination against women in other areas of economic and social life in order to ensure, on a basis of equality of men and women, the same rights, in particular:

(a) The right to family benefits;

(b) The right to bank loans, mortgages and other forms of financial credit;

(c) The right to participate in recreational activities, sports and all aspects of cultural life.

Article 14

1. States Parties shall take into account the particular problems faced by rural women and the significant roles which rural women play in the economic survival of their families, including their work in the non-monetized sectors of the economy, and shall take all appropriate measures to ensure the application of the provisions of the present Convention to women in rural areas.

2. States Parties shall take all appropriate measures to eliminate discrimination against women in rural areas in order to ensure, on a basis of equality of men and women, that they participate in and benefit from rural development and, in particular, shall ensure to such women the right:

(a) To participate in the elaboration and implementation of development planning at all levels;

(b) To have access to adequate health care facilities, including information, counselling and services in family planning;

(c) To benefit directly from social security programmes;

(d) To obtain all types of training and education, formal and non-formal, including that relating to functional literacy, as well as, inter alia, the benefit of all community and extension services, in order to increase their technical proficiency;

(e) To organize self-help groups and co-operatives in order to obtain equal access to economic opportunities through employment or self employment;

(f) To participate in all community activities;

(g) To have access to agricultural credit and loans, marketing facilities, appropriate technology and equal treatment in land and agrarian reform as well as in land resettlement schemes;

(h) To enjoy adequate living conditions, particularly in relation to housing, sanitation, electricity and water supply, transport and communications.

Part IV

Article 15

1. States Parties shall accord to women equality with men before the law.

2. States Parties shall accord to women, in civil matters, a legal capacity identical to that of men and the same opportunities to exercise that capacity. In particular, they shall give women equal rights to conclude contracts and to administer property and shall treat them equally in all stages of procedure in courts and tribunals.

3. States Parties agree that all contracts and all other private instruments of any kind with a legal effect which is directed at restricting the legal capacity of women shall be deemed null and void.

4. States Parties shall accord to men and women the same rights with regard to the law relating to the movement of persons and the freedom to choose their residence and domicile.

Article 16

1. States Parties shall take all appropriate measures to eliminate discrimination against women in all matters relating to marriage and family relations and in particular shall ensure, on a basis of equality of men and women:

(a) The same right to enter into marriage;

(b) The same right freely to choose a spouse and to enter into marriage only with their free and full consent;

(c) The same rights and responsibilities during marriage and at its dissolution;

(d) The same rights and responsibilities as parents, irrespective of their marital status, in matters relating to their children; in all cases the interests of the children shall be paramount;

(e) The same rights to decide freely and responsibly on the number and spacing of their children and to have access to the information, education and means to enable them to exercise these rights;

(f) The same rights and responsibilities with regard to guardianship, wardship, trusteeship and adoption of children, or similar institutions where these concepts exist in national legislation; in all cases the interests of the children shall be paramount;

(g) The same personal rights as husband and wife, including the right to choose a family name, a profession and an occupation;

(h) The same rights for both spouses in respect of the ownership, acquisition, management, administration, enjoyment and disposition of property, whether free of charge or for a valuable consideration.

2. The betrothal and the marriage of a child shall have no legal effect, and all necessary action, including legislation, shall be taken to specify a minimum age for marriage and to make the registration of marriages in an official registry compulsory.

Selected Bibliography

Allen, Ben T. *Preventing Sexual Harassment on Campus: Policies and Practices for Higher Education.* Washington, D.C.: College and University Personnel Association, 1995.

Altman, Andrew. "Making Sense of Sexual Harassment Law." *Philosophy and Public Affairs* 25, no. 1 (Winter 1996): 36–64.

American Association of University Professors. "Consensual Relations Between Faculty and Students," and "Sexual Harassment: Suggested Policy and Procedures for Handling Complaints." *Academe* (July/August 1995): 62–64.

American Association of University Women. *Hostile Hallways: The AAUW Survey on Sexual Harassment in America's Schools.* Washington, D.C.: American Association of University Women Educational Foundation, 1993.

Baugh, S. Gayle. "On the Persistence of Sexual Harassment in the Workplace." *Journal of Business Ethics* 16 (1997): 899–908.

Berdahl, Jennifer L., Vicki J. Magley, and Craig R. Waldo. "The Sexual Harassment of Men? Exploring the Concept with Theory and Data." *Psychology of Women Quarterly* 20 (1996): 527–547.

Bingham, Shereen G., ed. *Conceptualizing Sexual Harassment as Discursive Practice.* Westport, Conn.: Praeger, 1994.

Bouchard, Elizabeth. *Everything You Need to Know About Sexual Harassment.* New York: Rosen, 1997.

Brant, Clare, and Yun Lee Too, eds. *Rethinking Sexual Harassment.* London: Pluto Press, 1994.

Bravo, Ellen, and Ellen Cassedy. *The 9 to 5 Guide to Combating Sexual Harassment.* New York: John Wiley & Sons, 1992.

Browne, Kingsley R. "Title VII as Censorship: Hostile-Environment Harassment and the First Amendment." *Ohio State Law Journal* 52 (1991): 481–550.

Chamallas, Martha. "Feminist Constructions of Objectivity: Multiple Perspectives in Sexual and Racial Harassment Litigation." *Texas Journal of Women and Law* 1 (1992): 95–142.

Chrisman, Robert, and Robert L Allen, eds. *Court of Appeal: The Black Community Speaks Out on the Racial and Sexual Politics of Clarence Thomas vs. Anita Hill.* New York: Ballentine Books, 1992.

Christensen, F. M. "'Sexual Harassment' Must Be Eliminated." *Public Affairs Quarterly* 8 (1994): 1–17.

Copeland, Lois, and Leslie R. Wolfe. *Violence Against Women as Bias Motivated Hate Crime: Defining the Issues.* Washington, D.C.: Center for Women Policy Studies, 1991.

Cornell, Drucilla. *The Imaginary Domain: Abortion, Pornography, and Sexual Harassment.* New York: Routledge, 1995.

Culbertson, Amy L., Paul Rosenfeld, and Carol E. Newell. *Sexual Harassment in the Active-Duty Navy: Findings from the 1991 Navy-Wide Survey.* San Diego, Calif.: Navy Personnel Research and Development Center, 1993.

Dank, Barry M., and Roberto Refinetti, eds. *Sexual Harassment and Sexual Consent,* in *Sexuality and Culture,* vol. 1. New Brunswick, N.J.: Transaction Publishers, 1997.

Dooling, Richard. *Blue Streak: Swearing, Free Speech, and Sexual Harassment.* New York: Random House, 1996.

Dziech, Billie Wright, and Linda Weiner. *The Lecherous Professor: Sexual Harassment on Campus,* 2nd ed. Urbana: University of Illinois Press, 1990.

Epstein, Deborah. "Can a 'Dumb Ass Woman' Achieve Equality in the Workplace? Running the Gauntlet of Hostile Environment Harassing Speech." *Georgetown Law Journal* 84 (1996): 399–451.

Eskenazi, Martin, and David Gallen, eds. *Sexual Harassment: Know Your Rights.* New York: Carroll & Graf, 1992.

Estlund, Cynthia. "Freedom of Speech in the Workplace and the Problem of Discriminatory Harassment." *Texas Law Journal* 75 (1997).

Estrich, Susan. "Sex at Work." *Stanford Law Review* 43 (1991): 813–861.

Farley, Lin. *Sexual Shakedown: The Sexual Harassment of Women on the Job.* New York: MacGraw-Hill/Warner Books, 1978.

Feary, Vaughana Macy. "Sexual Harassment: Why the Corporate World Still Doesn't 'Get It.'" *Journal of Business Ethics* 13 (1994): 649–662.

Fitzgerald, Louise F., Sandra L. Shullman, Nancy Bailey, Margaret Richards, Janice Swecker, Yael Gold, Mimi Ormerod, and Lauren Weitzman. "The Incidence and Dimensions of Sexual Harassment in Academia and the Workplace." *Journal of Vocational Behavior* 32 (1988): 152–175.

Gallop, Jane. "Feminism and Harassment Policy." *Academe* (September–October 1994): 16–23.

————. *Feminist Accused of Sexual Harassment.* Durham, N.C.: Duke University Press, 1997.

Gardner, Carol Brooks. *Passing By: Gender and Public Harassment.* Berkeley: University of California Press, 1995.

Gerdes, Louise I., ed. *Sexual Harassment: Current Controversies.* San Diego, Calif.: Greenhaven Press, 1999.

Gutek, Barbara A. *Sex and the Workplace: The Impact of Sexual Behavior on Women, Men, and Organizations.* San Francisco: Jossey-Bass, 1985.

————. "How Subjective Is Sexual Harassment? An Examination of Rater Effects." *Basic and Applied Social Psychology* 17 (1995): 447–467.

————, and Mary P. Koss. "Changed Women and Changed Organizations: Consequences of and Coping with Sexual Harassment." *Journal of Vocational Behavior* 42 (1993): 28–48.

Hajdin, Mane. "Sexual Harassment in the Law: The Demarcation Problem." *Journal of Social Philosophy* 25, no. 3 (1994): 102–122.

————. "Sexual Harassment and Negligence." *Journal of Social Philosophy* 28, no. 1 (1997): 37–53.

Hill, Anita. *Speaking Truth to Power.* New York: Doubleday, 1997.

Hill, Anita Faye, and Emma Coleman Jordan, eds. *Race, Gender, and Power in America: The Legacy of the Hill–Thomas Hearings.* New York: Oxford University Press, 1995.

Holmes, Robert L. "Sexual Harassment and the University." *The Monist* 79, no. 4 (1996): 499–518.

Kaser, Joyce. *Honoring Boundaries: Preventing Sexual Harassment in the Workplace.* Amherst, Mass.: Human Resources Development Press, 1995.

Larkin, June. *Sexual Harassment: High School Girls Speak Out.* Toronto: Second Story Press, 1994.

LeMoncheck, Linda. *Dehumanizing Women: Treating Persons as Sex Objects.* Lanham, Md.: Rowman & Littlefield, 1985.

————. "Feminist Politics and Feminist Ethics: Treating Women as Sex Objects." In Robert M. Stewart, *Philosophical Perspectives on Sex and Love,* pp. 29–38. New York: Oxford University Press, 1995.

————, and Mane Hajdin. *Sexual Harassment: A Debate.* Lanham, Md.: Rowman & Littlefield, 1997.

Levy, Anne, and Michele Antoinette Paludi. *Workplace Sexual Harassment.* New York: Prentice Hall, 1996.

MacKinnon, Catharine A. *Sexual Harassment of Working Women: A Case of Sex Discrimination.* New Haven, Conn.: Yale University Press, 1979.

Morris, Celia. *Bearing Witness: Sexual Harassment and Beyond: Everywoman's Story.* Boston: Little, Brown, 1994.

Morrison, Toni, ed. *Race-ing Justice, En-gendering Power: Essays on Anita Hill, Clarence Thomas, and the Construction of Social Reality.* New York: Pantheon, 1992.

Office of the Inspector General. *The Tailhook Report: The Official Inquiry into the Events of Tailhook '91.* New York: St. Martin's Press, 1993.

Paglia, Camille. "The Strange Case of Clarence Thomas and Anita Hill." In *Sex, Art, and American Culture,* pp. 46–48. New York: Vintage Books, 1992.

Paludi, Michele A., ed. *Sexual Harassment on College Campuses: Abusing the Ivory Power.* Albany: State University of New York Press, 1996.

————, and Richard B. Barickman, eds. *Academic and Workplace Sexual Harassment: A Resource Manual.* Albany: State University of New York Press, 1991.

Patai, Daphne. *Heterophobia: Sexual Harassment and the Future of Feminism.* Lanham, Md.: Rowman & Littlefield, 1999.

Paules, Greta Foff. *Dishing It Out: Power and Resistance Among Waitresses in a New Jersey Restaurant.* Philadelphia: Temple University Press, 1991.

Petrocelli, William, and Barbara Kate Repa. *Sexual Harassment on the Job: What It Is and How to Stop It,* 4th ed. Berkeley, Calif.: Nolo Press, 1999.

Reardon, Kathleen Kelley. *They Don't Get It, Do They? Communication in the Workplace—Closing the Gap Between Men and Women.* Boston: Little, Brown, 1995.

Roberts, Melinda A. "Sexual Harassment, the Acquiescent Plaintiff, and the 'Unwelcomeness' Requirement." In Dana E. Bushnell, ed., *"Nagging" Questions: Feminist Ethics in Everyday Life,* pp. 105–122. Lanham, Md.: Rowman & Littlefield, 1995.

Roiphe, Katie. *The Morning After: Sex, Fear, and Feminism on Campus.* Boston: Little, Brown, 1993.

Rutter, Peter. *Understanding and Preventing Sexual Harassment: The Complete Guide.* New York: Bantam Books, 1997.

Sandler, Bernice R., and Robert J. Shoop, eds. *Sexual Harassment on Campus: A Guide for Administrators, Faculty, and Students.* Boston: Allyn & Bacon, 1998.

Schultz, Vicki. "Reconceptualizing Sexual Harassment." *Yale Law Journal* 107, no. 6 (April 1998): 1683–1805.

"Sexual Harassment." *Journal of Social Issues* 51 (1995).

Siegal, Deborah L. *Sexual Harassment: Research and Resources,* 3rd ed., revised by Marina Budhos. New York: National Council for Research on Women, 1995.

Skaine, Rosemarie. *Power and Gender: Issues in Sexual Dominance and Harassment.* Jefferson, N.C.: McFarland, 1996.

Smitherman, Geneva, ed. *African American Women Speak Out on Anita Hill–Clarence Thomas.* Detroit, Mich.: Wayne State University Press, 1995.

Stein, Laura W. *Sexual Harassment in America.* Westport, Conn.: Greenwood [Publishing Group], 1999.

Sterba, James P. *Justice for Here and Now.* New York: Cambridge University Press, 1998.

———. "Sexual Equality in the Workplace Would Reduce Sexual Harassment," in Louise I. Gerdes, ed., *Sexual Harassment: Current Controversies,* pp. 123–130. San Diego, Calif.: Greenhaven Press, 1999.

Stockdale, Margaret S., ed. *Sexual Harassment in the Workplace: Perspectives, Frontiers, and Response Strategies.* Thousand Oaks, Calif.: Sage, 1996.

Sumrall, Amber Coverdale, and Dena Taylor, eds. *Sexual Harassment: Women Speak Out.* Freedom, Calif.: Crossing Press, 1992.

Swisher, Karen L., ed. *At Issue: What Is Sexual Harassment?* San Diego, Calif.: Greenhaven Press, 1995.

Tannen, Deborah. *Talking from 9 to 5: Women and Men in the Workplace: Language, Sex and Power.* New York: Avon Books, 1994.

Thomas, Alison M., and Celia Kitzinger, eds. *Sexual Harassment: Contemporary Feminist Perspectives.* Buckingham, U.K.: Open University Press, 1997.

U.S. Merit Systems Protection Board. *Sexual Harassment of Federal Workers: An Update.* Washington, D.C.: U.S. Government Printing Office, Office of Merit Systems Review and Studies, 1988.

Wall, Edmund, ed. *Sexual Harassment: Confrontations and Decisions.* New York: Prometheus Books, 1992.

Webb, Susan L. *The Global Impact of Sexual Harassment.* New York: MasterMedia, 1994.

———. *Step Forward: Sexual Harassment in the Workplace: What You Need to Know!* 2nd ed. New York: MasterMedia, 1997.

Wells, Deborah L., and Beverly J. Kracher. "Justice, Sexual Harassment, and the Reasonable Victim Standard." *Journal of Business Ethics* 12 (1993): 423–431.

Young, Cathy. "Groping Toward Sanity." *Reason* (August/September 1998).

Selected Online Resources

Equal Employment Opportunity Commission (EEOC) *http://www.eeoc.gov/*

Feminist Majority Foundation. *Sexual Harassment Resources http://www.feminist.org/911/harass.html*

The Legal Information Institute at Cornell Law School. *Employment Discrimination: An Overview*
http://fatty.law.cornell.edu/topics/employment_discrimination.html

National Organization for Women (NOW). *NOW's Issue Report on Sexual Harassment*
http://www.now.org/issues/harass/index.html

9 to 5, National Association of Working Women. *Sexual Harassment: What Every Woman Needs to*
Know http://www.cs.utk.edu/~bartley/other/9to5.html